American History: Recent Interpretations

BOOK I: TO 1877

AMERICAN HISTORY:

Edited by ABRAHAM S. EISENSTADT *Brooklyn College*

New York, Established 1834

Recent Interpretations

BOOK I: TO 1877

THOMAS Y. CROWELL COMPANY

First Printing, January, 1962
Second Printing, July, 1962

Library of Congress Catalog Card Number: 62-10281

Designed by Laurel Wagner

Manufactured in the United States of America
by The Cornwall Press, Inc.

Preface

This collection is designed to meet the need for supplementary readings in basic courses in American history. The need for such readings is clear enough. A textbook has, after all, the limitations of its author's knowledge and approach. A class in history requires the stimulus of different views and expert knowledge, both of which may be found in a book of collateral readings. Such a book affords, moreover, a satisfactory answer to the question of how to bring large groups of students in touch with a wide range of literature and opinion under conditions of limited library facilities.

The basic problem in editing a book of supplementary readings is to define what one seeks to achieve and how one seeks to do it. The editing of this book has been guided by the following purposes:

The collection as a whole undertakes to present the newer viewpoints in American history. All too frequently the textbook is based on approaches that have to be substantially modified if not altogether discarded. The selections in this book, on the other hand, date almost entirely from 1945—for the greater part, indeed, from 1950. They constitute in this way an anthology of American historical writing since World War II. They indicate the newer directions of American historical thought.

The selections have been drawn, wherever possible, from a broad field of periodicals which include the following:

Agricultural History
American Archivist
American Heritage
American Historical Review
American Quarterly
American Scholar
Atlantic Monthly
British Journal of Sociology
Business History Review
Church History
Columbia University Forum
Current History
Indiana Magazine of History

Journal of Economic History
Journal of the Illinois State Historical Society
Journal of Negro History
Journal of Religion
Journal of Southern History
Marine Corps Gazette
Mississippi Valley Historical Review
New England Quarterly
Pacific Historical Review
Pennsylvania Magazine of History and Biography
Perspectives USA

Political Science Quarterly
Proceedings of the American Anti-
quarian Society
Proceedings of the American Philo-
sophical Society
Proceedings of the National Con-
ference on Social Welfare
Proceedings of the South Carolina
Historical Association

Sewanee Review
Theology Today
U.S. Naval Institute Proceedings
Virginia Quarterly Review
Western Political Quarterly
William and Mary Quarterly
World Politics
Yale Review

It is in the rich essay literature of such periodicals that the new American history is being defined. It is in this essay literature, too, that the contributions of the foremost historians will often be found at their condensed and argumentative best. Though clearly of great importance, these writings are usually inaccessible to the class. Many college libraries do not have the wide collection of periodicals from which the readings in this volume have been taken; and even if they did, it would be very difficult, if not impossible, for large classes to use them at any given time. In the relatively few instances where selections were taken from recent books, the reason has generally been that these selections recommended themselves as clearly preferable to what was afforded by the periodicals.

The anthology consists entirely of complete essays. Each selection is a self-contained unit. The excerpts and fragments that usually make up a book of readings have been avoided. In composing an anthology of essays the purpose has been to do justice to their writers by letting them speak their minds fully on subjects on which they are authorities, without the arbitrary interruption of an editor. The desire has also been to do justice to the instructor and his students by letting them read and analyze in its entirety a noteworthy essay by a major historian on an important issue in the American past.

The choice of a particular essay has been made for one or more definite reasons. The essay is concerned with a major problem, development, or individual in American history. It summarizes the findings of an expert in the specific area of his research. It is often revisionist in approach. It is well written. It presents a provocative thesis, designed to stimulate the mind of the student and the discussion of the class. It has, as Carl Becker put it, something to say and says it in its own way.

The essays as a whole seek to present history as wider in scope than merely past politics. In order to underscore the historian's interest in all aspects of human activity, the editor has included a relatively larger number of selections dealing with economic, social, religious, and intellectual developments in the American past.

Introductory notes have been written for all of the essays. The notes tell about the contribution and approach of the historian who wrote each essay. They define the nature and importance of the subject with which the essay is concerned. They suggest lines of inquiry about the subject, both in its particular context in the American past and in the broader frame of American historical development. The effort has been to see a historical issue in its significance for our own times, not only for the purpose of using the student's interest in the present as a point of departure for his study of the past but also to encourage him to see the present in its deeper perspective as a phase of the past in evolution. The effort has also been to throw open to the student the challenging questions posed by the study of history —such questions, for example, as whether the past is to be explained by determinism or by accident, what the nature and meaning of causation are, how much the great man influences the course of historical development, and whether or not an objective truth about the past can be attained. In terms of its introductory notes, therefore, the collection may be used as a "problems" approach to the study of the American past and may serve also as a primer for the study of the historical discipline.

The attempt has been made throughout to include articles of a high level of competence and interest and to represent as many approaches, to canvass as many problems, and to seek as catholic an orientation toward the whole American past as is possible. The footnotes that originally appeared with the essays have, as a rule, been omitted for reasons of length; in a few instances, however, where the theme of the essays is historiographical, the footnotes have, by necessity, been retained. Full information is given with each essay concerning the journal from which it has been taken, and the footnotes accompanying the essay may, of course, be readily consulted there. Obvious typographical errors have been corrected and abbreviations have been spelled out, but all stylistic preferences have been retained.

It is hoped that this volume will afford the student a broad and deep outlook on the American past as well as a real sense of the vitality of its study today. It is also hoped that he will thereby be encouraged to seek out its wider reaches and dimensions on his own.

A.S.E.

November, 1961

Acknowledgments

The editing of this anthology depended at every turn upon the assistance, cooperation, and good will of many persons. I am particularly indebted to Professors Herman Ausubel and John Hope Franklin for their very helpful counsel and ideas. The introductory notes owe much to the suggestions of my colleagues at Brooklyn College: Dean Albertson, Abraham Ascher, Richard O. Cummings, David Boroff, Margaret R. Furcron, Thomas B. Furcron, and Hans L. Trefousse. In the task of selecting the articles comprising this anthology out of an enormous repository of periodicals, I was served generously and patiently by the librarians of Brooklyn College, Bowdoin, Dartmouth, and of the American History Division of the New York Public Library. To several members of the Crowell Company I am especially grateful: to Mr. John T. Hawes, for his many good suggestions and his encouragement; to Mrs. Marian Reiner, for her ready, cheerful, and very capable assistance; to Mrs. Susan La Farge, for her help in moving the anthology through all stages of production; and to Mr. Nov Grano, for his expert advice. Making a book is so much a domestic enterprise that I am pleased, finally, to express my gratitude for the help given me by my family, in general, and, in particular, by my mother and my wife.

A. S. E.

FOR ELIZABETH, LAURA, JONATHAN

Contents

Imperial Problems and Revolution

3   NATIONAL GROWTH AND CIVIL WAR, 1783–1877

The Republic of the Founding Fathers

Politics in an Expanding Democracy

Society in Ferment

Civil War and Reconstruction

I

The Study and Writing of American History

1 *Allan Nevins*

NEW LAMPS FOR OLD IN HISTORY

The study of American history extends an invitation and a challenge. Even at first glance one can see that here is an epic drama, extending over some three and a half centuries, in which the frontiers of life are pushed from the Atlantic seaboard across a continent, from primitive and far-flung settlements to the advanced and teeming society of our own times. It is exciting to contemplate the larger themes of the drama as they unfold, the struggle of a transplanted civilization with the American wilderness, the rebellion against the British dominion, the growth of a democratic and materialistic society, the gigantic war between the North and the South, the industrialization of American life, the advent of the United States to world power. It is no less exciting to contemplate the titanic figures who move through the scenes of the drama, giving it all the human qualities of magnanimity, striving, friendship, success, despair, frustration, and hope.

The study of the American epic also presents a challenge. Several questions require careful consideration, if the study is to have any value. What, to begin with, do we mean by history? What is to be gained from the study of the American past? What qualifications do we need in order to undertake such a study? To what extent will it yield us a true picture of what actually occurred? To what extent is history an art, to what extent a science? Of what utility will our knowledge of the past be in our modern world?

Some of these questions are answered in the following essay by Allan Nevins, who, after his retirement as De Witt Clinton Professor of American History at Columbia University, became senior research associate at the Henry E. Huntington Library in San Marino, California. Professor Nevins is particularly well qualified to answer the larger questions about the nature and study of American history. He has written and edited more than fifty volumes canvassing virtually every major era of our past, and is presently engaged in work on a multi-volume study of the nation from the Mexican War through the age of Reconstruction. Professor Nevins's achievement has been recog-

Reprinted with permission from the *American Archivist*, XVII (January, 1954), 3–12.

nized in many ways: he has been president of the American Historical Association; he has served as Harmsworth Professor of American History at Oxford; he has twice won the Pulitzer Prize in biography. His particular interest and ability in opening up to the novice all the tasks and rewards of studying the past are especially evident in his volume entitled *The Gateway to History* (1938). The same interest and ability are apparent too in the essay below, in which Professor Nevins analyzes the problem of how and why the American past is being freshly explored and newly interpreted by succeeding generations.

There are many reasons for the study of American history. If, as Professor Nevins suggests, the present touches on our view of the past, it is also true that the past touches on our view of the present. Our study will afford us a better ability to meet the problems which now confront us. Seeing them in deeper perspective, we will understand them in fuller measure. We will get a truer sense of the substance and proportion of the present act of the American drama if we examine more extensively and more analytically the acts which have already been played.

One curious thing about history, as Guedalla said, is that it really happened. Another curious fact about history is that while it was happening, nobody really understood its meaning.

John Fiske, pausing one day in his young manhood before the window of Little, Brown in Boston, saw a volume within entitled "Pioneers of France in the New World" and noted that its author was identified as the man who had written "The Conspiracy of Pontiac." He remembered that when that earlier volume appeared, he had wondered whether Pontiac was a barbarous chieftain of medieval Europe. He recalled also that some teacher at Harvard had once expressed the view that the French and Indian War was a dull squabble of no real significance to students of history. Passing on, Fiske wondered why anyone should write about French pioneers in America. He lived to pen an essay on Francis Parkman which not only placed that author at the head of American historians (where he yet stands) but recognized that the epic significance of the struggle of Britain and France for the mastery of North America—a significance which Parkman had first expounded—could hardly be overstated. An interpretation of our continental history which nowadays we assume no child could miss had been beyond the grasp of the brilliant young John Fiske in the 1860's.

This idea that history can ever be so well written that it does not need rewriting can be held only by those foolish people who think that history can ever ascertain exact truth. It cannot. We can go further than the assertion of that truism: we can say, "Fortunate for history that it cannot ascertain exact truth!" If history were a photograph of the past it would be flat and uninspiring. Happily, it is a painting; and like all works of art, it fails of the highest truth unless imagination and ideas are mixed with the paints. A hundred photographs of London Bridge look just alike and convey altogether a very slight percentage of the truth, but Turner's Thames and Whistler's Thames, though utterly different, both convey the river with a deeper truth.

All parts of our history are always being rewritten; no segment of it, from 1492 to 1952, is not now in need of vigorous rewriting. Whenever an expert applies himself to the scrutiny of a special area, he at once sounds a lusty call for more searching exploration of the terrain. Douglas Freeman, carrying Washington through the Revolution, agreed with Bernard Knollenberg, writing a history of that war, that every part of the Revolutionary struggle needs the most searching re-examination and the boldest reinterpretation. Merrill Jensen states in the preface to his study of the Confederation that the entire period 1783–89 demands a study that will embrace every State and every act of Congress. There are men who believe that the historical study of the Civil War period has but just begun—and they are right. Margaret Leech, just completing a study of the McKinley administration, is convinced that a hundred research workers should be set to exploration of the dark nooks and secret crannies of the time.

"In vain the sage, with retrospective eye," writes Pope, "would from the apparent what conclude the why." The three main reasons why history constantly needs reinterpretation include something more than the impossibility of ever learning all the truth about all the motives and actions of the past.

The chief of the three reasons is the need of every generation for a reinterpretation to suit its own preconceptions, ideas, and outlook. Every era has its own climate of opinion. It thinks it knows more than the preceding era; it thinks it takes a wider view of the universe. Every era, too, is affected by cataclysmic events which shift its point of view: the French Revolution, the Metternichian reaction, the movement for national unification in Italy, the United States, and Germany, the apogee of Manchester liberalism, and so on down to the multiple crisis of our atomic age. We see the past through a prism which glows and sparkles as new lights catch its facets. Much of the rewriting of history is a readjustment to this prism. George Bancroft's spectrum was outmoded a few years after his laborious "last revision"; Charles A. Beard's begins to be outworn today, for we possess what Beard would have called a new frame of reference.

As a second reason, new tools of superior penetrative power are from time to time installed in the toolshed of even our rather unprogressive race of historians. Our council for research in the social sciences (it should be studies) justly emphasizes the value of overlapping disciplines. Much could be said for the contention that the best historians nowadays are prepared in some other field than that of history. Thus Wesley Clair Mitchell, the historian of the greenbacks, of business cycles, and of the ebb and flow of economic activity, whose National Bureau of Economic Research inspired so much fruitful historical writing, was trained as an economist. (He also was trained by John Dewey, who gave courses under all sorts of titles, but "every one of them dealt with the same subject— how we think.") Beard was trained as a political scientist. Parrington was trained as a student of literature. Carl Becker was trained in European history but wrote in the American field. James Henry Breasted was first trained in theology, a fact which stood him in good stead when this pioneer of Egyptology in America began to trace the development of conscience and religion in the ancient East. Not one historian in fifty knows as much as he should of the tool called statistics, or of psychology, or of economic geography, or of ecology. The kinship between Halford J. Mackinder, the geographer, and Frederick J. Turner, the historian, in loosing seminal ideas showed what the geographer could learn from history and the historian from geography.

But the third great reason why history is rewritten is simply because the constant discovery of new materials necessitates a recasting of our view of the past. We might think that this would one day cease, but it never does. Everyone who has laboriously mapped any historical subject knows how steadily the dust of new facts falls upon that map, blurring some lines and defining new ones. Happy are those who live to rewrite their books, as even Parkman rewrote one of his—"LaSalle and the Great West." One would have said that all the materials for a history of the Revolution had been assembled in print by the innumerable agencies, local, State and national, devoted to that effort, but Freeman assures us that the great depositories like the Massachusetts Historical Society, the American Philosophical Society, and the main State libraries, bulge with unstudied documents. One would have said that all the material for the history of the Confederate War Office had been studied and restudied; but, behold: the diary of the third officer of that department, Kean, is suddenly deposited in the University of Virginia, and we find a complete reassessment of the Southern military administration possible.

Thus the idea that history is photography is set at naught. It is art; it constantly requires a new mixture of pigments, new points of view, new manipulation of light and shade; and as an art it presents an endless chal-

lenge to the writer who perceives that the highest truth of history will always transcend a statement of fact; that indeed, historical fact is but a
foundation for the truth won by imagination and intellectual power.

The best history is always interpretive, but this does not mean that the
best history is consciously or ostentatiously interpretive. The work of the
historical masters, from Thucydides to Trevelyan, illustrates the fact that
interpretation is most effective when implicit rather than explicit. The true
historical attitude is a search for truth about a situation, force, or event—
the War of 1812, the abolitionist impulse, Pearl Harbor—which slowly,
painfully, accurately, dredges up an unforeseen interpretation. That is,
history properly operates by the inductive, not the deductive, method.
The merit of an Olympian historian like Parkman is that he says, in effect:
"Let us collect and collate all the relevant facts, and find what conclusions
emerge from their impartial analysis." The cardinal weakness of a controversial historian like Beard is that he repeatedly gave the impression—perhaps falsely—of having said to himself: "Let us take this provocative theory
of the fact, and see how impressive an array of facts we can collect in its
support." Ideas in history, that is, should be applied in subordination to the
ascertainment of all the facts, and not in control of the ascertainment of
one picked body of facts. Hence it is that nothing could be more absurd
than to try to predict in advance the interpretations to be applied to our
history by future writers—who will certainly go their own way. But we
may legitimately make some guesses as to the general drift of some of the
new interpretations lying ahead of us.

As American history lengthens and the past falls into longer perspective, we tend not so much to discard major interpretations entirely as to
place new ones beside them; not so much to substitute one simple synthesis
for another as to embrace old monistic views in a new and complex synthesis. Let us take a sweeping view of the first century of our national
history, 1775–1875. In that tremendously variegated and baffling sea of
events, forces, personalities, tendencies, and fortuities, let us assume that
three great dominant developments lift themselves above all others.

These three—let us assume—are the establishment of American independence, political, economic, and finally cultural, from Europe; the westward
movement for the conquest and development of the continent; and the
abolition of slavery and a Southern way of life in a civil war which vindicated national unity. Some students, to be sure, would select other elements
in our historical fabric, but three special students out of five and nine lay
readers out of ten would, I believe, choose these. Now it is evident to a
cursory view that each of the three lent itself at first to a simple monistic
interpretation, expounded in the work even of subtle historians, and that
within one or two generations this simple view of the past was replaced by

a dual or multiple interpretation. What had been a flat telescopic image was given depth and reality by a stereopticon lens.

The Revolution seemed to our primitive historians, down to and including George Bancroft, simply a political upheaval; richly interesting as it was, it was the epic story of the establishment of political liberty in a new nation in a new world, as a guiding torch to all mankind. Before long, however, historians doubled the lens. They showed that the Revolution was a social no less than a political convulsion; that the internal transformation of America was quite as significant as the external; that a broad sequence of changes was set in motion, or rather accelerated, which rolled inexorably on through the Jeffersonian and Jacksonian eras. Some of this truth was visible to that early historian Richard Hildreth, who was as realistic as he was conservative; more of it to Moses Coit Tyler and John Bach McMaster; and all of it to a later school headed by J. Franklin Jameson, Parrington, and others.

The westward movement and the taming of the continent were first treated in terms of the transforming impact of man on nature; the expulsion of the Indian and wild beast, the hewing out of pioneer farms, the building of roads, and the ultimate planting of school and factory where the fur trader had trod. Then arose the eminent historian who perceived an equally rich meaning in the impact of nature, the wilderness, upon man; who explained how the frontier converted the European into an American, how it transformed men of caste-ridden minds into belligerently democratic individualists, how it manufactured nationalists out of separatists, and how, in short, it altered the whole pattern of thought, emotion, and conduct. This binocular view of the westward march was infinitely more interesting and arresting than the old monocular view. Parkman, Justin Winsor, Reuben Gold Thwaites, Edward Eggleston, Theodore Roosevelt, H. H. Bancroft, had been roughly accurate in their delineation of the westward thrust, but their interpretation had lacked depth and distinctness. When Turner substituted his perceptive and penetrating image of the frontier for this flat photograph, it flashed into life, color, and meaning; and behind Turner came a new body of writers who saw with his eyes.

To Hermann Von Holst the abolition of slavery seemed to mark the climax of 70 years of national life. America, to this German of Lithuanian birth, this hater of Russian and Prussian tyrannies, was the home of freedom and democracy; and the development and exemplification of these two inestimable gifts had been its principal mission in the world. But Liberty in America had suffered from a cancerous social institution—slavery,—which sadly impaired her usefulness in the sisterhood of nations and threatened her very life. This interpretation possessed more validity than some recent writers have been willing to allow; indeed, within limits it was entirely valid. But it was too obvious, and it left too many historical phenomena of the period unexplained. The antagonism of North and South by 1860 transcended slavery, even though the conflict over slavery was certainly its central element. The simple monistic view of our great upheaval in the middle of the nineteenth century had to be amplified.

Hence arose the interpretation of that upheaval as one which included conflicts of economic interest, of philosophies of life, and of ingrained prejudice; a conflict between the eighteenth-century and the nineteenth-century mind; a conflict between the nascent industrialism of the North and the entrenched agrarianism of the South. Such an interpretation had been adumbrated by Southern politicians and publicists like Yancey during the war; it was stated with emphasis by a Southern historian, Percy A. Greg, soon after Appomattox. It had the merit of both widening and deepening the canvas. It demonstrated the links which joined Thaddeus Stevens, the antislavery covenanter, with Thad Stevens, the ironmaster, and Thad Stevens, the high-tariff legislator. It used as a constructive interpretation and not as a cloak for our political shortcomings and errors or as a means of glozing over the hideous blot of slavery, it had immeasurable value.

So much for three great developments in American history: the severance from Europe, the conquest and settling of the continent, and the elimination of slavery and the State rights doctrine as retarding agencies in our national growth. The character of a fourth great development, accomplished and sealed in the last 50 years of our national life, can hardly be missed. On that new phase of our history, too, general agreement will perhaps be found. We have become first a great world power, and then the great world power. We have moved first into the open arena of world affairs, and then into the very center of that arena. We now view our national past from the vantage point of this new turn and with the changed perspective which it gives us.

Just as John Fiske saw our history from 1607 to 1789 as an evolutionary preparation for the gift to the world of practical democracy and the Anglo-American principle of self-government in the shape of our Constitution and Federal system, just as Von Holst saw the whole period from 1776 to 1861 as a preparation for the vindication of human liberty and national unity, so now we have historians who view our whole national life as an unconscious preparation for the time when we should become Protector of the Faith for all democratic peoples; when, having turned away from Western European affairs until we gained first place among the nations, we returned to them as the pivot and support of Western European civilization. These writers regard American history not in terms of the Western continent but in terms of an Atlantic community. We find, indeed, that we never left that community; that the Seven Years War was our first world war, the Revolution our second; that we have but awakened to our consciousness of a global role. And when these historians write of our national future, they speak not of short-term objects, but of what Lincoln called "man's vast future."

This tremendous change of the past 40 or 50 years—this emergence of America to the leadership of the Western World—will undoubtedly affect our children's children, and the long generations to come, in the most sweeping way. It will loom up, in time to come, as tremendously as the great changes which preceded it—as the Revolution, internal and external, the American conquest of the frontier and the frontier's conquest of the American, the death of slavery, and the birth of machine industry. But the full significance of this development will not become evident until it, too, is given the dual or multiple interpretation that historians gave these older developments. We shall not understand its essential character until all the accompanying phenomena, social, economic, and intellectual, have been analyzed, and some mind as electric as Parrington's and as penetrating as Turner's has pierced nearer its heart. When then will be its significance? That is a question we cannot answer; it is for the oncoming generation of historians.

My own guess is that this great development by which America has been projected into world leadership, with all the exhilarations and perils, the opportunities and costs of that position, will in some fashion be connected, by future interpreters, with the advent of an age of mass action, mass production, and mass psychology in American life. From being one of the most unorganized, the most invertebrate of nations, in 1860, we have grown into the most powerfully and efficiently organized people on the globe. Our population of 155,000,000 disposes of its resources through such mass combinations, political, social, and economic, as mankind never saw before. Our thinking in 1865 was still individual thinking; today it is largely mass thinking, shaped and colored by mass media of unparalleled and sometimes dismaying potency—press, radio, television, cinema. No one can go to what were recently primitive frontier communities in America—say Texas and California—without being struck, and a little appalled, by the complexity and efficiency with which they have organized their life. It was our mass production which won the two last world wars; it is our genius for making big organizations work which has built the means for saving Western democracy since the latest world war. Our national outlook, once that of the individualistic pioneer, has become a social outlook. Without this pervasive internal change, our new position in the world would have been impossible.

The striking shift in our character and our world position in the last half century of course has some direct results, already visible, in our interpretation of history. We are evincing a greater militancy in asserting the virtues of our political and social system. The apologetic attitude of the years of the Great Depression is gone. We can henceforth be more confident and more energetic in asserting that our way of life, called decadent by our enemies, has proved itself historically to be freer, more flexible, and more humane than any other in history. We can be as emphatic and frank as ever in describing our past weaknesses, from slavery to slums, but we shall insist more rigorously on the fundamental healthiness of our system and on its proved ability to mend its defects and give us a constantly self-regenerating society.

We shall also evince, I think, a tendency to insist more emphatically on the fundamental unity of the United States with Western Europe and the various other nations sprung from Western Europe. All kinds of Western institutions and virtues now find their principal stronghold in the United States. The literature written in the English tongue increasingly has its main center of vitality in America, a fact well recognized by the London *Times* Literary Supplement. The Roman Catholic Church, like the Protestant churches, finds its chief springs of wealth and power in the United States. The Atlantic Community, as many publicists term it, has taken the place of the former division between Europe and the Americas. Oldtime quarrels between America and Western Europe have lost a great part of the significance which was once attached to them. What does the War of 1812 count for, compared with the maintenance and growth of the political, social, and cultural ties that have made the English-speaking nations so nearly a unity? The nationalistic view of our history will increasingly be replaced by the international view, treating America as part of a great historic civilization with the Atlantic its center, as the Mediterranean was the center of the ancient world; with the tides of population, power, and influence first moving from Europe to America, and then beginning to flow in the opposite direction.

We may look forward also to a more appreciative attitude toward our material strength and to a more scientific treatment of the factors which have created this material power. In the past our historians were apologetic about our love of the dollar, our race to wealth, our interest in material objects; they deprecated our worship of size and deplored our boastfulness about steel tonnage, grain production, and output of machinery. Clio, with her tradition of devotion to moral values, was scornful of any others. Our writers in general—for the historians but followed the poets, the novelists, and the dramatists—intimated that America had grown too fast, too coarsely, too muscularly; they exalted the rural virtues as against industrial might, the rarefied air of the study as against the smoky atmosphere of the mill.

Without denying that many accompaniments of our swift industrialization were unhappy, we can now assert that this historical attitude was erroneous. The nation grew none too fast. We can see today that all its wealth, all its strength, were needed to meet a succession of world crises —and we still dwell in a crisis era. Had we applied restrictions to keep our economy small, tame, and timid, we would have lost the First World War. Had the United States not possessed the mightiest oil industry, the greatest steel industry, the largest automotive factories, the most efficient machine-tool industry, the best technological schools, and the most ingenious working force in the world, we would indubitably have lost the Second World War. Were we significantly weaker today in technical skills, in great mills and factories, and the scientific knowledge which gave us priority with the atomic bomb and hydrogen bomb, all Western Europe would be cowering —we ourselves would perhaps be cowering—before the knout held by the Kremlin. The architects of our material growth—the men like Whitney, McCormick, Westinghouse, Rockefeller, Carnegie, Hill, and Ford—will yet stand forth in their true stature as builders of a strength which civilization found indispensable. As that realization spreads, industrial archives like that created in Dearborn by the vision of the Ford Motor Company will take their place as equal in importance to the political and cultural archives so long indispensable to students of our past.

It will yet be realized that the industrial revolution in the United States came none too soon and none too fast; and that the ensuing mass-production revolution, as yet so little understood by Americans, was not born a day too early. That is a fact which may well be stated in this birthplace of mass production—Detroit. It is a fact well appreciated in Manchester and London, in Paris and Berlin, and in Moscow. We shall also come to realize that the turmoil and human suffering which inescapably accompanied the industrial revolution and the mass-production revolution were not after all a tremendous price to pay for their benefits. The price was smaller in the United States than in foreign lands. The industrial revolution cost less in human travail here than it did in England, where it first came to birth; less than in Germany or Japan; far less than it is costing in Russia. Here is a wide field for the rewriting of American history and for the re-education of the American people, a field in which all archivists may contribute their due share.

Our material might, to be sure, is valuable only as it supports and carries to victory great moral ideas, only as it buttresses a civilization in which spiritual forces are predominant. But the fundamental difference between the democratic world and the totalitarian world lies precisely in the superior position which we give to moral and spiritual values. It is we, not our enemies, who have the right to talk about what Lincoln called man's vast future, for we really value men as individual souls. Behind our dreams of man's vast future, we mobilize an unconquerable strength. In time, when future historians look back on this period, which to us is so full of struggle, sacrifice, and anxious uncertainty, they will perhaps give it an interpretation of exalted character. They may say: "The era in which the United States, summoning all its strength, led democracy in winning the First World War, the Second World War, and the ensuing struggle against the Communist tyranny, was one of the great eras of history. It stands invested with all the radiance of the Periclean era, the Elizabethan era, and the era of Pitt and the long struggle against Napoleon."

II

Colonization and
Revolution, to 1783

COLONIAL BEGINNINGS

2 *Oliver La Farge*

MYTHS THAT HIDE THE AMERICAN INDIAN

It is fair enough that a study of the American past should begin with a study of the first Americans—the Indians. Even a minimal consideration of their society and achievements is all too frequently omitted from courses in American history. This omission is regrettable, because it deprives the student of an opportunity of seeing history in its full breadth as the study of contrasting cultures in evolution. It is regrettable too because the student's knowledge of the North American Indian tends to remain at the level of myths that have been questionably collected and inadequately explored.

The following essay by Oliver La Farge will serve admirably as an introduction both to the distinctive features of Indian culture and to the myths about it that we have fashioned for our own convenience. Mr. La Farge is a highly qualified guide to this subject, having devoted his creative life to a concern with the present and past of the American Indian. It is a deep and warm concern, variously reflected in his novels, his career as a professional anthropologist, and his activities in organizations interested in the problems and welfare of American Indians today.

The root question about any myth in history is why it grew. The question becomes all the more challenging if the myth has undergone substantial change. Why, for example, did the first European settlers regard the red man as noble and why did their descendants regard him as ruthless? The image of the noble Indian must, as Mr. La Farge explains, have served the need of the explorers and colonizers. Similarly, the image of the ruthless Indian must have served the need of an independent nation seizing control of a continent and having to justify the seizure. To wage war, one must have an enemy and the enemy

Reprinted with permission of the author from *American Heritage, The Magazine of History,* VII (October, 1956), 5–9, 103–7.

must, whatever else, arouse enmity. In the war for the land, the Indian was made over into an unqualified agent of barbarism and treachery. Only when the war had finally been won, in the later decades of the nineteenth century, could the myth be given up. Only then could the understanding begin to spread that the Indian had been seen too plainly and too starkly, that he had belonged to a variety of cultures, that the cultures had been in a constant process of evolution and inter-action, and that they had been far removed from complete barbarism.

Mr. La Farge clears away the myths by portraying the three In-dian areas—Southeast, Southwest, and Northwest Coast—which had achieved the highest cultural level at the time the white man came to settle in North America. He does more than explain the various pat-terns into which Indian societies formed themselves; he provides a broad view of cultures in interplay. Mr. La Farge canvasses the effects of Meso-America upon North America as well as the reciprocal im-pact of Indian and European ways. In proceeding to the study of American history and of a culture which is so markedly European in its origins and evolution, one cannot but profit by keeping this larger cultural picture in mind.

Ever since the white men first fell upon them, the Indians of what is now the United States have been hidden from white men's view by a number of conflicting myths. The oldest of these is the myth of the Noble Red Man or the Child of Nature, who is credited either with a habit of flowery oratory of implacable dullness or else with an imbecilic inability to con-verse in anything more than grunts and monosyllables.

That first myth was inconvenient. White men soon found their pur-poses better served by the myth of ruthless, faithless savages, and later, when the "savages" had been broken, of drunken, lazy good-for-nothings. All three myths coexist today, sometimes curiously blended in a schizo-phrenic confusion such as one often sees in the moving pictures. Through the centuries the mythical figure has been variously equipped; today he wears a feather headdress, is clothed in beaded buckskin, dwells in a tepee, and all but lives on horseback.

It was in the earliest period of the Noble Red Man concept that the Indians probably exerted their most important influence upon Western civilization. The theory has been best formulated by the late Felix S. Cohen, who, as a profound student of law concerning Indians, delved into early white-Indian relations, Indian political economy, and the white men's view of it. According to this theory, with which the present writer agrees, the French and English of the early Seventeenth Century encountered, along the East Coast of North America from Virginia southward, fairly advanced tribes whose semi-hereditary rulers depended upon the acquiescence of

their people for the continuance of their rule. The explorers and first settlers interpreted these rulers as kings, their people as subjects. They found
that even the commonest subjects were endowed with many rights and
freedoms, that the nobility was fluid, and that commoners existed in a
state of remarkable equality.

Constitutional monarchy was coming into being in England, but the
divine right of kings remained firm doctrine. All European society was
stratified in many classes. A somewhat romanticized observation of Indian
society and government, coupled with the idea of the Child of Nature, led
to the formulation, especially by French philosophers, of the theories of
inherent rights in all men, and of the people as the source of the sovereign's
authority. The latter was stated in the phrase, "consent of the governed."
Both were carried over by Jefferson into our Declaration of Independence
in the statement that "all men are created equal, that they are endowed by
their Creator with certain unalienable Rights" and that governments derive
"their just powers from the consent of the governed. . . ."

Thus, early observations of the rather simple, democratic organization
of the more advanced coastal tribes, filtered through and enlarged by the
minds of European philosophers whose thinking was ripe for just such
material, at least influenced the formulation of a doctrine, or pair of doctrines, that furnished the intellectual base for two great revolutions and
profoundly affected the history of mankind.

In the last paragraph I speak of "the more advanced" tribes. Part of
the myth about the first Americans is that all of them, or most of them,
had one culture and were at the same stage of advancement. The tribes
and nations that occupied North America varied enormously, and their
condition was anything but static. The advent of the white men put a
sudden end to a phase of increasingly rapid cultural evolution, much as if
a race of people, vastly superior in numbers, in civilization, and above all
in weapons, had overrun and conquered all of Europe in Minoan times.
Had that happened, also, the conquerors would undoubtedly have concluded, as so many white men like to conclude about Indians, that that
peculiar race of light-skinned people was obviously inferior to their own.

Human beings had been in the New World for at least 15,000 years.
During much of that time, as was the case in the beginning everywhere,
they advanced but little from a Palaeolithic hunting culture. Somewhere
around 2,500 B.C. farming began with the domestication of corn either in
Peru or in Meso-America[1] in the vicinity of western Guatemala. Farming
brought about the sedentary life and the increased food supply necessary
for cultural progress. By the time of the birth of Christ, the influence of
the high cultures, soon to become true civilizations, in Meso-America was

[1] Meso-America denotes the area in which the highest civilizations north of Peru
developed, extending from a little north of Mexico City into Honduras.

beginning to reach into the present United States. Within the next 1,500 years the Indians of parts of North America progressed dramatically. When the white men first landed, there were three major centers of high culture: the Southeast-Mississippi Valley, the Southwest, and the Northwest Coast. None of the peoples of these regions, incidentally, knew about war bonnets or lived in tepees.

The Southeast-Mississippi Valley peoples (for brevity, I shall refer to the area hereafter simply as "Southeast") seem to have had the strongest influences from Meso-America, probably in part by land along the coast of Texas, in part by sea across the Gulf of Mexico, whether direct from Mexico or secondhand through the peoples of the West Indies. There is a striking resemblance between some of their great earthen mounds, shaped like flat-topped pyramids, with their wood-and-thatch temples on top, and the stone-and-mortar, temple-topped pyramids of Meso-America. Some of their carvings and engravings strongly suggest that the artists had actually seen Meso-American sculptures. The full list of similarities is convincingly long.

There grew up along the Mississippi Valley, reaching far to the north, and reaching also eastwards in the far south, the high culture generally called "Mound Builder." It produced a really impressive art, especially in carving and modeling, by far the finest that ever existed in North America. The history of advancing civilization in the New World is like that of the Old—a people develops a high culture, then barbarians come smashing in, set the clock part way back, absorb much of the older culture, and carry it on to new heights. A series of invasions of this sort seems to have struck the Mound Builders in late prehistoric times, when they were overrun by tribes mainly of Muskhogean and Iroquoian linguistic stock. Chief among these were the ancestors of the well-known Five Civilized Tribes—the Seminoles, Creeks, Choctaws, Chickasaws, and Cherokees. When white men first met them, their culture was somewhat lower than that of the earlier period in the land they occupied. None the less, they maintained, in Florida, Alabama, Mississippi, Louisiana, and Georgia, the highest level east of the Rockies. A late movement of Iroquoian tribes, close relatives of the Cherokees, among them the Iroquois themselves, carried a simpler form of the same culture into Pennsylvania, New York, Ohio, and into the edge of Canada.

All of these people farmed heavily, their fields stretching for miles. They were few in a vast land—the whole population of the present United States was probably not over a million. Hunting and fishing, therefore, were excellent, and no reasonable people would drop an easy source of abundant meat. The development of their farming was held in check quantitatively by the supply of fish and game. They farmed the choice land, and if the fields began to be exhausted, they could move. They moved their habitations somewhat more freely than do we, but they were anything but nomadic. The southern tribesmen lived neither in wigwams nor tepees, but in houses with thatched roofs, which in the extreme south often had no walls. They had an elaborate social structure with class distinctions. Because of their size, the white men called their settlements "towns." The state of their high chiefs was kingly. They were a people well on the road towards civilization.

The Natchez of Mississippi had a true king, and a curious, elaborate social system. The king had absolute power and was known as the Sun. No ordinary man could speak to him except from a distance, shouting and making obeisances. When he went out, he was carried on a litter, as the royal and sacred foot could not be allowed to touch the ground. The Natchez nation was divided into two groups, or moieties: the aristocracy and the common people. The higher group was subdivided into Suns (the royal family), Nobles, and Honored Ones. The common people were known simply as Stinkers. A Stinker could marry anyone he pleased, but all the aristocrats had to marry out of their moiety, that is, marry Stinkers. When a female aristocrat married a Stinker man, her children belonged to her class; thus, when a Sun woman married a Stinker, her children were Suns. The children of the men, however, were lowered one class, so that the children of a Sun man, even of the Sun himself, became Nobles, while the children of an Honored One became lowly Stinkers.

This system in time, if nothing intervened, would lead to an overwhelming preponderance of aristocrats. The Natchez, however, for all their near-civilization, their temples, their fine crafts and arts, were chronically warlike. Those captives they did not torture to death they adopted, thus constantly replenishing the supply of Stinkers (a foreigner could become nothing else, but his grandchildren, if his son struck a royal fancy, might be Suns).

The Indians of the Southeast knew the Mexican-West Indian art of feather weaving, by means of which they made brilliant, soft cloaks. The Sun also wore a crown of an elaborate arrangement of feathers, quite unlike a war bonnet. In cloak and crown, carried shoulder-high on a litter, surrounded by his retainers, his majesty looked far more like something out of the Orient than anything we think of ordinarily when we hear the word "Indian."

The Natchez were warlike. All of the southeasterners were warlike. War was a man's proper occupation. Their fighting was deadly, ferocious, stealthy if possible, for the purpose of killing—men, women, or children, so long as one killed—and taking captives, especially strong males whom one could enjoy torturing to death. It is among these tribes and their simpler relatives, the Iroquois, that we find the bloodthirsty savage of fiction, but the trouble is that he is not a savage. He is a man well on the road towards civilization.

With the Iroquois, they shared a curious pattern of cruelty. A warrior expected to be tortured if captured, although he could, instead, be adopted, before torture or at any time before he had been crippled. He entered into it as if it were a contest, which he would win if his captors failed to wring a sign of pain from him and if he kept taunting them so long as he was conscious. Some of the accounts of such torture among the Iroquois, when the victim was a member of a tribe speaking the same language and holding to the same customs, are filled with a quality of mutual affection. In at least one case, when a noted enemy proved to have been too badly wounded before his capture to be eligible for adoption, the chief, who had hoped that the man would replace his own son, killed in battle, wept as he assigned him to his fate. At intervals between torments so sickening that one can hardly make one's self read through the tale of them, prisoner and captors exchanged news of friends and expressions of mutual esteem. Naturally, when tribes who did not hold to these customs, including white men, were subjected to this treatment it was not well received.

This pattern may have come into North America from a yet more advanced, truly civilized source. The Mexicans—the Aztecs and their neighbors—expected to be sacrificed if they were captured, and on occasion might insist upon it if their captors were inclined to spare them. They were not tortured, properly speaking, as a general rule, but some of the methods of putting them to death were not quick. What we find in North America may have been a debasement of the Mexican practices developed into an almost psychopathic pleasure among people otherwise just as capable of love, of kindness, of nobility, and of lofty thoughts as any anywhere —or what the conquistadores found in Mexico may have been a civilized softening of earlier, yet more fearful ways. The Aztecs tore fantastic numbers of hearts from living victims, and like the people of the Southeast, when not at war said "We are idle." They were artists, singers, dancers, poets, and great lovers of flowers and birds.

The Iroquois and Muskhogeans had a real mental sophistication. We observe it chiefly in their social order and what we know of their religions. The Iroquois did not have the royalty and marked divisions of classes that we find farther south, but their well-organized, firmly knit tribes were what enabled them, although few in numbers, to dominate the Algonkians who surrounded them. The Iroquois came nearer to having the matriarchy that popular fable looks for among primitive people than any other American tribe. Actual office was held by the men, but the women's power was great, and strongly influenced the selection of the officers.

Five of the Iroquois tribes achieved something unique in North America, rare anywhere, when in the Sixteenth Century they formed the League of the Five Nations—Senecas, Onondagas, Mohawks, Cayugas, and Oneidas —to which, later, the Tuscaroras were added. The league remained united and powerful until after the American Revolution, and exists in shadowy form to this day. It struck a neat balance between sovereignty retained by each tribe and sovereignty sacrificed to the league, and as so durable and effective a union was studied by the authors of our Constitution.

The league was founded by the great leader Hiawatha. Any resemblance between the fictional hero of Longfellow's poem and this real, dead person is purely coincidental. Longfellow got hold of the name and applied it to some Chippewa legends, which he rewrote thoroughly to produce some of the purest rot and the most heavy-footed verse ever to be inflicted upon a school child.

The Iroquois lived in "long houses," which looked like extended Quonset huts sheathed in bark. Smaller versions of these, and similarly covered, domed or conical structures, are "wigwams," the typical housing of the Northeast. Many people use the word "wigwam" as synonymous with "tepee," which is incorrect. A tepee, the typical dwelling of the Plains Indians of a later period, is a functional tent, usually covered with hides or, in recent years, canvas, and one of its essential features is that it is the shelter of constantly mobile people. A tepee, incidentally, is about the most comfortable tent ever invented, winter or summer—provided you have two or three strong, competent women to attend to setting it up and striking it.

The great tribes we have been discussing showed their sophistication in a new way in their response to contact with Europeans. Their tribal organizations became tighter and firmer. From south to north they held the balance of power. The British success in establishing good relations with many of them was the key to driving the French out of the Mississippi area; to win the Revolution, the Americans had to defeat the Iroquois, whose favor up to then had determined who should dominate the Northeast. The southern tribes radically changed their costume, and quickly took over cattle, slaves, and many arts. By the time Andrew Jackson was ready to force their removal, the Cherokees had a stable government under a written constitution, with a bicameral parliament, an alphabet for writing their language, printing presses, a newspaper, schools and churches.

Had it not been for the white men's insatiable greed and utter lawlessness, this remarkable nation would have ended with a unique demonstration of how, without being conquered, a "primitive" people could adapt itself to a new civilization on its own initiative. They would have become a very rare example of how aborigines could receive solid profit from the coming of the white men.

After the five Civilized Tribes were driven to Oklahoma, they formed a union and once again set up their governments and their public schools. Of course we could not let them have what we had promised them; it turned out that we ourselves wanted that part of Oklahoma after all, so once again we tore up the treaties and destroyed their system. None the less, to this day they are a political power in the state, and when one of their principal chiefs speaks up, the congressmen do well to listen.

The tribes discussed until now and their predecessors in the same general area formed a means of transmission of higher culture to others, east and west. Their influence reached hardly at all to the northwards, as north of the Iroquois farming with native plants was difficult or impossible. On the Atlantic Coast of the United States the tribes were all more or less affected. Farming was of great importance. Even in New England, the status of chiefs was definite and fairly high. Confederacies and hegemonies, such as that of the Narragansetts over many of the Massachusetts tribes, occurred, of which more primitive people are incapable. Farther south, the state of such a chief as Powhatan was royal enough for Europeans to regard him as a king and his daughter as a true princess.

To the westward, the pattern of farming and sedentary villages extended roughly to the line that runs irregularly through Nebraska and Kansas, west of which the mean annual rainfall is below twenty inches. In wet cycles, there were prehistoric attempts to farm farther west, and in historic times the Apaches raised fair crops in the eastern foothills of the southern tip of the Rockies, but only the white men combined the mechanical equipment and the stupidity to break the turf and exhaust the soil of the dry, high plains.

An essay as short as this on so large a subject is inevitably filled with almost indefensible generalizations. I am stressing similarities, as in the case of the Iroquois-Southeast tribes, ignoring great unlikenesses. Generalizing again, we may say that the western farmers, whose cultures in fact differed enormously, also lived in fairly fixed villages. In the southern part, they built large houses covered with grass thatch. At the northwestern tip of the farming zone we find the Mandans, Hidatsa, and Crows, who lived in semi-subterranean lodges of heavy poles covered with earth, so big that later, when horses came to them, they kept their choice mounts inside. These three related, Siouan-speaking tribes living on the edge of the Plains are the first we have come to whose native costume, when white men first observed them, included the war bonnet. That was in the early Nineteenth Century; what they wore in 1600, no one knows.

The western farmers had their permanent lodges; they also had tepees. Immediately at hand was the country of the bison, awkward game for men on foot to hunt with lance and bow, but too fine a source of meat to ignore. On their hunting expeditions they took the conical tents. The size of the tepees was limited, for the heavy covers and the long poles had to be dragged either by the women or by dogs. Tepee life at that time was desirable only for a short time, when one roughed it.

The second area of Meso-American influence was the Southwest, as anthropologists define it—the present states of New Mexico and Arizona, a little of the adjacent part of Mexico, and various extensions at different times to the north, west, and east. We do not find here the striking resemblances to Meso-America in numbers of culture traits we find in the Southeast; the influence must have been much more indirect, ideas and objects passing in the course of trade from tribe to tribe over the thousand miles or so of desert northern Mexico.

In the last few thousand years the Southwest has been pretty dry, although not as dry as it is today. A dry climate and a sandy soil make an archaeologist's paradise. We can trace to some extent the actual transition from hunting and gathering to hunting plus farming, the appearance of the first permanent dwellings, the beginning of pottery-making, at least the latter part of the transition from twining and basketry to true weaving. Anthropologists argue over the very use of the term "Southwest" to denote a single area, because of the enormous variety of the cultures found within it. There is a certain unity, none the less, centering around beans, corn, squashes, tobacco, cotton, democracy, and a preference for peace. Admitting the diversity, the vast differences between, say, the Hopi and Pima farmers, we can still think of it as a single area, and for purposes of this essay concentrate on the best-studied of its cultures, the Pueblos.

The name "Pueblo" is the Spanish for "village," and was given to that people because they lived—and live—in compact, defensible settlements of houses with walls of stone laid up with adobe mortar or entirely of adobe. Since the Spanish taught them how to make rectangular bricks, pure adobe construction has become the commoner type. They already had worked out the same roofing as was usual in Asia Minor and around the Mediterranean in ancient times. A modern Pueblo house corresponds almost exactly to the construction of buildings dating back at least as far as 600 B.C. in Asia Minor.

The Pueblos, and their neighbors, the Navahos, have become well enough known in recent years to create some exception to the popular stereotype of Indians. It is generally recognized that they do not wear feathers and that they possess many arts, and that the Pueblos are sedentary farmers.

Farming has long been large in their pattern of living, and hunting perhaps less important than with any people outside the Southwest. Their society is genuinely classless, in contrast to that of the Southeast. Before the Spanish conquest, they were governed by a theocracy. Each tribe was tightly organized, every individual placed in his niche. The power of the theocracy was, and in some Pueblos still is, tyrannical in appearance. Physical punishment was used to suppress the rebellious; now more often a dissident member is subjected to a form of being sent to Coventry. If he be a member of the tribal council, anything he says at meetings is pointedly ignored. If he has some ceremonial function, he performs it, but otherwise he is left in isolation. I have seen a once self-assertive man, who for a time had been a strong leader in his tribe, subjected to this treatment for several years. By my estimation he lost some thirty pounds, and he became a quiet conformist.

The power of the theocracy was great, but it rested on the consent of the governed. No man could overstep his authority, no one man had final authority. It went hard with the individual dissident, but the will of the people controlled all.

The Pueblos had many arts, most of which still continue. They wove cotton, made handsome pottery, did fine work in shell. Their ceremonies were spectacular and beautiful. They had no system of torture and no cult of warfare. A good warrior was respected, but what they wanted was peace.

The tight organization of the Pueblo tribes and the absolute authority over individuals continues now among only a few of them. The loosening is in part the result of contact with whites, in part for the reason that more and more they are building their houses outside of the old, solid blocks of the villages, simply because they are no longer under constant, urgent need for defense.

It is irony that the peace-loving southwestern farmers were surrounded by the worst raiders of all the wild tribes of North America. Around A.D. 1100 or 1200 there began filtering in among them bands of primitives, possessors of a very simple culture, who spoke languages of the Athabascan stock. These people had drifted down from western Canada. In the course of time they became the Navahos and the Apaches. For all their poverty, they possessed a sinew-backed bow of Asiatic type that was superior to any missile weapon known to the Southwest. They traded with the Pueblos, learned from them, stole from them, raided them. As they grew stronger, they became pests. The Navahos and the northeastern branch of the Apaches, called Jicarilla Apaches, learned farming. The Navahos in time became artists, above all the finest of weavers, but they did not give up their raiding habits.

These Athabascans did not glorify war. They made a business of it. Killing enemies was incidental; in fact, a man who killed an enemy had to be purified afterwards. They fought for profit, and they were about the only North Americans whose attitude towards war resembled that of the professional soldier. This did not make them any the less troublesome.

The last high culture area occupied a narrow strip along the Pacific Coast, from northern California across British Columbia to southern Alaska, the Northwest Coast culture. There was no Meso-American influence here, nor was there any farming. The hunting and fishing were so rich, the supply of edible wild plants so adequate, that there was no need for farming—for which in any case the climate was unfavorable. The prerequisite for cultural progress is a food supply so lavish that either all men have spare time, or some men can specialize in non-food-producing activities while others feed them. This condition obtained on the Northwest Coast, where men caught the water creatures from whales to salmon, and hunted deer, mountain sheep, and other game animals.

The area was heavily forested with the most desirable kinds of lumber. Hence wood and bark entered largely into the culture. Bark was shredded and woven into clothing, twined into nets, used for padding. Houses, chests, dishes, spoons, canoes, and boats were made of wood. The people became carvers and woodworkers, then carried their carving over onto bone and horn. They painted their houses, boats, chests, and their elaborate wooden masks. They made wooden armor, including visored helmets, and deadly wooden clubs. In a wet climate, they made raincloaks of bark and wore basketry hats, on the top of which could be placed one or more cylinders, according to the wearer's rank. The chiefs placed carvings in front of their houses that related their lineage, tracing back utlimately to some sacred being such as Raven or Bear—the famous, so-called totem poles.

I have said that the finest prehistoric art of North America was that of the Mound Builders; in fact, no Indian work since has quite equaled it—but that is, of course, a matter of taste. The greatest historic Indian art was that of the Northwest Coast. Their carvings, like the Mound Builder sculptures, demand comparison with our own work. Their art was highly stylized, but vigorous and fresh. As for all Indians, the coming of the white men meant ruin in the end, but at first it meant metal tools, the possession of which resulted in a great artistic outburst.

Socially they were divided into chiefs, commoners, and slaves. Slaves were obtained by capture, and slave-raiding was one of the principal causes of war. Generosity was the pattern with most Indians, although in the dry Southwest we find some who made a virtue of thrift. In the main, a man was respected because he gave, not because he possessed. The Northwest Coast chiefs patterned generosity into an ugliness. A chief would invite a rival to a great feast, the famous potlatch. At the feast he would shower his rival and other guests with gifts, especially copper disks and blankets woven of mountain sheep wool, which were the highest units of value. He might further show his lavishness by burning some possessions, even partially destroy a copper disk, and, as like as not, kill a few slaves.

If within a reasonable time the other chief did not reply with an even larger feast, at which he gave away or destroyed double what his rival had got rid of, he was finished as a chief—but if he did respond in proper form, he might be beggared, and also finished. That was the purpose of the show. Potlatches were given for other purposes, such as to authenticate the accession of the heir to a former chief, or to buy a higher status, but ruinous rivalry was constant. They seem to have been a rather disagreeable, invidious, touchy people. The cruelty of the southeasterners is revolting, but there is something especially unpleasant about proving one's generosity and carelessness of possessions by killing a slave—with a club made for that special purpose and known as a "slave-killer."

The Meso-American culture could spread, changing beyond recognition as it did so, because it carried its food supply with it. The Northwest Coast culture could not, because its food supply was restricted to its place of origin.

North and east of the Northwest Coast area stretched the sub-Arctic and the plains of Canada, areas incapable of primitive farming. To the south and east were mountains and the region between the Rockies and the Coastal ranges called the Great Basin. Within it are large stretches of true desert; most of it is arid. Early on, Pueblo influences reached into the southern part, in Utah and Nevada, but as the climate grew drier, they died away. It was a land to be occupied by little bands of simple hunters and gatherers of seeds and roots, not strong enough to force their way into anywhere richer.

In only one other area was there a natural food supply to compare with the Northwest Coast's, and that was in the bison range of the Great Plains. But, as already noted, for men without horses or rifles, hunting bison was a tricky and hazardous business. Take the year 1600, when the Spanish were already established in New Mexico and the English and French almost ready to make settlements on the East Coast, and look for the famous Plains tribes. They are not there. Some are in the mountains, some in the woodlands to the northeast, some farming to the eastward, within the zone of ample rainfall. Instead we find scattered bands of Athabascans occupying an area no one else wanted.

Then the white men turned everything upside down. Three elements were most important in the early influence: the dislodgment of eastern tribes, the introduction of the horse, and metal tools and firearms. Let us look first at the impact on the centers of high culture.

White men came late to the Northwest Coast, and at first only as traders. As already noted, early contact with them enriched the life of the

Indians and brought about a cultural spurt. Then came settlers. The most advanced, best organized tribes stood up fairly well against them for a time, and they are by no means extinct, but of their old culture there are now only remnants, with the strongest survivals being in the arts. Today, those Indians who are in the "Indian business," making money from tourists, dress in fringed buckskin and war bonnets, because otherwise the tourists will not accept them as genuine.

The tribes of the Atlantic Coast were quickly dislodged or wiped out. The more advanced groups farther inland held out all through colonial times and on into the 1830's, making fairly successful adjustments to the changed situation, retaining their sovereignty, and enriching their culture with wholesale taking over of European elements, including, in the South, the ownership of Negro slaves. Finally, as already noted, they were forcibly removed to Oklahoma, and in the end their sovereignty was destroyed. They remain numerous, and although some are extremely poor and backward, others, still holding to their tribal affiliations, have merged successfully into the general life of the state, holding positions as high as chief justice of the state supreme court. The Iroquois still hold out in New York and in Canada on remnants of their original reservations. Many of them have had remarkable success in adapting themselves to white American life while retaining considerable elements of their old culture. Adherents to the old religion are many, and the rituals continue vigorously.

The British invaders of the New World, and to a lesser degree the French, came to colonize. They came in thousands, to occupy the land. They were, therefore, in direct competition with the Indians and acted accordingly, despite their verbal adherence to fine principles of justice and fair dealing. The Spanish came quite frankly to conquer, to Christianize, and to exploit, all by force of arms. They did not shilly-shally about Indian title to the land or Indian sovereignty, they simply took over, then granted the Indians titles deriving from the Spanish crown. They came in small numbers—only around 3,000 settled in the Southwest—and the Indian labor force was essential to their aims. Therefore they did not dislodge or exterminate the Indians, and they had notable success in modifying Indian culture for survival within their regime and contribution to it.

In the Southwest the few Spaniards, cut off from the main body in Mexico by many miles of difficult, wild country, could not have survived alone against the wild tribes that shortly began to harry them. They needed the Pueblo Indians and the Pueblos needed them. The Christian Pueblos were made secure in their lands and in their local self-government. They approached social and political equality. During the period when New Mexico was under the Mexican Republic, for two years a Taos

Indian, braids, blanket, and all, was governor of the territory. Eighteen pueblos survive to this day, with a population now approaching 19,000, in addition to nearly 4,000 Hopis, whose culture is Pueblo, in Arizona. They are conservative progressives, prosperous on the whole, with an excellent chance of surviving as a distinctive group for many generations to come. It was in the house of a Pueblo priest, a man deeply versed in the old religion as well as a devout Catholic, that I first saw color television.

The Spanish, then, did not set populations in motion. That was done chiefly from the east. The great Spanish contribution was loosing the horses. They did not intend to; in fact they made every possible effort to prevent Indians from acquiring horses or learning to ride. But the animals multiplied and ran wild; they spread north from California into Oregon; they spread into the wonderful grazing land of the high Plains, a country beautifully suited to horses.

From the east, the tribes were pressing against the tribes farther west. Everything was in unhappy motion, and the tribes nearest to the white men had firearms. So the Chippewas, carrying muskets, pushed westward into Minnesota, driving the reluctant Dakotas, the Sioux tribes, out of the wooded country into the Plains as the horses spread north. At first the Dakotas hunted and ate the strange animals, then they learned to ride them, and they were off.

The Sioux were mounted. So were the Blackfeet. The semi-civilized Cheyennes swung into the saddle and moved out of the farming country onto the bison range. The Kiowas moved from near the Yellowstone to the Panhandle; the Comanches came down out of the Rocky Mountains; the Arapahos, the Crows, abandoning their cornfields, and the Piegans, the great fighting names, all followed the bison. They built their life around the great animals. They ate meat lavishly all year round; their tepees, carried or dragged now by horses, became commodious. A new culture, a horse-and-bison culture, sprang up overnight. The participants in it had a wonderful time. They feasted, they roved, they hunted, they played. Over a serious issue, such as the invasion of one tribe's territory by another, they could fight deadly battles, but otherwise even war was a game in which shooting an enemy was an act earning but little esteem, but touching one with one's bare hand or with a stick was the height of military achievement.

This influx of powerful tribes drove the last of the Athabascans into the Southwest. There the Apaches and the Navahos were also mounted and on the go, developing their special, deadly pattern of war as a business. In the Panhandle country, the Kiowas and Comanches looked westward to the Spanish and Pueblo settlements, where totally alien peoples offered rich plunder. The Pueblos, as we have seen, desired to live at peace. The original Spanish came to conquer; their descendants, becoming Spanish-

Americans, were content to hold what they had, farm their fields, and graze their flocks. To the north of the two groups were Apaches and Utes; to the east, Kiowas and Comanches; to the south, what seemed like unlimited Apaches; and to the west the Navahos, of whom there were several thousands by the middle of the Seventeenth Century.

The tribes named above, other than the Kiowas and Comanches, did not share in the Plains efflorescence. The Navahos staged a different cultural spurt of their own, combining extensive farming with constant horseback plundering, which in turn enabled them to become herdsmen, and from the captured wool develop their remarkable weaving industry. The sheep, of course, which became important in their economy, also derived from the white men. Their prosperity and their arts were superimposed on a simple camp life. With this prosperity, they also developed elaborate rituals and an astoundingly rich, poetic mythology.

The Dakotas first saw horses in 1722, which makes a convenient peg date for the beginning of the great Plains culture. A little over a hundred years later, when Catlin visited the Mandans, it was going full blast. The memory of a time before horses had grown dim. By 1860 the Plains tribes were hard-pressed to stand the white men off; by 1880 the whole pattern was broken and the bison were gone. At its height, Plains Indian culture was brittle. Materially, it depended absolutely on a single source of food and skins; in other aspects, it required the absolute independence of the various tribes. When these two factors were eliminated, the content was destroyed. Some Indians may still live in tepees, wear at times their traditional clothing, maintain here and there their arts and some of their rituals, but these are little more than fringe survivals.

While the Plains culture died, the myth of it spread and grew to become embedded in our folklore. Not only the Northwest Coast Indians but many others as unlikely wear imitations of Plains Indian costume and put on "war dances," to satisfy the believers in the myth. As it exists today in the public mind, it still contains the mutually incongruous elements of the Noble Red Man and the Bloodthirsty Savage that first came into being three centuries and a half ago, before any white man had ever seen a war bonnet or a tepee, or any Indian had ridden a horse.

3 *Roy F. Nichols*

ENGLISH ORIGINS OF AMERICAN POLITICS

That America is a child of Europe in general and of England in particular is a cliché of textbooks in American history. But an understandable concern with the progeny leads the textbooks to a regrettable neglect of the progenitor. The story of the transit of cultures from the
English motherland to the eastern seaboard of the North American
continent is thus only partly told. Hardly enough attention is paid to
the sound advice of our colonial historians, and especially of one of
the greatest of them, Charles M. Andrews, that American history
ought to begin at home—in England.

The special virtue of the following essay by Professor Roy F.
Nichols is that it heeds this advice. Dean of the Graduate School of the
University of Pennsylvania, Professor Nichols is most widely known
for his works on the Democratic party during the decade before the
Civil War. He was invited to serve as Pitt Professor of American History and Institutions at Trinity College, Cambridge, during the year
1948–49, and it was then that he developed his interest in the English
origins of American politics.

In explaining these origins, the essay which follows undertakes to
answer a series of interrelated questions: What profound changes were
at work in English religious ideas and institutions during the sixteenth
century? How was an essentially religious development transmuted
into one of great political consequence? How did social and economic
discontent contribute to the newer political orientation of the English
people? What significance did these tendencies have for the society
founded at the beginning of the seventeenth century in America? Professor Nichols opens his analysis with the ideas of the Reformation
which were stirring in early sixteenth-century England. He pursues his
theme with a discussion of the religious policy of the Tudors, the
interplay of religious and political sentiments within parishes, the expression of this interplay in Parliament, the role of the Puritans, the
impact of social and economic problems, and the broadcasting of the
newer ideas by means of English expansion to distant parts of the
world. In his excellent portrayal of the ferment of sixteenth-century
England, Professor Nichols discloses how a medieval country was
transformed into the matrix of American democracy.

The transformation and its aftermath are part of a historical
process which poses many challenging problems. What was the effect

Reprinted with permission from *The Pennsylvania Magazine of History and
Biography*, LXXVI (January, 1952), 5–29.

of environment, for example, upon the evolution of the liberal ideal for which the radical Protestants in England were fighting? Was it not inevitable that within the American context the ideal would become, as Edmund Burke put it, "the dissidence of dissent"? To what degree was this same ideal the cause of a century of revolution in England and how much was it transformed by the pressure of already established institutions and ideas during the course of that century? One cannot probe very far into the English origins of American politics without also asking about the nature and importance of non-English origins. One would wish to know, moreover, to what extent the growth of English radical Protestantism was part of larger European developments which would be linked to it in the formation of American political ideals and institutions.

These are the challenging questions implicit in what Professor Nichols is saying. The problem, then, is not merely one of understanding the birth of an idea. It is also one of understanding the transformation of the idea—to use Ariel's words, its "sea change into something rich and strange."

I

In the ancient English university town of Cambridge at the opening of the sixteenth century was an inconspicuous place of public entertainment known as the White Horse Inn. This hostelry stood back from the High Street, not far from Queen's College and separated from King's by the narrow filth of Plute's Lane. It had the advantage for certain purposes of being off the beaten track. Those wishing to enter unobserved might approach it, particularly in the dark of night, from the rear along the Backs where flowed the silent Cam, and slip in by a side door. To a number of alert Cambridge students who were discussing new and forbidden ideas in 1521, the White Horse Inn was a convenient gathering place for clandestine meetings.

For ten years there had been increasing intellectual curiosity at the University about the new concepts which were destined to change much in English life. The Dutch teacher Erasmus, who had been in residence at Queen's for three fruitful years, had opened the minds of many who heard his lectures on the meaning of the New Testament. These followers of Erasmus undertook to read the Bible with new understanding and inspiration. Recently, the more revolutionary ideas preached by Luther had come out of Germany, and his writings had become a center of discussion. Since the German preachments attacked the government and practices of the Church, Henry VIII, who was not only King of England but also Defender of the Faith, refused to tolerate such heresies. Luther's works, therefore, had been burned at St. Paul's in London in May, 1521, and not long after, during the Easter term, at Cambridge. Cambridge scholars were forbidden to read Luther's books.

But ideas were not easily killed in Cambridge. A vigorous group among the scholars and students were East Anglians, who had come across the fens and broads from Norfolk and Suffolk, bringing with them a sturdy atmosphere of independence and turbulence. Some had come from the cathedral city of Norwich.

Norwich, the capital of Norfolk, was encircled by a low range of hills in the valley of the Wensom where the river Yare joins its kindred stream. Even as late as the thirteenth century the city still stood at the head of a great estuary to which vessels put in from the German ocean. It was a natural landing place for Dutch and German traders and in earlier days had been the favorite approach of Teutonic invaders.

Dominated by its magnificent cathedral, and protected by its castle, Norwich had lived a feverish, frequently disturbed existence. For East Anglia, stretching out into the German ocean and separated from the rest of the realm by marshes and fenlands, was a corner far removed from most of England. The inhabitants of this region had been conditioned by their danger and their isolation into a headstrong and truculent people. Indeed, its lords had made it even more remote by building across the narrow isthmus of firm, dry land connecting it with England a great rampart, called the Devil's Dyke.

Religious and political activity were pronounced in East Anglia—it was said that there was a church in Norwich for every week in the year. Outside the city in a hollow beneath the hill on which St. Leonard's Priory stood was a spot known as the Lollard's Pit, where religious reformers had been martyred by fire. It was at Norwich, too, that Wat Tyler had raised his standard of revolt. The students from this enterprising and vital society who came across the fenland to Cambridge were not men to give up ideas merely because of royal fiat.

Norfolk men from Corpus, from Trinity Hall, and from Gonville's College picked their way silently in the dark through "detestable and filthy" Plute's Lane to enter the White Horse Inn by the hidden door. Here in "Little Germany," as it was called, under the chairmanship of a Norfolk cleric, Robert Barnes, prior of the community of Augustan friars at Cambridge, they discussed the new religious concepts. The Norfolk men were prepared for these ideas, since some of them had already received an indoctrination from German merchants, supercargoes, and ship captains who put into Great Yarmouth and came on to Norwich. They were also aware that the Oxford scholar Tyndale was working on an English translation of the Bible, and it is possible that Tyndale may have visited with them. Thus they were ready to talk, and the more they talked over the newly interpreted words of the Gospels, the more they realized how far the Church had departed from them. There must be reform, they concluded, well knowing that the whole force of hierarchy, government, and social inertia would be against them. One of the youths who left the White House charged with the burning impress of new ideas to return to Norwich was known affectionately as "Little Bilney."

In his home county Bilney sought to distribute the New Testament in English and went among the people sharing his revolutionary thoughts. His superior, Bishop Nix, could tolerate no such activity, and in 1531 brave Bilney was burned to death in the Lollard's Pit. But the flames that destroyed Bilney's body, however, lighted another torch that was to flare so all could see.

Once again the spirit of religious zeal for reform was abroad—heresy, some called it—like that which had last been stirred by the Lollards in the fourteenth and fifteenth centuries. The White Horse Inn gatherings had counterparts elsewhere; the spirit of Lollardy driven underground began to respond, and other fires were set. All told, these primarily religious influences were to open a new epoch in political behavior.

In this era to come, society was to participate in its own governance on a grander scale than men had heretofore dreamed. The power of those governing was to be limited and directed by public opinion to a degree hitherto unknown. The will of a haphazard variety of citizens of high and low degree was to be expressed and recorded by mechanisms which were constantly to be adjusted, augmented, and rebuilt, which were ever to be the object of restudy and experiment, particularly by those who sought devices that might more accurately capture and record the popular will. The right of humble individuals who had no claim to distinction to express opinions about those in power and to have a voice not only in shaping their policies, but also in determining whether they were to continue to exercise power, although not altogether a new concept in the world, had hardly been experimented with in any large population. Experiments were now to begin on a grand scale.

This democratic ideal burst forth in England with some force in the sixteenth century and was re-emphasized at a time and under conditions which permitted experiment in the America just discovered. The active, inquiring scholars from East Anglia, gathered around their table in the Cambridge inn, represented an attitude which was to become more frequently discernible in England in the sixteenth century and to which American Democracy was to owe much of its essential quality.

What these men were investigating, clothed as it was in religious terms, was a new concept of the relation of the individual to society—a concept which would shortly involve the question of the nature and power of government and the source of its authority. A new politics based upon new types of thought and action was in the making. The extent to which

new institutional concepts and behavior patterns could be experimented
with was enlarged, yet at the same time it was limited by the characteristics of English politics. It was eventually realized that the full force of
these ideas and attitudes could be developed only in an environment in
which institutions were less crystallized than in England. America was to
prove a convenient laboratory.

II

The ideas discussed by the scholars at the White Horse and circulated by
men like Bilney were of revolutionary purport. In reality, they questioned,
if not too apparently, the long-accepted pattern of English social order
and aroused antagonistic and divisive attitudes. The resulting controversy
was to create a new political behavior, the central mechanism of which
would be a kind of democratic partisanship. Ideas emphasizing the independence, the worth, and the equality of individuals as children of God
and joint heirs with Christ, challenged the prevailing modes of political
and social thought and organization. For English society had long been
stratified, each man born to a station in which he was supposed to remain.
It was intended that he accept his lot and follow the ancient patterns
which divided classes into the elite and the unprivileged.

The ecclesiastical hierarchy played a leading part among the elite because the Church was the accepted master of man's conduct and could
prescribe his destiny; the Church was even more implanted in his life
than the government. By confession, penance, and admonition, the Church
did much to define his status in this life and assign it in the next. Through
the seven sacraments the Church kept intimate watch over his life from
birth to death. He was to worship the mystery of the Trinity and give
implicit obedience to the priesthood; between God and man were the
hierarchy, the images, the vestments, the incense, the Latin chants—even
His Word was kept in Latin. Man could gain access to God only through
intercession.

At the beginning of the sixteenth century, many Englishmen were
dissatisfied with this religious situation. As they became increasingly
aware of the New Learning and humanism of the Renaissance and the
new exaltation of the independence and capacity of man, they became
less inclined to their subordinate status. Other dissatisfactions, however,
were more concrete and less subtle: the clergy too often were lax in their
behavior and careless of their responsibilities; some clergymen, particularly
those in monasteries, had acquired great wealth and had capital hoards as
well as landed estates. Corrupt and surfeited with wealth, the Church was
believed by some to be unworthy of its social power and influence. Furthermore, churchmen, bound to Rome, were often foremost in government. Much English money went to Rome, and English foreign policy and

even domestic affairs were shaped for the interests of the Papacy. The Church, therefore, seemed to frustrate or hinder at least three concepts of the day—humanism, capitalism, and nationalism.

Change of some sort became inevitable, and Henry VIII was shrewd enough to realize it and turn it to his advantage. A little more than a decade after the burning of the books and the White Horse meetings, the Crown and Parliament sufficiently associated themselves with the Lutheran revolt to nationalize the Church, assume control of its organization, and seize much of its property. But the English government paid little heed to the doctrinal controversies which were so much a part of the Protestant revolt in western Europe, and left matters of doctrine and liturgy much as they had been under the Roman order. It was in this field, however, that those who were not content with limited changes began to challenge the government.

Too many were familiar with the ideas of Luther, Zwingli, Calvin and other leaders of the Continental Reformation to be satisfied with the narrow limits of the doctrinal changes which the English government had made in the first half of the century. Opportunity for any further progress altered decidedly, however, when Mary ascended the throne and sought to restore the Church to its full Roman relationship. So intense was her zeal that several hundred Protestants who refused to accept the old order were burned at the stake. Many of the leaders of the Henrician and Edwardian reforms migrated to the Continent to mobilize and plan at Frankfurt, Zurich, Geneva and elsewhere. Others went "underground" to organize "resistance." But upon Mary's death and the accession of Elizabeth, the political potentialities of the religious situation began to be realized.

During the Marian exile many gained experience in new and independent forms of church organization and government. One group had established a congregation at the Weissfrauenkirche in Frankfurt, another at Strassburg. In Zurich a third group of leaders had lived in Pastor Bullinger's manse under the shadow of the Grossmünster. At Geneva others had listened to Calvin preach at the great cathedral, or had listened to their own ministers, notably John Knox, at the Temple de l'Auditoire close by. They had corresponded, visited, counseled, engaged in controversy, and some had written propaganda books which had a furtive circulation in England. They had openly questioned royal authority and justified popular resistance to tyranny. John Ponet, erstwhile Bishop of Winchester, published *A Short Treatise of Politike Power*. Christopher Goodman wrote *How Superior Powers Oght To Be Obeyd*, which seconded and re-enforced Ponet's argument, and John Knox blew his *First Blast of the Trumpet against the Monstrous Regiment of Women*. The more radical of the exiles had worked out a new church organization, in which pastors and elders were to have much more importance in the general governance of the English Church and presumably much more freedom of action in ordering the form of worship. Preaching was to supersede liturgy in importance. The exiles were eagerly awaiting the day when they might return to England to admonish a new sovereign and to advise how best to put their ideas into effect; they expected the chief seats in a new hierarchy which would "Genevate" the Church of England.

No sooner had word of Mary's death reached the Protestant cities on the Continent than the exiles hurried back to England hoping to receive from Elizabeth the authority to set up their new order. Their plan—a basic constitutional change—was to diminish the royal power and the authority of the bishops in matters ecclesiastical. But Elizabeth was her father's daughter; she was of no mind to tolerate such radical changes.

She was, indeed, in a difficult position. Her father's excesses, her brother's minority reign, her sister's religious and matrimonial alliance with Rome and Spain had all weakened popular confidence in the throne. The monarchy was shaky. Elizabeth knew that vigorous religious re-organization, such as the exiles had in mind, would stir up strife which she could ill afford. Hence, she realized she must act with caution. She herself had slight interest in religion, but she well understood that she had to maintain her own place and strengthen her power in religious matters. She realized also that placing the parishes in charge of independent priests and elders would take from her hands valuable instruments of government and would create a situation which might be difficult, if not impossible, for her and her bishops to control.

As soon as Elizabeth was proclaimed Queen in November, 1558, a battle of propaganda began. The restored Roman bishops of Mary's reign had anticipated what was coming and had sought to organize against it. At Mary's funeral one of her prelates had warned the throng that "The wolves would be coming out of Geneva . . . and have sent their books before, full of pestilent doctrines, blasphemy and heresy, to infect the people." The Roman bishops and their priests continued earnest in their preaching. Other priests who wished for a return of the Edwardian liturgy urged a middle way, while the returning exiles and the emerging underground forces sought a new order. Nor was preaching confined to the churches. Religious enthusiasts without parishes or pulpits, "gospellers," as they were called, were exhorting wherever they could gain a circle of listeners. Elizabeth, fully realizing the danger of this, decided that Parliament, not the pulpit, was to be the forum. In December, by royal proclamation, she forbade preaching; religious services were to be solely liturgical for the time being. Forthwith she summoned Parliament.

Like her father, Elizabeth was clever in understanding the uses of Parliament. When that body met she discovered that there was in the Commons a strong exile group ardently interested in the effort to Genevate the

Church. On the other hand, she found a Catholic party in the House of Lords where Mary's bishops attended in force. Elizabeth moved skillfully to secure the repeal of the return to Rome, which Mary had obtained after so much difficulty. English nationalism wanted no Romish control. The Queen would have been content merely to restore things as her father had left them, but, pushed by the exiles, she had to accept provisions which acknowledged her as Supreme Governor of the Church, not its Supreme Head, and an Act of Uniformity prescribing a new English prayer book. A bill which would have enabled Elizabeth to restore those bishops and priests who had been deprived of their positions during Mary's day failed by reason, probably, of the Catholic influence in the House of Lords.

Despite this compromise, Elizabeth did gain the ecclesiastical power which her father had had, but she was cautious in using it. She contented herself with sending commissioners throughout England to administer the oath, which, of course, could not be taken by Mary's Catholic leaders, although most of the lesser clergy accepted it. Elizabeth now could begin to appoint her bishops. Once again the word was caution, and men of moderate views willing to co-operate with the Queen received the most important positions.

The moderate policy of the Crown and Parliament was a grievous disappointment to many. Those sharing the ideas of the exiles refused to be content and began a course of action which was to have repercussions decidedly political in character. Controversy over policy, over basic institutional patterns, was going to permeate the realm.

III

Each parish in this period became a potential seat of controversy in which religion and politics were thoroughly intermingled. The institution of religion was so vitally connected with the life of most people in every community that almost everyone had an opinion about it and expressed it. Undoubtedly in some parishes the Church became a center of debate and of something akin to politics, for the essence of politics is the expression of opinion about power and policy governing the behavior of society. Many Englishmen had something to say and did not believe in hiding their lights under bushels.

Although the theme of the controversy was religious, it was also markedly political, because there was no very clear distinction between state and church. In fact, so closely were they connected that the parish was the fundamental unit and instrument both of civil government and ecclesiastical polity. The Church of God was not only the seat of worship, it was also, in the rural districts at least, the seat of government. There the vestry meetings were held, there the churchwardens assessed some of the local taxes. Then, too, other religious institutions—the priories, monasteries, chantries and guilds—had been an integral part of the civic life of the people. Charity had been dispensed, sickness cared for, and recreation provided by these agencies; people had looked to them so long for so much.

Now basic changes were in process. Monasteries, chantries, and guilds had been disbanded. The Church had been nationalized. There were new ideas about the service. Many were no longer interested in adoring mysteries and blindly obeying priestly injunctions: they had begun reading the Bible, now available in English; they wanted to hear expository preaching. All told, there was much to talk about, and most of it was controversial. Naturally, it was to be in the parish that the greater part of this controversy was to take place. Something very like politics began to permeate the vestry.

The center of the most active controversy was the nature of the church service. Should the images be torn out, should candles and incense be abandoned? Should the altar become a communion table and be placed in the center of the church? Should the rood and screen be pulled down and the crucifix laid aside? Should the priests abandon vestments? Should they preach more? All these questions produced differences of opinion, and when it came time to choose the churchwardens, there might well be contests dictated by such differences of opinion.

It must not be forgotten that the questions of who should direct vestry policy and who should be churchwardens were coming to mean more in community life just about this time. Originally, vestries had merely managed the minutiae of keeping the church in repair, of providing proper vestments and supplies for the service. For these expenses the churchwardens had levied rates or taxes, but now new functions were added. When the monasteries and charitable guilds were eliminated by the government, those who had taken care of the poor were deprived of their means. Furthermore, such economic policies as enclosing small farms to make sheep pastures and debasing the coinage had caused unemployment, higher prices, and more poverty. Some new provision had to be made for poor relief, and in Elizabeth's reign this responsibility was assigned to the parishes. The churchwardens and the justices of the peace were now required to support the unfortunate by assessment. The parishes were also given the new obligation of maintaining highways. Thus the churchwardens and vestrymen became economically as well as religiously responsible, and ambitions for securing these offices may have become more active.

The center of parish discussion and often its leader was, of course, the clergyman. Here, too, was to be found a diversity of opinion. The decades since the first new religious policies instituted by Henry VIII's government had witnessed a considerable change in the personnel of the clergy:

some had fled, others had been forced out of their offices, and, more important, perhaps, fewer young men had undertaken to enter the priesthood. Thus when a parish priest died, there was frequently no successor at hand. There was, in fact, in the early days of Elizabeth's reign, such a dearth of clergymen that "many of the laity who were competently learned, and of sobriety and good religion, were appointed to read the service in the churches." This opened the way for more lay participation in parish governance; often laymen were moved to preach and to give their views on the controversial issues of order and doctrine. Elizabeth, as we have seen, soon forbade them to preach, but their zeal was not always bound by this order.

Early in Elizabeth's reign a number of the exiles resumed their livings and sought to lead their parishioners in the new ways. Some of them appeared without vestments and used the Geneva prayer book. Their activities were encouraged during the 1560's when a number of French Huguenots and Dutch Protestants fled from the Continent and brought their experiences to aid the parishioners. Many of the new Tudor nobility and country gentlemen, rivals of the old Catholic families, were in sympathy with the religious changes, and as they had "livings" to bestow, gave them to clergymen and divinity students of Geneva sympathy. Upon occasion there was tumult and forceful expression.

In tempestuous Norwich these differences of opinion reached such a pitch that in the cathedral itself five of the prebendaries put on an antiritual demonstration, marched into the choir, shouted down the singers and finally broke up the organ. At another time a Puritan student fresh from Cambridge got up in the midst of evensong and read a new form of service. The controversy was heightened by the fact that the local country gentry in Norfolk did not like Puritanism, which they associated with the influx of foreigners into Norwich, there being 4,000 Flemings in the town. An antiforeign conspiracy was begun to drive them out.

Now and then "crazy" prophets rode the streets of Norwich claiming to speak God's messages. Anabaptists and members of a sect known as the Family of Love were fervent in their professions, opposing baptism of children and proclaiming that the godly could not sin. Other sectarians appeared who went so far as to advocate communism in goods and disbelief in sin and the law.

All this variety of new doctrine and custom was arousing widespread popular interest, giving people opinions which they were increasingly intent upon expressing. There was, consequently, a greater determination to increase the activity of laymen in parish government. The civil magistrates, well aware of this trend, realized that the new popular interest in government was a force to be reckoned with. The magistrates found themselves frequently in a strange position, because in many instances they were en-

deavoring to take over functions which had hitherto belonged to ecclesiastical courts. Some of their perquisites also brought them into close association with church vestries, since the magistrates as local gentry often
possessed the right to appoint priests to local parishes. Parishes themselves
were gaining more power over the appointment of their clergymen. Occasionally, influential parishioners purchased the right to bestow livings
from local landholders. In other cases, parish authorities assumed such
rights on the ground that the right recently held by neighboring abbeys had
lapsed when those foundations had been abolished by Henry VIII. Such
enterprising and independent parishes were usually interested in appoint-
ing priests of the new school.

Parish independence and increased lay participation in management
and discussion were encouraged by a new feature appearing in this troubled
time. The lack of educated clergy had led certain of the authorities in
cathedrals and large town parishes to organize discussion groups to which
the less-educated clergy and interested laymen might come for information, scriptural interpretation, or religious doctrine. This activity was
called "prophesying." Frequently, on some weekdays, large groups of interested people from the surrounding region would come in to listen or
to ask questions. This procedure naturally encouraged expression, argument, and controversy. Before long the implications of such free discussion
became disturbing, and Elizabeth and some of her bishops tried to discourage it. But it was too congenial to those who were becoming increasingly articulate on religion, and some of the bishops and many clerics encouraged the practice. These prophesyings strengthened the Puritan
tendency to manage parish affairs locally, upon occasion in defiance of
central authority.

But local enterprise went farther than this. The old practice of operating underground in complete independence was continued. Groups who
were dissatisfied with local parish conditions seceded, and Elizabeth had only
been seven years on the throne when independent organization began. The
custom during the terror of Mary of meeting in private houses or secular
buildings was resumed; people formed their own organizations, elected
their officers, chose their pastors, and drafted covenants or constitutions.
Such clandestine groups were illegal and invited punishment, but their
members were not afraid of being sent to jail. Later in Elizabeth's reign
they suffered banishment and some were even burned to death. These
liberals had the intelligence, the faith, and the courage for independent
action.

A great divisive issue was before the English people, an issue of more
general appeal than any other since the Norman Conquest. This issue was
charged with all kinds of emotional power, involving not only questions
of intimate personal concern in this world, but in the next as well. Could

government compose this issue by law, administrative practice, and influence? Government had tried several experiments since the issue was presented, but to date none had succeeded very long. There are certain popular attitudes which do not yield readily to government fiat.

IV

The ensuing struggle was to be fought out not only in the parishes, but it was to rise constantly in Parliament and create new patterns of political behavior in that body. The arrangement which Elizabeth worked out with her first Parliament was too moderate to satisfy the new zealots. Those who desired more fundamental changes, even though they concentrated their first efforts in the parishes, were inevitably going to raise the issue again in Parliament. Those who wished greater changes naturally sought a hearing in the national law-making body.

The method of parliamentary election in Elizabeth's time was still simple. The shire representatives were elected by all those males who possessed a forty-shilling freehold, and they came together at the call of the sheriff at the shire hall in the county town and there voted viva voce. As a matter of fact, local noblemen and country gentlemen generally nominated these "knights of the shire," there was seldom a contest, and all an election amounted to was a shout of approval by a few freeholders.

On the rare occasions when there was a contest it generally arose from local rivalry among the country gentry. Then, as in feudal days, the freeholders would rally around rival family standards as contesting landholders, who felt that the family honor was at stake, made their appeals. Such contests were often the expression of ancient feuds.

Some embryonic political methods had been developed. Although there was a prejudice against open canvassing, there was some discreet letter writing. Upon occasion a committee might be formed which would seek to enlist the interest of various men of standing and influence. Some candidates had friends and agents who went among the freeholders, threatening dispossession of their houses if they did not vote as they should. Outsiders could be brought in; a gentleman from a neighboring shire might come over with followers. Then, too, voters could be made by giving individuals small parcels of land on the understanding that they would relinquish them after the day of the election.

The climax of such politics came on election day. Since voting was done only in the shire town, freeholders had to come in to the shire hall where the election was held at eight in the morning. Because of the early hour, it was necessary at times to find lodging and board for those who must come far, and a wise candidate would hire an inn to see that his retainers had a place to eat and sleep. If the agent of one could secure all the inn accommodations, he had a great advantage. That shire halls were generally small presented another hazard. On election day each side tried to secure possession of its limited space; when the sheriff put the names, the viva voce response for the one controlling the hall would be overwhelming. Again, if the sheriff was favorable to a candidate, his influence might be the deciding factor, for when the result appeared to be close, the sheriff was supposed to poll the crowd. Each man had to give his name, his vote, and, if challenged, swear that he was worth at least forty shillings. Sheriffs were even known to adjourn elections and reconvene them in unexpected locations or to falsify returns. This sort of politics was not typical, for contests were rare, but such things did happen.

Election procedures in the shires were not duplicated in the boroughs. Custom, in fact, varied from borough to borough, and any description which implies uniformity is misleading. There was not even any common definition of a voter. The democratic procedures which seemed to be emerging in some boroughs during the later Middle Ages had quite generally given way to oligarchic control. The borough government composed of local magistrates sitting usually as two houses frequently chose the members of Parliament. These councils, which had originally been elected either by popular assemblies or by the trade guilds, had for the most part become close corporations which filled vacancies as they occurred. It had therefore become the custom in many such towns for the mayor and council to choose the members of Parliament without reference to popular will. On occasion their procedure might be complex. In one borough, for instance, the mayor named four burgesses. These four named four more, and the eight then named an additional four. In turn, these twelve men—six aldermen and six members from the lower house—chose two members of Parliament, usually from among the members of the borough council.

Thus the choice of members of Parliament rested largely in the hands of local magnates either in country or town. With the rise of religious differences, their opinions had great weight; the Queen and her ministers realized full well that they must be sure of the support of these local leaders. Members of the royal council cultivated them, particularly after Puritans began to appear in Parliament, and cabinet members undertook to correspond with men of local influence, seeking their support for favored candidates.

When candidates were returned favorable to the Queen's interest, they exercised their functions under ministerial direction. Puritan members found themselves frustrated, since the Crown prepared the agenda and could and did forbid the consideration of Puritan measures. Nothing like an Opposition to the Crown was tolerated in Parliament in the early years of Elizabeth's reign. But Peter Wentworth and William (?) Strickland resented her prohibition and protested. Strickland was for a time excluded from the House by the Privy Council, and Wentworth more than once went to the Tower. They and their friends took on some semblance of a party, and although they secured little legislation, they did finally secure some status in the course of Elizabeth's reign. In the end, the Queen recognized an Opposition and tolerated it sufficiently to allow members to speak against royal policy.

The growth of the Puritan movement saw an increase of Puritan influence in Parliament, which was aided even by the government itself. From the beginning of her reign there had been an important group of the Queen's advisers friendly to religious reform—men like Burghley, Walsingham, and others, many of them men who had recently risen in rank and fortune. The older families and the nobility tended to remain Catholic, but those whom Henry, Edward, and Elizabeth had ennobled and often enriched from the confiscated property of the Church, were apt to be Protestant, and, as events developed, tended to show Puritan interest. A group of Elizabeth's advisers had a sympathy for the Puritans which she herself entirely lacked. This support was significant where the question of Parliamentary support for Puritan measures was concerned. Since many constituencies could be persuaded by prominent members of the government circle to accept candidates named by them, this practice served to increase the size of the Puritan bloc and to give it a sense of importance and security.

v

Despite this advantage, however, it was evident that the Puritan interest in Parliament would usually be helpless against the Queen's command. Consequently, the Puritans realized that they would have to operate independently of Parliament. They therefore proceeded to organize to reform religion within the parishes, despite the Queen's displeasure and without benefit of political sanction. On a realm-wide basis they used techniques of planning, promoting, propaganda and organization which look surprisingly like modern political methods. In effect they were unconsciously creating a political organization for ostensibly nonpolitical purposes and were developing habits of behavior which their descendants were to find useful in America.

This tendency to organize and, in effect, to form parties had begun on the Continent. Among the English exiles, particularly in Frankfurt, there had been an Episcopal faction and a reform faction. Although the reformers had been defeated in Frankfurt and some of them had gone to Geneva, those at Zurich and Strassburg took vital interest in their differences of opinion and at times attempted either to arbitrate or direct them. When they returned to England at Elizabeth's succession, the exiles did not forget what they had learned.

Some of these men were still living in 1572 when the Puritans began to organize, and one of them, Anthony Gilby, became a leader in the Puritan campaign. He with John Field, Thomas Wilcox, and several others met in London during the session of Parliament to frame and promote legislation and to organize support for it. They urged a Presbyterian form of church government in which clergymen and elders would manage the parishes and send delegates to synods which would in turn rule the Church. Their principal item of propaganda was a pamphlet, *An Admonition to the Parliament*, which obtained wide circulation and stimulated replies in similar form from the Anglican hierarchy. This central committee organized correspondence and encouraged the formation of synods or classes which some of the enthusiasts had already experimented with along Genevan lines. For their temerity, some, including Field, went to jail. But behind the walls of Newgate Prison Field continued to act as a kind of national secretary of the party and to direct propaganda. These men accomplished nothing in Parliament at the time, but their efforts in some localities bore fruit.

For ten years they labored manfully and by 1583 were ready for a new trial of strength. In that year, shortly after the Puritan-Presbyterians were able to hold their first general conference at Cambridge, their talents were stimulated by a new move on the part of the Queen. Elizabeth had appointed John Whitgift, sometime Master of Trinity and Vice-Chancellor of Cambridge, as Archbishop of Canterbury in 1583. He had been the principal author of counterpropaganda in the preceding decade, and he now undertook to enforce conformity to the Anglican system of worship and doctrine. This once more aroused the political genius of the Puritan-Presbyterian group. Field again took over the task of corresponding and organizing secretary. His purpose now was to organize resistance to Canterbury's subscription test for religious uniformity, which all pastors were urged to refuse to sign. A great stream of petitions began to pour in upon Canterbury and Elizabeth's Puritan-minded Council; lawyers attacked Whitgift's proceedings, and the common law courts were not loath to use every quibble to hamper the operation of his ecclesiastical court. In addition to all this, a modified English version of the Geneva prayer book was prepared and printed.

In 1584, and during a meeting of Parliament in 1585, several convocations of Puritan-Presbyterian members met. They established a lobby in London, and during Parliamentary sessions met nightly with their Parliamentary members. William the Silent had recently been assassinated in the Netherlands and hatred of the Roman Catholics was at a new high. The Queen's safety was feared for and the Puritan members of Elizabeth's Council were particularly solicitous. This concern led the Council to persuade the Archbishop to accept a compromise which would forestall the displacement of many Puritan divines in their parishes. The Puritans themselves quickened their own efforts.

In 1585 these efforts took on the aspect of a political campaign to elect a friendly Parliament. Puritan leaders prepared propaganda statistics to show how many parishes were vacant or occupied by the unlearned and the unfit. They began working on a legislative program for the new Parliament, and they were also thinking along the lines of what would in another time become the party platform. A general conference, not unlike an early or embryonic party convention, was held at Cambridge in July.

When the new Parliament assembled in 1586, the results of these efforts were apparent. There was a larger and more defined Puritan group, which sat together in the House, caucussed and dined together, and acted in unison. Again they had the aid of a Popish plot, for it was during this Parliament that Mary Queen of Scots was executed. With the Scottish problem apparently solved, Peter Wentworth and his associates sought to secure legislation authorizing a Presbyterian reorganization. This the Queen forbade. Wentworth raised in ten pertinent questions the matter of the privileges of the House of Commons. For this he was sent to the Tower, ostensibly for organizing a Puritan lobby in synod form.

The Puritans again failed to accomplish anything in the way of law, but their leaders did complete the Book of Discipline which was finally approved at a synod held at St. John's College, Cambridge, in September, 1589, during the Stourbridge Fair. This "Disciplina Ecclesiae," the Puritan Discipline, was in effect a statement of principles for political as well as ecclesiastical action. It outlined a theocratic system of pastors and elders ruling according to the laws of God. Despite the almost unlimited power given to the pastors and officers elected by the congregation, it was stipulated that "in all the greater affairs of the church, as in excommunicating of any and in choosing and deposing of church members, nothing may be concluded without the knowledge and consent of the church [congregation]." In this statement lies one of the germs of American Democracy.

While those who sought to reorganize the Church and to curb the power of the Queen and bishops had accomplished little that can be found in the statutes of the realm, they had gained an influential place in government and society. They had protected themselves from any very active government prosecution. The Queen's punitive measures were reserved almost exclusively for secessionists like the Brownists, Separatists, and the more radical sectarians who defied the Church and left it. Such persons were placed under the ban and were liable for banishment or execution. Under this threat some fled to Holland at various times and in their congregational meetings at Amsterdam and Leiden developed ideas of political independence and self-government that were to be potent in America.

The Puritan-Presbyterian group ceased to be very active politically in

the closing years of Elizabeth's reign. But some of them who had been engaged in the more political aspects of the movement, organization, propaganda and lobbying did not forget their craft and were ready to act again
in the days of the Stuarts. They had likewise circulated ideas about limiting central authority and enlarging popular government. They had become
familiar with and had spread a concept of society of equal men who were
mutually responsible, which they urged as an improvement upon the older
concept of a stratified society with fixed status. They had stirred among the
people a new interest in Parliament and had given to some of its members
a sense of representing the people. Furthermore, it should be remembered
that ministers who had been deprived of their parishes by Elizabeth and her
bishops in some instances became tutors and teachers, and thus communicated to a new generation ideas of individual worth and public responsibility which had their influence upon the next generation from whom were
to come the founders and directors of the New England across the sea.

VI

The controversies of the sixteenth century which made their contributions
to the evolving political behavior of the English people were not altogether religious in their origin and vocabulary. There were others which
also contributed to the growing body of political argument stirring men to
organize pressure upon government. These sprang more directly from prevailing social and economic discontents.

Population increases were beginning to strain social stability. The rise
had been gradual but steady for more than a century, and now the increase
made labor cheap and land dear. Landlords were under pressure in an age
of rising prices to increase rents and were tempted by the growing cloth-
making industry to devote much of their land to sheep-grazing rather than
to crops. Then, too, rising prices in agricultural produce led many to see
the opportunities in commercial farming. The enterprising sought to establish large farms producing market crops, thus doing away with ancient
customs of subsistence farming on small holdings.

Normal economic activity was further disturbed by the policies of
Henry VIII and his government. His seizure of church lands caused a considerable redistribution of property. Much of it was sold, and in the course
of the transactions more money came into active circulation. Henry then
debased the currency, and the price level, already climbing because of increased silver mining in Germany, was raised still further. Such fluctuations
in prices and values stimulated speculation and business activity.

These social and economic changes were accompanied by rural unrest.
Many farmers were dispossessed, more were affected by increased rents;
prices rose faster than the wages paid to farm labor. Despite the fact that
many farmers prospered from the rising prices of their produce, many a

rural area was the scene of unhappiness and bitter discontent. Turbulent East Anglia was to be the scene of violence. There the dispossessed and the impoverished were vocal. There, also, many were upset by religious controversy and by the disarrangement of old customs caused by the suppression of the religious guilds.

In the midst of this clamor there appeared a leader, Robert Kett, who in 1549 rallied a host of some 16,000 men on Mousehold Heath outside of Norwich. His headquarters were established in the ruins of St. Leonard's Priory. In protest against the herding of large flocks on the common pasture by the great landlords, Kett's followers slaughtered 20,000 sheep. Enclosure hedges were torn down, some local landlords were plundered, and a few of the gentry were brought into camp. At the foot of a great tree, thereafter known as the Reformation Oak, Kett dispensed rude justice, meting out penalties against the land monopolists.

The revolt was short-lived; King Edward's guardian sent troops to put it down. In essence it had not been so different from the uprisings of Wat Tyler and Jack Cade in previous centuries. Fortunately, its violence was not to become too general a tradition in Democracy. Its significance at this time lies in the fact that it called attention to abuses suffered by the poor, and in the name of divine and social justice called loudly for reform. This thread of social consciousness in government has been very prominent in the design of American Democracy, and the fact that it was being emphasized in the sixteenth century on the eve of the American migration makes it appropriate to note the contrary types of political doctrine unravelling from it.

Those speaking in behalf of the displaced and hard-pressed were formulating a doctrine of greater equality, more social justice, and even wealthsharing to be secured by petition under threat of resort to arms. This ideology created a counterphilosophy akin to the later laissez-faire ideas based upon acceptance of the will of God. Its proponents maintained that there were sufficient opportunities for the thrifty—"many meane men's children cometh honestly up." Doctrines of equality, it was charged, appealed only to the idle and envious, who, by seeking a new order in which it was not possible for all to be rich, would inaugurate a system under which every man would be poor. Rather should the less fortunate pray to God and protest to the King, remembering that poverty was ordained of God, a trial to make man patient. Thus was set a pattern of thinking which was to form the basis of many a later political controversy.

VII

English political expression in the sixteenth century was not confined to religious and socio-economic discussion, nor was English political inventiveness limited to such instruments of political action as were in use during

these controversies. English energy and enterprise were carrying Englishmen to distant parts of the world, where they were assuming such responsibilities as would give impetus to the creation of a talent which was to contribute much to the development of Democracy. This talent was the
capacity to adapt or to create political mechanisms and administrative devices, particularly as part of the process of organizing new societies in
places far distant from England.

In the 1570's and 1580's England was first confronted with the problem
of sending Englishmen to America to set up some sort of permanent establishment. Such a problem required decisions of management and government which started the weaving of other patterns of American politics.

When English enterprisers began to think of a political structure for
America, they found certain experiences available upon which they could
draw. Experiments in the establishment of English practice in self-government outside the realm had been going on for three hundred years, starting
in the thirteenth century when certain English merchants broke away from
the domination of the foreign traders who were then supplying England
and sought to direct an independent line of export. These merchants were
interested in selling wool, tin, and hides to the Low Countries across the
Channel. Known as the Merchants of the Staple, they secured a concession
through Edward I from the authorities of Antwerp to establish a staple or
warehouse and offices, and a group of English traders thus set up in business for themselves in Antwerp. They had the right of self-government under the supervision of the London Merchants of the Staple; they elected a
mayor and governed themselves within their compound in Antwerp politically as well as commercially.

Early in the fifteenth century, after the Staple had moved to Calais,
Henry IV granted a charter to the Merchant Adventurers who were to
operate in the north European countries. Under this charter the Adventurers elected their own governors and made laws for themselves. A half-
century later, Edward IV gave a charter to the merchants operating in the
Low Countries, defining their procedure for electing a governor and a
court of twelve justiciars, as well as setting forth their legislative powers.
This charter also provided that their laws must be approved by the Crown.

In Elizabeth's reign such precedents were useful. Far-seeing merchants
noted the advantages Spain was reaping from her interests in the New
World and from her control of southern and eastern trade routes. Goaded
by England's lack of capital, her merchants were moved to seek sources of
gold and eastern commodities by operating to the northeast, and some even
thought of the northwest as a route to the Orient.

So it was that in 1553 a group of London merchants formed "The
Mysterie and Companie of the Marchants Adventurers for the discoverie
of regions, dominions, islands and places unknown." An expedition was

sent to Russia or Muscovy to establish contact with the East. The venture was so promising that under the leadership of Sebastian Cabot, son of the famous American discoverer, the first English joint-stock company to operate the Russian franchise was formed. On February 6, 1555, the charter forming the Muscovy Company passed the seals, giving the Company a monopoly of all franchises and prescribing a form of organization of great significance in the history of American Democracy.

The fellowship, *i.e.*, the stockholders, in the corporation were required to meet periodically to choose a "court" to operate their company. This court was to be presided over by Cabot as governor during his lifetime and after his death was to be headed by two governors. With them were to be associated twenty-eight other persons elected annually, four consuls, and twenty-four assistants. A quorum of the court was to consist of the governor, two consuls, and twelve assistants, or if the governor was away, three consuls and twelve assistants. The court or the Company was empowered to make orders for the governing of trade.

The Muscovy Company, although granted the franchise to venture to America by the northwest, did not take advantage of this portion of its liberties, but some of the stockholders who frequented Muscovy House caught the spirit of a new adventure. One of these, Sir Humphrey Gilbert, had had the idea of exploration and the establishment of American outposts as early as 1566, just at a time when French Protestants were trying to establish a settlement in Florida and the mariners Hawkins and Stukely were bringing back reports of Spanish and French activities in America. Gilbert's interest was for a time deflected by a governmental assignment to help extend English control in Ireland by military force and colonization. It was in Ireland that he met the sea dog Martin Frobisher, who was anxious to explore American waters for a northwest passage.

When Gilbert returned to England in the 1570's he tried to interest his Muscovy associates and other private interests in Frobisher's scheme of exploration and in his own plans of colonization. Finding his Muscovy friends were not at all interested in giving him support for an enterprise independent of their monopoly, he next sought to interest the government. Sir Henry Sidney, the Earl of Warwick, and Lord Burghley were enlisted to bring pressure upon the Muscovy Company on his behalf, and at length the Privy Council urged the Muscovy directors to co-operate. This was of no avail, however, until Michael Lock, the chief capitalist of the Company, was converted. With the blessing of the Muscovy Company, Gilbert set out to sell shares to finance his plan, but only the final heavy investment by Lock himself made the venture possible. Frobisher made three voyages and found enough ore in Greenland to cause the Queen to charter the Cathay Company and to contribute £1,000 toward what she hoped would be a mining town and a trade station on a new northwest route to the Far East.

While this enterprise was developing under Frobisher, Gilbert planned a colony more to the south, and in 1578 received from the government a charter "for inhabiting and planting our people in America." He was given authority to exercise jurisdiction over a region within two hundred leagues of wherever he fixed his capital. Gilbert labored on his colony for five years and made two voyages on its behalf. During the second voyage he landed on Newfoundland and actually began a settlement, but it all came to nought since he was lost at sea returning to England in 1583. His half-brother Sir Walter Raleigh, however, carried on and was given a patent in 1584 to settle much farther south in a region called Virginia. He sent settlers to what is now North Carolina, and on the island of Roanoke sought to establish government by incorporating his settlers in the fashion of an English municipality, as "The Governor and Assistants of the City of Raleigh in Virginia." His governor was to have twelve assistants and was to rule as an English municipal council.

Raleigh's ventures also failed, but several steps had been taken toward laying the foundation of American colonization. The Crown had been unable to undertake empire building directly or at its own expense; the donation of a few hundred pounds was all that government would give. But the Crown did encourage private enterprise to establish outposts. It granted charters or patents to individual enterprisers, decreeing that they could create societies in the form of trading posts designed to be governed as English municipalities, and that they should have land at their disposal with which to encourage settlement and possible speculation. The government withheld for itself a share of all treasure discovered. But it was the individual enterpriser who was to assume the burden of the great venture and to be creative in adapting or inventing such political institutions as would be necessary for management and governance.

Thus in the sixteenth century Englishmen were becoming familiar with the operation of many of the basic ideas which were to shape American Democracy. The worth of the individual, freedom of expression, government with some reference to popular will, respect for social justice, and the partnership between government and men willing to adventure much for the commonweal—all these concepts flourished in the minds of many enterprisers when they began to think of a new society in America.

4 *Louis B. Wright*

IMPERIAL PROSPERITY

FROM SOUTHERN PLANTATIONS

A man's reach, wrote Browning, should exceed his grasp, or what's a heaven for? History ought to be as much concerned with man's reach as with his grasp. It ought to consider the heaven in men's lives no less than their earth. If history is the record of what men have thought and done, then their hopes are as properly a part of the record as their achievements. Unfortunately, only their successes tend to live after them; the visions they could not fulfil are "oft interred with their bones." History tends to concentrate on plans that were realized. It does not linger over actions which, however significant in their day, did not for various reasons become part of the more permanent ways of society.

Here is the particular appeal and importance of the following essay by Dr. Louis B. Wright, Director of the Folger Shakespeare Library of Washington, D.C. Dr. Wright has achieved wide reputation as a historian of American colonial society, his interest centering largely on its English sources and connections. His contribution consists not only in his own appraisals of colonial culture but also in his excellent editions of important primary materials.

In the spring of 1951, Dr. Wright delivered a series of lectures at Alabama College on the theme of *The Colonial Search for a Southern Eden.* He wished to relive with Englishmen of the sixteenth and seventeenth centuries the persistent dream they had of establishing profitable colonies in the Southern region of the Atlantic seaboard. In the second of his lectures, which is reprinted here, Dr. Wright directs his attention to the enthusiastic plans of Elizabethans and Jacobeans for the colony of Virginia. What they hoped and what actually occurred were, however, very different things.

But it is the special theme of Dr. Wright's essay that both are essential components of the past. What man proposed and nature disposed has to be understood no less than what nature and other historical factors helped realize. Only through such understanding can one appreciate the fullness of the American adventure.

If the delusion of quick riches from the discovery of gold died hard as Englishmen contemplated the resources of America, another dream almost as

Reprinted with permission from Louis B. Wright, *The Colonial Search for a Southern Eden* (University: University of Alabama Press, 1953), pp. 21–39.

intoxicating took its place. Indescribable good things might be found in the vegetable and animal kingdoms, and prosperity and plenty would flow from the fields and streams of the New World. Even more exciting to many an Englishman nursing his gout or other ailment was the belief that curative herbs of wondrous potency were to be had overseas for the picking. Since 1577, English readers had been wistfully contemplating a book called *Joyfull Newes Out Of The Newe Founde Worlde*, translated by a merchant named John Frampton from the Spanish of Nicholas Monardes. This volume assured the public that cures for most of the ills of mankind would be forthcoming from America. And that portion of America most productive of desirable products was the southern region. In popular belief the sun-drenched climates were most like paradise and would produce all of the good things which man had possessed before the fall of Adam. Both California and Florida still employ press agents to keep that doctrine alive.

In the 1560's someone in contact with Spanish America, probably John Hawkins, introduced tobacco, believed to be a strong and beneficent medicine, and its use set in motion a chain reaction which had far-reaching effects on the development of the British Empire. Also introduced soon thereafter were other vegetable products, notably potatoes, both white and sweet, which proved to be valuable supplements to the diet. In addition to their food value, physicians assured potato-eaters that this food had other virtues including the power to stimulate the affections of tender love. The price of potatoes responded accordingly.

Men had once thought of America as a series of gold mines; now they began to talk of the country as one vast herb garden or plantation of good things, especially those vegetables and fruits which grew in tropical climates. Ponce de Leon had believed that Florida would reveal a fountain of youth. More prosaic Anglo-Saxons contented themselves with an array of new herbs, fruits, gums, and drugs which might confer some of the same benefits. The early promotional literature is filled with extravagant descriptions of Nature's abundance in the land to the south.

The bounty of Nature would provide the commodities, said propagandists and pamphleteers, to make England prosperous. The unpeopled land across the seas would also make a place for the surplus population and create a market for more English goods. The English have been called a "nation of shopkeepers"—a nation whose primary interest is business and commerce. We Americans have attained our own commercial civilization by a natural inheritance. This instinct for commerce—as contrasted with the mere search for treasure—is evident from the earliest proposals for English expansion in the New World.

The first book describing Virginia, for example, gives an excellent statement of the mercantilist point of view and follows it with an enumeration of the multitude of merchantable commodities by which Virginia would enrich itself and the mother country. This work, *A briefe and true report of the new found land of Virginia* (1588), by Thomas Hariot, a scientific observer, is worth our attention for the way it emphasized a point of view which dominated English policy for the next two centuries. The first chapter of the book, Hariot promises, "will make declaration of such commodities there alreadie found or to be raised, which will not onely serue the ordinary turnes of you which are and shall bee the planters and inhabitants, but such an ouerplus sufficiently to bee yelded, or by men of skill to bee prouided, as by way of trafficke and exchaunge with our owne nation of England, will enrich your selues the prouiders, those that shal deal with you, the enterprisers in general, and greatly profit our owne countrey men, to supply them with most things which heretofore they haue bene faine to prouide, either of strangers or of our enemies: which commodities for distinction sake, I call Merchantable."

The notion of a self-sufficient closed commercial empire, which would not need to buy from strangers and enemies, was to grow stronger with the passing years. Already Hariot in 1588 thought he had discovered in Virginia (really the coast of what is now North Carolina) a source for some of the exotic commodities which England was to seek, usually in vain, during the next century.

Significantly Hariot begins his chapter of "merchantable" commodities with a discussion of silk, for silk had to be imported from Asia, or bought from Italians, Frenchmen, Portuguese, or Spaniards. In contemporary thinking, its purchase represented a great drain on the economy.

Silk was to be a greater will-o'-the-wisp than gold mines had ever been. From Raleigh's colony to the settlement of Georgia, the imperial economy would demand the production of silk, and always success evaded the planners. Englishmen unhappily had to pay dearly for an extravagant fashion which made courtiers and gentlemen rustle in silk doublets and hose. Even after the eighteenth century had introduced a more subdued fashion in dress for men, satin and taffeta gowns for women consumed an enormous yardage of silk. One has only to look at a few portraits of ladies by Gainsborough, Reynolds, and Romney to realize that even if the world of fashion was small, it took thousands of yards of silk to clothe it. At the time of Oglethorpe's project for settling Georgia, England's annual silk bill averaged approximately £500,000 sterling, and for the preceding century and a half England had been paying huge sums for this fabric.

Hariot thought that Virginia would soon supply silk for home consumption and for commerce. He had observed a silk-fibred grass similar to a type common in Persia "which is in the selfe same climate as Virginia, of which very many of the silke workes that come from thence into Europe are made." He also was hopeful of worm silk, for "in manie of our iourneyes we founde silke wormes fayre and great" and "there is no doubt but if art be added in planting of mulberry trees and others fitte for them in commodious places . . . there will rise as great a profite in time to the Virginians, as thereof doth now to the Persians, Turkes, Italians, and Spaniards." A warm climate like that of Persia was what Hariot thought he had found in Virginia, and undoubtedly the products which the Levant Company and the East India Company had brought from the East would soon be flowing from the New World.

Among the merchantable commodities which Hariot believed Virginia could produce were many others which England had imported: drugs and rare gums, oils, wine, cedar wood, furs, iron, copper, alum, pitch, tar, rosin and turpentine. Among the drugs was sassafras, a fragrant shrub used to this day as a folk remedy. Sassafras tea, drunk in April and May, is supposed to cure spring fever. So highly was it prized by the early seventeenth century that many cargoes of sassafras were shipped back to English markets.

Second only to silk in the volume of money required for its purchase was wine. Foreigners from the warmer countries, notably Portugal and Spain, had long profited from English thirst, and English merchants looked forward hopefully to colonies in a climate where grape vines would flourish. Consequently Hariot's observations on the grapes of Virginia stirred new hope: "There are two kinds of grapes that the soile doth yeeld naturally: the one is small and sowre of the ordinarie bignesse as ours in England: the other farre greater & of himselfe lushious sweet. When they are planted and husbanded as they ought, a principall commoditie of wines by them may be raised." The big luscious grapes were muscadines or scuppernongs, and Hariot's words were at least partially prophetic, for though wine-making never succeeded in bolstering the economy of Virginia, homemade scuppernong wine has comforted many a Southerner from that day to this.

The promise of wine production in Virginia impressed other early travellers some of whom were even more enthusiastic than Hariot. William Strachey, for example, writing about 1610, comments that "we have eaten there as full and lushious a grape as in the villages between Paris and Amiens, and I have drunck often of the rathe [early] wine, which Doctor Bohune and other of our people have made full as good, as your French British wyne. Twenty gallons at a time have bene sometimes made without any other helpe then by crushing the grape with the hand, which letting to settle five or six daies, hath in the drawing forth proved strong and headdy. Unto what perfection might not these be brought by the art and industry of manie skillful vineroones [vignerons], being thus naturally good."

Like the desire for silk production, the hope of growing grapes and making wine for commerce persisted for many generations. At the beginning of the eighteenth century Robert Beverley made elaborate attempts to produce wine commercially at his plantation in King and Queen County, Virginia. He was scarcely more successful than others had been. John Fontaine, a French Huguenot, with characteristic French logic, accounted for Beverley's failure by pointing out that he followed Spanish instead of French methods in wine production.

Most of the early writers on English expansion had the mercantilist point of view and realized that the greatest profits eventually would come from the colonial production of raw materials which England had to buy outside of what today we would call the "sterling area." Captain John Smith in 1606 emphasized the commercial possibilities of Virginia: "Muscovia and Polonia [Russia and Poland] doe yearely receive many thousands for pitch, tarre, sope-ashes, Rosen, Flax, Cordage, Sturgeon, Masts, Yards, Wainscot, Firres Glasses and such like; also Swethland [Sweden] for Iron and Copper. France in like manner for wine, Canvas, and Salt. Spaine as much for Iron, Steele, Figges, Reasons [raisins], and Sackes [wine]. Italy with Silkes and Velvets consumes our chiefe Commodities. Holland maintaines it selfe by fishing and trading at our owne doores." Virginia, Smith assured the reader, could provide all of these commodities within the scope of a hundred miles, "either ready provided by nature, or else to be prepared were but industrious men to labour."

The Muscovy Company which imported from the Baltic forests most of the naval stores required by English vessels was at the mercy of the whims of Russia, which was as difficult to deal with in the seventeenth century as it is in the twentieth. One thing our own diplomats ought to know is that Russian behavior is historically consistent, whether the ruler be Ivan the Terrible or Joseph Stalin. If the magnificent forests of Virginia could supply all of the needs of the royal navy and English shipping, that service alone would justify the expense of colonization. For various reasons Virginia's forests did not meet expectations for forest products, but eventually the long leaf pines of South Carolina and Georgia supplied a profitable trade in rosin and turpentine—valuable commodities in international trade to this day.

So important was the colonization of the earthly paradise in Virginia by Englishmen that the endeavor became a patriotic crusade. The Virginia Company enlisted the services of the clergy, a very good substitute in the seventeenth century for the British Broadcasting Company. Preachers extolled the virtues of Virginia in the pulpit and pictured the new country as little short of celestial in its promise. For example, the Reverend Daniel Price, a fashionable London preacher and chaplain to Prince Henry, delivered a sermon on May 28, 1609 which is typical of the clergy's extravagant praise of Virginia. Published by authority of the Virginia Company under the title of *Saul's Prohibition Staide . . . with a reproofe of those that traduce the Honourable Plantation of Virginia. Preached in a Sermon Commaunded at Pauls Crosse* (1609), this sermon condemned to hell all those who libelled Virginia and pictured the new country as "the Barne of Britaine, as Sicily was to Rome, or the Garden of the world as was Thessaly, or the Argosie of the world as is Germany." Virginia, said Price, would soon surpass Persia, Tyre, Babylon, Arabia, Spain, and other countries, ancient and modern, in the supply of spices, silks, dyes, oils, rare woods and other precious commodities. Moreover, investors in this godly enterprise would have an insurance not vouchsafed other speculators, for God himself would grant them an "vnspeakable blessing" for bringing the message of salvation to the Indians. "You will make . . . A Sauadge country to become a sanctifyed Country; you will obtaine their best commodities; they will obtaine the sauing of their Soules; you will enlarge the boundes of this Kingdome, nay the bounds of heauen."

Here openly asserted with ecclesiastical authority is the statement of profit in the saving of heathen souls for Protestant Christianity with the distinct implication that Virginia is presently to be a corner of heaven itself. English travellers in the nineteenth century were to ridicule Americans for their bumptiousness in declaring that the United States was "God's country," as if it had the special favor of the Deity. That assertion was made in the early seventeenth century by Daniel Price and scores of other pious promoters of English colonization.

The Virginia Company and later the royal authorities under James I and Charles I took steps to see that Virginia became a source of the commodities which were causing the greatest drain of cash into foreign pockets, namely silk and wine. The newly-established House of Burgesses in 1619, on instructions from London, passed a law that every man in Virginia owning land should plant six mulberry trees annually for seven years to nourish silk worms. The mulberry trees flourished all right but the worms suffered from sundry mishaps. Just when it looked as if the infant industry would get a start, rats destroyed the cocoons.

King James himself busied his royal brain with schemes to encourage silk production. Already religious refugees from France and other Continental countries had set up silk-spinning and weaving shops in England and the King hoped to produce the raw silk for this hopeful industry in his new colony of Virginia. To promote this enterprise—and some others almost as important—he instructed one John Bonoeil, a Frenchman in charge of the Royal silk works, to compile a treatise. When the book was done, James himself wrote a preface and the whole thing was published under the title of *His Maiesties Gracious Letter To The Earle of South-Hampton, Treasurer, and to the Councell and Company of Virginia heere: commanding the present setting vp of Silkworkes, and planting of Vines in Virginia. . . . Also a Treatise of the Art of making Silke: Or, Directions for the mak-*

ing of lodgings, and the breeding, nourishing, and ordering of Silkewormes, and for the planting of Mulbery trees, and all other things belonging to the Silke Art. Together with instructions how to plant and dresse Vines, and to make Wine, and how to dry Raisins, Figs, and other fruits, and to set Oliues, Oranges, Lémons, Pomegranates, Almonds, and many other fruits, &c. And in the end, a Conclusion, with sundry profitable remonstrances to the Colonies. Set foorth for the benefit of the two renowned and most hopefull Sisters, Virginia and the Summer-Ilands. By Iohn Boneil Frenchman, seruant in these imployments to his most Excellent Maiesty of Great Brittaine, France, Ireland, Virginia, and the Summer-Ilands. Published by Authority (1622). With all the weight of the Crown behind it, this treatise ought to have been effective, but like government efforts in the promotion of analogous enterprises in later times, it failed. Recently we have read in the newspapers about British efforts to relieve the shortage of fats at home by raising groundnuts [peanuts] in Africa and the enormous losses incurred, and of the plan to produce poultry and eggs for home consumption on African farms. From King James' time to Mr. Attlee's, the government has had ill-luck in promoting these enterprises of imperial benefit. Ignorance, weather, and pests often confound the dreams of statesmen.

King James' letter prefatory to Bonoeil's treatise is indicative of the seriousness with which the government viewed the necessity of producing silk and wine within the empire. "Whereas We vnderstand that the Soyle in Virginia naturally yeeldeth store of excellent Mulberry trees," wrote the English Solomon, "We haue taken into Our Princely consideration the great benefit that may grow to the Aduenturers and Planters, by the breed of Silkewormes, and setting vp of Silkeworkes in those parts. And therefore of Our gracious Inclination to a designe of so much honour and aduantage to the publike, Wee haue thought good, as at sundry other times, so now more particularly to recommend it to your speciall care, hereby charging and requiring you to take speedy order, that our people there vse all possible diligence in breeding Silkewormes, and erecting Silkeworkes, and that they rather bestow their trauell in compassing this rich and solid Commodity then in Tobacco, which besides much vnnecessary expence, brings with it many disorders and inconueniences. And for as much as Our Seruant, Iohn Bonoeil hath taken paines in setting downe the true vse of the Silkeworme, together with the Art of Silkemaking, and of planting Vines, and that his experience and abilities may much conduce to the aduancement of this business; We doe hereby likewise require you to cause his directions, both for the said Silkeworkes and Vineyards, to bee carefully put in practice thorowout our Plantations there, that so the worke may goe on cheerfully, and receiue no more interruptions nor delayes."

To his royal majesty, it must have seemed simple to decree the production of these commodities which would redress the balance of trade with the rest of the world, but unhappily, about the time Bonoeil's book reached Virginia, the Indians fell on the settlements in the terrible massacre of 1622, a calamity which nearly wiped out the colony. For several years, the Virginians were more concerned about survival than with King James' plans for the empire.

It is worth noting that the King here makes an attack in passing on the production of tobacco, a commodity which he had condemned the year after he ascended the throne in *A Counter Blaste To Tobacco* (1604). Having gone on record as opposed to the use of tobacco, the King felt obliged to continue his hostility. Already, however, signs indicated that tobacco might prove the most profitable crop produced in Virginia.

About 1612, John Rolfe began to experiment with the growing of tobacco. Within four years it had become a staple crop and was planted even in the streets and marketplace of Jamestown. The use of tobacco had already taken such a firm hold on Englishmen that in 1614 it was estimated that England's annual tobacco bill amounted to £200,000 sterling and someone complained in Parliament that even preachers smelled of smoke and poor men each night spent a large portion of their daily wages on pipe tobacco. Even though King James might not approve, it was clear that here was a product which would have to be produced within the empire or else the drain on the economy would be almost as great as that for silk and wine.

Some tobacco was produced in England, but before Rolfe's experiments most of it had come from Spain, to the distress of English imperialists. In 1620 one Edward Bennett published *A Treatise deuided into three parts touching the inconueniences that the Importation of Tobacco out of Spaine hath brought into this Land*. Using some of the same arguments made by the advocates of silk culture, Bennett urged the production of tobacco within the empire. "The maine decay of Trade," he pointed out, "and the chiefe cause that hindreth the importation of Bullion out of Spaine is Tobacco, for there is consumed by all computation, yearely in this Land, three hundred thousand weight." The Spanish tobacco trade, Bennett argues, has hindered the development of Virginia and the Bermudas. The encouragement of tobacco production in these colonies, he asserts, would create prosperity and establish a strong bulwark against Spain. Incidentally, Bennett insisted that the Spaniards were very uncleanly in the way they handled their tobacco. He is probably the first to use a theme which tobacco advertisers in a later time appear to have found effective.

The popularity of tobacco and its potentialities for the trade of England had not been anticipated by the economic planners who were slow to realize that at last a luxury product had been discovered which could be produced within the frame of empire. Once that fact was demonstrated, the government took steps to see that England reaped the maximum benefits from the tobacco trade. Government regulations from the time of James I onward forbade the growing of tobacco in England itself and decreed that tobacco grown in the colonies should be shipped directly to English ports for processing. Thus the government reaped a substantial revenue from duties and brought in a product in great demand in the foreign trade. The sale of tobacco abroad, even in competition with Spanish and Dutch tobacco, helped to offset the unfavorable cash position created by purchases of non-empire products like silk and wine.

The production of tobacco, which had come into English trade almost by the backdoor, occupied a place of first importance in the imperial economy in the later seventeenth and eighteenth centuries. So profitable was the trade that many merchants of London and Bristol devoted themselves exclusively to it, and the production of tobacco was the main concern of planters in Virginia, Maryland, and in a portion of the Carolinas. Such a concentration was not without its penalties because a crop failure, or a glut of the market by overproduction, might cause a widespread financial disaster. Wise leaders in the colonies argued earnestly against the hazards of the one crop system, a system which has often been the ruin of the South, but profits were large in good years, and the pressures were great, both at home and abroad, to raise more and more tobacco. When the Reverend James Blair at the end of the seventeenth century was arguing with the Board of Trade that they should help establish a college to save the souls of Virginians, Sir Edward Seymour, a Lord of the Treasury, exclaimed, "Souls? Damn your souls! Make tobacco!" To the empire builders, tobacco was more important even than salvation, and they prized the tobacco colonies on the Chesapeake above those sometimes recalcitrant and always competitive offspring to the north.

Tobacco was an ideal commodity from the point of view of the seventeenth- and eighteenth-century mercantilists. It was produced in the raw state in the colonies; it was shipped from the colonies to the mother country, paying an export tax in the colony and an import tax at home; and it could be processed in England to become a lucrative article of export. Furthermore it could be raised with unskilled labor, such labor as could be supplied by African slaves, themselves an article of profitable commerce to the Royal African Company. The usefulness of the rawest slaves from the west coast of Africa in the tobacco fields of Virginia, Maryland, and Bermuda helped to fasten a system of labor and a racial problem upon the Southern colonies which had evil consequences persisting to our own day.

Although the very success of tobacco as a money crop was a hindrance to the production of other desired commodities, the planners did not abandon hope that Virginia would eventually compete with France, Spain, Italy, Persia, and the East Indies in exotic products. The distribution of

John Bonoeil's treatise in 1622 was accompanied by orders from the Virginia Company commanding efforts to produce silk and wine. Skilled artisans from Southern Europe came to Virginia to instruct the settlers in these crafts, and experimentation led some Virginians to believe as late as 1649 that silk and wine would supersede in time tobacco in popular favor, but their optimism was ill-founded. The profits from sugar in Barbados induced a few planters to try to plant sugar cane, but nothing came of this. The grapes, lemons, oranges, ginger, and figs, recommended to the planters, likewise failed, and tobacco ruled supreme. In 1705 Robert Beverley the historian complained that Virginians were so entrapped in the one crop system and so lacking in enterprise that they would not even use their abundant timber for making their own wooden ware but instead imported it from England. By this time, however, the Board of Trade in London had come to approve of Virginia and Maryland's complete concentration upon tobacco, which fitted well with mercantile theory. They would try elsewhere to produce the other desired materials.

One of the commodities which international trade in the Elizabethan period had popularized, and which England now wanted to produce, was sugar. Sugar like silk was a product which cost England cash, cash which went to Italian, Spanish, and Portuguese producers. In early times, Englishmen had depended on the bees to provide their sweets, and many ancient recipes specified honey for sweetening. But in the sixteenth century, trade with the Canary and Madeira Islands brought sugar into fairly common use. By the early seventeenth century it was an essential.

Sugar was believed to have great curative values and to be a preservative of health. John Gerard, the herbalist, asserted that "It drieth and cleanseth the stomacke, maketh smooth the roughness of the breast and lungs, cleareth the voice, and putteth away hoarseness, the cough, and all sournesse and bitternesse." And a seventeenth century physician had a saying that

> If Sugar can preserve both Pears and Plumbs,
> Why can it not preserve as well our Lungs?

Even if sugar had not possessed these healing virtues, it was pleasant to the taste and Englishmen even used it to qualify their drinks. But England was not a sugar-producing nation, and the government was troubled.

Sugar canes had been taken from the Canaries to Brazil and had flourished. From Brazil, sugar cane had spread to the Spanish islands of the West Indies. Perhaps Englishmen might find a place where they too could produce sugar. About 1640 conditions on Barbados forced the planters there to think of a crop to take the place of tobacco. Stimulated by the demand for tobacco on the European market, the Barbadians had raised more of the weed than they could sell. Faced with bankruptcy because of the glut of the tobacco market, they were ready to try anything and sugar cane looked promising. The cane grew so luxuriantly on Barbados that within a short time sugar had superseded tobacco as the principal industry on that island, and it quickly spread to other British territory in the Caribbean.

On the mainland of North America English planters had no success with sugar cane in the colonial period. But Barbados became a sugar paradise. Since sugar making required expensive equipment, only those planters with large capital could operate the plantations and refineries. Consequently many of the smaller planters, who had done well with tobacco, had to leave Barbados in search of greener pastures. Many of them came to South Carolina and helped to establish the economy of that colony on a sound basis, as we shall see later.

The sugar making of Barbados was so profitable in imperial trade that by 1675 over four hundred vessels were engaged in the transport of sugar and molasses. A by-product of molasses, rum, became a national drink and another commodity enormously important in international commerce. The sugar islands were so prized by the mother country that when the Peace of Paris in 1763 ended the Seven Years War, some English politicians wanted to allow France to retain Canada on condition that she cede the French islands in the West Indies to Great Britain.

These French West Indian possessions had proved so enormously valuable as sources of sugar and molasses that English merchants were anxious to obtain them. The demand for rum had long outstripped the capacity of Barbados and the other British islands to supply the necessary raw material, namely molasses, but nevertheless England tried to prevent the colonies from developing an independent trade with the French West Indies. As early as 1733, England passed the first Molasses Act to restrict the trade to the British possessions and succeeded only in stimulating wholesale smuggling between the French islands and New England, where the manufacture of rum had become an important factor in the Northern colonies' prosperity. This disrespect for imperial regulations by the Northern colonies was one more reason why the home government found the Southern colonies more to their liking.

By the middle of the seventeenth century, England has succeeded in developing two profitable tropical products within the empire, namely tobacco and sugar. The cash which these commodities brought into England confirmed still further the belief held by many of the mercantile imperialists that the most desirable colonies would be those established in the South. Pleased with the profits from tobacco and sugar, Englishmen for the next century continued their endeavor to find a modern counterpart of the Garden of Eden in the warmer parts of America where they might yet produce all of those exotic commodities which had previously defied the best efforts of their statesmen.

5 *Perry Miller*

ERRAND INTO THE WILDERNESS

History is a narrative of social self-consciousness. It is the cumulative story of how and why one generation's sense of purpose has been altered by that of the next generation. It deals with the fundamental questions facing men in society: what they construe to be their identity, the goals they set for their existence, the ways in which they hope to achieve them, the awareness they have of failing to do so.

No group offers the student a more challenging and fascinating means of exploring these questions and gaining the larger perspective of history which they open than the Puritans who came to settle English America during the 1630's and who were so important in molding its values and institutions during the course of the seventeenth century. Conscious of their purpose, the Puritans regarded themselves as having been sent on an "errand into the wilderness." But what exactly was this errand? How was it interpreted by the first generation of Puritans? How did they translate it into the terms of civil and religious polity? How did the sense of their errand change among the second and third Puritan generations? What accounts for it? How was it reflected in the jeremiads of their ministers?

These are the questions answered in the following essay by Perry Miller, Professor of American Literature at Harvard. Professor Miller's larger interest is in the intellectual history of New England during the seventeenth and early eighteenth centuries and during the decades before the Civil War. His works on the earlier period include a superb trilogy on the intellectual anatomy of New England during its first century: *Orthodoxy in Massachusetts, 1630–1650* (1933), *The New England Mind: The Seventeenth Century* (1939), and *The New England Mind: From Colony to Province* (1953). The essay below first appeared in *The William and Mary Quarterly* (January, 1953) and subsequently in a collection of essays which carried its title: *Errand into the Wilderness* (1956). In it, Professor Miller explores the changing attitude of the Puritans toward their purpose and their movement

Reprinted by permission of the publishers from Perry Miller, *Errand into the Wilderness* (Cambridge, Mass.: The Belknap Press of Harvard University Press), pp. 2–15. Copyright 1956 by the President and Fellows of Harvard College. This essay appeared originally in *The William and Mary Quarterly*, Third Series, X (January, 1953), 3–19.

from a vision which had been universal to one which was becoming merely American.

The essay has a double importance. It extends our knowledge about the Puritans and therefore our understanding of them. It restores the Puritans to the premises and realities of the seventeenth century and thus gives renewed validity to their purpose and their actions. In this respect, the essay, and for that matter the rest of Professor Miller's brilliant contribution, may be seen as part of the larger effort of our generation to come to terms with, indeed to rehabilitate, the Puritans. The historian of the late nineteenth and early twentieth centuries saw the Puritans as intolerant, unlearned, inflexible, severe, strait-laced, sexually constricted, unchanging—Calvinist in the worst sense of the word. In recent decades, however, historians have been adopting a less monolithic and more favorable outlook. Samuel Eliot Morison, for example, has stressed the intellectual and educational attainments of the Puritans, Clifford K. Shipton their contributions to American democracy, Alan Simpson their real sense of inspiration and enthusiasm, Perry Miller their larger philosophy and its validity and vitality in the world of the seventeenth century.

Professor Miller's essay is important, moreover, for its bearing on the question of a philosophy for our own times. What, indeed, is our sense of purpose? What do we understand to be the ends of existence and by what means do we seek to attain them? What are the circumstances around us shaping our view of ends and means? What are our jeremiads and how valid are the charges our consciences level against us? Do we still, in any wise, have a covenant with God? If, as Professor Miller suggests, we found ourselves alone with America in the seventeenth century, have we restored ourselves to Europe in the twentieth? Or is the essence of our problem that, having made America a mission for ourselves, we are now seeking to make it one for the world? And if, throughout its history, America has been on an errand, what was it in the generations following the Puritans, and what is it today?

It was a happy inspiration that led the staff of the John Carter Brown Library to choose as the title of its New England exhibition of 1952 a phrase from Samuel Danforth's election sermon, delivered on May 11, 1670: *A Brief Recognition of New England's Errand into the Wilderness*. It was of course an inspiration, if not of genius at least of talent, for Danforth to invent his title in the first place. But all the election sermons of this period— that is to say, the major expressions of the second generation, which, delivered on these forensic occasions, were in the fullest sense community expression—have interesting titles; a mere listing tells the story of what was happening to the minds and emotions of the New England people: John Higginson's *The Cause of God and His People In New-England* in 1663,

William Stoughton's *New England's True Interest, Not to Lie* in 1668, Thomas Shepard's *Eye-Salve* in 1672, Urian Oakes's *New England Pleaded With* in 1673, and, climactically and most explicitly, Increase Mather's *A Discourse Concerning the Danger of Apostasy* in 1677.

All of these show by their title pages alone—and, as those who have looked into them know, infinitely more by their contents—a deep disquietude. They are troubled utterances, worried, fearful. Something has gone wrong. As in 1662 Wigglesworth already was saying in verse, God has a controversy with New England; He has cause to be angry and to punish it because of its innumerable defections. They say, unanimously, that New England was sent on an errand, and that it has failed.

To our ears these lamentations of the second generation sound strange indeed. We think of the founders as heroic men—of the towering stature of Bradford, Winthrop, and Thomas Hooker—who braved the ocean and the wilderness, who conquered both, and left to their children a goodly heritage. Why then this whimpering?

Some historians suggest that the second and third generations suffered a failure of nerve; they weren't the men their fathers had been, and they knew it. Where the founders could range over the vast body of theology and ecclesiastical polity and produce profound works like the treatises of John Cotton or the subtle psychological analyses of Hooker, or even such a gusty though wrongheaded book as Nathaniel Ward's *Simple Cobler*, let alone such lofty and rightheaded pleas as Roger Williams' *Bloudy Tenet*, all these children could do was tell each other that they were on probation and that their chances of making good did not seem very promising.

Since Puritan intellectuals were thoroughly grounded in grammar and rhetoric, we may be certain that Danforth was fully aware of the ambiguity concealed in his word "errand." It already had taken on the double meaning which it still carries with us. Originally, as the word first took form in English, it meant exclusively a short journey on which an inferior is sent to convey a message or to perform a service for his superior. In that sense we today speak of an "errand boy"; or the husband says that while in town on his lunch hour, he must run an errand for his wife. But by the end of the Middle Ages, errand developed another connotation: it came to mean the actual business on which the actor goes, the purpose itself, the conscious intention in his mind. In this signification, the runner of the errand is working for himself, is his own boss; the wife, while the husband is away at the office, runs her own errands. Now in the 1660's the problem was this: which had New England originally been—an errand boy or a doer of errands? In which sense had it failed? Had it been despatched for a further purpose, or was it an end in itself? Or had it fallen short not only in one or the other, but in both of the meanings? If so, it was indeed a tragedy, in the primitive sense of a fall from a mighty designation.

If the children were in grave doubt about which had been the original errand—if, in fact, those of the founders who lived into the later period and who might have set their progeny to rights found themselves wondering and confused—there is little chance of our answering clearly. Of course, there is no problem about Plymouth Colony. That is the charm about Plymouth: its clarity. The Pilgrims, as we have learned to call them, were reluctant voyagers; they had never wanted to leave England, but had been obliged to depart because the authorities made life impossible for Separatists. They could, naturally, have stayed at home had they given up being Separatists, but that idea simply did not occur to them. Yet they did not go to Holland as though on an errand; neither can we extract the notion of a mission out of the reasons which, as Bradford tells us, persuaded them to leave Leyden for "Virginia." The war with Spain was about to be resumed, and the economic threat was ominous; their migration was not so much an errand as a shrewd forecast, a plan to get out while the getting was good, lest, should they stay, they would be "intrapped or surrounded by their enemies, so as they should neither be able to fight nor flie." True, once the decision was taken, they congratulated themselves that they might become a means for propagating the gospel in remote parts of the world, and thus of serving as steppingstones to others in the performance of this great work; nevertheless, the substance of their decision was that they "thought it better to dislodge betimes to some place of better advantage and less danger, if any such could be found." The great hymn that Bradford, looking back in his old age, chanted about the landfall is one of the greatest passages, if not the very greatest, in all New England's literature; yet it does not resound with the sense of a mission accomplished—instead, it vibrates with the sorrow and exultation of suffering, the sheer endurance, the pain and the anguish, with the somberness of death faced unflinchingly:

May not and ought not the children of these fathers rightly say: Our fathers were Englishmen which came over this great ocean, and were ready to perish in this wilderness; but they cried unto the Lord, and he heard their voyce, and looked on their adversitie . . . .

We are bound, I think, to see in Bradford's account the prototype of the vast majority of subsequent immigrants—of those Oscar Handlin calls "The Uprooted": they came for better advantage and for less danger, and to give their posterity the opportunity of success.

The Great Migration of 1630 is an entirely other story. True, among the reasons John Winthrop drew up in 1629 to persuade himself and his colleagues that they should commit themselves to the enterprise, the economic motive frankly figures. Wise men thought that England was overpopulated and that the poor would have a better chance in the new land. But Massachusetts Bay was not just an organization of immigrants seeking advantage and opportunity. It had a positive sense of mission—either it was sent on an errand or it had its own intention, but in either case the deed was deliberate. It was an act of will, perhaps of willfulness. These Puritans were not driven out of England (thousands of their fellows stayed and fought the Cavaliers)—they went of their own accord.

So, concerning them, we ask the question, why? If we are not altogether clear about precisely how we should phrase the answer, this is not because they themselves were reticent. They spoke as fully as they knew how, and none more magnificently or cogently than John Winthrop in the midst of the passage itself, when he delivered a lay sermon aboard the flagship *Arbella* and called it "A Modell of Christian Charity." It distinguishes the motives of this great enterprise from those of Bradford's forlorn retreat, and especially from those of the masses who later have come in quest of advancement. Hence, for the student of New England and of America, it is a fact demanding incessant brooding that John Winthrop selected as the "doctrine" of his discourse, and so as the basic proposition to which, it then seemed to him, the errand was committed, the thesis that God had disposed mankind in a hierarchy of social classes, so that "in all times some must be rich, some poor, some highe and eminent in power and dignitie; others mean and in subjeccion." It is as though, preternaturally sensing what the promise of America might come to signify for the rank and file, Winthrop took the precaution to drive out of their heads any notion that in the wilderness the poor and the mean were ever so to improve themselves as to mount above the rich or the eminent in dignity. Were there any who had signed up under the mistaken impression that such was the purpose of their errand, Winthrop told them that, although other peoples, lesser breeds, might come for wealth or pelf, this migration was specifically dedicated to an avowed end that had nothing to do with incomes. We have entered into an explicit covenant with God, "we haue professed to enterprise these Accions vpon these and these ends"; we have drawn up indentures with the Almighty, wherefore if we succeed and do not let ourselves get diverted into making money, He will reward us. Whereas if we fail, if we "fall to embrace this present world and prosecute our carnall intencions, seekeing great things for our selves and our posterity, the Lord will surely breake out in wrathe against us be revenged of such a periured people and make us knowe the price of the breache of such a Covenant."

Well, what terms were agreed upon in this covenant? Winthrop could say precisely—"It is by a mutuall consent through a specially overruleing providence, and a more than ordinary approbation of the Churches of Christ to seeke out a place of Cohabitation and Consorteshipp under a due forme of Government both civill and ecclesiasticall." If it could be said thus concretely, why should there be any ambiguity? There was no doubt whatsoever about what Winthrop meant by a due form of ecclesiastical government: he meant the pure Biblical polity set forth in full detail by the New Testament, that method which later generations, in the days of increasing confusion, would settle down to calling Congregational, but which for Winthrop was no denominational peculiarity but the very essence of organized Christianity. What a due form of civil government meant, therefore, became crystal clear: a political regime, possessing power, which would consider its main function to be the erecting, protecting, and preserving of this form of polity. This due form would have, at the very beginning of its list of responsibilities, the duty of suppressing heresy, of subduing or somehow getting rid of dissenters—of being, in short, deliberately, vigorously, and consistently intolerant.

Regarded in this light, the Massachusetts Bay Company came on an errand in the second and later sense of the word: it was, so to speak, on its own business. What it set out to do was the sufficient reason for its setting out. About this Winthrop seems to be perfectly certain, as he declares specifically what the due forms will be attempting: the end is to improve our lives to do more service to the Lord, to increase the body of Christ, and to preserve our posterity from the corruptions of this evil world, so that they in turn shall work out their salvation under the purity and power of Biblical ordinances. Because the errand was so definable in advance, certain conclusions about the method of conducting it were equally evident: one, obviously, was that those sworn to the covenant should not be allowed to turn aside in a lust for mere physical rewards; but another was, in Winthrop's simple but splendid words, "we must be knit together in this worke as one man, wee must entertaine each other in brotherly affection." We must actually delight in each other, "always having before our eyes our Commission and community in the worke, our community as members of the same body." This was to say, were the great purpose kept steadily in mind, if all gazed only at it and strove only for it, then social solidarity (within a scheme of fixed and unalterable class distinctions) would be an automatic consequence. A society despatched upon an errand that is its own reward would want no other rewards: it could go forth to possess a land without ever becoming possessed by it; social gradations would remain eternally what God had originally appointed; there would be no internal contention among groups or interests, and though there would be hard work for everybody, prosperity would be bestowed not as a consequence of labor but as a sign of approval upon the mission itself. For once in the history of humanity (with all its sins), there would be a society so dedicated to a holy cause that success would prove innocent and triumph not raise up sinful pride or arrogant dissension.

Or, at least, this would come about if the people did not deal falsely with God, if they would live up to the articles of their bond. If we do not

perform these terms, Winthrop warned, we may expect immediate manifestations of divine wrath; we shall perish out of the land we are crossing
the sea to possess. And here in the 1660's and 1670's, all the jeremiads (of
which Danforth's is one of the most poignant) are castigations of the people
for having defaulted on precisely these articles. They recite the long list of
afflictions an angry God had rained upon them, surely enough to prove
how abysmally they had deserted the covenant: crop failures, epidemics,
grasshoppers, caterpillars, torrid summers, arctic winters, Indian wars,
hurricanes, shipwrecks, accidents, and (most grievous of all) unsatisfactory
children. The solemn work of the election day, said Stoughton in 1668, is
"Foundation-work"—not, that is, to lay a new one, "but to continue, and
strengthen, and beautifie, and build upon that which has been laid." It had
been laid in the covenant before even a foot was set ashore, and thereon
New England should rest. Hence the terms of survival, let alone of prosperity, remained what had first been propounded:

> If we should so frustrate and deceive the Lords Expectations, that his
> Covenant-interest in us, and the Workings of his Salvation be made to cease,
> then All were lost indeed; Ruine upon Ruine, Destruction upon Destruction
> would come, until one stone were not left upon another.

Since so much of the literature after 1660—in fact, just about all of it—
dwells on this theme of declension and apostasy, would not the story of
New England seem to be simply that of the failure of a mission? Winthrop's dread was realized: posterity had not found their salvation amid
pure ordinances but had, despite the ordinances, yielded to the seductions
of the good land. Hence distresses were being piled upon them, the
slaughter of King Philip's War and now the attack of a profligate king
upon the sacred charter. By about 1680, it did in truth seem that shortly no
stone would be left upon another, that history would record of New England that the founders had been great men, but that their children and
grandchildren progressively deteriorated.

This would certainly seem to be the impression conveyed by the assembled clergy and lay elders who, in 1679, met at Boston in a formal
synod, under the leadership of Increase Mather, and there prepared a report on why the land suffered. The result of their deliberation, published
under the title *The Necessity of Reformation*, was the first in what has
proved to be a distressingly long succession of investigations into the civic
health of Americans, and it is probably the most pessimistic. The land was
afflicted, it said, because corruption had proceeded apace; assuredly, if the
people did not quickly reform, the last blow would fall and nothing but
desolation be left. Into what a moral quagmire this dedicated community
had sunk, the synod did not leave to imagination; it published a long and

detailed inventory of sins, crimes, misdemeanors, and nasty habits, which makes, to say the least, interesting reading.

We hear much talk nowadays about corruption, most of it couched in generalized terms. If we ask our current Jeremiahs to descend to particulars, they tell us that the republic is going on the rocks, or to the dogs, because the wives of politicians aspire to wear mink coats and their husbands take a moderate five per cent cut on certain deals to pay for the garments. The Puritans were devotees of logic, and the verb "methodize" ruled their thinking. When the synod went to work, it had before it a succession of sermons, such as that of Danforth and the other election-day or fast-day orators, as well as such works as Increase Mather's *A Brief History of the Warr With the Indians*, wherein the decimating conflict with Philip was presented as a revenge upon the people for their transgressions. When the synod felt obliged to enumerate the enormities of the land so that the people could recognize just how far short of their errand they had fallen, it did not, in the modern manner, assume that regeneration would be accomplished at the next election by turning the rascals out, but it digested this body of literature; it reduced the contents to method. The result is a staggering compendium of iniquity, organized into twelve headings.

First, there was a great and visible decay of godliness. Second, there were several manifestations of pride—contention in the churches, insubordination of inferiors toward superiors, particularly of those inferiors who had, unaccountably, acquired more wealth than their betters, and, astonishingly, a shocking extravagance in attire, especially on the part of these of the meaner sort, who persisted in dressing beyond their means. Third, there were heretics, especially Quakers and Anabaptists. Fourth, a notable increase in swearing and a spreading disposition to sleep at sermons (these two phenomena seemed basically connected). Fifth, the Sabbath was wantonly violated. Sixth, family government had decayed, and fathers no longer kept their sons and daughters from prowling at night. Seventh, instead of people being knit together as one man in mutual love, they were full of contention, so that lawsuits were on the increase and lawyers were thriving. Under the eighth head, the synod described the sins of sex and alcohol, thus producing some of the juiciest prose of the period: militia days had become orgies, taverns were crowded; women threw temptation in the way of befuddled men by wearing false locks and displaying naked necks and arms "or, which is more abominable, naked Breasts"; there were "mixed Dancings," along with light behavior and "Company-keeping" with vain persons, wherefore the bastardy rate was rising. In 1672, there was actually an attempt to supply Boston with a brothel (it was suppressed, but the synod was bearish about the future). Ninth, New Englanders were betraying a marked disposition to tell lies, especially when selling anything. In the tenth place, the business morality of even the most righteous left everything to be desired: the wealthy speculated in land and raised prices excessively; "Day-Labourers and Mechanicks are unreasonable in their demands." In the eleventh place, the people showed no disposition to reform, and in the twelfth, they seemed utterly destitute of civic spirit.

"The things here insisted on," said the synod, "have been oftentimes mentioned and inculcated by those whom the Lord hath set as Watchmen to the house of Israel." Indeed they had been, and thereafter they continued to be even more inculcated. At the end of the century, the synod's report was serving as a kind of handbook for preachers: they would take some verse of Isaiah or Jeremiah, set up the doctrine that God avenges the iniquities of a chosen people, and then run down the twelve heads, merely bringing the list up to date by inserting the new and still more depraved practices an ingenious people kept on devising. I suppose that in the whole literature of the world, including the satirists of imperial Rome, there is hardly such another uninhibited and unrelenting documentation of a people's descent into corruption.

I have elsewhere endeavored to argue that, while the social or economic historian may read this literature for its contents—and so construct from the expanding catalogue of denunciations a record of social progress—the cultural anthropologist will look slightly askance at these jeremiads; he will exercise a methodological caution about taking them at face value. If you read them all through, the total effect, curiously enough, is not at all depressing: you come to the paradoxical realization that they do not bespeak a despairing frame of mind. There is something of a ritualistic incantation about them; whatever they may signify in the realm of theology, in that of psychology they are purgations of soul; they do not discourage but actually encourage the community to persist in its heinous conduct. The exhortation to a reformation which never materializes serves as a token payment upon the obligation, and so liberates the debtors. Changes there had to be: adaptations to environment, expansion of the frontier, mansions constructed, commercial adventures undertaken. These activities were not specifically nominated in the bond Winthrop had framed. They were thrust upon the society by American experience; because they were not only works of necessity but of excitement, they proved irresistible— whether making money, haunting taverns, or committing fornication. Land speculation meant not only wealth but dispersion of the people, and what was to stop the march of settlement? The covenant doctrine preached on the *Arbella* had been formulated in England, where land was not to be had for the taking; its adherents had been utterly oblivious of what the fact of a frontier would do for an imported order, let alone for a European mentality. Hence I suggest that under the guise of this mounting wail of sinfulness, this incessant and never successful cry for repentance, the Puritans launched themselves upon the process of Americanization.

However, there are still more pertinent or more analytical things to be said of this body of expression. If you compare it with the great productions of the founders, you will be struck by the fact that the second and third generations had become oriented toward the social, and only the social, problem; herein they were deeply and profoundly different from their fathers. The finest creations of the founders—the disquisitions of Hooker, Shepard, and Cotton—were written in Europe, or else, if actually penned in the colonies, proceeded from a thoroughly European mentality, upon which the American scene made no impression whatsoever. The most striking example of this imperviousness is the poetry of Anne Bradstreet: she came to Massachusetts at the age of eighteen, already two years married to Simon Bradstreet; there, she says, "I found a new world and new manners, at which my heart rose" in rebellion, but soon convincing herself that it was the way of God, she submitted and joined the church. She bore Simon eight children, and loved him sincerely, as her most charming poem, addressed to him, reveals:

> If ever two were one, then surely we;
> If ever man were loved by wife, then thee.

After the house burned, she wrote a lament about how her pleasant things in ashes lay and how no more the merriment of guests would sound in the hall; but there is nothing in the poem to suggest that the house stood in North Andover or that the things so tragically consumed were doubly precious because they had been transported across the ocean and were utterly irreplaceable in the wilderness. In between rearing children and keeping house she wrote her poetry; her brother-in-law carried the manuscript to London, and there published it in 1650 under the ambitious title, *The Tenth Muse Lately Sprung Up in America*. But the title is the only thing about the volume which shows any sense of America, and that little merely in order to prove that the plantations had something in the way of European wit and learning, that they had not receded into barbarism. Anne's flowers are English flowers, the birds, English birds, and the landscape is Lincolnshire. So also with the productions of immigrant scholarship: such a learned and acute work as Hooker's *Survey of the Summe of Church Discipline*, which is specifically about the regime set up in America, is written entirely within the logical patterns, and out of the religious experience, of Europe; it makes no concession to new and peculiar circumstances.

The titles alone of productions in the next generation show how concentrated have become emotion and attention upon the interest of New England, and none is more revealing than Samuel Danforth's conception of an errand into the wilderness. Instead of being able to compose abstract treatises like those of Hooker upon the soul's preparation, humiliation, or exultation, or such a collection of wisdom and theology as John Cotton's *The Way of Life* or Shepard's *The Sound Believer*, these later saints must, over and over again, dwell upon the specific sins of New England, and the more they denounce, the more they must narrow their focus to the provincial problem. If they write upon anything else, it must be about the half-way covenant and its manifold consequences—a development enacted wholly in this country—or else upon their wars with the Indians. Their range is sadly constricted, but every effort, no matter how brief, is addressed to the persistent question: what is the meaning of this society in the wilderness? If it does not mean what Winthrop said it must mean, what under Heaven is it? Who, they are forever asking themselves, who are we?—and sometimes they are on the verge of saying, who the Devil are we, anyway?

This brings us back to the fundamental ambiguity concealed in the word "errand," that *double entente* of which I am certain Danforth was aware when he published the words that give point to the exhibition. While it was true that in 1630, the covenant philosophy of a special and peculiar bond lifted the migration out of the ordinary realm of nature, provided it with a definite mission which might in the secondary sense be called its errand, there was always present in Puritan thinking the suspicion that God's saints are at best inferiors, despatched by their Superior upon particular assignments. Anyone who has run errands for other people, particularly for people of great importance with many things on their minds, such as army commanders, knows how real is the peril that, by the time he returns with the report of a message delivered or a bridge blown up, the Superior may be interested in something else; the situation at headquarters may be entirely changed, and the gallant errand boy, or the husband who desperately remembered to buy the ribbon, may be told that he is too late. This tragic pattern appears again and again in modern warfare: an agent is dropped by parachute and, after immense hardships, comes back to find that, in the shifting tactical or strategic situations, his contribution is no longer of value. If he gets home in time and his service proves useful, he receives a medal; otherwise, no matter what prodigies he has performed, he may not even be thanked. He has been sent, as the devastating phrase has it, upon a fool's errand, than which there can be a no more shattering blow to self-esteem.

The Great Migration of 1630 felt insured against such treatment from on high by the covenant; nevertheless, the God of the covenant always, remained an unpredictable Jehovah, a *Deus Absconditus*. When God promises to abide by stated terms, His word, of course, is to be trusted; but then, what is man that he dare accuse Omnipotence of tergiversation? But if any such apprehension was in Winthrop's mind as he spoke on the *Arbella*, or in the minds of other apologists for the enterprise, they kept it far back and allowed it no utterance. They could stifle the thought, not only because Winthrop and his colleagues believed fully in the covenant, but because they could see in the pattern of history that their errand was not a mere scouting expedition: it was an essential maneuver in the drama of Christendom. The Bay Company was not a battered remnant of suffering Separatists thrown up on a rocky shore; it was an organized task force of Christians, executing a flank attack on the corruptions of Christendom. These Puritans did not flee to America; they went in order to work out that complete reformation which was not yet accomplished in England and Europe, but which would quickly be accomplished if only the saints back there had a working model to guide them. It is impossible to say that any who sailed from Southampton really expected to lay his bones in the new world; were it to come about—as all in their heart of hearts anticipated —that the forces of righteousness should prevail against Laud and Wentworth, that England after all should turn toward reformation, where else would the distracted country look for leadership except to those who in New England had perfected the ideal polity and who would know how to administer it? This was the large unspoken assumption in the errand of 1630: if the conscious intention were realized, not only would a federated Jehovah bless the new land, but He would bring back these temporary colonials to govern England.

In this respect, therefore, we may say that the migration was running an errand in the earlier and more primitive sense of the word—performing a job not so much for Jehovah as for history, which was the wisdom of Jehovah expressed through time. Winthrop was aware of this aspect of the mission—fully conscious of it. "For wee must Consider that wee shall be as a Citty upon a Hill, the eies of all people are uppon us." More was at stake than just one little colony. If we deal falsely with God, not only will He descend upon us in wrath, but even more terribly, He will make us "a story and a by-word through the world, wee shall open the mouthes of enemies to speake evill of the wayes of god and all professours for Gods sake." No less than John Milton was New England to justify God's ways to man, though not, like him, in the agony and confusion of defeat but in the confidence of approaching triumph. This errand was being run for the sake of Reformed Christianity; and while the first aim was indeed to realize in America the due form of government, both civil and ecclesiastical, the aim behind that aim was to vindicate the most rigorous ideal of the Reformation, so that ultimately all Europe would imitate New England. If we succeed, Winthrop told his audience, men will say of later plantations, "the lord make it like that of New England." There was an elementary prudence to be observed: Winthrop said that the prayer would arise from subsequent plantations, yet what was England itself but one of God's plantations? In America, he promised, we shall see, or may see, more of

God's wisdom, power, and truth "then formerly wee have beene acquainted with." The situation was such that, for the moment, the model had no chance to be exhibited in England; Puritans could talk about it, theorize upon it, but they could not display it, could not prove that it would actually work. But if they had it set up in America—in a bare land, devoid of already established (and corrupt) institutions, empty of bishops and courtiers, where they could start *de novo*, and the eyes of the world were upon it—and if then it performed just as the saints had predicted of it, the Calvinist internationale would know exactly how to go about completing the already begun but temporarily stalled revolution in Europe.

When we look upon the enterprise from this point of view, the psychology of the second and third generations becomes more comprehensible. We realize that the migration was not sent upon its errand in order to found the United States of America, nor even the New England conscience. Actually, it would not perform its errand even when the colonists did erect a due form of government in church and state: what was further required in order for this mission to be a success was that the eyes of the world be kept fixed upon it in rapt attention. If the rest of the world, or at least of Protestantism, looked elsewhere, or turned to another model, or simply got distracted and forgot about New England, if the new land was left with a polity nobody in the great world of Europe wanted—then every success in fulfilling the terms of the covenant would become a diabolical measure of failure. If the due form of government were not everywhere to be saluted, what would New England have upon its hands? How give it a name, this victory nobody could utilize? How provide an identity for something conceived under misapprehensions? How could a universal which turned out to be nothing but a provincial particular be called anything but a blunder or an abortion?

If an actor, playing the leading role in the greatest dramatic spectacle of the century, were to attire himself and put on his make-up, rehearse his lines, take a deep breath, and stride onto the stage, only to find the theater dark and empty, no spotlight working, and himself entirely alone, he would feel as did New England around 1650 or 1660. For in the 1640's, during the Civil Wars, the colonies, so to speak, lost their audience. First of all, there proved to be, deep in the Puritan movement, an irreconcilable split between the Presbyterian and Independent wings, wherefore no one system could be imposed upon England, and so the New England model was unserviceable. Secondly—most horrible to relate—the Independents, who in polity were carrying New England's banner and were supposed, in the schedule of history, to lead England into imitation of the colonial order, betrayed the sacred cause by yielding to the heresy of toleration. They actually welcomed Roger Williams, whom the leaders of the model had kicked out of Massachusetts so that his nonsense about liberty of conscience would not spoil the administrations of charity.

In other words, New England did not lie, did not falter; it made good everything Winthrop demanded—wonderfully good—and then found that its lesson was rejected by those choice spirits for whom the exertion had been made. By casting out Williams, Anne Hutchinson, and the Antinomians, along with an assortment of Gortonists and Anabaptists, into that cesspool then becoming known as Rhode Island, Winthrop, Dudley, and the clerical leaders showed Oliver Cromwell how he should go about governing England. Instead, he developed the utterly absurd theory that so long as a man made a good soldier in the New Model Army, it did not matter whether he was a Calvinist, an Antinomian, an Arminian, an Anabaptist or even—horror of horrors—a Socinian! Year after year, as the circus tours this country, crowds howl with laughter, no matter how many times they have seen the stunt, at the bustle that walks by itself: the clown comes out dressed in a large skirt with a bustle behind; he turns sharply to the left, and the bustle continues blindly and obstinately straight ahead, on the original course. It is funny in a circus, but not in history. There is nothing but tragedy in the realization that one was in the main path of events, and now is sidetracked and disregarded. One is always able, of course, to stand firm on his first resolution, and to condemn the clown of history for taking the wrong turning: yet this is a desolating sort of stoicism, because it always carries with it the recognition that history will never come back to the predicted path, and that with one's own demise, righteousness must die out of the world.

The most humiliating element in the experience was the way the English brethren turned upon the colonials for precisely their greatest achievement. It must have seemed, for those who came with Winthrop in 1630 and who remembered the clarity and brilliance with which he set forth the conditions of their errand, that the world was turned upside down and inside out when, in June 1645, thirteen leading Independent divines—such men as Goodwin, Owen, Nye, Burroughs, formerly friends and allies of Hooker and Davenport, men who might easily have come to New England and helped extirpate heretics—wrote the General Court that the colony's law banishing Anabaptists was an embarrassment to the Independent cause in England. Opponents were declaring, said these worthies, "that persons of our way, principall and spirit cannot beare with Dissenters from them, but Doe correct, fine, imprison and banish them wherever they have power soe to Doe." There were indeed people in England who admired the severities of Massachusetts, but we assure you, said the Independents, these "are utterly your enemyes and Doe seeke your extirpation from the face of the earth: those who now in power are your friends are quite otherwise minded, and doe professe they are much offended with your proceedings."

Thus early commenced that chronic weakness in the foreign policy of Americans, an inability to recognize who in truth constitute their best friends abroad.

We have lately accustomed ourselves to the fact that there does exist a mentality which will take advantage of the liberties allowed by society in order to conspire for the ultimate suppression of those same privileges. The government of Charles I and Archbishop Laud had not, where that danger was concerned, been liberal, but it had been conspicuously inefficient; hence, it did not liquidate the Puritans (although it made halfhearted efforts), nor did it herd them into prison camps. Instead, it generously, even lavishly, gave a group of them a charter to Massachusetts Bay, and obligingly left out the standard clause requiring that the document remain in London, that the grantees keep their office within reach of Whitehall. Winthrop's revolutionaries availed themselves of this liberty to get the charter overseas, and thus to set up a regime dedicated to the worship of God in the manner they desired—which meant allowing nobody else to worship any other way, especially adherents of Laud and King Charles. All this was perfectly logical and consistent. But what happened to the thought processes of their fellows in England made no sense whatsoever. Out of the New Model Army came the fantastic notion that a party struggling for power should proclaim that, once it captured the state, it would recognize the right of dissenters to disagree and to have their own worship, to hold their own opinions. Oliver Cromwell was so far gone in this idiocy as to become a dictator, in order to impose toleration by force! Amid this shambles, the errand of New England collapsed. There was nobody left at headquarters to whom reports could be sent.

Many a man has done a brave deed, been hailed as a public hero, had honors and ticker tape heaped upon him—and then had to live, day after day, in the ordinary routine, eating breakfast and brushing his teeth, in what seems protracted anticlimax. A couple may win their way to each other across insuperable obstacles, elope in a blaze of passion and glory—and then have to learn that life is a matter of buying the groceries and getting the laundry done. This sense of the meaning having gone out of life, that all adventures are over, that no great days and no heroism lie ahead, is particularly galling when it falls upon a son whose father once was the public hero or the great lover. He has to put up with the daily routine without ever having known at first hand the thrill of danger or the ecstasy of passion. True, he has his own hardships—clearing rocky pastures, hauling in the cod during a storm, fighting Indians in a swamp—but what are these compared with the magnificence of leading an exodus of saints to found a city on a hill, for the eyes of all the world to behold? He might wage a stout fight against the Indians, and one out of ten of his fellows might perish in the struggle, but the world was no longer interested. He would be reduced to writing accounts of himself and scheming to get a publisher in London, in a desperate effort to tell a heedless world, "Look, I exist!"

His greatest difficulty would be not the stones, storms, and Indians, but the problem of his identity. In something of this sort, I should like to suggest, consists the anxiety and torment that inform productions of the late seventeenth and early eighteenth centuries—and should I say, some thereafter? It appears most clearly in *Magnalia Christi Americana*, the work of that soul most tortured by the problem, Cotton Mather: "I write the Wonders of the Christian Religion, flying from the Depravations of Europe, to the American Strand." Thus he proudly begins, and at once trips over the acknowledgment that the founders had not simply fled from depraved Europe but had intended to redeem it. And so the book is full of lamentations over the declension of the children, who appear, page after page, in contrast to their mighty progenitors, about as profligate a lot as ever squandered a great inheritance.

And yet, the *Magnalia* is not an abject book; neither are the election sermons abject, nor is the inventory of sins offered by the synod of 1679. There is bewilderment, confusion, chagrin, but there is no surrender. A task has been assigned upon which the populace are in fact intensely engaged. But they are not sure any more for just whom they are working; they know they are moving, but they do not know where they are going. They seem still to be on an errand, but if they are no longer inferiors sent by the superior forces of the Reformation, to whom they should report, then their errand must be wholly of the second sort, something with a purpose and an intention sufficient unto itself. If so, what is it? If it be not the due form of government, civil and ecclesiastical, that they brought into being, how otherwise can it be described?

The literature of self-condemnation must be read for meanings far below the surface, for meanings of which, we may be so rash as to surmise, the authors were not fully conscious, but by which they were troubled and goaded. They looked in vain to history for an explanation of themselves; more and more it appeared that the meaning was not to be found in theology, even with the help of the covenantal dialectic. Thereupon, these citizens found that they had no other place to search but within themselves—even though, at first sight, that repository appeared to be nothing but a sink of iniquity. Their errand having failed in the first sense of the term, they were left with the second, and required to fill it with meaning by themselves and out of themselves. Having failed to rivet the eyes of the world upon their city on the hill, they were left alone with America.

6 *Bernard Bailyn*

COMMUNICATIONS AND TRADE:
THE ATLANTIC IN THE SEVENTEENTH CENTURY

Americans in the seventeenth century were located on the frame of an
Atlantic world. The ocean no less than the land defined their existence.
Land has so much fashioned our history since 1776 that we tend to
forget how much the ocean fashioned it before 1776. The frontier of
the colonists was not only terrestrial but oceanic. It was indeed only
by means of their commercial lifelines across the ocean that they were
able to master the land. No less significant, the oceanic trade posited
the central characteristics of their society.

It is this impact of trade on colonial life which Professor Bernard
Bailyn of Harvard University considers in the following article. Professor Bailyn, one of the most promising of America's younger historians, has written an excellent study of *The New England Merchants
of the Seventeenth Century* (1955). Social history in the broadest
sense, the work is concerned with the relevance of family ties, status
mobility, religious connections, and the course of politics to the economic interests of the mercantile group. In the article below, Professor
Bailyn seeks to answer several important questions about the role of
transoceanic trade in the colonial world. What was the larger structure
of England's commercial system? What part did kinship play in Atlantic trade? How did trade help shape the character of colonial urban
development? How did the advent of an English official class in the
colonies affect the merchant community?

In his answers, Professor Bailyn adds a dimension to the story of
American origins in the seventeenth century. He provides a view of
the larger Atlantic world without which our colonial past is only
partly seen. He construes history as a complex of forces that is at
once economic, social, and political. And he reminds us that this
complex, and indeed all history, may ultimately be understood only
in terms of people and their interrelations.

In the first half of the seventeenth century the northern mercantile nations
of Europe followed Spain and Portugal in flinging their commercial frontiers westward to the New World. By the end of the century they had

Reprinted with permission from *The Journal of Economic History*, XIII (Fall,
1953), 378–87.

surpassed the Iberian nations in western trade and made of the Atlantic basin a single great trading area. Their economic enterprises created not only a crisscrossing web of transoceanic traffic but also a cultural community that came to form the western periphery of European civilization. The members of this community were widely separated, scattered across three thousand miles of ocean and up and down the coasts of two continents. But the structure of commerce furnished a communication system that brought these far-flung settlements together. The same structure proved to be a framework upon which certain important elements in colonial society took form. My purpose is to sketch certain characteristics of the Atlantic colonies in the seventeenth century which relate to these social consequences of commercial growth.

The formative period of northern Atlantic trade was the second third of the seventeenth century. In those years there were important commercial developments on the American continent by the English, the Dutch, and the French; but the swiftest advance took place in the Caribbean. "After 1625," A. P. Newton writes, "swarms of English and French colonists poured like flies upon the rotting carcase of Spain's empire in the Caribbean, and within ten years the West Indian scene was changed forever." The Lesser Antilles became a battleground of the expanding European empires. The island of St. Christopher in the Leewards was jointly possessed by the French and English; Barbados, Nevis, Antigua, and Montserrat were indisputably English; Guadeloupe and Martinique were French; and Curaçao, St. Eustatius, and Tobago were in the hands of the Dutch.

The feverish activity that lay behind these developments resulted from the belief of numerous Europeans that wealth could be readily extracted from the places in the New World with which they were acquainted. But for every success there were a dozen failures. Hopes were held for commercial designs that strike us now as ill-conceived, even stupid. Yet to contemporary merchants, cautious men who built fortunes on their ability to judge investments shrewdly, they were at least as promising as the schemes that succeeded.

Remarkable only for its subsequent fame but typical in its results was the Plymouth Company's colony at the mouth of the Sagadahoc River in New Hampshire. Behind the failure of this venture lay the belief that exploiters of North America, like those of Asia, had only to build coastal trading factories, to which throngs of natives would haul precious piles of goods to exchange for tinkling bells and snippets of bright cloth. English merchants invested approximately £15,000 in the Lynn Ironworks, which collapsed within two decades of its promising start in the early 1640's. At least three major fur companies foundered on the belief that the heartland of American pelts lay in the swampy margins of a mythical "Great Lake of the Iroquois," from which were supposed to flow all the main rivers emptying into the Atlantic. The Virginia settlements after the mid-twenties gradually gained a solid economic base, but only after a decade and a half of continuous failure. In the Caribbean islands, experimentation in all sorts of commodities preceded and accompanied the development of sugar as a staple crop.

Patterns of trade were established, of course, around the poles of successful economic ventures, and it was, therefore, only after the broad wave of failures had receded, leaving behind clear indications of natural possibilities, that the commercial system in its familiar form became evident.

The result was a network of trading routes woven by the enterprises of merchants, shipmasters, and colonists representing all the leading mercantile nations of western Europe. The character of each nation's involvement in the web of traffic was determined largely by the resources it controlled and its place in European affairs. Holland's concentration on the carriage of other nations' goods shaped its position; the commerce of France came to rest upon Canadian furs and West Indian sugar; England's position was determined by the very variety of her colonial products and of the interests of her merchants.

The form of England's commercial system was an interlocked group of irregular circles linking the fixed points of port towns in the British Isles, Newfoundland, the American mainland, the West Indies, the Wine Islands, and the continent of Europe. Outward from the larger ports in the British Isles flowed shipping, manufactures, and investments in colonial property, the enhanced value of which returned as colonial products to be sold at home or abroad. No important part of this flow was self-sufficient. Merchants in the colonies, who profited by injecting into the flow goods of their ownership which would be carried one or more stages closer to the ultimate resolution, became important agents in maintaining the efficiency of this mechanism. Their commerce was not independent, and if it appeared to be so to some of them that was because the efficiency of the system permitted them to operate successfully within a limited area. A breakdown in any major part of the mechanism affected all other parts. When, at the outbreak of the American Revolution, the link between England and her colonies was broken, the whole system, in so far as it affected the colonial merchants, was destroyed.

To contemporaries, the commercial system, which we may describe in abstract, geometrical terms, was not something impersonal existing above men's heads, outside their lives, to which they attached themselves for purpose of trade. Unconcerned with abstract economic forces, they knew that their trade was the creation of men and that the bonds that kept its parts together were the personal relationships existing among them.

Overseas commerce in the seventeenth century was capricious. Arrangements were interminably delayed by the accidents of sailing. Demand fluctuated almost incalculably, as one unforeseen crop failure could create a market which the arrival of a few ships could eliminate overnight. Reliable factors and correspondents were, therefore, of paramount importance, for the success of large enterprises rested on their judgment. In such a situation the initiation and continuance of commerce demanded deep personal commitments between people separated by hundreds of miles of ocean. How could such commitments be made? Not, in these early years, by impersonal correspondences between men brought into temporary contact by complementary business needs. The logic of the situation demanded that they follow pre-existent ties of blood or long acquaintance.

To a striking degree first commercial contacts were secured by the cement of kinship. Very frequently brothers, sons, and "in-laws" became the colonial agents of their European relatives. In the middle years of the seventeenth century a number of European—especially English and French —trading families spread out over the Atlantic world. Sons of Londoners seeking their fortunes entered trade in the West Indies and drew on their London connections who were themselves anxious to profit from the importation of colonial goods. Thus Richard Povey, brother of the famous London merchant-politician Thomas Povey, looked after the family interests in Jamaica, while another brother, William, attended to affairs in Barbados. Not infrequently the same family had other relatives on the American mainland who joined in the growing enterprise. The Winthrop family, starting with representatives in England and Massachusetts, ended with ties to Rhode Island, New London and Hartford, Connecticut, Teneriffe in the Canaries, and Antigua in the West Indies. Typical of the reports by young Samuel Winthrop of his progress in securing the last-named contacts are these sentences from a letter of 1648 to his father:

> Captain Clement everet a Justice of peace [in St. Christopher], who being our country man and hearing our name vsed me verry Courtiously, and assisted me much in my law suites which were there verry many. Justice Froth, who was of your acquantance in England (as he informes me), was his Granfather. I haue left in his handes my busines in St. Christpors.

Jean Bailly of La Rochelle conducted his West Indian trade through two relatives in the Caribbean islands, especially Clerbaut Bergier in Martinique. But the most complete family commercial system of which we have any knowledge is that of the Hutchinsons; it is an almost ideal type of this sort of arrangement.

The Hutchinson family trading unit was based upon the continuous flow of manufactures exported from London by the affluent Richard Hutchinson to his brothers Samuel and Edward and his nephews Elisha and Eliakim in Boston, Massachusetts. They, together with Thomas Savage, who had married Richard's sister, retailed the goods in the Bay area and, through middlemen, sold also to the inland settlers. They conducted a large trade with the West Indies, sending provisions and cattle in exchange for cotton and sugar which they sold for credit in London. This West Indian trade of the Hutchinsons was largely handled for them by Peleg Sanford of Portsmouth, Rhode Island, whose mother was another sister of Richard and who was, hence, cousin and nephew of the Boston merchants of the family. Peleg, who had started his career as a commercial agent in the West Indies, exported their horses and provisions to Barbados where they were sold by his brothers, the Barbadian merchants William and Elisha Sanford.

The Hutchinsons with their Rhode Island and West Indian relations formed a self-conscious family group which considered it unfortunate but not unnatural that Edward Hutchinson should go to jail, as he did in 1667, as a consequence of his support of his nephew Peleg in a law suit.

Since commerce was so dependent upon personal relationships, the weaving of a network of correspondences was greatly facilitated by the migrations within the colonial area. Many mainland settlers transplanted themselves to the Carribean islands and became factors in the West Indies for the merchant friends they had left behind. On the other hand, several merchants were involved in the movement of people among and out of the West Indies, and some of them became residents of the continental colonies. Thus, John Parris, a relative of the New Englander John Hull, moved from the West Indies to Boston where he engaged in large operations in an attempt to stock his Barbados plantation with slaves. Men who moved south to the Indies or north to the continent carried with them friendships and a knowledge of affairs in their old home towns which were used in broadening the foreign contacts of the colonial merchants.

A further consequence of the personal nature of commercial ties in this early period was the consistency, long before mercantilist legislation became effective, with which Frenchmen and Britishers dealt with their fellow nationals in trade. Correspondences with foreigners were difficult to establish and maintain. To British colonials in this period, it seemed that little reliance could be placed on the bonds of Frenchmen who desired nothing more than the collapse of the British settlements in the New World. In long-distance transactions Englishmen preferred to deal with their relatives and friends who, if necessary, could be brought to law in the British courts far more easily than could Frenchmen. Richard Wharton, one of the most enterprising colonial merchants of the seventeenth century, failed to extend his contacts into the French West Indies because of his inability to secure reliable French correspondents. The later enforcement of mercantilist legislation was greatly facilitated by this early tendency of overseas merchants to favor connections with, if not relatives or old friends, at least fellow countrymen.

Through channels of trade created by personal ties among Europeans scattered about the Atlantic world flowed not only physical commodities but the human communications that related the settlers to European life. The orbits of commerce formed by lines drawn between the fixed points of correspondents helped shape the character of urban development and the structure of society in the colonial settlements.

On the American continent, as certain trading centers became poles in the primary cycles of trade, others slipped back toward ruralism. In the passage of generations the communities involved in the major orbits came into closer cultural relations with Europe than they did with some of the neighboring backwoods villages. The Boston merchants' meeting place in their Townhouse Exchange was in every way, except geographically, closer to the "New-England walke" on the London Exchange than to the market places of most inland towns. Study of any of the continental trading regions reveals the varying degrees of provincialism that followed the solidification of the routes of commerce.

In New England, the most important commercial center in North America during the seventeenth century, Boston, with its excellent harbor and access to the provincial government and to flourishing agricultural markets, became the major terminus of traffic originating in Europe. With the exception of Salem and Charlestown, the other promising mercantile centers of the 1630's and 1640's fell back into secondary economic roles and relative seclusion from the cultural life of the Atlantic community. Plymouth, which had been the first trading center east of Manhattan, was described in 1660 as "a poor small Towne now, The People being removed into Farmes in the Country," and New Haven, whose optimistic merchant leaders had laid out "stately and costly houses," was "not so glorious as once it was," with its "Merchants either dead or come away, the rest gotten to their Farmes." This is not to say that these essentially rural districts had no trade. On the contrary, there were men in the Connecticut River towns and along Long Island Sound who managed a considerable exchange of goods; but their dealings were different from those of the Bostonians. Engaged in secondary orbits of trade, they sent small but steady flows of local produce only to other American colonies or occasionally to the West Indies. The Connecticut River grandees were, like the younger Pynchon, primarily landed squires and only secondarily merchants. The few men in the small coastal villages who did devote themselves primarily to trade operated within a commercial sphere subordinate to that of the Bostonians and the Dutchmen.

Life in the inland areas and in the minor ports came to differ significantly from that in the commercial centers in direct contact with Europe. While Boston and New York assumed characteristics of British provincial outports and while their leading residents groped for an understanding of their place as colonials in British society, towns like Scarborough, Maine, and Wethersfield, Connecticut, became models of new types of communities; and their inhabitants, restricted in experience to the colonial world, came to lack the standards by which to measure or even to perceive their provincialism. Fashion, patterns for styles of living, and the emulative spirit of provincialism followed the routes of trade, which, throughout the colonial world, became important social boundaries.

This fact became particularly evident in the last third of the century when national rivalries, both military and economic, required the presence of official representatives in the colonies from the home countries. These officers, civil and military, settled for the most part in the large trading centers, close to the main objects of their supervision. Their presence in what might be called the focuses of the primary trading orbits had a most important social consequence. These home country representatives were quickly surrounded by a number of Europeans new to the colonies: men seeking careers in the quickly expanding colonial administrations. Customs functionaries, lesser bureaucrats, fortune hunters in official positions— these newcomers, grouped around the chief European representatives, came to constitute colonial officialdom, which in all the main colonial ports became a major social magnet for the residents. For not only did it represent cosmopolitan fashion and political influence, but, in its access to those who controlled government contracts and who wielded the weapon of customs regulations, it offered great economic opportunities.

Toward these groups, therefore, moved every colonial with ambition and the slightest hope of success. The threshold of officialdom became a great divide in the society of the commercial towns. Next to this principle of association, "class," in the traditional European sense, was meaningless. In Europe the word "merchant" meant not only an occupation but a status and a way of life. In America, where, as Madam Knight discovered in her famous journey of 1704, they gave the title of merchant to every backwoods huckster, trade was not so much a way of life as a way of making money, not a social condition but an economic activity. Similarly, how could the well-known American mariner, Captain Cyprian Southack, be prevented from describing himself, as he did on occasion, as "gent."?

The limits of officialdom, however, were palpable. No merchant would confuse failure with success in obtaining favors from customs officials or in gaining contracts for provisions and naval stores. It was well worth a merchant's noting, as Samuel Sewall did in his *Diary*, that he was not invited to the governor's dinner parties or to the extravagant funerals staged by the members of his group.

It was as true in the seventeenth century as it is now that the introduction of an important new social barrier necessarily intrudes upon a variety of interests. The advent of officialdom was attended by upheavals throughout the Atlantic world. Wherever we turn in this period we find evidence of social dislocation as successful resident entrepreneurs came to terms with this important new force in the colonial world.

One of the first successful agricultural districts in Carolina was Albemarle County. Behind the barrier of shifting sand bars that blocked Albemarle Sound to all but the most shallow-draft ocean-going vessels lived, in the 1670's, approximately 3,000 settlers—farmers, coastal backwoodsmen, many of them tough, stubborn refugees from better-organized communities. Their one cash crop was tobacco, of which they prepared nearly one million pounds a year. This they disposed of to northerners on peddling voyages in exchange for the commodities they needed. The Navigation Law of 1673 levied duties on tobacco at the port of lading, and Albemarle, like all other commercial centers, was soon visited by a customs collector. The settlers resisted, fearing an increase in the price of goods if their tobacco was taxed, and they forced the governor to remit to the traders three farthings in every penny taken. In 1677 the appointment of an imperious collector of customs determined to enforce the law led to a rebellion of the settlers headed by one John Culpeper. Until the legal authorities could regain control, Culpeper acted as collector, formed a temporary government, and barred the royal comptroller and surveyor of the customs at Albemarle from the exercise of his office.

Culpeper's rebellion, though it was soon quelled and finds little mention in American history, was a significant event. It is a simplified example of what was taking place throughout the colonies. We do not yet have a full account of Leisler's rebellion which kept New York in turmoil for two years. But when we do, it will be found that it was in great part the culmination of resentments that accompanied the introduction of English officialdom into that province. Leisler's career, in fact, can only be understood against the background of family rivalries that grew up around this pre-eminent principle of association. Edmund Andros, famous for his difficulties as the governor of the Dominion of New England, had a less notorious but equally important reign as the Duke of York's governor in New York. In this position he precipitated social differences among the merchants who resisted when they could not take advantage of his influence. He was finally recalled on charges of excessive fee-taking and profiteering.

The rebellion of 1689, which overthrew his administration of the Dominion of New England, divided the northern merchants on lines not of ideology but of interests defined by the degree of proximity to officialdom. No ideology, no religious belief, no abstract political principle or party loyalty separated the Boston merchants Richard Wharton and Charles Lidget, but in 1689 they were on opposite sides of the political fence. Lidget ended up in the Boston jail with Andros because his connections, inherited from his father who had built the family fortune on the timber he sold to the Navy mast contractors, linked him to the leaders of the official group. Wharton died in the midst of his fight for the removal of Andros whose favor he had been denied. The fact that Lidget was one of the founders of the first Anglican Church in New England does not indicate a religious or ideological orientation different from Wharton's. The latter, if he was not an active Anglican, certainly was not a dissenter. Both men married heiress daughters of nonconformist New Englanders.

In the West Indies the same principle was at work during most of the seventeenth century. But toward the end of the century controversies touched off by the intrusion of officialdom diminished in the islands as a consequence of the consolidation of large plantations and the growth of absenteeism. The resident nonofficial population became less active politically as the large planters returned to the home country, leaving their estates in the hands of managers and agents. But battles over the economic benefits of political and social advantage were not ended; they were merely transferred to London where they punctuated the history of the West India interest.

By the end of the century this principle of association in the commercial centers was deeply woven into the fabric of American society. Its importance did not diminish thereafter. Recently, Oliver Dickerson in his book *The Navigation Acts and the American Revolution* destroyed a number of myths by pointing out the importance of what he called "customs racketeering." From his researches it appears that the merchant group was as deeply divided on the eve of the Revolution as it was in 1689. Both John Hancock and Thomas Hutchinson were leading Boston merchants, but the former was clearly victimized by the strategy of the Hutchinson-Bernard clique which controlled the channels of prerogative. And in South Carolina, Henry Laurens, probably the richest merchant in the southern colonies, whose mercantile connections were with the opponents of the King's Friends, suffered equally from the rapacity of the official group.

Further study of the merchants as a social group may reveal that this principle of association, which emerged as an important social force when the nations of Europe undertook to draw together the threads of trade spun by seventeenth-century entrepreneurs, was a major determinant of the movement that led to Revolution.

COLONIAL SOCIETY IN THE
EIGHTEENTH CENTURY

7 Chester E. Eisinger

THE FARMER IN THE
EIGHTEENTH CENTURY ALMANAC

The image we Americans have of ourselves reflects the meaning and direction of American life. The image is a compound of what is real and of the hopes with which we invest what is real. Thus, what we see in the national mirror is part fact, part fancy. The myths we live by, no less than the realities, are important factors in the things we do and in the way we go. The study of American history must therefore be concerned with the changing image we have had of ourselves and with the reasons why it has changed.

What view of itself did the agrarian society of the eighteenth century take? This is the question posed by Chester E. Eisinger, Professor of English at Purdue University. For the answer, Professor Eisinger has made a wide canvassing of the almanacs which enjoyed great vogue and popularity among Americans at that time. The almanac is a particularly felicitous source of information about agrarian values and the American image. Dangling near the fireplace, it was endlessly consulted for its information about sunrises and sunsets, for its homely advice, for its simple poetry. It served as an eighteenth-century combination of *Reader's Digest* and Edgar Guest, of *Ladies' Home Journal* and Dr. Spock. It was full of preachment and morality; it prescribed details for the good life; it commended farmers for the simplicity of their ways and the ruggedness of their individualism; it encouraged a do-it-yourself society to continue doing it. If to work is to pray, then farm work afforded its own morality. The almanac, as Professor Eisinger stresses, spoke for more than

Reprinted with permission from *Agricultural History*, XXVIII (July, 1954), 107–12.

agrarian virtues. In an age when America was an open and mobile frontier of Europe, it was inevitable that Americans should define the differences between themselves and Europeans. In their image of themselves, Americans stressed their freehold tenures, their equality, their abundance, their freedom, their independence. The parts of the image made a whole which Professor Eisinger aptly calls agrarian nationalism.

The image is a challenging one. It elicits both interest and interrogation. What part of the image of the farmer in the eighteenth century almanac was fact, what part fancy? How did this image contrast with that given us by such notable visitors as Crèvecoeur and Kalm? In what ways did this image reflect larger political, social, and economic developments? In what ways did it influence them? In what way does this image explain some of the values which lie deep in our tradition: our sense of difference from the European world, our isolationism, our individualism, our respect for the frontier, our belief that we are a frontier people?

In studying the image of the eighteenth-century farmer, one wonders inevitably about its meaning for today. If a generic portrait could be found in an age when most Americans were farmers, could such a portrait be found today? And what would it show? To what extent have the virtues of the farmer's life subsisted, to what extent have they been lost? To what extent, for example, is suburbia the homage that an industrial America is paying to the idyl of a lost agrarian world? To what extent has the American now come to identify himself with the European because of the challenge of the non-Western world? Some components of the national portrait are currently being stressed. The American is escaping from freedom; he is other-directed rather than inner-directed; he is a member of the growing white-collar class; he is under the governance of a power elite; he is being homogenized by mass culture. The portrait is the joint product of professional sociologists and social psychologists and it is fair to ask if they are not also professional Jeremiahs. Are there no redeeming virtues in the American image today?

Ultimately, the question we come upon is the role of such an image in the national life. The image serves a purpose. It speaks a wish. It expresses a disappointment. It compensates for a sense of inadequacy. It sets a goal. It affords a blending of reality and myth in which the myth intensifies some of the reality and also blurs some of it out. It nominates the national heroes and permits the nation to become heroic by identifying itself with them. It defines what is American in contradistinction to what is foreign. In whatever mirrors we may see it—almanacs, magazines, novels, newspapers, radio, television—the national image is that sufficient reflection of reality which we call truth and by which we live our daily lives. In its changing forms, it sums up the self-consciousness of our changing generations. As such, it is a vital part of the American past.

In recent decades, scholarship has revealed the value of the old farmer's almanac for social and intellectual history. Even a cursory examination of these little books shows how they acted as cultural carriers in the eighteenth century, disseminating knowledge about the new science, the new religion, and the new politics. But since the almanacs were compiled primarily, if not uniquely, for the farmer, the question arises: what knowledge and what ideas did they convey about the farmer and agriculture? It is to the answer of this obvious but hitherto neglected question that the present paper addresses itself.

Quite simply, the answer is that the almanac, a mirror of its time, reflected the American acceptance in the eighteenth century of what I have called elsewhere the freehold concept, a notion that became for the American imagination of the nineteenth century a belief that here in our West was the Garden of the World, a fructifying belief that made of the yeoman farmer the archetypal American and advanced the settlement of western lands. Partly myth and partly fact, the freehold concept rests on holding land in freehold tenure, and includes the propositions that men have a natural right to the land; ownership of it gives them status and a stake in society, as well as social and economic security; agriculture is the most productive form of labor, and it is conducive to moral and physical health; the agrarian way of life stimulates and makes possible individualism and self-reliance; the farmer is the backbone of democracy whom the government must support. This complex of ideas had wide currency among eighteenth century writers; its principal champions were Franklin, Jefferson, and St. Jean de Crèvecoeur. These men, like their contemporaries who shared a belief in the freehold concept, saw in agrarianism a key that would open to them the quality and aspiration of the society about them. Generally speaking, the almanacs accepted the agrarian view of eighteenth century life in America and conveyed it to their readers, thus fulfilling their function as media of popular culture.

Hardly as a matter of an interpretation of society, but simply as a useful practice, the almanacs, one would assume, would be full of practical advice to farmers. This assumption should apply especially to an eighteenth century almanac, published at the dawn of scientific farming when agricultural reformers like Arthur Young and Jared Eliot were beginning to make themselves heard. Curiously enough, such practical materials appeared only sporadically in the almanacs and obviously had no special importance in the editorial scheme. The early Leeds almanac is an illuminating example. In the 1687 issue Daniel Leeds announces that he is a student of agriculture, and he runs a section on "Short Rules in Husbandry." This appears annually, giving information on such matters as the dates of sowing and harvesting and the making of cider. But the section is omitted in 1694, and from that date to the end of the almanac's career in the early eighteenth century there are only scattered references to farming. The student of agriculture had turned to other interests. Leeds is more typical in this respect than Richard Saunders' *Poor Richard Improved*, which published advice in virtually every issue after 1762 on such subjects as preventing smut, raising silkworms, increasing corn crops, or cultivating vines for wine. One would guess that pragmatic American editors and readers alike would welcome such aids to improvement, but the evidence in the majority of the almanacs does not support such a conclusion. Strangely enough, in this area the almanacs seem to have disregarded an opportunity to interest and serve the farmer.

Apparently, however, the almanac editor felt his reader would be interested in pastoral poetry, for he published an inordinate amount of it. It is a paradoxical comment on the American mind of the period that the almanacs should have neglected the practical aspects of farming in favor of verse celebrating rural harvests and rural pleasures. This poetry, I think it fair to say, constitutes an indirect eulogy of the farmer. It is a means of assuring him of his own importance and good fortune and of the valuable role he plays in society. These appear to me to have been the self-consciously agrarian motives of the almanac makers in using pastoral verse. Furthermore, such verse incorporated several typically agrarian themes. Primitivism is one of the fundamental assumptions in these pastorals, as it is in all agrarianism. The poets insisted on singing of the rustic youth "brown with meridian toil,/Healthful and strong"; or on pointing out the virtues of sweating in the field while making hay. They enumerated the pleasures of country life, "void of care" where "Woods, and op'ning Fields,/With purling Streams to harmless Joys invite"; rural pastimes are invariably innocent. Another theme is domestic felicity which distinguishes the countryman from the great men whose minds are filled with "anxious Pain":

> The Farmer in his Cot enjoys more Bliss,
> With's little Children climbing for a Kiss.

Of course the idyllic note is frequently sounded; here it is in a poem of provincial pride celebrating the development of New England.

> From Savage Deserts rise our green Retreats
>
> . . . . .
>
> *Great Britain's* Glory buds and blossoms here:
> Ye Gods in *Rome*, what have ye more to do?
> *Elysium* in *New England* waits for you.

The final paragraph, in a kind of prose poem on "Spring," published in 1799, summarizes the whole pastoral spirit in associating agricultural life with the golden age that must have existed before the fall of man.

The industrious tiller of the ground now rises to behold the beauties of the morn—to breathe the fragrance of nature, and to be entertained by the airy choirs, which, in animated strains, sing their morning hymns. With the enlivening sun he begins his pleasing task—unwrecked with care, and unperplexed with doubt, he joins his simple song to the varied music of the day. Let none consider the culture of the ground as an ignoble employment: It was the business originally assigned to man: It was his business, and his pleasure, when all his passions were harmonious, and every wish was innocent.

Most often encountered in the pastoral verse is the cornucopia theme, which displays an intense preoccupation with the abundance of the crops. Not only is there a constant reiteration of the idea of plenty, but also this theme is presented to the almost inevitable accompaniment of the chuckling sense of triumph that signalizes man's victory over nature. The great enemy is winter, for it brings the possibility of freezing and starving. The desideratum is security: warmth and sufficient food. The pastoral is not only an expression of exultation but a paean to the farmer whose success in the art of cultivation has forced the fear of want farther and farther into the distance. The farmer becomes in this context the founder and carrier of civilization; Prometheus joins hands with Ceres. The importance of these pastoral themes for America lies in the fact that the conflict described was intensely felt in America, a relatively new country, and the significant role of the farmer in it was immediately discernible.

These considerations, then, lend an authoritative ring of conviction to the poet's statement that there is no "greater heaven on earth" than watching the last load of the harvest come home. They give us real sympathy with the satisfaction of the full barn:

> Now Ceres crowns the barns with plenty;
> Joyful farmers view their store:
> Be happy men, let this content ye,
> Nor dread the winter [storms] no more.

The same sentiment is found in "The Joys of Harvest," which tells how the damsels and swains celebrate the end of their harvest toils with a dance. The swain, as if carried away in some pagan rite, always turns his eyes in rapture toward the harvest, the reward that crowns all his toil.

When we turn to other aspects of agrarianism in the almanacs, we find some support for the foregoing view of the pastorals. Agriculture is regarded as the basis for all society and the source of all progress, and it is the one indispensable industry. No almanacs I have examined contradict this view. Although not all almanacs are concerned with these matters, many of them contain relevant evidence; a sampling will reveal the general pattern. Note then, this couplet which Eben W. Judd used:

> HAIL agriculture! by whose parent aid,
> The deep foundations of our states are laid. . . .

In 1786 Judd had published a brief essay, "Agriculture," which touched upon many of the most significant aspects of the freehold concept:

Nothing can more fully prove the ingratitude of mankind (a crime often charged upon them, and often denied) than the little regard which the disposers of honorary rewards have paid to *Agriculture;* which is treated as a subject so remote from common life, by all those who do not immediately hold the plough, or give fodder to the ox, that there is room to question, whether a great part of mankind has yet been informed that life is sustained by the fruits of the earth.

Agriculture not only gives riches to a nation, but the only riches we can call our own, and of which we need not fear either deprivation or diminution.

Of nations, as of individuals, the first blessing is independence. Neither the man nor the people can be happy, to whom any human power can deny the necessaries, or conveniencies of life. There is no way of living without foreign assistance, *but by the product of our own land improved by our own labour.* Every other source of plenty is perishable or casual.

Here the central position of agriculture in the national life and in the economy is affirmed by arguments similar to those used by the Physiocrats in France. Another Physiocratic notion—that agriculture is the only source of wealth—is also suggested. The democratic ideas of political and economic independence are linked to agriculture, while the traditional atomistic and isolationist attitude, which has since the eighteenth century been associated with agricultural areas in this country, also emerges in this passage.

Nathaniel Ames, maker of perhaps the most distinguished almanac of his time, also devoted thought to agrarianism. In 1761 he printed this Physiocratic aphorism: "Husbandry is the Philosopher's Stone which turns Trees, Fruits, Earth, Iron & Water into Gold." A few years later in the introductory paragraph to a discussion of the use of marl as a fertilizer, Ames underlines some of the ideas Judd had used. ". . . the Kingdoms of the Earth, and the Glory of the World will be transplanted into AMERICA: But the Study and Practice of Agriculture must go Hand in Hand with our Increase. . . ." R. B. Thomas, who issued *The Farmer's Almanack*, displayed more consistent interest in the freehold concept than any other almanac maker of the century. He too should be heard on this score: "The cultivation of the earth . . . [is] the most useful and necessary employment in life." Agriculture is "the art which supports, supplies, and maintains all the rest." And Richard Saunders developed all these ideas in an essay "On Husbandry," preceded by this quatrain:

> To render service, and perfection give
> To this great *Art*, by which all others live:
> To twine the laurel round the farmer's brow,
> And learn to *use*—to *venerate* the PLOUGH.

No employment is more beneficial than agriculture, Saunders tells us. Poets have celebrated it; the leaders of antiquity have followed it. He relates the story of Cincinnatus and exalts Washington as the modern counterpart. Furthermore, husbandry is advantageous because it converts a barren desert into an area of "smiling meads, fertile fields, and numerous flocks and herds." We cannot praise too highly, Saunders concludes, those enterprising farmers who, blest with liberty, brought civilization to this country and set it on the road to glory.

Many of these grandiose generalizations about the role of agriculture in society reveal the spirit of agrarian nationalism that was widespread in America; it is this manifestation of the freehold concept that we may now specifically consider. Patriotic pride could be readily expressed in agricultural terms, since two factors, the availability of land and farming under freehold tenure, gave attractive opportunity to those who were denied it in Europe. Furthermore, the social and political tone of colonial, and later democratic, America was conducive to a more independent and free rural life than could be enjoyed anywhere else. In fact, that freehold tenure which evokes so much praise from Americans and visiting foreigners alike seems to have nourished those qualities of independence, individualism, and love of freedom which constitute the democratic manner and were eventually written into the democratic dogma.

Early expressions of agrarian nationalism appear in the almanacs before one can legitimately talk about American nationalism, but they reflect even well before the Revolution a consciousness of the differences between America and Europe that indicates a conviction of the superiority of American place and custom. In his *Almanack for . . . 1693*, Daniel Leeds has a few lines voicing the confident hope that the produce of American farms will not be the victim of those twins of Old World tyranny, the church and the military.

> Winter we now forget, green Grass we see,
> In Woods and Fields, and Leaves on every Tree.
> The Planters Hopes nor thrifty Husbands Tillage
> Becomes not here the Priest nor Souldiers Pillage.

Fifty years later Titan Leeds glories in the freedom from oppression that marks the American farmer who is happy because bounteous Providence allows him "With his own hands Paternal Grounds to Plow"; he is secure from the "Cheats of Law," "Nor does [he] the Affronts of Palaces endure." In a poem "On Publick Spirit" that runs throughout the 1752 issue of *Poor Richard Improved*, Franklin predicts that America will develop into a great country. Contributing to its growth will be those "Sons of Mis'ry" from Europe who come here to populate the land and enjoy its blessings, where

> Allotted Acres (no reluctant Soil)
> Shall prompt their Industry and pay their Toil.

Characteristic of agrarian nationalism is the open invitation to share the bounty of a fruitful earth and a desire to impugn the social institutions of Europe as they affect the agricultural classes. Thus Judd quotes David Humphreys, who tells us that love of independence prompts the European pilgrim to labor in the soil; having escaped "vassall'd woes," he will find a quiet farm home here. It was obvious that the freehold was superior to serfdom.

For the freehold meant independence, which was another source of nationalistic pride and also a positive good in itself. The almanac makers recognized that the farmer embodied more completely than any other class of citizens in the New World the democratic virtues of independence and equality, and that he loved liberty and was able to live more freely than others. "The Contented Farmer" in Ames' Almanac for 1761 says,

> I eat, drink, and sleep, and do what I please,
> The King in his Palace can only do these.

This freedom and this rather aggressive egalitarianism are hallmarks of the freehold concept. The farm was recognized in explicit terms as a source of "independence and affluence" by Richard Saunders. The same author published a vigorous and a self-conscious agrarian statement on liberty in his *Poor Richard Improved . . . 1771:*

> Who'd know the Sweets of Liberty?
> 'Tis to climb the Mountain's Brow,
> Thence to discern rough Industry,
> At the Harrow or the Plough;
> 'Tis where my Sons their Crops have sown,
> Calling the Harvest all their own,
> 'Tis where the Heart to Truth allied,
> Never felt unmanly Fear;
> 'Tis where the Eye, with milder Pride,
> Nobly sheds sweet Pity's Tear,
> Such as AMERICA yet shall see,
> These are the sweets of Liberty.

Much earlier Franklin had praised the farmer's lot in a poem called, appropriately, "The Farmer."

> O happy he! happiest of mortal Men!
> Who far remov'd from Slavery, as from Pride,
> Fears no Man's Frown, nor cringing waits to catch
> The gracious Nothing of a great Man's Nod;
> . . . . . .

Tempted nor with the Pride nor Pomp of Power,
Nor Pageants of Ambition, nor the Mines
Of grasping Av'rice, nor the poison'd Sweets
Of pamper'd Luxury, he plants his Foot
With Firmness on his old paternal Fields,
And stands unshaken.

The dignity of man, in which Franklin takes a justifiable pride, is guaranteed by the security of the freehold.

Full ownership of the paternal fields was ever a theme emphasized and enjoyed by Americans who cherished their liberties. Land was always available in America; after the French and Indian war, Ames thought, it might be had for nothing in some areas. Free land offered the farmer wonderful opportunity but just as important was the nature of the tenure: "We hold our Lands under no other Lord but He who gave the Land of *Canaan* to *Abraham*. . . . In a long address to the husbandmen of America, written a few years later, Ames is discussing the practical aspects of farming; he points out that we must raise crops for export in order to increase our wealth. "We are not tenants but *lords* of the soil, and may live as genteel, tho' not in such splendour, as lords . . ." by increasing our trade, diligence, and industry.

These prideful sentiments have an obvious corollary: the independent farmer should be the master of his political destiny. Ames asserts the responsibility of the farmer to participate in government, and suggests that he become, in a sense, a politician. But strangely enough, he is alone in this opinion. Other almanacs feel that the farmer should stick to his plough. This is a significant deviation from the general pattern of eighteenth century agrarianism in the almanacs. It should be added that the only other idea in the freehold concept that does not appear is the notion that men have a natural right to the land.

These two deficiencies in the almanac's total coverage of the freehold concept are in reality the exceptions that prove the validity of the thesis here, namely, that the almanac reflected the American acceptance of the concept. For while it is indeed curious that there was not a more vigorous and original contribution to agrarian thought in the almanacs, it is nevertheless clear that the bulk of the propositions that make up the freehold concept were cordially received and advanced by almanac makers. Their championship of this concept reveals them as spokesmen for the farmer and prophet of the agricultural wealth and destiny of our nation.

8 *Carl Bridenbaugh*

ONE HUNDRED YEARS OF URBAN GROWTH

What has been the role of the city in directing the course of American history? Our culture is so largely urban today that it is hard to realize that during the greater part of our history we were a rural people and that most of human history has been lived in the village and the farm rather than in the city. Figures on the distribution of population between city and country do not tell the whole story, however. The metropolis has throughout the course of history exercised an impact on the polity of states that is out of all proportion to the actual numbers of its inhabitants. It is an impact which can be traced in a variety of examples: Athens in the Periclean Age, Rome under the emperors, Florence in the age of the Medici, Madrid under the Habsburgs, Paris under the Bourbons, London in the Victorian Age, New York in the twentieth century.

It would be a misunderstanding of our colonial history, suggests Professor Carl Bridenbaugh of the University of California, to minimize the importance of the urban centers that flourished before the Revolution, despite, again, their relatively small percentage of total population. Bringing the urban aspect of early American history into proper perspective has, indeed, been the particular contribution of Professor Bridenbaugh in his two most significant works: *Cities in the Wilderness* (1938, 1955) and *Cities in Revolt* (1955). Professor Bridenbaugh has extended our knowledge of the dimensions of colonial society through his other works as well, including *Rebels and Gentlemen: Philadelphia in the Age of Franklin* (1942), *The Colonial Craftsman* (1950), and *Myths and Realities: Societies of the Colonial South* (1952).

The essay that follows is the final chapter of *Cities in the Wilderness*. Professor Bridenbaugh's portrait of the major urban centers of the colonial period—Boston, Newport, New York, Philadelphia, and Charles Town—highlights four significant aspects of their history: their physical growth, their economic activities, their handling of social problems, and their cultural traits and attainments.

Framing the five colonial cities in a larger perspective, Professor Bridenbaugh comes up with several challenging observations. Commercial wealth, more than any other factor, determined why and how the towns grew. The problems they faced were generally similar and so too were the ways in which they solved them. The American cities based their solutions upon European examples, adapting the examples to fit in with American circumstances. The transcending importance of the colonial cities was that they "were centers of the transit of civilization from the Old World to the New." They represented a distinct aspect of American life, different at once from the rural hinterlands of the tidewater regions and from the primitive advancing thrusts of the frontier. The five urban centers played a major role in the political, social, and intellectual activities of the colonial period and particularly in the tense drama which reached its climax in the American Revolution.

Professor Bridenbaugh's observations invite further thought. How far, for example, may one argue an urban interpretation of the American past as a counterpoise to the long familiar frontier interpretation? The writings of such historians as Constance Green, Bessie L. Pierce, Arthur M. Schlesinger, Bayrd Still, and Richard Wade, to cite some examples, would suggest that cities have profoundly affected the entire course of our history. What factors were responsible for the growth of cities after the colonial period? What problems did cities face and how did they meet them? How much did the problems they faced and the ways they solved them differ from those of urban centers in other areas of the Western world?

Living in the age of the megalopolis, the super-city, with its teeming millions and its sprawling suburban empire, we are naturally concerned with understanding the nature of our own urban culture. We are concerned to know the patterns and problems of the exploding metropolis—how it is housing its citizens, weaving its transportation network, resolving its racial tensions, renovating its slums, cleaning up its politics, entertaining its masses, educating its children, relating itself to the problems of the state, the nation, and the world. With the preponderant majority of America's population of over 180,000,000 concentrated in the great metropolitan areas, these are matters well worth our concern and our investigation.

The first hundred years of town history on the American continent witnessed the foundation and gradual development of a truly urban society. The story of American life is customarily regarded as a compound of sectional histories, and in the early colonial period two sections are commonly considered,—the tidewater and the frontier. Yet the tidewater was itself divided, and if we consider the sections as social and psychological rather than as purely geographical entities, it is possible to distinguish three of them,—the rural, agricultural society of the countryside; the restless, advancing society of the frontier; and the urban, commercial society of the larger seaports. Beginning as small specks in the wilderness, the five communities grew from tiny villages into towns, and finally attained the status of small cities. With other village communities of similar interests and outlook which multiplied and grew in the eighteenth century, they emerged as a social and economic "section" extending the length of the Atlantic seaboard, and exhibiting definite urban characteristics in striking contrast to rural farming districts and wilder regions of the frontier. Life in urban areas produced its own peculiar problems to be faced, and the urban viewpoint, based upon continuous close contacts with Europe, derived less from agriculture than from trade. Commercially minded town society looked to the East rather than the West, and was destined from the first to serve as the connecting link between colonial America and its Old World parents.

The future of the colonial towns became immediately evident from the conditions surrounding their birth. Designed as trading communities, they were established on sites most favorable for the pursuit of commerce. They were the western outposts of European commercial expansion in the seventeenth century. City-dwellers from the Old World formed the larger proportion of early town populations, and from the start commercial relations with England or Holland were maintained. Most significantly, the founding process occurred at a time when western Europe, under Dutch and English leadership, was gradually outgrowing and casting off the limitations of medieval feudal economy. Colonial towns grew to maturity in the era of world expansion attending the emergence of modern capitalism, and being new communities, with few irrevocably established customs or traditions, they frequently adapted themselves to the economic drift with more ease and readiness than did the older cities of England. Moreover, the colonizing movement was itself an expression of early capitalistic activity. It called forth organized rather than individual efforts and resources, created new and wider markets for economic development, and opened up seemingly unlimited territories for imperialistic exploitation. It thus produced a marked effect upon Old World economy, accelerating the breakdown of local units of business, and facilitating the formation of larger and more complex organizations of commerce and finance.

The problems which confronted town-dwellers in America were not only those of urban communities, but of a pioneer society as well. Urban development depends largely upon community wealth, and upon the willingness of the group to devote portions of it to projects for civic betterment, or to consent to taxation for this purpose. To a considerable extent the nature of town governments and the extent of authority vested in them conditioned the expenditure of town wealth for community enterprises. Here the colonists were hampered by the traditional nature of the charters of medieval English municipal corporations, whose limitations ill accorded with circumstances in seventeenth and eighteenth century America, especially with the imperious demands for expansion and immediate activity in the New World. In New England towns a new political organization, the town meeting, developed, which exhibited considerable efficiency in the handling of urban problems. This institution was more immediately susceptible to social wants and requirements than were the aristocratic, self-perpetuating corporations founded in America after the example of English municipal governments. Its greater powers of local taxation, and the fact that it placed the spending of public moneys and the enactment of civic ordinances in the hands of those directly affected by these operations, made it a far more effective form of government for dealing with community problems. These problems were the greater, because in the first century of their history the five colonial seaports enjoyed a much more rapid physical growth than did the cities of contemporary Europe. The individual enterprise of American town-dwellers, and the commercial expansion and prosperity they achieved, aided in the solution of these problems of town living, but much of the efficiency and success which attended their efforts may be attributed to the emergence in the New World of a relatively high sense of civic responsibility in the early eighteenth century, at a time when public consciousness in Europe had receded to an extremely low ebb.

The towns were primarily commercial communities seeking treasure by foreign trade, and their economic vitality and commercial demands led to their early breaking the narrow bonds of medieval economic practice to forge ahead on uncharted but highly profitable commercial adventures. All five, during the first century, developed from simple manorial organizations, completely dependent upon European connections, into full-fledged commercial centers, only partially tied to England, and in many cases competing with British cities for a share of imperial traffic. Boston entered early into the West Indian provision trade, thereby setting an example for other American commercial communities. Soon Massachusetts mariners were seeking to monopolize the colonial carrying traffic in ships of their own building, and the profits of carrier and middleman became the basis of the Bay town's prosperity. Her priority in this field gave her an advantage which other seaports did not begin to overcome until the fourth decade of the eighteenth century. A further foundation for urban economic prosperity lay in the existence of an expanding frontier society with its great need for manufactured products. This made possible an earlier development of the towns as distributing centers for a wide hinterland than was the case with English cities like Bristol, Norwich and Exeter, and became in this first century as important a factor in the economic growth of New York, Philadelphia and Charles Town as in that of the New England metropolis. As a producer of staple goods for exchange in trade, Boston, with its limited back country, was at a disadvantage. More fortunate were New York with its flour and furs, Philadelphia, with its great staples of wheat, meat and lumber, and Charles Town, which after 1710 found prosperity in the important South Carolina crops of rice and indigo. Eventually the communities enjoying this sound economic backing rose to threaten the supremacy of Boston in colonial trade, while Newport and Philadelphia cut heavily into the Bay town's West India commerce. In the eighteenth century also Newport attained importance in shipbuilding and the slave trade. By 1742 Boston merchants were facing a period of relative decline, while their competitors in other colonial towns found the volume and profits of their traffic steadily mounting.

Continual increase in the volume of colonial trade and enlargement of the territory served by the towns led to a greater complexity in commercial relations. In the early years merchants performed all types of business, but toward 1700 their functions began to be more specialized. Retail merchandising having definitely emerged by 1700, the great merchant now dealt chiefly with larger operations of exporting, importing and wholesaling, leaving much of the small trade to the shopkeeper. Demands of trade had by 1710 necessitated the issuance of paper currency in most of the colonies, and the establishment of the colonial post office to serve intercolonial communication. Growing business further led to the creation of insurance offices and some extension of credit facilities. Profits from trade, originally completely absorbed in shipbuilding ventures and industries subsidiary to shipping, now began to create a surplus which sought investment in land, or, in some communities, in the development of certain forms of manufacturing.

Economic prosperity thus made possible the rise of colonial cities. It led to physical expansion of town boundaries, and facilitated dealing with urban problems by corporate effort. Wealth wrung from trade, more than any other single factor, determined the growth of a town society, in which urban amusements and a colonial culture might thrive. This is not, however, to force the history of urban America within the narrow bounds of an exclusively economic interpretation. Social and intellectual development are dependent upon and conditioned by economic progress, but they are not its necessary and inevitable result. They are altered, encouraged or stifled by the action and influence of material forces, but they are not necessarily caused or even initiated solely by economic factors.

When we consider American urban society, apart from its economic aspects, we find it characterized by certain problems affecting it as a unit, and with which as a unit it had to deal. Such problems in general, or collective attempts for their control and regulation, are either absent from or unimportant in rural or frontier societies, but in the case of our urban section they are present, in rudimentary form at least, from its inception. They persist and grow with the maturing of that section, and the means taken for dealing with them further differentiate the urban from other types of society.

Logically, the first of these problems to appear are the physical, and of these the most immediate was housing. As in rural regions this remained for the most part an individual problem, and there are only a few cases on record where even indirectly, by sale or subdivision of land or by encouragement of artisans, the community stepped in to relieve a housing shortage. On the other hand, the laying out and maintaining of a highway system constituted a problem, perhaps the first, which transcended private initiative. Not that the community at any time scorned the assistance of private enterprise; a favorite device, at Boston and elsewhere, throughout the colonial era, was by remission of taxes or grant of other privileges to encourage individuals to open up streets and undertake paving operations for public use at their own charge. But from the beginning public authorities indicated the location of roads, supervised the opening up of new ones, ordered their clearing or partial paving by abutters, and strove to prevent encroachments upon them. At Philadelphia and Charles Town, where some prior power had surveyed and planned the thoroughfares, the first task of local authorities was light; it was more arduous in other communities, where there was no preliminary plan, and where the design had constantly to be expanded and altered to keep pace with town growth. The problems accompanying the mere existence of a highway system,—paving, cleaning and upkeep,—called for full exercise of municipal authority. Sometimes the community exacted from each inhabitant a yearly amount of labor on the streets; in other cases it hired this labor and paid for it outright. In either case it had to levy special taxes, for materials or labor or both. To insure some cleanliness in the streets, it passed mandatory ordinances restricting the conduct of townsmen, impressed the services of carters, and employed public funds for the hire of scavengers. Further to protect the public ways, it restricted and regulated the traffic upon them, especially the weight of cart loads and the width of their wheels. Less necessary but desirable improvements in the highways, like the construction of drains, first came about through private demand and initiative, but as the civic power matured and public funds became available, these too became public functions and responsibilities. In either the municipal or the individual approach to highway problems the towns had good precedent in the Mother Country. In actual execution, especially with regard to refinements like paving and drainage, they seem in some cases to have gone beyond contemporary English cities. With a few exceptions, this generalization does not apply to the corporation governed towns, or to the unfortunately ungoverned metropolis of South Carolina.

Highways may be said to constitute the most rudimentary of public utilities, but there were others,—bridges, wharves, and engineering projects, —of which colonial townsfolk almost immediately felt the need. In the beginning, while municipal authority was politically and financially feeble, these were almost solely the product of private enterprise, but with the gradual tendency of town development they became increasingly matters of public concern. Following Old World precedent, bridges were conceived as parts of the highway system, and hence undoubtedly under public control, but they were usually constructed and operated by private persons or companies, under grant from local or provincial authorities. As the century progressed, in a few cases, notably at Philadelphia and Boston, town governments directly managed the operation and upkeep of bridges. Land reclamation projects, and harbor facilities like lighthouses, pursued a similar history. In the case of wharves, they were either a municipal or a private concern. Most towns maintained a minimum of public docking facilities, while more ambitious wharf projects, like the Long Wharves of Boston and Newport, were only within the capacity of private capital. At Philadelphia public docking facilities were so excellent as to discourage employment of private capital in their erection; at New York, so poor as to require it. Toward the end of the era, when the demands of trade began to make regular transportation between communities desirable, stage and freight routes, too, were operated by private capital, under license, usually from the provincial government.

Fire constitutes a threat especially dangerous to urban communities, and as buildings in colonial towns were from the beginning placed close together, its imminence was immediately felt. The combatting and prevention of fire called forth more than individual efforts from the start. Municipal ordinances required the keeping of fire fighting equipment by all townsmen, regulated their chimneys, forbade bonfires, fireworks, and the housing of explosives in crowded areas. Public authorities had also to make direct outlays for fire fighting equipment of their own, and hire companies for its care and operation. In Boston, Philadelphia and Newport private societies for the protection of property during fires were organized to supplement public agencies. Similarly, water supply for fire uses was a matter of public concern and regulation. Boston, with its crowded streets and buildings of inflammable construction, and its willingness to spend public money and energy for public welfare, was in general far in the forefront with regard to its fire defenses, but by the end of the first century all towns possessed fire engines of the latest European model, and fire fighting regulations equal or superior to those of the average English town.

A distinctive urban function grew in part out of the fire hazards of crowded sections,—the enactment of building regulations. Only public authority could specify the nature of legal building materials as did Boston after the fire of 1679 and the South Carolina Assembly after the Charles Town fire of 1740. Exercise of municipal powers was also necessary to prevent imperfect construction and dangerous neglect of town chimneys and hearths. In addition, conditions of urban congestion led to party-wall regulations like those of Boston and Philadelphia.

Another, more subtle class of problems, those which involved the personal relationships of inhabitants, affected town society from its inception. Intensified by the peculiar conditions of urban life, they required collective rather than individual efforts and powers for their control. Old World experience had taught town-dwellers the immediate need for means of preserving the public peace in settled communities, and the early appearance of constables in all towns supplied the traditional response to that need. For their security after nightfall the towns appointed bellmen or watchmen of varying degrees of efficiency. New York, after developing a highly effective nocturnal police in the seventeenth century, allowed this institution to languish from unwillingness to devote the necessary public funds thereto; other towns were slower in supplying the need, though somewhat more successful by the end of the first century. Efficiency of the watch was in direct ratio to the availability of public funds for its support,—impressment of a citizen's watch having revealed its inadequacy by the turn of the century,—and here the New England towns, with their powers of local taxation, were at a distinct advantage. There are numerous instances, during periods of unusual danger or disturbance like wars or epidemics, when the towns entirely failed in their efforts to preserve nocturnal peace, and their functions had to be taken over by the military arm of the provincial government.

Existence of crime and disorder early became a community concern in urban settlements. Here invitations to lawbreaking existed in the inequalities of weath and opportunity, and materials for its perpetration in the diverse and unruly elements of town and seaport society. The concentration of people, many of them hardworked and underprivileged, also made for mob disorders, which increased in violence and frequency with the growth of the towns. Presence of sailors, blacks, foreigners, paupers, unpopular religious sects, interlopers in trade, profiteers, and rival political factions, all provided increasing incentives for disorder and violence as the period progressed. Town society clearly soon passed beyond the stage where individual efforts or the force of public opinion could deal with this problem; rather it required the sanctions of the law. Provincial governments passed legislation, and municipal authorities enacted ordinances outlawing offenses against society. Riot acts were drawn up by colonial assemblies, and the local constabulary did its best to round up and confine the perpetrators of disorder and violence. In general, the towns could do little to remove the causes of criminality, and the solution of this peculiarly vexing problem of city life remained as remote in the seventeenth and eighteenth centuries as today.

For punishments, colonial authorities followed a number of Old World precedents, favoring especially the speediest and least expensive methods, —fines, floggings, public humiliation, restitution of stolen goods, and, occasionally, mutilation. In general, their criminal codes were less brutal than those of contemporary Europe. Efforts to make the whole community a partner in the work of law enforcement appeared in the division with informers of the proceeds from fines. Prisons were still generally places of detention for those awaiting trial, though imprisonment as punishment for crime seems to have become more widespread as the period advanced, and save in the case of debtors was probably somewhat more in use in the colonies than in the Old World. The frequency of jail breaks indicates the inefficiency of all colonial prisons, and their inadequacy suggests the absence of more vicious criminal types that troubled older societies. Yet colonial prisons were probably no more inadequate than those of contemporary England, and certainly far less squalid and brutal. Save in the case of Philadelphia in the eighteenth century, the rudimentary penology of the times made no distinction between various classes of offenders, and absence of prison facilities led to frequent misuse of alms and workhouses, wherein pauper and lawbreaker were housed together.

Offenses against the moral and ethical standards which society imposes appear more flagrant in the comparative populousness and congestion of urban environments, and early forced themselves upon the attention of colonial communities. In addition, the psychology of the times made many aspects of the regulation of conduct, manners and dress a legitimate province for the public authority. Early appearance of prostitution in the towns shocked authorities into decreeing harsh penalties for it and similar offenses. With its increasing prevalence in a society which included growingly diverse and uncontrollable elements, they seem everywhere to have become less concerned with the actual offense than with the fear lest the illegitimate offspring become charges to the community. Drunkenness was a prevailing vice, and in all towns the authorities and the better elements fought to eradicate it. Excellent tavern legislation in several of the towns reduced this offense to a minimum, but illegal sale of liquor, and misuse of the legitimate product, continued to baffle municipal authority throughout the period. Sabbath legislation in every town,—as strict in the Anglican South as in Puritan New England,—attempted to insure the sacred character of the Lord's Day. Gambling, card-playing, loitering, idleness, extravagance in dress and behavior, and evidence of frivolity came under the ban of public regulation, either through colony or municipal authority, or as at Philadelphia through the dominant religious group. Especially at Boston and Philadelphia many seemingly innocent amusements suffered from the disapproval of a stern and narrow religion, which served as a powerful and useful supplement to the civic power.

The existence and effects of crime and immorality are intensified in urban communities; so, too, the problem of pauperism. Reports of travelers as to the absence of poverty from colonial towns can only be regarded as comparatively true, for in each town numbers of those unable to care for themselves soon constituted a problem of which the community had to take cognizance. The generally excellent methods with which the towns met this problem indicate a considerable sense of civic maturity and responsibility. New York and Charles Town favored the out-relief method through most of the period, but Boston and Philadelphia had by the end of the century well-regulated and practically self-supporting workhouses, and Newport maintained an adequate almshouse. Considerable direct relief had to be granted, especially at Boston, and in all towns save New York private or religious organizations supplemented the public work of poor relief. Methods to forestall the growth of poverty were devised, such as compulsory apprenticeship of poor children, exclusion of strangers without obvious means of livelihood, and, especially in the New England towns, restriction of immigration. In times of particular stress special devices had to be resorted to, as the distribution of corn or firewood, or a temporary embargo on export of necessary commodities. At Boston, where the problem of poverty became acute in the 1670's and was never thereafter absent, careful registration of all aliens and dependents prevailed, and a public granary was maintained.

The general health, which in rural regions may be privately cared for, early became in urban communities a matter for public concern, and municipal ordinances soon restricted the conduct of inhabitants in matters which might affect the general well-being. Location of wells and privies, and of slaughterhouses and tan pits which might become public nuisances, removal of dumps and disposal of refuse were all subjects of municipal regulation. Similarly, public authorities directed inhabitants in their behavior during epidemics, and enacted quarantine regulations in an attempt to prevent visitations of infectious disease. Toward the end of the century excellent isolation hospitals appeared in several of the towns, erected and operated by the municipality. Despite failure in this period of all attempts to regulate the practice of medicine by town or colony, the medical profession in the towns attained a relatively high development for the times.

In their approach to the physical and social problems of urban life the towns were imitators, not originators. The townsmen came to America with a fund of European experience from which they seldom deviated, and new methods as they employed them had usually first to cross the Atlantic. Poor relief and tavern legislation were directly imported from Great Britain, and the towns might conceivably have done better with their police problem had not Old World precedent served them so exclusively as a guide. Yet it may be said that in several cases there are distinct improvements in the thoroughness with which old methods were employed, and which may usually be traced to the individual civic pride of townsmen, reflected in their municipal governments. This is especially true of communities which enjoyed the town meeting form of government, where, as we have seen, the direct demands of townspeople could effect greater thoroughness and efficiency in dealing with town business, but even in the corporation governments of America there is less indifference to the public welfare than may be noted in contemporary England or Europe. Visitors were impressed with the excellence of poor relief at Boston and Philadelphia, and with Philadelphia's model prison. Fire defences in the towns were a combination of English and Dutch examples, and, especially at Boston, probably unsurpassed for their time. Solution of urban problems in colonial towns was continually hampered by lack of public funds or of necessary authority for obtaining them,—the sad decline of New York's excellent watch is an illustration,—but it was assisted, where public power failed, either politically or financially, by an encouraging growth of civic consciousness among private individuals and non-political organizations. Establishment of private agencies for charity, education, fire protection, improvement of morals, and the like, and the appearance of individual benefactors to the public welfare of the community, in an age not distinguished for civic virtue or interest, is a remarkable and significant accomplishment of town society in colonial America.

Having as they all did a common model and experience, colonial towns exhibit a remarkable similarity in the solution of their urban problems. There are many instances of the failure of a community to provide the usual and accepted necessary solution, but, with the possible exception of Philadelphia's eighteenth century prison, hardly a single example of the development by one town of a unique institution. By the time that local divergences from the original plan might have been expected to appear, communication had sufficiently improved to permit of one town's borrowing from the successful experience of another. The same holds true for privately initiated supplements of municipal endeavor. The Scot's Charitable Society and the Fire Society appear in Boston, copied from European models, and at a later date are further copied by other American towns. In the eighteenth century, because of its long experience in dealing with urban problems, the greater efficiency of its form of government, and its willingness to spend public money for the public good, Boston became the great example, with respect to municipal institutions, for other towns on the continent, but it enjoyed no monopoly of this function. New Yorkers had the fire defences of Philadelphia held up to them as a model, Bostonians were shamed by the excellence of Philadelphia's market, while Charlestonians tried to fashion their city government after the example of the corporation of New York. By the end of the period under review this inter-city exchange of experience had resulted in a striking similarity in municipal institutions, as well as a fairly uniform level of their development. Boston, for the reasons enumerated above, was probably still somewhat in advance in matters of social and material concern, though with its humanitarian agencies Philadelphia was running a close second. Charles Town, within the limits of its governmental incapacity, dealt in fairly efficient fashion with its problems; at Newport, a lesser development of these problems had not yet necessitated any great display of urban consciousness. Even at New York, where political factionalism, a selfish corporation, and the difficulty of amalgamating two languages and nationalities prevented a consistent and devoted attempt to solve the problems of urban living, a comparison of its municipal life with that of older provincial cities of the British Empire would not have resulted in discredit to the former.

The accumulation of economic resources and their concentration in urban units, their direction in commercial ventures which attracted and supported large populations within these units, and the problems of providing for the physical and social well-being of those who thus became city-dwellers, all these aspects of urban development succeeded in bringing forth in America a distinctive society. In constitution, spiritual life, recreational activities, and intellectual pursuits it differed from types of society to be found in other sections of the continent. In respect neither to national origins nor to economic status of their inhabitants did the towns long remain homogeneous. Settled originally by people of the same nation, usually of the same locality, they soon came to include children of other European countries and of another race. Early in their history there could be found small groups of Scots in Boston, French Huguenots in Boston, New York and Charles Town, Welsh in Philadelphia, and a few Jews in every town. Many Germans settled in the 1680's in the environs of Philadelphia, and New York from the time of the first English occupation presented the problem of two peoples, each with their own language, schools and churches, living side by side under government by the numerically weaker group. This incipient cosmopolitanism flowered with the renewed immigration of the early eighteenth century, when all towns received numbers of Scotch-Irish, and the middle and southern cities, especially Philadelphia, large accessions of German exiles. For the most part these strangers were allowed to settle peaceably in colonial towns, whose economic expansion enabled them easily to absorb the newcomers, and though recent arrivals seldom attained social recognition or overcame the barrier of language where it existed, still there was little nativism and small emphasis on the superior advantages of Anglo-Saxon nativity. Such bountiful immigration did, however, lead to many restrictions, especially in the north, where the labor market was well supplied and the poor rates overburdened, to establishment of special churches and social organizations, and in Philadelphia, at least, to common use of the German language in business transactions. By far the greater problem was created by the presence of African Negroes in all towns. In Boston and Newport, where they were used mainly as house servants, and where many of them were free, the problem was negligible. They were subject to various discriminatory rules, such as those which required them to work out their obligations to the community in menial labor rather than by watch or militia duty. But at New York and Charles Town their greater numbers kept constantly present the fear of servile insurrection. At the former town they were the unfortunate objects of such waves of hysteria as the Negro Conspiracy of 1741, and at Charles Town, where they at times equalled the white population in numbers, a severe slave code kept them in subjection.

Social stratification further differentiated urban society from the easy democracy of the back country, where any man might own land and all must work with their hands. Distinctions between the well-to-do and the not-so-rich were perhaps relatively unimportant in the beginning, when society was still so fluid that luck or diligence might elevate a man above his fellows in a short time, but with the accumulation of wealth and economic power in the hands of a few, and the coming in of numbers of artisans, indentured servants and immigrant laborers, class lines tightened and society crystallized into easily recognizable categories of better, middling, and poorer sorts. In all towns native aristocracies were commercial in origin, even at Charles Town where they later sought land as a basis for social distinction. They consolidated their position by means of wealth from successful trading ventures, collecting thereby social prestige and political influence. They lived grandly, dressed gaily, kept horses and coaches, and employed the labor of the less fortunate. The commercial, political and social leadership of the towns was in their hands. Later, as urban life became more sophisticated, they contributed to the development of secular amusements and to the relaxation of earlier strict moral codes. They gained further brilliance by alliance with representatives of British officialdom in America. Below them the middle class, professional people, tradesmen and artisans, lived comfortably but more plainly, enjoying in prosperous times many of the good things of life, but in hard times feeling the pinch far more than did their wealthy neighbors. Steady laborers might know periods of prosperity, but many of them could be squeezed out by the vicissitudes of the economic cycle. They performed the menial labor of the towns, enlisted as common seamen, and constituted a group from which much urban poverty and disorder were recruited. Negro and Indian slaves, mere unprivileged pieces of property, rounded out the caste system as it developed itself in metropolitan America.

Save Newport, each of the towns had originally been dedicated to a dominant Protestant religious organization, but after a century of growth diversity, indifference and actual unbelief came to characterize the religious scene. The complexities of town society were in large measure responsible for this development, for different national or social groups soon evolved their favored sects and denominations. When the ministry could no longer speak with one voice to all elements of town populations, it lost much of its influence, both social and clerical, and the appearance of agnosticism and irreverence was rapid. In general, at the end of the first century, Anglicanism was in all towns the religion of officials and aristocrats; Quakerism and Congregationalism, which had once in their own localities enjoyed this favored position, had joined the ranks of middle class religions, which further included Baptists and Presbyterians; while for the common man a religious refuge was just appearing in the enthusiastic, emotional revivalism of Whitefield. Absence of devotion penetrated all classes; the poorer sort were largely indifferent to the attractions of religion, freethinking characterized such middle class groups as Franklin's Junto, and aristocrats indulged a fashionable Deism. In contrast, a stern and uniform religious fundamentalism for a much longer time characterized the rural communities of the countryside.

Much of their power the quasi-established churches had attained in an age when religious concerns so dominated men's thoughts as to exclude many other aspects of life. But the commercial success of colonial towns altered this singleness of outlook by acquainting townsmen with the delights of secular grandeurs and providing money for their enjoyment. As the age advanced the church step by step gave way before the institution of more attractive secular recreations. Most successful of these, appearing very early and appealing to all classes, was the tavern. Instituted originally as a necessary convenience for strangers and travelers, it soon showed itself to be the resort of all classes of townsmen, the place where they conducted much of their business and where much of their social life was passed. In the eighteenth century coffee houses became as in England the rendezvous of business men and the scene of many commercial transactions. Taverns served not only as places of casual conviviality, but as headquarters for the multifarious clubs into which town social life gradually organized itself. They also offered opportunities for cards, billiards and games of chance, and housed the many traveling shows and exhibitions which the better transportation of the eighteenth century made possible.

Games, contests, tavern recreations, and public celebration of holidays constituted the entertainment of the common man, but for the aristocrats mounting wealth and sophistication were creating more elaborate forms of amusement. To the hearty private dinners and occasional excursions of early days succeeded great public banquets, dances and balls, musical entertainments, and finally, in two of the towns, dramatic presentations. Gradually the commercial aristocracy of the towns, combining with royal officials, evolved a society whose entertainments were artificial, costly, sophisticated and exclusive. But for aristocrat or common man, the vicarious amusements that money could buy, and their variety and attractiveness, differentiated town society from that of the countryside with its simpler, spontaneous pleasures, and tended to draw town-dwellers away from a strict and narrow conception of life as a duty and a task. Copied as they were from the recreations of English society, they also tended to make social life in the towns more like that of the metropolis.

A final characteristic of town society was that it offered to its members a wider intellectual opportunity and challenge than was possible to the man whose life was bounded by his fields or by the hard necessity of clearing away the forest. From earliest childhood opportunities for education, free or otherwise, were open to the town-dweller. Especially was this true of the poor, whose educational needs were largely cared for by religious societies, charity schools, or compulsory apprenticeship. This last system enabled youth of the poorer classes to equip themselves for a trade. In other strata of society young men might fit themselves for business at private vocational schools, for a place in society with private masters, or for higher education for a learned profession at public or private Latin schools or with a private tutor. Young women, too, in the towns might purchase instruction in various fields of learning or merely in the polite arts of feminine society. Also, in the northern English towns, Boston, Newport and Philadelphia, there was from the start a tradition of scholarliness and of respect for intellectual achievement. It followed that a society so trained, constantly in contact by ship with Europe, was alive and ready to adopt the intellectual fashions of the age. Hence, in this first century of American life, most of the intellectual activity, in science, literature and the arts, and what intellectual progress there was, took place in the towns. Only there were there material and opportunity for such activity. And rather than regard the results of that progress with condescension, we should, with James Franklin's subscriber, wonder at the contrary. In comparison with the Augustan Age of eighteenth century London, intellectual and social life in the colonies may seem bare and sterile, but in comparison with the intellectual barrenness of provincial life in England itself, its cultivation and sophistication appear revealed. Urban culture in the eighteenth century was provincial culture at its best, nourished during this period of faltering imitation, which had to precede that of native accomplishment, by constant contact with the vital intellectual currents of England and Europe.

In these various ways the developments of a hundred years of life under relatively urban conditions created a society at once distinct from that of rural regions, whether tidewater or back country, and even further removed from that of the westward reaching frontier. The communal attitude toward the solution of the physical and social problems of diversified populations dwelling together in close propinquity, and the constantly widening outlook which material progress, commercial expansion, and contact with the larger world of affairs made possible, were its distinguishing characteristics. In general, this society was more cooperative and social, less individualistic in its outlook toward problems of daily life, far more susceptible to outside influences and examples, less aggressively independent than the society of frontier America. At the same time it was more polished, urbane, and sophisticated, more aware of fashion and change, more sure of itself and proud of its achievements, more able to meet representatives from the outside world as equals without bluster or apology than the rural society of the colonial back country. Because its outlook was eastward rather than westward, it was more nearly a European society in an American setting. It had appropriated various points on the American continent and transformed them as nearly as possible into likenesses of what it had known at home. It was itself less transformed in the process than might have been expected, because the contact with the homeland never ceased, but rather increased with the passage of years. Its importance to American life as a whole was therefore great. Here were centers of the transit of civilization from Old World to New,—five points at the least through which currents of world thought and endeavor might enter, to be like other commodities assimilated and redistributed throughout the countryside. It was well for the future of national America that its society should not remain completely rural and agricultural, isolated and self-sufficient, ignorant of outside developments and distrustful of new ideas from abroad, as it might well have done had there been no cities. Instead, the five towns provided the nucleus for a wider and more gracious living in the New World.

9 *Edwin S. Gaustad*

SOCIETY AND THE GREAT AWAKENING
IN NEW ENGLAND

Of the sequence of dramas which make up human history none is perhaps more dramatic than that of man's faith and its periodic renewal. The way in which it is renewed is never the same, nor are the causes and consequences of its renewal. It is the need for understanding the various ways in which man has pursued the same goal of seeking his God and revitalizing his faith which challenges and interests the stu-

Reprinted with permission from *The William and Mary Quarterly*, Third Series, XI (October, 1954), 566–77.

dent of history. There are many questions to be answered. Each touches ultimately upon times that try men's souls.

Such times of trial, certainly, were the 1740's, when the deep and wide revival known as the Great Awakening swept through the American colonies. Appealing to a primitive sense of faith and salvation, evangelical in its fervor and doctrine, capturing the hearts and minds of tens of thousands, bypassing if not quite undoing formal religions and established orthodoxies, it was clearly the most important movement of its kind in the colonial period. Inevitably, therefore, the Great Awakening has become a focus of attention for historians. Inevitably, too, it has been variously understood as the patterns of historical understanding have themselves varied.

Herein may be found at least two reasons for the value of the following essay by Edwin Scott Gaustad, professor of humanities and philosophy at the University of Redlands in California. It is, for one thing, an illuminating commentary on the Great Awakening itself; as such, appearing in 1954, it was a forerunner of the study on *The Great Awakening in New England* which Professor Gaustad brought out in 1957. The essay is, secondly, a revealing commentary on the historical writings about the movement. Professor Gaustad takes exception to the view that the Great Awakening was limited to certain social classes and to certain geographical areas. In this respect, what he is saying is part of a wider rejection of the school of Beard and Turner, a school that has until recently exercised considerable influence upon American historical writing. His rejection can be properly understood, therefore, if it is related to the critical reconsiderations of the colonial and early national periods being made by such historians as Robert E. Brown, Edmund S. Morgan, Douglass Adair, Cecelia M. Kenyon, and Richard B. Morris.

The exciting phenomenon of the Great Awakening will suggest questions to the critical inquirer that relate both to its uniqueness and to its similarity to other religious outpourings. What factors have been responsible for spiritual resurgence in any age, and what for the Great Awakening in particular? What developments had produced the decline in religious feeling that preceded the Great Awakening? To what exent was it the product of great leaders, to what extent did the latter no more than tap deeper currents that had been welling up? What relevance did the Great Awakening have to the larger political, economic, and social developments of its times? What impact did it have upon subsequent developments not merely of a religious nature, but also political, social, and economic? To what degree was it not a single revival, but a whole complex of related revivals? If it was the latter, what were its different causes, courses, and consequences?

Beyond the many questions of this sort lies the deeper one of man's faith. What is its nature, what are its sources? To what degree is it consonant with science, to what degree is it antagonistic? Is man more prone to seek God in times of troubles? If so, what is he seeking, what are the troubles that are besetting him, who is the God he seeks? The student of history will have more than superficial interest in answering these questions. They are important for an understanding of earlier ages. They are central to an understanding of our own.

Contemporaries of the turbulent religious upheaval which took place in New England in the years 1740 to 1742 described it as a "great and general awakening." Later historians, less ready to admit either its greatness or its generality, have in concert described the revival as limited to this area or that, to this social class exclusive of that, and as brought about by this or that socio-economic force. We have come a long way from "the economic interpretation of religion," when all felt obliged to excuse the obtrusion of churches and pious sentiments by explaining that this sheep's clothing of religion concealed an economic wolf within. Yet the phenomenon known as the Great Awakening is of such proportions as to lead to its interpretation as something other than a religious movement.

It would be folly to suggest that the Awakening was completely divorced from the culture of eighteenth-century New England, from the shortage of specie, from the growth of trade, from the greater leisure and less crudity of life, from the vigilant struggles for popular representation and the increasing degree of political independence. To admit its connection with these secular developments is, however, vastly different from cataloguing the revival as a "deep-rooted social movement," as a lower-class uprising, or as "a revolt of the backcountry producers." John Chester Miller viewed the movement as riding on the wave of hostility between rich and poor created by the Land Bank uproar, and producing a full and permanent cleavage between the social classes. The uninhibited and fervent James Davenport, according to Miller, divided the

social classes much as during the Land Bank fervor. The Opposers were joined by more and more of the wealthy and educated as Davenport carried the Great Awakening down to a lower stratum and preached the gospel of discontent and levellism. . . . This conviction among the common people that they had been singled out by God for salvation and that the Opposers—the upper classes—were for the most part damned gave class feeling a new twist in Massachusetts.

Though this theory probably serves as a useful counterweight to that other tenacious myth that "the elect" and "the élite" were synonymous terms in colonial New England, it does not do justice to the historical evidence concerning the revival itself. Indeed, John Miller begins his discussion with a question that begs the question: "What caused the Great Awakening to split up the Congregational church and cut a swath between rich and poor, stimulating the hostility that already divided them?"

This identification of the anti-revivalists with the upper classes is made by Perry Miller, who declares the list of subscribers to Chauncy's *Seasonable Thoughts* to be "a roster of antirevivalists and also a social register." Eugene E. White writes of the revival as one of the "deep-rooted social movements," a "social phenomenon," "confined to the cities and the settled areas of the East." More recently, Richard D. Mosier views it as an affair not of the cities, but of the rural areas, "a revolt of the backcountry producers from the stringent controls of the mercantile aristocracy which ruled from afar"; the Awakening was also anti-clerical and anarchical, "the first step in a movement which culminates in the American Revolution." And Clinton Rossiter, speaking of the Great Awakening in all the colonies, writes as follows: "It appealed primarily to the poor and despised; it revolted the well-born, well-educated, and well-to-do." These are statements of faith.

There is, on the contrary, abundant evidence that this religious turmoil was in fact "great and general," that it knew no boundaries, social or geographical, that it was both urban and rural, that it reached both lower and upper class. The geographical non-particularity of the Great Awakening is readily established, though it is necessary to distinguish it from the earlier series of revivals emanating from Northampton. Beginning in 1734 and continuing for two or three years, these revivals were largely a frontier phenomenon, concentrated along the banks of the Connecticut River from Northfield to Saybrook Point. They arose under the influence of Jonathan Edwards and the "surprising conversions" which took place in Northampton. To them, but only to them, the term "frontier revivalism" can with propriety be applied, and not to the Great Awakening, which began after the earlier revivals were "very much at a Stop" and the initial phase of which occurred rather in the coastal than in the inland area. Edwards regarded the two movements as quite distinct, speaking of the revivalism early in 1741 as "the beginning of that extraordinary religious commotion, through the land. . . ." In the frontier revivals, no churches were split, no clergy were offended, no flagrant itineracy occurred, no elaborate apologetic was necessary, no legislation was provoked, and no vast array of abusive epithets came into use.

The Awakening itself began when, on September 14, 1740, the proud, portly, and pompous George Whitefield arrived at Newport to preach (he tells us) with "much Flame, Clearness and Power. . . . The People were exceedingly attentive. Tears trickled down their Cheeks. . . ." His arrogance passed for conviction, his sentiment for piety, his superficiality for simplicity, and his moving rhetoric for inspiration. And wherever the youthful Anglican went, so did the Awakening. It spread from Newport to Bristol to Boston, and northeast to Roxbury, Marblehead, Ipswich, Newbury, Hampton, Portsmouth, and York. It moved west of Boston into

Concord, Sudbury, Worcester, Leicester, Brookfield, and Northampton; thence south, through Springfield, Suffield, Windsor, Hartford, and New Haven; and southwest, through Milford, Stratford, Fairfield, and Stamford. In less than two months, the tour of New England by "the Grand Itinerant" was over. From the many areas left shaking, tremors reached out to meet each other, and to move all that lay between.

At the small town of Harvard, about forty miles west of Boston, "God was pleased . . . to rouze and awaken sleepy Sinners," this being done without the intervention of any itinerants or "Strangers." On November 23, 1741, all heaven broke loose in Middleborough, Massachusetts. "I have written Accounts of seventy-six that Day struck, and bro't first to inquire what they should do to escape condemnation." Their joyful pastor, Peter Thacher, further notes that from that time on, there was "an uncommon Teachableness among my People." In Wethersfield, Connecticut, Eleazar Wheelock reported late in 1741 that "the Lord bowed the heavens and Came Down upon a Large assembly in one of the Parishes of the town the Whole assembly Seam'd alive with Distress. . . ." Gilbert Tennent, who followed Whitefield in a tour of New England, observed that at Charlestown "multitudes were awakened, and several had received great consolation, especially among the young people, children and Negroes." He recorded also a general "shaking among the dry bones" at Harvard College, while in New Haven the concern was considerable and "about thirty students came on foot ten miles to hear the word of God." In brief, it is simply not possible to draw any meaningful lines on a map of New England in order to distinguish where in 1741 the revival was and where it was not. It was a phenomenon not alone of the back country or exclusively of the cities, of the coast or of the frontier. From Stamford, Connecticut, to York, Maine, from Danbury to Northfield (the New England Dan to Beersheba), there had been a great and general awakening.

In 1742, six Boston ministers testified that these "uncommon religious Appearances" were found "among Persons of all Ages and Characters." Another Boston clergyman, the fiery Presbyterian John Moorhead, extolled "the wonderful things which God is adoing, and has already Manifested amongst Indians, Negros, Papists and Protestants of all Denominations." Though somewhat extreme, Moorhead's observation points to the truly universal character of the Awakening. If it reached Indians, Negroes, and even Quakers, is it possible that it extended also to the upper classes?

It has never seemed urgently necessary to offer proof of lower-class participation in the revival, perhaps because of the finality of such a quotation as the following, which describes James Davenport and his Boston listeners:

Were you to see him in his most violent agitations, you would be apt to think, that he was a Madman just broke from his Chains: But especially had you seen him returning from the Common after his first preaching, with a large Mob at his Heels, singing all the Way thro' the Streets . . . attended with so much Disorder, that they look'd more like a Company of Bacchanalians after a mad Frolick, than sober Christians who had been worshipping God. . . .

A strong image such as this lingers long in the imagination, causing Davenport and his large mob, in retrospect, to seem the epitome of the Awakening. Even in those surveys of New England's revival where Davenport is not regarded as its personification, he is given disproportionate emphasis. There was no Davenport party. By the ardent supporters of the revival he was judged, in the middle of 1742, to be "deeply tinctur'd with a Spirit of Enthusiasm," and unworthy to be invited "into our Places of publick Worship"—this from the ministers who diligently worked in behalf of the "great and glorious work of God." Indeed, the friends of the Awakening feared him more than its foes, for they recognized in him the potential for discrediting the entire movement. Thomas Prince, joyfully describing the successes of the revival in Boston, tells of Davenport's coming in these words: "And then through the providence of the sovereign God, the wisdom of whose ways are past finding out, we unexpectedly came to an unhappy period, which it exceedingly grieves me now to write of. . . ." His fellow Presbyterian, Gilbert Tennent, himself repeatedly condemned for going to rash and intemperate extremes, denounced Davenport's technique as "enthusiastical, proud, and schismatical." Further, in the summer of 1742, a Connecticut court found Davenport "disturbed in the rational Faculties of his Mind," while a Massachusetts court declared him *non compos mentis*. To be sure, if Davenport represented anything at all, it would be of a lower order. The point is, however, that he was the spokesman for no class or party, and least of all is he a symbol of the Great Awakening as a whole.

When Whitefield departed from Boston on his first New England tour, the *Evening-Post* editorialized that "the Town is in a hopeful way of being restor'd to its former State of Order, Peace and Industry." Three days later, a letter, appearing in the *News-Letter*, deplored this attitude, affirming that "the Generality of sober and serious Persons, of all Denominations among us (who perhaps are as much for maintaining Order, Peace and Industry as Mr. Evening-Post and Company) have been greatly Affected with Mr. Whitefield's Plain, Powerful, and Awakening Preaching. . . ." Were the "sober and serious" actually reached by the revival? Benjamin Colman, of the Brattle Street Church, wrote Whitefield that after Tennent's visit to Boston "great Additions are made to our Churches. . . . Many of them among the Rich and Polite of our Sons and Daughters. This week the overseers of our Colleges have appointed a Day of Prayer and Humiliation with thanksgiving, for the Effusion of the Spirit of God. . . ." The phrase, "especially among young people," often occurs in contemporary accounts of the revival, suggesting a greater concentration of "concern" in that generation. But that the movement followed class lines, there is no indication.

With reference to the colleges, of which Colman spoke and of whose social standing there can be little question, their sympathies would have remained with the Awakening had not Whitefield heedlessly insulted them. Yale and Harvard both cheerfully heard the leading exponents of the movement, and some of the instructional staff left their posts to carry the word. An effective deterrent to their support was this remark, published in Whitefield's *Journal:* "As for the Universities, I believe it may be said, their Light is become Darkness, Darkness that may be felt, and is complained of by the most godly Ministers." Whitefield sought to mitigate the effect of this unwarranted affront by writing a letter in July, 1741, "To the Students, &c. under convictions at the colleges of Cambridge and New-Haven," declaring that "It was no small grief to me, that I was obliged to say of your college, that 'your light was become darkness;' yet are ye now become light in the Lord." The damage had already been done; nevertheless, not until 1744 did Harvard issue a formal testimony against Whitefield, Yale following suit in 1745. Even then, it must be noted, the testimony was "Against the Reverend Mr. George Whitefield, And his Conduct" and not against the revival in general. Yale and Harvard graduates alike continued to bear the main responsibility in furthering the "extraordinary Work of God."

Pro-revivalism was in no way the equivalent of social egalitarianism. One of the sins for which Jonathan Edwards reproved his young people was their spending much time in "frolicks," without having "any regard to order in the families they belonged to. . . ." There was a large measure of social consciousness in Edwards's Northampton parish, as later events even more clearly revealed; yet the church could hardly be regarded as outside the scope of the Awakening. Ebenezer Parkman of Westborough, a peerless social conservative, was fully sympathetic with the revival at the same time that he complained in horror that the young men of the lower classes had the presumption to adorn themselves with "Velvet Whoods." Gilbert Tennent, often represented as a leveller and "a Man of no great Parts or Learning," had in fact received from his father no mean education in Hebrew, the classics, and theology, and could move easily in any stratum of society.

In Boston, then if not now, the upper reaches of New England society were concentrated. And that city's support of the revival was an effective force in the entire movement. When Whitefield first came to town, he was "met on the Road and conducted to Town by several Gentlemen."

Later in the week, he dined with the governor, Jonathan Belcher, with whom he enjoyed a most cordial relationship. Of Boston's four newspapers, three were either favorable to the Awakening or successfully maintained some degree of neutrality. Only Timothy Fleet's rather coarse *Evening-Post* was openly opposed to the revival, and even this paper did not dare to swim against the tide of public feeling until near the end of 1742, when the movement had already begun to ebb.

The established clergy of New England's capital were preponderantly pro-revivalist or New Light: the proportion was three to one. Of the three divines hostile to the Great Awakening, only Charles Chauncy was open and active in his opposition, and he did not begin a deliberate refutation of the revival until 1743. Throughout 1741, Chauncy allowed himself to be carried along in the main current of the movement, even to the point of telling sinners that they "hang, as it were, over the bottomless pit, by the slender thread of life, and the moment that snaps asunder, you sink down into perdition. . . ." As late as May of 1742, Chauncy declared, "There are, I doubt not, a number in this land, upon whom God has graciously shed the influence of his blessed Spirit. . . ." So that during the height of the Awakening, 1740 to 1742, its most able and prodigious opponent sounded much like Jonathan Edwards himself. The two remaining Old Lights or "Opposers" among Boston's established clergy, both of the Mather family, published nothing concerning the religious excitement, though they privately expressed their disdain of the affair. Samuel Mather, son of Cotton, was dismissed from Second Church in 1741 because, among other reasons, of his negative attitude toward the Awakening and his reluctance to participate in it. In a vain attempt at reconciliation, Mather promised "to beware of any thing in my sermons or conversation which may tend to discourage the work of conviction and conversion among us." Mather Byles, grandson of Increase and first pastor of the Hollis Street Church, succeeded in avoiding any public controversy over the revival. Though publishing a sermon in 1741 on *Repentance and Faith The Great Doctrine of the Gospel of Universal Concernment*, Byles' position—religious and political—was unalterably conservative, and his sympathies were thoroughly Old Light.

Except for three wavering neutrals, the other Boston ministers vigorously, tirelessly, promoted the revival. The city's senior pastor at this time was Benjamin Colman, of Brattle Street Church. A great friend to institutions of higher learning and widely respected abroad as well as at home for his erudition, Colman received the degree of Doctor of Divinity in 1731 from the University of Glasgow. Liberal and learned, he did not hesitate to "play the Artillery of Heaven against the hardy Sons of Vice," and in 1741 he happily reported that "The Work of God with us goes on greatly . . . our crowded serious Assemblies continue, and great Additions are made to our Churches." Following Whitefield's initial visit, Colman spoke at Boston's first evening lecture of the pleasure it gave the ministers to see "in the Weeks past, Old and Young, Parents and Children, Masters and Servants, high and low, rich and poor together, gathering . . . to the Doors and Windows of our Places of Worship. . . ." Benjamin Colman is certainly to be regarded as a constant friend of the Awakening—though, just as certainly, he is to be distinguished from such fanatics as James Davenport and Andrew Croswell. His position, however, was rather one of discrimination than of moderation. He had even shown great interest in the earlier Northampton revival, corresponding with Edwards and others connected with it, passing on to his friends abroad news of religious awakenings in the colonies, and urging Edwards to write the *Faithful Narrative of Surprising Conversions*. The first minister of New England to correspond with Whitefield, he was instrumental in bringing the latter to that area. With much zeal and sincere concern, he favored and furthered the revival to the very end, seeking, like Edwards, to discourage the excesses and abnormalities as no proper part of the true display of God's grace.

William Cooper, Colman's associate since 1715, joined with his colleague in praising "the remarkable Work of Grace begun, and I hope going on amongst us; the eminent Success which God has been pleas'd to give to his preached Gospel of late; the surprizing Effusion of the Holy Spirit, as a Spirit of Conversion to a blessed Number. . . ." At First Church, there was no such harmony. Chauncy's opposition was offset by the approbation of his associate, Thomas Foxcroft, of what he called the "Pauline Spirit and Doctrine remarkably exemplify'd among us." Thomas Prince and Joseph Sewall of Old South Church were eminently successful in making that church a vital center of revival activity. Prince, Boston's foremost reporter of the Awakening, was largely responsible for the creation of the disorganized but important *Christian History*, the first specifically religious magazine in the colonies, the purpose of which was to give accounts of the "surprizing and . . . extensive Revivals." Although it was ostensibly edited by Thomas Prince, Junior, the magazine's enemies were probably correct in declaring the elder Prince to be the power behind the pen. Joseph Sewall, who looked upon the revival as itself a means or channel of grace, inveighed against "every Thing that hath a Tendency to quench his [God's] Spirit, and obstruct the Progress and Success of his good Work." John Webb, senior minister at New North Church, vividly portrayed Christ entreating reluctant sinners in this time of concern to seek and receive the saving grace. His colleague, Andrew Eliot, in 1743 signed a testimony favoring the Great Awakening, noting only that itineracy had not been sufficiently protested against. Samuel Checkley of New South Church, who in 1741 preached on the topic "Little children brought

to Christ," was among the same group of signers. And Joshua Gee of
Second Church, having reproved the cool indifference of his associate,
Samuel Mather, exploded with bitterness when in 1743 a group of ministers issued a testimony against errors and disorders in the Awakening without making "an open Acknowledgment of the late remarkable Effects of a
gracious Divine Influence in many of our Churches." Gee succeeded in
calling a gathering of ninety New England ministers who were "persuaded
there has of late been a happy Revival of Religion," and in issuing a favorable witness to the revival signed by sixty-eight divines and attested to by
forty-three others unable to attend the meeting.

The division of Boston's Congregational clergy in this turbulent period
is, therefore, as follows: nine New Light, three Old Light, three neutral.
Five churches were pro-revivalist (Brattle Street, Old South, Second, New
North, and New South); New Brick and West were neutral; Hollis Street
was anti-revivalist; and First was divided. The city's one Presbyterian
church, with John Moorhead as pastor, was as determined in its support
of the Awakening as the one Baptist church was in its opposition. One
segment of Boston society did hold aloof: namely, that which attended
the city's three Anglican churches. But respectability, in eighteenth-century New England at least, was not wholly identified with Anglicanism.
Even as it is impossible to fix any meaningful geographical boundaries to
the sweep of the Awakening, so the attempt to limit its sway or ascribe its
rise to any single social class proves misleading.

As the revival declined and the "distinguishing names of reproach"
came to be employed more freely and less gently, theological and ecclesiastical factions hardened, sometimes producing divisions that were
social—in Connecticut, even political. With the increase in animosities,
reports of revivalism were dismissed as "stupid Bombast Stuff," and Ezra
Stiles in 1760 described the period of the revival as a time when "Multitudes were seriously, soberly and solemnly out of their wits." A Connecticut divine summarized the effects of the movement as follows:

Antinomian Principles are advanc'd, preach'd up and printed;—Christian Brethren have their Affections widely alienated;—Unchristian Censoriousness and
hard judging abounds, Love stands afar of, and Charity cannot enter;—Many
Churches and Societies are broken and divided. . . . Numbers of illiterate Exhorters swarm about as Locusts from the Bottomless Pit. . . .

As such reports came to abound, it seemed plausible, if not desirable, to
describe the revival as socially suspect from the beginning, as carried along
by a disinherited, rural debtor class. It is, however, tendentious history
that sees New England's religious upheaval of 1740 to 1742 as something
less than "a great and general awakening."

10 *Beverly McAnear*

COLLEGE FOUNDING IN THE
AMERICAN COLONIES, 1745–1775

Education is philosophy. What we see in the classroom is a view of life. The view expresses a complex of values. It defines a culture. Education is one of the means by which a culture sustains and explains itself. It accommodates the young to prevalent values and institutions; and it justifies those values and institutions as a valid response to the deeper questions that man has always asked about himself. To the degree that the daily conditions of life change, philosophy and education will also change. The school will adapt its program to new conditions.

This can be seen clearly from the following article by Dr. Beverly McAnear, who has written extensively on colonial society and, in particular, on colonial education. In the eighteenth century, culture was entering upon a new phase. Population was increasing rapidly. English America was settling into an established order of religious diversity and toleration. The religious order was, paradoxically, being more securely established by the spread of more secular and rational philosophies. Wealth was accumulating, larger urban centers were emerging, social groups were becoming defined and stratified. The urgent dictates of the wilderness were beginning to yield to ways which were more leisurely and sophisticated.

Inevitably these changing conditions articulated themselves in different educational forms and values. Colonial colleges increased considerably in number and substantially reformulated their curricula. Dr. McAnear addresses himself to some larger questions concerning these developments. What particular factors occasioned the founding of new colleges during the period 1745–1775? What were the tangible problems the founders faced and how did they resolve them? What were the consequences of the great mid-eighteenth-century expansion in colonial higher education?

Similar questions suggest themselves concerning developments in higher education today, for we are clearly in a new age of college founding and expansion. In what ways are the forms and substance of American higher education undergoing change and for what reasons? Touching as it does upon America's image and role in world affairs, the change is of great importance.

Reprinted with permission from *The Mississippi Valley Historical Review*, XLII (June, 1955), 24–44.

In the year 1745 there were but three colleges in all of British North America. Yet by the beginning of the Revolution the virus that Ezra Stiles labeled "College Enthusiasm" had so widely infected the American colonists that seven new colleges had been firmly established; plans had been laid for three more which were to open during the Revolution; and at least six abortive projects had been undertaken by responsible people. Thus by 1776 every province and nearly every popular religious sect was planning and had arranged for financial backing for a school of its own. In addition to the older three—Harvard, Yale, and William and Mary—those actually giving instruction were: Dartmouth College in New Hampshire; the College of Rhode Island, now Brown University; King's College, from which Columbia University has descended; Queen's College, soon to bear the name of Rutgers; the College of New Jersey, destined to become Princeton University; the Academy and College of Philadelphia, still living as the University of Pennsylvania; and Newark Academy, ultimately to reappear as the University of Delaware.

This interest in the founding of colleges coincided with a growth of the spirit of rationalism that sought intellectual stimulation in sources other than theological—a spirit eagerly capitalized on by college promoters who urged the establishment of non-sectarian institutions. Sectarian discussion, such as the Old Light–New Light controversy, further spurred on the founding of colleges consecrated to the religious approach of the partisans. Finally, college founding was helped along by the years of prosperity after 1748, which made fund raising easier, and by the growth of civic and humanitarian spirit, which provided the stimulus. Between 1745 and 1765 most of the campaigns were organized by Yale graduates; after 1765 College of New Jersey men began to take the lead. Men educated in Great Britain and some who were not college men were also among the founders of the new colleges. Except for the role of Harvard graduates in the founding of Dartmouth and the part played by the College of Philadelphia in the establishment of Newark Academy, the graduates of the other American colleges did not figure prominently in the movement.

Regardless of their educational background, college promoters became interested in advancing higher education through affiliation either with a library company or with a church. Most organizers—and they were the most successful—were ministers interested in the advancement of their own sect. Clerical leaders campaigned for Dartmouth, Queen's, New Jersey, Newark, and, in their final stages of organization, for Rhode Island and King's. The reasons emphasized by clerics for establishing colleges were to educate ministers, to raise the level of general culture and morals through the influence of the clerical alumni, and to convert the Indians. They maintained that a college was a religious society whose basic and chief duty was to train its students to be religious and moral men. The study of nature was to be subservient to the inculcation of religion; the one was only a threshold to the other, and religious instruction therefore was to be emphasized. They freely promised toleration to all Protestant Trinitarian sects, but they demanded clerical administration and the dominance of one sect.

Those promoters identified with one of the library companies were usually laymen, often without much formal education. Colleges and libraries were at that time a natural conjunction of interests, for some of the library companies were originally designed as organizations which would not only circulate books but which would also provide popular lecture courses, particularly on scientific subjects. Men affiliated with libraries were concerned with the foundation of Rhode Island, King's, and Philadelphia, and with abortive proposals for colleges at Newport and Charleston. They argued that a college should properly be considered a civil society committed to the duty of training youths for service to the commonwealth, and the value of any type of training was to be measured according to its ultimate usefulness to the graduates in civil life. The best attribute of an educated man was an independent mind; free inquiry was therefore to be encouraged and religious instruction prohibited. To assure freedom, religious toleration and non-sectarianism were to be maintained, and even direct state control was proposed.

To their basic appeal for support each group of promoters added virtually the same arguments. College alumni would provide superior public servants and the very presence of the college and its faculty would raise the cultural level of the province. The students' love of their native province would be protected against the alienation that might result from new attachments formed during their school years in distant parts, and thus the best minds of the colony would be saved for the service of their birthplace. Money would not flow out of the province to enrich the residents of college towns in other provinces. And, finally, a local school would provide a less expensive education for ambitious sons of residents.

Almost inevitably a movement to launch a college aroused religious and political rivalries. Many of the quarrels concerned the sectarian affiliation of the proposed college; and in these contests the Anglicans and Presbyterians were the most combative. In addition to their involvement in the Old Light–New Light controversy raging in the Calvinistic churches, some of the schools became involved in provincial or imperial political questions which had nothing to do with higher education, and some college promoters were confronted with the monopolistic claims of institutions already established. Once aroused by these contentions, factions which had been aligned in the opening days of a college lived on to blight its growth. These feuds account in great measure for the failure of all the newer colleges to gain annual provincial appropriations, and they caused the failure of many of the proposals for new colleges even though neither money nor public interest was lacking.

Factional division usually began with a dispute over the terms of a charter of incorporation and the nomination of the first trustees. Incorporation was necessary to protect the institution's property and to permit the granting of degrees; and the religious loyalties of the trustees usually determined the ecclesiastical affiliation of the college. The founders of New Jersey and Dartmouth objected so stubbornly to the inclusion of royal officers of Anglican faith among the trustees that they were almost denied their charters. A furious battle over the method of organization of the college cost King's thousands of pounds of endowment and all hope of future provincial support.

In drafting their charters, King's, Dartmouth, and Queen's used the College of New Jersey charter of 1748 as a model; Rhode Island drew upon the Harvard and Yale charters, in addition to New Jersey's; and Newark turned to the charter of Pennsylvania. Ironically, no one seems to have known at the time whether the colonial governors had the power to grant charters of incorporation and therefore whether the college charters were valid.

The building lot for the college was invariably provided by a public or semi-public organization in order to attract the college to its town. The difficulties that New Jersey College experienced in its attempts to secure a sizable sum in four different New Jersey villages indicate that the custom was not well established in the 1740's. But it caught on quickly, and Queen's was embarrassed by bids from New Brunswick, Tappan, and Hackensack, while Rhode Island felt obliged to hold an auction to terminate five months of competitive controversy.

As soon as money was available, a college hall, containing classrooms and a dormitory, was erected. To supervise construction, some colleges relied on artisans or amateur architects, but Rhode Island, New Jersey, and Philadelphia retained the services of the Philadelphia architect and builder, Robert Smith. The plans drawn by Smith and William Shippen, a physician and amateur architect of Philadelphia, were repeated elsewhere and virtually created in America the collegiate Georgian style. Essentially their design was an adaptation of that for King's College, Cambridge University. During the twenty-five years before the Revolution, five of these schools spent approximately £15,000 sterling for the erection or remodeling of buildings. "This they chose to do," President John Witherspoon of the College of New Jersey wrote, "though it wasted their Capital, as their great Intention was to make effectual Provision, not only for the careful Instruction, but for the regular Government of the Youth." A pretentious building was also desirable because it afforded publicity, and its inclusion of dormitory space and commons reduced student expenses.

The cost of the original hall invariably reduced the college to a state of near insolvency. Indeed, Philadelphia and Rhode Island invested in their buildings literally the last penny in the till. As a result, trustees tended to limit the materials for classroom demonstrations in physics, surveying, and astronomy. Thanks to the persistence of their presidents, however, by 1775 the scientific instruments of King's, New Jersey, and Philadelphia were equal to or better than those possessed by Harvard, Yale, and William and Mary. The other new colleges owned little or no scientific apparatus.

A greater handicap was the inadequacy of libraries. By the time of the Revolution, the Harvard library, with more than 4,000 volumes, was probably the largest college library in the colonies. Yale was not far behind, but William and Mary must have had less than 3,000. While Philadelphia, King's, and New Jersey, with perhaps 2,000 books each, made at least a respectable showing, library facilities at the other newly established institutions were either virtually or completely non-existent.

Nearly all the books in the libraries of the newer colleges had been presented: none customarily bought more than occasional titles. The only important purchases were three consignments for New Jersey, one of which was so costly that the trustees deemed it an extravagance and charged the bill to the president. To make matters more difficult, these libraries were largely the gifts of benevolent clergymen, and the weight of theology hung heavy upon them. "But few modern Authors, who have unquestionably some Advantages above the immortal ancient, adorn the Shelves," wrote a college official in 1760. "This Defect is most sensibly felt in the Study of Mathematics, and the Newtonian Philosophy." Philadelphia and New Jersey sought to remedy matters by assessing the students a library fee, but the income must have been small.

By the time the trustees of a college had built the hall and provided furniture, scientific equipment, and a library, they had invested approximately £5,000—perhaps the equivalent of $350,000 today. By 1776 the physical properties of all the infant colleges probably represented the expenditure of something approaching £25,000—an investment which produced virtually no income, since students' rents could hardly have paid for maintenance.

In assembling a faculty, the trustees were apt to seek a president who had been trained in a British university, but since the necessary income was often lacking they were forced to be content with the product of an American college. The president bore the heaviest share of the burden of the school. He did a good part of the teaching and conducted the college's religious exercises. He was also the chief and sometimes the only administrative officer, and he was obliged to gather money and recruit students. To supplement his income, he often served as the pastor of a neighboring church. Such arrangements were discouraged by the trustees, however, and as the college grew more prosperous, pressure was placed on the president to confine himself to college affairs.

The other members of the faculty (seldom more than three) were usually younger men destined within a few years to be clergymen. Most were American trained, though Anglican schools secured some British-educated tutors. Lack of money prevented the hiring of a more stable, better trained faculty, since almost any profession promised greater returns and better social status. The hardest position to fill was that of the science instructor. Few men with the necessary training were to be found in the colonies, and hence the post was often vacant. Each instructor normally was assigned a given class of students to whom he imparted knowledge on all subjects except the natural sciences. This arrangement demanded, however, that a faculty member undertake a considerable degree of specialization of subject matter, because the curricula emphasized given branches of learning in different years.

One of the president's most perplexing tasks was the enrollment of students. To an even greater extent than the present-day college, colonial institutions relied upon income from tuition to provide vitally needed revenue. But to recruit students, it was necessary to popularize the value of higher education. Prior to 1745 not many parents in the British North American colonies sent their sons to college. This was especially true for the Middle Colonies. To attract public attention, some use was made of printed publicity. Ministers were pressed to act as recruiting agents for the college identified with their sect. Alumni, especially where they were schoolmasters or pastors, were able to help the recruiting for New Jersey, but most of the other colleges were too young to have many graduates.

The overwhelming majority of entrants were attracted by the college nearest their homes. The difficulty and expense of travel, the emotional complications inherent in distant separation from home, and local pride perhaps influenced students and furnished talking points for recruiting agents. But provincialism could be defeated if a distant college offered a cheaper education. Those colleges which grew most rapidly and attracted most students from other provinces were those which charged least. New Jersey and Rhode Island had the lowest charges, and Eleazer Wheelock permitted some Dartmouth students to work for their expenses. Hence these three colleges showed the most rapid increase in enrollment. Apparently New Jersey was also aided by its custom of admitting applicants as juniors, thus waiving costly residence at college for the first two or three years of a boy's work. Philadelphia and King's were the most expensive and therefore always had small student bodies, largely drawn from their immediate vicinity.

Despite ardent campaigning, the enrollment in all these infant colleges was small. The opening class in any of them could hardly have been more than five to eight boys. Succeeding classes naturally increased enrollment, and the prosperous years of the early 1770's greatly aided recruitment. Even so, most of the newer schools prior to the Revolution had at best an attendance of only forty or fifty students. By all odds, the most successful was New Jersey, which grew to an enrollment of about one hundred. Yet, despite this rapid growth, New Jersey was still smaller than her older rivals, for after 1755 the student bodies of Harvard and Yale had often exceeded one hundred and fifty. Approximately four sevenths of all college students of 1775 were enrolled in the three oldest institutions.

Upon appearance at college, the prospective student was required to pass an entrance examination, usually administered by the president. The requirements of the new colleges seem to have been copied from those of Yale; for Rhode Island, King's, and New Jersey the requirements were almost identical. Essentially, the test demanded ability to translate elementary Latin and Greek and a knowledge of arithmetic—this last being a contemporary innovation. It is doubtful that an applicant was ever sent home, though sometimes extra work was prescribed.

Many of the students admitted were mere boys. From 1750 to 1775 the median age of the entrants at Yale was only sixteen or seventeen; at Philadelphia it was sixteen; and at King's only fifteen. Eleven- and twelve-year-old freshmen were not unknown, and John Trumbull satisfied the Yale entrance examination at the age of seven years and five months. Because of the competition for students the colleges were in danger of becoming grammar schools. As a step toward remedying this difficulty, the governors of King's in 1774 ruled that after the admission of the class of 1778 entrance would be refused any applicant younger than fourteen "except upon account of extraordinary qualifications."

As a general rule, only freshmen were admitted. Though there were exceptions in every college, only Dartmouth, New Jersey, and possibly Philadelphia made a practice of admitting students to advanced standing. These boys had usually studied with a minister because such a training was less expensive than college residence. For admission to advanced standing, the college required payment of fees for the earlier years and passage of an entrance examination. The examination seems to have been largely a formality. Writing to a friend, one such candidate at New Jersey reported: "After examinations on the usual *authors*, when I and they, who were examined with me, received admission into the junior-class, we were told, that we should have been examined on the *Roman antiquities*, if it had not been forgotten." Witherspoon disliked the system and unsuccessfully sought to abolish it.

Rhode Island, King's, and New Jersey also patterned their curricula after the Yale model, a program that reflected the course of study developed in the English dissenting academies. Actually colleges, these institutions had broken away from complete concentration upon the classics and Aristotelianism and had instituted Newtonianism, social sciences, and modern languages. All four colleges required the same course of studies in the first two years: principally Latin, Greek, and Hebrew. That they assigned much more time to these subjects than did the English academies indicates an effort to repair the deficiencies of their matriculants who, compared to their English counterparts, were retarded about a year and a half. In the final two years, the American colleges emphasized natural sciences, mathematics, and metaphysics. President Samuel Johnson at King's apportioned three fourths of the time of juniors and seniors to mathematics and the natural sciences, while Yale provided but one year, and Rhode Island and New Jersey considerably less than a year. To complete the studies for the senior year, Yale provided metaphysics and divinity, and New Jersey and Rhode Island oratory, composition, and almost certainly divinity. This difference in emphasis is partly explained by the desire of the dissenting colleges to train preachers and in part by the lack of scientific equipment and instructors. All devoted some time to logic, ethics, geography, and public speaking.

At Philadelphia a more independent approach to the curriculum was undertaken by President William Smith, who was influenced by Dr. Samuel Johnson, the great English writer, and by Robert Dodsley's *Preceptor*. Nonetheless, the subjects prescribed by Smith were much the same as those offered elsewhere, except that he placed much greater stress upon oratory and the social sciences and did not regularly offer courses on religion.

Between 1765 and 1775 the American institutions showed great capacity to adapt their curricula to trends appearing in the English academies. Stress was placed on English grammar and composition by requiring polished written translations and original products of the students' pens, and greater weight was placed on oratory. English literature, however, was never taught formally. Some schools began to offer modern foreign language as electives, and with their growing popularity classes in Hebrew were deserted. Greater attention was also paid to history by Witherspoon at New Jersey and by President James Manning at Rhode Island, though, as was the case in England, apparently only ancient history was taught. In brief, during these thirty years the college moved to some degree from ancient to modern languages, from divinity to the social sciences, and from metaphysics to natural sciences. Only Dartmouth and King's seemed to find the older ideas the better.

Most colleges organized their courses into a four-year curriculum. Smith, however, instituted at Philadelphia the then current English innovation of a three-year college. In actual fact, Philadelphia's program of study was abbreviated by pushing back into the academy some of the courses taught elsewhere to college freshmen. Newark also seems to have required only three years' residence, but similar experiments in truncation by Witherspoon at New Jersey and Manning at Rhode Island were soon abandoned.

Classes began early and lasted through the day, punctuated by morning and evening prayers. Instruction was based upon recitations from and elaborations of textbooks, though the lecture method was used by some presidents in teaching the seniors. The college library was rarely used by undergraduates, and New Jersey claimed distinction for its policy of encouraging seniors to browse in the library. To stimulate scholarship, King's, New Jersey, and Philadelphia set up prizes to be awarded for excellence in specified subjects, and Manning wanted to adopt the plan at Rhode Island. But the system proved ineffective, and it was allowed to die.

Regular attendance, payment of fees, and proper deportment—or due regret for improper deportment—seemed almost invariably to yield a diploma on the scheduled day. "To the frequent scandal, as well of religion, as learning," wrote a contemporary critic, "a fellow may pass with credit through life, receive the honors of a liberal education, and be admitted to the right hand of fellowship among the ministers of the gospel. . . . Except in one neighbouring province, ignorance wanders unmolested at our colleges, examinations are dwindled to mere form and ceremony, and after four years dozing there, no one is ever refused the honors of a degree, on account of dulness and insufficiency." In 1756 there were 172 students enrolled at Yale, and all but seven eventually received degrees. Elsewhere, virtually automatic progress by the student likewise seems to have been the rule; only at King's and Philadelphia was the mortality rate high.

All the younger colleges claimed to be non-sectarian and insisted that full religious toleration was granted to all Protestants. Therefore all were advertised as "free and Catholic" or as "Catholic, Comprehensive, and liberal." Nevertheless, all students were required to take courses in divinity or the Bible, and all attended college prayers twice a day. College laws also required attendance at church on Sunday. Tolerance demanded that the student be permitted to attend the church of his own choice, though in some instances there was only one church in town. Thus while sectarians could and did freely accuse each other of proselytizing, none could charge these college administrators of ignoring the injunction laid down by one of their trustees that *"Liberty* be not made a Cloak of *Licentiousness."*

Most students lived in the college hall, two or three to a room or suite of rooms. Meals were served in the college refectory, usually situated in the basement of the college hall. The only important meal came at mid-day; it consisted essentially of meat and potatoes. The evening meal was based upon left-overs from noon, and breakfast brought only bread and butter. While this community life was recommended by the college authorities, many students preferred the more expensive but freer method of boarding out in adjacent homes. Such freedom, however, sometimes created special problems of discipline.

Relations between the faculty and the students seem to have been reasonably good, although there were, of course, exceptions. Provost William Smith, of Philadelphia, gained a reputation for harshness; Eleazer Wheelock, of Dartmouth, ruled with the care but without the indulgence of a father; and Robert Harpur, the science instructor at King's, was hated and tormented on general principles. But the newer colleges were free of the student riots which occurred at Harvard and Yale.

The students found their college days profitable and enjoyable, and letters written after graduation to former schoolmates bore the impress of nostalgia. Extracurricular activities revolved around clubs devoted to literary and bibulous exercises. Oratory was perhaps the most popular interest, and students sharpened their oratorical prowess in nightly practice for the seniors' grand performance on commencement day. Singing and the writing of verse were also fashionable; and the score for the New Jersey commencement of 1762 is one of the earliest examples of college music now extant. In their songs and some of their poetry the students frequently gave expression to sentiments which suggest that college pride had already been born.

However valuable students found college life to be, their fathers regarded the expense of maintenance with no little concern. During the years between 1746 and 1772 the charges of the College of New Jersey for room, board, and tuition—£9 per year—were the lowest of any college. But college fees gradually increased, and after 1772 an economical parent found that the lowest bill, £12, was presented by the College of Rhode Island. The highest annual charges made by any of the newer colleges were those of King's—£18. And room, board, and tuition, of course, represented only a fraction of a student's total expenses. Firewood, candles, and washing cost £3 more; books and stationery, clothing and travel, and pocket money, too, increased the cost. Thus in 1775 the lowest cost of educating a boy ranged from £25 to £35 a year; it might easily amount to £55 or even more for spendthrifts. But the highest expense in America was mild compared to charges in England, where advanced education cost over £100 annually.

For colonial days these were large sums in terms of personal cash income. An able carpenter with good employment earned about £50 a year; a captain in the royal army, £136; a college instructor, £100; and a good lawyer, £500. Some relief was afforded by the extension of credit, and only too often greater relief was gained by parents who defaulted payment of the indebtedness. A little money for needy students was raised through church collections and subscriptions by the Baptists at Rhode Island and the Presbyterians at New Jersey. But none of the infant colleges had annually appointed scholars, and it appears that only at Dartmouth did any number of students work to pay their expenses. Therefore, sooner or later, the father had to pay, and clearly only the well-to-do could easily afford to do so. Indeed, some contemporary commentators believed that only the sons of the wealthy should go to college.

The greatest problem faced by the college administrators was that of getting the money necessary to keep the college open, for students' fees paid only a small part of the cost of a boy's education. In their search for the requisite funds, promoters of the new colleges found that tapping the provincial treasury yielded only a trickle of cash. Harvard, Yale, and William and Mary all had been given both grants and annual subventions by their respective provincial governments or by the King. Among the newer colleges, only Dartmouth, King's, and Philadelphia were voted money from public treasuries, and King's alone was treated generously. None ever received an annual public subsidy, despite repeated applications.

Appeals to the general public by means of subscription lists and lotteries brought some funds, and occasional bequests added more; but the receipts from these sources were usually needed to meet recurring deficits. To gain capital for investment, efforts were made to raise funds in Europe and the West Indies. Between 1745 and 1775 the seven new colleges received well over £72,000 in gifts from thousands of people solicited by hundreds of well-wishers. Over the same period approximately two sevenths of these funds were invested in income-producing endowment; about three sevenths were used in meeting current operating expenses; and the remaining two sevenths were absorbed in the erection of buildings. With the exception of King's, which was able to meet its running expenses with the income from its investments, all were operating on deficit budgets after 1770; and at the same time the raising of funds for colleges became increasingly difficult.

The most obvious effect of the work of the pioneer educators who were responsible for the establishment and operation of these newer colleges was the great increase in the number of college-trained men in the colonies. From 1715 through 1745 the three older colleges graduated about fourteen hundred men, but in the following thirty-one years over thirty-one hundred gained bachelors' degrees in British North America. Almost nine hundred of these degrees (28 per cent of the total number) were granted by the seven new colleges. These schools therefore were responsible for about half the increase of college-trained men during these decades.

Behind the growing interest in college attendance was increasing economic prosperity. Each advance in college enrollment followed by three or four years the initial point on a rise of the index of commodity prices. Mounting colonial wealth aided the establishment of colleges in provinces from which the older colleges had drawn few students. Probably over 90 per cent of the graduates of Harvard, Yale, and William and Mary came from eastern New Hampshire, Massachusetts, Connecticut, and Virginia. Rhode Island and the middle provinces were relatively fallow fields, and to the boys in those areas the younger colleges represented opportunity. Therefore, the advance in enrollment beginning in 1769 redounded to the advantage of the newer rather than the older colleges, and from 1769 through 1776 they graduated approximately 40 per cent of the bachelors of arts.

This sudden popular interest in a college degree brought repeated demands that college bills should not be so high as to exclude the sons of the less well-to-do. This insistence sprang in part from a belief that the duty of the college was to open the gates of opportunity to youths of merit regardless of their fathers' social and economic position. One of the college propagandists argued: "The great Inducement to Study and Application . . . is the Hope of a Reward adequate to the Expence, Labour and Pains, taken. In Countries where Liberty prevails, and where the Road is left open for the Son of the meanest Plebeian, to arrive at the highest Pitch of Honours and Preferments, there never will be wanting such Emulation, and of Course great Men. . . . Such at this Day, is Great Britain." Some extended the argument, maintaining that all classes of society needed some type of education beyond that of the common school.

These democratic concepts of education were being applied at the time to a class society which it was assumed educated men would buttress. Such efforts as were made to reduce the barrier of high cost came from the dissenting colleges. Groups of dissenters in England had long aided poor students financially, and the Baptists and Presbyterians in America followed the custom. Furthermore, ministers were badly needed in the colonies and usually they could be recruited only among the sons of farmers. A costly education, therefore, would handicap the Presbyterian and Baptist churches. Inevitably the administrators of dissenting colleges were forced to yield to pressure to keep their fees down, and hence their graduates included a goodly number of sons of artisans and farmers of modest means. Thus the requirements of religious sects gave effect to the demand for democratization of higher education.

One concern of this increased interest in higher education was the improvement of professional training. New Jersey was the first of the younger colleges to build a curriculum designed to train preachers, and it is not surprising, therefore, that about half of the pre-Revolutionary graduates of New Jersey entered the ministry. Rhode Island and Newark followed New Jersey's precedent, and President Smith at Philadelphia read lectures in divinity as a special course for candidates for the ministry. Through the influence of President Witherspoon, New Jersey was also the first of the new colleges to introduce formal graduate training in divinity, a program already long established at William and Mary.

Philadelphia in 1765 and King's in 1767 undertook to supply professional training in medicine, though on an undergraduate level. But physicians had a poor economic and social status, and so the medical schools were never overflowing with students. By 1776, Philadelphia had graduated but ten students and King's twelve. Perhaps it was as well, for one of the abler graduates of King's recommended in his thesis the prescription of a specific he had not the courage to administer.

This advance in educational standards also influenced the legal profession, and in 1756 the New York bar began to demand college work as a requisite for admission. By 1776 one third of those entitled to plead before the provincial courts held the degree of bachelor of arts. Formal training in civil law, the common law, or municipal law was never undertaken in any colonial college, although King's, Philadelphia, and the advocates of the proposed college at Charleston all dreamed and planned for the establishment of such courses.

The colleges likewise raised the standards of secondary education. Throughout the period, criticism of the preparation of college matriculants was constant, and, in an effort to gain more satisfactory material, all the new colleges maintained their own grammar schools. These secondary schools were also essential to the colleges as "feeders" of matriculants. As the years passed, the number of independent grammar schools in the middle and southern provinces increased sharply, and the graduates of the newer colleges, particularly New Jersey, were in great demand as masters.

These college founders also made significant contributions to colonial interdependence. Hundreds of students crossed provincial boundaries to enroll in their alma maters. Half of Newark's enrollment came from provinces other than Delaware; 40 per cent of Philadelphia's from homes outside of Pennsylvania. New Jersey attracted men from North Carolina and Massachusetts. So heavy a migration was a significant change, for the three older colleges had drawn nearly all their students from relatively restricted areas. In the years immediately preceding the Revolution, students migrating northward were passed by northern-born graduates, particularly of Yale and New Jersey, moving to southern provinces. In Virginia and North Carolina, New Jersey men began a new cycle of college founding. Thus the younger colleges stimulated interprovincial migration of able men, trained in much the same intellectual pattern.

The history of higher education during these three decades, then, is dominated by the establishment of successful colleges and the development of promotional techniques. Each successive college was founded more easily and with better planning than its predecessors; problems were foreseen and precedents were available and accepted. Once opened, they carried on until subjected to military interference during the Revolution. These colleges significantly increased the cultural level of the population and raised the educational standards of the professions. The founders advanced the practice and idea of democratic higher education. They transplanted the essentials of the educational system of the English dissenting academies and saw the system take root; and virtually the entire task had been the accomplishment of men born and bred in America. They believed that they were strengthening the bonds of an empire in which America should be subsidiary, not subordinate to England. From the beginning many had hoped the colleges would further the creation of cultural autonomy in America. In 1770, for example, Ezra Stiles tabulated the various degrees granted by the several American colleges and concluded: "Thus all the learned degrees are now conferred in the American Colleges as amply as in the European Colleges." As the colonial epoch closed, many Americans proudly felt that they had achieved educational self-reliance.

IMPERIAL PROBLEMS AND REVOLUTION

11 Curtis P. Nettels

BRITISH MERCANTILISM AND THE ECONOMIC
DEVELOPMENT OF THE THIRTEEN COLONIES

In their attempt to understand the causes of the American Revolution, historians have turned inevitably to an analysis of British mercantilism. It, after all, was the matrix of colonial life. For more than a century, it provided a framework for imperial relations. In analyzing the matter, historians have addressed themselves to a few basic questions. What impact did mercantilist policy have upon colonial economic development? Even if it was adverse, did it necessarily cause the American Revolution? And if it was not adverse, what did cause the Revolution?

Historians have been far from agreed in their answers. Some, like George Louis Beer and Lawrence Henry Gipson, have argued that British mercantilism was essentially favorable to the colonies; but it was the utter defeat of the French by the British in North America which, paradoxically, freed the colonies from their need for imperial support and encouraged them to seek independence. Some, like Oliver M. Dickerson and Lawrence A. Harper, have argued that British mercantilist policy was economically advantageous to the colonies but that blundering administration of the policy after 1763 precipitated revolution. Some, like Louis M. Hacker, have argued that inherent in English mercantilism was an ever-increasing conflict of interests between English merchant capitalism and colonial merchant capitalism and that this conflict resulted inevitably in the American Revolution.

Reprinted with permission from *The Journal of Economic History*, XII (Spring, 1952), 105–14.

In the following essay, Professor Curtis P. Nettels of Cornell University brings his extensive knowledge of early American history to a discussion of this important problem. His many writings include a monograph on *The Money Supply of the American Colonies Before 1720* (1934), an appraisal of *George Washington and American Independence* (1951), and a comprehensive survey of the colonial period entitled *The Roots of American Civilization* (1938). In the essay below, Professor Nettels analyzes the guiding premises of British mercantilist policy in the pre-revolutionary age, considering in his analysis a few central questions. How did that policy contribute to the growth of colonial wealth? What, moreover, was its impact on the economic development of the Southern colonies? Of the Middle and Northern colonies? How did British policy after 1763 lead to revolution?

Although Professor Nettels does not reduce the coming of the Revolution to the constraint of economic determination, there can be no doubt that he sees it as the product of economic constraint. The question for the student of history is to understand the difference between the two, with regard both to the history of the Revolution and to history in general. The question, moreover, is whether colonial man lived by economic laws alone or whether other motives impelled his larger actions. To answer both questions is also to understand better the actions of men in a revolutionary epoch such as our own.

Mercantilism is defined for this discussion as a policy of government that expressed in the economic sphere the spirit of nationalism that animated the growth of the national state in early modern times. The policy aimed to gain for the nation a high degree of security or self-sufficiency, especially as regards food supply, raw materials needed for essential industries, and the sinews of war. This end was to be achieved in large measure by means of an effective control over the external activities and resources upon which the nation was dependent. In turn, that urge impelled the mercantilists to prefer colonial dependencies to independent foreign countries in seeking sources of supply. If the state could not free itself completely from trade with foreign nations, it sought to control that trade in its own interest as much as possible. To realize such objectives, mercantilism embraced three subordinate and related policies. The Corn Laws fostered the nation's agriculture and aimed to realize the ideal of self-sufficiency as regards food supply. State aids to manufacturing industries, such as the protective tariff, sought to provide essential finished goods, including the sinews of war. The Navigation Acts were intended to assure that foreign trade would be carried on in such a way as to yield the maximum advantage to the state concerned.

Since the mercantilist states of Europe lacked the resources for complete self-sufficiency, they could not free themselves from dependence on foreign supplies. Economic growth therefore increased the importance of external trade, and the preference for colonies over foreign countries intensified the struggle for dependent possessions. The importance in mercantilism of a favorable balance of trade and of a large supply of the precious metals is a familiar theme. We need only to remind ourselves that the mercantilists considered it the duty of government to obtain and to retain for the nation both a favorable trade balance and an adequate stock of gold and silver. To this end the state should help to build up a national merchant marine and should foster domestic manufacturing industries. The chief means of procuring raw materials, a favorable trade balance, and an ample supply of the precious metals was that of exporting high-priced manufactured goods and shipping services.

Despite its emphasis on government action, mercantilism was not socialism. In England, the system invoked the initiative and enterprise of private citizens. It encouraged the merchants, shippers, and manufacturers by conferring benefits upon them and by identifying their private interests with the highest needs of the state. So close was this identification that one may properly regard the theory of mercantilism as a rationalization of the special interests of dominant groups of the time. The mercantilist policy was an expression of an accord between landowners and merchant-capitalists in alliance with the Crown.

Is it possible to measure the influence of government on the economic development of an area? Whether such influence be large or small, it must necessarily be only one factor at work in the process of economic change. The range of influence of even the most powerful government is limited, whereas economic activity is world-wide in its scope and ramifications. Thus far no scheme of statecraft has succeeded in bending all the members of the perverse human family to its designs. To many students of economic affairs it may seem futile to attempt to isolate and to measure the effect of only one factor in the immensely intricate, varied, and shifting activities that are involved in the development of a large area, such as the thirteen colonies. But perhaps such an effort may serve a purpose. It at least stimulates thought, which is essential to intellectual growth, and growth—not final answers or ultimate solutions—is all that one can expect to attain in this world of perpetual change.

To begin with, we note that the thirteen colonies experienced a phenomenal development during the 150 years in which they were subject to the regulating policies of English mercantilism. Adam Smith said in 1776:

A nation may import to a greater value than it exports for half a century, perhaps, together; the gold and silver which comes into it during all this time may be all immediately sent out of it; its circulating coin may gradually decay, different sorts of paper money being substituted in its place, and even the debts, too, which it contracts with the principal nations with whom it deals, may be gradually increasing; and yet its real wealth, the exchangeable value of the annual produce of its lands and labor, may, during the same period, have been increasing in a much greater proportion. The state of our North American colonies, and of the trade which they carried on with Great Britain, before the commencement of the present disturbances, may serve as a proof that this is by no means an impossible supposition.

To what extent did English mercantilism contribute to this "real wealth"—this "exchangeable value of the annual produce of . . . lands and labor?" Lands and labor. Two of the most fundamental factors in the growth of the thirteen colonies were the character of the people and the nature of the land and resources to which they applied their labor. The connecting link between the two that gave the thirteen colonies their unique character was the system of small individual holdings that came into being, usually at the start of settlement. It provided a strong incentive to labor and was therefore a major factor in their development. Crèvecoeur spoke of "that restless industry which is the principal characteristic of these colonies," and observed: "Here the rewards of . . . [the farmer's] industry follow with equal steps the progress of his labor; his labor is founded on the basis of nature, self-interest, can it want a stronger allurement . . . ? As farmers they will be careful and anxious to get as much as they can, because what they get is their own."

Although the land system of the thirteen colonies has not usually been considered an element of mercantilism, yet it was not divorced from it. Why did the English Government grant to its colonies a benefit that was not commonly bestowed on settlers by the other colonizing powers? Small holdings inspired the colonists to work; their labor expanded production; and increased production enlarged English commerce. The resulting trade was more susceptible to control by the state than a comparable trade with foreign countries would have been. For this reason, the colonial land system may be regarded as an expression of mercantilist policy. Viewed in this light, mercantilism contributed directly to the growth of the settlements.

Such also was the effect of the policy of England with reference to the peopling of its part of America. The government opened the doors to immigrants of many nationalities and creeds. Its liberality in this respect was unique. It harmonized with the mercantilist doctrine. The Crown admitted dissenters and foreigners in order to expand colonial production and trade. Such immigrants were, to a large extent, industrious, progressive, and energetic. Their productivity was stimulated by the climate of freedom in which they lived—a climate that was made possible in good measure by the indulgence of the government. The resulting growth of

English trade served the needs of the state as they were viewed by the mercantilists.

We shall next consider the effects of specific mercantilist laws and government actions on the economic development of the thirteen colonies. It appears at once that such laws and actions did not create or sustain any important industry or trade in Colonial America. The major economic pursuits of the colonies grew out of, and were shaped by, the nature of the resources of the land, the needs of the settlers, and the general state of world trade in the seventeenth century. No important colonial activity owed its birth or existence to English law. The statutes and policies of mercantilism, with an exception or two, sought to control, to regulate, to restrain, to stimulate, or to protect. In the great majority of instances it was not the role of the government to initiate, to originate, to create. All the important mercantilist laws were adopted in response to a development that had occurred. They undertook to encourage, or to regulate, or to suppress some industry, practice, or trade that had been initiated by private citizens and which they had proved to be profitable. When the origins of enterprise in America are considered, it appears that every important industry got its start by reason of the natural resources of an area, by virtue of the demand for a product, or because of such factors of trade as transportation or location. Ordinarily, the government did not subject a colonial activity to regulation by law until it had proved itself to be profitable. In Virginia, for instance, the government did not initiate the tobacco industry or attempt to stimulate its early development. Rather, the Crown sought to discourage it. After it had taken root under the influence of general economic conditions, the government stepped in to regulate it. The major Navigation Act was passed in response to the success of the Dutch in world commerce. The English Government did not legislate against certain industries in the colonies until they had grown of their own accord to the extent that they menaced their English counterparts. The currency policy which England applied to its colonies was worked out not in a vacuum but in answer to practices in which the colonists were engaging.

The effects of mercantilist laws naturally depended upon their enforcement. Since they almost invariably sought to prevent something that the colonists had found to be profitable, the task of enforcement was difficult. It required the exercise of force and vigilance.

In a general way, the government attained a reasonable success in its efforts to enforce the policies that bore directly on the southern mainland colonies, whereas the principal acts which were designed for the Middle Colonies and New England could not be made effective.

The program for the plantation area embraced several policies. The Navigation Act of 1661 excluded from its trade all foreign merchants and foreign vessels. By the terms of the Staple Act of 1663 the planters must buy most of their manufactured goods from England. Slaves must be bought from English slave traders. The area must depend upon English sources for capital and credit, and the planters could not avail themselves of legal devices in order to ease their burdens of debt.

The government made a strenuous effort to enforce these policies. The decisive action centered in the three Dutch wars between 1652 and 1675. The defeat of the Dutch drove them from the southern trade and enabled the English merchants to hold it as in a vise. After 1665 the development of the plantation colonies proceeded in conformity with the tenets of mercantilism. The effect was to retard that development, since the planters were subjected to a virtual English monopoly and were denied the benefits of competitive bidding for their crops and the privilege of buying foreign goods and shipping services in the cheapest market.

Certain conditions of the period 1675 to 1775 favored the English mercantilists in their efforts to enforce the southern policy. The geography of the Chesapeake country made it easy to exclude foreign vessels, since the English navy had to control only the narrow entrance to the bay in order to keep foreign vessels from reaching the plantations. That the tobacco ships had to move slowly along the rivers made concealment impossible for interlopers. Secondly, there was the factor of debt. Once a planter had become indebted to an English merchant, he was obliged to market his crops through his creditor in order to obtain new supplies. Hence he lost the advantage of competitive bidding for his export produce. And finally, the four wars with France, 1689–1763, served to rivet the plantation area to Britain, as mercantilism intended. The British navy provided convoys for the tobacco ships, and the expenditures of the Crown in America for military purposes provided the planters with additional buying power for English goods, thereby increasing their dependence on British merchants, vessels, and supplies.

By reason of the acts of government, the economic development of the southern colonies exhibited after 1665 about as clear an example of effective political control of economic activity as one can find. The trade of the southern colonies was centered in Britain. They were obliged to employ British shipping, to depend on British merchants, and to look only to British sources for capital and credit. They were not permitted to interfere with the British slave trade. British investments enjoyed a sheltered market in that the Crown excluded the foreign investor from the area and prohibited the colonists from taking any legal steps that would impair the claims of British creditors. The resulting dependence of the plantation country gave it a strongly British character, retarded its development, fostered discontent, and goaded the planters to resistance and revolt.

The initial enforcement of the Navigation Acts in the 1660's reduced the profits of the tobacco planters and forced them to cut the costs of production. Slavery was the answer. Appropriately at this time the English Government undertook to furnish its colonies with an ample supply of slaves. The planters were obliged to buy them on credit—a main factor in reducing them to a state of commercial bondage. The English government forbade the planters to curtail the nefarious traffic. American slavery was thus one of the outstanding legacies of English mercantilism. That resolute foe of English mercantilist policy, George Washington, subscribed to the following resolve in 1774: "We take this opportunity of declaring our most earnest wishes to see an entire stop forever put to such a wicked, cruel, and unnatural trade."

In another sense the Navigation Act of 1661 had a discernible effect on American development. It stimulated the shipbuilding and shipping industries in New England and the Middle Colonies. It did not, however, create those industries. But the English Government drove the Dutch from the trade of English America before English shipping could meet the full needs of the colonies. The Navigation Act gave to English colonial shipbuilders and shipowners the same privileges that were given to English shipbuilders and shipowners. Undoubtedly this favored treatment spurred on the shipping industries of New England. Shipbuilding flourished there, since the colonial builders were permitted to sell their product to English merchants, and New England shipowners could employ their American-built vessels in the trade of the whole empire. New England benefited directly from the expulsion of the Dutch from the trade of English America. After New England's shipbuilding industry had become fully established (and had proved itself more efficient than its English rival) the British Government refused to heed the pleas of British shipowners who wished to subject it to crippling restraints.

English policy for the plantation area was essentially negative. It did not originate enterprises. With one exception it did not attempt to direct economic development into new channels. The exception appears in the bounty granted for indigo—a form of aid that made the production of that commodity profitable and sustained it in the lower South until the time of the Revolution, when the industry expired with the cessation of the bounty.

The policies that affected the Middle Colonies and New England differed materially in character and effect from the policies that were applied to the South. The northern area received the privilege of exporting its chief surplus products—fish, meats, cereals, livestock, lumber—directly to foreign markets. As already noted, the northern maritime industries flourished under the benefits conferred upon them by the Navigation Acts. Freedom to export the staples of the area in company with vigorous shipbuilding and shipping industries induced the northerners to engage in a varied foreign trade. This outcome, however, was in part a result of certain restrictive measures of the English Government. It prohibited the importation into England of American meats and cereals, thereby forcing the colonists to seek foreign markets for their surplus.

The resulting trade of the northern area—with southern Europe, the Wine Islands, Africa, and the foreign West Indies—did not prove satisfactory to the English mercantilists. It built up in the colonies a mercantile interest that threatened to compete successfully with English traders and shipowners. It carried with it the danger that the northerners might nullify those features of the Navigation Acts which aimed to center most of the trade of English America in England. Nor did their reliance on foreign trade prove to be entirely satisfactory to the colonists. In time of war, their vessels were exposed to the depredations of the French. The English navy could not protect the diverse northern trades with convoys, as it protected the simpler, more concentrated commerce of the plantation area. The wartime disruption of the northern trade deprived the area of the foreign money and products that in peacetime its merchants carried to England for the purpose of buying English goods for the colonial market. The resulting decline of the exportation of English merchandise was then deplored by the English mercantilists. Unable to procure finished goods in England, the northerners were driven to manufacture for themselves. Thence arose what the mercantilists regarded as a fatal danger— the prospect that the colonies would manufacture for themselves, decrease their purchases in England, and produce a surplus of finished goods that would compete with English wares in the markets of the world.

To avoid this danger, the English mercantilists devised their major experiment in state planning of the early eighteenth century. They undertook to foster the production of naval stores in the Middle Colonies and New England. Such products would be sent directly to England as a means of paying for English goods. They would divert the colonists from domestic manufacturing and free them from their dependence on diverse foreign trades. They would transform the commerce of the northern area in such a way that it would resemble that of the plantation area—a simple, direct exchange of American raw products for English finished goods.

The naval-stores program was constructive in intent. The government sought to shape the development of the northern area, thereby solving a serious problem. But the policy failed. It did not stimulate the production of naval stores in the northern area sufficiently to provide it with adequate payments for English goods, or to divert the northerners from their foreign trades, or to halt the trend toward home manufacturing.

This failure led the mercantilists to embrace a purely negative policy. As the trade of the northern area with the foreign West Indies increased, the English Government undertook to stop it altogether. Such was its intent in imposing upon the colonies the Molasses Act of 1733. But that effort did not succeed. Again, a mercantilist policy failed to bear its expected fruit.

The early policies of mercantilism had a marked effect on the growth of the northern area. But the result turned out to be unpleasing to the English authorities. Their endeavors to give a new direction to the development of the area failed completely after 1700. A problem had arisen for which English mercantilism never found a solution.

The main element in this problem was the trend in the northern area toward domestic manufacturing. Since that trend menaced all the essentials of mercantilism, the English Government did its best to thwart it. Thus there was no more important ingredient in English policy than the determined effort to retard or prevent the growth in America of industries that would produce the sort of goods that England could export at the greatest profit. Such, chiefly, were cloth, ironware, hats, and leather goods. The effectiveness of the laws and orders against colonial manufacturing is a subject of dispute. It is difficult to prove why something did not happen. If the colonies were slow in developing manufacturing industries, was it the result of English policy or of other factors? The writer believes that English policies had a strong retarding influence. The barriers erected were extensive and formidable. British statutes restrained the American woolen, iron, and hat industries. The colonies could not impose protective tariffs on imports from England. They could not operate mints, create manufacturing corporations, or establish commercial banks—institutions that are essential to the progress of manufacturing.

It was easier to enforce a policy against American fabricating industries than a policy that aimed to regulate maritime trade. A vessel could slip in and out of the northern ports. A manufacturing plant and its operations could not be concealed, unless, as in later times, it was engaged in mountain moonshining. The exposure of factories to the gaze of officials undoubtedly deterred investors from building them in defiance of the law.

New industries in an economically backward country commonly needed the positive encouragement and protection of government. It was the rule of mercantilism that handicaps to home manufacturing should be overcome by tariffs, bounties, and other forms of state aid. Such stimuli were denied to the colonies while they were subject to English mercantilism. Not only was the imperial government hostile; equally important, the colonial governments were not allowed to extend assistance to American promoters who wished to establish industries on the basis of efficient, large-scale operations.

An important aspect of the influence of state policy is its effect on the attitude of the people who are subjected to its benefits and restraints. The colonists as a whole were not seriously antagonized by the British imperium prior to 1763. Its most detrimental policy—that of the Molasses Act—was not enforced. In time of war (which meant thirty-five years of the period from 1689 to 1763) the military expenditures of the Crown in America helped to solve the most crucial problem of the colonies by supplying them with funds with which they could pay their debts and buy needed supplies in England. The shipbuilders and shipowners of the northern area shared in the national monopoly of imperial trade. Underlying all policy and legislation was the extremely liberal action of the English Government in making land available to settlers on easy terms and of admitting into the colonies immigrants of diverse nationalities and varied religious faiths.

After 1763 the story is different. The colonies no longer received the sort of easy money that they had obtained from military expenditures during the wars. Instead, they were called upon to support through British taxes the defense establishment that was to be maintained in America after the war. Britain now abandoned its old liberal practice regarding land and immigration and replaced it with restrictive measures suggestive of the colonial policies of France and Spain. The Crown proceeded to enforce with vigor all the restraints it had previously imposed on colonial enterprise. Most of the features of the imperial rule that had placated the colonists were to be done away with. Not only were the old restraints to be more strictly enforced, they were to be accompanied by a host of new ones. The policies of Britain after 1763 merely intensified the central difficulty of the trade of the colonies. How might they find the means of paying for the manufactured goods that they must buy from England? If they could not get adequate returns, they would have to manufacture for themselves.

In its total effect, British policy as it affected the colonies after 1763 was restrictive, injurious, negative. It offered no solutions of problems. In the meantime, the colonists, having lived so long under the rule of mercantilism, had become imbued with mercantilist ideas. If the British imperium would not allow them to grow and expand, if it would not provide a solution of the central problem of the American economy, the colonists would have to take to themselves the right and the power to guide their economic development. They would find it necessary to create a new authority that would foster American shipping and commerce, make possible the continued growth of settlement, and above all stimulate the growth of domestic manufacturing industries. Thus another result of English mercantilism was the American Revolution and the creation thereafter of a new mercantilist state on this side of the Atlantic.

12 *Richard B. Morris*

BENJAMIN FRANKLIN'S GRAND DESIGN

Many were the causes of the American Revolution. One of the most important, certainly, was the inability of Anglo-American statesmen to solve the problems of a growing empire in terms which would be satisfactory both to the mother country and to the colonies. The new conditions of the mid-eighteenth century called for greater cooperation among the colonies and for a redistribution of authority between the center and the localities. Herein is to be found the great importance of the congress of colonial delegates at Albany in June, 1754, and of the grand design which Benjamin Franklin submitted to them for a colonial union and for a new federal relationship between the colonies and the mother country. Why had the congress met? What were the articles of Franklin's plan? Would Anglo-American statesmen accept a plan for resolving imperial problems? And if they would not, what might their refusal mean for the future course of the empire?

These are the questions to which Richard B. Morris, Gouverneur Morris Professor of History at Columbia University, addresses himself in the following essay. Professor Morris has written and edited many works dealing with early American history. He is also co-editor (with Henry Steele Commager) of The New American Nation Series. His essay on Franklin's plan of union raises challenging problems for investigation and interpretation in regard to the whole pattern of developments within the eighteenth-century British Empire. What factors were creating tensions within the Empire? If, as Professor Morris suggests, a central problem in government is to define the respective areas of authority and liberty, how had imperial authorities dealt with this problem before the Albany Congress and how did they deal with it afterwards? Could the adoption of Franklin's plan indeed have averted the American Revolution? To what extent was the failure to adopt the plan a failure of Anglo-American statesmen, to what extent was it a matter beyond their control or influence? By extending his consideration of these problems to other times and areas, the student may gain insight into the disruption not only of the great British Empire of the eighteenth century but also of empires which preceded it or have flourished since its day.

Reprinted with permission from *American Heritage, The Magazine of History,* VII (February, 1956), 5-7, 106-9.

In one of the world's great success stories Ben Franklin adverts to a resounding failure with which his name is associated. Quoting from
Dryden's rendition of a Juvenal *Satire*, he counsels us:

> Look round the habitable world: how few
> Know their own good, or, knowing it, pursue!

Franklin's brain child, the Albany Plan of Union, failed of adoption
because neither the colonists nor the mother country knew their own
good. "Such mistakes are not new," the scientist-statesman reflects in his
Autobiography. "History is full of the errors of states and princes." The
best measures of statesmanship, he shrewdly remarks, are seldom "adopted
from previous wisdom, but forced by the occasion."

One of the richest opportunities the study of history affords statesmen
is the chance to learn from past failures in shaping policy for present
realities. From the failure to ratify the Albany Plan of Union, for which
British and American statesmen must share the blame, a good deal was
salvaged, perhaps more by the Americans than the British. When it came
to applying the lessons learned at Albany to setting up their own federal
system, the Americans showed that the experience was by no means
wasted. On the other hand, the unwillingness of the British government
to set up a truly federal system at a decisive period cost Britain a large
slice of her old empire. Eventually Britain did apply the lessons of federalism learned at Albany, but by then America had been irretrievably lost
to her.

The Albany Plan of Union was a grand design of statesmanship, the
kind that is envisioned perhaps not more than once a century. It was
devised to deal specifically with the first of a series of crises in the relations between Great Britain and her North American colonies.

In the summer of 1754 the shadow of France's aggressive intentions
lay darkly over the British Empire in America. Already a young lieutenant colonel of the Virginia militia had met the enemy at the forks of the
Ohio, routed a French reconnaissance party, and, while the Albany Congress was still in session, had been obliged to surrender to a larger French
force. The following year that young officer was to secure tragic proof
of the inadequacy of Britain's military preparations and of the formidable
capacity of her enemy to wage war. The experience George Washington
gained on the Monongahela served his country well at a later day.

The French and Indian War, or the Seven Years' War as it was called
when it spread from America to Europe, to Africa, to India and to the
seven seas, was really a clash of two world empires. In the American
colonies England's military security rested in no small part upon her traditional alliance with the Iroquois, the Six Confederated Nations. But the
bonds between England and her Indian allies had been stretched to the

breaking point as the Iroquois observed with increasing alarm the rising military might of France.

The Iroquois saw the French using the interlude between Queen Anne's and King George's Wars to expand on the Mississippi and in the Illinois country. Their tension mounted when the French boldly established Fort Niagara on Lake Erie as a bastion against them. To the Six Nations the alliance with England seemed to have less and less military value. As the French became more aggressive the Six Nations moved toward neutrality.

The English erected Fort Oswego on Lake Ontario. They dispatched to the Six Nations their old friend William Johnson, Indian trader and honorary sachem of the Mohawks. But these measures fell short of guaranteeing continued Iroquois loyalty. Already some of the tribes had forged close French ties.

With a world war in the offing, glaring defects in the British colonial system were apparent equally to the Indians and the British government. No unified policy had been established. Each colony acted for itself. Regional and sectional differences made it virtually impossible to reach agreement with the Indians on a number of outstanding issues.

These imperial problems were uppermost in the mind of the Board of Trade when, in September, 1753, it instructed Sir Danvers Osborne, governor of New York, to summon an intercolonial conference to restore friendship with the Iroquois and to determine whether the colonies would "enter into articles of union and confederation with each other for the mutual defense of His Majesty's subjects and interests in North America, as well in time of peace as war." The order never reached Osborne. Suicide, brought on by private grief, ended his brief career in the province, and the letter was placed in the hands of Lieutenant Governor James De Lancey, who had assumed Osborne's duties.

At long last, on June 19, 1754, 24 delegates from seven of the fourteen continental colonies assembled in the old city hall of the compact Dutch fortress town of Albany. Under one roof were assembled a remarkable group of colonial statesmen, a group predisposed toward a liberal solution of political problems and not given to taking orders. While there was no official presiding officer, James De Lancey chaired the sessions he attended. De Lancey had long been feuding with the more liberal-minded Livingston faction, and had earned a reputation, not entirely deserved, of being the leader of the prerogative party in New York, the party which supported the Crown, the governor, and the other royal officials against the pretensions of the assembly.

Massachusetts sent a five-man delegation, including one of her most distinguished sons. He was Thomas Hutchinson, then a member of the provincial council, later chief justice and Tory lieutenant governor. Rhode Island dispatched Chief Justice Stephen Hopkins, whose election the very next year to the governorship marked a shift in power in that colony from the Newport to the Providence faction. Connecticut's Deputy Governor William Pitkin headed that delegation. He had already gained a reputation as a champion of colonial rights against the royal prerogative.

The strongest delegations came from New York and Pennsylvania. In addition to De Lancey, New York was represented by William Johnson, most deeply versed of all the delegates in Indian problems and most beloved by the Iroquois. Johnson advocated fraternization toward the red man and carried it out in his own private life. He was slated to become superintendent of Indian affairs and was to compile a formidable military record in the French and Indian War, a record which won him a knighthood. Two other prerogative men were in the New York delegation. They were the lawyers Joseph Murray and John Chambers. Another delegate was William Smith, a member of the governor's council and a leader of the liberal or anti-prerogative party.

Pennsylvania sent a formidable delegation, including John Penn, grandson of William Penn, a member of the proprietary family and later to become lieutenant governor. Accompanying him were Richard Peters, secretary of the province, Isaac Norris, speaker of the assembly, and Benjamin Franklin, then postmaster general of the colonies and a member of the legislature.

Franklin had already established his reputation. Then in his forty-ninth year, Franklin at Albany was to demonstrate his right to rank with the most constructive political thinkers of his century.

A crisis brought these minds together. A later crisis would divide them. Some, like Thomas Hutchinson and John Penn, became loyalists; others, like Hopkins and Franklin, led the rebellion against the Crown. But in the year 1754 they all considered it to be feasible for the colonies to work in cooperation with the British government. Some even went so far as to regard the interests of the empire as paramount to those of their own sections and provinces. That time never came again.

The primary business of the Albany Congress was the making of a firm treaty with the Iroquois. In all, 150 Indian chiefs attended. They spared no pains to point out to the English their defenseless condition. Most eloquent perhaps was Chief Hendricks of the Mohawks. "Look at the French," he declared. "They are men. They are fortifying everywhere. But—we are ashamed to say it—you are like women." Taking a stick and throwing it behind his back, he asserted: "You have thus thrown us behind your back and disregarded us."

Soothing words, vague promises and bribes headed off what had threatened to be an explosive situation. On behalf of all the delegates De Lancey gave a chain belt to the Indians, signifying that the colonies were acting jointly with the entire body of the Six Nations. Then New York, Pennsylvania and Connecticut each held separate sessions with the Indians. When the Iroquois chiefs left the conference they were in a far happier frame of mind than when they came. Thirty wagonloads of presents, including guns, may well have contributed to their more cheerful mood on departure. The English had good reason to feel that the old Indian alliance had been re-established on a firm basis.

While these talks with the Indians were in progress, the delegates debated the question "whether a Union of all the Colonies is not at present absolutely necessary for their security and defence." They unanimously agreed that such a union was imperative, and a committee consisting of one member appointed by each delegation was set up at once to prepare and receive plans of union.

Now the idea of a union of the colonies was by no means novel. As far back as 1643 a notable step in that direction had been taken when the New England Confederation was formed. In that federation delegates from all the New England colonies except Rhode Island were empowered to decide on war and peace, to enact laws for the protection of the colonies, and to levy as well as collect taxes. The New England Confederation functioned down to the revocation of the Massachusetts charter in 1684. It had performed its greatest service in directing colonial military operations in King Philip's Indian war.

During the early intercolonial wars various plans for troop quotas were proposed. That original imperial thinker, the humanitarian William Penn, in 1697 had advocated an intercolonial assembly under a royal commissioner, but with an extremely limited jurisdiction.

Proposals for union kept cropping up. In 1751 Archibald Kennedy, a defense-conscious official who was receiver-general (tax collector) of New York and a member of the governor's council, proposed an intercolonial confederacy to hearten the Indians and curb the French. Meeting annually, the commissioners were to have power to supervise military affairs. Perhaps most significant, in the light of the later Albany Plan, was Kennedy's suggestion that the confederacy be established by act of Parliament.

Kennedy sent his ideas on to Benjamin Franklin, who seized upon them with enthusiasm. It would be a very strange thing, he wrote the New Yorker, if Six Nations of ignorant savages should be capable of forming a union that had subsisted for ages, and yet a like union should be impracticable for ten or a dozen English colonies to whom it was necessary. Going further than Kennedy, Franklin at this time proposed an intercolonial government, to be set up by voluntary action on the part of the colonies.

En route to Albany in 1754 Franklin stopped off in New York City to discuss with his friend Kennedy and with James Alexander, a noted colonial attorney and long a leader of the anti-prerogative forces, the refurbished plan of union which he had first evolved, at Kennedy's prompting, three years earlier. As Alexander wrote Cadwallader Colden, their talk had turned on the difficulty of forming a union without "affecting our liberties on the one hand, or being ineffectual on the other." Thus, in the late spring of 1754, these three colonial thinkers came to grips with the crucial problem raised by any design of government—that of liberty versus authority.

In addition to seeking the support of influential persons, Franklin recognized the necessity of rallying public opinion behind the plan. Before leaving Philadelphia he had prepared for his newspaper, the *Pennsylvania Gazette*, an article pointing out the need for union and stressing the fact that "our enemies have the great advantage of being under one direction, with one council, and one purse." Datelined Philadelphia, May 9, his article was illustrated by one of the very earliest cartoons in American journalistic history, a woodcut of a snake separated into parts, representing the colonies, with the motto beneath it: "JOIN OR DIE"— a device that was employed again at the start of the American Revolution.

Franklin's plan was so much bolder in conception than various other plans which were advanced, and so much better conceived for the purposes at hand, that it caught on at once. In fact, the "Plan of Union" as it was finally adopted at the Albany Congress was essentially based upon the "Short Hints Towards a Scheme for Uniting the Northern Colonies," which Franklin had prepared in advance of the congress and talked over with Kennedy and Alexander.

But there was one significant difference between Franklin's first proposal of 1751 and the later one embraced in the "Short Hints." The new plan was to be imposed by parliamentary authority. A thorough realist, Franklin by now saw no hope of achieving union through voluntary action on the part of the colonies. Perhaps no move better typifies the temper of the Albany Congress than the vote of that assembly on this particular proposal. Every delegate except three from Connecticut and two from Pennsylvania voted in favor of having Parliament legislate a federal union into existence. Twenty years later a number of these very same men, chief of them Franklin himself, were to deny Parliament's authority either to tax or to legislate for the colonies.

In conference Franklin's "Short Hints" underwent some minor revisions. His original plan provided for a governor-general, appointed and paid by the Crown, who was to have a veto over all acts of the grand council, in addition to executive powers. Except for changing the name from governor-general to president-general and adding to his authority the power to make Indian treaties and to declare war and peace with the advice and consent of the grand council, the executive in the final plan remained substantially as Franklin had proposed it. The legislature was to consist of a grand council to be chosen triennially by the assemblies of the colonies in numbers proportionate to the taxes paid into the general treasury.

Although the proportions of the first grand council were fixed in the final plan, provision was made that in later elections representation was to be based upon taxation rather than population. However, the fact that Franklin had conferred the power of election upon the assemblies rather than the more aristocratic and prerogative-minded governors' councils constituted a notable democratic innovation. Franklin's plan set up a general treasury for the united colonies. So did the final plan, which also provided for a union treasurer in each colony.

One of the most important areas reserved for the proposed continental government was the West. The Albany Plan would have given the federal government the power to deal with the problems of defense, to raise arms, build forts, equip vessels of war, regulate the Indians, and administer territorial expansion. The final plan authorized the president-general and council to make laws for regulating the new settlements until they were formed into particular governments.

That these proposals were meant to curb the power of the original colonies over the western lands is perfectly clear from a representation to the King in Council, drawn up by Thomas Hutchinson and adopted at the congress. This imperialistic document urged that "the bounds of these Colonies which extend to the South Sea, be contracted and limited by the Alleghenny or Apalachian mountains." The Albany Plan, combined with the representation of that congress, would in effect have written off the trans-Appalachian claims of colonies like Virginia, and in fact was embodied in the Royal Proclamation of 1763.

Perhaps equally significant is the authority which the plan conferred upon the continental government to levy taxes. Finally, the continental government was empowered to make laws concerning matters within its jurisdiction, but such laws were to be submitted to the King in Council for approval or disallowance. If not disallowed within three years after submission, they were to remain in force.

At the Albany Congress the only real opposition to the Plan of Union seems to have been offered by the Connecticut delegates. They made various objections. They felt that the territory was too large to administer and that it would be dangerous to unite under one head a population so rapidly growing. They objected to the president-general's veto and found that the power of levying taxes was "a very extraordinary thing" and ran counter to the rights of Englishmen. Some slight opposition was also made by De Lancey, who would have preferred to lodge with the colonial governors a veto on the election of representatives to the grand council.

But both Franklin and Pownall assert that the plan was unanimously adopted at the conference, and Thomas Hutchinson on his return to Massachusetts so informed the press. Hence, the Connecticut delegates must have abstained from casting a negative vote.

In America public opinion was never sufficiently aroused to put the plan across. The Connecticut assembly went on record opposing its adoption. New Jersey, which did not attend the congress, held that the plan adversely affected its constitution. The Pennsylvania assembly, despite Franklin's own prestige, voted it down without discussion. The Massachusetts assembly debated the plan at length and then defeated it. In short, with the exception of New York, whose legislature went on record favoring the proposal, every assembly which considered the plan turned it down.

In England the Albany Plan received as frigid a reception as in America. The Board of Trade submitted the plan to George II without comment, but the Privy Council took no action. Lord Halifax, head of the Board of Trade, urged instead a thoroughly undemocratic scheme of union, with a permanent revenue as its paramount objective. Other plans, like Cadwallader Colden's hereditary council of landholders in America in imitation of the House of Lords, contemplated sweeping revisions in the colonial charters, even the setting up of three regional unions. Such plans would not have enlarged colonial self-government, but delimited it.

Many years later Franklin pithily summed up the rejection of his plan on both sides of the water.

"The crown disapproved it," he pointed out, "as having too much weight in the democratic part of the constitution, and every assembly as having allowed too much to prerogative; so it was totally rejected." In short, the thinking of the men who met at Albany in 1754 was too bold for that day. In evolving the Plan of Union Franklin had shown himself to be an imperial-minded thinker who placed the empire above individual states' rights.

During the discussion over the ratification of the Albany Plan Franklin's own pen was not idle. Governor Shirley of Massachusetts proposed a drastic revision of the Albany Plan. He would have permitted Parliament to tax the colonies directly and have excluded the colonists from all share in the choice of the grand councilors.

In a stinging rebuttal Franklin pointed out that "compelling the colonies to pay money without their consent would be rather like raising contributions in an enemy's country than taxing of Englishmen for their own public benefit. It would be treating them as conquered people, and not as true British subjects."

These words of Franklin penned in 1754 forecast the constitutional arguments of the American colonists when, in 1765, Parliament for the first time instituted direct taxation of the colonies. The Stamp Act, which provoked the calling of another congress in New York—this one without permission of the Crown—touched off the great controversy which was fated to end in war. Had it been put in operation the Albany Plan would very likely have obviated the necessity for Parliament to levy taxes for the military defense and administration of the colonies.

Perhaps the British government recognized its mistake in failing to adopt the plan, but not until long after the Revolution had broken out and military currents were running adverse to the mother country. Following Burgoyne's defeat at Saratoga the British government instructed the Carlisle Peace Commission to concede to the colonies, if necessary, "Congress as a permanent institution so long as it did not infringe the sovereignty of Parliament." But America was by then irrevocably committed to independence and the offer was flatly rejected. In fact, the federal principle embodied in the Albany Plan would not be accepted by Great Britain for another half century, and then it was still another colonial revolt, this time in Canada, which converted the government to federalism.

For Americans the failure of statesmanship in 1754 was a lesson that was not soon forgotten. The Albany Plan constituted the basic core of that federal system that came into effect with the First Continental Congress. Even the notion that such a plan might keep the colonies in the empire was not lightly abandoned. At the First Congress the conservative Pennsylvanian and later loyalist, Joseph Galloway, proposed a watered-down version of the Albany Plan of Union, virtually identical with Franklin's plan except in one respect. He proposed that *both* Parliament and the intercolonial council should be empowered to legislate for the colonies, each to have a negative on the other. Again, it is significant of the temper of the year 1774 that this proposal was narrowly defeated by a vote of six states to five.

Despite the defeat of Galloway's proposal the old Albany Plan was not allowed to die. In June, 1775, as a delegate to the Second Continental Congress, Franklin proposed a plan of confederation substantially based on the Albany Plan. This plan substituted for the strong provision granting the powers of taxation to the grand council a proposal to allow Congress the right to make requisitions. But the new plan pointed toward national sovereignty in the large powers it conferred on Congress in other respects, powers extending to all matters "necessary to the general welfare." The proposal was shelved. After independence was declared the government was administered by congressional committees, and their meddlesome incompetence severely taxed the patience of the commander in chief.

As finally adopted, the Articles of Confederation incorporated a number of the ideas of the Albany Plan, including the control of the West by the federal government. Nevertheless, it continued the voting equality of the states which had been established by the First Congress. Again Franklin tried to introduce the idea of representation in proportion to population, but again he lost. The Articles set up a union of limited powers between equal sovereign states. By failing to go as far as the Albany Plan in limiting state sovereignty, the Articles of Confederation fell far short of what the delegates at Albany had proposed 24 years earlier.

But at least in one respect, the Congress of the Confederation did achieve one of the principal objectives of the Albany Plan—federal control of the western territories. The Northwest Territory Ordinance of 1787, in which Congress set up a government for the territories and laid down principles for the admission of new states, was a triumph for the federal dreamers at Albany.

Ultimate recognition of the practicality of the Albany Plan was attained at the Constitutional Convention. If you substitute a president for a president-general and add a second house you will find that in substance the Albany Plan was embodied in the federal Constitution.

Consider some of the basic concepts of the Albany Plan. The members of the council were to have been elected by the legislatures of the various colonies in the same manner in which United States senators were provided for in the Constitution. The colonies were represented as colonies, as in the Senate, yet a proportionate and varying representation was adopted, as we find in the House of Representatives. True, the system of proportionate representation which was finally adopted was based more appropriately on the democratic principle of population. Each of the powers granted the council were specifically given to Congress by the Constitution, except the power to purchase Indian lands and make new colonies of the land so acquired. Had these powers been spelled out in the Constitution, Jefferson might have been spared some anxious moments at the time of the Louisiana Purchase.

Writing in 1789, when the new federal government had become effective, Franklin indulged some speculations about the significance of the great failure of 1754. In a magazine article in which he analyzed his old Plan of Union, he made these observations:

> On reflection, it now seems probable, that, if the foregoing plan, or something like it, had been adopted and carried into execution, the subsequent sepa-

ration of the colonies from the mother country might not so soon have happened, nor the mischiefs suffered on both sides have occurred, perhaps during another century. For the colonies, if so united, would have really been, as they then thought themselves, sufficient to their own defense; and, being trusted with it, as by the plan, an army from Britain, for that purpose, would have been unnecessary. The pretences for framing the Stamp Act would then not have existed, nor the other projects for drawing a revenue from America to Britain by acts of parliament, which were the cause of the breach, and attended with such terrible expense of blood and treasure; so that the different parts of the empire might still have remained in peace and union.

Of all the failures of British-American statesmanship, this first major failure may well have had the most momentous consequences for the world.

13 *Lawrence Henry Gipson*

THE AMERICAN REVOLUTION AS AN AFTERMATH OF THE GREAT WAR FOR THE EMPIRE, 1754-1765

When did the American Revolution begin? To set a date is at once to explain its nature and suggest its causes. It is clear enough that hostilities between the mother country and her mainland colonies became overt and very sharp after the Treaty of Paris in 1763. But what did this state of affairs signify? Were these hostilities the outcropping of tensions that had been long in growth and that were deeply imbedded in British colonial policy? Or were they more immediately the product of the peace concluded by Britain and France and of the war that had preceded it? Just what had been the nature of that war? Each of these questions relates closely to the larger one of what the Revolution was all about.

The answer given by Professor Lawrence Henry Gipson of Lehigh University is certainly one of the most impressive of our age. Professor Gipson's nine volumes on *The British Empire before the American Revolution* (1936-56) establish him as the scholar par excellence of the late colonial period. While his subject is broad and his interests manifold, he is concerned in particular with explaining the changing conditions within the great British Empire of the mid-century and the ways in which these led to the first successful colonial revolution of modern times. The explanation is indeed absorbing, deriving as it does from Professor Gipson's considered opinion that, for the larger part, imperial conditions had been favorable to the colonies.

Reprinted with the permission of the author and publisher from *The Political Science Quarterly*, LXV (March, 1950), 86-104.

In the following essay, Professor Gipson presents some of the challenging conclusions to which his long researches have led him. He shows that the French and Indian War was in fact part of a great imperial war. He explores at close range the origins of the war and, in particular, the desire of the British to secure and protect their North American colonies. He indicates how problems born in war grew immensely in peace. And he stresses above all that the terms of peace played no small part in precipitating a revolt that might otherwise not have come.

Professor Gipson belongs to a school of historians that has argued for a thorough hearing of the British cause in the American Revolution and that has found the cause to have had considerable merit. In raising doubts, moreover, about the cause of the revolutionaries, these historians have put a different light upon the nature and meaning of the Revolution. Belonging ourselves to the conservative order of the modern age, when the colonial system throughout the world is in revolt and new nations are emerging rapidly and in abundance, we would do well to ponder the suggestions of Professor Gipson concerning that earlier age when we revolted against our own colonial status and struck out for national independence.

Great wars in modern times have too frequently been the breeders of revolution. The exhausting armed struggles in which France became engaged in the latter half of the eighteenth century led as directly to the French Revolution as did the First World War to the Russian Revolution; it may be said as truly that the American Revolution was an aftermath of the Anglo-French conflict in the New World carried on between 1754 and 1763. This is by no means to deny that other factors were involved in the launching of these revolutionary movements. Before proceeding with an analysis of the theme of this paper, however, it would be well to consider the wording of the title given to it.

Words may be used either to disguise or to distort facts as well as to clarify them, but the chief task of the historian is to illuminate the past. He is faced, therefore, with the responsibility of using only such words as will achieve this broad objective of his calling and to reject those that obscure or defeat it. For this reason "the French and Indian War," as a term descriptive of the conflict to which we have just referred, has been avoided in this essay as well as in the writer's series on the *British Empire before the American Revolution.* This has been done in spite of the fact that it has been employed by most Americans ever since the early days of our Republic and therefore has the sanction of long usage as well as the sanction of American national tradition assigning, as does the latter, to the Revolutionary War a position of such commanding importance as to make all other events in American history, preceding as well as following it, quite subordinate to it. In contrast to this traditional interpretation of our history one may affirm that the Anglo-French conflict settled nothing less than the incomparably vital question as to what civilization—what complex cultural patterns, what political institutions—would arise in the great Mississippi basin and the valleys of the rivers draining it, a civilization, whatever it might be, surely destined to expand to the Pacific seaboard and finally to dominate the North American continent. The determination of this crucial issue is perhaps the most momentous event in the life of the English-speaking people in the New World and quite overshadows in importance both the Revolutionary War and the later Civil War, events which, it is quite clear, were each contingent upon the outcome of the earlier crisis.

A struggle of such proportions, involving tremendous stakes, deserves a name accurately descriptive of its place in the history of the English-speaking people, and the title "the French and Indian War," as suggested, in no way fulfills this need. For the war was not, as the name would seem to imply, a conflict largely between English and French New World colonials and their Indian allies, nor was it localized in North America to the extent that the name would appear to indicate. In contrast, it was waged both before and after an open declaration of war by the British and French nations with all their resources for nine years on three oceans, and much of the land washed by the waters of them, and it ultimately brought in both Spain, allied to France, and Portugal, allied to Great Britain. While it involved, it is true, as the name would connote, wilderness fighting, yet of equal, if not of greater, importance in assessing its final outcome was the pouring forth of Britain's financial resources in a vast program of shipbuilding, in the equipment and support of the British and colonial armies and the royal navy, and in the subsidization both of allies on the European continent and of the colonies in America. If it also involved the reduction of the fortress of Louisbourg, Fort Niagara, Fort Duquesne, Quebec and Montreal in North America, each in turn to fall to British regulars aided by American provincial troops, these successes, of great significance, were, in fact, really contingent upon the resounding British naval victories in the Mediterranean, off the Strait of Gibraltar, in the Bay of Biscay, and elsewhere, that brought about the virtual extinction of the French navy and merchant marine and thereby presented to France— seeking to supply her forces in Canada and elsewhere with adequate reinforcements and matériel—a logistical problem so insoluble as to spell the doom of her North American empire and of her possessions in India and elsewhere.

If the term "the French and Indian War" meets none of the requirements of accurate historical nomenclature, neither does the term "the Seven Years' War"—a name appropriately enough employed by historians to designate the mighty conflict that raged for seven years in Germany before its conclusion in the Treaty of Hubertusburg in 1763. The principals in this war were Prussia, allied with Great Britain, Hanover, Brunswick and Hesse, facing Austria, most of the Holy Roman Empire, Russia and Sweden, all allied with France and receiving subsidies from her. Although George II, as King of Great Britain and Elector of Hanover, in the treaty of 1758 with Frederick of Prussia, promised not to conclude peace without mutual agreement with the latter, and although large subsidies were annually paid to Prussia as well as to the other continental allies out of the British treasury and troops were also sent to Germany, it must be emphasized that these aids were designed primarily for the protection of the King's German Electorate. In other words, the British alliance in no way supported the objectives of the Prussian King, when he suddenly began the German war in 1756 by invading Saxony—two years after the beginning of the Anglo-French war. In this connection it should be borne in mind that throughout the Seven Years' War in Germany Great Britain remained at peace with both Russia and Sweden and refused therefore to send a fleet into the Baltic in spite of the demands of Frederick that this be done; nor were British land troops permitted to assist him against Austria, but only to help form a protective shield for Hanover against the thrusts of the French armies. For the latter were determined not only to overrun the Electorate—something that they succeeded in doing—but to hold it as a bargaining point to be used at the conclusion of hostilities with Great Britain, a feat, however, beyond their power of accomplishment. Closely related and intertwined as were the two wars, they were, nevertheless, distinct in their beginning and distinct in their termination.

Indeed, while British historians at length were led to adopt the nomenclature applied by German and other continental historians to all hostilities that took place between 1754 and 1763 in both the Old and New Worlds, American historians, by and large in the past, have rejected, and rightly so, it seems, the name "the Seven Years' War" to designate specifically the struggle during these years in North America with the fate of that continent at stake; so likewise many of them have rejected, as equally inadmissible, the name "the French and Indian War." Instead, the late Professor Osgood employed the title "the Fourth Intercolonial War," surely not a good one; George Bancroft called the war "the American Revolution: First Phase," still more inaccurate in some respects than the names he sought to avoid; Francis Parkman, with the flare of a romanticist, was at first inclined to call it "the Old French War" but finally, under the influence of the great-man-in-history thesis, gave to his two remarkable volumes concerned with it the totally misleading name, *Montcalm and Wolfe;* finally, John Fiske, the philosopher-historian, as luminous in his views as he was apt to be careless in the details of historical scholarship, happily fastened upon the name "the Great War." In the series on the *British Empire before the American Revolution* the writer has built upon Fiske's title and has called it "the Great War for the Empire" in order to emphasize not only the fact that the war was a very great conflict both in its scope and in its lasting effects, as Fiske saw it with clearness, but also, as a war entered into specifically for the defense of the British Empire, that it was by far the most important ever waged by Great Britain to this end.

It may be pointed out that later charges, especially by American writers, that the war was begun by Great Britain with less worthy motives in mind, are not supported by the great mass of state papers and the private correspondence of British statesmen responsible for making the weighty decisions at the time—materials now available to the student which the writer has attempted to analyze in detail in the two volumes of his series that appeared under the title of *Zones of International Friction, 1748–1754.* In other words, the idea that the war was started as the result of European balance-of-power politics or by British mercantilists for the purpose of destroying a commercial rival and for conquering Canada and the French West Indies, and for expelling the French from India, rather than for the much more limited and legitimate objective of affording the colonies and particularly the new province of Nova Scotia and the Old Dominion of Virginia protection against the aggressive aims of France, must be dismissed by students brought face to face with impressive evidence to the contrary.

The development of the war into one for the military mastery of the North American continent came with the growing conviction on the part of the British ministers that nothing short of this drastic step would realize the primary aims of the government in arriving at the determination, as the result of appeals from the colonies for assistance, to challenge the right of French troops to be planted well within the borders of the Nova Scotia peninsula and at the forks of the Ohio. One may go as far as to state that the acquisition of Canada—as an objective sought by mercantilists to contribute to the wealth of Great Britain—would have seemed fantastic to any contemporary who had the slightest knowledge of the tremendous financial drain that that great possession had been on the treasury of the French King for over a century before 1754. Moreover, the motives that ultimately led, after much searching of heart, to its retention after its conquest by Great Britain were not commercial but strategic and had primarily in view the security and welfare generally of the older American colonies.

In view of these facts, not to be confused with surmises, the name "the Great War for the Empire" seems to the writer not only not inappropriate but among all the names heretofore applied to the war in question by far the most suitable that can be used by one concerned with the history of the old British Empire, who seeks earnestly to maintain that standard of exactness in terminology, as well as in other respects, which the public has a right to demand of him.

The description just given of the motives that led to the Great War for the Empire, nevertheless, runs counter, as suggested, to American national tradition and most history that has been written by American historians in harmony with it. This tradition had a curious beginning. It arose partly out of Pitt's zealous efforts to energize the colonies to prosecute the war most actively; but there also was another potent factor involved in its creation. Before the conclusion of hostilities in 1763 certain powerful commercial interests—centered particularly at Newport, Rhode Island, Boston, New York City, and to a less extent in Philadelphia—in a desire to continue an enormously lucrative trade with the French West Indies, and therefore with the enemy, all in the face of Pitt's determination to keep supplies from the French armed forces operating in the New World, began to express themselves in terms that implied that the war was peculiarly Great Britain's war and only incidentally one that concerned her colonies and that the French, really friendly to the aspirations of British colonials, were opposed only to the mercantilistic ambitions of the mother country. By 1766—just twelve years after the beginning of the war and three years after its termination—this extraordinary tradition had become so well established that Benjamin Franklin, astonishingly enough, could actually assert in his examination before a committee of the House of Commons:

> I know the last war is commonly spoke of here as entered into for the defence, or for the sake of the people of America; I think it is quite misunderstood. It began about the limits between Canada and Nova Scotia, about territories to which the crown indeed laid claim, but were not claimed by any British colony. . . . We had therefore no particular concern or interest in that dispute. As to the Ohio, the contest there began about your right of trading in the Indian country, a right you had by the Treaty of Utrecht, which the French infringed . . . they took a fort which a company of your merchants, and their factors and correspondents, had erected there to secure that trade. Braddock was sent with an army to retake that fort . . . and to protect your trade. It was not until after his defeat that the colonies were attacked. They were before in perfect peace with both French and Indians. . . .

By the beginning of 1768 the tradition had been so extended that John Dickinson—voicing the popular American view in his highly important *Letters from a Farmer in Pennsylvania*, No. VIII—felt that he not only could affirm, as did Franklin, that the war was strictly Britain's war and fought for selfish purposes, but could even insist that the acquisition of territory in North America as the result of it "is greatly injurious to these colonies" and that they therefore were not under the slightest obligation to the mother country.

But to return to the last phases of the Great War for the Empire. The British customs officials—spurred into unusual activity in the face of Pitt's demand for the strict enforcement of the Trade and Navigation Acts in order to break up the pernicious practice of bringing aid and comfort to the enemy—were led to employ writs of assistance for the purpose of laying their hands upon goods landed in American ports and secured in exchange for American provisions sent for the most part either directly or indirectly to the French West Indies. Although in the midst of hostilities, most of the merchants in Boston showed bitter opposition to the writs and equally ardent support of James Otis' declaration made in open court in 1761 that Parliament, acting within the limits of the constitution, was powerless to extend the use of these writs to America, whatever its authority might be in Great Britain. The importance of this declaration lies not so much in its immediate effect but rather in the fact that it was indicative of the line of attack that not only Otis would subsequently follow but also the Adamses, Hawley, Hancock, and other popular leaders in the Bay colony during the developing crisis, in the laying down of constitutional restrictions upon the power of Parliament to legislate for America. Further, it is clear that, even before the Great War for the Empire had been terminated, there were those in the province who had begun to view Great Britain as the real enemy rather than France.

Just as definitely as was the issue over writs of assistance related to the war under consideration was that growing out of the twopenny acts of the Virginia Assembly. In search of funds for maintaining the frontier defensive forces under the command of Colonel George Washington, the Assembly was led to pass in 1755 and 1758 those highly questionable laws as favorable to the tobacco planters as they were indefensibly unjust to the clergy. Even assuming the fact that these laws were war measures, and therefore in a sense emergency measures, it was inconceivable that the Privy Council would permit so palpable a violation of contractual relations as they involved. The royal disallowance of the laws in question opened the way for Patrick Henry, the year that hostilities were terminated by the Peace of Paris, not only to challenge in the Louisa County courthouse the right of the King in Council to refuse to approve any law that a colony might pass that in its judgment was a good law, but to affirm that such refusal was nothing less than an act of tyranny on the part of the King. It was thus resentment at the overturning of Virginia war legislation that led to this attack upon the judicial authority of review by the Crown—an authority exercised previously without serious protest for over a century. It should also be noted that the Henry thesis helped to lay the foundation for the theory of the equality of colonial laws with those passed by Parliament, a theory of the constitution of the empire that most American leaders in 1774 had come to accept in arguing that if the King could no longer exercise a veto over the acts of the legislature of Great Britain, it was unjust that he should do so over those of the colonial assemblies.

But the most fateful aftermath of the Great War for the Empire, with respect to the maintenance of the historic connection between the mother country and the colonies, grew out of the problem of the control and support not only of the vast trans-Appalachian interior, the right to which was now confirmed by treaty to Great Britain, but of the new acquisitions in North America secured from France and Spain. Under the terms of the royal Proclamation of 1763, French Canada to the east of the Great Lakes was organized as the Province of Quebec; most of old Spanish Florida became the Province of East Florida; and those areas, previously held by Spain as well as by France to the west of the Apalachicola and to the east of New Orleans and its immediate environs, became the Province of West Florida. The Proclamation indicated that proper inducements would be offered British and other Protestants to establish themselves in these new provinces. With respect to the trans-Appalachian region, however, it created there a temporary but vast Indian reserve by laying down as a barrier the crest of the mountains beyond which there should be no white settlement except by specific permission of the Crown.

The Proclamation has been represented not only as a blunder, the result largely of carelessness and ignorance on the part of those responsible for it, but also as a cynical attempt by the British ministry to embody mercantilistic principles in an American land policy that in itself ran counter to the charter limits of many of the colonies and the interests in general of the colonials. Nevertheless, this view of the Proclamation fails to take into account the fact that it was the offspring of the war and that the trans-Appalachian aspects of it were an almost inevitable result of promises made during the progress of hostilities. For both in the Treaty of Easton in 1758 with the Ohio Valley Indians, a treaty ratified by the Crown, and in the asseverations of such military leaders as Colonel Bouquet, these Indians were assured that they would be secure in their trans-Appalachian lands as a reward for deserting their allies, the French. As a sign of good faith, the lands lying within the bounds of Pennsylvania to the west of the mountains, purchased by the Proprietors from the Six Nations in 1754, were solemnly released. Thus committed in honor in the course of the war, what could the Cabinet Council at its termination do other than it finally did in the Proclamation of 1763? But this step not only was in opposition to the interests of such groups of land speculators as, for example, the Patrick Henry group in Virginia and the Richard Henderson group in North Carolina, both of whom boldly ignored the Proclamation in negotiating with the Cherokee Indians for land grants, but also led to open defiance of this imperial regulation by frontiersmen who, moving beyond the mountains by the thousands, proceeded to settle within the Indian reserve—some on lands previously occupied before the beginning of the late war or before the great Indian revolt in 1763, and others on new lands.

The Proclamation line of 1763 might have become an issue, indeed a most formidable one, between the government of Great Britain and the colonials, had not the former acquiesced in the inevitable and confirmed certain Indian treaties that provided for the transfer of much of the land which had been the particular object of quest on the part of speculators and of those moving westward from the settled areas to establish new homes. Such were the treaties of Hard Labor, Fort Stanwix, Lochaber, and the modification of the last-named by the Donelson agreement with the Cherokees in 1771. Nor did the regulation of the trans-Appalachian Indian trade create serious colonial irritation, especially in view of the failure of the government to implement the elaborate Board of Trade plan drawn up in 1764. The same, however, cannot be said of the program put forward by the ministry and accepted by Parliament for securing the means to maintain order and provide protection for this vast area and the new acquisitions to the north and south of it.

Theoretically, it would have been possible for the government of Great Britain to have dropped onto the lap of the old continental colonies the entire responsibility for maintaining garrisons at various strategic points in North America—in Canada, about the Great Lakes, in the Ohio and Mississippi valleys, and in East and West Florida. In spite, however, of assertions made by some prominent colonials, such as Franklin, in 1765 and 1766, that the colonies would be able and were willing to take up the burden of providing for the defense of America, this, under the circumstances, was utterly chimerical, involving, as it would have, not only a vast expenditure of funds but highly complicated inter-colonial arrangements, even in the face of the most serious inter-colonial rivalry such as that between Pennsylvania and Virginia respecting the control of the upper Ohio Valley. The very proportions of the task were an insuperable obstacle to leaving it to the colonies; and the colonies, moreover, would have been faced by another impediment almost as difficult to surmount—the utter aversion of Americans of the eighteenth century, by and large, to the dull routine of garrison duty. This was emphasized by the Massachusetts Bay Assembly in 1755 in its appeal to the government of Great Britain after Braddock's defeat to send regulars to man the frontier forts of that province; the dispatches of Colonel George Washington in 1756 and in 1757 respecting the shameful desertion of militiamen, ordered to hold the chain of posts on the western frontier of Virginia in order to check the frightful French and Indian raids, support this position, as does the testimony in 1757 of Governor Lyttelton of South Carolina, who made clear that the inhabitants of that colony were not at all adapted to this type of work. The post-war task of garrison duty was clearly one to be assumed by regulars held to their duty under firm discipline and capable of being shifted from one strategic point to another as circumstances might require. Further, to be effective, any plan for the defense of the new possessions and the trans-Appalachian region demanded unity of command, something the colonies could not provide. Manifestly this could be done only through the instrumentalities of the mother country.

The British ministry, thus confronted with the problem of guaranteeing the necessary security for the extended empire in North America, which it was estimated would involve the annual expenditure of from three to four hundred thousand pounds for the maintenance of ten thousand troops—according to various estimates made by General Amherst and others in 1764 and to be found among the Shelburne Papers—was impelled to raise the question: Should not the colonials be expected to assume some definite part of the cost of this? In view of the fact that it was felt not only that they were in a position to do so but that the stability of these outlying possessions was a matter of greater concern and importance generally to them, by reason of their proximity, than to the people of the mother country three thousand miles away, the answer was in the affirmative. The reason for this is not hard to fathom. The nine years of war had involved Britons in tremendous expenditures. In spite of very heavy taxation during these years, the people were left saddled at the termination of hostilities with a national debt of unprecedented proportions for that day and age of over one hundred and forty million pounds. It was necessary not only to service and to retire this debt, in so far as was possible, but also to meet the ordinary demands of the civil government and to maintain the navy at a point of strength that would offer some assurance that France and Spain would have no desire in the future to plan a war to recover their territorial losses. In addition to all this, there was now the problem of meeting the charges necessary for keeping the new possessions in North America under firm military control for their internal good order and for protection from outside interference.

It may be noted that before the war the British budget had called for average annual expenditures of six and a half million pounds; between the years 1756 and 1766 these expenditures mounted to fourteen and a half million pounds a year on the average and from the latter date to 1775 ranged close to ten million pounds. As a result, the annual per capita tax in Great Britain, from 1763 to 1775, without considering local rates, was many times the average annual per capita tax in even those American colonies that made the greatest contribution to the Great War for the Empire, such as Massachusetts Bay and Connecticut—without reference to those colonies that had done little or nothing in this conflict, and therefore had accumulated little in the way of a war debt, such as Maryland and Georgia. The student of the history of the old British Empire, in fact, should accept with great reserve statements to the contrary—some of them quite irresponsible in nature—made by Americans during the heat of the controversy, with respect to the nature of the public burdens they were obliged to carry in the years preceding the outbreak of the Revolutionary War. In this connection a study of parliamentary reimbursement of colonial war expenses from 1756 to 1763 in its relation to public debts in America between the years 1763 and 1775 is most revealing. As to American public finance, all that space will here permit is to state that there is abundant evidence to indicate that, during the five-year period preceding the outbreak of the Revolutionary War, had the inhabitants of any of the thirteen colonies, which therefore included those of Massachusetts Bay and Virginia, been taxed in one of these years at the average high per capita rate that the British people were taxed from 1760 to 1775, the proceeds of that one year's tax not only would have taken care of the ordinary expenditures of the colony in question for that year but also would have quite liquidated its war debt, so little of which remained in any of the colonies by 1770. Well may John Adams have admitted in 1780 what was equally true in 1770: "America is not used to great taxes, and the people there are not yet disciplined to such enormous taxation as in England."

Assuming, as did the Grenville ministry in 1764, the justice of expecting the Americans to share in the cost of policing the new possessions in North America, the simplest and most obvious way, it might appear, to secure this contribution to a common end so important to both Americans and Britons was to request the colonial governments to make definite grants of funds. This was the requisition or quota system that had been employed in the course of the recent war. But the most obvious objections to it were voiced that same year by Benjamin Franklin, who, incidentally, was to reverse himself the following year in conferring with Grenville as the Pennsylvania London agent. In expressing confidentially his personal, rather than any official, views to his friend Richard Jackson on June 25, 1764 he declared: "Quota's would be difficult to settle at first with Equality, and would, if they could be made equal at first, soon become unequal, and never would be satisfactory." Indeed, experience with this system in practice, as a settled method of guaranteeing even the minimum essential resources for the end in view, had shown its weakness and utter unfairness. If it could not work equitably even in war time, could it be expected to work in peace? It is, therefore, not surprising that this method of securing even a portion of the funds required for North American security should have been rejected in favor of some plan that presented better prospects of a definite American revenue.

The plan of last resort to the ministry was therefore to ask Parliament to act. That Grenville, however, was aware that serious objections might be raised against any direct taxation of the colonials by the government of Great Britain is indicated by the caution with which he approached the solution of the problem of securing from America about a third of the total cost of its defense. The so-called Sugar Act first of all was passed at his request. This provided for import duties on certain West Indian and other products. Colonial import duties imposed by Parliament, at least since 1733, were no innovation. But the anticipated yield of these duties fell far short of the desired one hundred thousand pounds. He therefore, in introducing the bill for the above Act, raised the question of a stamp duty but requested postponement of parliamentary action until the colonial governments had been consulted. The latter were thereupon requested to make any suggestions for ways of raising an American fund that might seem more proper to the people than such a tax. Further, it would appear—at least, according to various London advices published in Franklin and Hall's *Pennsylvania Gazette*—that proposals were seriously considered by the Cabinet Council during the fall of 1764 for extending to the colonies representation in Parliament through the election of members to the House of Commons by various colonial assemblies. However, it is quite clear that by the beginning of 1765 any such proposals, as seem to have been under deliberation by the ministry, had been put aside when Grenville at length had become convinced that representation in Parliament was neither actively sought nor even desired by Americans. For the South Carolina Commons House of Assembly went strongly on record against this idea in September 1764 and was followed by the Virginia House of Burgesses in December. In fact, when in the presence of the London colonial agents the minister had outlined the objections raised by Americans to the idea of such representation, no one of them, including Franklin, was prepared to deny the validity of these objections. That he was not mistaken in the opposition of Americans at large to sending members to Parliament, in spite of the advocacy of this by James Otis, is clear in the resolutions passed both by other colonial assemblies than the ones to which reference has been made and by the Stamp Act Congress in 1765. Indeed, in 1768 the House of Representatives of Massachusetts Bay went so far in its famous Circular Letter framed in opposition to the Townshend duties as to make clear that the people of that colony actually preferred taxation by Parliament without representation to such taxation with representation.

When—in view of the failure of the colonial governments to suggest any practicable, alternate plan for making some contribution to the post-war defensive program in North America—Grenville finally urged in Parliament the passage of an American stamp bill, he acted on an unwarranted assumption. This assumption was—in paraphrasing the minister's remarks to the colonial agents in 1765—that opposition to stamp taxes, for the specific purpose in mind, would disappear in America both in light of the benefits such provision would bring to colonials in general and by reason of the plain justice of the measure itself; and that, in place of opposition, an atmosphere of mutual goodwill would be generated by a growing recognition on the part of Americans that they could trust the benevolence of the mother country to act with fairness to all within the empire. Instead, with the news of the passage of the act, cries of British tyranny and impending slavery soon resounded throughout the entire eastern Atlantic American seaboard. What would have been the fate of the empire had Grenville remained in office to attempt to enforce the act, no one can say. But as members of the opposition to the Rockingham ministry, he and his brother, Earl Temple, raised their voices—one as a commoner, the other as a peer—in warning that the American colonies would inevitably be lost to the empire should Parliament be led to repeal the act in the face of colonial resistance and the pressure of British merchants. Had Parliament determined, in spite of violence and threats of violence, to enforce the act, it might have meant open rebellion and civil war, ten years before it actually occurred. Instead, this body decided to yield and, in spite of the passing of the so-called Declaratory Act setting forth its fundamental powers to legislate on all matters relating to the empire, suffered a loss of prestige in the New World that was never to be regained.

But the Stamp Act was not the sole object of attack by colonials. To many of them not only the Sugar Act of 1764 but the whole English prewar trade and navigation system was equally, if not actually more, obnoxious. Indeed, the unusual energy displayed by the navy and the customs officials, spurred into action by Pitt during the latter years of the war—bringing with it the condemnation in courts of vice-admiralty of many American vessels whose owners were guilty of serious trade violations, if not greater crimes—generated a degree of antagonism against the whole body of late seventeenth- and early eighteenth-century restrictions on commercial intercourse such as never had previously existed. It is not without significance that the greatest acts of terrorism and destruction during the great riot of August 1765 in Boston were directed not against the Massachusetts Bay stamp distributor but against those officials responsible for encouraging and supporting the enforcement, during the late war, of the various trade acts passed long before its beginning in 1754. The hatred also of the Rhode Island merchants, as a group, against the restrictions of the navigation system as well as against the Sugar Act of 1764, remained constant. Moreover, in December 1766 most of the New York merchants, over two hundred in number, showed their repugnance to the way that this system was functioning by a strongly worded petition to the House of Commons in which they enumerated an impressive list of grievances that they asked to be redressed. Even Chatham, the great friend of America, regarded their petition "highly improper: in point of time most absurd, in the extent of their pretensions, most excessive; and in the reasoning, most grossly fallacious and offensive." In fact, all the leading men in Great Britain supported the system of trade restrictions.

Nevertheless, the determination of the government—in view especially of the great financial burdens that the late war had placed upon the mother country—to enforce it now much more effectively than had been done before 1754, and to that end in 1767 to pass appropriate legislation in order to secure funds from the colonies by way of import duties so that public officials in America might be held to greater accountability when paid their salaries by the Crown, could have only one result: the combined resistance of those, on the one hand, opposed to any type of taxation that Parliament might apply to America and of those, on the other, desiring to free the colonies of hampering trade restrictions.

The suggestion on the part of the Continental Congress in 1774 that Americans would uphold the British navigation system, if exempted from parliamentary taxation, while a shrewd gesture to win support in England, had really, it would seem, no other significance. For it is utterly inconceivable that the Congress itself, or the individual colonial governments, could have set up machinery capable of preventing violations of the system at will on the part of those whose financial interests were adversely affected by its operation. Moreover, it is obvious that, by the time the news had reached America that Lord North's ministry had secured the passage of the coercive acts—for the most part directed against Massachusetts Bay for the defiant destruction of the East India Company's tea —leading colonials, among them Franklin, had arrived at the conclusion that Parliament possessed powers so very limited with respect to the empire that without the consent of the local assemblies it could pass neither constitutional nor fiscal legislation that affected Americans and the framework of their governments. It is equally obvious that this represented a most revolutionary position when contrasted with that held by Franklin and the other delegates to the Albany Congress twenty years earlier. For it was in 1754 that the famous Plan of Union was drawn up there and approved by the Congress—a plan based upon the view that Parliament, and not the Crown, had supreme authority within the empire, an authority that alone was adequate in view of framers of the Plan to bring about fundamental changes in the constitutions of the colonies in order legally to clothe the proposed union government with adequate fiscal as well as other powers.

In accounting for the radical change in attitude of many leading colonials between the years 1754 and 1774 respecting the nature of the constitution of the empire, surely among the factors that must be weighed was the truly overwhelming victory achieved in the Great War for the Empire. This victory not only freed colonials for the first time in the history of the English-speaking people in the New World from dread of the French, their Indian allies, and the Spaniards, but, what is of equal significance, opened up to them the prospect, if given freedom of action, of a vast growth of power and wealth with an amazing westward expansion. Indeed, it is abundantly clear that a continued subordination of the colonies to the government of Great Britain was no longer considered an asset in the eyes of many Americans by 1774, as it had been so judged by them to be in 1754, but rather an onerous liability. What, pray tell, had the debt-ridden mother country to offer in 1774 to the now geographically secure, politically mature, prosperous, dynamic, and self-reliant offspring along the Atlantic seaboard, except the dubious opportunity of accepting new, as well as retaining old, burdens? And these burdens would have to be borne in order to lighten somewhat the great financial load that the tax-payers of Great Britain were forced to carry by reason of obligations the nation had assumed both in the course of the late war and at its termination. If many Americans thought they had a perfect right to profit personally by trading with the enemy in time of war, how much more deeply must they have resented in time of peace the serious efforts made by the home government to enforce the elaborate restrictions on commercial intercourse? Again, if, even after the defeat of Colonel Washington at Great Meadows in 1754, colonials such as Franklin were opposed to paying any tax levied by Parliament for establishing a fund for the defense of North America, how much more must they have been inclined to oppose such taxation to that end with the passing in 1763 of the great international crisis?

At this point the question must be frankly faced: If France had won the war decisively and thereby consolidated her position and perfected her claims in Nova Scotia, as well as to the southward of the St. Lawrence, in the Great Lakes region, and in the Ohio and Mississippi valleys, is it at all likely that colonials would have made so fundamental a constitutional issue of the extension to them of the principle of the British stamp tax? Would they have resisted such a tax had Parliament imposed it in order to provide on an equitable basis the maximum resources for guaranteeing their safety, at a time when they were faced on their highly restricted borders by a militant, victorious enemy having at its command thousands of ferocious redskins? Again, accepting the fact of Britain's victory, is it not reasonable to believe that, had Great Britain at the close of the triumphant war left Canada to France and carefully limited her territorial demands in North America to those comparatively modest objectives that she had in mind at its beginning, there would have been no very powerful movement

within the foreseeable future toward complete colonial autonomy—not to
mention American independence? Would not Americans have continued to
feel the need as in the past to rely for their safety and welfare upon
British sea power and British land power, as well as upon British resources generally? In other words, was Governor Thomas Hutchinson
of Massachusetts Bay far mistaken when, in analyzing the American situation late in 1773, he affirmed in writing to the Earl of Dartmouth:

> Before the peace [of 1763] I thought nothing so much to be desired as the
> cession of Canada. I am now convinced that if it had remained to the French
> none of the spirit of opposition to the Mother Country would have yet ap-
> peared & I think the effects of it [that is, the cession of Canada] worse than all
> we had to fear from the French or Indians.

In conclusion, it may be said that it would be idle to deny that most
colonials in the eighteenth century at one time or another felt strongly
the desire for freedom of action in a wider variety of ways than was
legally permitted before 1754. Indeed, one can readily uncover these strong
impulses even in the early part of the seventeenth century. Yet Americans
were, by and large, realists, as were the British, and under the functioning
of the imperial system from, let us say, 1650 to 1750 great mutual
advantages were enjoyed, with a fair division, taking everything into consideration, of the financial burdens necessary to support the system.
However, the mounting Anglo-French rivalry in North America from 1750
onward, the outbreak of hostilities in 1754, and the subsequent nine years
of fighting destroyed the old equilibrium, leaving the colonials after 1760 in
a highly favored position in comparison with the taxpayers of Great
Britain. Attempts on the part of the Crown and Parliament to restore by
statute the old balance led directly to the American constitutional crisis,
out of which came the Revolutionary War and the establishment of
American independence. Such, ironically, was the aftermath of the Great
War for the Empire, a war that Britons believed, as the Earl of Shelburne
affirmed in 1762 in Parliament, was begun for the "security of the British
colonies in N. America. . . ."

14 *Edmund S. Morgan*

THE AMERICAN REVOLUTION:
REVISIONS IN NEED OF REVISING

The American Revolution is central to our national ideal. The image which the nation has of itself at once defines and is defined by the way it came into existence. But the image is a changing one. The birth of the American nation is variously seen, and what is seen is in no small measure a reflection of the problems and prepossessions of the present. One age has construed the Revolution as a struggle for liberty, another as a defense of property, and still a third as a somewhat regrettable explosion brought on by extremists on both sides. The concerns of the present have been turning the kaleidoscope of our revolutionary past.

It is this matter of changing interpretations of the American Revolution which concerns Professor Edmund Sears Morgan of Yale University. Professor Morgan established himself as an authority on the revolutionary period in *The Stamp Act Crisis: Prologue to Revolution* (1953), which he wrote in collaboration with his wife, Helen M. Morgan. He has canvassed the whole period in *The Birth of the Republic* (1956), a volume that is excellent for its brevity, its wit, its clarity, and its viewpoint. Here Morgan addresses himself squarely to the basic questions about the Revolution: What was its nature? What were its causes? To what extent was it justified?

His answer marks, in effect, the return of the Whig or patriotic approach to American historical writing. This approach found its greatest expression in the writings of George Bancroft during the middle and latter decades of the nineteenth century. For the last half-century or more, historians have put the American cause to the most severe questioning, abjuring patriotism as the last refuge of the scholar. With Morgan, however, the Revolution becomes again a struggle for freedom from British tyranny, a search for principles, indeed, a "people's war." The Americans of that generation he tends to see as uniformly patriotic, and the motives impelling them he tends to see as uniformly lofty.

How does Morgan's interpretation reflect the problems and prepossessions of our own times? Perhaps a clue may be found in the fact that the ultimate concern of our nation today is that ideal of freedom which it is seeking to retain and defend in a world increas-

Reprinted with permission from *The William and Mary Quarterly*, Third Series, XIV (January, 1957), 3-15.

ingly unfree. The liberal ideal is central to our institutions, and an age in which its survival is being challenged is also one which will contemplate and applaud its early struggles.

In the essay below, Professor Morgan poses questions to each of the major interpretations of the American Revolution which have been current during the past half-century. How valid, he asks, are the views of those who found that the First British Empire was run fairly and benevolently? How accurate is the social and economic interpretation, in the light of which the Fathers were founding fortunes rather than liberty? And what is to be said of Sir Lewis B. Namier's approach, which sees English politics in local and personal terms and has the effect of damning the Whigs and faintly praising George III? All these interpretations, insists Professor Morgan, fail to answer basic questions about the Revolution. More than that, they raise difficult questions for each other.

But Professor Morgan raises questions for himself no less than for others. Is he being fair, for example, to say that historians who saw the old colonial system as essentially non-oppressive of the Americans before 1763 would necessarily condone its operation after that date? Is Morgan fair in denying that different social and economic interests were factors in causing different American attitudes toward the British program and toward each other? To what extent is he correct in suggesting that Americans were united in principle and action? To what extent is he correct in suggesting that unless we explain the mind of the great leaders, like Washington, Adams, Jefferson, and Franklin, we explain nothing of the nature and causes of the Revolution? Is it valid to identify all of the Revolution with them? Is it fair to presume that if any one of the interpretations which Morgan questions does not entirely explain the Revolution that it does not do so at least in part? May not one believe that Professor Morgan's views and those he criticizes are not mutually exclusive, but rather supplementary in explaining a highly complex series of developments?

The interpretation we settle on is a matter of great importance. For in our view of the nature and causes of the American Revolution we are defining something more than the birth of a nation. We are defining as well what has become of the nation since its birth and what it is today.

During the past fifty years three ideas have inspired research into the history of the eighteenth century in America and England. The earliest of these to appear, and the most fruitful of results, was the idea that American colonial history must be seen in the setting of the British Empire as a whole. We are all familiar today with the new insights and new discoveries that have grown out of this view: the great works of George Louis Beer and Charles McLean Andrews, the monumental synthesis of Professor Lawrence Gipson, which now approaches its culmination. This has been a great idea, and it has done more than any other to shape our understanding of the colonial past.

A second idea, which has affected in one way or another most of us who study colonial history, is that the social and economic divisions of a people will profoundly influence the course of their history. This idea received early application to American history in Carl Becker's study of New York politics on the eve of the Revolution and in Charles Beard's *An Economic Interpretation of the Constitution*. New York politics before the Revolution, Becker said, revolved around two questions, equally important, the question of home rule and that of who should rule at home.[1] Subsequent historians have found in Becker's aphorism a good description of the Revolutionary period as a whole. The conflict between different social groups now looms as large in our histories of the Revolution as the struggle against England. Like all seminal ideas, this one has sometimes been used as a substitute for research instead of a stimulus to it. Historians have been so convinced of the importance of social and economic divisions that they have uttered the wildest kind of nonsense, for example, about the social and economic basis of a religious movement like the Great Awakening of the 1740's. The view has nevertheless been productive of important new insights and new information.

The third idea, although it has had scarcely any effect as yet on the study of American history, has furnished the principal impetus to recent research in British history. It is a more complex idea, growing out of the discoveries of Sir Lewis Namier. The effect of these discoveries has been to attach a new importance to local as opposed to national forces. "It has been the greatest of Sir Lewis Namier's achievements," says Richard Pares, "to exhibit the personal and local nature of political issues and political power at this time."[2] Namier and his disciples, of whom Pares is the most notable, have destroyed the traditional picture of British politics in the age of the American Revolution. During this period, they tell us, there were no political parties in the modern sense, nor were there any political factions or associations with any principle or belief beyond that of serving selfish or local interests. The Rockingham Whigs, who made such a display of their opposition to the repressive measures against the colonies, were no different from the other squabbling factions except in their hypocritical pretense of standing for broader principles. And George III owed his control over Parliament not to bribery and corruption but simply to his constitutional position in the government and to his skill as a politician

---

[1] Carl Becker, *The History of Political Parties in the Province of New York, 1760–1776* (Madison, Wis., 1909), p. 22.

[2] Richard Pares, *King George III and the Politicians* (Oxford, 1953), p. 2.

during a time when the House of Commons lacked effective leaders of its own.

Each of these three ideas, the imperial, the social or economic, and the Namierist, has had a somewhat similar effect on our understanding of the American Revolution. That effect has been to discredit, in different ways, the old Whig interpretation. The imperial historians have examined the running of the empire before the Revolution and pronounced it fair. The Navigation Acts, they have shown, were no cause for complaint. The Board of Trade did as good a job as could be expected. The Admiralty Courts were a useful means of maintaining fair play and fair trade on the high seas. Indeed, Professor Gipson tells us, the old colonial system "may not unfairly be compared to modern systems of state interference with the liberty of the subject in matters involving industry and trade, accepting the differences involved in the nature of the regulations respectively. In each case, individuals or groups within the state are forbidden to follow out lines of action that, while highly beneficial to those locally or personally concerned, are considered inimical to the larger national objectives."[3] In the light of such imperial benevolence and farsightedness, the unwillingness of the Americans to pay the trifling contribution demanded of them in the sixties and seventies becomes small and mean, and the resounding rhetoric of a Henry or an Otis or an Adams turns into the bombast of a demagogue.

The social and economic interpretation does nothing to redeem the fallen Revolutionary patriots but rather shows them up as hypocrites pursuing selfish interests while they mouth platitudes about democracy and freedom. Their objections to parliamentary taxation are reduced to mere tax evasion, with the arguments shifting as the character of the taxes shifted. Their insistence on freedom and equality is shown to be insincere, because in setting up their own governments they failed to establish universal suffrage or proportional representation. They were, it would appear, eager to keep one foot on the lower classes while they kicked the British with the other.

Namier and his followers have little to say about the American revolutionists but devote themselves to scolding the English Whigs. Though the Namierists generally achieve a sophisticated objectivity with regard to persons and parties, they sometimes seem fond of beating the Whigs in order—one suspects—to displease the Whig historians. For example, the unflattering portrait of Charles James Fox that emerges from Richard Pares's brilliant study must surely be read in part as a rebuke to Sir George Otto Trevelyan, or rather to those who have accepted Trevelyan's estimate of Fox. This deflation of Fox and Burke and the other Rockingham

[3] Lawrence H. Gipson, *The British Empire before the American Revolution,* III (Caldwell, Idaho, 1936), 287.

Whigs, while accomplished with scarcely a glance in the direction of the colonies, nevertheless deprives the American revolutionists of a group of allies whose high-minded sympathy had been relied upon by earlier historians to help demonstrate the justice of the American cause.

By the same token the righteousness of the Americans is somewhat diminished through the loss of the principal villain in the contest. George III is no longer the foe of liberty, seeking to subvert the British constitution, but an earnest and responsible monarch, doing his job to the best of his abilities. And those abilities, we are told, while not of the highest order, were not small either. George, in fact, becomes a sympathetic figure, and one can scarcely escape the feeling that the Americans were rather beastly to have made things so hard for him.

While the imperial, the economic, and the Namierist approaches have thus contributed in different ways to diminish the prestige of the American Revolution and its promoters, it is a curious fact that none of the ideas has produced any full-scale examination of the Revolution itself or of how it came about. The imperial historians have hitherto been occupied primarily in dissecting the workings of the empire as it existed before the Revolutionary troubles. Although their works have necessarily squinted at the Revolution in every sentence, the only direct confrontations have been brief and inconclusive.

The social and economic interpretation has been applied more extensively to different aspects of the Revolution, but surprisingly enough we still know very little about what the social and economic divisions actually were in most of the colonies and states at the time of the Revolution. Professor Schlesinger's analysis of the role of the merchant class[4] remains a fixed point of knowledge at the opening of the period, and Charles Beard's *Economic Interpretation of the Constitution* is a somewhat shakier foundation at the close of it, reinforced, however, by the work of Merrill Jensen.[5] Historians have bridged the gap between these two points with more assurance than information. There are, it is true, several illuminating studies of local divisions but not enough to warrant any firm conclusions about the role of economic and social forces in the Revolution as a whole. After thirty years we are only a little closer to the materials needed for such conclusions than J. Franklin Jameson was in 1926.

The Namierist approach, as already indicated, has been confined to events in England rather than America. Though the effect of such investigations has been to exonerate George III and discredit the English Whigs, the Revolution has not been a primary issue for Namier or Pares. One

[4] Arthur M. Schlesinger, *The Colonial Merchants and the American Revolution* (New York, 1918).

[5] Merrill Jensen, *The Articles of Confederation* (Madison, Wis., 1940); *The New Nation* (New York, 1950).

student of Professor Namier's, Eric Robson, made a preliminary excursion into the subject but confined his discussion primarily to military history.[6] And while Professor Charles Ritcheson has treated the place of the Revolution in British politics,[7] the implications of Namier's discoveries for developments on this side of the water remain unexplored.

Thus while the new ideas and new discoveries have altered our attitudes toward the American Revolution, they have done so for the most part indirectly, almost surreptitiously, without coming up against the Revolution itself. There is need for intensive and direct examination of all phases of the Revolution in the light of each of these ideas, and we may expect that in the next few years such examinations will be made. Professor Gipson has already begun. I should like to suggest, however, that we need not only to examine the Revolution in the light of the ideas but also to re-examine the ideas in the light of the Revolution; and in doing so we need also to examine them in relation to each other.

The Revolution is one of those brute facts which historians must account for, and it is a fact of central importance for ascertaining the meaning and limits of the three ideas we are discussing. I believe that each of the three needs revisions and will take them up in order.

While everyone will acknowledge the importance of the imperial idea and of the discoveries made under its influence, the net effect of that idea has been to emphasize the justice and beneficence of the British imperial system as it existed before the Revolution. May we not therefore pose a question to the imperial historians: if the empire was as fairly administered as you show it to have been, how could the Revolution have happened at all? In their preliminary skirmishes with this problem, imperial historians have frequently implied that the American revolutionists were moved, in part at least, by narrow or selfish views and stirred up by evil-minded agitators. But if historians are to sustain such a view in any full-scale consideration of the Revolution, they face a very difficult task: they must explain men like George Washington, John Adams, Thomas Jefferson, and Benjamin Franklin as agitators or as the dupes of agitators, or as narrow-minded men without the vision to see beyond provincial borders. After all due allowance is made for patriotic myopia, this still seems to me to be an impossible undertaking. Anyone who studies the Revolution can scarcely emerge without some degree of admiration for the breadth of vision that moved these men. In twenty-five years they created a new nation and endowed it with a government that still survives and now has the longest continuous history of any government in existence outside of England.

<hr>

[6] Eric Robson, *The American Revolution in its Political and Military Aspects* (London, 1955).

[7] Charles Ritcheson, *British Politics and the American Revolution* (Norman, Okla., 1954).

The idea that they were narrow-minded simply will not wash. Nor is it possible to see them as the dupes of their intellectual inferiors. Samuel Adams, Patrick Henry, and James Otis may perhaps be cast as demagogues without seeming out of place, but not the giants of the period. If the British government could not run the empire without bringing on evils that appeared insufferable to men like Washington, Jefferson, John Adams, and Franklin, then the burden of proof would seem to be on those who maintain that it was fit to run an empire.

When the imperial historians are ready to attempt the proof, they must face a second task: they must explain away the character which the Namierist historians have given to the British statesmen of the period. The Namierists, as already indicated, have emphasized the parochial character of English politics in this period. They have cut the Whigs down to size, but they have cut down everyone else on the British political scene likewise. If Parliament was dominated by local interests, what becomes of imperial beneficence and farsightedness?

The whole effect of the Namierist discoveries, so far as the colonies are concerned, must be to show that British statesmen in the 1760's and 1770's, whether in Parliament or in the Privy Council, were too dominated by local interests to be able to run an empire. There was no institution, no party, no organization through which imperial interests, as opposed to strictly British interests, could find adequate expression. In fact the Namierist view and the view of the imperial historians are directly at odds here: though neither group seems as yet to be aware of the conflict, they cannot both be wholly right, and the coming of the Revolution would seem to confirm the Namierist view and to cast doubt on the imperialist one. The achievements of the revolutionists and the failures of the British statesmen suggest in the strongest possible terms that it was the Americans who saw things in the large and the British who wore the blinders. If this is so, may it not be that the case for the beneficence and justice of the British Empire before the Revolution has been overstated?

In response to our argument *ad hominem* the imperialists may summon the aid of the economic interpretation to show that the Americans, however high-toned their arguments, were really moved by economic considerations of the basest kind. We may, however, call these considerations basic rather than base and offer our previous character witnesses against the economists too. There is no time to plead to every indictment here, but one may perhaps answer briefly the strongest yet offered, that of Charles Beard, and then suggest how the economic interpretation needs revision. Though Beard expressly disclaimed that his economic interpretation was the whole story, he gave not merely a one-sided view but a false one. All the evidence that Beard extracted from the records of the Constitutional Convention points toward the sordid conclusion that the delegates who held public securities also held undemocratic political views, motivated consciously or unconsciously by the desire to protect their investments. Beard consistently overlooked contradictory evidence. I will cite only two examples.

The first is his treatment of Roger Sherman, the delegate to the Constitutional Convention from Connecticut. Sherman, he notes, had risen from poverty to affluence and held nearly eight thousand dollars worth of public securities. Sherman's corresponding political philosophy he represents by the following statement: "Roger Sherman believed in reducing the popular influence in the new government to the minimum. When it was proposed that the members of the first branch of the national legislature should be elected, Sherman said that he was 'opposed to the election by the people, insisting that it ought to be by the state legislatures. The people, he said, immediately should have as little to do as may be about the government. They want information and are constantly liable to be misled.' "[8]

The quotation certainly supports Beard's view, but Beard failed to indicate what Sherman said at other times in the convention. On June 4, four days after the speech Beard quotes, Sherman was against giving the President a veto power, because he "was against enabling any one man to stop the will of the whole. No one man could be found so far above all the rest in wisdom." On June 21 he argued again for election of the House of Representatives by the state legislatures, but after election by the people had been decided upon, spoke for annual elections as against triennial, because "He thought the representatives ought to return home and mix with the people." On August 14 he was in favor of substantial pay for congressmen, because otherwise "men ever so fit could not serve unless they were at the same time rich."[9] Whatever explanation may be offered for these views, they suggest a much broader confidence in the people than might be inferred from the single remark by which Beard characterized the man.

It cannot be said that the statements which Beard neglected are concerned with an aspect of Sherman's views not relevant to the problem Beard was examining: they are certainly as relevant as the statement he did quote. His treatment of Pierce Butler, the delegate from South Carolina, is similar. Beard notes that Butler held public securities and that he argued for apportionment of representation according to wealth.[10] He neglects to mention that Butler, in spite of his security holdings, opposed full payments of the public debt, "lest it should compel payment as well to the

---

[8] Charles Beard, *An Economic Interpretation of the Constitution of the United States* (New York, 1913), pp. 213–214.

[9] *Records of the Federal Convention of 1787*, ed. Max Farrand (New Haven, 1911–37), I, 99, 362; II, 291.

[10] Beard, *Economic Interpretation*, pp. 81–82, 192.

Blood-suckers who had speculated on the distresses of others, as to those who had fought and bled for their country."[11] The statement is relevant, but directly opposed, to Beard's thesis.

It requires only a reading of the Convention debates to see that Beard's study needs revision.[12] But the trouble with the economic interpretation, as currently applied to the whole Revolutionary period, goes deeper. The trouble lies in the assumption that a conflict between property rights and human rights has been the persistent theme of American history from the beginning. It was undoubtedly the great theme of Beard's day, and Beard was on the side of human rights, where decent men belong in such a conflict. From the vantage point of twentieth-century Progressivism, he lined up the members of the Constitutional Convention, found their pockets stuffed with public securities, and concluded that they were on the wrong side.

It was a daring piece of work, and it fired the imagination of Beard's fellow progressives.[13] Vernon L. Parrington has recorded how it "struck home like a submarine torpedo—the discovery that the drift toward plutocracy was not a drift away from the spirit of the Constitution, but an inevitable unfolding from its premises." As a result of Beard's work, Parrington was able to see that "From the beginning . . . democracy and property had been at bitter odds."[14]

Parrington went on to construct his own image of American history in these terms, and he too had a powerful influence. Together he and Beard virtually captured the American past for Progressivism, a performance all the more remarkable when we consider that they did not enlist the revered founding fathers of the Constitution on their side.

It is time, however, that we had another look at the conflict between human rights and property rights; and the Revolutionary period is a good place to begin, for however strong the conflict may later have become, it was not a dominant one then. Anyone who studies the Revolution must notice at once the attachment of all articulate Americans to property. "Liberty and Property" was their cry, not "Liberty and Democracy." In the face of the modern dissociation of property from liberty, historians have often felt that this concern of the revolutionists for property was a rather shabby thing, and that the constitutional principles so much talked

[11] Farrand, *Records*, II, 392.

[12] Robert E. Brown's *Charles Beard and the Constitution* (Princeton, 1956) appeared too late to be of use in preparation of this paper, but the reader will find in it abundant additional evidence of deficiencies in Beard's use of the Convention records.

[13] See Douglass Adair, "The Tenth Federalist Revisited," *William and Mary Quarterly*, 3d Ser., VIII (1951), 48–67; Richard Hofstadter, "Beard and the Constitution: The History of an Idea," *American Quarterly*, II (1950), 195–213.

[14] Vernon L. Parrington, *Main Currents in American Thought* (New York, 1927–30), III, 410.

of, before 1776 as well as afterward, were invented to hide it under a more attractive cloak. But the Americans were actually quite shameless about their concern for property and made no effort to hide it, because it did not seem at all shabby to them. The colonial protests against taxation frankly and openly, indeed passionately, affirm the sanctity of property. And the passion is not the simple and unlovely passion of greed. For eighteenth-century Americans, property and liberty were one and inseparable, because property was the only foundation yet conceived for security of life and liberty: without security for his property, it was thought, no man could live or be free except at the mercy of another.

The revolutionists' coupling of property with life and liberty was not an attempt to lend respectability to property rights, nor was it an attempt to enlist the masses in a struggle for the special privileges of a small wealthy class. Property in eighteenth-century America was not associated with special privilege, as it came to be for later generations. Land was widely owned. A recent investigation has demonstrated that in Massachusetts, a key state in the Revolution, nearly every adult male could meet the property qualifications for the franchise.[15] We hear much from modern historians about the propertyless masses of the Revolutionary period, but it is altogether improbable that the mass of Americans were without property.

The Americans fought England because Parliament threatened the security of property. They established state constitutions with property qualifications for voting and officeholding in order to protect the security of property. And when the state governments seemed inadequate to the task, they set up the Federal government for the same purpose. The economic motive was present in all these actions, but it was present as the friend of universal liberty. Devotion to security of property was not the attitude of a privileged few but the fundamental principle of the many, inseparable from everything that went by the name of freedom and adhered to the more fervently precisely because it did affect most people so intimately.

What we have done in our social and economic interpretations of the Revolution is to project into eighteenth-century America a situation which existed in the nineteenth and early twentieth centuries, when property and the means of production became concentrated in the hands of a few, when liberty if it was to exist at all had to get along not only without the aid of property but in opposition to it. We seem now to be approaching a period when property, in another form, may again be widely distributed and may again become the friend rather than the enemy of liberty. Whether such is the case or not, as historians we should stop

15 Robert E. Brown, *Middle-Class Democracy and the Revolution in Massachusetts, 1691-1780* (Ithaca, N.Y., 1955).

projecting into the eighteenth century the particular economic and social antagonisms that we have found in later generations. We may still believe that the American Revolution was in part a contest about who should rule at home, but we should beware of assuming that people took sides in that contest according to whether or not they owned property. And we should totally abandon the assumption that those who showed the greatest concern for property rights were not devoted to human rights.

The challenge of the Revolution to the Namier school of historians is less direct and less crucial, but it does pose one or two questions which these historians seem not to have confronted. The first is whether the new judgment of George III has not raised that monarch's reputation a little too high. Granted that George was neither the fool nor the knave he has hitherto been thought, granted that he was moved by a desire to maintain parliamentary supremacy rather than regal supremacy, it is nevertheless true that under his leadership England lost an important, if not the most important, part of her empire. The loss was not inevitable. All the objectives of the Americans before 1776 could have been attained within the empire, and would have cost the mother country little or nothing. George undoubtedly received a good deal of assistance from other politicians in losing the colonies, but the contention of the Namierists has been that the King still held a position of central responsibility in the British government in the 1760's and 1770's, a responsibility which they have shown that he shouldered and carried. If he was responsible then he must be held responsible. He must bear most of the praise or blame for the series of measures that alienated and lost the colonies, and it is hard to see how there can be much praise.

The other question that the Revolution poses for the Namierists may be more fundamental. Virtually no one in British politics, they argue, had any political principles that reached beyond local or factional interests. The argument, though convincingly presented, presumes a consistent hypocrisy or delusion on the part of the Whig opposition. It may be that the Whigs were hypocritical in their attack on George III and their support of the Americans. But if so why were they hypocritical in just the way they were? Why did they appeal to principles of government that later won acceptance? Can we be sure that it was only in order to attack their opponents? Can we be sure they were on the right side for the wrong reasons? I do not pretend to know the answers to these questions, but I am not quite comfortable about judgments of history in which people are condemned for being prematurely antimonarchical.

What I would suggest in conclusion is that the Whig interpretation of the American Revolution may not be as dead as some historians would have us believe, that George Bancroft may not have been so far from the mark as we have often assumed. Is it not time to ask again a few of the old questions that he was trying to answer? Let us grant that local interests were the keynote of British politics; we must still ask: how did the Americans, living on the edge of empire, develop the breadth of vision and the attachment to principle which they displayed in that remarkable period from 1763 to 1789? While English politics remained parochial and the empire was dissolving for lack of vision, how did the Americans generate the forces that carried them into a new nationality and a new human liberty?

The answer, I think, may lie in a comparatively neglected field of American scholarship. During the past fifty years our investigations of the colonial period have been directed primarily by the imperial idea and the social and economic one. We have seen the colonists as part of the empire or else we have seen them as the pawns of sweeping economic and social forces. What we have neglected is the very thing that the English have been pursuing in the study of their institutions. We have neglected, comparatively speaking at least, the study of local institutions, and it is in such a study that we may perhaps discover the answer to the fundamental question that moved Bancroft, the question of how a great nation with great principles of freedom was forged from thirteen quarrelsome colonies. What kind of institutions produced a Jefferson, a Madison, a Washington, a John Adams? Not imperial institutions certainly. The imperial machinery had no place for Americans except in performing local services. No American ever sat on the Board of Trade or the Privy Council. Few Americans ever came in contact with imperial officers. It was in local American institutions that these men gained their political experience.

Two generations ago Herbert Baxter Adams thought he had the clue to the question of where American liberty began, and he put a host of graduate students to work studying the local institutions of the colonies. As we all know, they did not find precisely what Adams was looking for, but they produced a prodigious number of studies, which are still the principal source of historical information about many colonial institutions. Some have been superseded by more recent scholarship, but we need more new studies of this kind, which will take advantage of what we have learned since Adams's time about the imperial setting and about social and economic forces.

We need to know how the individual's picture of society was formed. We need to study the social groupings in every colony: towns, plantations, counties, churches, schools, clubs, and other groups which occupied the social horizons of the individual colonist. We need to study political parties and factions in every colony. We need to study the way government worked at the local level. We need to study the county courts and the justices of the peace. We need to study the distribution of land and other forms of wealth from decade to decade and from place to place.

We need to know so elementary a thing as the history of representation and the history of taxation in every colony. We have always known that the Revolution had something to do with the phrase, "no taxation without representation," and yet, after two generations of modern scholarship, how many scholars have studied the history of taxation in the colonies? Who really knows anything about the history of representation?

Without abandoning what we have gained from the imperial idea and from economic interpretations, we must dissect the local institutions which produced the American Revolution, the institutions from which were distilled the ideas that enabled men of that age to stand as the architects of modern liberty. The task has not been wholly neglected. A number of scholars have been quietly working at it. I will not attempt to name them here, but their discoveries are sufficient to show that this is the direction which scholarship in colonial history should now take and that the rewards will not be small.

III

*National Growth and
Civil War, 1783–1877*

III

THE REPUBLIC OF THE
FOUNDING FATHERS

15 *Adrienne Koch*

PHILOSOPHER-STATESMEN OF THE REPUBLIC

The veneration of the founding fathers has come full circle in our day. They have been taken out of the historiographic pillory. They are no longer men of questionable democracy, psychology, or class interests. They are libertarians, men of vision, beginners of the American experiment. As such they are the subject of many sympathetic biographies. Even more are they the subject of immense editions of collected works. And there is reason enough for Americans today to consecrate and hallow their ground. The essence of current American history is the defense of the ideal of freedom and the rights of the individual against totalitarianism and the absence of these rights. Never has the nation so unanimously been drawn back to its ideological beginnings, as in our present struggle for survival.

Herein consists the importance of the following essay by Professor Adrienne Koch of the University of California at Berkeley. A long-time student of the founding fathers and author of an illuminating study of *Jefferson and Madison* (1950), Professor Koch centers her attention on the contribution to the republic of four of the greatest of their generation: Jefferson, Madison, John Adams, and Hamilton. Their principles, she feels, "almost define the range of our national ideology—our objectives, our character as a people, our economic and social patterns, our 'Americanism.'" In her attempt to define these principles, Professor Koch is also attempting to answer some very significant questions. What were the defining characteristics of the republican ideal which was central to the political philosophy of late eighteenth-century America? To what extent did each of the four men

Reprinted with permission from *The Sewanee Review*, LV (July, 1947), 384–6, 392–405. Copyright 1947 by the University of the South.

in question subscribe to this ideal? What basic principle did each contribute to the newly founded republic? What differences of morality were there among the four? How did the variety of their ideas make possible, as Professor Koch suggests, the existence and endurance of the republic?

In saying that the republic of the founding fathers has not been with us since the age of Jackson, Professor Koch is raising questions about them, about us, and about the interim period. What accounts for their remarkable political contribution? How much was it a product of their talent, how much a product of their times? What has become of that talent? Is it not true of American political development that the nation was conceived in genius and has grown and continued to exist in mediocrity? Why is the quality of leadership that was the rule then the exception now? How far and why has their vision of a republic of virtue with an educated citizenry not been realized?

Nothing would have better revealed the poverty of later political development to the Founding Fathers than the fact that they were gathered into a pantheon and that their principles were pronounced dogma. The generation of Jefferson builded better than they hoped but worse than they knew, because they knew that each age had to adapt to the changing times the deeper principles of American republicanism. What would they have said, one wonders, of a generation which made eternal vigilance of eighteenth-century ideas the price of twentieth-century liberty? Is it not fair to believe that the American political tradition which they began could be made vital only by the understanding that in each age there must be new fathers and a new founding?

I

The founding fathers were men of remarkably broad interests with an uncanny aptitude for political analysis and for the adaptation of theories to practice. There are some who describe this phenomenon as no more than the heritage of humanism which the American enlightenment merely re-embodied. Certainly the statesmen who shaped the Republic in its first form were confronting essentially the same issues as those formulated by the Renaissance humanists: the attempt to reconcile speculative thinking on the nature of man with the immediate task of creating a new political and social order. They differed from More, Erasmus, and their fellows in that these modern humanists were under more pressure to apply their theories to the urgent task at hand. But there is something breath-taking about the re-embodiment of broad humanist principles in a struggling and relatively unsophisticated people, beset on every side by the problems of living. The "fathers" therefore deserve either spontaneous admiration or informed respect, whether we study their ideas and actions as we find them, or trace their intellectual heritage to another age.

Of the first statesmen of the Republic, four—Jefferson, Madison, John Adams, and Hamilton—trained their sights higher than did any others. Addressing themselves to more than practical considerations, they seemed to be genuinely inspired by the historical uniqueness of the experience open to them, to launch a new civilization on a large scale. In final outcome, they proved equal to the challenge of planning republican government, and they could only have become so because they tried to understand not only the buried sources of power, but the moral objectives of good government. In a sense they were, as Hamilton once contemptuously declared, "speculative" thinkers and "empirics." Even Hamilton himself belonged to the company he criticized, for he, with the others, assessed what he already found in existence as social habit and political tradition; he built upon that which was already "given"; and recommended, according to his lights, the best direction of change.

Jefferson, the greatest of them all, was conspicuously devoted to the theory and practice of good government. Further, he was actively critical of his own *methods* of establishing political judgments, and he was intellectually prepared to examine the logical, philosophical, scientific, or sentimental elements in his views of society. He learned to style himself an "ideologist," by which term he meant to identify himself with his friends, the French philosophers, who had founded a school of thought known as "Ideology" in the Napoleonic period. Hamilton, Madison, and Adams as well as Jefferson contributed characteristic ways of thought, individual tempers of belief which were to be important not only in the era of the Republic but for America thenceforth. The principles of the four philosopher-statesmen taken together almost define the range of our national ideology—our objectives, our character as a people, our economic and social patterns, our "Americanism."

The challenge of creating a new form of government gave rise to an atmosphere of intellectual adventure, in which the Platonic vision of the philosopher-king could for one brief period take on American reality. "Until philosophers take to government, or those who now govern become philosophers," Plato had boldly written, "so that government and philosophy unite, there will be no end to the miseries of states." In the timeless analogy of the cave in the *Republic,* the philosophers who struggle to free themselves from the chains of ignorance and superstition make their way to the light outside. They see the truth. Loving its clarity, they would bask in its light. But the thought of the chained multitude below gives them no rest, and they understand, as Platonic seekers of truth must, that they can not fail to carry glimmerings of light to the poorer minds who inhabit the cave.

The four great philosopher-statesmen of the American "Enlightenment" conform admirably to the Platonic pattern. They grope in authentic Platonic fashion for the true principles of social order, accepting the responsibility of administering the affairs of their less far-sighted fellow men; yet they reject the Platonic ideal as an explicit inspiration. They are willing to exemplify it if they must; but justify it, direct from its ancient source, never. Plato, even for Jefferson who had the most developed philosophic predilections of the group, was too full of metaphysical flights and trances to prove sympathetic to the common-sense orientation of the new nation. In any event the double drive of philosophy and leadership, thought and action, vision and its fortifying concrete detail is heeded by Jefferson, Madison, Adams, and even Hamilton. From the time of Franklin to the present this double drive has dictated a double destiny for the American nation and a dualistic orientation for its literature. In the great period of American political literature, both forces were present without fatal conflict, and lend a peculiar divided charm and predictive importance to this body of writing.

II

The ideology of American democracy began its career with a set of political principles termed "Republican." Although John Adams was quick to warn of the shifting meanings of the term "republic," it became a fixed pole of political reference in American political theory, directly contraposing that other pole, Monarchy, against which the Revolution had been waged. Adams himself believed in republican doctrine and, like the other political leaders of his day, made standard references to the ancient republics as the historical alternative to monarchy and to feudal hierarchic society. Almost everyone in early America agreed on the minimal connotation of the term, either explicitly or by implication. Like late eighteenth-century philosophers elsewhere, they understood that a republic was a government which derived its power from the people "originally," referred back to the people for an ultimate court of appeal in "crucial" questions transcending the ordinary affairs of legislation, and exercised its granted powers through representatives chosen by a majority of the voting citizens. In theory, at least, these voting citizens were further supposed to represent the "will of the people," and while they confided specific powers to their representatives, it was understood that a republic was essentially a government of laws rather than of men.

Were one to try to locate the maximum adherence to this republican ideal, one could project an imaginary political line with the left terminal point designating "maximum faith" and the right terminal point "minimum faith." We should then have to place Jefferson at the left and Hamilton at the right. John Adams accordingly must occupy the middle ground, to the left of Hamilton and the right of Jefferson; but he is also to the right of Madison, who is closer to Jefferson on most fundamental

political matters—although it is important to note that Madison is sometimes closer to Hamilton in economic questions than is either Adams or
Jefferson.

Had Jefferson written no more than the initial draft of the *Declaration of Independence* he would probably have earned his place on the
radical left of our American political line. The achievement of the *Declaration*, if it proves nothing else, certainly established its author's title to
the greatest pen in the patriotic cause. Certain contemporaries, either
through faulty judgment or through jealousy of Jefferson's ability to
fashion a line of fundamental national policy that could sing itself into
the country's ears, challenged the author on the score of "originality."
Madison was incensed for he knew that it was absurd to cavil thus. "The
object," he protested, "was to assert not to discover truths, and to make
them the basis of the Revolutionary Act. The merit of the Draught could
only consist in a lucid communication of human Rights, a condensed
enumeration of the reasons for such an exercise of them, and in a style
and tone appropriate to the great occasion, and to the spirit of the American people." But if the content of the *Declaration* is not enough to establish Jefferson in his pre-eminence on the left, there is the *Notes on the
State of Virginia* (1784), the first American book to become an accidental
"expatriate," published in England and France in pirated versions before it
reached print in the country of its origin. This series of informal essays
ranges far and wide over disputed questions in philosophy, science, politics, and morals, and is the natural discourse of a born humanistic rationalist. Proud of his friend's prowess as a thinker, Madison once observed
that Jefferson was "greatly eminent for the comprehensiveness and fertility of his genius, for the vast extent and rich variety of his acquire-
ments; and particularly distinguished by the philosophic impress left on
every subject which he touched." And then as if the *Notes* had come to
mind, Madison hastened to add: "Nor was he less distinguished from an
early and uniform devotion to the cause of liberty, and systematic preference of a form of Government squared in the strictest degree to the
equal rights of man."

Indeed, although Madison had been a friend, follower, and co-worker
of Jefferson's for many years when he wrote this tribute, it is notable
that in all the advancing and receding waves of historical interpretation
the residual significance of Jefferson's contribution to the American tradition has grown rather than diminished. Of American presidents, this
statesman of the "Enlightenment" most closely approximates the Platonic
philosopher-king. No other incumbent of the presidency, and no other
of the liberal philosophic spirits of his age—many-sided men like Franklin,
Benjamin Rush, and Thomas Cooper—could match Jefferson's happy
union of learning, independence, and competent judgment in diverse fields

such as social morality, government, education, natural science, agriculture, and the arts. What Washington began to do for the American personality by example and by the sheer weight of personal decency and leadership, Jefferson moulded into an intellectualized ideal of social order. The entire development of American affairs, as the definition of our national ideology, is consequently more indebted to Jefferson than it is to any other single man.

This is not to say that Jefferson was an illustration of that *cliché*, the crusader of eighteenth-century enlightenment who preached the gross "goodness" of man and the inevitable rational progress of society. Jefferson, who never wearied of reading history—he knew excellently the classical and the best of modern historians—had come to recognize the hazards of evil in human as in social affairs. He had so acute an awareness of the consequences of entrenching evil men in public positions that he concluded no society would be safe without an informed, alert citizenry participating actively in government. Devoted to human possibilities of growth, he out-distanced the faith of the other philosopher-statesmen— although Madison and Adams both had their areas of hope and solid, if less generous, funds of goodwill. Another way of viewing the difference between Jefferson and all others is to recognize his philosophy of education for what it was—a conscious "ideological" program to create right-thinking, tolerant citizens whose management of local affairs would be but a neighborly orientation for their wise judgment and activity in the affairs of the Union. It was a program fitted to practical needs and political responsibilities, and yet attuned to the highest cultivation of the arts, the sciences, and *belles lettres*.

If it was Jefferson who recommended the fullest participation in political control, just as he sustained the greatest confidence in the educability of the American people, it was Hamilton who had most concern for government as a *force*, who saw little to worry about in its suppressive intrusions upon local or personal "rights." It must be understood that the whole of the political "line" ranging from Jefferson to Madison to Adams and to Hamilton operated within *realistic* limits. Each statesman feared different contingencies, each phrased his hopes in typical or unique terms, each seized upon symbols of approbation or aversion sympathetic to his own personality and to the range of his ideational life. One might almost conclude: *therefore*, the republic was made possible— through the very variety and divergence of the founders' visions, ideas, and wishes.

Hamilton, for instance, saw very clearly the vast economic potentialities of America if the government would ally itself on the side of those who possessed large fortunes and legislate in the direction of the expansion of financial and commercial activities. In the "people" Hamilton bought virtually no stock. He thought they might listen to a debate and repeat with fair accuracy another man's line of argument, but they were by and large susceptible to the flatteries and the manipulations of natural politicians. Indeed, when left to his own selfish and irrational devices, the "great beast" might actually retard the productive energy of the nation, rather than build it up.

It was some time after Hamilton's memorable project of the *Federalist* (1787–88)—that lucid exposition of constitutional republican government, not always consistent in its internal logic, but always impressive in its powerful defense of the need for national unity—that he began to voice his gloomiest thoughts about the survival of the republican experiment in self-government. "It is yet to be determined by experience whether it be consistent with that stability and order in government which are essential to public strength and private security and happiness" he wrote in 1792, having already tasted the strength of Jefferson's principled opposition. He seemed eager to give voice to his fear that republicanism might not "justify itself by its fruits." His progress tory-wise away from what he had called "the fair fabric of republicanism . . . modelled and decorated by the hand of federalism" was complete. In this short-sightedness Hamilton showed himself less of a philosopher and less of a statesman than one would desire. Were it not for the towering importance of certain of his administrative and governmental principles, Hamilton's temperament and the transparency of his self-interest would hardly qualify him as a philosopher-statesman. But there is great penetration in his theory that the extension of national prerogative is indispensable for achieving internal uniformity and efficiency in a genuinely "central" government. And there is undeniable truth in his perception that this is the first essential of defense against foreign powers. Another realistic principle of capitalist development appreciated by Hamilton early in the nation's life was that it was a direct obligation of the government to foster the development of the productive resources and activities of the nation—by whatever combination of interests might prove effective. The first of these principles figures in Hamilton's masterful *First Report on the Public Credit* (1790), when he unhesitatingly decides that "If the voice of humanity pleads more loudly in favor of some [classes of creditors] than of others, the voice of policy, no less than of justice, pleads in favor of all." The second principle is the key argument of Hamilton's classical treatise on protectionism, the *Report on Manufactures* (1791).

By a peculiar concentration of interest, Hamilton attained a definiteness in the body of his belief which sounds surprisingly modern in tone. Read today, his justification of strong efficient government comes close to a native American defense of totalitarian political management. But clever though his analysis was, it did not succeed in reconciling the two inseparable demands of prospering republicanism: national power, exercised to the full by an unimpeded, energetic central administration, and mature responsibility vested in the people of a free society.

The conservatism and legalism of John Adams and Madison explain almost as much about the success of the American republic as they do about the absence of these names from most of the emotional appraisals of the early American tradition. Adams was a testy man, given to incalculable fits of temper that could shake his soul and harden his behavior to the utmost expression of stubbornness. Madison was naturally prudent, neither commanding in person nor captivating in his imaginative vistas. He did not permit himself the occasional exaggerations of the genius which he himself detected in Jefferson, while Adams, unlike Hamilton, *never* lost sight of his high duty to guard the national interest and subordinate his own political welfare to the paramount needs of the American republic. Adams was therefore saved from the extravagancies of Hamiltonian ambition. Since the "mean," in politics, is not golden, not, at any rate, in the "memory of the race," both Adams, the unorthodox federalist, and Madison, the conservative republican, paid the political price of hewing to the Aristotelian middle. Without Adams, the preservation of the dignified ideal of lawful, responsible government and a great example of Bolingbroke's ideal "Patriot King" who comes to guard like an "angel" the destiny and the long-range interests of his country might not have been realized. Without Madison, the amelioration of factional (including "class") strife would not so early have been made a governmental objective, nor would the allocation of sovereign power in the federal and in state contexts have found so subtle an expositor.

The surety of republican foundations, one might say, depended upon the Jeffersonian "left," with its key insights that the preservation of individual freedom and the moral development of cooperative society were the ultimate objectives of free society. It depended upon the Hamiltonian "right" with its knowledge that governments need effective organization and the power which comes from having the substantial productive and financial forces in the nation solidly united behind the administration. The stability of the Republic and its true course depended much upon the labors of Madison, with his realistic conviction that the main purpose of a government is the protection of the many and diverse economic interests into which every country is divided—and with his belief that this protection can be accomplished through a limited, federal republic capable of preventing the monopolistic dictation of one faction or combine over the people of the nation. The experienced conclusion of the elder Adams, that republicanism would not dispel disparities of wealth and station and the aristocracies which there entail, was a grave note of warning. When Adams added that the chief function of wise governors would be to protect the separate but "balanced" powers delegated to them, by compact with the people, in order to prevent tyranny, chaos, or the anarchy of the impassioned mob, he further safeguarded the Republic from what the ancients had been pleased to characterize as the "inevitable" degeneration of the good society.

The main task of republican government, in the long view of John Adams, appeared to be the prevention of excessive power in the hands of any one group. Believing that "vice and folly are so interwoven in all human affairs that they could not, possibly, be wholly separated from them without tearing and rending the whole system of human nature and state," Adams had to put his trust in the rare statesmanlike leaders who would possess wisdom to formulate just laws, and discipline to abide by them. ᴵAdams thought the network of checks and balances would defeat the ambitious and power-hungry few who might design to capture government for their private ends, and would ensure fair representation of the interests of every region in the nation, thereby allowing the propertied and "responsible" citizens who were the mainstay of each region a voice in governmental affairs. By these devices, he thought he could make the most of fallible human nature. A republic, devoted to the interests of the people and operating through their own representatives, should be the outcome of these precautionary mechanisms! Adams accordingly thought his own republicanism as firm as that of anyone, including the leader of the Republican party, his good friend and occasional enemy, Thomas Jefferson, who, in Adams' opinion, differed from himself only in that he was for "liberty and straight hair. I thought curled hair was as republican as straight."

Madison's starting point was less psychological and more sociological. It began with the observed differences in group interests, differences which he took to calling "factions." Factions for Madison were special-interest groups arising out of the fundamental conflict present in every society between those who are rich and maintain their riches, and those who are poor and struggle to relieve their condition. "All civilized societies are divided into different interests and factions" he wrote in the interesting year of 1787, "as they happen to be creditors or debtors—rich or poor—husbandmen, merchants or manufacturers—members of different religious sects—followers of different political leaders—inhabitants of different districts—owners of different kinds of property, etc." The advantage of modern republicanism over other governments Madison expected to find in its ability to impede the full force of factional combinations, preventing them from controlling the state, and from usurping the rights of one or more minorities. Madison as a Virginian feared the added danger that the majority (the North) might suppress the rights of the minority (the South), contending in a letter to Jefferson that "Where the real power in a government lies, there is the danger of oppression. In our Governments the real power lies in the majority of the Community, and the invasion of private rights is chiefly to be apprehended, not from acts of Government contrary to the sense of its constituents, but from acts in which the Government is the mere instrument of the major number of the constituents." Madison thus called to the attention of all men the inflexible requirement that democracies protect the civil rights of minorities from the real or reported "will" of the majority.

Madison and Adams made more of property rights than Jefferson did, but neither of them deserted the democratic theories of natural rights, popular sovereignty, limited government, anti-monarchism and anti-aristocracy. Nor did the two conservatives ever approach Hamilton's justification of plutocracy. Both Adams and Madison inclined to the ideal of a republic which was economically agrarian at base, but supplemented by mercantile and manufacturing interests. Madison perhaps a little more than Adams realized the vital role of credit and of government-financed expansion of the country's natural resources and communications—the role which John Adams' son, John Quincy Adams, was to develop fully in his program of "Internal Improvement." Theoretically, therefore, it was Hamilton, of doubtful birth, who thought most exclusively of the moneyed interests of the country, partly because he saw in them the source of national strength, while Jefferson, graceful and learned "landed esquire," cared most deeply about the widespread independent well-being of the "people," farmers and laborers included. Adams and Madison, each aristocratic in taste in the typical styles of Massachusetts and Virginia, but far from dazzling in the family fortunes to which they were born, were actively promoting a scheme of society favorable to widespread middle-class prosperity and power.

III

The ethical theories of these men were influential factors upon the political and economic views they maintained. Save for the four philosopher-statesmen of the Republic, the American character might never have been given more than haphazard or perfunctory significance. Jefferson, Madison, and John Adams all understood the importance of character for those who would be leaders in a republic, and Hamilton sometimes did and sometimes paid only lip-service to the ideal. Jefferson and Madison and Adams advocated that "the purest and noblest characters" (Madison's phrase) should serve as the people's representatives, since they alone would do so from the "proper motives." Because these men dedicated themselves to the cause of their country before they consulted their immediate personal needs, the inceptive principles of the American republic betoken seekers of truth and wisdom, and good citizens in the Roman sense, rather than mere men of office.

Jefferson, perceiving that government was necessary for the release of man's fullest potentialities, liked to speak of it as of secondary or instrumental value—a habit which was later perversely construed to mean that government was "evil." The range of realistic political choice for Jefferson lay entirely between repressive government and republicanism, and he identified the essence of republicanism as "action by the citizens in person in affairs within their reach and competence, and in all others by representatives, chosen immediately, and removable by themselves. . . ." For this reason, a republic was the "only form of government that is not eternally at open or secret war with the rights of mankind." To achieve republican freedom, citizens must pay a price, the wakefulness of "eternal vigilance," and, therefore, a citizenry trained in the principles of government, an *educated* citizenry, is the indispensable support of freedom.

Thus, subtly and indirectly, a moral climate had been postulated for the America in which republicanism was to be tried. Benevolence and moral sense, self-created will rather than coercive force, are the dynamic daily agents in free society as well as the purely *theoretical* factors of its ethics. "Natural" moralism is opposed to the reputed "natural" rule of force, which Jefferson saw as the breeder of authoritarian society, whether of "kings, hereditary nobles, and priests" or, in the language of our own day, of leaders, demagogues, and commissars. Jefferson's agrarianism, so often made the catch-word for his variety of democracy, is in reality a by-product of an almost sentimental preference for the simplicity of classical republicanism joined to the supposed purity of "primitive" Christianity. Yet when Jefferson realized that the evolution of his nation demanded the self-sufficiency and expansion of her manufacture and trade —when he perceived that free society would be jeopardized if it were unable to defend itself on the high seas—he protested that "he . . . who is now against domestic manufacture, must be for reducing us either to dependence . . . or to be clothed in skins, and to live like wild beasts in dens and caverns. I am not one of these; experience has taught me that manufactures are now as necessary to our independence as to our comfort. . . ." Despite this, Jefferson's instinctive trust reposed in the fair and free interchange of nation with nation, as in citizen with citizen— which is to say that he was a man of peace, conceiving productive society basically as a peaceful society, an earnest judgment in which he was fully joined by James Madison.

Economically and politically, to Hamilton's expert eye the softer fringe of social morality was not a subject for enthusiasm nor even for *belief*. "The seeds of war are sown thickly in the human breast," Hamilton had written, and the rivalry that precipitated wars, in his view,

stemmed partly from "the temper of societies," and partly from the human
disposition to "prefer partial to general interest." Coming to terms with
self-interested reality was accordingly Hamilton's basic preoccupation,
whether that "reality" meant strong armies and navies for defense against
foreign powers, or a strong system of national credit. In an ultimate separation of himself from his idealistic associates, whom he termed "political
empirics," Hamilton in an important unfinished paper called "Defence of
the Funding System" (1795), identified the "true" politician as one who
"takes human nature (and human society its aggregate) as he finds it, a
compound of good and ill qualities, of good and ill tendencies, endued
with powers and actuated by passions and propensities which blend enjoyment with suffering and make the causes of welfare the causes of misfortune." Afraid to warp this fundamental human complex by urging a
happiness not suited to it, the true politician supposedly aims at the social
measures designed to "make men happy according to their natural bent,
which multiply the sources of individual enjoyment and increase national
resources and strength." The great objective of the statesman should thus
be to find the cement for compounding diverse elements of a state into a
"rock" of national strength.

Governments would not need to be afraid to take power, Hamilton
believed, could they strip themselves of false attitudes of modesty. In the
logic of economic stability and national expansion, of credit and appropriations and "sound policy" versus the misguided pleadings of "common
humanity," Hamilton saw an unanswerable imperative: to wit, that the
"sacred" right of property must be defended by the laws and by the
constitutions of the land and that even the non-propertied groups in the
community should protect property rights lest the "general principles of
public order" be subverted.

John Adams, the self-styled "John Yankee" who could not bear to
kowtow to "John Bull"—nor for that matter to any foreign power—seems
more at home in Jefferson's and Madison's company than he is with Hamilton, the "boss" of his own party. Without Adams, the democratic
precedent of the New England meeting-hall, the training green, and the
system of self-support for local schools, churches, and cultural institutions
might have spoken only with muffled voice in the American tradition.
The political "virtues" of Massachusetts even Jefferson commended,
pointing to that state as the best exponent of the theme that knowledge is
power. In Adams' championship of New England, there is a nucleus of
national pride useful and perhaps necessary to a rising nation. To this
Adams personally added the dignified appeal that however much republican government consisted of equal laws justly administered, it further
required consistent benevolence and encouragement for the arts and sciences. Almost a humanist, but never quite freed of a Puritan sense of guilt

and sin, Adams privately reveled in the classics just as Jefferson did. The late correspondence which flourished between Adams and Jefferson as the two aged statesmen with great *éclat* enacted the roles of sages in retirement is a phenomenon of tireless learning and peppery jest, joined in a correspondence the like of which is not known elsewhere in the annals of American statesmen.

IV

Such were the philosopher-kings of the American "Enlightenment." However often they may have erred—in description, in prognosis, in emphasis, and sometimes in behavior as statesmen—they seem to have possessed that rare wisdom about human and political affairs which never quite exhausts its power to suggest. On occasions, it restores its own original vitality and suffices to sanction an important change in national or international policy. We know that in the curious reversals of history, the truths of an age are likely to suffer sea-change. As Lincoln pointed out, the maxim "all men are created equal," once thought a self-evident truth, is termed a "self-evident lie" once we have "grown fat, and lost all dread of being slaves ourselves." So it may be with the far-ranging insights and veridical principles of the philosopher-statesmen of the Republic. Since the advent of the Jacksonian age—a "calamitous" presidency in Madison's prediction—the objectives of tempered democracy have been often ignored or ingeniously misinterpreted. As the letters and state papers of the Republican era again come under review, it is apparent that democratic ideology can still benefit by its own articulate original. The foundation of our national literature is present here, as well in the practical literature of ideas as in the imitative experiments of the deliberately "literary" work of the day.

16 *Henry Steele Commager*

THE CONSTITUTION:

WAS IT AN ECONOMIC DOCUMENT?

As the most important document in the history of the United States, the Constitution of 1787 inevitably presents to historians the challenge of interpretation. Inevitably it raises questions about its meaning in the world of the 1780's and about the purposes and interests which guided

Reprinted with permission from *American Heritage, The Magazine of History,* X (December, 1958), 58–61, 100–3.

the Founding Fathers in drawing it up. The most important answer to such questions, surely, was given by Charles A. Beard in *An Economic Interpretation of the Constitution* (1913). Accepted without significant challenge for some four decades, Beard's *Interpretation* has come under widespread criticism during the 1950's. Beard has been questioned regarding the way he has used his evidence. He has also been questioned regarding the assumptions he made about the Founding Fathers.

In the following essay, Henry Steele Commager tests Beard's *Interpretation* by referring it to the actual provisions of the Constitution. The subject lies squarely within the province of Professor Commager's interest. Author and editor of a vast number of books on American history, Professor Commager has been largely concerned with the history of American ideas and with political and constitutional ideas above all. At present Professor of American History and American Studies at Amherst, he has also taught at Columbia University, has lectured in many foreign universities, has written (with Samuel Eliot Morison) one of the most popular texts in American history, and is co-editor (with Richard B. Morris) of The New American Nation Series.

What Professor Commager says in the essay below will elicit many questions from the student about the changing outlook of historians not only toward the Constitution but also toward other major acts and actors in our past. Why does the outlook of historians change? In what respects is an economic interpretation of history limited? In what respects is it justified? What is the relevance here of Beard's assertion that he was offering his *Interpretation* as merely one way of looking at the Constitution? How much more valid than an economic interpretation is a political one? If Beard construed the Constitution in the light of his times, to what extent may we be construing it in the light of ours? Why have we come to approve where he had earlier come to doubt? To what extent are our respective views mutually exclusive, to what extent are they basically reconcilable? In a very profound sense, the Constitution began and has defined the characteristics of the American experience. Its making demands our closest study.

By June 26, 1787, tempers in the Federal Convention were already growing short, for gentlemen had come to the explosive question of representation in the upper chamber. Two days later Franklin moved to invoke divine guidance, and his motion was shunted aside only because there was no money with which to pay a chaplain and the members were unprepared to appeal to Heaven without an intermediary. It was not surprising that when James Madison spoke to the question of representation in the proposed legislature, he was conscious of the solemnity of the occasion. We are, he said, framing a system "which we wish to last for ages" and one that might "decide forever the fate of Republican Government."

It was an awful thought, and when, a few days later, Gouverneur Morris spoke to the same subject he felt the occasion a most solemn one: even the irrepressible Morris could be solemn. "He came here," he observed (so Madison noted),

as a Representative of America: he flattered himself he came here in some degree as a Representative of the whole human race: for the whole human race will be affected by the proceedings of this Convention. He wished gentlemen to extend their views beyond the present moment of time; beyond the narrow limits . . . from which they derive their political origin. . . .

Much has been said of the sentiments of the people. They were unknown. They could not be known. All that we can infer is that if the plan we recommend be reasonable & right; all who have reasonable minds and sound intentions will embrace it . . .

These were by no means occasional sentiments only. They were sentiments that occurred again and again throughout the whole of that long hot summer, until they received their final, eloquent expression from the aged Franklin in that comment on the rising, not the setting, sun. Even during the most acrimonious debates members were aware that they were framing a constitution for ages to come, that they were creating a model for people everywhere on the globe; there was a lively sense of responsibility and even of destiny. Nor can we now, as we contemplate that Constitution which is the oldest written national constitution, and that federal system which is one of the oldest and the most successful in history, regard these appeals to posterity as merely rhetorical.

That men are not always conscious either of what they do or of the motives that animate them is a familiar rather than a cynical observation. Some 45 years ago Charles A. Beard propounded an economic interpretation of the Constitution—an interpretation which submitted that the Constitution was *essentially* (that is a crucial word) an economic document—and that it was carried through the Convention and the state ratifying conventions by interested economic groups for economic reasons. "The Constitution," Mr. Beard concluded, "was essentially an economic document based upon the concept that the fundamental private rights of property are anterior to government and morally beyond the reach of popular majorities."

At the time it was pronounced, that interpretation caused something of a sensation, and Mr. Beard was himself eventually to comment with justifiable indignation on the meanness and the vehemence of the attacks upon it—and him. Yet the remarkable thing about the economic interpretations is not the criticism it inspired but the support it commanded. For within a few years it had established itself as the new orthodoxy, and those who took exception to it were stamped either as professional patriots—perhaps secret Sons or Daughters of the Revolution—or naïve academicians who had never learned the facts of economic life.

The attraction that the economic interpretation had for the generation of the twenties and thirties—and that it still exerts even into the fifties —is one of the curiosities of our cultural history, but it is by no means an inexplicable one. To a generation of materialists Beard's thesis made clear that the stuff of history was material. To a generation disillusioned by the exploitations of big business it discovered that the past, too, had been ravaged by economic exploiters. To a generation that looked with skeptical eyes upon the claims of Wilsonian idealism and all but rejoiced in the frustration, it suggested that all earlier idealisms and partiotisms— even the idealism and patriotism of the framers—had been similarly flawed by selfishness and hypocrisy.

Yet may it not be said of *An Economic Interpretation of the Constitution* that it is not a conclusion but a point of departure? It explains a great deal about the forces that went into the making of the Constitution, and a great deal, too, about the men who assembled in Philadelphia in 1787, but it tells us extraordinarily little about the document itself. And it tells us even less about the historical meaning of that document.

What were the objects of the Federal Convention? The immediate objects were to restore order; to strengthen the public credit; to enable the United States to make satisfactory commercial treaties and agreements; to provide conditions in which trade and commerce could flourish; to facilitate management of the western lands and of Indian affairs. All familiar enough. But what, in the light of history, were the grand objects of the Convention? What was it that gave Madison and Morris and Wilson and King and Washington himself a sense of destiny?

There were two grand objects—objects inextricably interrelated. The first was to solve the problem of federalism, that is, the problem of the distribution of powers among governments. Upon the wisdom with which members of the Convention distinguished between powers of a general and powers of a local nature, and assigned these to their appropriate governments, would depend the success or failure of the new experiment.

But it was impossible for the children of the eighteenth century to talk or think of powers without thinking of power, and this was a healthy realism. No less troublesome—and more fundamental—than the problem of the distribution of powers, was the problem of sanctions. How were they to enforce the terms of the distribution and impose limits upon all the governments involved? It was one thing to work out the most ideal distribution of general and local powers. It was another thing to see to it that the states abided by their obligations under the Articles of Union and that the national government respected the autonomy of the states and the liberty of individuals.

Those familiar with the Revolutionary era know that the second of these problems was more difficult than the first. Americans had, indeed, learned how to limit government: the written constitutions, the bills of rights, the checks and balances, and so forth. They had not yet learned (nor had anyone) how to "substitute the mild magistracy of the law for the cruel and violent magistracy of force." The phrase is Madison's.

Let us return to the *Economic Interpretation*. The correctness of Beard's analysis of the origins and backgrounds of the membership of the Convention, of the arguments in the Convention, and of the methods of assuring ratification, need not be debated. But these considerations are, in a sense, irrelevant and immaterial. For though they are designed to illuminate the document itself, in fact they illuminate only the processes of its manufacture.

The idea that property considerations were paramount in the minds of those assembled in Philadelphia is misleading and unsound and is borne out neither by the evidence of the debates in the Convention nor by the Constitution itself. The Constitution was not *essentially* an economic document. It was, and is, *essentially* a political document. It addresses itself to the great and fundamental question of the distribution of powers between governments. The Constitution was—and is—a document that attempts to provide sanctions behind that distribution; a document that sets up, through law, a standing rule to live by and provides legal machinery for the enforcement of that rule. These are political, not economic functions.

Not only were the principles that animated the framers political rather than economic; the solutions that they formulated to the great questions that confronted them were dictated by political, not by economic considerations.

Here are two fundamental challenges to the Beard interpretation: first, the Constitution is primarily a document in federalism; and second, the Constitution does not in fact confess or display the controlling influence of those who held that "the fundamental private rights of property are anterior to government and morally beyond the reach of popular majorities."

Let us look more closely at these two contentions. The first requires little elaboration or vindication, for it is clear to all students of the Revolutionary era that the one pervasive and overbranching problem of that generation was the problem of imperial organization. How to get the various parts of any empire to work together for common purposes? How to get central control—over war, for example, or commerce or money—without impairing local autonomy? How, on the other hand, preserve personal liberty and local self-government without impairing the effectiveness of the central government? This was one of the oldest problems in political science, and it is one of the freshest—as old as the history of the Greek city-states; as new as the recent debate over Federal aid to education or the Bricker amendment.

The British failed to solve the problem of imperial order; when pushed to the wall they had recourse to the hopelessly doctrinaire Declaratory Act, which was, in fact, a declaration of political bankruptcy; as Edmund Burke observed, no people is going to be argued into slavery. The Americans then took up the vexatious problem. The Articles of Confederation were satisfactory enough as far as the distribution of powers was concerned, but wholly wanting in sanctions. The absence of sanctions spelled the failure of the Articles—and this failure led to the Philadelphia Convention.

Now it will be readily conceded that many, if not most, of the questions connected with federalism were economic in character. Involved were such practical matters as taxation, the regulation of commerce, coinage, western lands, slavery, and so forth. Yet the problem that presented itself to the framers was not whether government should exercise authority over such matters as these; it was *which* government should exercise such authority—and how should it be exercised?

There were, after all, no anarchists at the Federal Convention. Everyone agreed that *some* government had to have authority to tax, raise armies, regulate commerce, coin money, control contracts, enact bankruptcy legislation, regulate western territories, make treaties, and do all the things that government must do. But where should these authorities be lodged—with the state governments or with the national government they were about to erect, or with both?

This question was a political, not an economic, one. And the solution at which the framers arrived was based upon a sound understanding of politics, and need not be explained by reference to class attachments or security interests.

Certainly if the framers were concerned primarily or even largely with protecting property against popular majorities, they failed signally to carry out their purposes. It is at this point in our consideration of the *Economic Interpretation of the Constitution* that we need to employ what our literary friends call *explication du texte*. For the weakest link in the Beard interpretation is precisely the crucial one—the document itself. Mr. Beard makes amply clear that those who wrote the Constitution were members of the propertied classes,[1] and that many of them were personally involved in the outcome of what they were about to do; he makes out a persuasive case that the division over the Constitution was along economic lines. What he does not make clear is how or where the Constitution itself reflects all these economic influences.

Much is made of the contract clause and the paper money clause of the Constitution. No state may impair the obligations of a contract—whatever those words mean, and they apparently did not mean to the framers quite what Chief Justice Marshall later said they meant in *Fletcher v. Peck* or *Dartmouth College v. Woodward*. No state may emit bills of credit or make anything but gold and silver coin legal tender in payment of debts.

These are formidable prohibitions, and clearly reflect the impatience of men of property with the malpractices of the states during the Confederation. Yet quite aside from what the states may or may not have done, who can doubt that these limitations upon the states followed a sound principle—the principle that control of coinage and money belonged to the central, not the local governments, and the principle that local jurisdictions should not be able to modify or overthrow contracts recognized throughout the Union?

What is most interesting in this connection is what is so often overlooked: that the framers did not write any comparable prohibitions upon the United States government. The United States was not forbidden to impair the obligation of its contracts, not at least in the Constitution as it came from the hands of its property-conscious framers. Possibly the Fifth Amendment may have squinted toward such a prohibition; we need not determine that now, for the Fifth Amendment was added by the *states* after the Constitution had been ratified. So, too, the emission of bills of credit and the making other than gold and silver legal tender were limitations on the states, but not on the national government. There was, in fact, a lively debate over the question of limiting the authority of the national government in the matter of bills of credit. When the question came up on August 16, Gouverneur Morris threatened that "The Monied interest will oppose the plan of Government, if paper emissions be not

---

[1] "A majority of the members were lawyers by profession.

"Most of the members came from towns, on or near the cost, that is, from the regions in which personalty was largely concentrated.

"Not one member represented in his immediate personal economic interests the small farming or mechanic classes.

"The overwhelming majority of members, at least five-sixths, were immediately, directly, and personally interested in the outcome of their labors at Philadelphia, and were to a greater or less extent economic beneficiaries from the adoption of the Constitution."

Beard, *An Economic Interpretation of the Constitution.*

prohibited." In the end the Convention dropped out a specific authorization to emit bills of credit, but pointedly did not prohibit such action. Just where this left the situation troubled Chief Justice Chase's Court briefly three-quarters of a century later; the Court recovered its balance, and the sovereign power of the government over money was not again *successfully* challenged.

Nor were there other specific limitations of an economic character upon the powers of the new government that was being erected on the ruins of the old. The framers properly gave the Congress power to regulate commerce with foreign nations and among the states. The term commerce—as Hamilton and Adair (and Crosskey, too!) have made clear—was broadly meant, and the grant of authority, too, was broad. The framers gave Congress the power to levy taxes and, again, wrote no limitations into the Constitution except as to the apportionment of direct taxes; it remained for the most conservative of Courts to reverse itself, and common sense, and discover that the framers had intended to forbid an income tax! Today, organizations that invoke the very term "constitutional" are agitating for an amendment placing a quantitative limit upon income taxes that may be levied; fortunately, Madison's generation understood better the true nature of governmental power.

The framers gave Congress—in ambiguous terms, to be sure—authority to make "all needful Rules and Regulations respecting the Territory or other Property" of the United States, and provided that "new states may be admitted." These evasive phrases gave little hint of the heated debates in the Convention over western lands. Those who delight to find narrow and undemocratic sentiments in the breasts of the framers never cease to quote a Gouverneur Morris or an Elbridge Gerry on the dangers of the West, and it is possible to compile a horrid catalogue of such statements. But what is significant is not what framers said, but what they did. They did not place any limits upon the disposition of western territory, or establish any barriers against the admission of western states.

The fact is that we look in vain *in the Constitution itself* for any really effective guarantee for property or any effective barriers against what Beard calls "the reach of popular majorities."

It will be argued, however, that what the framers feared was the *states*, and that the specific prohibitions against state action, together with the broad transfer of economic powers from state to nation, were deemed sufficient guarantee against state attacks upon property. As for the national government, care was taken to make that sufficiently aristocratic, sufficiently the representative of the propertied classes, and sufficiently checked and limited so that it would not threaten basic property interests.

It is at this juncture that the familiar principle of limitation on governmental authority commands our attention. Granted the wisest distribution of powers among governments, what guarantee was there that power would be properly exercised? What guarantees were there against the abuse of power? What assurance was there that the large states would not ride roughshod over the small, that majorities would not crush minorities or minorities abuse majorities? What protection was there against mobs, demagogues, dangerous combinations of interests or of states? What protection was there for the commercial interest, the planter interest, the slave interest, the securities interests, the land speculator interests?

It was Madison who most clearly saw the real character of this problem and who formulated its solution. It was not that the people as such were dangerous; "The truth was," he said on July 11, "that all men having power ought to be distrusted to a certain degree." Long before Lord Acton coined the aphorism, the Revolutionary leaders had discovered that power corrupts. They understood, too, the drive for power on the part of individuals and groups. All this is familiar to students of *The Federalist*, No. 10. It should be familiar to students of the debates in Philadelphia, for there, too, Madison set forth his theory and supported it with a wealth of argument. Listen to him on one of the early days of the Convention, June 6, when he is discussing the way to avoid abuses of republican liberty—abuses which "prevailed in the largest as well as the smallest [states] . . ."

. . . And were we not thence admonished [he continued] to enlarge the sphere as far as the nature of the Government would admit. This was the only defence against the inconveniences of democracy *consistent with the democratic form of Government* [our italics]. All civilized Societies would be divided into different Sects, Factions & interests, as they happened to consist of rich & poor, debtors and creditors, the landed, the manufacturing, the commercial interests, the inhabitants of this district or that district, the followers of this political leader or that political leader, the disciples of this religious Sect or that religious Sect. In all cases where a majority are united by a common interest or passion, the rights of the minority are in danger. . . . In a Republican Govt. the Majority if united have always an opportunity [to oppress the minority. What is the remedy?] The only remedy is to enlarge the sphere, & thereby divide the community into so great a number of interests & parties, that in the first place a majority will not be likely at the same moment to have a common interest separate from that of the whole or of the minority; and in the second place, that in case they should have such an interest, they may not be apt to unite in the pursuit of it. It was incumbent on us then to try this remedy, and . . . to frame a republican system on such a scale & in such a form as will controul all the evils which have been experienced.

This long quotation is wonderfully eloquent of the attitude of the most sagacious of the framers. Madison, Wilson, Mason, Franklin, as well as Gerry, Morris, Pinckney, and Hamilton feared power. They feared power whether exercised by a monarch, an aristocracy, an army, or a majority, and they were one in their determination to write into fundamental law limitations on the arbitrary exercise of that power. To assume, as Beard so commonly does, that the fear of the misuse of power by majorities was either peculiar to the Federalists or more ardent with them than with their opponents, is mistaken. Indeed it was rather the anti-Federalists who were most deeply disturbed by the prospect of majority rule; they, rather than the Federalists, were the "men of little faith." Thus it was John Lansing, Jr., of New York (he who left the Convention rather than have any part in its dangerous work) who said that "all free constitutions are formed with two views—to deter the governed from crime, and the governors from tyranny." And the ardent Patrick Henry, who led the attack on the Constitution in the Virginia Convention—and almost defeated it—complained not of too little democracy in that document, but too much.

The framers, to be sure, feared the powers of the majority, as they feared all power unless controlled. But they were insistent that, in the last analysis, there must be government by majority; even conservatives like Morris and Hamilton made this clear. Listen to Hamilton, for example, at the very close of the Convention. Elbridge Gerry, an opponent of the Constitution, had asked for a reconsideration of the provision for calling a constitutional convention, alleging that this opened the gate to a majority that could "bind the union to innovations that may subvert the State-Constitutions altogether." To this Hamilton replied that

There was no greater evil in subjecting the people of the U.S. to the major voice than the people of a particular State. . . . It was equally desirable now that an easy mode should be established for supplying defects which will probably appear in the New System. . . . There could be no danger in giving this power, as the people would finally decide in the case.

And on July 13, James Wilson, another staunch Federalist, observed that "The majority of people wherever found ought in all questions to govern the minority."

But we need not rely upon what men said; there is too much of making history by quotation anyway. Let us look rather at what men did. We can turn again to the Constitution itself. Granted the elaborate system of checks and balances: the separation of powers, the bicameral legislature, the executive veto, and so forth—checks found in the state constitutions as well, and in our own democratic era as in the earlier one—what provision did the framers make against majority tyranny? What provisions did they write into the Constitution against what Randolph called "democratic licentiousness"?

They granted equality of representation in the Senate. If this meant that conservative Delaware would have the same representation in the upper chamber as democratic Pennsylvania, it also meant that democratic Rhode Island would have the same representation as conservative South Carolina. But the decision for equality of representation was not dictated by considerations either economic or democratic, but rather by the re-calcitrance of the small states. Indeed, though it is difficult to generalize here, on the whole it is true that it was the more ardent Federalists who favored proportional representation in both houses.

They elaborated a most complicated method of electing a Chief Ex-ecutive, a method designed to prevent the easy expression of any majority will. Again the explanation is not simple. The fact was that the framers did not envision the possibility of direct votes for presidential candidates which would not conform to state lines and interests and thus lead to dissension and confusion. Some method, they thought, must be designated to overcome the force of state prejudices (or merely of parochialism) and get an election; the method they anticipated was a preliminary elimination contest by the electoral college and then eventual election by the House. This, said George Mason, was what would occur nineteen times out of twenty.[2] There is no evidence in the debates that the complicated method finally hit upon for electing a President was designed either to frustrate popular majorities or to protect special economic interests; its purpose was to overcome state pride and particularism.

Senators and Presidents, then, would not be the creatures of democ-racy. But what guarantee was there that senators would be representatives of property interests, or that the President himself would recognize the "priority of property"? Most states had property qualifications for office holding, but there are none in the Federal Constitution. As far as the Constitution is concerned, the President, congressmen, and Supreme Court justices can all be paupers.

Both General Charles Cotesworth Pinckney and his young cousin Charles, of South Carolina, were worried about this. The latter proposed a property qualification of $100,000 (a tidy sum in those days) for the Presidency, half that for the judges, and substantial sums for members of Congress. Franklin rebuked him. He was distressed, he said, to hear any-thing "that tended to debase the spirit of the common people." More sur-

[2] It has happened twice: Jefferson vs. Burr (1801) and J. Q. Adams vs. Clay, Jackson, and Crawford (1825).

prising was the rebuke from that stout conservative, John Dickinson. "He doubted," Madison reports, "the policy of interweaving into a Republican constitution a veneration for wealth. He had always understood that a veneration for poverty & virtue were the objects of republican encouragement." Pinckney's proposal was overwhelmingly rejected.

What of the members of the lower house? When Randolph opened "the main business" on May 29 he said the remedy for the crisis that men faced must be "the republican principle," and two days later members were discussing the fourth resolution, which provided for election to the lower house by the people. Roger Sherman of Connecticut thought that "the people should have as little to do as may be about the Government," and Gerry hastened to agree in words now well-worn from enthusiastic quotation that "The evils we experience flow from the excess of democracy." These voices were soon drowned out, however. Mason "argued strongly for an election . . . by the people. It was to be the grand depository of the democratic principle of the Govt." And the learned James Wilson, striking the note to which he was to recur again and again, made clear that he was for "raising the federal pyramid to a considerable altitude, and for that reason wished to give it as broad a basis as possible." He thought that both branches of the legislature—and the President as well, for that matter—should be elected by the people. "The Legislature," he later observed, "ought to be the most exact transcript of the whole Society."

A further observation is unhappily relevant today. It was a maxim with John Adams that "where annual elections end, there tyranny begins," and the whole Revolutionary generation was committed to a frequent return to the source of authority. But the framers put into the Constitution no limits on the number of terms which Presidents or congressmen could serve. It was not that the question was ignored; it received elaborate attention. It was rather that the generation that wrote the Constitution was better grounded in political principles than is our own; that it did not confuse, as we so often do, quantitative and qualitative limitations; and that—in a curious way—it had more confidence in the intelligence and the good will of the people than we seem to have today. It is, in any event, our own generation that has the dubious distinction of writing into the Constitution the first quantitative limitation on the right of the majority to choose their President. It is not the generation of the framers that was undemocratic; it is our generation that is undemocratic.

It is relevant to note, too, that the Constitution contains no property qualification for voting. Most states, to be sure, had such qualifications—in general a freehold or its equivalent—and the Constitution assimilated such qualifications as states might establish. Yet the framers, whether for reasons practical or philosophical we need not determine, made no serious efforts to write any property qualifications for voting into the Constitution itself.

The question of popular control came up clearly in one other connection as well: the matter of ratification. Should the Constitution be ratified by state legislatures, or by conventions? The practical arguments for the two methods were nicely balanced. The decisive argument was not, however, one of expediency but of principle. "To the people with whom all power remains that has not been given up in the Constitutions derived from them" we must resort, said Mason. Madison put the matter on principle, too. "He considered the difference between a system founded on the Legislatures only, and one founded on the people, to be the true difference between a *league* or *treaty* and a *Constitution*." Ellsworth's motion to refer the Constitution to legislatures was defeated by a vote of eight to two, and the resolution to refer it to conventions passed with only Delaware in the negative.

Was the Constitution designed to place private property beyond the reach of majorities? If so, the framers did a very bad job. They failed to write into it the most elementary safeguards for property. They failed to write into it limitations on the tax power, or prohibitions against the abuse of the money power. They failed to provide for rule by those whom Adams was later to call the wise and the rich and the wellborn. What they did succeed in doing was to create a system of checks and balances and adjustments and accommodations that would effectively prevent the suppression of most minorities by majorities. They took advantage of the complexity, the diversity, the pluralism, of American society and economy to encourage a balance of interests. They worked out sound and lasting political solutions to the problems of class, interest, section, race, religion, party.

Perhaps the most perspicacious comment on this whole question of the threat from turbulent popular majorities against property and order came, *mirabile dictu,* from the dashing young Charles Pinckney of South Carolina—he of the "lost" Pinckney Plan. On June 25 Pinckney made a major speech and thought it important enough to write out and give to Madison. The point of departure was the hackneyed one of the character of the second branch of the legislature, but the comments were an anticipation of De Tocqueville and Lord Bryce. We need not, Pinckney asserted, fear the rise of class conflicts in America, nor take precautions against them.

The genius of the people, their mediocrity of situation & the prospects which are afforded their industry in a Country which must be a new one for centuries are unfavorable to the rapid distinction of ranks. . . . If equality is . . . the leading feature of the U. States [he asked], where then are the riches & wealth whose representation & protection is the peculiar province of this permanent body [the Senate]. Are they in the hands of the few who may be called rich; in the possession of less than a hundred citizens? certainly not. They are in the great body of the people . . . [There was no likelihood that a privileged body would ever develop in the United States, he added, either from the landed interest, the moneyed interest, or the mercantile.] Besides, Sir, I apprehend that on this point the policy of the U. States has been much mistaken. We have unwisely considered ourselves as the inhabitants of an old instead of a new country. We have adopted the maxims of a State full of people . . . The people of this country are not only very different from the inhabitants of any State we are acquainted with in the modern world; but I assert that their situation is distinct from either the people of Greece or of Rome . . . Our true situation appears to me to be this—a new extensive Country containing within itself the materials for forming a Government capable of extending to its citizens all the blessings of civil & religious liberty—capable of making them happy at home. This is the great end of Republican Establishments. . . .

＼Not a government cunningly contrived to protect the interests of property, but one capable of extending to its citizens the blessings of liberty and happiness—was that not, after all, what the framers created?

17 *Alpheus T. Mason*

THE NATURE OF OUR
FEDERAL UNION RECONSIDERED

If the American genius is politics, its masterpiece is the Constitution. Now enveloped in sanctity and myth, the Constitution was in its day a practical solution of a real problem. Seen in perspective, the problem has been inherent in all of American experience, from the planting of the colonies in the seventeenth century to the pre-eminence of the United States in world affairs in the twentieth. In an essentially federal order, whether of a British metropolis and her colonies or of an American national government and its states, the basic question is how to adjust the conflicting claims to jurisdiction of the center and of the localities. In an order posited on broadly democratic concepts, the question is also whether power resides in all the people acting as a national community or whether it resides only in the people acting

Reprinted with the permission of the author and publisher from *The Political Science Quarterly*, LXV (December, 1950), 502-21.

through their localities: through, in the American instance, their colonial or state governments.

How did the Constitution resolve these questions? What sort of federal union did the Founding Fathers think they had fashioned? Their thought is brought under a revealing light in the following essay by Alpheus T. Mason, McCormick Professor of Jurisprudence at Princeton University and author of several important volumes on American political and legal history. Professor Mason discloses how the two great writers of *The Federalist Papers*, James Madison and Alexander Hamilton, proceeded from contradictory premises concerning the source of power in the Constitution and concerning, therefore, the essential nature of the republic they were establishing. The contradiction, Professor Mason explains, made the course from Philadelphia in 1787 to Fort Sumter in 1861 a direct and inevitable one. One need not look elsewhere for the causes of the Civil War.

His explanation is a challenging one. Yet may not one question his view that the difference of political premises must certainly have ended in conflict? The Civil War came only because deeper historical conditions—social, economic, psychological—had invested the difference of premises with compelling interest, vitality, and passion. Indeed, the student must see the long-range problem of relations between the center and the localities from the time of Jamestown until today within the context of these deeper conditions.

Doing so, he will understand that the mother country and the colonies comprised a federal order, *de facto*, before the attempt at imperial reforms was made during the 1760's. He will understand how the American Revolution was the rejection in one decade of a central jurisdiction which the Founding Fathers were, paradoxically, constrained to establish for themselves in another decade. He will understand how the transformation of a loosely joined agrarian society into one more closely knit by commerce, industry, and finance in turn transformed a theory affirming local sovereignty into one affirming the sovereignty of the nation.

The conflict over jurisdiction which runs through the American past may serve the student as a mirror to the national experience. In that conflict, he will find reflected the larger image of a people in growth, contention, and change. The Constitution of 1787 will offer him a dramatic reflection, at a critical moment, of this image.

The thinking of any age, including our own, tends to be pervaded by the illusory notion that human beings are at some final crossroads or other, that men must choose and choose quickly between extreme alternatives. Thereafter, the ceaseless struggle which had heretofore racked mankind presumably ends, and society sinks at last into the normalcy of peace. Even the politically astute James Madison sometimes spoke in apocalyptic terms. The Philadelphia Convention, as he saw it in 1787, was deciding "forever the fate of Republican Government. . . ." "The two extremes before us," he said, "are a perfect separation and a perfect incorporation of the 13 States. In the first case they would be independent nations subject to no law, but the law of nations. In the last, they would be mere counties of one entire republic, subject to one common law." Subsequent proceedings proved that the possibilities were far less narrow, various compromises being achieved, even on the most controversial issues. Yet these remarkable successes did not preclude future controversy or bring national repose. The Constitution provided only the basis on which the nation could resume the march of history—a workable makeshift perhaps to avoid "civil war," as Hamilton suggested, ". . . dismemberment of the Union and monarchies in different portions of it."

For their achievement, the Founding Fathers have not always been applauded. They have, on occasion, been accused of writing into the Constitution itself an irreconcilable ambiguity. In the struggle over ratification, strategic considerations drove the contestants to minimize or to exaggerate, thus making the evidence as to the Constitution's meaning less than clear-cut. To allay the fears of opponents, advocates of ratification, especially Madison, said things which, in later years, proved embarrassing to him and misleading to scholars. Certain of the Constitution's enemies turned alarmist, portraying the proposed national charter in the most extreme terms. That is why substantial support for the revolutionary changes wrought by the Philadelphia Convention comes especially from those vigorously opposing ratification—Samuel Adams, Patrick Henry, Richard Henry Lee, Luther Martin, among others.

The upshot was that the Constitution, a "bundle of compromises," as someone has described it, was neither altogether satisfactory, nor crystal clear, to its enemies or its supporters. To friends of union and energetic government, like Hamilton, it was bitterly disappointing; to defenders of the "sovereign" states, it made for a "consolidated system," one "consolidated government" calculated to be as obnoxious as that the colonists had thrown off in 1776. Jefferson's position is distinguishable from that of both Federalists and anti-Federalists. Particular provisions of the document impressed him less than the Constitution's demonstration of reason as the solvent of varying interests and divergent points of view. "I am captivated," he wrote James Madison, December 20, 1787, "by the compromise of the opposite claims of the great and little States, of the last to equal, and the former to proportional influence."

But was not the accommodation of interests Jefferson saw, or thought he saw, reflected in the Constitution more apparent than real? Did not both sides make concessions, and yet couch what had been surrendered in language so equivocal as to disguise the Constitution's true import? Obviously the Constitution did not draw the boundary line between the general government and the states, nor indicate the source from which its powers were derived, so distinctly clear as to escape sharp diversities of opinion, protracted controversy, and finally civil war. Did not the Founding Fathers, with noble motives and good intentions, plant in the Constitution itself a time bomb that, after 1860, burst the nation asunder in civil war?

Examination of this question proceeds on the generally accepted view that slavery was the occasion, not the cause, of the Civil War. Basically that conflict arose out of irreconcilable differences as to the nature of the union. Any number of issues, besides slavery, might easily have provoked the holocaust—tariffs, regulation of interstate commerce, national taxing power, and so on. Indeed, dispute over certain of these matters had carried the nation more than once to the very brink of open conflict. Before the slavery issue matured to the explosive stage, Lincoln himself set this tragic aspect of the war in clear perspective: "I would save the Union. . . . If I could save the Union without freeing any slave, I would do it; and if I could save it by freeing all the slaves, I would do it. . . ." This is but another way of saying that at bottom the war grew out of bitter differences as to the nature of the organism the Founding Fathers had brought into being during the years 1787 to 1789.

Was the Constitution, as John Taylor, John C. Calhoun and others fiercely maintained, a compact of states, or was it rooted in what Hamilton called "that pure, original fountain of all legitimate authority"—*"The Consent of The People"*? One answer to these questions may be found in dry-as-dust documents; the other is written in blood. The first answer is deeply embedded in the vast record accumulated during the framing and ratification of the Constitution. When prolonged debate and bitter controversy failed to yield a conclusive verdict, the contestants carried this baffling poser of political theory to the battlefield to be settled by the arbitrament of the sword. Let us first consider the contemporary record.

If there be any single proposition to which Americans, since 1776, have been dedicated, it is this: that the people have a right to change their government, "laying its foundations on such principles, and organizing its powers in such form, as to them should seem most likely to effect their Safety and Happiness." The Declaration of Independence averred that the people alone were the rightful source of legitimate authority. The opening sentence of that document speaks of the "one people" dissolving the "political bands which have connected them with another." By that act one people of thirteen united states "assumed among the Powers of the earth, the separate and equal station to which the Laws of

Nature and of Nature's God entitled them." "Civil liberty," Benjamin Hichborn declared, March 5, 1777, is "not a government by laws, made agreeable to charters, bills of rights or compacts." It is a "power existing in the people at large," the power "to alter or annihilate both the mode and essence of any former government," "for any cause or for no cause at all, but their own sovereign pleasure."

James Wilson called this (and many others agreed with him) "the leading principle in politics and that which pervades the American constitutions." Never before put into practice, this theory—that "Supreme power resides in the people"—so clearly expounded in the writings of "the great Locke," had been working itself in the minds of men for many ages. In 1776, Americans declared themselves free and independent states, by authority of the whole people. "The distinctions between Virginians, Pennsylvanians, New Yorkers, and New Englanders are no more," Patrick Henry had told the First Continental Congress in 1774. "I am not a Virginian, but an American. . . . All distinctions are thrown down. All America is thrown into one mass." "It is only in our united Character as an Empire," George Washington wrote Governor William Livingston, June 12, 1783, "that our Independence is acknowledged, that our power can be regarded, or our Credit supported, among foreign Nations." Lincoln echoed Washington (as did a host of nationalist orators during the intervening years) in his first inaugural address, proclaiming that "The Union is much older than the Constitution."

Under this nationalist theory, the Articles of Confederation were but a step, as inconsistent as they were important, toward union. This was "an experiment of inestimable value, even by its failure," John Quincy Adams remarked in 1836. "It taught our fathers the lesson, that they had more, infinitely more to do than merely to achieve their Independence by War. That they must form their social compact upon principles never before attempted upon earth." To deal effectively with the national exigencies following Yorktown it had been as necessary in 1787 as in 1776 "to go," as James Wilson said on the floor of the Philadelphia Convention, "to the original powers of Society"—the people. The Convention, in short, was a revolutionary body, acting in accordance with the proposition that "all authority is derived from the people." The Declaration of Independence and the Constitution are thus "parts of one consistent whole." Each rests fundamentally on the natural right of a people to dislodge or alter their government and to reinstitute such new forms as they see fit.

But to assert this doctrine against a tyrannical mother country was one thing; to ground new institutions of government in such a high-toned principle was something else. In his address of 1787 to the people of the United States, Dr. Benjamin Rush observed:

There is nothing more common than to confound the terms of the *American Revolution* with those of the *late American War*. The American War is over: but this is far from being the case with the American revolution. On the contrary, nothing but the first act of the great drama is closed. It remains yet to establish and perfect our new forms of government; and to prepare the principles, morals, and manners of our citizens for these forms of government, after they are established and brought to perfection. . . . Patriots of 1774, 1775, 1776—heroes of 1778, 1779, 1780! come forward! your country demands your services!—Philosophers and friends to mankind, come forward! your country demands your studies and speculations!

THE REVOLUTION IS NOT OVER!

Before 1787 Dr. Rush's theory—that the American colonies constituted "one people" and the continuing nature of the revolution initiated in 1776—was widely recognized and accepted. This notion, "in itself so simple," John Quincy Adams wrote in 1836, "addressed itself at once so forcibly to the reason, to the imagination, and to the benevolent feelings of all, that it can scarcely be supposed to have escaped the mind of any reflecting man from Maine to Georgia." And yet, when this elemental doctrine was projected and acted upon in the Philadelphia Convention, it stirred "State Sovereignties, corporate feudal baronies, tenacious of their own liberty, impatient of a superior and jealous, and disdainful of a paramount Sovereign, even in the whole democracy of the nation." The people, that is to say, could exert themselves negatively and unitedly against the tyrannous oppression of Great Britain, but when that same ultimate authority moved constructively in the face of well-nigh insurmountable internal complexities, vested interests and political prejudice were profoundly aroused.

It was generally recognized that, to achieve the energy necessary for an effective national government, extensive restrictions would have to be imposed upon the corporate action of states, passionately claiming to be independent and sovereign. It was also recognized that such "binding ligaments," as John Quincy Adams said, could be properly imposed by "no earthly power other than the People themselves." "Federal liberty is to States," James Wilson observed in the Philadelphia Convention, "what civil liberty is to private individuals. And States are not more unwilling to purchase it, by the necessary concession of their political sovereignty, than the savage is to purchase civil liberty by the surrender of the personal sovereignty which he enjoys in a State of nature."

What, then, was the nature of the change effected by the Constitution? Did it merely continue and guarantee, as Luther Martin insisted at the Philadelphia Convention, the relationship of "sovereign," "independent" states existing under the Articles of Confederation; or did it, as James Wilson and others maintained, by deriving authority from the people, preclude (at least in theory) any possibility of thereafter inter-posing the states against national authority? The answer to these ques-tions falls into two parts. There is, on the one hand, the reply of advocates of ratification, like James Wilson and Alexander Hamilton; and, on the other, the view of opponents of the Constitution, such as Richard Henry Lee and Samuel Adams.

Under the Randolph Plan the government established was to be "para-mount to the state constitutions." "Can an individual retain his equality," James Wilson argued on the floor of the Pennsylvania ratifying conven-tion, "when he becomes a member of civil government? He cannot. . . . As little can a sovereign state," Wilson reasoned, "when it becomes a mem-ber of the federal government." Hamilton was equally emphatic. The Constitution of 1787 was intended to scotch forever that "gross heresy . . . that a *party* to a *compact* has a right to revoke that *compact.*" Emanating from "We the People of the United States," the Constitution transformed a "League of Friendship," a "loose alliance," into a government. In pro-viding for national authority, acting on indivduals rather than on states, the Constitution of 1787 substituted a government of law for one whose only instrument had been prayerful requisition or force. "This . . . is not a government founded upon compact," James Wilson told the Pennsyl-vania ratifying convention. "It is founded upon the power of the peo-ple. . . . The power both of the general government, and the state gov-ernments, under this system, are acknowledged to be so many emanations of power from the people."

Ironically enough, impressive support for this nationalistic theory came from the Constitution's most rabid opponents. "It is, in its very *introduction*, declared to be a compact between the people of the United States as individuals," Luther Martin complained, "and it is to be ratified by the *people* at large, in their capacity *as individuals.*" All this, Martin explained, "would be quite right and proper, if there were *no State gov-ernments*, if *all the people* of this continent were in a *state of nature*, and we were forming one *national government* for *them as individuals.*" "The Constitution is an ordinance," Richard Henry Lee protested, "not of the people of New Hampshire," and so on, but of "the people of America." "What right had they to say, *We the people* . . . instead of, *We the states?*" Patrick Henry inquired in the Virginia ratifying convention. "The question turns, sir, on that poor little thing—the expression, We, the Peo-ple, instead of the States of America. . . . Here is a resolution as radical as that which separated us from Great Britain."

Responding December 3, 1787 to Richard Henry Lee, who had sent him a copy of the "new Constitution," Samuel Adams voiced similar senti-ments and opposed ratification for the same reason:

I am not able to conceive why the Wisdom of the Convention led them to give the Preference to the former [national government] before the latter [sovereign states]. If the several states in the Union are to become one entire Nation, under one Legislature, the Powers of which shall extend to every Subject of Legislation, and its Laws be supreme and control the whole, the Idea of Sovereignty in these States must be lost.

"Whether the Constitution be good or bad," George Mason said, going to the heart of the matter, "it is a national government, and no longer a confederation."

The Constitution was intended, its friends insisted (and on this basic point its enemies agreed), to remedy the congenital defect that had plagued the central government under the Articles of Confederation—that "it never had a ratification by the People." Hamilton argued emphatically that by "extending to the individuals" it would slay the "political monster"—*"imperium in imperio."*

How, in the face of historical evidence so abundantly conclusive; how, in a debate where the participants were agreed as to the revolutionary character of the Constitution of 1787, could the doctrine that our fundamental law was a mere compact between sovereign states, the doctrine boldly asserted by Jefferson in the Kentucky Resolutions of 1798, by Madison in the Virginia Resolutions of 1799—the doctrine acted upon by the slave states—receive any credibility at all? How could our "leading principle in politics . . . that the supreme power resides in the people," the doctrine so universally accepted in 1787, be converted into the self-stultifying notion that the Constitution was a compact of independent, sovereign entities? How could states' rights advocates, John C. Calhoun in particular, claim for entities called states a prerogative that belongs, under our theory of government, only to people or populations? How, in short, could the highest political capacity of the people be transmuted into the capacity of corporate bodies—the states? Investigation of these questions leads ultimately to James Madison. In the divisive effort culminating in civil war, all major participants on the side of disunion derived essential support from him.

The position of Madison on the nature of the Constitution and of the Union, also as to the scope of the powers granted the national government, stands in bold contrast to the clear-cut views of the Constitution's major supporters as well as of its radical opponents. In *Federalist* No. 39, Madison maintained:

The Constitution is to be founded on the assent and ratification of the people of America, given by deputies elected for the special purpose. . . . This assent and ratification is to be given by the people, not as individuals composing one entire nation, but as composing the distinct and independent States to which they respectively belong. It is to be the assent and ratification of the several States, derived from the supreme authority in each State—the authority of the people themselves. The act, therefore, establishing the Constitution, will not be a *national*, but a *federal* act. . . . Each State, in ratifying the Constitution, is considered as a sovereign body, independent of all others, and only to be bound by its own voluntary act. In this relation, then, the new Constitution will, if established, be a *federal*, and not a *national* Constitution.

Madison labored the point; for him the distinction was fundamental. Yet Hamilton passed it over lightly in essay 9 as "a distinction, more subtle than accurate. . . ."

For Madison the task of the Convention was not to abolish the Articles of Confederation but "to reduce" them. He spells out his meaning in *Federalist* No. 40: "The truth is, that the great principles of the Constitution proposed by the Convention may be considered less as absolutely new, than as the expansion of principles which are found in the articles of Confederation." The Father of the Constitution elaborated his thought further in *Federalist* No. 45, dealing specifically with the nature and scope of national power: "The change which it [the Constitution] proposes consists much less in the addition of NEW POWERS to the Union than in the invigoration of its ORIGINAL POWERS." The powers of the new government, he said, "are few and defined."

The sharpness of the contrast between Madison and his collaborator, Hamilton, grew out of basic disagreement as to the source from which the powers of the national government emanated. For Hamilton the Articles of Confederation, being fatally defective, must be destroyed, liquidated, not merely "reduced." "The evils we experience do not proceed," he wrote, in *Federalist* No. 15, "from minute or partial imperfections, but from fundamental errors in the structure of the building, which cannot be amended otherwise than by an alteration in the first principles and main pillars of the fabric." The capital infirmity of the existing system was congenital—"it never had ratification by the People." To avoid the "gross heresy" that a "party to a compact has a right to revoke that compact, the fabric of American empire ought to rest on the solid basis of *The Consent of The People.*" In essay 15 he had portrayed the Constitution as the proper corrective of "the great and radical vice"—"legislation for states . . . as contradistinguished from the individuals of which they consist." There follows his classic expression of nationalistic doctrine:

If we are unwilling to be placed in this perilous situation; if we still will adhere to the design of a national government, or, which is the same thing, of a superintending power, under the direction of a common council, we must resolve to incorporate into our plan those ingredients which may be considered as forming the characteristic difference between a league and a government; we must extend the authority of the Union to the persons of the citizens,—the only proper objects of government.

"The great bulk of the citizens of America are with reason convinced" Hamilton observed in *Federalist* No. 84, "that Union is the basis of their political happiness." "We have neither troops, nor treasury, nor government," he had remarked in *Federalist* No. 15. Having thus "reached almost the last stage of national humiliation," should we permit, he inquired, "that sacred knot which binds the people of America together to be severed or dissolved by ambition or by avarice, by jealousy, or by misrepresentation?"

It followed, in consequence, that the powers granted the national government by the proposed Constitution had to be new and "undefined"—indeed, undefinable in view of the great interests committed to the care of the national government. Far from possessing, as Madison asserted, only "a few and defined powers," the national government possessed "all the power which a free people *ought to delegate to any government.*"

Nor was the vigor of the new government to be applied so exclusively, as Madison suggested, in the field of foreign relations. Hamilton conceived of the "Union," and of the central government as an essential force in domestic affairs as well—especially as a "barrier against domestic faction and insurrection." "A government ought to contain in itself every power requisite to the full accomplishment of the objects committed to its care . . . free from every other control but a regard to the public good and to the sense of the People." It would be, Hamilton argued, "both unwise and dangerous to deny the federal government an unconfined authority, as to all those objects which are intrusted to its management."

"Let us at last break the fatal charm," Hamilton pleaded dramatically in *Federalist* No. 15, "which has too long seduced us from the paths of felicity and prosperity." "Let us not attempt," he reiterated in *Federalist* No. 23, "to reconcile contradictions, but firmly embrace a rational alternative." Hamilton's exhortations might well have been addressed to his *Federalist* collaborator, Madison.

Some one has characterized the personality of the *Federalist* as "split." It would perhaps be closer to the mark to call it schizophrenic. The major authors not only disagreed on basic issues but, at certain points, Madison was in disagreement with himself, embracing the Hamiltonian theory that the Constitution emanates from the people, as well as his collaborator's theory of the broad and "unconfined" scope of national authority. For the most part, however, Madison saw the Constitution as resting precisely on those flimsy foundations Hamilton cited as incurably defective.

These equivocal views of the Father of the Constitution, expressed in a series of essays designed to win ratification, provided the leaders of nullification and secession with exactly the formula, the destructive ammunition, they used in their abortive attempt to blow up the Union. Nor is this all. Madison's theory that the Constitution emanates from and was ratified by "the people . . . comprising the distinct and independent states" is the more extraordinary because of its novelty. In 1787, "People of the States" and "People of the United States" were not antagonistic conceptions, as Madison's interpretation in *Federalist* No. 39 implies. The polar concepts familiar to the men of that day—"States" and "People," "Governments" and "People"—had been inherited from John Locke. The term "State" usually meant, as Dr. Johnson said, in the Philadelphia Convention, "districts of people forming one Political Society." "Governments" were universally regarded as properly the creations of people, and the term "People" meant an aggregation of individuals endowed with the natural right to determine their form of government. The state and federal governments were, as Madison said in *Federalist* No. 46, but "different agencies and trustees of the people." A "constitution" represented a fresh manifestation of the inexhaustible, inalienable right of people to govern themselves. In this sense the Philadelphia Convention of 1787 had assembled "to raise," as John Quincy Adams observed in 1839, "the marble palace of the people to stand the test of time."

In the years after 1798, Madison's explosively novel theory became the stock in trade of anti-Federalist leadership; it was the central idea on which nullificationists and secessionists built their ill-fated case. Madison himself employed it in the Virginia Resolutions, declaring that the powers of the federal government are derived from

the compact to which the States are parties . . . and that, in case of a deliberate, palpable, and dangerous exercise of other powers not granted by the said compact, the States who are parties thereto, have the right and are in duty bound to interpose for arresting the progress of the evil, and for maintaining within their respective limits the authorities, rights, and liberties appertaining to them.

The year before, Jefferson had asserted in his Kentucky Resolutions that the Constitution was a compact of states, and that, "as in all other cases of compact among parties having no common judge, each party has an equal right to judge for itself, as well of infractions as of measures of redress."

John Taylor of Caroline County, Virginia, gleefully appropriated Madison's theory in his vehement attack on Hamilton's and Marshall's nationalistic views of the Constitution and of the Union. Taylor's intellectual gymnastics, however, were mixed with legerdemain. Opponents of the Constitution, as we have seen, vigorously attacked it, primarily because its provisions made, as they said, for a "consolidated government." After

1820, Taylor, drawing heavily from Madison's numbers of the *Federalist*, held that the Convention had rejected the idea of "consolidation" and of national supremacy, and John Marshall, notwithstanding this decisive repudiation, had achieved the forbidden end by judicial interpretation! In other words, a secessionist position, otherwise difficult, if not impossible, to maintain, was made comparatively easy by James Madison, whose numbers of the *Federalist* supplied John Taylor with the authoritative ammunition he leveled against Hamilton's and Marshall's doctrines of national supremacy.

It was not, however, until 1861 that the slave states cut loose. Then enlisting Madison's authority they held that the Constitution emanated from the sovereign states, that they therefore had the rights to interpose their judgment against any acts of the national government deemed by them unauthorized, and that they might therefore secede from the Union. It was on this theory, entangled with ethics and economics, that the South went on to Harper's Ferry, Shiloh and Appomattox.

One need not accuse the Father of the Constitution of instigating the Civil War—he died in 1836—but one may venture the suggestion that his numbers of the *Federalist* papers planted the verbal bomb that, after 1861, flared tragically. The ambiguity lay not so much in the Constitution as in what he said about it. One may reach this conclusion, and still be "captivated," as Jefferson was, "by the compromise [or semblance of it] of the opposite claims of the great and little states." It may be that this was an occasion that called for the sort of equivocation in which Madison so freely indulged. It may be that his equivocal views were rooted in far more wisdom than the comparatively greater forthrightness of his collaborator, Hamilton; for, without Madison's concessions to rampant state loyalties, there may not have been any Constitution of 1787. One may recall that Hamilton himself in 1780 shied off from his own suggestion that the Congress under the Articles of Confederation, in order to cope with the crisis, might assert and exercise discretionary power—power adequate to deal with national exigencies. This course then seemed "too bold an expedient." That is why he advocated calling a convention as the safer course.

Nevertheless the grim verdict at Appomattox repudiated Madison as conclusively as the record of 1787–89. A theory of the Union which reason had proved powerless to resolve was finally established by resort to force. Washington had suggested war as a possibility when he (according to Gouverneur Morris' recollections) told the Convention: "It is too probable that no plan we propose will be adopted. Perhaps another dreadful conflict is to be sustained. . . ." And yet, even after the first shots were fired on Sumter and secession was a fact, Lincoln still searched for a theory of the Union that would go deeper than the great constitutional debates then rife. He finally hit upon an idea suggested in 1774, ironically enough, by Patrick Henry, that the

Union is perpetual . . . much older than the Constitution. It was formed, in fact, by the Articles of Association in 1774, . . . matured and continued by the Declaration of Independence in 1776. It was further matured by the Articles of Confederation in 1778. And finally, in 1787, one of the declared objectives for ordaining and establishing the Constitution was "to form a more perfect union."

These successive efforts proved to be in vain, but eight years after Lincoln made his pronouncement the United States Supreme Court adopted his reasoning, almost his very words. Chief Justice Chase, holding that Texas had failed in its attempt to secede, said:

Union of the States never was a purely artificial and arbitrary relation. It began among the colonies . . . and received definite form, and character, and sanction from the Articles of Confederation. By these the Union was solemnly declared to be "perpetual" . . . the Constitution was ordained "to form a more perfect union." It is difficult to convey the idea of indissoluble unity more clearly than by these words.

And so, through Washington, Hamilton, Marshall and Lincoln, this, the organic view of the Union conceived of as rooted in the consent of the people, had steadily advanced. Repeatedly tested by pen, and, finally, by musket, the Union was at last seen, not as "a purely artificial and arbitrary relation," but as fused, in Chief Justice Chase's words, "out of common origin, mutual sympathies, kindred principles, similar interests, and geographical relations." Justice Holmes, himself a soldier in Lincoln's army, reinforced this nationalist theory of the Union in a Supreme Court opinion in 1919:

When we are dealing with words that are also a constituent act, like the Constitution of the United States, we must realize that they [the framers] have called into life a being the development of which could not have been foreseen completely by the most gifted of its begetters. It was enough for them to realize or to hope, that they had created an organism; it has taken a century and cost their successors much sweat and blood to prove that they created a nation.

After Sumter, reason could no longer serve as the instrument for achieving the ends of nationalist statesmanship. Thus, union, like the Constitution itself, had to be "extorted from the grinding necessities of a reluctant nation."

18 *Broadus Mitchell*

ALEXANDER HAMILTON AS FINANCE MINISTER

If there was any central problem confronting the new government, it was the financial one; and if there was any central person acting for the new government, it was the first Secretary of the Treasury, Alexander Hamilton. No one was more conscious than he of the experiment in politics which the new nation was attempting; no one was more aware that the national tree would grow as the institutional twigs would be bent by the first administrators of the newly organized republic. The role he played in defining the dimensions of American government has been surpassed by only a few presidents and perhaps not at all by any other member of the cabinet since his day.

What that role was has been analyzed by the latest and certainly the most competent of his biographers, Broadus Mitchell. In his long and active career, Professor Mitchell has taught at the Johns Hopkins University, Occidental College, and Rutgers University, and has written a number of books, dealing in the main with American economic history. Appearing in 1957 and subtitled *Youth to Maturity—1755–1788,* the first volume of Professor Mitchell's biography of Hamilton, like the essay below, stresses Hamilton's importance for his own and for later times.

An estimate of Hamilton invariably evokes an estimate of Jefferson, who is generally regarded as his antagonist in the debate over the national purpose and how to pursue it. Yet in their differences regarding the policies to be pursued by the new government, Jefferson and Hamilton are more accurately seen as complementary protagonists of the larger republican and national idea. It should not be forgotten that Hamilton was of the same libertarian philosophy as Jefferson, a spokesman for the rights of minorities and individuals (see Harold C. Syrett, "Alexander Hamilton: History by Stereotype," *The New-York Historical Society Quarterly,* January, 1959). A political economist in the true sense, Hamilton saw his problem as one of using financial means to achieve national security and growth. His program was a rejection of laisser faire, and it is an error to regard him as a disciple of Adam Smith; national independence, he felt, could be secured only through the active participation of government. In this sense, says Mitchell, he was a collectivist and a mercantilist. Whatever faults he may have had as Secretary of the Treasury, his probity cannot be questioned. He

Reprinted with permission from *Proceedings of the American Philosophical Society,* CII (April, 1958), 117-23.

represented not privilege but public good. The course he charted for the role of the national government in public life is the one which, without infringement upon individual liberty, has actually been followed since his day.

In reading Professor Mitchell's essay, one cannot avoid the larger questions which hang perennially over the study of American history, some indeed over the study of all history. How much does the individual make the times, how much do the times make the individual? Did the opportunities within a new government create the figure of a Hamilton, or did Hamilton create his own opportunities? What economic policies would the new nation have pursued if Robert Morris, Washington's first choice for the Treasury post, had accepted, thus denying the position to Hamilton, the second choice? To what extent, if at all, should government participate in the development of the national economy? In what way should particular economic interests (in Hamilton's day, the commercial and the agrarian) be related to each other, and what special considerations ought to be extended them? What should be the respective roles, in promoting national economic growth, of the central government and of the localities?

These questions reveal the contribution which Alexander Hamilton offers to current thought. He urges the importance of the experiments in viability being performed by the many new nations of the world today, much as he urged the importance of his own nation's experiment in the 1790's. He summarizes the self-consciousness with which a new state defines both its social philosophy and the way to achieve it.

One is helped in finding his way through the fierce, often bitter controversies of the Federalist period if he has it constantly in mind that Hamilton was, as Wolcott said, "of the first endowments of mind." Some of his contemporaries, acting in the same scenes, possessed more varied knowledge. His formal schooling was compressed into little more than four years. Without patrimony, from boyhood he was thrown largely on his own resources. His relatively short career (cut off at the age of forty-nine) was incessantly occupied with action, most of it not in his private but in the public behalf. Five years of his early twenties, when ideally a thinker would be accumulating diversified informational inventory, he devoted to exacting military service. He never realized his hope of visiting Europe. He had the least opportunity to browse in books, to learn to play a musical instrument, or to lean and loaf at his ease, inviting his soul.

Thus, in the commonly accepted meaning of the term (perhaps denoting mental mellowness) he was not the same philosopher as others to whom we may point. The remarkable feature is that in scraps of time he snatched so much from books, and managed to be so aware of cultural undercurrents. Imagination he was blessed with, a perfect well-spring of optimistic foresight. This *esprit* must ever remain a mystery; is it born of physical vigor, of nervous vitality, of emotional generosity? Does this native verve grow from evidence received, or does it find its own proofs? Dynamism, combined with cheerfulness and good will, does not make a man a sage, but tends in that direction.

Whatever the judgment on the completeness of Hamilton's mental stock, nobody ever denied his acuteness and analytical capacity. Remembering this in surveying his policies as finance minister, one does well to give him the benefit of the doubt on controversial points. He made mistakes of several sorts, more largely personal and political than fiscal, but as a rule his superior wits saved him from following infatuations. Some to which he yielded he afterward forswore with excellent candor and firmness. In the Treasury he did not, could not commit the blunder of supposing that the sinking fund would grow automatically by compounding interest on securities bought up and retired. The fund must expand from revenue alone. Any ambiguity in his language which has induced critics to fancy the reverse should be cancelled by confidence in his good head. The elder Pitt, whose example influenced Hamilton, may be similarly exculpated.

Instances of villains with brains are not wanting. But one feels assured that Hamilton's high intelligence—leave aside his code of honor—would have protected him against improprieties in administration of the country's finances. He knew that he was not in public life for the moment; he had settled purposes that needed time in the nurture. This is ascribing his integrity to the most utilitarian motive. It is easier and juster to lift it to the moral plane. In the heats of party conflict he could not escape the accusation of favoring his friends or, worse, of placating his enemies by betraying his official trust. I may say at once that no evidence of this exists. First, presumption is against it. For the quarter century of his greatest activity he lived in intimacy with Washington, for long periods in daily, almost hourly contact, and he ever enjoyed Washington's approval. He left the Treasury, as even the cynical Talleyrand observed, to make a living for his family. After sitting at the receipt of a nation's customs, and in spite of unremitting industry in his profession, he died insolvent. Congressional investigation, upon which he insisted when it seemed ready to be abandoned by its promoters, cleared him of any wrongdoing. Finally, as is recalled if one knows anything about Hamilton, he proclaimed in print his private lapse in adultery to blast a charge of public malfeasance. We have his letter to Henry Lee, no less friendly than firm, refusing to disclose Treasury information for speculative advantage. He buttressed, if he did not devise, the system of internal checks of one Treasury officer upon another.

This is presumptive evidence. In addition, accusation, busy in his day and since, has not been able to produce from Treasury records or the transactions of businessmen or speculators who stood to profit by privileged knowledge, any proof of the Secretary's complicity. William Constable, as revealed by his letters, in the weeks when Hamilton's first "budget" (Report on the Public Credit, January 9, 1790) was impending, sought opportunities to "be with" Hamilton and also Wolcott. His object was to obtain secret information, but his reports to Andrew Craigie and others show that he came away no wiser than he went, which, however, was tolerably wise, for he was no fool in drawing reasonable inferences from the necessities of the case, and from his experience of Hamilton's prior principles. Indeed, Craigie and his correspondents, some months earlier, seemed to take for granted redemption of the debt in the hands of the holders if Hamilton was appointed Secretary of the Treasury.

Further inquiry may convict Hamilton of passive guilt perhaps in choosing, or more particularly in retaining William Duer as his assistant in the Treasury. Duer was a schemer, and not without success until his enthusiastic indiscretion and secret corruptions caught up with him, landing him in debtor's prison. Before that, and while still outwardly in high feather, he had left the Treasury at his own wish, but with Hamilton's approval. His known machinations, legal if not laudable, do not concern us for themselves. Nor is there room for doubt that in furthering his private engagements, which we have in his own handwriting, he abused, or intended to abuse, his official position. There is no evidence that Hamilton was a partner in these plans to enrich American and European speculators at the expense of unsuspecting sellers and buyers of securities. The question is whether we are to fasten on Hamilton the fault not of complicity but of complacence in the face of Duer's doings.

Here I must apply my own maxim that little escaped Hamilton's notice, and that he was apt in inference from what he knew. The Treasury staff, while larger than that of other departments, was small, and Duer was nominally next to Hamilton in authority and closest to him in association. The suspicious point out that Duer was a relative, by marriage, of Hamilton's wife. Further, Hamilton always befriended Duer—spoke well of him to Robert Morris, the Superintendent of Finance, when Duer was purchasing agent for the army in New York, brought him into the Treasury, later cautioned him against running into speculative disaster, still later solicited his temporary release from jail. All of this looks like too great indulgence of Duer's misdeeds. On the other hand, Duer was recommended by previous experience and character. He had been a patriot in civil and military posts, had been secretary of the Board of Treasury under the Confederation, and was generally credited with financial ingenuity, which presumably would be serviceable in the new national government. Other plausible endorsements might be mentioned.

It is not profitable to conjecture, but in the light of what is now known and which may not be soon or ever amplified, my guess is that Hamilton too far tolerated Duer in the bosom of the Treasury. As Hamilton was responsible for the honorable functioning of the department, he should earlier have prompted Duer's departure, if that is what happened, for the good of the service. On the other hand, not to excuse Hamilton, allowing he was at fault, but to round out the situation, several circumstances may be had in mind. Hamilton was himself excessively occupied in the short period of Duer's tenure, organizing his office, preparing and then defending his momentous first report to Congress. Speculation in public debt was not new; it had been active since 1787, rose conspicuously only when the report was submitted, and not until later, when panic threatened, did Hamilton look on speculation as harmful to the country's credit. Further, it was a period when men who esteemed their own motives had more difficulty than now, and less help from the public conscience, in keeping the line between official trust and private benefit. Members of the old Board of Treasury had been privy to Duer's deviousness while in their midst. Finally, supposing that Hamilton early learned of Duer's duplicity, he may have judged that an open scandal from his exposure would have been more harmful to the public credit—or, if you like, to the administration, though that would have been much the same thing —than handling the case with a little patience. This last gains some credence from the fact that later, when Hamilton received a complaint of Duer's conduct in the Treasury, he explained that Duer had been some time out of office, and let it go at that.

I am not expected, before this Society, to retell the story of Hamilton's fiscal proposals and of his conduct of the Treasury between September, 1789, and January, 1795. I beg your attention to a few features which may be less familiar and to an overall estimate of his aims and services.

It would be a mistake to suppose that Hamilton in his earlier period was political scientist, eager to tighten constitutional bonds, and that after he was installed in the Treasury he became economist, bent upon restoration of the country's credit and advance of its material prosperity. The fact is that there was no alteration in his object to create a strong nation, from the time when he broached plans to James Duane and Robert Morris a decade before for political and economic renovation. Only after assuming charge of the Treasury did he command fiscal and monetary tools with which to rear the structure which the Constitution promised and which he had envisioned all along. In the Treasury his economic devices drew breath from and in turn animated his political purposes. Throughout, he was the political economist in the original and true meaning of the term. He practiced statecraft for the energizing of the economy; he promoted production and exchange of goods and services for the benefit of the body politic. Those who differed with his Treasury policies were quick to perceive and to attack the political design with which he informed his fiscal proposals, for example in the assumption of state debts and establishment of the Bank of the United States. His critics were accurate in their swift recognition of his political incentives, though their broad opposition to his measures and readiness to brand them as of class or party inspiration showed less wisdom. Still, on the whole, we may accept the Secretary of the Treasury at his enemies' estimate.

If anything, Hamilton was more the prophet and practitioner of government than he was the patron of finance, trade and manufactures. In a young country, of enormous potential resources, but sparsely populated, overwhelmingly agricultural and extractive in its pursuits, and fractioned into conflicting political and economic divisions, organization became his dearest object. Public action must come before private. Capital could be secured and varied enterprise stimulated by the fostering care of federal government. He knew that what we call national wealth, in its origin and maintenance, is not material (land, labor, capital, consumption goods), but is exceedingly immaterial. It is capacity for economic processes. This means cooperation under conditions of self-discipline, safety of persons and property, and stability.

Dependence upon government as the engine of economic growth, appropriate in Hamilton's America, had been relaxed and was soon to be abandoned in Europe, notably in Britain of Adam Smith, James Watt, and the Industrial Revolution, and in France of the Physiocrats, *laissez faire*, and the tricolor. I do not need to remind that these had suffered from too much government in economic life—over-regulation, protected monopolies, pestiferous taxation. There the era was ripe for freedom, appeal to natural law, individual self-interest, competition rather than controls. Though these cries rang in Hamilton's ears, he was convinced that America was in the stage to be benefited by governmental promotion and protection. Without these encouragements our business community and citizens generally lacked the capital, confidence, and experience for sure and rapid advance. While he expected that impetus supplied by resourceful central government would raise up private enterprise, so far lessening extension of governmental responsibility in the economy, he can scarcely be described as the apostle of Adam Smith. He understood and was influenced by the *Wealth of Nations*, but considered that America could apply the theory of that work only at some day in the future.

It will be recalled that Hamilton prefaced several of his Treasury reports with persuasive short essays forestalling objections and arguing the merits of his proposals. Particularly in the Report on Manufactures, 1791, he must be circumspect in rearing a rival, as many thought, to the agricultural interest. Almost all property in this country was in land and its appurtenances, including slaves to the southward where lay, besides, the greatest suspicion of central authority. He was obliged to show, tactfully, how industry—protected industry—presented a vigorous claim, not least because it would benefit farmers. But his tenderness toward the extractive economy (which was a way of life too) was induced by inhibitions of most of his hearers, was not his own preference. Appreciating the basic importance of agriculture, he did not yield in his design to produce a quickening variety in activities, which would require public prompting.

So much for his general purpose. What of his practical, institutional means toward equipping a competent nation? Out of disorder, debt, and not a little discouragement flowing from the recent business depression, he must rouse the country to system and progress. He was sustained by his faith that America's advance in union, security, and wealth would be rapid, proliferating in every direction. This sure insight armed him to attack obstacles which others believed were more serious if not insuperable. The debt is the plainest case in point. Seventy-five or eighty millions total (leaving aside the Continental currency which was past rescue) could be promptly discharged once the country addressed itself to the task. Hamilton did better. The debt would be the means of its own payment. He would turn the bane into a blessing.

He had to begin amidst the detritus of Revolution and Confederation. He had to discover what the debt was, and how divided, before he could present it (partly estimated even so) for candid acknowledgment. The debt, including accumulated interest, must be funded, offering a fair option for voluntary conversion. The new securities were to issue to the actual holders of the old. Any discrimination in favor of original holders, who had parted with public paper for however small a fraction of its nominal value, would be fatal to Hamilton's plan. In the debates in the House, genuine solicitude for justice to deserving losers was mixed with a deal of declamation pleading for old soldiers, their widows and orphans, and castigating heartless speculators. Madison's argument for discrimination was the most thoughtful, perhaps the sincerest.

But Hamilton and his champions could not hearken. Unless the precedent was established of honoring the debt in the hands of the holders, evidences of it would not be certainly transferable. Unless transferable the securities would not serve in a degree as currency, more importantly as the basis for loans which would result in more currency and varied investment. Only so could we mount upon the debt to a higher station. It was charged at the time and has been repeated since that Hamilton, in his insistence, was callous to the cries of suffering and cunningly courted the support of speculators and the wealthy generally. That they were gainers there is no doubt. But their profit was not his purpose.

Mr. Parrington, in his vigorous sketch, has said that it is not necessary to do more than scan Hamilton's writings to know his spirit and aims. One is allowed to suspect that Parrington has followed his own advice. I pause over this admission of partial examination before pronouncing judgment not because this influential critic is the worst offender, for he is not. A thorough reading of Hamilton leaves a different impression from that received by too many. He was not the tactician of privilege, but the advocate of the public good. He was the patriot, not the partisan. In a state of political confusion and economic immaturity, men who commanded means and business talents must in any case play a crucial role. If these were attracted as allies, government would gain in solidity and capacity. So would the capitalists and enterprisers. This was in itself a proper object. But more than that, their efforts would be directed, by government policing as well as promotion, into channels calculated to serve the entire community.

John Adams and Alexander Hamilton were of similar principles but dissimilar personalities. After eyeing each other appraisingly, they worked together uneasily until their hostility became scandalous. Under these circumstances neither would be expected to give a sympathetic report of the other. Adams recorded that Hamilton shouldered his work on associates in the Treasury while he disported himself in society. The remark is worth exploring because the full truth is revealing. In all likelihood Tench Coxe helped Hamilton with the Report on Manufactures. Coxe had the development of industry near his heart, and aided that cause in numerous important ways. Probably he had charge of collecting and afterward cast into form the information on the state of manufactures in the country. That part of the report is distinct from the argumentative prologue. Coxe, deeply imbued with the utility of rounding out the economy by adding factories to fields, may have presented this thesis in outline or more fully for the opening of the document. We shall know only when the body of Coxe's papers, now in private hands, shall become available. Hamilton sought the advice of informed and trusted men on means of restoring the public credit. William Bingham, of Philadelphia, who had unusual knowledge from observation in England and participation in the founding of the Bank of North America, answered Hamilton's inquiry at special length. Some have suggested that Bingham supplied the pattern of Hamilton's funding scheme. Their expedients corresponded at important points, but did not coincide at others. A part of what Bingham urged, Hamilton had advocated earlier. Stephen Higginson, of Boston, was another that offered approximations to Hamilton's devices. We must not forget that the financial program to be broached by the Treasury formed the conversation of business and public men in the autumn of 1789, and that administration policy when announced had been anticipated in main features. Oliver Wolcott, Jr., who was chosen by Hamilton for the Treasury staff because he was expert in accounting matters, theory as well as practice, worked out detailed plans for administration of the funding and conversion operation. We have in his hand his departmental reports to the Secretary which provoke admiration. Besides, much that flowed between Hamilton and his subordinates has left no trace that we can identify. These assignments of the Secretary to his assistants are just what one would expect to find, for everything was to be done in a short space, and Hamilton would not fail to apportion the tasks that required talent as well as the routine demanding industry and accuracy.

If anything, Hamilton took too much of the burden of the Treasury upon himself, detail in addition to foremost policy formations. His manuscripts show this. The main reports are in his hand, sometimes in several drafts which record the elaboration, less frequently the alteration of his ideas. Many particular directions and queries in the administration of the Treasury, likewise in his hand, concern detail but were far from routine. Procedures at the custom houses must be as nearly as possible correct, for what was practiced at that initial stage would set precedents, and unworkable rules would plague the government into the future. For the same reason he referred questions in the interpretation of the laws to Richard Harison, United States Attorney at New York. This was correspondence which Hamilton could not delegate. Hamilton's personal discharge of his duties in the Treasury becomes more remarkable when we remember their variety. He must not only strike out bold plans for the rescue of credit, establishment of a mint, provision of currency, promotion of manufactures, commencement of a military academy, and organization of the coast guard. He must also conduct the day-to-day operation of the most far-flung department of the new federal government. Obstruction of collection of the excise in the western country transcended ordinary administrative vexations, required his preparation of the punitive military expedition to Pittsburgh, which he accompanied, and distracted him in the political controversy which ensued.

This would have been enough, but he engineered his measures through Congress. He was floor leader off the floor. This legislative management, which critics thought unbecoming, was reduced by the competence and loyalty of Federalists in the House, notably Boudinot, Ames, and William Smith. His and their efforts would have been spared in part, by no means entirely, if Hamilton had been allowed to give his reports in person, or had been called in later to answer questions. Much that entered into the protracted and exacerbated debates could have been cleared up and put by. Though Hamilton's power of written statement has hardly ever been exceeded, numerous members were honestly confused by the novelty of the subject matter, particularly in the reports of 1790 on credit and bank, and would have profited by oral exchanges with the Secretary. Of course certain major policy questions, fiscal and constitutional, required legislative discussion. Objections disingenuously raised would have been exploited anyhow. Further, in investigations in the House, 1793–1794, into his official conduct, which were principally party-inspired, Hamilton was obliged to defend himself by prodigious labors. Under pressure of time, which his opponents purposely made exigent, he must summarize and analyze Treasury accounts over a span of years, not to speak of the verbal argument which informed these exhibits. He could have spared himself these pains, at least in part, had he made annual reports on Treasury operations. This he omitted to do, and that is clearly a count against the wisdom of his procedure.

Besides all else, while we are naming over his accumulating occupations, he had to give cabinet counsel. In addition, his enthusiasm (some said aggrandizing meddling) took him into responsibilities which he should have been content to leave in the hands of other ministers. In judging of this, one must be mindful how keenly he felt the opportunity and need for framing good central government policy at the outset. All but nominally, he was the chief minister of state under the President, if only because so much, in the nature of the case, involved the Treasury.

Finally, closing this subject of Hamilton's personal discharge of his Treasury duties, particularly the devising of plans embodied in major reports, it may be mentioned that the day of government ghost writers was not yet. If ghosts penned the lines signed with others' names, often in that spectral company was Hamilton. A variety of instances of his deft service for friends could be given, including Henry Laurens' resignation of the presidency of the Old Congress, Baron von Steuben's plea for reimbursement of his Revolutionary expenses, and, not least, Hamilton's part in Washington's Farewell Address. If he found time to furnish thoughts and words to those who sought his aid, would he have neglected to speak for himself in his closest concerns?

It is recorded of Mrs. Hamilton that she related, at an advanced age, how her husband struck off in a single night his celebrated defense of the constitutionality of the Bank of the United States. President Washington, according to the story, brought the adverse opinions of Jefferson and of Randolph to Hamilton's home, thinking it suitable that he should examine these for his rebuttal. The Secretary of the Treasury retired to his study and did not emerge until his counter-argument was finished. Somewhere along the line, in the memory of Mrs. Hamilton or of her narrator, the composition of this document was too much compressed. For we know from the manuscript itself and from his letters to Washington that the work was spread over a week. Even so, this reduces the impossible to the extraordinary. Allowing that Hamilton had been revolving the project of the bank in his mind for a decade, had broached it anew in one recent report and given it elaborate statement in another, his claim for its constitutionality is one of his finest performances, both in the lesser matter of its vibrant language and the superior one of its bold conception. The idea of implied powers in the Constitution was not entirely new in his own mouth or in the observations of others. But he now applied the doctrine with compelling candor.

We have noticed that in Hamilton's plans and executions as finance minister the political was entangled with the fiscal. The one was imbued with the other. This took on the highest dignity when he declared the supremacy of the central government within its sphere and defined that sphere liberally. The rule for interpretation of the Constitution must be that of reason, beckoned forward by developing social need as well as restrained by the letter of the law. He declared frankly that between illegitimate extension of federal authority and too cautious limitation of it lay a penumbra. Here was room for honest difference of opinion, depending upon information, experience, and what was expected to be useful in federal-state relations. He gave the federal power the benefit of the doubt.

Hamilton himself, besides his agency in inspiring the calling of the Constitutional Convention, had made contribution to the framing of the basic law. He had helped render it ampler in scope than it would have been without his proposals, formally rejected though these were. But nothing that anybody wrote into the document was more enlivening than what he read into it in establishing the propriety of a national bank. This institution that he defended, as handmaiden of the Treasury, as the source of a reliable paper currency, was serviceable, but the principle that supported it, applied through the years, was to make the Constitution a living instrument. Hamilton's generous view of the opportunities and duties of the central power is repeatedly vindicated in the history of America. There have been delays in this constitutional progress, with temporary reversals later repented. But manifestly Hamilton's forecast of our actual national development has been borne out. He feared the centrifugal tendencies, fostered the centripetal forces. Enough have cried that Hamilton did not sufficiently cherish local autonomy, with its friendliness to variety in ways of life and its guarantees of liberty itself. That argument will go on, as I hope it shall, forever. We have it now in an Arkansas guardsman one day, under state orders, barring pupils from a school, and the next day, under national command, ushering them into their classrooms. The proof of Hamilton's forecast is in the event. Hugely growing population, quick-

ened communications, scale and standardization of production have multiplied our common concerns, thereby increasing our reliance on national decisions. Most Americans agree that these, in the secular trend, have not
imperiled our freedom, but have enlarged it.

A related subject, imbedded in Hamilton's fiscal policy, is his successful
plea for federal assumption of the state Revolutionary debts. In his report,
the fiscal reasons prompting this were foremost—simplicity, avoidance of
competition between taxing jurisdictions, and consequent larger yield from
revenue sources. Federal assumption of the state debts would benefit not
only state but federal creditors. There is no occasion for questioning his
sincerity in giving precedence to fiscal uniformity and economy. He knew
only too intimately the mischiefs of the contest between states and Congress for revenue during the war and under the Confederation. As a member of Congress he had failed in protracted efforts to secure for the central
government an independent income from a 5 per cent import duty. In the
report he merely hinted at what promptly became the staple of debate,
namely, that if all creditors looked to the national authority that would
have their loyalty.

Opponents, jealous for state importance, were not to miss the implications of any proposal that tended to magnetize the central power. Having
lost on the issue of a discrimination in favor of original holders who had
alienated their federal securities, they would make a more determined
stand for the rights of states which had met a large part of their own
indebtedness or were in the course of doing so. As the controversy waxed,
and threatened to go irrevocably against him, Hamilton was bound to accept the dispute in the political terms chosen by his critics. The effectiveness of the federal government, and future viability of the Union as he
saw it, hung in the balance.

Hence his saving agreement with Jefferson whereby northern votes
would be found to place the capital on the Potomac and southern votes
would be changed to carry the assumption. I see no reason to suppose that
the exchange was other than genuine and deliberate on the part of both
principals. Each must persuade followers to produce the required vote.
Their meeting ground was the good of the country under the Constitution. Each sacrificed something for this worthy object. It has regularly
been said that Hamilton did not care where the capital was placed geographically, that consequently he made an empty gift for an essential gain.
On the other hand, in his last term in the Old Congress, where the place-
ment of the capital obsessed the members, he showed at least a decent regard for the claims of New York or for another northern site which his
friends would approve. He had that much local or regional attachment,
though it is true that he did not put his heart into the fight with anything
like the vehemence shown by Madison on the other side. Jefferson on his

part surely understood the unwillingness of his southern compatriots to concede the assumption. The only fault was in the sequel, when Jefferson, after Hamilton's death, represented himself as having been deceived into a measure for which he was blamed.

Seeking to follow the career of Hamilton, I have never seen much profit in pursuing the rancors that developed between him and Jefferson, at least not for their own sake. Numbers of chroniclers, in gleeful partisanship for one champion or the other, have revived these disputes. The bitterness was genuine at the time, and knowledge of its different occasions is illuminating for the historian. Aside from satisfying this curiosity, the quarrels between them are of minor moment compared to the contributions made by both to our national beginnings. A superb combined achievement was in progress. On the one hand, the rights of man, newly proclaimed, were to be nourished. On the other hand, the practicability of these rights was to be tested in the experiment of constructing a firm nation. It was in this second behalf that Hamilton strove. Perhaps the body of the people, as afterward understood, would have found expression and risen to power without Hamilton's preparatory efforts for economic solvency and political unity. What we have is the grateful story as it unfolded.

19 *James Morton Smith*

THE SEDITION LAW, FREE SPEECH,

AND THE AMERICAN POLITICAL PROCESS

In the cold war that dominates our age, the conflict, as we see it, is between a free world and a captive one. We see the United States as sharing with its Western allies a legacy of freedom. For us the legacy is clearly defined in the first ten amendments to our constitution; and of these our most valued possession, perhaps, is the first, which seeks to insure the right of free speech and a free press. In the popular outlook toward the cold war, not too much consideration is given to the degree to which the free world is captive and the captive world free. Nor, for that matter, is consideration given to the fact that the United States was not so much conceived in liberty as in the struggle to achieve it. In its early years, indeed, the founders of the republic were sharply divided over the constitutional guarantees of free

Reprinted with permission from *The William and Mary Quarterly*, Third Series, IX (October, 1952), 497-511.

speech and free press. During the late 1790's, at a time of very strained relations with France, a bitter domestic conflict was fought between the Federalists and the Republicans regarding the nature and applicability of these guarantees. Only as a result of the attempt and failure of the Federalists to enforce their Sedition Law were the concept and practice of free speech and free press amplified to the point of their present importance in the American political process.

It is this crucial development which is discussed by Professor James Morton Smith in the following essay. Currently Editor of Publications of the Institute of Early American History and Culture at Williamsburg, Professor Smith is the author of *Freedom's Fetters*, the first of a two-volume appraisal of the Alien and Sedition Laws and the response which they evoked. Professor Smith quite rightly regards his subject as an important phase in the evolution of the American civil-liberties tradition. In the essay which follows, he assesses the influence of the Sedition Law in shaping the republican process, and in so doing he answers several relevant questions. What, to begin, were the provisions of the Sedition Law and the circumstances which occasioned its enactment? What was the English common-law concept of seditious libel and what theory of government did it express? What were the respective views of the Federalists and of the Republicans regarding public criticism of officeholders? How was the Sedition Law enforced? To what extent were the theory and practice of the Sedition Law in conflict with the principles of the American Revolution? What was the importance of the election of 1800? What significance did the Sedition Law and its defeat have for the American political process?

No one will deny the importance for that process of establishing the principle that the governed may criticize and control the governors through the instruments of free speech and a free press. It is no less important for us, however, to understand to what extent this principle is practiced today, to what extent it should be practiced, and whether indeed it is a valid one for our times. The extent of its practice would certainly depend on the degree to which our speech and our press are free. One would not have to look very far for evidences of serious limitations upon such freedom in recent years: the widespread use of wiretapping to build up cases against political suspects, the Congressional investigations of individuals believed to be "Communist" or "subversive" in government agencies and in colleges and universities, the widespread discharge of government officials for purposes of "security," the filling of dossiers with evidence of questionable validity, the blacklisting of movie, radio, and TV performers, the banning of books and individuals by controllers of opinion in various communities throughout the United States. It is clear now that the dominion of McCarthyism during the early 1950's meant the decline of free speech and press; what is not so clear is that the demise of McCarthy may have given further life to a less virulent McCarthyism. Even under the best conditions, however, a free press is only a press which is free to the interests and prerogatives of its publisher. Free speech, moreover, is no guarantee that a public which is free to speak will do so. Is our political process characterized by public opinion or is it more truly characterized by public indifference?

An ultimate question for the student of history is whether or not the principle of the liberty of opinion is a valid one for our times. Perhaps the survival of our national system is at too critical a stage to permit free public criticism. Perhaps the dangers facing us are, in the language of Justice Holmes, too clear, too present. If so, may we not be holding on to the appearance of liberty when the times have long since invalidated its reality? What, indeed, is to become of a system of liberty in a world that is transforming itself by totalitarianism? Can the ideas of a liberty-seeking Atlantic community of the eighteenth century serve the needs of the power-seeking revolutionary world of the twentieth? These are the questions we must ask and seek to answer in exploring with Professor Smith that earlier period of our history when the American tradition of civil liberties was first being established.

Popular government rests on the right of the public to choose between opposing views. Since an informed public opinion is vital to republican government, freedom of expression is necessary for the formation of that opinion. If people cannot communicate their thoughts to one another without running the risk of prosecution, no other liberty can be secure because freedom of speech and of the press are essential to any meaning of liberty. The years between 1798 and 1801 afford the first instance under the Constitution in which American political leaders faced the problem of defining the role of public criticism in a representative government. This paper deals with the solution which the Federalists proposed and acted upon and the response of the American people to it.

I

After the revelations of Talleyrand's duplicity in the XYZ affair, President John Adams called for unanimity in framing a defense program against France. When the Jeffersonian Republicans balked at some of the measures that pointed toward war rather than a negotiated settlement, the long-standing Federalist fear of fractional strife led them openly to identify their old political opponents not only as pernicious democrats but also as pro-French traitors. To insure unanimity of action against the French Directory, the Federalists launched a systematic legislative program directed against the opposition party.

The Alien and Sedition Laws have been described as "an effective weapon against what was deemed an especially pernicious and dangerous form of domestic opposition in time of war." Only the Alien Enemy Law, however, was made contingent upon a declaration of war. The rest of these ill-fated acts were designed to deal with domestic political opposition in time of peace. They were political devices which topped the levee erected by the Federalists to withstand the rising tide of Republicanism. Both the Naturalization and the Alien Friends Laws represented a growing distrust not only of aliens but also of the people in general; both acts were designed to restrict the growth of the opposition party. The Sedition Law, aimed directly at the Democratic-Republicans, was the capstone of the internal security program of the Federalist party.

Section one of the statute punished conspiracies and combinations to impede the operation of federal laws and set the penalty at not more than five years in prison and a $5,000 fine. The second section dealt solely with verbal opposition, providing penalties for any person, citizen or alien, making any "false, scandalous and malicious" statements against the President, either house of Congress, or the government with intent to defame them, or to bring them into contempt or disrepute, or to excite against them the hatred of the good people of the United States. The maximum penalty was two years imprisonment and a $2,000 fine.

The law allowed the truth of the critical remarks to stand as an absolute defense against the charge of sedition and specified that the jury, not the judge, should decide whether the words used violated the law. Finally, the law was to expire not at the termination of the diplomatic crisis with France but with the expiration of President Adams' term of office.

II

The view which the law takes of the offense of publishing and uttering seditious words depends upon the attitude held as to the relation of the rulers to the people. Are the people the superiors of the rulers, or are the rulers the superiors of the people? The first view holds that sovereignty resides with the people and not with the government. The so-called rulers are the elected agents and servants of the people, who may discuss questions relating not only to government policy but also to punishment or dismissal of dishonest, inadequate, or unpopular agents. If anyone disagrees with the faultfinding, they may advocate the cause of the agents. The most that can happen is the replacement of the agent with another more to the people's liking.

The criminal law of seditious libel which emerged in England during the seventeenth and eighteenth centuries developed at a time when the accepted view made the rulers the superiors of the people. By virtue of their exalted positions, the rulers were considered the wise and good guides of the country. Authority therefore had to be approached with proper decorum. Mistakes might be pointed out in respectful petitions, but whether the rulers were mistaken or not, no censure could be leveled against them. The people could not make adverse comments in conversation, in clandestine pamphlets, or later in newspapers. The only lawful method of presenting grievances was through their lawful representatives in the legislature, who might be petitioned in an orderly and dignified manner.

This view made words punishable, because to find fault with the government tended to undermine the respect of the people for it and to reduce its dignity and authority. The "bad tendency" test, moreover, presumed that criticism tended to overthrow the state. There was no need to prove any intention on the part of the defendant to produce disaffection or to excite an insurrection; it was enough if he intended to publish the blame. The law of seditious libel was thus the product of the view that the government was master.

III

It was to this English common-law concept that the Federalists turned for their model. Even so, they attempted to adapt the authoritarian practice to the basic realities of popular government by working out a compromise between the rights of the authorities and the rights of the people. An aristocratic party which deplored political democracy, they based their defense of the right of authorities to freedom from public criticism, paradoxically enough, on the fact that the American government rested on the consent of the governed. They contended that the election of officials by the people demonstrated the confidence which the people had in those officers. Once these officials had been elevated by the people to the highest offices in the land, they became the "constituted authorities" who ran things until the next election. Thus, the Federalists exalted the officeholder above the mass of the citizens. It was a greater offense to criticize one of the rulers than it was to criticize one of the people themselves, because the rulers partook of the majesty of the whole people.

The Federalist theory of government, moreover, held that the right of political participation was not the province of all men but the prerogative of a chosen few. As Jay put it, "those who own the country are the most fit persons to participate in the government of it." The Sedition Law was consistent with the Federalist concept of an elite ruling class. Thinking that the stability of American society depended on "the few, the rich, and the well born," they opposed any criticism which might threaten their positions as rulers by undermining public confidence in their administration. Because they had been in power since the adoption of the Constitution, they looked upon themselves as the peculiar guardians of the nation's welfare. By identifying their administration with the government, and the government with the Constitution, the Federalists concluded that criticism of their administration was an attempt to subvert the Constitution and to overthrow the government.

The Republicans agreed that the government of the United States rests on the people, but they widened the concept of "public confidence" to coincide with "public opinion." Elected officials could lose the confidence of the people as well as gain it. To continue to merit public confidence, their measures must meet public approval. Public opinion was not a cyclical phenomenon which appeared every two years to be registered at the polls. It was in the continual process of formulation and could be conveyed constitutionally in speeches or in the press. The people did not vote themselves out of further political participation by the act of voting in elected officials. They were free to examine the conduct of the authorities; they could denounce it as well as praise it. They did not have to wait until election time to withdraw their confidence from an agent whom they decided was unworthy of it.

The Republicans based their arguments against the law on the ground that it destroyed "the responsibility of public servants and public measures to the people." Madison specifically condemned the law, because it exposed the United States, "which acquired the honour of taking the lead among nations towards perfecting political principles," to the disgrace of retreating "towards the exploded doctrine that the administrators of the Government are the masters and not the servants of the people."

IV

Although the Federalists asserted that the Sedition Law was declaratory of the English common law, they also announced that it mitigated the rigors of the law as expounded by Blackstone. It made the intent of the speaker, as well as the tendency of his words, an essential element in the crime of seditious libel. Moreover, it allowed truth as a justification and made the jury the judge of the criminality of the utterances. Of what value to the accused were these three procedural safeguards?

The interpretation which the courts put on the truth provision made it worse than useless as an aid to the defendant. Under the rulings handed down by the judges of the Supreme Court on circuit, this supposed safeguard actually reversed the normal criminal law presumption of innocence. Instead of the government having to prove that the words of the accused were false, scandalous, and malicious, the defendant had to prove that they were true. As Judge Samuel Chase put it, the accused had to prove all of his statements "to the marrow. If he asserts three things and proves but two," the jurist said, "he fails in his defense, for he must prove the whole of his assertions to be true." This is a clear illustration of the doctrine of presumptive guilt; in practice, the courts presumed the defendant guilty until he proved himself innocent.

Moreover, the accused was required not only to prove the truth of every word in every statement but, in some instances, to prove an entire count in an indictment by the same witness. Even though the statement contained more than one point, the defendant could not introduce different witnesses to prove different points. According to Judge Chase, this practice would have been "irregular and subversive of every principle of law."

What was the effect of the clause requiring that bad intent should be proved? In every case, the government prosecutors and the judges presumed the bad intent of the speaker from the bad tendency of the words. Moreover, it was the tendency of the words to find fault with elected officials which was penalized and not the intent to cause violence. The courts narrowed the legal test of criminality to the pre-Revolutionary common-law test; persons were punished if the tendency of their words was to undermine public confidence in the elected officials and thus to render it less likely that they might be re-elected.

Finally, the function of the trial jury was reduced almost to that of a rubber stamp. It is evident from the replies of grand juries to charges from federal judges and from the verdicts of the trial juries that both were Federalist-dominated, if not made up exclusively of Federalists. The strictness with which the trial judges restricted defense challenges of jurors virtually prevented any challenges for political bias, and led to extensive criticism of the courts. Congressman Matthew Lyon, the first victim of the law, claimed that all of his trial jurors were chosen from towns which were hostile to him. The Callender case, however, is the only one in which it can be proved positively that the trial jury was Federalist to a man. Whether the juries were deliberately packed or not, they were usually chosen by the federal marshal, who was a Federalist and who became the keeper of the prisoner upon conviction. In no event can the juries be called impartial. Indeed, Beveridge observes that "the juries were nothing more than machines that registered the will, opinion, or even inclination of the national judges and the United States District Attorneys. In short, in these prosecutions, trial by jury in any real sense was not to be had."

Under the Sedition Law, the jury was to decide on the criminality of the utterance; one of its vital functions was to decide on the intent of the speaker. The proper duty of the court in sedition cases was to aid the jury in reaching a decision, by instructing it on what the law was in one set of circumstances or in another. The judges were given no power to pass on the facts of publication or intent. In practice, however, they determine the intent of the defendant.

In the trial of Thomas Cooper, a leading Republican publicist, Judge Chase ruled that the defendant's effort to prove the truth of his publication demonstrated his bad intent. The defendant's attempt to utilize the legal defense allowed by the Sedition Law, the judge declared, "showed that he intended to dare and defy the Government, and to provoke them, and his subsequent conduct satisfies my mind that such was his disposition. For he justifies the publication, and declares it to be formed in truth. It is proved to be his publication."

Thus the judge ruled, and directed the jury to find, that Cooper had published the words and that he had done so with a wicked intent. "Take this publication in all its parts," he told the jury, "and it is the boldest attempt I have known to poison the minds of the people." It was poison not because it incited the people to force and violence but because it criticized President John Adams in an election year, tending to defeat his campaign against Thomas Jefferson. In short, the instruction of the judges made verdicts of guilty virtually inevitable.

To summarize, then, the clause on truth was nullified by the courts, the right of the jury to decide the criminality of the writing was usurped by the presiding judges, and the test of intent was reduced to the seventeenth-century common-law test of bad tendency. Without these procedural safeguards, the Sedition Law was almost a duplicate of the English common law of seditious libel. Since intent was presumed from tendency, the test of criminality became the same: the tendency of the words to bring rulers into disrepute.

Every man convicted under the Sedition Law was fined and imprisoned for political expressions critical of the administration in power. Indeed, the chief enforcement effort was tied directly to the campaign of 1800. As the contest between Jefferson and Adams approached, Secretary of State Timothy Pickering made systematic plans for action against the leading Republican papers in the United States. The opposition press was led by five papers—the Philadelphia *Aurora*, the Boston *Chronicle*, the New York *Argus*, the Richmond *Examiner*, and the Baltimore *American*. Because of their strategic geographical location and their able editorial direction, these gazettes circulated widely. Nor was their influence confined to their subscription lists. In those days before the communications revolution, the smaller newspapers consisted largely of material reprinted from the important journals. Thus, a blow at any of the "big five" Republican presses would be a severe setback to the Democratic-Republican party in 1800.

In the summer of 1799, Pickering launched a campaign to prosecute every one of the leading Republican papers which either had not been prosecuted under the Sedition Law or which had no cases pending against it. He took personal charge of the proceedings against William Duane, editor of the *Aurora*, and received the approval of President Adams. Since the *Chronicle* had been chastised, the secretary omitted Boston but wrote identical directives to the district attorneys in New York, Richmond, and Baltimore instructing them to scrutinize the Republican papers issued in their cities and to prosecute them for any seditious libels against the President or any federal official.

The timing of these communiqués is important. They were written early in August, 1799, so that the district attorneys would have time to bring indictments at the September or October term of circuit court. Even if the trial had to be postponed until the April or May term in 1800, as was the case against the New York *Argus*, it would still come in time to silence the papers or their editors during the campaign of 1800. As a result of Pickering's efforts, suits were brought against every one of the "big five" Republican journals except the Baltimore *American*. Moreover, four other Republican newspapers of lesser importance were prosecuted, and three were forced out of business.

In every case in which the law was enforced, a political crime was punished for the same reason that all political crimes have ever been punished—for expressions of discontent with the authorities. As Professor Schofield has pointed out, the sedition cases clearly demonstrated "the great danger . . . that men will be fined and imprisoned, under the guise of being punished for their bad motives, or bad intent and ends, simply because the powers that be do not agree with their opinions, and spokesmen of minorities may be terrorized and silenced when they are most needed by the community and most useful to it, and when they stand most in need of the protection of the law against a hostile, arrogant majority."

The evidence is conclusive that the Sedition Law, as enforced, reduced the limits of speech and press in the United States to those set by the English common law in the days before the American Revolution. This was the standard advocated by the Federalists who enacted the law, and it was the standard applied by the Federalist judges who interpreted the law.

v

The basic question, then, is this: is the pre-Revolutionary rule the guide to the liberties protected by the First Amendment? Is the bad tendency test compatible with free and open discussion of public affairs by the people? Formulated in an age of authority, the common-law doctrine of seditious utterances was anti-republican to the core. When Blackstone wrote his *Commentaries*, in 1769, he was trying to describe the law as it then existed. Although prior censorship had expired seventy-five years before he wrote, the government continued to institute numerous sedition prosecutions. Blackstone discussed the importance of a free press in a free state, but he insisted that liberty of the press meant only that no restraints could be laid upon writings prior to their publication.

This definition, however, legalized suppression any time after the moment of publication; the most vital or the most harmless discussion of public policy could be punished if it was obnoxious to the authorities. Common law asserted the right of the state to punish true statements about public magistrates, if they tended to expose them to public hatred, contempt, and ridicule. Sir James Fitzjames Stephen has observed that the practical enforcement of the law of seditious libel in England "was wholly inconsistent with any serious public discussion of political affairs." As long as it was recognized as the law of the land, any political discussion existed only by sufferance of the government.

By following this British precedent, which held that liberty of the press was conferred on the British people by the government when Parliament failed to extend the Licensing Act in 1695, the Federalists subscribed to the authoritarian view that the government is the master, not the servant, of the people.

VI

The American Revolution culminated in the formulation and establishment in the United States of a form of government which rested on the will of the governed. Growing out of the natural-rights philosophy of the seventeenth and eighteenth centuries, this revolutionary theory of government was founded on the principle that governments are instituted to secure, among other things, the liberties of the individual. A written Constitution established a limited government, which was barred from invading these "inalienable rights."

The meaning of the First Amendment did not crystallize in 1791, when the Bill of Rights was added to the Constitution. Not until the years from 1798 to 1801, when the Sedition Act was debated and enforced, did the limits of liberty of speech and of the press become an issue which focused attention squarely on its definition as a part of the American experiment in self-government. The first thing to be kept in mind in determining the meaning of the First Amendment is that it was added by the people as a further bulwark guarding civil liberties in the United States from governmental interference. Moreover, the liberties protected by the First Amendment were those prevailing not in England but in the United States.

One of the political catalysts of the American Revolution was the effort of the British to subdue the popular press in colonial America. This attempt was twofold. Under the Stamp Act of 1765, a prohibitive tax was placed on the paper used by the press. Had this law been executed, it would have forced out of circulation the inexpensive press, thus suppressing colonial discussion of politics in the popular papers. A second method used to crush colonial opposition to ministerial policies was an accelerated use of the law of seditious libel. Indeed, when George III issued his proclamation of rebellion against the American colonies, he gave as its official title "A Proclamation, By the King, for Suppressing Rebellion and Sedition."

There are several important pronouncements prior to the debates of 1798 which indicate that liberty of the press in the post-Revolutionary United States meant more than the English common-law rule. Many of the colonial publications on political affairs were considered seditious and even treasonable under the common law and its loose administration by the King's judges. That one of the objects of the American Revolution was to abolish the common-law restriction on liberty of the press, especially on political discussion, is illustrated by one of the addresses framed by the first Continental Congress in 1774.

In a letter addressed to the inhabitants of Quebec, Congress enumerated five rights basic to a free government. One of these was liberty of the press. "Besides the advancement of truth, science, morality, and arts in general," its importance consisted "in its diffusion of liberal sentiments on the administration of Government, its ready communication of thought between subjects, and the consequential promotion of union among them, whereby oppressive officers are shamed or intimidated into more honourable and just modes of conducting affairs."

This statement of liberty of the press specifically denies the right of the government to censure remarks because of their tendency to bring magistrates into public shame and contempt. Indeed, it asserts the opposite right of criticizing administrative officials chosen by the "free and full consent" of the governed.

The Declaration of Independence, of course, was the classic repudiation of the idea that the government was the master of the people. The Virginia bill for establishing religious freedom, written by the author of the Declaration, is another Revolutionary document which sets forth a philosophical justification of the right of a person to intellectual freedom. The preamble includes a declaration for individual liberty not only in the field of religion, but also in the field of civil affairs.

To suffer the civil magistrate to intrude his powers into the field of opinion [it reads] and to restrain the profession or propagation of principles on supposition of their ill tendency, is a dangerous falacy [*sic*], which at once destroys all religious liberty, because he being of course judge of that tendency, will make his opinions the rule of judgment, and approve or condemn the sentiment of others only as they shall square with or differ from his own; that it is time enough for the rightful purposes of government for its officers to interfere when principles break out into overt acts against peace and good order; and finally, that truth is great and will prevail if left to herself; that she is the proper and sufficient antagonist to error, and has nothing to fear from the conflict unless by human interposition disarmed of her natural weapons, free argument and debate; errors ceasing to be dangerous when it is permitted freely to contradict them.

The basic doctrine of this bill, which Jefferson always ranked next to the Declaration of Independence, was its rejection of the bad tendency test in the field of opinion. It announced the right of an individual to choose his beliefs, religious or political, free from compulsion.

One of the strongest statements made in 1798 on the American meaning of liberty of the press was contained in the reply of the Federalist envoys to France in answer to Talleyrand's protest against remarks in the American press critical of the Directory. "The genius of the Constitution," wrote Marshall, Pinckney, and Gerry, in a passage which their fellow Federalists ignored, "and the opinion of the people of the United States, cannot be overruled by those who administer the Government. Among those principles deemed sacred in America, among those sacred rights considered as forming the bulwark of their liberty, which the Government contemplates with awful reverence and would approach only with the most cautious circumspection, there is no one of which the importance is more deeply impressed on the public mind than the liberty of the press."

All these statements went much farther than the Blackstonian theory which held that liberty of the press prevented only government censorship. Although they all agreed that the absence of censorship was an important part of that freedom, they also asserted the right of the people to participate in free and full discussion of public affairs. They were declarations based on American experience, not on British precedents. They rejected the authoritarian view that the rulers are the superiors of the people.

VII

The Alien and Sedition Laws played a prominent role in shaping the American tradition of civil liberties. Based on the concept that the government was master, these laws provoked a public response which clearly demonstrated that the people occupied that position. The severity of the Sedition Law failed to prevent the "overthrow" of the Adams administration by the Jeffersonian "disorganizers." Indeed, the law furnished a ready text which the Republicans used to incite the American people to legal "insurgency" at the polls; the election resulted in the repudiation of the party which tried to protect itself behind the Sedition Law. The defeat of the Federalists illustrates the common understanding that the First

Amendment abolished the English common-law crime of seditious libel, of which the Sedition Law was merely declaratory.

The adherence of the people to the Republicans marked the beginning of a new political era. As John Adams himself pointed out, the election resulted in the "revolution of 1801": the Age of Federalism was at an end. Public opinion had never been without its influence on the conduct of government, but it had been grudgingly acknowledged by the Federalists. It now became the basis of American democratic development. As early as 1794, Madison had stated concisely what has since become the traditional American view: "If we advert to the nature of Republican Government, we shall find that the censorial power is in the people over the Government, and not in the Government over the people."

In his first inaugural address, Jefferson made this his main theme. Referring to the election of 1800 as a "contest of opinion" which had been decided by "the voice of the nation," the new President reasserted the right of the people "to think freely and to speak and to write what they think." Although he stoutly defended the right of the majority to rule, he cautioned that its will "to be rightful must be reasonable. The minority," he declared, "possess their equal rights, which equal law must protect, and to violate would be oppression." In a passage which condemned the Sedition Law without naming it, he restated the fundamental principle of the American experiment in popular government:

If there be any among us who would wish to dissolve this Union or to change its republican form, let them stand undisturbed as monuments of the safety with which error of opinion may be tolerated where reason is left free to combat it. I know, indeed, that some honest men fear that a republican government can not be strong, that this Government is not strong enough; but would the honest patriot, in the full tide of successful experiment, abandon a government which has so far kept us free and firm on the theoretic and visionary fear that this Government, the world's best hope, may by possibility want energy to preserve itself? I trust not. I believe this, on the contrary, the strongest Government on earth. I believe it the only one where every man, at the call of the law, would fly to the standard of the law, and would meet invasions of the public order as his own personal concern. Sometimes it is said that man can not be trusted with the government of himself. Can he, then, be trusted with the government of others? Or have we found angels in the forms of kings to govern him? Let history answer this question.

20 *Reginald Horsman*

WESTERN WAR AIMS, 1811–1812

In looking at the long arc of American development from the achievement of independence to the Civil War, one has perforce to find a place for the War of 1812. There is an imperative connection between knowing what the war was about and knowing what the whole period was about. The one defines the nature and importance of the other.

But then what exactly was the War of 1812? By and large, answers to this question have fallen into three broad categories. One view, expressed by Madison in his war message to Congress and widely accepted by historians during the nineteenth century, is that the Americans were fighting to protect their maritime rights and preserve their national honor. A second is that they were agrarian imperialists intent upon getting new lands in general and Canada in particular. A third is that they wished to remove the Indian threat to their frontiers and could do it only by defeating Great Britain, the friend and instigator of the Indians. In explaining the War of 1812, we have been better able to understand why Americans should have fought for land and security than for honor and maritime rights, particularly since the shipping interests of the Northeast did not want war at all. For this reason, the prevalent explanation during the past few decades has been that the war sprang from material interests, from the Western desire to protect its frontiers and to add to its domain.

There is of course another possible explanation. There may have been a close connection between Western interests and maritime rights. The connection has been suggested by a few historians but never extensively pursued. It is carefully explored in the following essay by Professor Reginald Horsman of the University of Wisconsin (at Milwaukee). In pursuing his thesis, Professor Horsman undertakes to answer several relevant questions. Why may it be argued that the war was a distinctly commercial one? What were the interests of the South and of the West in the export trade? To what extent did the Indian policy and the accession of Canada figure in the pro-war speeches of the War Hawks? What connection was there, finally, between the national pocket and the national pride and how could touching the American in the first become a sufficient basis for ruffling him in the second?

There is such a dramatic unleashing of forces after the War of

Reprinted with permission from *Indiana Magazine of History*, LIII (March, 1957), 1–18.

1812 that the relevance of the war to the forces must be understood. By contrast, the quarter-century before 1815 seems hardly as constructive and expansive as that which followed. Why? Perhaps the appearance is somewhat deceiving. Or perhaps the national energy expressed itself in laying foundations and building institutions. Perhaps, too, a nation conceived in liberty and dedicated to the pursuit of happiness could not conceivably be free or happy in an age of global war between Britain and France, one into which were swept all the states of the Atlantic world.

In itself, the war would not seem, at first sight, to have been of commanding importance. The military and naval battles have neither the primitive heroism of the American Revolution nor the bitter tragedy of the Civil War. When seen in perspective, however, the war stands out as a watershed of profound social and political change. Its nature and causes afford us a significant view of that larger arc of American development from 1776 to 1861.

It is an interesting paradox that a war of such insignificant proportions as that of 1812 should have produced such controversy concerning its causes. Nineteenth century historians, with a unanimity more characteristic of that century than of this, in general accepted the view that the war was essentially a struggle to defend American neutral rights and the national honor against the aggressions of Great Britain. In the present century this unanimity has been shattered. Historian after historian has placed his own particular interpretation on the events preceding the outbreak of war in June, 1812.

Of all the works produced during these years, undoubtedly the most influential has been Julius Pratt's *Expansionists of 1812*, published some thirty years ago.[1] Professor Pratt stated in his introduction that he only intended to examine one set of causes of the war,[2] but this has not prevented later historians from according the work an importance far out of proportion to this statement. Pratt's main thesis was that a factor of primary significance in the causes of the war was the western demand that the British, accused of instigating Indian troubles, should be expelled

[1] Julius W. Pratt, *Expansionists of 1812* (New York, 1925). For earlier attempts to modify the nineteenth century interpretations of the war, see D. R. Anderson, "The Insurgents of 1811," American Historical Association *Annual Report*, 1911 (Washington, 1913), I, 165-176; Howard T. Lewis, "A Re-Analysis of the Causes of the War of 1812," *Americana*, VI (1911), 506-516, 577-585; Christopher B. Coleman, "The Ohio Valley in the Preliminaries of the War of 1812," *Mississippi Valley Historical Review*, VII (1920), 39-50; Louis M. Hacker, "Western Land Hunger and the War of 1812: A Conjecture," *ibid.*, X (1924), 365-395. It was only with the publication of Pratt's work that attempts at a western interpretation of the war achieved general acceptance.

[2] Pratt, *Expansionists of 1812*, 14.

from Canada. This, he argued, was matched by a southern demand for the
Floridas for agrarian, commercial, and strategic reasons. Thus the northern and southern Republicans arrived at an understanding that the acquisition of Canada on the north was to be balanced by the annexation of the
Floridas on the south.[3]

Since the publication of Pratt's work in 1925 his ideas have exerted a
constant influence upon historians—so much so that two standard works
on American diplomatic history, Bemis and Bailey,[4] both base their final
conclusions regarding the origins of the war on Professor Pratt's thesis.
Samuel F. Bemis, after dealing mainly with maritime questions, concludes
that the War of 1812 was finally caused by a western expansionist urge
rather than solely by the grievances of neutral rights and impressment,
and as authority for this statement refers to Pratt.[5] Thomas A. Bailey,
after a more balanced presentation of the origins of the conflict, states
that the presence of Canada probably tipped the scales in favor of war.[6]
Nevertheless, in spite of these recent acceptances of Pratt's western expansionist theories, his ideas have not gone unchallenged since 1925.

The most relevant criticisms came in 1931 in two articles by George
Rogers Taylor on agricultural conditions in the Mississippi Valley in the
years preceding the War of 1812.[7] Taylor argued that the westerners
were suffering a commercial depression, and that they had a vital interest
in British commercial regulations. He endeavored to show that it was not
necessary to seek non-commercial motives to explain the western attitude
toward the war. These ideas received remarkably little attention during
the remainder of the 1930's, though Bernard Mayo in his excellent study
of the young Henry Clay enthusiastically endorsed many of Taylor's
views.[8]

It was not until 1941, with the publication of Warren H. Goodman's
article on the historiography of the origins of the war, that it was possible
to find conveniently summarized the various conflicting theories which
had been advanced by historians.[9] In this article, the most significant con-

[3] *Ibid.,* 12–13.

[4] Samuel Flagg Bemis, *A Diplomatic History of the United States* (3d ed., New
York, 1953); Thomas A. Bailey, *A Diplomatic History of the American People* (4th
ed., New York, 1950).

[5] Bemis, *Diplomatic History,* 156–157.   [6] Bailey, *Diplomatic History,* 136.

[7] George Rogers Taylor, "Prices in the Mississippi Valley Preceding the War of
1812," *Journal of Economic and Business History,* III (1930), 148–163; Taylor, "Agrarian Discontent in the Mississippi Valley Preceding the War of 1812," *Journal of
Political Economy,* XXXIX (1931), 471–505.

[8] Bernard Mayo, *Henry Clay: Spokesman of the New West* (Boston, 1937). This
work contains one of the best discussions of the origins of the war, though it has received scant attention from historians.

[9] Warren H. Goodman, "The Origins of the War of 1812: A Survey of Changing
Interpretations," *Mississippi Valley Historical Review,* XXVIII (1941), 171–186.

tribution to the problem in recent years, Goodman surveyed the changing interpretations of the war and reasoned that both the advocates of maritime rights as well as of expansionist theories had been too extreme in their views. In his opinion the importance of the northwestern desire to annex Canada to prevent Indian depredations, and of the southern desire to annex Florida, had been overestimated, and the articles by Taylor on agricultural conditions in the Mississippi Valley deserved more attention.[10]

Goodman's plea for a more balanced viewpoint has not had any marked effect on historians in the years since 1941. The major contribution of this period has been Alfred L. Burt's study of the relations of Britain, her North American colonies, and the United States between 1783 and 1818.[11] Professor Burt in this careful study of the diplomacy of the period returned, in some measure, to a nineteenth century view of the war. He argued that the questions of neutral rights and impressment formed the essence of the conflict, and he rejected Pratt's theories concerning peculiarly western aims. Taylor's opinions regarding the depression in the Mississippi Valley were not considered in Burt's arguments, though he briefly pointed out the importance of the commercial depression in the southern states in arousing anger against England.[12] This southern aspect of the origins of the war received more detailed treatment in July, 1956, in an article by Margaret K. Latimer on South Carolina as a protagonist of the conflict.[13] Miss Latimer contended that South Carolina favored the war against England because of the depressed state of her export trade in cotton. She also briefly suggested that the West saw in war the solution of its commercial difficulties.[14]

Professor Pratt has not allowed the various attacks on his theories to go unchallenged. Both in his 1941 review of Burt's volume,[15] and in his general history of American foreign policy, published in 1955,[16] he restated his opinions concerning the importance of particular western demands. He has not, however, offered anything essentially new, though he now acknowledges that depressed agricultural conditions were a factor in American anger.[17] Professor Pratt still stands by the theories which he first produced some thirty years ago.

There still remains therefore considerable divergence on this question of the origins of the War of 1812, and of why the West so enthusi-

---

[10] *Ibid.*, 180–185.

[11] Alfred L. Burt, *The United States, Great Britain, and British North America, from the Revolution to the Establishment of Peace after the War of 1812* (New Haven, 1940).   [12] *Ibid.*, 211–224, 305–310.

[13] Margaret Kinnard Latimer, "South Carolina—A Protagonist of the War of 1812," *American Historical Review*, LXI (1956), 914–929.   [14] *Ibid.*, 928.

[15] *American Historical Review*, XLVII (1941), 87–89.

[16] Julius W. Pratt, *A History of United States Foreign Policy* (New York, 1955).

[17] *American Historical Review*, XLVII (1941), 88.

astically gave its support to the war measures. The three main streams of opinion, exemplified by the views of Pratt, Taylor, and Burt, in turn show the war-supporters as eager to revenge Indian depredations by the conquest of Canada, desperate and angry owing to the loss of overseas markets for their goods, and burning with patriotic anger at British aggressions, particularly impressment. The tendency of other historians in studying this confused topic is either to list divergent reasons for war without any attempt at division into degrees of importance, or to choose one reason and to relegate the others to a position of relative insignificance. Yet, in spite of this confusion, it does seem possible to create some pattern from this jigsaw of neutral rights, agricultural depression, expansionism, and fear of Indian attack, and to assess the relative importance of causes.

The question of overseas markets for American produce is undoubtedly basic to the problem of why the West and the South led America to war in 1812. The factor that originally led historians to seek non-commercial causes for the conflict was that in the vote for war in Congress, the Northeast, the foremost commercial and shipping area, was the section opposed to the conflict.[18] This, however, is not a reason for supposing that non-commercial factors were the primary cause of the war. The fact is that the shippers of New England, engaged in an extensive wartime carrying trade, were able, in spite of British restrictions, to make a considerable profit.[19] They were quite prepared to condone British practices and oppose war with that country as long as these profits were available. They realized that they had much to lose by war. Abstract questions of neutral rights bore little weight with the commercial New Englander waxing rich in spite of all foreign restrictions.

The case was much different in the West and South. These areas harbored the producers not the carriers. They were not concerned with the vast profits of the carrying trade but with the more marginal question of selling their produce. The South, it is commonly agreed, depended to a great extent on her export of tobacco and cotton, but in the case of the West there has been disagreement. Writers have, on occasion, taken the view that as the West was in a primitive agricultural state it was not concerned with the matter of exporting its produce.[20] It is true that the West was not engaged in an extensive overseas export trade, but the fact that its overseas exports were small made it all the more essential that this trade should not be interrupted. The farmer of the West needed purchasing

18 See Charles O. Paullin and John K. Wright, *Atlas of the Historical Geography of the United States* (Washington, 1932), 109.

19 Samuel E. Morison, *The Maritime History of Massachusetts* (Boston, 1941), 191.

20 See, for example, Hacker, "Western Land Hunger...," *Mississippi Valley Historical Review*, X, 366.

power for his land, for manufactured articles, and for small luxuries in his home and diet.[21] This fact has been brought out by Taylor in his two articles, and he also shows, by a careful consideration of the prices for western produce at New Orleans, that in the years from 1808 to 1812 the Mississippi Valley was in a period of agricultural depression. At a time when costs were remaining stationary or even rising, the prices which farmers could obtain for their produce were falling rapidly.[22]

The important fact, however, is not that there was a depression but that the westerners attributed this depression to British commercial restrictions. Throughout the debates of the Twelfth Congress in 1811 and 1812 it is apparent that westerners and southerners were convinced that the British were ruining the overseas market. Frequently, in works stressing western expansionist urges as the basic cause for war, the words of Henry Clay and Richard M. Johnson of Kentucky, of Peter B. Porter of western New York, and of Felix Grundy of Tennessee, have been quoted. These men have been taken as living proofs of the dominating urge of the West to take Canada and subdue the Indians. A careful consideration of their speeches in Congress shows, however, that though they spoke with feeling and eloquence of the atrocities of the Indians and of taking Canada, the *dominating* themes of their speeches were the questions of maritime rights, especially the right to export American produce.

On December 6, 1811, Peter B. Porter opened the debate on the report of the Foreign Relations Committee,[23] of which he was chairman. He stated: "The committee thought that the Orders in Council, so far as they go to interrupt our direct trade, that is, the carrying of the productions of this country to a market in the ports of friendly nations, and returning with the proceeds of them—ought to be resisted by war."[24] He was maintaining, in no uncertain terms, that the United States should fight for the right to sell her produce. His brother War Hawks gave him full support. The greatest War Hawk of them all, Henry Clay, contended that, "to-day we are asserting our right to the direct trade—the right to export our cotton, tobacco, and other domestic produce to market."[25] Clay was echoing the sentiments of his fellow Kentuckian, Richard M. Johnson, who, as far back as April 16, 1810, had argued that there was no doubt that America had just cause of hostility: "At this moment France and Great Britain have decrees in force, which regulate at their pleasure the exportation of our own produce—the produce of our own soil and

---

[21] Taylor, "Prices in the Mississippi Valley . . . ," *Journal of Economic and Business History,* III, 148.   [22] *Ibid.,* 154–163.

[23] On the Foreign Relations Committee were a group of ardent war-supporters: John C. Calhoun, Joseph Desha, Felix Grundy, John A. Harper, and Peter B. Porter. The report of the committee was presented on November 29. *Annals of Congress,* 12th Cong., 1st Sess., 373–377.   [24] *Ibid.,* 414.   [25] *Ibid.,* 601, Dec. 31, 1811.

labor."[26] This was not a question of the westerners urging war to defend the carrying trade of New England, but the westerners claiming the right to export the produce of their own area. Felix Grundy of Tennessee, who is regarded as one of the most fervent Indian haters and supporters of the drive for Canada said, on December 9, 1811, that the point of contention between the United States and Great Britain "is the right of exporting the productions of our own soil and industry to foreign markets."[27]

The westerners received full support in this connection from their allies of the South, and it would appear that this unity stemmed from a common interest in the sale of their produce. Robert Wright from Maryland stated on December 11, 1811, after a violent attack on British restrictions on American trade, that "we are to look for the cause of the reduction of the prices of our cotton and tobacco in the political and commercial history of Europe."[28] John C. Calhoun, talking of the people of the South, said that "they see in the low price of the produce, the hand of foreign injustice."[29]

This commercial desire of the war party did not go unnoticed by the opposition. Historians favoring the western expansionist theory have been fascinated by John Randolph of Virginia,[30] who so passionately denounced the westerners for seeking a war of aggression. A favorite quotation is his famous "we have heard but one word—like the whip-poor-will, but one eternal monotonous tone—Canada! Canada! Canada!"[31] It is forgotten that in his wandering half-demented diatribes Randolph attributed practically every reason for desiring war to the War Hawks. Other less vehement, but perhaps more sane, members of the opposition saw other motives behind the desires of the war party. On December 13, 1811, Adam Boyd of New Jersey stated bluntly: "You go to war for the right to export our surplus produce—tobacco, cotton, flour, with many other articles."[32] Daniel Sheffey of Virginia, in a long and penetrating speech on January 3, 1812, came to this conclusion: "No! the nominal repeal of the Orders in Council is not your object. It is the substantial commercial benefit which you conceive will follow that act, that forms the essence of the controversy. The unmolested commerce to France and her dependencies is the boon for which you are going to war. This is the real object, disguise it as you will."[33] Such observations of the opposition may of course have been completely unfounded, but it is at least possible to give

26 *Ibid.*, 11th Cong., 2d Sess., 1869.

27 *Ibid.*, 12th Cong., 1st Sess., 424; see also *ibid.*, 487–503.

28 *Ibid.*, 470.   29 *Ibid.*, 482, Dec. 12, 1811; see also *ibid.*, 682.

30 See, for example, Pratt, *Expansionists of 1812*, 141–144; Hacker, "Western Land Hunger . . . ," *Mississippi Valley Historical Review*, X, 376.

31 *Annals of Congress*, 12th Cong., 1st Sess., 533, Dec. 16, 1811.

32 *Ibid.*, 521.   33 *Ibid.*, 623.

them as much weight as the exponents of the expansionist theories give to the utterances of Randolph.

In the West itself there seems much evidence that the representatives in Congress were only reflecting the views of their constituents. Bernard Mayo in his biography of Clay states, after an examination of Kentucky newspapers, that "unprecedented hard times" caused by Britain's illegal monopoly was the constant theme of distressed farmers in this period from 1810 to 1812.[34] On December 10, 1811, the *Reporter* of Lexington, Kentucky, stated: "It appears that our government will at last make war, to produce a market for our Tobacco, Flour, and Cotton."[35] A particularly significant series of petitions was presented to Congress from Mississippi Territory in September and November, 1811.[36] There were two petitions from the inhabitants of the territory, and one from the territorial legislature. All the petitions requested that the payment of instalments on the petitioners' land should be deferred until a later date, owing to a lack of specie. The petitioners stated that they were dependent upon foreign commerce for money, and that the price of cotton had been so reduced that they could not discharge the annual expenses of their families, much less pay for their lands. All three petitions attributed this to the destructive effects of foreign restrictions upon American commerce. The petition of November 11 admirably summarized the importance of foreign commercial regulations to this area of the West: "The Severe pressure of the times arising From the unjust Edicts of Foreign Governments, and the unpresedented State of the world. . . the Violation of the legitimate and well Established Rights of neutral Commerce on the high seas, to which the Belligerents of Europe have resorted Are not confin'd in their Destructive consequences to the Commercial enterprize of our Country—But their effects are seen and Felt among the humble Cultivators of the Soil—Who Depend for the reward of their laborious Occupations on an Oppertunity to convey the Surpless Products of their Industry to Those Countries in which they are consumed."[37]

There seems little doubt that the West, through its representatives in Congress and on the frontier itself, had a vital interest in its export market, and that it was attributing the loss of this market and the subsequent decline in prices primarily to British commercial restrictions. It is not surprising then that in Congress in 1811 and 1812 the western representatives spoke vigorously of the need to defend American maritime rights—this

[34] Mayo, *Henry Clay*, 382–383.

[35] *Reporter* (Lexington, Kentucky), Dec. 10, 1811, quoted in Taylor, "Agrarian Discontent . . . ," *Journal of Political Economy*, XXXIX, 500.

[36] Clarence E. Carter (ed.), *The Territorial Papers of the United States*, VI, *The Territory of Mississippi: 1809–1817* (Washington, 1938), 226–227, 238–240, 241–242.

[37] *Ibid.*, 239.

was not, as the advocates of the expansionist theories would maintain, simply a façade, hiding the real western desire to conquer Canada; it was a genuine feeling that if the West and South were to have a market for their produce British restrictions would have to be resisted.

In reading works such as Pratt it is possible to obtain the impression that the War Hawks talked constantly of Canada and of the Indians, and ignored maritime questions. This was not the case; by far the greater part of the argument of the War Hawks was devoted to attacking British maritime depredations. They had a material interest in doing this, and what is more they had a genuine feeling that American national honor was suffering from British action at sea. Many of these men were young[38] and proud, and were willing to combine the principles of self-interest and honor. They felt anger at the British regulations which they thought had produced the commercial distress, and they felt anger at all the other British infringements of American rights. Only a quarter of a century before, the United States had struggled for independence against a country which now ignored this new-won freedom. The leaders of these War Hawks were young men who had been raised on the traditions of the War of Independence. The older generation, well represented by Jefferson and Madison, were "first generation revolutionaries"—men who had gambled for independence, had won, and were in their later years little inclined to risk their winnings in an uncertain war with England. Henry Clay and his young allies were the "second generation revolutionaries"— young men who were willing to take chances with the hard-won gains of their parents. They had grown to manhood hearing oft-repeated tales of the War of Independence, but they themselves had long been compelled to suffer without retaliation the constant infringement of American rights. The generation of the War Hawks had come of age during a period in which American seamen were being taken from American ships, and in which Britain had attempted to tell America how and what she should export. It is not surprising that when to these acts was added growing agricultural distress there was an ever-increasing cry for war.

The report of the Foreign Relations Committee of November 29, 1811,[39] recommending war preparations for the United States, concerned itself exclusively with maritime matters. This report, which bluntly stated that the time for submission was at an end, objected bitterly to British commercial regulations and to the practice of impressment. It summarized the essential cause of complaint against Great Britain with the argument

---

[38] Ages of some of the War Hawks when Congress met: William Lowndes. 20; John C. Calhoun, 29; George M. Troup, 32; Israel Pickens, 31; Henry Clay, 34; Felix Grundy, 34; Langdon Cheves, 36. See James L. Harrison (ed.), *Biographical Directory of the American Congress: 1774–1949* (Washington, 1950).

[39] *Annals of Congress,* 12th Cong., 1st Sess., 373–377.

that the United States claimed the right to export her products without losing either ships or men.[40] The arguments of the War Hawks in the ensuing debates clearly followed the lines of reasoning laid down in this report. Their leaders agreed that war was necessary against Britain for the defense of American maritime interests and honor. Richard M. Johnson of Kentucky speaking on December 11, 1811, certainly discussed Canada, as quoted by Pratt,[41] but previously he had stated: "Before we relinquish the conflict, I wish to see Great Britain renounce the piratical system of paper blockade; to liberate our captured seamen on board her ships of war; relinquish the practice of impressment on board our merchant vessels; to repeal her Orders in Council; and cease, in every other respect, to violate our neutral rights; to treat us as an independent people."[42]

In speech after speech the War Hawks echoed Johnson's sentiments.[43] Orders in Council, illegal blockades, impressment, and the general terms of neutral rights and national honor dominated their arguments. Clay himself stated on December 31, 1811: "What are we not to lose by peace?—commerce, character, a nation's best treasure, honor!"[44] Clay's whole argument in this speech was for the necessity of war to defend American maritime rights.

The letters of the War Hawks appear to support their public utterances. George W. Campbell, Senator from Tennessee, wrote to Andrew Jackson that it is "difficult to perceve [sic] how war can be avoided, without degrading the national character, still lower. . . . For there is no ground to expect G. Britain will abandon her system of depredation on our commerce, or her habitual violations of the personal rights of our citizens in the impressment of our seamen."[45] George M. Troup of Georgia wrote to Governor David B. Mitchell on February 12, 1812, denouncing all further temporizing or indecision. He wanted either war or an open abandonment of the contest—nothing else would satisfy the just expectations of the southern people, "who have been bearing the brunt of the restrictive system from the beginning."[46] William Lowndes of South Carolina was confident in December, 1811, that unless England repealed her Orders in Council, there would be war before the end of the session.[47] These westerners and southerners were vitally interested in maritime ques-

[40] *Ibid.*, 376.   [41] Pratt, *Expansionists of 1812*, 52.

[42] *Annals of Congress*, 12th Cong., 1st Sess., 457.

[43] *Ibid.*, 425, 467–475, 483–490, 502, 509, 517–518, 637, 658, 678–691.

[44] *Ibid.*, 599.

[45] Campbell to Jackson, Dec. 24, 1811, John Spencer Bassett (ed.), *The Correspondence of Andrew Jackson* (6 vols., Washington, 1926–1933), I, 212.

[46] Troup to Mitchell, Feb. 12, 1812, Edward J. Harden, *The Life of George M. Troup* (Savannah, 1859), 107.

[47] Lowndes to his wife, Dec. 7. 1811, Harriott Horry (Rutledge) Ravenel, *Life and Times of William Lowndes of South Carolina* (Boston, 1901), 90.

tions, and showed a very real awareness of the long years of British depredations upon American commerce.

Pratt's thesis that a factor of primary importance in producing the war was the desire of the westerners to prevent Indian troubles by expelling the British from Canada, has exerted such influence that it requires careful investigation. Some writers, notably Louis Hacker in his article on western land hunger, and Burt in his detailed study of this period, have attempted to eliminate the Indian problem as a factor in persuading the westerners to demand war.[48] It would seem from the available evidence that these writers are wrong in completely ignoring the Indian factor. Though it seems likely that the dominant motives of the West were related to British maritime actions, the importance, in certain areas, of the fear of British instigation of the Indians should not be underestimated. It seems likely in fact that, particularly after Tippecanoe, the suspected British backing of Indian depredations was of definite importance in bringing matters to a head, and in convincing the already aroused westerners that some warlike action against Great Britain was needed.

There is no doubt that the presence of hostile Indians on the frontier was of great importance to the westerners. Any careful study of the records of this period inevitably leads one to that conclusion. The debates of the Twelfth Congress and the territorial papers of Indiana, Michigan, and Louisiana-Missouri, have constant references to the Indian problem.[49] One has only to read the letters of Governor William Henry Harrison of Indiana to the War Department to realize the extent to which the thinking of certain areas of the West was dominated by this factor.[50]

Even more important from the point of view of this study is that there was no doubt in the minds of the settlers that the British were instigating the action of the Indians. On July 31, 1811, the citizens of Vincennes, Indiana, adopted a series of resolutions to petition the President regarding the danger from the Indians. The third of these petitions stated: "That we are fully convinced that the formation of this combination headed by the Shawanese prophet, is a British scheme, and that the agents of that power are constantly exciting the Indians to hostility against the United States."[51]

---

[48] Hacker, "Western Land Hunger . . . ," *Mississippi Valley Historical Review*, X, 372–374; Burt, *United States and Great Britain*, 305–310.

[49] See the debates of the Twelfth Congress *passim*, especially those of December, 1811; also, Carter, *The Territorial Papers of the United States*, VIII, *The Territory of Indiana, 1810–1816* (Washington, 1939); X, *The Territory of Michigan, 1805–1820* (Washington, 1942); XIV, *The Territory of Louisiana-Missouri, 1806–1814* (Washington, 1949).

[50] Logan Esarey (ed.), *Messages and Letters of William Henry Harrison* (2 vols., Indianapolis, 1922); this is Volume VII of the Indiana Historical *Collections*.

[51] *Ibid.*, 541.

In August the *Kentucky Gazette* stated that "we have in our possession information which proves beyond doubt, the late disturbances in the West to be owing to the too successful intrigues of British emissaries with the Indians."[52] The encounter at Tippecanoe on November 7, 1811, crystallized this western sentiment and convinced the settlers that British intrigues were bringing desolation to the frontier. Whatever the British policy was in reality, the American settlers undoubtedly were convinced that it was inciting the Indians to aggressive warfare.

The fact that the frontiersmen connected the British and the Indians is no reason for supposing that the prevention of this alliance was the *dominating* motive in the vote of Congress for war in 1812. This view fails to take into consideration several relevant facts. In the first place, the core of the feeling against the Indians was in the exposed northwest frontier—in the Indiana, Michigan, and Illinois territories, and it should be remembered that these areas had no vote in Congress. It is true, of course, that the anger against the supposed British inciting of the Indians was felt deeply outside the immediately exposed area—Kentucky was much incensed at the Indian depredations and Kentuckians fought and were killed at Tippecanoe;[53] also Andrew Jackson wrote from Tennessee offering Harrison the use of his forces after that encounter.[54] Yet, it is essential to realize that of the 79 votes for war in the House only a total of nine votes came from the states of Kentucky, Tennessee, and Ohio, while a total of 37 came from the South Atlantic states of Maryland, Virginia, North and South Carolina, and Georgia. Pennsylvania, a state of limited frontier area by this period, alone provided 16 votes for war.[55] There is no doubt that the *leaders* of the movement for war were often westerners, whether from the Ohio Valley, frontier New Hampshire, or western New York, but the actual vote for war depended on non-frontiersmen. The Indian menace undoubtedly influenced frontier areas, and in some was the dominating factor, but it seems unlikely that the large vote for war in non-frontier areas was inspired by a desire to protect the northwest frontier from Indian depredations. The importance of the argument concerning Indians in the Congressional debates of 1811 and 1812 has been greatly overestimated. British encouragement of the Indians was discussed in the war debates but it was discussed in connection with other factors. A reference to the murderous savages urged on by the

[52] *Kentucky Gazette*, August 27, 1811, quoted in Ellery L. Hall, "Canadian Annexation Sentiment in Kentucky Prior to the War of 1812," *Register of the Kentucky State Historical Society*, XXVIII (1930), 375.

[53] *Annals of Congress*, 12th Cong., 1st Sess., 425–426.

[54] Jackson to William Henry Harrison, Nov. 30, 1811, Bassett, *Correspondence of Andrew Jackson*, I, 210.

[55] See *Annals of Congress*, 12th Cong., 1st Sess., 1637, for list of voters; Paullin and Wright, *Atlas of Historical Geography*, 109, gives an analysis of the vote for war.

British provided a fine emotional climax to any speech, but it would appear that the argument which united the 79 representatives of diverse sections to vote for war was the more generally applicable one of the need to sell produce in order to live.

Arising out of the Indian problem is the important question of the demand for Canada. It may well be asked that if the dominant motive for war was not a desire to shatter the Anglo-Indian alliance, how can the fervent demand for the conquest of Canada be explained? The two theses explaining the demand for Canada which have received the most general support are those of Hacker and Pratt. Hacker[56] saw the reason for this, and for war itself, in a desire for Canadian land. Pratt disagreed with him and, in a subsequent article, effectively demonstrated the weaknesses in Hacker's argument.[57] Pratt considered, of course, that the demand for Canada arose from the supposed British instigation of the Indians. This view is worthy of careful consideration. Indeed it appears that in the case of certain areas—particularly the Indiana and Michigan Territories—the desire to quench support for the Indians was probably the dominating wish in the minds of the settlers in 1811 and 1812. Yet, while it is true that much of the debating of the Twelfth Congress was concerned with plans for the conquest of Canada, it would appear that in general these aims were not primarily inspired by a desire to prevent British support of the Indians.

Burt, in his detailed work on Britain, America, and Canada, suggests, without detailed elaboration, that the conquest of Canada was anticipated as the seizure of a hostage rather than as the capture of a prize.[58] It would seem from the debates in Congress that this was indeed the case. The key fact is that almost exclusively in their speeches the War Hawks first considered the *reasons* why war was necessary, and dwelt on maritime grievances, and then, when turning to the *methods* of waging war, discussed the question of invading Canada. It is true that the war party saw in the conquest of Canada an opportunity to prevent further Indian depredations, but there seems no reason to believe that this was in itself a sufficient reason for the war party to achieve such general support in 1812. The various sections of the United States were not sufficiently altruistic for the South Atlantic states to demand war and the conquest of Canada for the purpose of relieving the Northwest from Indian attacks. Yet, the demand for Canada entered into the speeches of the southerners as it did into the speeches of the western War Hawks. Pratt explained this away by contending that there was a sectional bargain, by which the

56 See footnote 1.

57 Julius W. Pratt, "Western Aims in the War of 1812," *Mississippi Valley Historical Review*, XII (1925), 36–50.

58 Burt, *United States and Great Britain*, 310.

South was to obtain Florida, and the West, Canada; but, as Goodman and Burt clearly show,[59] and as is apparent in the debates in Congress, the demand for Florida was a comparatively negligible factor in the actual demand for war. There seems little evidence to support the thesis that the South supported the demand for Canada in return for western support of southern claims to Florida.

Calhoun, the young South Carolinian, clearly stated the reasons for southern support of Canadian conquest, and helped to explain the general attitude of the war party, in a speech on December 12, 1811. In answering Randolph's taunt that the Canadas bore no relation to American shipping and maritime rights he stated: "By his system, if you receive a blow on the breast, you dare not return it on the head; you are obliged to measure and return it on the precise point on which it was received. If you do not proceed with mathematical accuracy, it ceases to be just self-defence; it becomes an unprovoked attack."[60] This gives the essence of the matter. Once the War Hawks had decided they wanted war, they were obliged to face the problem of where they could injure their mighty foe. At sea it seemed that there was little hope. Britain's vast navy, which had swept France from the seas, was to be matched against a handful of American frigates. Apart from the activities of American privateers there seemed little hope of waging effective war against Britain on the sea. The conquest of Canada was the obvious, if not the only method of injuring Britain. Clay's speech of February 22, 1810,[61] has been quoted as one of the first appeals for the conquest of Canada: "The conquest of Canada is in your power" are words of joy to the expansionist historian.[62] Yet these words were said after Clay had discussed British mercantile spoilations, and after he had stated that as peaceful measures had failed it was time for resistance by the sword. He then tried to convince the weak and vacillating Eleventh Congress that war against Great Britain was practicable, and that injury could be inflicted upon their enemy: "It is said, however, that no object is attainable by war with Great Britain. In its fortunes, we are to estimate not only the benefit to be derived to ourselves, but the injury to be done the enemy. The conquest of Canada is in your power."[63]

Members of the war party in the Twelfth Congress echoed these words of Clay. Two representatives of North Carolina—Israel Pickens and William R. King—summarized the essential reasoning behind the demand for Canada. King on December 13, 1811, stated that he was not enamored

[59] Goodman, "Origins of the War of 1812," *Mississippi Valley Historical Review,* XXXIII, 180–181; Burt, *United States and Great Britain,* 306.

[60] *Annals of Congress,* 12th Cong., 1st Sess., 481.

[61] *Ibid.,* 11th Cong., 2d Sess., 579–582.

[62] See Pratt, *Expansionists of 1812,* 40.

[63] *Annals of Congress,* 11th Cong., 2d Sess., 580.

of conquest but that this war had been forced upon America: "We cannot, under existing circumstances, avoid it. To wound our enemy in the most vulnerable part should only be considered."[64] Pickens, less than a month later, answered the opposition that though the contemplated attack on the British Provinces is called a war of offense, "when it is considered as the only mode in our reach, for defending rights universally recognised and avowedly violated, its character is changed."[65] Even calm and honest Nathaniel Macon of Virginia, whose opinion can surely be given as much weight as the impassioned and half-mad Randolph of the same state, contended that the war which the United States was about to enter was not a war of conquest—"Its object is to obtain the privilege of carrying the produce of our lands to a market"—but he considered that no war could long continue to be merely one of defense.[66] The War Hawks called for attack upon Canada because it was the only certain way they knew of attacking Britain.

Peaceful restriction had apparently failed and the West and South resolved to fight the British in the only area in which she appeared to be vulnerable, her North American provinces. Perhaps the most adequate summary by a westerner of why the West wanted to fight was that given by Andrew Jackson on March 12, 1812, when, as commander of the militia of the western district of Tennessee, he issued a call for volunteers from this area. In this document, if in no other, one would expect to see reflected the ideas and aspirations of the people of the West; a commander calling for volunteers does not use unpopular arguments. Under the heading, "For what are we going to fight?", Jackson wrote these words: "We are going to fight for the reestablishment of our national charector [sic], misunderstood and vilified at home and abroad; for the protection of our maritime citizens, impressed on board British ships of war and compelled to fight the battles of our enemies against ourselves; to vindicate our right to a free trade, and open a market for the productions of our soil, now perishing on our hands because the *mistress of the ocean* has forbid us to carry them to any foreign nation; in fine, to seek some indemnity for past injuries, some security against future aggressions, by the conquest of all the British dominions upon the continent of north america."[67]

The coming of war in 1812 was not a sudden event; it was the culmination of a long series of injuries and insults, of checks to American commerce, and of the infringement of American rights. The United States, under the leadership of Jefferson and Madison, repeatedly attempted to defend her rights by peaceful economic coercion. Yet, almost inevitably, a breaking point was reached. The time came when, with na-

---

[64] *Ibid.,* 12th Cong., 1st Sess., 519.
[65] *Ibid.,* 646, Jan. 4, 1812.   [66] *Ibid.,* 663, Jan. 4, 1812.
[67] Bassett, *Correspondence of Andrew Jackson,* I, 221–222.

tional honor at its lowest ebb, and large sections of agricultural America suffering depression, any war seemed preferable to a dishonorable and unprofitable peace. The young War Hawks who urged war in 1811 and 1812 had grown up in this atmosphere of the oppression of American rights, and with apparently nothing to gain by peace, urged America to fight for the right to exist as a fully independent nation. Considering the period through which they had grown to manhood, it is not surprising that they demanded war to preserve American commerce, neutral rights, and honor, and that, in order to revenge themselves upon their enemy, they proposed the invasion of Canada. The suspected British instigation of the Indians was an added irritant, but if Great Britain had pursued a conciliatory maritime policy towards the United States, it seems extremely unlikely that there would have been war between the two countries. The fundamental cause of the War of 1812 was the British maritime policy which hurt both the national pride and the commerce of the United States.

POLITICS IN AN
EXPANDING DEMOCRACY

21 *Samuel Flagg Bemis*

THE MONROE DOCTRINE: DIPLOMATIC
BACKGROUND, PRONOUNCEMENT, AND EFFECT,

1815–1826

The Monroe Doctrine is probably the most important pronouncement in the history of American foreign policy. It evolved from half a century of relations between the United States and the great European powers and chartered the course of those relations for more than a century to come. It asserted the central role of the United States in the history of the Western Hemisphere.

The traditional account of the Monroe Doctrine has certain limitations. It fails to show how far the United States was pursuing both practical goals and political ideals. It does not sufficiently explain the diplomatic involvements that formed the context of the doctrine. And it does not clearly indicate that the effective author of the Monroe Doctrine was John Quincy Adams. These limitations are corrected in the following account by Samuel Flagg Bemis, who recently retired as Sterling Professor of Diplomatic History and Inter-American Relations at Yale University. Without doubt the foremost authority in our day on American diplomatic history and twice the recipient of the Pulitzer Prize, Professor Bemis has tended in his many writings to focus his interest on the early national period. The Monroe Doctrine stands naturally and prominently in the line of his primary interest.

The diplomatic goal of the United States during that early period,

From *The Latin American Policy of the United States*, copyright, 1943, by Samuel Flagg Bemis. Reprinted by permission of Harcourt, Brace & World, Inc.

it may be said, was to insure its independence by securing its borders and to secure its borders by expanding them. This purpose explains, as Professor Bemis says, the Congressional resolution of 1811 against the transfer of American territory by one foreign power to another. It explains, also, the so-called Transcontinental Treaty of 1819, whereby the United States acquired the Floridas and set a new boundary between Spanish dominions and its own, from the Atlantic Ocean to the Pacific. It is certainly the basis for understanding how the Monroe Doctrine sought, first, to prevent the European powers from acting against the rebellious American colonies of Spain, thereby safeguarding the United States, and, second, to provide our country with the opportunities which would open up with the prevention of such European action.

The Monroe Doctrine is a particular through which the generality of American diplomacy may be studied. If the governing premises of our foreign relations in 1823 were territorial security and expansion, what were they before and what have they been since? What are they today? If the Monroe Doctrine was the gauntlet which a revolutionary republican order threw down to an established monarchical one, to what extent may the diplomacy of today also be seen as a conflict between a revolutionary order and an established one? How much have international relations been altered by new conditions of warfare, how much have they been altered by other conditions, such as the emergence of the totalitarian state? If John Quincy Adams played so important a role in defining the Doctrine, what were the roles of other outstanding men in producing great diplomatic developments? One cannot ask about the role of the individual in diplomatic history without also asking about the larger circumstances which shape diplomacy in any age. What was the complex of social and economic forces which the Monroe Doctrine expressed? How did the changing nature of those forces change the nature of the doctrine during the century after its pronouncement? What socio-economic complex does our diplomacy express today?

That our diplomacy has changed since 1823 there can be no doubt. The order we speak for is not exclusively republican. The premises we sustain are far from being revolutionary. We have become deeply involved in European wars. Looking at the course of our diplomatic history since the Monroe Doctrine, we ought to take some account of what change has occurred and why.

The initial Latin American policy of the United States had been to make sure that during the disruption of the Spanish Empire a more powerful European rival monarchy should not step into Spanish provinces contiguous to or close to the United States in such a way as to threaten its independence, security, and vital interests, the most vital interest after independence and security being that of continental expansion. The thesis of the preceding chapters is that the independence and the territorial integrity of the United States and its Manifest Destiny—using the phrase in its most proper sense: the opportunity to found a Continental Republic by expanding through to the other ocean—depended upon the fate of the Spanish borderlands of Florida and Texas, and ultimately of the island of Cuba. This inspired the lucky Louisiana procurement. It provoked the Florida question. It produced the notable No-Transfer Resolution of January 15, 1811. It resulted in the unsuccessful war with Great Britain of 1812–1815. It elicited the skillful diplomacy of John Quincy Adams and the magnificent achievement of the Transcontinental Treaty. It looked to the territorial basis of the United States of today.

To say that the original Latin American policy of the United States was dominated by self-interest plainly predicated is not to agree that it was devoid of political idealism. In guiding itself by the compass of national interest the Government was yielding to a natural magnet that animates all nations without exception. In following the polestar of independence and republican government it was pursuing political ideals so dear to the people as to have produced their nationhood. In championing the independence and liberties of the republican New World against the intrusions of the monarchical Old World it was upholding both its own interests and its own ideals, which were the interests and ideals of both American continents. In the Monroe Doctrine, as promulgated in the year 1823, there was a perfect union of interest and ideal. That doctrine expressed for the Western Hemisphere the final fruitage in policy of the Era of Emancipation: the independence of the republican New World and its separation from the wars and power-politics of monarchical Europe. I say it expressed the republican independence of the New World; it by no means guarded it effectively or guaranteed it, neither at the time of its pronouncement nor for a long time to come.

Occasionally a twentieth-century historian, usually writing in the Spanish language and well aware of the transcendent significance of the pristine Monroe Doctrine as a dictum of America for the Americans, would forsooth capture for President Monroe's original message a Spanish or a Latin American origin, particularly the non-colonization principle and the concept of two distinct and separate spheres of politics, American versus European. Such writers point to certain historical but isolated expressions of theory that by no means prevailed in their day. Thus the Spanish friar Francisco de Vitoria, exploring in the sixteenth century the theory of sovereignty and the relations of sovereigns to each other and to peoples, maintained piously that America and its aboriginal peoples could not be the object of occupation or colonization by Christian sovereigns, that is to say, by European powers. Nevertheless they were conquered and colonized. Again, the Emperor Charles V in 1519, with great convenience to himself and his Spanish heirs, promulgated a law, ratified by Philip II in 1563 and by Charles II in 1681, declaring the inviolability and indivisibility and non-alienability forever of the American possessions and peoples of the Crown of Castile. But portions of them, like Louisiana and the Floridas, were subsequently ceded to other powers. In 1750 Spain and Portugal settled their boundary dispute in South America by a treaty which stipulated that in case of war between themselves in Europe they would remain neutral in their dominions in America. Notwithstanding this treaty the two monarchies did fight again in South America, and that soon. Such writers cite with more force a proposition conceived by John Adams in the Continental Congress that the United States should stipulate in any treaty of alliance the untouchability of the continent of North America by a European power, even an ally against Great Britain.

Interesting as it may be to compare these ideas with the principles of the Monroe Doctrine—(1) non-colonization, (2) abstention of the United States from the wars of European powers in matters relating to themselves, (3) America for the Americans—it is enough to say that none of them prevailed at the time of their utterance, except John Adams's proposal, and that on North American initiative in the Franco-American alliance of 1778. The idea of abstention from European wars and entanglements was the product of the diplomatic experience of the Anglo-American Revolution and the relations of the United States with Europe during the ensuing wars of the French Revolution. The principle that the New World was closed to further European colonization had its roots in the menace of territorial transfer to which we have given so much attention in the previous chapters, and in the desire to keep territory in this Hemisphere free from the commercial restrictions of European colonial systems.

It was the relationship of legitimist Europe to Spain and to revolutionary Spanish America, and the predicament of British diplomacy after the peace settlement of 1815 that provoked the Monroe Doctrine in full concept. From a village capital on the banks of the Potomac River, President James Monroe in 1823 proclaimed to the world the two principles already noted, of non-colonization and abstention plus the added dictum, a corollary of the doctrine of abstention from Europe, the nonintervention of European powers in the affairs of the New World. To the European situation we must now turn.

British policy after the overthrow of Napolean and the Treaty of Vienna embraced these principal objectives: (1) international appeasement and repose, meanwhile the recuperation and development of the triumphant British Empire and the expansion of markets for the new English manufactures thrown up by the Industrial Revolution; (2) as necessary for the first objective, the enforcement of the specific purpose of the Quadruple

Alliance (Austria, Great Britain, Prussia, Russia) as confirmed and restated in 1815: to maintain the peace of Europe by preventing another revolutionary irruption of France; (3) to countenance the institution of monarchy but without intervening to protect particular monarchs against internal revolutions except in France for the one purpose here noted, for despite their sympathy for repression of revolution everywhere the ruling Tory classes could not safely deny the origin of the English dynasty and government in the Revolution of 1688; (4) to preserve in Europe the balance of power so favorable to British prestige and influence not only on that continent but also all over the world; (5) to prevent the rise of any rival empire that might challenge the absolute supremacy of Britain on the seas.

Britain's continental allies, on the other hand, would fain use the Quadruple Alliance to repress revolution wherever it might raise its head against a legitimist divine-right ruler. For this purpose Alexander I of Russia proclaimed in 1815 the Holy Alliance, signed originally by himself, the King of Prussia, and the Emperor of Austria, and promptly adhered to by all the absolute monarchs and potentates of Europe except for the Sultan of Turkey, who was not a Christian; the Pope, who was a Christian but not an hereditary prince; and the Prince Regent of Great Britain, who was a nominal Christian and an hereditary prince but not an absolute monarch—he had to content himself with a personal letter to the Czar applauding the principles of the Holy Alliance without binding his government, which was responsible only to Parliament.

For the first few years, that is, until after the Conference of Aix-la-Chapelle of 1818, Lord Castlereagh, Foreign Minister of Great Britain (1812–1822) and draftsman of the diplomatic bond that united the Four, was able to hold the Quadruple Alliance to its strict purpose as interpreted by his government; but in 1820 the continental allies got out of British control when liberal revolutions based on the sovereignty of the people and representative government took place in Spain, Naples, Piedmont, Portugal, and threatened to break out all over Europe, even in England itself. At the Conferences of Troppau-Laibach (1820–1821) the Holy Allies, despite the dissent of Great Britain, gave a mandate to Austria to put down revolution in Naples and in Piedmont lest it spread to their own states. At the Conference of Verona in 1822 they overrode British opposition and approved French military intervention in Spain to tear up the new constitution there and restore the absolute authority of Ferdinand VII. They even announced that if Great Britain (ally of Spain since the Peninsular War) should take the side of the Spanish constitutionalists they would come to the aid of France.

Castlereagh had failed in his task of holding the Quadruple Alliance to the compass of British policy. Overburdened by the immense responsibilities and labors of his office, his reason faltered and he made way with his own life, on the eve of the Conference of Verona. His great rival, George Canning, never a believer in European conferences, succeeded him (1822–1827). France invaded Spain. Britain's army of the Napoleonic wars no longer existed, and the fleet was powerless to stop a continental force from crossing the Pyrenees. Moreover, the Prince Regent, the Duke of Wellington, and the Tory leaders sympathized with the French intervention as long as it limited itself to the suppression of revolution and did not extend its force beyond the boundaries of Spain.

With the Quadruple Alliance in ruins in Europe and the political front divided at home, the new Foreign Minister went as far as he could when he stated in the House of Commons that he hoped the Spanish constitutionalists would win: "Indifference we can never feel towards the affairs of Spain: and I earnestly hope and trust that she may come triumphantly out of the struggle." As hostilities broke out south of the Pyrenees, Canning communicated to the French Government, through a despatch (March 31, 1823) to the British Ambassador at Paris, a formal warning implying that war with England would follow if France (1) should establish a permanent military occupation of Spain, (2) should appropriate any portion of the Spanish colonies, (3) should violate the territorial integrity of Portugal. On the first and third of these points France had already given assurances, but she remained ominously silent about the Spanish colonies. Since the withdrawal of the allied army of occupation following the Congress of Aix-la-Chapelle, French policy had reassumed its traditional character of opposition to British plans both in the Old World and the New, and had begun to design independent monarchies under Bourbon princes and French influence for Spanish America.

Canning concluded his despatch of March 31, 1823, which significantly was published in England within five days after its signature, with a grave and measured statement of Great Britain's position, most instructive to the student of the origin of the Monroe Doctrine and the Latin American policy of the United States. It contained these words:

With respect to the Provinces in America, which have thrown off their allegiance to the Crown of Spain, time and the course of events appear to have substantially decided their separation from the Mother Country; although the formal recognition of those Provinces, as Independent States, by His Majesty, may be hastened or retarded by various external circumstances, as well as by the more or less satisfactory progress, in each State, towards a regular and settled form of Government. Spain has long been apprized of His Majesty's opinions upon this subject. Disclaiming in the most solemn manner any intention of appropriating to Himself the smallest portion of the late Spanish possessions in America, His Majesty is satisfied that no attempt will be made by

France, to bring under her dominion any of those possessions, either by conquest, or by cession, from Spain.

The Quadruple Alliance was dead. British diplomacy had been unable to keep it disciplined for the single purpose of preventing the resur-
rection of French power. How could the diplomatic defeat in Europe
now be compensated? Where else could Canning enlist support against
possible French intervention in the affairs of Latin America, first step perhaps in the revival of a French colonial empire and of French sea power?
The British Foreign Minister turned to the United States, where the situation seemed to be favorable to an Anglo-American entente.

Under Castlereagh's general policy of appeasement and repose, Anglo-
American relations had been steadily ameliorating, particularly in regard
to the vital territorial questions of North America. After the War of 1812
Great Britain had abandoned all connection with the Indians, all thought
of blocking the western expansion of the United States, at least to the
Rocky Mountains. The Rush-Bagot agreement of 1817, providing for
naval disarmament of the Great Lakes, confirmed this new attitude. The
treaty of 1818 of boundaries, navigation, and fisheries, was another evidence of the new policy of live and let live. Contemporaneously the
British attitude toward the Florida question evidenced a resolve not to
harass the continental position of the United States.

To be sure, the British Minister at Washington, Stratford Canning,
had objected excitedly to a bill proposed in Congress for a government
establishment at the mouth of the Columbia River, only to be told by
Secretary Adams that the United States would resist the claim of Great
Britain to any new colonial establishments on the North American continent; but this passage between the diplomatists seems to have been entirely upon the initiative of the British Minister, and his superiors preferred not to pursue it further. It is of interest to us here as the first
expression in diplomatic conversations of the non-colonization principle,
presently to find expression in the Monroe Doctrine. On the Northwest
Coast both the United States and Great Britain were protesting the attempt
of the Czar of Russia to extend his sovereignty southward to 51° North
Latitude and out into the high seas one hundred miles from shore, a claim
which gave Adams an opportunity again, and most pointedly, to assert his
non-colonization principle: "I told him [Baron Tuyll, the Russian Minister
at Washington] specially, that we should contest the right of Russia to
any territorial establishment on this continent, and that we should assume
distinctly the principle that the American continents are no longer subjects for *any* new European colonial establishments."

The opposing attitude of the United States and Great Britain as to
the independence of the new states of Latin America remained the out-

standing difference in policy. If Castlereagh had endeavored by talking vaguely about a possible Allied mediation, to hold off recognition by the United States of the Latin American republics, Great Britain though annoyed had made no protest when Monroe's Government had acknowledged their independence. Now the two powers had come to see almost eye to eye on the Holy Alliance and the possibility of European intervention in the New World.

The United States, like Great Britain, had declined to join the Holy Alliance, when so invited by the Russian Czar in 1820. In his instructions to Middleton, Minister to Russia, politely declining the invitation, John Quincy Adams, formulator of the non-colonization principle, expressed the other two major dicta of the Monroe Doctrine of 1823: abstention from European entanglements and wars, separation of the two political worlds of Europe and America. "The political system of the United States is . . . extra-European. To stand in firm and cautious independence of all entanglement in the European system, has been a cardinal point of their policy under every administration of their government from the peace of 1783 to this day. . . . It may be observed that for the repose of Europe as well as of America, the European and American political systems should be kept as separate and distinct from each other as possible."

The United States, like Great Britain, looked with apprehension upon the possibility of support by any European power to crumbling Spanish sovereignty in the New World. Canning's course in dealing with the Spanish question, particularly his published despatch of March 31, 1823, to France, added to the improved tone of Anglo-American feeling. "Even Adams has caught a something of the soft infection," reported the British Minister from Washington. The Secretary of State had mentioned to him that in separating herself from the councils and measures of the European alliance, Great Britain had avowed principles which were emphatically those of the United States and disavowed principles which the United States abhorred.

"This coincidence of principle," Adams took occasion to say, "connected with the great changes in the affairs of the world, passing before us, seemed to me a suitable occasion for the United States and Great Britain to compare their ideas and purposes together, with a view to the accommodation of great interests upon which they had heretofore differed."

Adams of course was referring to his desire for a settlement of long-standing issues between the two countries: suppression of the slave trade with its attendant controversy over visit and search, commercial intercourse with the British colonies, neutral rights and the freedom of the seas. He explicitly disavowed any idea of an alliance with Great Britain.

From this soft American infection, George Canning in London chose to divine a possibility of cooperation with Great Britain in opposing European intervention in Latin America. An opportunity came when Richard Rush, the United States Minister, casually asked about affairs on the Continent, and remarked that "should France ultimately effect her purpose of overthrowing the constitutional government in Spain, there was at least the consolation left, that Great Britain would not allow her to go further and stop the progress of emancipation in the colonies." The British note of March 31, 1823, to France, Rush judged, indicated that England would not remain passive.

In this transient remark Canning was quick to see an opening.

"What do you think your Government would say to going hand in hand with England in such a policy?" he asked Rush. "Not that any concert of action under it would become necessary, because I fully believe that the simple fact of our two countries being known to hold the same opinions would, by its moral effect, put down the intention on the part of France, if she entertains it. I base this belief upon the large share of the maritime power of the world which Great Britain and the United States share between them, and the consequent influence which the knowledge of their common policy, on a question involving such important maritime interests, present and future, could not fail to produce everywhere."

"I am unable to say in what manner my Government would look upon such a suggestion, . . ." Rush replied, "but I will communicate it in the same informal manner in which you have thrown it before me." Then he added acutely: "I can hardly do this to full advantage unless you will at the same time enlighten me as to the precise situation in which England stands in relation to those new communities and especially on the material point of acknowledging their independence."

Canning answered that Great Britain would not object to an accommodation between Spain and the colonies which might even secure to Spain commercial advantages not extended to other nations. Great Britain would not offer her mediation again, but would not interfere to prevent a compromise.

"Is Great Britain at this moment taking any steps," Rush asked more specifically, "or contemplating any which have reference to the recognition of these new communities, that being the point on which the United States would naturally feel most interest?"

"None whatever, as yet," admitted Canning, "but she is on the eve of taking one of a preparatory nature, which will leave her at large to recognize or not, according to the position of events at a future period."

The "preparatory step" which the British Government was then "on the eve of taking" proved to be the sending of consuls to Mexico, Colombia, Peru, Chile, and Buenos Aires, and commissioners of inquiry to Mexico and Colombia. The United States had sent consuls as early as 1811 and a commission of inquiry to South America in 1817. It had opened its ports to vessels bearing the flag of the new states from the beginning of their revolt; Great Britain did not do so until 1822. Now she still declined to recognize that independence which the United States had already acknowledged to the world.

This was the first of several conversations between the two men in August and September, 1823, during which Canning formally proposed in writing that the United States and Great Britain issue a joint declaration of policy in regard to the Spanish American question as follows:

1. We conceive the recovery of the Colonies by Spain to be hopeless.
2. We conceive the question of the recognition of them, as Independent States, to be one of time and circumstances.
3. We are, however, by no means disposed to throw any impediment in the way of an arrangement between them and the mother country by amicable negotiations.
4. We aim not at the possession of any portion of them ourselves.
5. We could not see any portion of them transferred to any other Power, with indifference.

The British Foreign Minister asked Rush if he had powers to sign a convention on this subject. In repeated conversations until September 26 he urged the desirability of such a joint pronouncement. He stated that he had just received "notice" that as soon as the French occupation of Spain was completed a conference of the Allies would be proposed to discuss the affairs of South America. The American Minister explained that he had no powers on the subject, but hinted that he might join in the proposed declaration *if* Great Britain would first recognize the independence of the Latin American republics. He made up his own mind to participate in the joint statement if Canning on his part would recognize the new republics as the United States had done. If such a step, under this condition, would benefit his own Government, well and good; if not, Government could disavow him. Rush was willing to risk his career for the independence of the New World.

A parallel or even joint recognition of independence is what Monroe's Administration had been suggesting to London ever since 1818, in order to detach Britain from her continental allies. Castlereagh consistently had avoided the proposal, that is, to underwrite the Latin American policy of the United States: namely, independence and republics. Canning was unwilling to substitute immediate recognition for point 2 of his memorandum. He insisted on leaving this vital question to "time and circumstances"—the most noncommittal formula any diplomat could conjure. Rush said that he must wait for instructions from his Government.

Soon the American Minister had misgivings about the wisdom of his hint to Canning. He became wary of the motives of Great Britain. They sprang, he suspected, from "the apprehensions which are now probably coming upon her, touching her own influence and standing through the formidable and encroaching career of these continental potentates. She at last perceives a crisis likely to come on, bringing with it peril to her own commercial prospects on the other side of the Atlantic, and to her political sway in both hemispheres. Hence probably some of her recent and remarkable solicitudes." He became convinced of this when Canning suddenly ceased to talk any more about the subject and begged Rush to regard it merely as a tentative inquiry rather than a formal proposal.

Canning, uncertain whether Rush could secure the assent of his government to the proposal, could not wait in the emergency for the correspondence to cross and recross the Atlantic. He therefore turned to direct conversations with the French Ambassador at London, Prince Polignac, and notified him that Great Britain would not allow France to intervene in the Spanish American provinces.

It was one thing for the French army, backed by the moral support of the Holy Allies, to penetrate the Pyrenees; it was another matter to cross the Atlantic to Spain's colonies. In the so-called Polignac Memorandum of October 9, 1823, which was a formal record of these conversations, the French Ambassador, speaking for his government, was obliged to agree:

That his Government believed it to be utterly hopeless to reduce Spanish America to the state of its former relation to Spain.

That France disclaimed, on Her part, any intention or desire to avail Herself of the present state of the Colonies, or of the present situation of France toward Spain, to appropriate to Herself any part of the Spanish Possessions in America. . . .

That She abjured, in any case, any design of acting against the Colonies by force of arms.

It was this British "ultimatum," which rested on the controlling force of the navy, that cut short any ambitious plans that France alone might have developed amidst the ruins of Spanish America. It did not, however, put a full quietus on plans for a conference of the Allies to consider the South American question. In the Polignac Memorandum France had by no means renounced a conference. In November, 1823, Ferdinand VII requested it. The Allies themselves were divided as to the wisdom of such a meeting. Russia, an American power, with a trading post as far south as California, was eager for a conference, and the Czar was willing as usual to lend himself to the common purpose of suppressing revolutions. But it is doubtful whether Alexander I would have agreed to any solution of the colonial question with England absent. Neither Austria nor Prussia had interests in America; consistent champions of the principle of legitimacy in

Europe itself they were apathetic about a conference for trans-Atlantic purposes and opposed to any program of intervention across the ocean. Had there been a conference it is not likely that it would have sanctioned any reconquest of Latin America. As Canning himself said, the news of the Monroe Doctrine gave the *coup de grâce* to the whole idea. There was no conference.

When President Monroe and his advisers discussed the import of Rush's despatches they did not know of this Polignac Memorandum, although the attitude of Great Britain might be divined from the earlier warning to France of March 31, 1823, or from Canning's proposal to Rush. The Government at Washington was excessively worried, during these weeks of deliberation, in October and November, over what were esteemed to be significant communications from the Russian Minister at Washington. The first of these announced that the Czar, in conformance with the principles of his allies, would not receive any agents whatsoever from any of the rebel governments in America. It suggestively expressed satisfaction that the United States, in recognizing the independence of those governments, had proclaimed its intention to continue neutral. A second note declared the Emperor's policy in general to be that of guaranteeing the tranquillity *of all the states of which the civilized world was composed—* this meant the supremacy of Spain over her colonies, the Minister explained, when pointedly asked by Adams at the President's request. To Monroe and his advisers, all except the perspicacious Secretary of State, it looked as though Alexander I intended to back up an intervention of the allied powers. Adams was reasonably confident that the British Government would oppose such a move even if the Allies could agree on it, which he considered unlikely. Canning's very proposal to the United States suggested that European intervention would not be likely. He realized that England had already separated from her allies of 1814.

The President and the other members of the Cabinet did not feel so easy about Europe as did the Secretary of State. Let us now turn to the deliberations in Monroe's Cabinet that took place after the President opened Richard Rush's despatches of the late summer of 1823.

The "crisis" implied by Rush's accounts of his interviews with Canning impressed President Monroe prodigiously. Upon receipt of Rush's despatches, which arrived in Washington a few days before Adams's return from a long visit to Massachusetts, Monroe sought the advice of two of the three elder statesmen and former Presidents: Thomas Jefferson and James Madison, both of whom had dealt with the great territorial problems that had arisen in North America from the disruption of the Spanish Empire. He did not consult the one other ex-President, John Adams, perhaps because that elder statesman's competent son would soon be at hand. To his fellow-Virginians Monroe declared that he believed the United States ought to accept the overture of Great Britain.

They agreed. Jefferson, who had been reading the Abbé DePradt's new book on *Europe after the Congress of Aix-la-Chapelle,* responded as follows:

> Our first and fundamental maxim should be never to entangle ourselves in the broils of Europe, our second never to suffer Europe to intermeddle with Cis-Atlantic affairs. America, North and South, has a set of interests distinct from those of Europe, and peculiarly her own. She should therefore have a system of her own, separate and apart from that of Europe. . . . Great Britain is the nation which can do us the most harm of any one, or all, on earth; and with her on our side we need not fear the whole world. With her then we should most sedulously cherish a cordial friendship; and nothing would tend more to knit our affections than to be fighting once more, side by side, in the same cause. Not that I would purchase even her amity at the price of taking part in her wars. But the war in which the present proposition might engage us, should that be its consequence, is not her war, but ours. It's [*sic*] object is to introduce and establish the American system, *of keeping out of our land all foreign powers,* of never permitting those of Europe to intermeddle with the affairs of our nations. It is to maintain our own principle, not to depart from it. . . .

Jefferson had considered carefully the coveted island of Cuba, when he pondered over Canning's fourth proposition: "That we aimed at no portion of the Spanish colonies for ourselves." The sage of Monticello felt that such a self-denial would be worth the price of making it, particularly because it would bind England too, and it would not necessarily prevent the annexation of a free Cuba some day to the United States.

Madison was entirely in favor of accepting the proposal of a joint Anglo-American pronouncement. He would even go a step farther: he suggested that the two powers join also in condemning French intervention in Spain and in a declaration on behalf of the revolted Greeks in southeastern Europe. "There ought not to be any backwardness," he thought, "in meeting her [Great Britain] in the way she has proposed. . . . Our co-operation is due to ourselves *and to the world:* and whilst it must ensure success in the event of an appeal to force, it doubles the chance of success without that appeal."

In the Cabinet all except Adams also favored the joint declaration. Secretary of War John C. Calhoun was the greatest alarmist of all. He thought this step necessary to detach Great Britain from the Holy Alliance—this certainly showed little comprehension of European politics of that day. If the United States remained neutral, he declared, Great Britain would join the intervention of the Holy Alliance—then after South America would come the turn of North America, in order to put down the original and most successful example of democratic rebellion. Attorney-General Wirt questioned the wisdom of committing the United States to any forceful resistance of intervention, whatever   pronouncement were made; he stressed the fact that the people would not fight for the independence of South America.

We may be sure that no member of the Administration, except possibly Calhoun, was in favor of war even in alliance with Great Britain. All agreed that the occasion called for a systematic exposition of foreign policy. It was the President's own suggestion that such a statement should be included in his forthcoming annual message to the Congress on the state of the Union. Then it would be an executive monologue rather than a part in a diplomatic dialogue which conceivably could be construed as a position taken in regard to a particular nation.

John Quincy Adams saw a catch in the British proposal. "The object of Canning," he said, "appears to have been to obtain some public pledge from the Government of the United States, ostensibly against the forcible interference of the Holy Alliance between Spain and South America; but really or especially against the acquisition to the United States themselves of any part of the Spanish-American possessions." He had in mind particularly Cuba and Texas, which might some day as free people seek annexation to the United States, but never to England. Already in April, 1823, Adams had extended the No-Transfer principle of 1811 (then limited to "territory adjoining the southern boundary of the United States") to the island of Cuba, which he felt must not only never pass into the possession of another European power, but also must some day be annexed to the United States if only by what he called the law of political gravitation. Thus did a patriotic and conscientious statesman, who so recently had won title for his country to the shore of the Pacific Ocean, launch the No-Transfer principle upon the seaways that would control the future naval communications between the two coasts of North America.

We know today that the motive of the Canning proposal was not *principally* to pledge the United States against the acquisition of further territory out of the dissolving Spanish Empire, although an incidental purpose certainly was just that, particularly as to Cuba. We have seen that his principal purpose was rather to make convenient use of the United States in the scale of world politics to balance against setbacks which British diplomacy had suffered from the continental Allies.

With shrewd instinct Adams sensed this. "I remarked," he records, "that the communications recently received from the Russian Minister, Baron Tuyl [*sic*], afforded, as I thought, a very suitable and convenient opportunity for us to take our stand against the Holy Alliance, and at the same time to decline the overture of Great Britain. It would be more candid, as well as more dignified, to avow our principles explicitly to

Russia and France, than to come in as a cock-boat in the wake of the British man-of-war."

In the end Adams's advice on this point prevailed. He further persuaded the President not to champion the Spanish or Greek revolutions in his message. He advised against all interference with the political concerns of Europe. He urged the President to express the hope and expectation that the European powers would equally abstain from any attempt to spread their principles in the American Hemisphere, or to subjugate by force any part of these continents to their will. On this last point, which coincided with the ideas of Jefferson, Adams was repeating an idea common to all the elder statesmen. Thus before the pronouncement of the Monroe Doctrine Adams had urged all three of its principal dicta: the non-colonization principle (which was original with him, although rooted in the No-Transfer principle and the North American territorial questions of the period); abstention from European wars and entanglements (which was instinctive with the statesmen of North American independence); and exclusion of Europe from the American Hemisphere, a new corollary of Washington's Farewell Address, which had crystallized during the many public discussions of policy that attended the revolution of the Spanish colonies. If we mean putting all these ideas together at the right time and pronouncing them with a strong republican tone, John Quincy Adams more than any other one man helped formulate the Monroe Doctrine in 1823. But President Monroe was responsible for the message, the Secretary of State deferred properly to the President's leadership, and the Doctrine appropriately bears Monroe's name.

Here is precisely what the original Monroe Doctrine said, in its principal passages, which are taken *verbatim et literatim* from the President's message of December 2, 1823:

At the proposal of the Russian Imperial Government, made through the Minister of the Emperor, residing here, a full power and instructions have been transmitted to the Minister of the United States at St. Petersburg, to arrange by amicable negotiation, the respective rights and interests of the two Nations on the North West Coast of this Continent. A similar proposal has been made by His Imperial Majesty, to the Government of Great Britain, which has likewise been acceded to. The Government of the United States has been desirous by this friendly proceeding, of manifesting the great value which they have invariably attached to the friendship of the Emperor, and their solicitude to cultivate the best understanding with his Government. In the discussions to which this interest has given rise, and in the arrangements by which they may terminate, the occasion has been judged proper, for asserting as a principle in which the rights and interests of the United States are involved, that the American Continents, by the free and independent condition which they have assumed and maintain, are henceforth not to be considered as subjects for future colonization by any European Power. . . .

It was stated at the commencement of the last session, that a great effort was then making in Spain and Portugal, to improve the condition of the people of those countries; and that it appeared to be conducted with extraordinary moderation. It need scarcely be remarked, that the result has been, so far, very different from what was then anticipated. Of events in that quarter of the Globe, with which we have so much intercourse, and from which we derive our origin, we have always been anxious and interested spectators. The Citizens of the United States cherish sentiments the most friendly, in favor of the liberty and happiness of their fellowmen on that side of the Atlantic. In the wars of the European powers, in matters relating to themselves, we have never taken any part, nor does it comport with our policy, so to do. It is only when our rights are invaded, or seriously menaced, that we resent injuries, or make preparation for our defense. With the movements in this Hemisphere we are of necessity more immediately connected, and by causes which must be obvious to all enlightened and impartial observers. The political system of the allied powers, is essentially different in this respect from that of America. This difference proceeds from that, which exists in their respective Governments, and to the defence of our own, which has been achieved by the loss of so much blood and treasure, and matured by the wisdom of their most enlightened citizens, and under which we have enjoyed unexampled felicity, this whole nation is devoted. We owe it therefore to candor, and to the amicable relations existing between the United States and those powers, to declare that we should consider any attempt on their part to extend their system to any portions of this Hemisphere, as dangerous to our peace and safety. With the existing Colonies or dependencies of any European power, we have not interfered, and shall not interfere. But with the Governments who have declared their Independence, and maintained it, and whose Independence we have, on great consideration, and on just principles, acknowledged, we could not view any interposition for the purpose of oppressing them, or controuling in any other manner, their destiny, by any European power, in any other light, than as the manifestation of a unfriendly disposition towards the United States. In the war between those new governments and Spain, we declared our neutrality, at the time of their recognition, and to this we have adhered, and shall continue to adhere, provided no change shall occur, which in the judgment of the competent authorities of this Government, shall make a corresponding change, on the part of the United States, indispensable to their security.

The late events in Spain and Portugal, show that Europe is still unsettled. Of this important fact, no stronger proof can be adduced, than that the allied powers should have thought it proper, on any principle satisfactory to themselves, to have interposed by force, in the internal concerns of Spain. To what extent, such interposition may be carried, on the same principle, is a question, in which all Independent powers, whose Governments differ from theirs, are interested; even those most remote, and surely none more so than the United States. Our policy in regard to Europe, which was adopted at an early stage of the wars which have so long agitated that quarter of the Globe, nevertheless re-mains the same, which is, not to interfere in the internal concerns of any of its powers; to consider the Government *de facto;* as the legitimate for us; to culti-vate friendly relations with it, and to preserve those relations by a frank, firm and manly policy, meeting in all instances, the just claims of every power; sub-mitting to injuries from none. But, in regard to those continents, circumstances are eminently and conspicuously different. It is impossible that the allied powers, should extend their political systems, to any portion of either continent, with-out endangering our peace and happiness, nor can anyone believe, that our Southern Brethren, if left to themselves, would adopt it of their own accord. It is equally impossible, therefore, that we should behold such interposition in any form with indifference. If we look to the comparative strength and resources of Spain and those new Governments, and their distance from each other, it must be obvious that she can never subdue them. It is still the true policy of the United States, to leave the parties to themselves, in the hope, that other powers will pursue the same course.

The text of the Monroe Doctrine itself has overshadowed the diplo-matic communications which were made at the time to Russia and to Great Britain. These were drafted by John Quincy Adams and discussed in Cabinet. The President as a result of the discussions modified them slightly, mostly for amenity's sake. Not published until many years later by historians, they fill out the picture of Latin American policy that was formulated in the historic deliberations of President Monroe's Cabinet.

The first of these was a formal note to the Russian Minister, Novem-ber 15, 1823. It acknowledged his communication of October 16 and in carefully courteous language explained why the United States, acting in its sovereign capacity on principles different from Russia's, had recognized the independence of the Latin American republics and received their agents. Later, November 27, 1823, John Quincy Adams read to the Baron von Tuyll a lengthy supplementary statement entitled "Observations on the Communications recently received from the Minister of Russia." The Government of the United States, explained the Secretary, while recogniz-ing the right of nations to establish and modify their own governments according to their own judgments, and while itself espousing the repub-lican principle, had not sought by the propagation of its own principles to disturb the peace or to intermeddle with the policy of any part of Europe. It had recognized the established independence of the former Spanish colo-nies and entered into political and commercial relations with them, "re-lations the more important to the interests of the United States, as the whole of those emancipated Regions are situated *in their own Hemisphere, and as the most extensive, populous and powerful of the new Nations are in their immediate vicinity; and one of them bordering upon the Ter-ritories of this Union.*" In the existing contest between these states and their mother-country it would remain neutral as long as the European powers did. "In the general declarations [of the Russian Minister] that the allied Monarchs will never compound, and never will even treat with the *Revolution* and that their policy has only for its object by *forcible* interposition to guaranty the tranquillity *of all the States of which the civilized world is composed*, the President wishes to perceive sentiments, the application of which is limited and intended in their results to be limited to the Affairs of Europe. That the sphere of their operations was not intended to embrace the United States of America, nor any portion of the American Hemisphere."

Finally, this statement to Russia ended with a declaration of policy that included a principle not wholly embodied in the text of the contemporary Presidential message, namely the No-Transfer principle: "That the United States of America, and their Government, could not see with indifference, the forcible interposition of any European Power, other than Spain, either to restore the dominion of Spain over her emancipated Colonies in America, or to establish Monarchical Governments in those Countries, or to transfer any of the possessions heretofore or yet subject to Spain in the American Hemisphere, to any other European power."

Is it not clear that the expanding territorial questions of the West and Far West, meaning simply *the Continental Republic*, were moving the President and his Secretary of State as they formulated these fundamental principles of foreign policy so vital to their native land?

The response to Canning's proposal to Rush was in the form of instructions by the Secretary of State to the Minister in London, dated November 29, 1823. These declared that the United States was in agreement with the points proposed by Canning *if* there were coupled to them a recognition of the independence of the Latin American states. Only on this basis would the United States be willing to move in parallel but separate action with Great Britain. "Should an emergency occur, in which a *joint* manifestation of opinion by the two governments may tend to influence the Councils of the European allies, either in the aspect of persuasion or of admonition, you will make it known to us without delay, and we shall according to the principles of our government, and in the forms prescribed by our Constitution, cheerfully join in any act by which we may contribute to support the cause of human freedom, and the independence of the South American nations."

This, of course, left to Congress responsibility for any possible joint action under the circumstances that might exist in the unknown future. It should be said that, because Canning had never referred again to his famous proposals, Rush did not even convey to him the sense of these instructions.

Nor was Adams willing to concert with Great Britain on the No-

Transfer Policy. In a separate instruction to Rush of November 30, devoted to the possibility of a European Congress on Spanish America, the Secretary stressed the policy of his country in recognizing the independence of the new states, and in opposing the transfer of sovereignty over American territory. "So long as Great Britain withholds the recognition of that [independence]," he stated, addressing himself to the idea of concert of policy with Great Britain, "we may, as we certainly do, concur with her in the aversion to the transfer to any other power of any of the Colonies in this Hemisphere, heretofore or yet, belonging to Spain; but the principles of that aversion, so far as they are common to both parties, resting only upon a casual coincidence of interests, in a national point of view *selfish* on both sides, would be liable to dissolution by every change of phase in the aspect of European politics."

The unexpected news of the Monroe Doctrine piqued Canning and nettled the continental chancelleries, despite their professions of indifference and contempt for it. Nevertheless financial securities of the new states rose on the London exchange, and those of Spain fell, as they did also in Paris, as soon as the message became known. After his settlement directly with Polignac, Canning successfully persuaded the United States to regard as confidential his proposal, or as he now chose to call it, his tentative "sounding" of Rush. He did not wish to enhance the prestige of the United States at Britain's expense in the eyes of the Latin American nations. He did not want them to know that the United States had insisted, as the price of any joint *démarche*, on Britain's recognition of the independence of their republics. He wished Great Britain to get exclusive credit in their eyes—and corresponding influence—for frustrating any conceivable European intervention. This is why the Monroe Doctrine vexed him so.

After the President's message reached Europe, the British Foreign Minister had the Polignac Memorandum lithographed and passed around to offset Monroe's statement and to help undo the diplomatic defeat suffered at the hands of Richard Rush and John Quincy Adams. But he soon learned to make the best of the new American doctrine ostensibly, and he even took some credit for it with his own diplomatic service. Unblushingly he allowed that the President had "assisted" him in safeguarding Latin America. "The effect of the ultra-liberalism of our Yankee cooperators," he wrote to his minister in Washington, "or the ultra-despotism of Aix-la-Chapelle allies, gives me just the balance that I wanted." Without the slightest diffidence he later personally assumed credit for the independence of the new states which American diplomacy had by then impelled Great Britain to recognize for her best interests. "I called the New World into existence," he boasted in 1826, "to redress the balance of the Old."

However distasteful the use of the pronoun, or unjustified the assertion itself, it revealed the *motive:* to use the United States for the purpose of British diplomacy in keeping the balance of power in Europe. The aim of American diplomacy was exactly the opposite: to keep the independent republics of the New World separated from the power-politics of Europe. Whatever the other motives of the Latin American policy of the United States, that aim remained constant.

In Latin America the liberal elements received the Monroe Doctrine most cordially. They did not fail immediately to perceive its useful diplomatic possibilities for themselves. Two governments, Brazil and Colombia, endorsed it. But the men who governed the new states realized that it was the British navy that counted more than the republican ideals of President Monroe. The conservative leaders, those distrustful of republicanism and leaning toward monarchy, in short the pro-British contingents, disliked the Doctrine. If there had been any original doubt in their minds about what governed the situation, it was removed when the United States declined the overtures of five of the new states either for actual alliance, as in the case of Chile (1824), Colombia (1824), and Brazil (1825), or assurance of contingent assistance, as requested by Mexico (1825) and the United Provinces of the Rio de la Plata (1826) for the enforcement of the Doctrine, and when it showed no enthusiasm for a general Pan American mutual defense pact such as was projected at the abortive inter-American conference at Panama in 1826, to which the United States sent delegates so belatedly that they failed to get there in time.

If the replies of the United States to these several solicitations were evasive, it must be noted that except in the case of Mexico the importunities were only nominally against the Holy Alliance; really it was the hope of each state to involve the United States in the existing war against the mother country, or in the instance of the United Provinces, in their war against Brazil.

Colombia was the first to inquire just how the United States intended to enforce the Doctrine, and to ascertain whether it could not be turned to some immediate advantage. Acting on instructions from his government, the Colombian Minister at Washington asked:

In what manner the Government of the United States intends to resist on its part any interference of the Holy Alliance for the purpose of subjugating the new Republics or interfering in their political forms: if it will enter into a Treaty of Alliance with the Republic of Colombia to save America in general from the calamities of a despotic system; and finally if the Government of Washington understands by foreign interference the employment of Spanish forces against America at the time when Spain is occupied by a French Army, and its Government under the influence of France and her Allies.

By this time the Polignac Memorandum was known in Washington. Everybody realized Spain could get no help in Europe.

Adams answered that the fact that Spain was occupied by France would not change the neutrality of the United States in regard to the employment of Spanish forces in America. The action which the United States might take in any future emergency would depend on Congress. As to the invitation for an actual alliance, the Secretary of State responded:

> As however the occasion for this resort [the President laying the matter before Congress] could arise only by a deliberate and concerted system of the allied Powers to exercise force against the freedom and independence of your Republic; so it is obvious that the United States could not undertake resistance to them by force of Arms, without a previous understanding with those European Powers, whose Interests and whose principles would secure from them an active and efficient co-operation in the cause—This there is no reason to doubt, could be obtained, but it could only be effected by a negotiation preliminary to that of any alliance between the United States and the Colombian Republic, or in any event coeval with it.

That is to say, in John Quincy Adams's own words, the effectiveness of the Monroe Doctrine depended not only upon Congress but also upon Great Britain. After such a statement it was not unnatural that the Latin American states leaned heavily on British patronage in the rivalry for prestige, trade, and influence that ensued between Great Britain and the United States. British predominance as a low-cost manufacturing nation and as a source of loans to the new governments also proved irresistible attractions.

Nothing is clearer from these diplomatic exchanges of the United States with some of the new states, and from debates in Congress, particularly on the Panama Congress, than the unilateral and non-binding character of the Doctrine. As President, John Quincy Adams would have been willing to have the United States delegates to Panama empowered to sign a convention affirming, as doctrines of inter-American public law, the principles of nonintervention and non-colonization, without any pledge to enforce them other than in the territory of each signatory. But the debates left no doubt that Congress was opposed even to this. Perhaps the best exposition of the equivocal force of the Doctrine is to be read in a despatch sent to the United States Minister in Buenos Aires, in 1828:

> The declaration of the late President [explained Secretary of State Henry Clay] was that of the head of the Executive Government of the United States. Although there is every reason to believe that the policy which it announced was in conformity with the opinion both of the nation and of Congress, the declaration must be regarded as having been voluntarily made, and not as

conveying any pledge or obligation, the performance of which foreign nations have a right to demand. When the case shall arrive, if it should ever occur, of such an European interference as the message supposes, and it becomes consequently necessary to decide whether this country will or will not engage in war, Congress alone, you well know, is competent, by our Constitution, to decide that question. In the event of such an interference, there can be but little doubt that the sentiment contained in President Monroe's message, would still be that of the People and Government of the United States.

Great Britan was no more willing than the United States to pledge herself, after the Polignac Memorandum, to help the new states of Latin America resist any future attack.

Historical scholars have agreed that there was no real danger of Allied intervention by force to restore Spanish America to Spain. Any conceivable danger that there might have been, from France, was stopped by the Polignac Memorandum. Because of this, there has been a tendency to dismiss the Monroe Doctrine as a mere trumpet-blast safely and somewhat impudently blown behind the protection of the British navy, and from that to conclude that it did no real good to Latin America.

This is an exaggerated and distorted view. We have observed that Monroe and his advisers did not know of the Polignac Memorandum. Canning had them scared. Except for John Quincy Adams they really feared that some sort of European mischief was afoot in the New World at the cost of republican independence, and even he was nervous. "I consider the cause of that country [South America], as essentially our own," wrote the President to Jefferson sending him a copy of the message just off the press. "That the crisis is fully as menacing, as has been supposed, is confirmd [sic] by recent communication, from another quarter [Russia]. . . ." Under these circumstances the announcement of the Monroe Doctrine was a courageous and independent act calculated to suit the policy of the United States rather than that of Great Britain. It is true that the Doctrine had no real force behind it. It was only a pronouncement, if you please, but it contained powerful words nevertheless, words that both served the immediate interests of the United States and exalted for the whole Hemisphere the ideals of independence and the sovereignty of the people. The immediate service to the New World of the Monroe Doctrine at the time of its origin was not in preventing European intervention against the independence of an American state but in galvanizing the preponderant *republican character* of the new states at the outset. In doing this it was loyal to the ideology of the Anglo-American Revolution and the French Revolution, both of which were anathema to the Holy Alliance and to Tory England. It would be a long time, if ever, before the United States would be in a position alone to make good all these words in the face of any conceivable challenge, but they did honor as they were uttered to the statesman who formulated them, to the President who spake them, to the republic which sponsored them, and to the New World which listened to them.

The Monroe Doctrine, following the earlier recognition by the United States of the republics of Latin America, had the effect of impelling Great Britain at last to recognize the independence of the new states *de jure* in 1825, despite their distasteful form of republican government. Her immediate consolation was the continuation of monarchy in Brazil after the separation from Portugal in 1822. British good offices in 1825 brought about a peaceful recognition by the King of Portugal of his son as Emperor of Brazil. "It was a blow," records the British authority, Professor Webster, "to the United States, which had sought by the inculcation of republican institutions and separation from Europe to enforce its own leadership of the New World." Later, in 1828, British diplomacy won another triumph by mediating successfully between Brazil and the United Provinces of the Plata to establish the independent Republic of Uruguay.

Following the Era of Emancipation the principal objective of the United States in dealing with the South American nations, and one of the purposes of its diplomacy with all of Latin America, was the negotiation of treaties of amity, commerce and navigation that would conform with the model Plan of 1776 for treaties with foreign powers, on which the general treaty structure of the nation rested. These principles were: reciprocal equality of commerce and navigation on the conditional most-favored-nation basis, and the mooted dicta of international law known as the Freedom of the Seas.[1] Great Britain had refused to accept such treaties with the United States, and after the Napoleonic period France and Russia had gone over to British practice. In her treaties with the Latin American nations Great Britain rejected the American dicta. Thus the treaties of the United States with the new republics during the period 1824 to 1854 were a distinct contribution to the new liberal order of trade, navigation and international law for the opening to foreign commerce of the British colonial empire and the eventual adoption of the Freedom of the Seas by the great naval powers in the Declaration of Paris of 1856. It was the Anglo-American Revolution of 1776 which began this political and economic liberation. The Industrial Revolution ensured its final success.

[1] These dicta were:

Free ships free goods, except for contraband of war.

Freedom of neutrals to trade between port and port of a belligerent, except for contraband of war.

A carefully defined and restricted list of contraband, expressly excepting naval stores and foodstuffs.

Blockades to be binding must be real, that is to say, maintained by a sufficient number of ships really to prevent access to an enemy port.

After 1826 South America ceased to have for the United States the dominant interest which had animated the nation since the War of 1812. Latin American policy focused again on continental borderlands that stood in the pathway of expansion to the Pacific Ocean, and then on the seaways and their island outposts that controlled the isthmian transit between the two ocean coasts of North America. This was a renewal and an extension of the great territorial questions of North America that had controlled that policy from the beginning.

22 *Bray Hammond*

JACKSON'S FIGHT WITH THE "MONEY POWER"

What was the nature of Jacksonian democracy? Beyond agreeing upon its significance in the process of American development, historians have tended to go their separate ways in answering this question. In his pamphlet, *Jacksonian Democracy*, Professor Charles Grier Sellers, Jr., of the University of California, finds that, depending on their own interests and frames of reference, historians have formulated three essentially different answers. A "patrician" school, drawn from Eastern middle or upper-middle-class interests and writing largely during the latter half of the nineteenth century, saw in Jacksonian democracy the origins of a deplorable vulgarity and corruption in American public life. After 1900, an "agrarian democratic" school, with Western and Southern middle-class backgrounds and guided by the hypotheses of Frederick Jackson Turner, rehabilitated Jacksonian democracy as an egalitarian movement of the common man. In recent years, a school of "urban" historians has emerged which, from the vantage of the New Deal and American industrial progress and problems, has seen Jacksonian democracy either as a contest for power between capitalists and non-capitalists or between old capitalists and new ones.

It is this last view which is presented in the following essay by Bray Hammond. A former assistant secretary of the Federal Reserve Board, Mr. Hammond is the author of *Banks and Politics in America* (1957), a fresh and imposing study of the political impact of business enterprise during the period from the Revolution to the Civil War. Because of its importance for his theme, the dramatic struggle between Andrew Jackson and the Second Bank of the United States draws the close attention of Mr. Hammond. In considering the nature and importance of the struggle, he arrives at an arresting and perspicacious analysis of what Jacksonian democracy was all about.

Reprinted with permission from *American Heritage, The Magazine of History,* VII (June, 1956), 9–11, 100–3.

He explains how Jackson himself was far from being a Jacksonian democrat. He explains how the advent of the Industrial Revolution created opportunities and problems which necessarily involved banks and politics. He explains how the attack on the Bank, generally regarded as a clear expression of Jacksonian democracy, in fact expressed the principles neither of Jackson nor of democracy.

Mr. Hammond's misgivings about the role of the Jacksonians in American economic development suggest questions about the role of other men in other times. It is a moot problem whether the economic values and policies which governed the building of American life are those which indeed should have governed. Touching as it does upon American life in our own age, the problem is no less moot today.

"Relief sir!" interrupted the President. "Come not to me, sir! Go to the monster. It is folly, sir, to talk to Andrew Jackson. The government will not bow to the monster. . . . Andrew Jackson yet lives to put his foot upon the head of the monster and crush him to the dust."

The monster, "a hydra of corruption," was known also as the Second Bank of the United States, chartered by Congress in 1816 as depository of the federal government, which was its principal stockholder and customer. The words were reported by a committee which called on President Jackson in the spring of 1834 to complain because he and Secretary of the Treasury Roger Taney had removed the federal deposits from the federal depository into what the Jacksonians called "selected banks" and others called "pet banks." The President was disgusted with the committee.

"Andrew Jackson," he exclaimed in the third person as before, "would never recharter that monster of corruption. Sooner than live in a country where such a power prevailed, he would seek an asylum in the wilds of Arabia."

In effect, he had already put his foot on the monster and crushed him in the dust. He had done so by vetoing a new charter for the Bank and removing the federal accounts from its books. So long as the federal Bank had the federal accounts, it had been regulator of the currency and of credit in general. Its power to regulate had derived from the fact that the federal Treasury was the largest single transactor in the economy and the largest bank depositor. Receiving the checks and notes of local banks deposited with it by government collectors of revenue, it had had constantly to come back on the local banks for settlements of the amounts which the checks and notes called for. It had had to do so because it made those amounts immediately available to the Treasury, wherever desired. Since settlement by the local banks was in specie, i.e., silver and gold coin, the pressure for settlement automatically regulated local bank lending; for the more the local banks lent, the larger the amount of their notes and checks in use and the larger the sums they had to settle in specie. This loss of specie reduced their power to lend.

All this had made the federal Bank the regulator not alone of the currency but of bank lending in general, the restraint it had exerted being fully as effective as that of the twelve Federal Reserve Banks at present, though by a different process. With its life now limited to two more years and the government accounts removed from its books, it was already crushed but still writhing.

The Jacksonian attack on the Bank is an affair respecting which posterity seems to have come to an opinion that is half hero worship and half discernment. In the words of Professor William G. Sumner, the affair was a struggle "between the democracy and the money power." Viewed in that light, Jackson's victory was a grand thing. But Sumner also observed—this was three-quarters of a century ago—that since Jackson's victory the currency, which previously had owned no superior in the world, had never again been so good. More recently Professor Lester V. Chandler, granting the Bank's imperfections, has said that its abolition without replacement by something to take over its functions was a "major blunder" which "ushered in a generation of banking anarchy and monetary disorder." So the affair stands, a triumph and a blunder.

During Andrew Jackson's lifetime three things had begun to alter prodigiously the economic life of Americans. These were steam, credit, and natural resources.

Steam had been lifting the lids of pots for thousands of years, and for a century or so it had been lifting water from coal mines. But only in recent years had it been turning spindles, propelling ships, drawing trains of cars, and multiplying incredibly the productive powers of man. For thousands of years money had been lent, but in most people's minds debt had signified distress—as it still did in Andrew Jackson's. Only now was its productive power, long known to merchants as a means of making one sum of money do the work of several, becoming popularly recognized by enterprising men for projects which required larger sums than could be assembled in coin. For three centuries or more America's resources had been crudely surmised, but only now were their variety, abundance, and accessibility becoming practical realities. And it was the union of these three, steam, credit, and natural resources, that was now turning Anglo-Saxon America from the modest agrarian interests that had preoccupied her for two centuries of European settlement to the dazzling possibilities of industrial exploitation.

In the presence of these possibilities, the democracy was becoming transformed from one that was Jeffersonian and agrarian to one that was financial and industrial. But it was still a democracy: its recruits were still men born and reared on farms, its vocabulary was still Jeffersonian, and its basic conceptions changed insensibly from the libertarianism of agrarians to that of *laissez faire*. When Andrew Jackson became President in 1829, boys born in log cabins were already becoming businessmen but with no notion of surrendering as bankers and manufacturers the freedom they might have enjoyed as farmers.

There followed a century of exploitation from which America emerged with the most wealthy and powerful economy there is, with her people the best fed, the best housed, the best clothed, and the best equipped on earth. But the loss and waste have long been apparent. The battle was only for the strong, and millions who lived in the midst of wealth never got to touch it. The age of the Robber Barons was scarcely a golden age. It was scarcely what Thomas Jefferson desired.

It could scarcely have been what Andrew Jackson desired either, for his ideals were more or less Jeffersonian by common inheritance, and the abuse of credit was one of the things he abominated. Yet no man ever did more to encourage the abuse of credit than he. For the one agency able to exert some restraint on credit was the federal Bank. In destroying it, he let speculation loose. Though a hard-money devotee who hated banks and wanted no money but coin, he fostered the formation of swarms of banks and endowed the country with a filthy and depreciated paper currency which he believed to be unsound and unconstitutional and from which the Civil War delivered it in the Administration of Abraham Lincoln thirty years later.

This, of course, was not Andrew Jackson's fault, unless one believes he would have done what he did had his advisers been different. Though a resolute and decisive person, he also relied on his friends. He had his official cabinet, largely selected for political expediency, and he had his "kitchen cabinet" for informal counsel. Of those advisers most influential with him, all but two were either businessmen or closely associated with the business world. The two exceptions were Major William B. Lewis, a planter and neighbor from Tennessee who came to live with him in the White House; and James K. Polk, also of Tennessee, later President of the United States. These two, with Jackson himself, constituted the agrarian element in the Jacksonian Administration. Several of the others, however, were agrarian in the sense that they had started as poor farm boys.

Martin Van Buren, probably the ablest of Jackson's political associates, was a lawyer whose investments had made him rich. Amos Kendall, the ablest in a business and administrative sense, later made the telegraph one of the greatest of American business enterprises and himself a man of wealth. He provided the Jacksonians their watchword, "The world is governed too much." He said "our countrymen are beginning to demand" that the government be content with "protecting their persons and property, leaving them to direct their labor and capital as they please, within the moral law: getting rich or remaining poor as may result from their own management or fortune." Kendall's views may be sound, but they are not what one expects to hear from the democracy when struggling with the money power.

Roger Taney, later Chief Justice, never got rich, but he liked banks and was a modest investor in bank stock. "There is perhaps no business," he said as Jackson's secretary of the treasury, "which yields a profit so certain and liberal as the business of banking and exchange; and it is proper that it should be open as far as practicable to the most free competition and its advantages shared by all classes of society." His own bank in Baltimore was one of the first of the pets in which he deposited government money.

David Henshaw, Jacksonian boss of Massachusetts, was a banker and industrialist whose advice in practical matters had direct influence in Washington. Henshaw projected a Jacksonian bank to take the place of the existing institution but to be bigger. (A similar project was got up by friends of Van Buren in New York and one of the two was mentioned favorably by Jackson in his veto message as a possible alternative to the existing United States Bank.) Samuel Ingham, Jackson's first secretary of the treasury, was a paper manufacturer in Pennsylvania and later a banker in New Jersey. Churchill C. Cambreleng, congressional leader of the attack on the Bank, was a New York businessman and former agent of John Jacob Astor. These are not all of the Jacksonians who were intent on the federal Bank's destruction, but they are typical.

There was a very cogent reason why these businessmen and their class generally wanted to kill the Bank of the United States. It interfered with easy money; it kept the state banks from lending as freely as they might otherwise and businessmen from borrowing.

New York, for example, was now the financial and commercial center of the country and its largest city, which Philadelphia formerly had been. The customs duties collected at its wharves and paid by its businessmen were far the largest of any American port, and customs duties were then the principal source of federal income. These duties were paid by New York businessmen with checks on New York banks. These checks were deposited by the federal collectors in the New York office of the Bank of the United States, whose headquarters were in Philadelphia and a majority of whose directors were Philadelphia businessmen. This, Amos Kendall observed, was a "wrong done to New York in depriving her of her natural advantages."

It was not merely a matter of prestige. As already noted, the United

States Bank, receiving the checks of the New York businessmen, made the funds at once available to the secretary of the treasury. The Bank had therefore to call on the New York banks for the funds the checks represented. This meant that the New York banks, in order to pay the federal Bank, had to draw down their reserves; which meant that they had less money to lend; which meant that the New York businessman could not borrow as freely and cheaply as they might otherwise. All this because their money had gone to Philadelphia.

Actually the situation was not so bad as my simplified account makes it appear. For one thing, the goods imported at New York were sold elsewhere in the country, and more money came to New York in payment for them than went out of the city in duties paid the government. But I have described it in the bald, one-sided terms that appealed to the local politicians and to the businessmen prone to grumbling because money was not so easy as they would like. There was truth in what they said, but it amounted to less than they made out.

New York's grievance was special because her customs receipts were so large and went to a vanquished rival. Otherwise the federal Bank's pressure on the local banks—all of which were state banks—was felt in some degree through the country at large. Wherever money was paid to a federal agency—for postage, for fines, for lands, for excise, for import duties—money was drawn from the local banks into the federal Bank. The flow of funds did not drain the local banks empty and leave them nothing to do, though they and the states' rights politicians talked as if that were the case. The federal Bank was simply their principal single creditor.

And though private business brought more money to New York and other commerical centers than it took away, the federal government took more away than it brought. For its largest payments were made elsewhere —to naval stations, army posts, Indian agents, owners of the public debt, largely foreign, and civilians in the government service throughout the country. In the normal flow of money payments from hand to hand in the economy, those to the federal government and consequently to the federal Bank were so large and conspicuous that the state banks involved in making them were disagreeably conscious of their size and frequency.

These banks, of course, were mostly eastern and urban rather than western and rural, because it was in eastern cities that the federal government received most of its income. Accordingly, it was in the eastern business centers, Boston, New York, Baltimore, and Charleston, that resentment against Philadelphia and the federal Bank was strongest. This resentment was intensified by the fact that the federal Bank's branch offices were also competitors for private business in these and other cities, which the present Federal Reserve Banks, very wisely, are not.

General Jackson's accession to the presidency afforded an opportunity to put an end to the federal Bank. Its charter would expire in seven years. The question of renewal was to be settled in that interval. Jackson was popular and politically powerful. His background and principles were agrarian. An attack on the Bank by him would be an attack "by the democracy on the money power." It would have, therefore, every political advantage.

The realities behind these words, however, were not what the words implied. The democracy till very recently had been agrarian because most of the population was agricultural. But the promoters of the assault on the Bank were neither agrarian in their current interests nor representative of what democracy implied.

In the western and rural regions, which were the most democratic in a traditional sense, dislike of the federal Bank persisted, though by 1829 it had less to feed on than formerly. Years before, under incompetent managers, the Bank had lent unwisely in the West, had been forced to harsh measures of self-preservation, and had made itself hated, with the help, as usual, of the state banks and states' rights politicians. But the West needed money, and though the Bank never provided enough it did provide some, and in the absence of new offenses disfavor had palpably subsided by the time Jackson became President.

There were also, in the same regions, vestiges or more of the traditional agrarian conviction that all banks were evil. This principle was still staunchly held by Andrew Jackson. He hated all banks, did so through a long life, and said so time after time. He thought they all violated the Constitution. But he was led by the men around him to focus his aversion on the federal Bank, which being the biggest must be the worst and whose regulatory pressure on the state banks must obviously be the oppression to be expected from a great, soulless corporation.

However, not all agrarian leaders went along with him. For many years the more intelligent had discriminated in favor of the federal Bank, recognizing that its operations reduced the tendency to inflation which, as a hard-money party, the agrarians deplored. Altogether, it was no longer to be expected that the agrarian democracy would initiate a vigorous attack on the federal Bank, though it was certainly to be expected that such an attack would receive very general agrarian support.

It was in the cities and within the business world that both the attack on the Bank and its defense would be principally conducted. For there the Bank had its strongest enemies and its strongest friends. Its friends were the more conservative houses that had dominated the old business world but had only a minor part in the new. It was a distinguished part, however, and influential. This influence, which arose from prestige and substantial wealth, combined with the strength which the federal Bank derived from the federal accounts to constitute what may tritely be called a "money power." But it was a disciplined, conservative money power and just what the economy needed.

But it was no longer *the* money power. It was rivaled, as Philadelphia was by New York, by the newer, more vigorous, more aggressive, and more democratic part of the business world.

The businessmen comprising the latter were a quite different lot from the old. The Industrial Revolution required more men to finance, to man, and manage its railways, factories, and other enterprises than the old business world, comprising a few rich merchants, could possibly provide. The Industrial Revolution was set to absorb the greater part of the population.

Yet when the new recruits, who yesterday were mechanics and farmers, offered themselves not only as laborers but as managers, owners, and entrepreneurs requiring capital, they met a response that was not always respectful. There was still the smell of the barnyard on their boots, and their hands were better adapted to hammer and nails than to quills and ink. The aristocrats were amused. They were also chary of lending to such borrowers; whereupon farmers' and mechanics' banks began to be set up. These banks found themselves hindered by the older banks and by the federal Bank. They and their borrowers were furious. They resisted the federal Bank in suits, encouraged by sympathetic states' rights politicians, and found themselves blocked by the federal courts.

Nor were their grievances merely material. They disliked being snubbed. Even when they became wealthy themselves, they still railed at "the capitalists" and "the aristocrats," as David Henshaw of Massachusetts did, meaning the old families, the Appletons and Lawrences whom he named, the business counterparts of the political figures that the Jacksonian revolution had replaced. Henshaw and his fellow Jacksonian leaders were full of virtue, rancor, and democracy. Their struggle was not merely to make money but to demonstrate what they already asserted, that they were as good as anyone, or more so. In their denunciation of the federal Bank, one finds them calling it again and again "an aristocracy" and its proprietors, other than the federal government, "aristocrats."

The Jacksonians, as distinct from Jackson himself, wanted a world where *laissez faire* prevailed; where, as Amos Kendall said, everyone would be free to get rich; where, as Roger Taney said, the benefits of banks would be open to all classes; where, as the enterprising exploiters of the land unanimously demanded, credit would be easy. To be sure, relatively few would be rich, and a good many already settling into an urban industrial class were beginning to realize it. But that consideration did not count with the Jacksonian leaders. They wanted a new order. But what they achieved was the age of the Robber Barons.

The attack on the old order took the form of an attack on the federal Bank for a number of reasons which may be summed up in political expediency. A factor in the success of the attack was that the president of the Bank, Nicholas Biddle, was the pampered scion of capitalists and aristocrats. He was born to wealth and prominence. He was elegant, literary, intellectual, witty, and conscious of his own merits. When at the age of 37 he became head of the largest moneyed corporation in the world he was wholly without practical experience. In his new duties he had to rely on brains, self-confidence, and hard work.

With these he did extraordinarily well. He had a remarkable grasp of productive and financial interrelations in the economy. The policies he formulated were sound. His management of the Bank, despite his inexperience, was efficient. His great weakness was naïveté, born of his ignorance of strife.

This characterization, I know, is quite contrary to the conventional one, which makes Biddle out a master of intrigue and craft such as only the purity of Andrew Jackson could overcome. But the evidence of his being a Machiavelli is wholly the assertion of his opponents, whose victory over him was enhanced by a magnification of his prowess. One of these, however, the suave Martin Van Buren, who knew him well and was a judge of such matters, ascribed no such qualities to him but instead spoke of the frankness and openness of his nature; it was in Daniel Webster that Van Buren saw wiliness.

Nicholas Biddle's response to the Jacksonian attack was inept. He was slow in recognizing that an attack was being made and ignored the warnings of his more astute friends. He expected the public to be moved by careful and learned explanations of what the Bank did. He broadcast copies of Jackson's veto message, one of the most popular and effective documents in American political history, with the expectation that people in general would agree with him that it was a piece of hollow demagogy. He entered a match for which he had no aptitude, impelled by a quixotic sense of duty and an inability to let his work be derogated. He engaged in a knock-down-drag-out fight with a group of experts as relentless as any American politics has ever known. The picture he presents is that of Little Lord Fauntleroy, lace on his shirt and good in his heart, running into those rough boys down the alley.

In his proper technical responsibilities Nicholas Biddle was a competent central banker performing a highly useful and beneficial task. It is a pity he had to be interrupted, both for him and for the economy. For him it meant demoralization. He lost track of what was going on in the Bank, he made blundering mistakes, he talked big. These things his opponents used tellingly against him. He turned from able direction of the central banking process to the hazardous business of making money, of which he knew nothing and for which his only knack lay in an enthusiastic appraisal of America's great economic future. In the end his Bank of the United States broke, he lost his fortune, he was tried on criminal charges (but released on a technicality), and he died a broken man.

This was personal misfortune, undeserved and severe. The more important victim was the American people. For with destruction of the United States Bank there was removed from an overexcitable economy the influence most effective in moderating its booms and depressions.

Andrew Jackson had vetoed recharter in 1832 and transferred the federal accounts to the pet banks in 1833 and 1834. The Bank's federal charter expired in 1836, though Nicholas Biddle obtained a charter from Pennsylvania and continued the organization as a state bank. The period was one of boom. Then in 1837 there was panic, all the banks in the country suspended, prices fell, and business collapsed. It was all Andrew Jackson's fault, his opponents declared, for killing the federal Bank. This was too generous. Jackson was not to blame for everything. The crisis was world-wide and induced by many forces. It would have happened anyway. Yet certainly Jackson's destruction of the Bank did not help. Instead it worsened the collapse. Had the Bank been allowed to continue the salutary performance of the years immediately preceding the attack upon it, and had it been supported rather than undermined by the Administration, the wild inflation which culminated in the collapse would have been curbed and the disaster diminished. Such a course would have been consistent with Jackson's convictions and professions. Instead he smote the Bank fatally at the moment of its best performance and in the course of trends against which it was needed most. Thereby he gave unhindered play to the speculation and inflation that he was always denouncing.

To a susceptible people the prospect was intoxicating. A continent abounding in varied resources and favorable to the maintenance of an immense population in the utmost comfort spread before the gaze of an energetic, ambitious, and clever race of men, who to exploit its wealth had two new instruments of miraculous potency: steam and credit. They rushed forward into the bright prospect, trampling, suffering, succeeding, failing. There was nothing to restrain them. For about a century the big rush lasted. Now it is over. And in a more critical mood we note that a number of things are missing or have gone wrong. To be sure, we are on top of the world still, but it is not very good bookkeeping to omit one's losses and count only one's gains.

That critical mood was known to others than Jackson. Emerson, Hawthorne, and Thoreau felt it. So did an older and more experienced contemporary of theirs, Albert Gallatin, friend and aide in the past to Thomas Jefferson, and now president of a New York bank but loyal to Jeffersonian ideals.

"The energy of this nation," he wrote to an old friend toward the end of Andrew Jackson's Administration, "is not to be controlled; it is at present exclusively applied to the acquisition of wealth and to improvements of stupendous magnitude. Whatever has that tendency, and of course an immoderate expansion of credit, receives favor. The apparent prosperity and the progress of cultivation, population, commerce, and improvement are beyond expectation. But it seems to me as if general demoralization was the consequence; I doubt whether general happiness is increased; and I would have preferred a gradual, slower, and more secure progress. I am, however, an old man, and the young generation has a right to govern itself. . . ."

In these last words, Mr. Gallatin was echoing the remark of Thomas Jefferson that "the world belongs to the living." Neither Gallatin nor Jefferson, however, thought it should be stripped by the living. Yet nothing but the inadequacy of their powers seems to have kept those Nineteenth-Century generations from stripping it. And perhaps nothing else could.

But to the extent that credit multiplies man's economic powers, curbs upon credit extension are a means of conservation, and an important means. The Bank of the United States was such a means. Its career was short and it had imperfections. Nevertheless it worked. The evidence is in the protest of the bankers and entrepreneurs, the lenders and the borrowers, against its restraints. Their outcry against the oppressor was heard, and Andrew Jackson hurried to their rescue. Had he not, some other way of stopping its conservative and steadying influence could doubtless have been found. The appetite for credit is avid, as Andrew Jackson knew in his day and might have foretold for ours. But because he never meant to serve it, the credit for what happened goes rather to the clever advisers who led the old hero to the monster's lair and dutifully held his hat while he stamped on its head and crushed it in the dust.

Meanwhile, the new money power had curled up securely in Wall Street, where it has been at home ever since.

23 *Charles M. Wiltse*

CALHOUN: AN INTERPRETATION

What was the age of Jackson all about? Historians today are far from agreed on its essential importance. Bray Hammond, as we have noted, finds it in the attempt to liberate business, to make available to the many the entrepreneurial opportunities that were being confined to the few. Professor Arthur M. Schlesinger, Jr., finds it in the attempt on the part of the other sections of society, including the laboring classes begotten by the new industrialism, to restrain the power of the business community. Professor Marvin Meyers finds it in the attempt to restore the virtues of an earlier republican society.

Looking through the eyes of John C. Calhoun, his biographer finds in the age of Jackson something else again. Author of an outstanding three-volume life of the great Southern leader, Charles M. Wiltse concludes, in the following essay, that Jacksonian politics were the politics of despotism and that Jackson himself was the despot. Events before the administrations of Jackson had made Calhoun apprehensive for the liberty of minority interests and had led him to formulate a doctrine of nullification. But events during those administrations confirmed his worst fears and persuaded him of the dire need for sustaining his doctrine.

Mr. Wiltse pursues his argument by addressing himself to the component questions which his appraisal of Calhoun undertakes to answer. What were the larger historical conditions which formed the matrix of Calhoun's thought? What were the tenets of his political philosophy in general and of his theory of the concurrent majority in particular? How did the activities of Jackson and his cohorts confirm Calhoun's fears for liberty and for the rights of minorities?

It is fair enough to say that Mr. Wiltse's analysis of Calhoun answers many significant questions but raises many others. To what extent, for example, was Calhoun's political philosophy a rationalization both of Southern economic interests and of his own personal ambitions? How can one otherwise explain his conversion from ardent nationalism to ardent sectionalism? To what extent does the theory of the concurrent majority, in seeking to preclude the tyranny of the majority, lead inevitably to the tyranny of the minority? How fair is Wiltse's view of Jackson, which, regarding him from the premises of Calhoun, magnifies that which seems to be high-handed and peremptory

Reprinted with permission from *Proceedings of the South Carolina Historical Association*, 1948, pp. 26–38.

and blurs out that which may have been sincerely and effectively liberal?

Calhoun's ideas represent a significant point in the route from 1787, when the Constitution was drawn up, to 1861, when the Civil War began. Social change had made infeasible the balance of jurisdiction between the central and state governments which the Founding Fathers had devised. The Southern problem was a real one. The South was fast becoming the prisoner of a system which it had helped create and to which for many decades it had held the key. Yet it is important to remember, as Professor Charles Sellers will remind us in a subsequent essay, that during this period not every Southern state was South Carolina and not every Southerner was John C. Calhoun. He was for the Southern problem a Jeremiah and a Cassandra. Many Southern leaders held substantially different convictions. The Civil War came only when Southern leadership arrived, as it did in 1860, at the viewpoint which Calhoun had assumed in 1830.

I

When the bitterly contested subtreasury bill was before the Senate early in 1838, Clay took occasion to upbraid Calhoun for his apostasy. Calhoun replied in kind, and Philip Hone, popular Whig merchant and former Mayor of New York, watching the scene from a seat on the Senate floor, noted a greater "degree of acrimony and ill-nature" than the occasion warranted. Hone was ready to excuse the South Carolina Senator, however, on the ground that he was unusually sensitive, "like all men whose position is doubtful in their own minds."

Hone was a shrewd observer and a good judge of human nature, but he was utterly wrong about Calhoun. Whatever his faults, however great his errors, Calhoun's position was never doubtful in his own mind. He sometimes arrived at his conclusions with baffling rapidity, but the most careful and mature reflection never shook his faith in his own logic. Throughout a lifetime of controversy, as he once confessed with masterly understatement to a friend, he remained "a good deal attached" to his own opinions, and "not so much disposed, perhaps, to take advice" as he ought to be. His insufferable cocksureness made enemies of men who should have been his friends, but it was also the measure of his leadership, for in times of stress and turmoil, men who doubt themselves tend to fall in behind those who have no doubts.

The quality of his intellect led Calhoun almost inevitably to generalize from his experience, and to set up his generalizations in the form of universal laws. His unshakable self-confidence, his unquestioning certainty that he was right, led him to evaluate the actions of others and in large measure to determine his own on the basis of these general principles. His own political philosophy, in short, was a framework upon which he hung his reading of history and in terms of which he interpreted the economic and political forces of his time. By the same token it is also a pattern which gives consistency and direction to a career that appeared to his enemies and often to his friends to be erratic and without principle. His course was not determined by simple reactions to people and events, but was rather derived from a system of philosophy into which people and events had first been neatly fitted and arranged. Calhoun's career will become more meaningful if we examine the major tenets of this system, and apply them as he did to the world in which he lived.

Calhoun belonged to an age of revolution, of intellectual ferment, of political and economic experimentation. He was born before the close of the American struggle for independence. When he was a precocious lad of six his father opposed ratification of the new Constitution of the United States, because it gave too much power to a central government. The French Revolution was the overshadowing fact of his youth. He was nearing maturity when Virginia rebelled against the autocracy of the Alien and Sedition Acts, and he had already entered preparatory school when the explosive force of that rebellion carried Thomas Jefferson to the presidency. He was in college when Bonaparte completed the transition from successful military commander to First Consul to Emperor, and we know from his letters that the young Carolinian watched the process and its aftermath with interest and concern.

Equally suggestive of conflict and upheaval is Calhoun's early political career. He entered public life at a time when his country was being forced to choose sides in a world-wide struggle for power. He sat in a war Congress and grappled there with the problems of foreign invasion and internal revolt. He saw, and encouraged, the rise of industry in the northern and middle states, but in the process he had ample opportunity to observe the interaction of economic forces and political events. From the vantage point of a Cabinet seat he witnessed the first sectional rift in the smooth surface of the Union, and he recognized the Missouri Compromise for what it was: an internal balance of power. It was an age of wonderful technological advances, which seemed to go hand in hand with crumbling social institutions; an age when active minds went back to fundamentals, and thinking men sought new interpretations of the world order.

Calhoun's own search for first principles undoubtedly began at an early stage of his career, but it was the fall of 1828 before he reduced his findings to orderly and systematic form in the *South Carolina Exposition.* Thenceforth he weighed every public measure in the same scale. He added illustrations from current politics or from history as he went along, but he found nothing to justify any basic modification in the general thesis. When his theory appeared in definitive form in the posthumous *Disquisition on Government* it was still essentially the same as it had been in its initial version, save for a greater completeness in its presentation. Like the authors of the *Federalist*, Calhoun drew freely from Hobbes and Harrington and Locke, but the significance of the doctrine thus derived lay not in its 17th century skeleton but in its contemporary dress, and in the use to which it was put.

II

Government, for Calhoun, was inseparable from human nature, and with respect to neither was he troubled by any Utopian illusions. His major premise, derived from what he called "universal experience," was that man cannot exist without some kind of government. The law of self-preservation requires that we pursue our own interests more assiduously than we pursue the welfare of others. The natural consequence is a tendency to conflict among individuals which would destroy society and make life impossible were it not controlled. The controlling force, what ever form it takes, is government. The powers of government, however, must be exercised by men, and they are therefore liable to abuse because of the same tendency in human nature that makes government necessary. Unless safeguarded in some fashion, the power given to the rulers to prevent injustice and oppression will be used by them to oppress the ruled.

This tendency to abuse of the powers of government could be successfully resisted, in Calhoun's view, only by the internal structure of the government itself. Governments so constructed that the ruled might resist the abuses of the rulers he called limited or constitutional governments. All others were absolute. In neither category did it make any difference whether the ruler was a single individual, an oligarchy, or a majority.

A constitutional government, as Calhoun visualized it, must be based on suffrage; but the right of suffrage alone is not enough to prevent absolutism. By means of popular elections the actual seat of power may be shifted from the rulers to the body of the community, but the abuse of power will not thereby be prevented unless the individual interests of the whole citizen body are the same. Where interests are many and varied, the right of suffrage merely intensifies the tendency to conflict, for each interest strives to gain control of the powers of government as a means of protecting itself. This leads to combinations and arrangements, until the whole community is divided into two hostile parties.

Indeed, the community would be so divided, even if interests were otherwise the same, by the action of the government alone. To fulfill its purpose government must be strong. It must, therefore, employ officers, collect taxes, and spend money in numerous ways. It is difficult if not impossible to collect taxes equally from the whole community, and they are never spent in equal proportions. The community will thus be divided into opposing interests by the fiscal action of the government alone. The majority, moved by the same self-interest as the individuals who compose it, will inevitably seek to aggrandize itself at the expense of the minority. The fact that, by means of the ballot, the two may change places only intensifies the tendency to conflict and disorder.

Suffrage, then, is not enough to prevent the abuse of power. There must be some other provision which will prevent any single interest or combination of interests from gaining exclusive control of the machinery of government. Calhoun's solution of the problem was the theory of the concurrent majority. Where the action of the government might affect the various portions of the community unequally, he would give to each portion, through its own majority, either a concurrent voice in the making of the laws, or a veto on their execution. To act at all the government would thus require the consent of the various interest groups of which it was composed. Its guiding principle would therefore be compromise, whereas the only principle underlying absolute governments is force.

Such, in broad outline, is Calhoun's system of political philosophy. The dogma of state sovereignty, with its correlatives of nullification and secession, was but an application of this more general doctrine, restated in terms of familiar American institutions. He found a classical basis for his theory in the separate representation of patricians and plebeians in ancient Rome, under a system that gave to each a veto on the acts of government, and a more recent illustration in the balance of classes in British parliamentary practice. In his own country he found that the basic distinction between interests, though still along economic lines, followed an essentially geographical pattern. They were not stratified as classes or estates, but were localized as sections or regions in terms of the prevalent source of livelihood, this in turn being based on climate and natural resources. The States were most nearly representative of this division, so it was to the States, in their character as members of a confederacy, that Calhoun accorded a concurrent veto power.

The controversies of the preceding three decades pointed the way so clearly to this particular application that it would have been the part of political wisdom to use it even if logic had directed otherwise. Ever since the Alien and Sedition Acts, and the countering resolutions from the legislatures of Kentucky and Virginia, a debate as to the true construction of the Constitution had been in progress. The Virginia school, for which both Jefferson and Madison had argued, held the instrument to be in fact a compact among independent sovereignties. From this it followed, under accepted principles of international law, that each party to the compact had a right to judge of its own powers, and to interpose to arrest a patent violation of the agreement. Calhoun's own intensive study during the summer and early fall of 1828 when he was preparing to write the *Exposition* convinced him of the validity of the compact theory, and served as his point of departure in his subsequent writings and speeches on the question. The Roman Tribunate had been established by agreement between warring factions. First the temporal lords and then the commons derived their equal power in Britain from contracts, signed and witnessed in due form. The concurrent veto—the great conservative principle of a society—did not just happen, but came into existence to protect each of the parties to a compact from violation by the others.

Having fitted the Constitution of the United States into its proper niche in his political philosophy, it was no difficult matter for Calhoun to reason that the House of Representatives was the organ of the numerical majority, but that the Senate, with its representation by States, was intended to give a concurrent voice to the various interests that made up the body politic. His own function in the Senate was thus to maintain the interests, economic and political, of South Carolina, and by extension the interests of the whole region of which the State was a part. He could change sides on major issues, he could change party allegiance, he could pursue a seemingly erratic course on any phase of public policy, and still be entirely consistent with his own political philosophy. He represented a minority interest, threatened with extinction by the action of a government in control of a numerical majority. Nor was it alone for South Carolina's benefit that he asserted her sovereignty against the weight of numbers. It was also for the good of the whole; for in that way alone, so he believed, could the Union endure.

III

The major tenets of this theory of the state—that governments tend to become absolute, that rulers tend to abuse their powers, that the honors and emoluments of government are in themselves enough to fix party lines and precipitate a struggle for power—all of these propositions were deductions from the nature of man. But they were far more than that. They were also obvious facts that anyone could see for himself in the day-to-day operations of the government of the United States. So clear were they to Calhoun that they gave validity to a theory otherwise abstract, and justified extremes that a man of less positive convictions might have hesitated to invoke.

History may be interpreted in many ways, according to the preconceptions of the historian, the material he elects to accept, and the sources he chooses to ignore. The age of Jackson may, indeed, have been the forerunner of later social movements in which the welfare of the common man was pitted against intrenched privilege and greed. Certainly Amos Kendall and Francis Blair, among the ablest if not the most truthful journalists of the century, strove mightily to provide the contemporary voter (and incidentally, posterity) with just such a picture. But to Calhoun, and unquestionably to a majority of the middle class of his day, Jackson's career was one unbroken march toward despotism. It proved every point in Calhoun's political theory, offered new and pertinent illustrations of the nature of the governmental process, and justified the most vigorous forms of opposition. Let us strip the Jackson era of its supporting propaganda, forget the idealism of the glosses that have been written on it, and look at it as nearly as we may with Calhoun's eyes.

The tools of power were ready to Jackson's hand when that extraordinary man took office, and his political lieutenants were thoroughly skilled in their use. The tools had been thoughtfully provided by unwitting rivals going back for nearly a decade. The four-year tenure law of 1820, conceived by the political genius William H. Crawford, was a potent engine for securing partisans. Under this innocent-looking statute district attorneys, officers of the customs service, registers of the land offices, naval agents, and a few less numerous officials were made removable at the will of the President. Their terms of office, moreover, were specifically limited to four years, so that as each presidential election rolled around, virtually the entire civilian personnel of the Federal Government would have to seek reappointment. The more numerous group of postal employees already served for limited periods, defined by the contracts under which the mails were carried.

The four-year law was in fact one element in a closely knit political machine that Crawford had built up on the foundations of the old Jefferson-Burr alliance, and which was expected to make him President in 1824. When ill-health thwarted Crawford's hopes, Martin Van Buren succeeded to control of the machine, which he deftly turned to the service of Andrew Jackson. John Quincy Adams, meanwhile, though he had less than a third of the popular vote, had been elected President early in 1825 by a House of Representatives in which tariff sentiment predominated. Immediately thereafter the leading exponent of the protective policy received the first place in the Cabinet, and the President propounded a legislative program whose maximum benefits would accrue to those states to which he owed his election. He did his best to divert former Crawford partisans to his own cause by judicious reappointments under the four-year law; and in the skillful hands of Secretary of State Henry Clay, the printing and other public contracts were given out with a view to Adams' re-election.

It was not the officeholders, however, but the beneficiaries of the tariff who made up the core of Adams' strength, and shortly before the election of 1828 he prepared to insure their loyalty with still higher duties. Calhoun was already in opposition, since his state and section were the primary victims of the administration policy. He had allied himself perforce with the Jacksonians, even though it brought him into the same camp as the bulk of the Crawford Radicals, his bitter foes of a few years earlier. Calhoun and other Southern followers of Jackson tried to block this new attempt to increase the tariff by introducing provisions deliberately obnoxious to Adams' New England supporters; but when the critical moment arrived Van Buren, Eaton, Benton, and others among the Jackson inner circle voted to pass the measure they had pledged themselves to defeat. The strength of the tariff interest had not been lost upon the Democratic managers, and with the election approaching in the fall, they made their own peace with the manufacturers. They courted both sides and won.

It was at this point that Calhoun wrote the *South Carolina Exposition.* To him, the relation between the dominant economic interest and the partisan majority was clear. In subtle, indirect, but entirely legal ways, the latter had been bought by the former. The government was already in the exclusive control of the stronger interest, and the destruction of the weaker, which was also his own, must inevitably follow, unless Jackson chose to cast the influence of his vast personal popularity into the opposite scale.

Jackson, surrounded as he was by some of the ablest party strategists ever produced in this or any other country, preferred to consolidate his power. His methods were simple, direct, and effective. He began by reappointing to office only known and proven partisans, and by removing those who were not whole-hearted in his cause in favor of men whose personal loyalty was undeviating. When the process of patronage distribution was well advanced, in December 1829, a New York paper devoted to Van Buren's interests announced its support of Jackson for a second term, and of Van Buren for the succession. From the beginning of his campaign, Jackson had been committed to a single term, but before another year was out his candidacy for re-election was acknowledged and a new "official" newspaper had been established in the capital to advance it. The Washington *Globe,* edited publicly by Blair and behind the scenes by Kendall, became thereafter an almost irresistible vehicle for party propaganda. Its financial support came from office-holders, who were required to subscribe for it—and pay in advance—or resign their places to men who would.

Another important milestone on Jackson's march to autarchy was the Maysville Road veto in 1830. The action was received with initial approbation in the South because it appeared to put an end to federal spending for public works. It could therefore be used as an argument for reducing the revenue, which meant the tariff. But it presently appeared, as other internal improvement bills received the President's approbation, that the question was still open. The only real change was that the use of public funds for improvement purposes was made subject in each case to the personal judgment of the executive. The Maysville Road was in Kentucky, whose legislature had sent Henry Clay to the Senate. Highways and canals in more compliant states might perhaps prove to be for national purposes.

Year after year McDuffie introduced into the House bills for tariff reduction in accordance with what he and Calhoun believed to be Jackson's pre-election pledge to South Carolina; and year after year they came to nothing. The vote was manipulated by the same economic interest that had elected Adams and now supported Jackson. The cost of manufactured products rose, the price of cotton fell, and Southern leaders, particularly the younger group in South Carolina, threatened revolt. So in July 1831 Calhoun restated his theory, with embellishments looking to positive action. He pointed out that although a substantial minority believed the tariff to be unconstitutional, the majority continued to pursue that policy to the economic ruin of the cotton states. So he claimed for the interest he represented a concurrent veto, but at the same time expressed his great preference for an adjustment of the point at issue by Congress.

Again the national legislature refused to make concessions, and in that refusal gave further evidence of the validity of Calhoun's premises. For there was actually strong sentiment in many parts of the country for tariff reduction, but to yield to it would have been to concede a political triumph to Calhoun. This neither Jackson nor Clay would do; so at the risk of civil war the Jacksonians and the National Republicans voted together to maintain a prohibitive scale of duties, lest the pretensions of a rival be advanced. Throughout the whole controversy the actions, motives, and purposes of Calhoun and his followers were deliberately misrepresented and distorted by Blair and his satellite editors to arouse public indignation against South Carolina and her leaders.

The issue was joined in the fall of 1832. Calhoun stated the case for state action to arrest the tariff in a letter to Governor Hamilton late in August. It was timed immediately to precede state elections whose outcome would determine whether South Carolina would interpose her sovereignty to restrain the protective system. Calhoun showed how the majority always has an interest in enlarging the powers of government, and how human nature itself would impel the rulers to oppress the ruled, unless they were in some manner prevented from so doing. Majority rule was in fact only rule by the stronger interest, whose cupidity and ambition would inevitably hasten the government along the road to absolutism. The only barrier lay in the original sovereignty of the states.

To those who lost money by the protective policy the argument was convincing. The Nullifiers won their two-thirds majority. The convention was duly called, and the tariffs of 1828 and 1832 were declared null and void within the limits of South Carolina.

Jackson's answer to nullification was a proclamation explicitly claiming for the Federal Government—which is to say, for the majority—precisely the powers that George III had claimed over the colonies in 1776: the power to judge of its own limits, to pass laws within those limits, and to compel obedience to those laws. The partisan majority then ratified these claims by voting to the President full control over army, navy, militia, and for all practical purpose public treasury, any or all of which might be used to assist in the collection of import duties in the rebellious state. An act, Calhoun called it, to "enforce robbery by murder." He did not doubt that Jackson, like Macbeth, saw in his dreams the vision of a crown.

The compromise of 1833 put an end for the time being to the controversy between South Carolina and the general government, but it impeded not at all Jackson's progress toward undisputed power. In the summer of 1832 the President had vetoed a bill renewing the charter of the Bank of the United States. The Bank threw its influence to Clay in the fall election, and for this political opposition, Jackson undertook to destroy the "monster of corruption" without waiting for its charter to expire. In the fall of 1833, with no economic justification and the flimsiest of legal pretexts, the public funds were removed from the custody of the Bank and placed with various State institutions where they were directly under executive control. Two Secretaries of the Treasury were dismissed before one who would sign the necessary order was found, and the action was deliberately timed to precede the meeting of Congress, so that it could not be blocked.

In the Senate, where Calhoun and Clay had temporarily joined forces against the administration, the removal of the deposits was denounced as the ultimate act of tyranny. Clay read from Plutarch the description of Caesar entering the Roman Treasury sword in hand. Calhoun showed that whatever the motive, the result in this case was the same. For the Roman had seized the public treasure to buy partisans with which to consolidate his power; and the public funds in the pet banks were being recklessly loaned out to speculators who were thereby converted into partisans. The Senate voted a resolution censuring the President. Jackson replied with a sharp protest, which the Senate refused to receive.

As of the spring of 1834 the record, in the eyes of Calhoun and those who thought with him, was something like this: First the patronage had been perverted, by instituting the general practice of removal from office without cause—the principle of the Albany Regency that "to the victors belong the spoils." The total number of employees and pensioners of the

Federal Government had doubled since 1825, and expenses exclusive of payments on the public debt, had likewise doubled, although the population increase was no more than 25 percent. The revenue had been enormously increased in the same interval, largely through a form of taxation which fell unequally on the different sections of the country, and the President had been given by a subservient Congress the power to perpetuate this inequality by military force. A large and unscrupulous press had been suborned to do the bidding of the party leaders. The public money had been removed without adequate reason or even plausible excuse from the depository established and safe-guarded by law, and had been placed in a group of favored banks where it was under the exclusive control of the executive. This money was being used by the banks that held it, not as a deposit but as capital, and the amount of it was loaned out three and four times over, the profits going to the pet banks and the loans going to partisans, present or prospective. Yet when the Senate condemned the final act of power, though it had sanctioned everything that went before, the President, in language skillfully chosen to inflame popular prejudices, accused the Senate of violating his rights. In the Cherokee case two years earlier Jackson had ignored a decision of the Supreme Court. Who but the most blinded partisan could fail to see in this challenge to the Senate the first step toward subverting the legislative arm as well?

All this would have been more than enough to convince men less predisposed in that direction than Calhoun that the Constitution was in fact a dead letter and Andrew Jackson a dictator of unrestrained power. But there was more to come. Jackson decreed that Martin Van Buren should be his successor, and a party convention made up of officeholders and pensioners unanimously ratified the choice. There was no subtlety about it. The President was openly and shamelessly designating his successor, and would use all the vast patronage at his command to insure the election of his favorite. To Calhoun it was as "open and palpable usurpation of the supreme executive power" as though it had been brought about by military force. Force had in fact been threatened for the collection of a relatively trifling debt from France, and that matter still hung fire early in 1836 when Van Buren's cause looked none too bright. So Jackson indulged once more in vigorous saber-rattling, until Calhoun thought him bent upon war to justify himself in accepting a third term. Napoleon was not the first who had risen to imperial estate through successful foreign war, nor was he likely to be the last.

Jackson also decreed that the resolution of censure should be expunged from the Senate Journal, and the faithful Benton, himself designated for the presidential succession at one remove, undertook the task. He was not "single-handed and alone" for long. The party machinery, reaching down to the smallest hamlet and out to the remotest reaches of a far-flung domain, was set in motion. Senators who had voted to condemn the President were marked for the slaughter, and those members of their State Legislatures who had supported them were the preliminary victims. Against each of these local representatives a campaign was waged on his home ground, with all the persuasions that a powerful and wealthy central government could command. In half a dozen states the political complexion of the legislature was changed, and Senators were "instructed" to expunge the hated judgment. Some obeyed, others resigned; but the result was the same. In less than three years the Senate majority was reversed, and Jackson was vindicated in January 1837. Not without reason Calhoun called it "the melancholy evidence of a broken spirit, ready to bow at the feet of power."

IV

To a generation accustomed to a liberal evaluation of the Jackson era, this picture will seem exaggerated and overdrawn. It was nevertheless the picture that a substantial and talented portion of King Andrew's subjects saw. Calhoun's writings and speeches only add more detail to the skeleton presented here. Substantially the same view will be found in the columns of Duff Green's *United States Telegraph,* of Richard Craillé's Richmond *Jefferson and Virginia Times,* and in many other anti-Jackson papers. It was ably and clearly expressed by many prominent actors on the scene, like John Tyler of Virginia, George Poindexter of Mississippi, Willie P. Mangum of North Carolina, even by Clay and Webster themselves. In literary form Judge Beverley Tucker's novel, *The Partisan Leader,* first published by Duff Green in 1836, traces the same forces through three hypothetical Van Buren administrations, and might have come even closer to prophesy than it did had not the panic of 1837 put an abrupt end, for the time being, to the hand-picked Jackson dynasty.

Calhoun's analysis of the political process was complete long before he gave his own support to Van Buren's program in the special session of 1837. The administration, through the normal reaction of the average man to economic catastrophe, had been thrown into the minority, and Calhoun knew that the interests of South Carolina were no safer in the hands of the Clay-Webster combination than they had been under Jackson or Adams. As the advocate of a special interest it was clearly his duty to go with whichever party was most likely to advance his cause.

The theory, to repeat, was fully matured before Jackson left office, every tenet of it having been in one way or another confirmed by the career of the Hero. It was thereafter a glass through which Calhoun observed the passing scene. The logcabin-and-hard-cider campaign of 1840 merely showed once more how partisans were lost when the well of patronage ran dry, and were won by promises, however specious. He had reasoned from the start that the struggle for place would tend to become more violent until control changed hands at every election, to be retained at last by force. He saw the partisan majority change with each election from Van Buren's day until his own death in 1850. Believing as he did that the need for new sources of political reward would force the partisan majority to seek new forms of power, he could hardly have been surprised at Polk's venture into aggressive war.

Had Calhoun been less sure of himself, less ready to pursue his own reasoning to the ultimate end, and less ingenious in fitting the facts as he saw them into the pattern as he himself had laid it down, he might perhaps have reached a different explanation of his times, and followed in consequence a different course. Being the type of man he was, and in the environment that was his, like Luther at the Diet of Worms, he could do no other. To him and to a majority of his generation liberty was the most precious possession of mankind. It was for liberty that a revolution had been fought and a new nation established—not to substitute after half a century the absolutism of a successful general for that of a demented British king. History, philosophy, and his own experience taught him that the natural tendency of government was to whittle away the sphere of liberty, and that this tendency could be resisted only by power. Calhoun was simply realist enough to know that the greatest power in any state, next to military might, is the organized power of its economic interests.

24 Charles Grier Sellers, Jr.

WHO WERE THE SOUTHERN WHIGS?

In our study of history we tend to use convenient schemes. The past is wrapped up in a tidy package. It becomes considerably more teachable if also considerably less true. One can better understand results that are known to follow if one has causes that clearly explain them. Nothing would more baffle the student or distress his mentor than to have an imperfect matching of causes and results.

A notable case in point is the analysis we give, in our courses and in our textbooks, of the coming of the Civil War. To account for a conflict so dire, so bloody, and so regrettable, we have settled upon causes that could lead into it clearly, cosmically, understandably, inevitably. The North and South must have been, for several decades, moving farther and farther apart into sharply defined attitudes of in-

Reprinted with permission from *The American Historical Review*, LIX (January, 1954), 335–46.

creasing mutual hostility. It would untidy our package and confuse our scheme to consider that the process had not been one of decades, that hostility was not ever increasing, and that, indeed, the attitudes were far from being clearly defined or clearly sectional.

That is the lesson we can learn from the following essay by Charles Grier Sellers, Jr., of the University of California. Professor Sellers is one of the younger scholars who are doing so much to restudy the complex pattern of politics during the decades after the War of 1812. He has contributed considerably to an understanding of those decades through his perceptive articles as well as through his fine biography of James K. Polk, the first volume of which appeared in 1957.

In the essay below, Professor Sellers asks us to reconsider Southern politics in the 1830's and 1840's. We may give up several of our stereotypes, he submits, if we look again and more closely at the program and activities of the Southern Whigs. We may find that we have erroneously projected the Solid South of the decades after the Civil War to those before it. We may find too that we may have to replace our clear and certain explanation of why the war came with one that is appreciably more complex and certainly less convenient.

Students of the Old South have spent much of their time in recent years dispelling myths about that fabled land of moonlight and magnolias. Our understanding of the social, intellectual, and economic life of the ante-bellum South has been considerably revised and immeasurably widened by the work of a large number of able scholars.

Political history, however, has been unfashionable, and one of the results has been the survival of a series of myths about the political life of the South in the 1830's and 1840's. The key myth may be called the myth of a monolithic South: a section unified as early as the 1820's in its devotion to state rights doctrines and its hostility to the nationalistic, anti-slavery, capitalistic North. The result of approaching ante-bellum history by way of Fort Sumter and Appomattox, this point of view found its classic statements in the apologias of Jefferson Davis and Alexander H. Stephens, but it was made respectable in the first generation of professional scholarship by such historians as Herman Von Holst and John W. Burgess. It colored such early monographs as U. B. Phillips' "Georgia and State Rights" and H. M. Wagstaff's *States Rights and Political Parties in North Carolina, 1776–1861*, and is to be seen in most of the more recent works on the pre-Civil War South. It has also given rise to the corollary myths that Calhoun was the representative spokesman and political leader of the South after about 1830, and that the Whig party in the South mainly reflected the state rights proclivities of the great planters.

These myths have been strengthened by Frederick Jackson Turner's sectional analysis of our early national history. Turner's approach has been extremely fruitful, but its sweeping application has tended to exaggerate differing sectional tendencies into absolute sectional differences. The application of geographic sectionalism to individual states, moreover, has fostered the further myth that political strife within the Old South was confined largely to struggles over intrastate sectional issues between up-country and low country, hill country and "black belt."

All of these myths have some basis in fact. They are, however, the product of a misplaced emphasis which has permeated nearly all the studies of pre–Civil War southern politics. Sectionalism and state rights have been made the central themes of southern political history for almost the entire ante-bellum period. Southern opposition to nationalistic legislation by Congress has been overemphasized. And the social, economic, and ideological lines of political cleavage within the slave states have been obscured. The early history of the Whig party below Mason and Dixon's line shows the character of these distortions.

It is too often forgotten that in the ante-bellum period the South had a vigorous two-party system, an asset it has never since enjoyed. Until at least the later 1840's, the voting southerner was much more interested in the success of his own party and its policies than in banding together with southerners of the opposite party to defend the Constitution and southern rights against invasion by the North. The parties were evenly matched and elections were bitterly contested. It was rare for any southern state to be regarded as absolutely safe for either party. Of the 425,629 votes cast in the slave states at the election of 1836, the Whigs had a majority of only 243 popular votes. In this and the three succeeding presidential elections, a total of 2,745,171 votes were cast, but the over-all margin, again in favor of the Whigs, was only 66,295, or 2.4 per cent of the total votes. In these four elections the Whigs carried a total of twenty-seven southern states and the Democrats twenty-six.

An equally close rivalry is evident in congressional representation. In the five congressional elections between 1832 and 1842, southern Democrats won an aggregate total of 234 seats, while their opponents captured 263. Whigs predominated among southern representatives in three of these five Congresses, and Democrats in two. In three of them the margin between the southern wings of the parties was five or less. We have then a picture of keen political competition, with a vigorous Whig party maintaining a slight ascendancy.

What did this Whig party stand for? The pioneer account of the southern Whigs was the essay by U. B. Phillips which, significantly, appeared in the *Festschrift* to Frederick Jackson Turner [New York, 1910]. This study shows Phillips' characteristic tendency to generalize about the entire South on the basis of conditions in his native Georgia. "The great central body of southern Whigs," he declares, "were the cotton producers, who were first state-rights men pure and simple and joined the Whigs from a sense of outrage at Jackson's threat of coercing South Carolina."

Two years after Phillips' essay appeared, Arthur C. Cole published his exhaustive monograph on *The Whig Party in the South*. Less than a third of the Cole volume is concerned with the period before 1844, when Whiggery was of greatest importance in the South, and he generally follows the Phillips interpretation of its origins. His account of the birth of the party devotes three pages to early National Republicanism in the South, twenty to the anti-Jackson sentiment aroused during the nullification crisis, and only four and a half to the fight over the national bank and financial policy. "Various interests," he says, "linked in political alliance with the few southerners whose interests and inclinations led to the support of latitudinarian principles, a still larger faction made up of those who supported constitutional doctrines on the opposite extreme and whose logical interests seemed to point against such an affiliation."

An analysis, however, of the record of the Twenty-second Congress (1831–1833) leads to somewhat different conclusions. It was this Congress which dealt with the tariff, nullification, and national bank questions, and it was during this Congress that the groundwork for the Whig party was laid. Of the ninety southerners in the House of Representatives, sixty-nine had been elected as supporters of Andrew Jackson, while twenty-one, nearly a fourth, were National Republicans. Of the sixty-nine Democrats, twenty-five were subsequently active in the Whig party. Eighteen of the latter were state rights Whigs, while seven were not identified with the state rights wing of the opposition. These twenty-five men then, together with the twenty-one National Republicans, may be regarded as representative of the groups which formed the Whig party in the South.

These incipient Whigs voted twenty-four to twenty-one in favor of the tariff of 1832, a measure denounced by state rights men and nullified by South Carolina. They also voted twenty-four to nineteen for the Force Bill, which was designed to throttle the nullifiers. This backing of administration measures was hardly a portent of an opposition state rights party. The real harbinger of Whiggery was the vote on the national bank bill, which this group supported twenty-seven to seventeen.

The Whig party actually took shape during the Twenty-third Congress (1833–1835), in which it gained the allegiance of fifty-two of the ninety-nine southern members of the House. They voted twenty-nine to sixteen in favor of rechartering the national bank and unanimously in favor of restoring the government deposits to Biddle's institution. By a closer vote of twenty-two to twenty they supported repairing and extending the Cumberland Road. In the Twenty-fourth Congress (1835–1837) the forty-eight Whig Representatives from the South divided thirty-eight to three in favor of Clay's bill to distribute the proceeds from sales of public lands to the states. Other votes showing similar tendencies might be cited, but enough has been said to suggest that, even in the beginning, a majority of southern anti-Jackson men were far from being state rights doctrinaires.

In the light of this record it is not so surprising that only a handful of southern Whigs followed Calhoun when he marched his supporters back into the Democratic household during Van Buren's administration. The record also prepares one for the increasing manifestations of nationalism among southern Whigs which Phillips and Cole found so difficult to explain. The southern wing of the party backed Clay almost unanimously for the Presidential nomination in 1840. Tyler's nomination for Vice President was more a sop to the disappointed Clay men, of whom Tyler was one, than a concession to the state rights proclivities of southern Whiggery, the reason usually given for his choice.

The nature of southern Whiggery had its real test when Tyler challenged Clay for leadership of the party. Of the fifty-five southern Whigs in the lower house of the Twenty-seventh Congress (1841–1843), only three stuck by the Virginia President and his state rights principles, whereas Mangum of North Carolina presided over the caucus which read Tyler out of the party, and southern Whig editors joined in castigating him unmercifully. Southern Whigs supported Clay's legislative program—repeal of the Subtreasury, a national bank, distribution, and tariff—by large majorities. Even the Georgians, Berrien, Toombs, and Stephens, defended the protective features of the tariff of 1842.

Having said so much to the point that the Whig party in the South did not begin as and did not become a state rights party, it is necessary to add that neither was it consciously nationalistic. State rights versus nationalism simply was not the main issue in southern politics in this period. It is readily apparent from the newspapers and correspondence of the time that, except for Calhoun and his single-minded little band, politicians in the South were fighting over the same questions that were agitating the North—mainly questions of banking and financial policy.

It is hard to exaggerate the importance of the banking question. State and federal governments, by their policy in this sphere, could cause inflation or deflation, make capital easy or difficult to obtain, and facilitate or hinder the marketing of staple crops and commercial activity generally. And by chartering or refusing to charter banks, they could afford or deny to the capitalists of the day the most profitable field of activity the economy offered.

The banking issue is the key to an understanding of southern as well as northern Whiggery. Merchants and bankers were most directly concerned in financial policy, but their community of interest generally included the other business and professional men of the towns, especially the lawyers, who got most of their fees from merchants, and the newspaper editors, who were dependent on the merchants for advertising revenues. The crucial point for southern politics, however, is that the large staple producers were also closely identified economically with the urban commercial groups. These were the principal elements which went into the Whig party.

The Whigs generally defended the national bank until its doom was sealed, then advocated a liberal chartering of commerical banks by the states, and finally, after the Panic of 1837, demanded a new national bank. The Democrats fought Biddle's institution and either favored state-operated banks to provide small loans for farmers, as distinguished from commercial banks, or tried to regulate banking strictly or abolish it altogether.

Much of the misunderstanding about the Whig party in the South may be traced to the technique of plotting election returns on maps. Such maps tell us much, but they may also mislead. They show, for example, that the "black belts" of the lower South were the great centers of Whig strength. This has led scholars to reason: (1) that the Whig party was a planters' party *par excellence*, (2) that planters were necessarily rigid state rights men, and (3) that the Whig party was, therefore, a state rights party. *Q. E. D.!*

What the maps do not illustrate, however, is the dynamics of the political situation—the elements of leadership, impetus, financing, and propaganda, which are the real sinews of a political organization. In the case of the Whig party, these elements were furnished mainly by the commercial groups of the cities and towns, with their allied lawyers and editors. Lawyers were the practicing politicians for both parties, but the greater incidence of lawyers among the Whigs is an indication of the commercial affiliations of the party. Seventy-four per cent of the southern Whigs who sat in Congress from 1833 to 1843 are identified as practicing attorneys, as compared with fifty-five per cent of the Democrats. In the lower house of the Tennessee legislature of 1839, farmers predominated, but a fourth of the Whigs were lawyers, as compared with only a tenth of the Democratic membership.

The size and importance of the urban middle class in the Old South has yet to be fully appreciated. As early as 1831, Nashville, for example, contained twenty-two wholesale houses and seventy-seven retail stores, not to mention numerous other businesses, such as the sixty taverns and tippling houses. Even the little county seat town of Gallatin, Tennessee, boasted in 1840 ten mercantile firms, a grocer, a merchant tailor, three hotels, five lawyers, five doctors, a paper and grist mill, and eighteen artisans' establishments of one kind or another.

Businessmen dominated the towns socially, economically, and politically, and the towns dominated the countryside. This was particularly true of the "black belts" of the lower South, since the great cotton capitalists of this region were especially dependent on commercial and credit facilities for financing and carrying on their extensive planting operations. In recognition of the urban influence on politics, congressional districts were commonly known by the names of the principal towns in each—as, for example, the Huntsville, Florence, Tuscaloosa, Montgomery, and Mobile disstricts in Alabama.

Other evidence points in the same direction. A large majority of the stockholders in Virginia banks in 1837 lived in the areas of heaviest Whig voting. The principal commercial towns of the state—Richmond, Petersburg, and Norfolk—gave unbroken Whig majorities throughout the period 1834–1840. In North Carolina twenty of the twenty-one directors of the two principal banks in 1840 were Whigs. The first Whig governor of North Carolina was a railroad president; the second was a lawyer, cotton manufacturer, and railroad president; and the third was one of the wealthiest lawyers in the state.

Similar party leadership obtained elsewhere. In Virginia, younger men of the type of John Minor Botts of Richmond and Alexander H. H. Stuart of Staunton actually directed the party of which Tyler and Tazewell were nominal leaders. Senators George A. Waggaman and Judah P. Benjamin were typical of the New Orleans lawyers who guided Louisiana Whiggery. Poindexter and Prentiss in Mississippi were intimately associated both personally and financially with the bankers and businessmen of Natchez. The Tennessee Whigs were led by John Bell, Nashville lawyer and iron manufacturer, who had married into the state's leading mercantile and banking house; Ephraim H. Foster, bank director and Nashville's most prominent commercial lawyer; and Hugh Lawson White, Knoxville lawyer, judge, and bank president.

This commercial bias of the Whig party did much to pave the way for the industrial development of the South after the Civil War. It was no accident that former Whigs provided a large part of the leadership for the business-minded Conservative-Democratic parties which "redeemed" the South from Republican rule and then proceeded to make the conquered section over in the image of the victorious North, often in the interest of northern capital.

Commercial considerations and the banking question did not, of course, determine political alignments in the Old South by themselves. Pro-tariff sentiment made for Whiggery among the sugar planters of Louisiana, the hemp growers of Kentucky, and the salt and iron manufacturers of western Virginia and Maryland. The more liberal policy of the Whigs toward internal improvements by both the state and federal governments won them support in landlocked interior sections and along the routes of projected transportation projects. And the fact that the Democrats generally championed a broadened suffrage, apportionment of congressional and legislative seats on the basis of white population, and other measures for extending political democracy, inclined propertied and conservative men to rally to the Whig party as a bulwark against mobocracy.

These factors, however, merely reinforced the commercial nature of southern Whiggery. The business orientation of the Whigs and the relative unimportance of their state rights wing become quite apparent if the party is described as it actually developed in the various states, rather than on the basis of general assumptions about southern politics.

A state by state analysis would indicate that, in the four border slave states and Louisiana, Whiggery was simply National Republicanism continued under a new name. The National Republicans were also strong in Virginia, but here they were joined in opposition to the Democrats by a body of state rights men alienated from Jackson by his attitude toward nullification. The National Republican and commercial wing of the party, however, was the dominant one, especially after the business-minded Conservative Democrats joined the Whigs on the Subtreasury question. In North Carolina and Tennessee, the Whig party was formed by the secession of pro-Bank men from the Democratic party, aided in Tennessee by the local popularity of Hugh Lawson White as a Presidential candidate in 1835–1836.

The state rights element was more conspicuous in the four remaining states of the lower South. But it was by no means the majority wing of the Whig party in all of them. Both Alabama and Mississippi had an original nucleus of pro-Clay, anti-Jackson men, and in both states the nullification episode caused a substantial defection from the Jackson ranks. In Mississippi, however, a greater defection followed the removal of government deposits from the national bank. The state rights men were clearly a minority of the opposition party, which elected an outspoken foe of nullification to the governorship in 1835 and sent the ardent Clay partisan, Seargent S. Prentiss, to Congress two years later.

The state rights defection seems to have been more important in Alabama, where it was led by the able Dixon H. Lewis. The Lewis faction, however, maintained only a tenuous connection with the regular Whigs, and in 1837 Lewis and his supporters followed Calhoun back into the Democratic party. The significant fact is that in neither Alabama nor Mississippi were the Whigs greatly weakened by the departure of Calhoun's admirers.

Only in South Carolina and Georgia did avowed state rights men make up the bulk of the anti-Jackson party. When the real nature of the new party alignments became apparent, the politicians of Calhoun's state gave proof of their sincerity (and of the Presidential aspirations of their chief) by moving back to the Democratic ranks at the first decent opportunity.

The principal Whig leader in Georgia was John M. Berrien, a Savannah lawyer and attorney for the United States Bank who had been forced out of Jackson's cabinet by the Peggy Eaton affair. At the time of the election of 1832, Jackson's Indian policy was so popular in Georgia that Berrien did not dare oppose the President openly. Instead, he went about stirring up anti-tariff and state rights sentiment, while secretly trying to prevent anti-Bank resolutions by the legislature. Immediately after Jackson's re-election, however, Berrien and his allies managed to reorganize the old Troup political faction as an openly anti-Jackson state rights party. In view of Berrien's pro-Bank attitude and his subsequent staunch support of Clay's policies, it seems probable that he was merely capitalizing on state rights sentiment to defeat Democratic measures which he opposed on other grounds. At any rate, the Georgia Whigs were soon arrayed against the Jackson financial program, and they held their lines nearly intact in the face of the desertion of state rights Whigs to the Democrats on the Subtreasury issue. By 1840 Berrien had brought his Georgia followers into close harmony with the national party.

This summary sketch of southern Whiggery raises, of course, more questions than it could possibly answer definitively. It has attempted to suggest, however, that preoccupation with the origins and development of southern sectionalism has led to distortions of southern political history in the 1830's and 1840's. Specifically, it is suggested:

That only John C. Calhoun and a small group of allied southern leaders regarded state rights as the most important issue in politics in this period.

That the southern people divided politically in these years over much the same questions as northern voters, particularly questions of banking and financial policy.

That the Whig party in the South was built around a nucleus of National Republicans and state rights men, but received its greatest accession of strength from business-minded Democrats who deserted Jackson on the Bank issue.

That the Whig party in the South was controlled by urban commercial and banking interests, supported by a majority of the planters, who were economically dependent on banking and commercial facilities. And finally,

That this alliance of the propertied, far from being inherently particularistic, rapidly shook off its state rights adherents and by 1841 was almost solidly in support of the nationalistic policies of Henry Clay.

There is a great need for intensive restudy of southern politics in the 1830's and 1840's, and particularly for critical correlation of local and national developments. The story as it comes from the contemporary sources is full of the resounding clash of solid interests and opposing ideologies, hardly having "the hollow sound of a stage duel with tin swords" which one historian seems to detect. And recent events should make the student wary of state rights banners, especially when raised by conservative men against national administrations not conspicuously devoted to the interests of the propertied.

25 *Norman A. Graebner*

MARITIME FACTORS IN THE OREGON COMPROMISE

A decade in history is seldom as integrated as mere chronology would seem to suggest or as the convenience of having the past neatly divided would seem to require. The 1840's, however, have about them a distinct unity. Clearly, this was the decade of expansion. The United States achieved virtually all of the borders that we have since then come to accept as its natural fulfillment. The Webster-Ashburton Treaty of 1842 defined the Maine boundary, Texas entered the Union in 1845, the Oregon Treaty of 1846 extended the northern boundary of the United States along the 49th parallel to the Pacific, and the war with Mexico added the great Southwest to the national domain.

Attention has naturally centered on the headlong thrust to the Pacific. Why did it occur at this time? Among the many factors responsible, which was the most important? What decided in particular the way in which the United States acquired its Pacific empire?

A noteworthy answer to these questions has been made by Professor Norman A. Graebner of the University of Illinois, who has established himself as an authority on the middle period of American history as well as on American foreign policy. In his *Empire on the Pacific: A Study in American Continental Expansion* (1955), Professor Graebner suggests that too much has been made, in explaining that expansion, of the role of American settlers in the Far West, of the spirit of manifest destiny, and of the consequences of the Mexican War. The movement to the Pacific was precise, calculated, and limited in its goals. Above all, it sought specific outlets on the Coast, in the hope that they would become foci for a great Far Western trade. The accession of land was entirely incidental to the accession of ocean ports. "Any interpretation of westward expansion beyond Texas," submits

Reprinted with the permission of the author and publisher from *Pacific Historical Review*, XX (November, 1951), 331-45.

Professor Graebner, "is meaningless unless defined in terms of commerce and harbors."

His interpretation of the Oregon compromise, which pushed the American frontier to the Pacific Ocean, is defined in precisely such terms in the following essay. Professor Graebner makes some very interesting points. He shows how widespread was the sentiment for compromise, how it focused on three specific harbors on the Pacific coast, how the relative strength of the particular program of compromise meant also the relative weakness of the general spirit of manifest destiny, and how the remarkable thing about the Oregon treaty was not so much why the Americans accepted the compromise as why the British did.

Professor Graebner's essay suggests many questions. How much did American expansion to the West proceed under the banner of national ideals, how much under the auspices of particular interests and private gain? Is it correct to set up a contrariety, as Professor Graebner's thesis does, between the manifest destiny of the United States and its pursuit of commerce, or has our destiny always been to be a nation of shopkeepers and tradesmen?

What did our Pacific advance signify diplomatically? Did it not mean that the Americas were recognized as the domain of the United States and that the independence guaranteed the Latin American republics by the Monroe Doctrine was itself dependent on the territorial and commercial ambitions of the colossus of the North? What were the consequences for our foreign relations of having become a Pacific power?

What was the impact of the great territorial advance of the 1840's upon our domestic affairs? What significance did it have for the nation's commerce and transportation? What did the opening up of a new empire of land mean for American values? To what extent, moreover, did it begin the course toward civil war? The milestones of that course —the Wilmot Proviso, the Compromise of 1850 and its failure, "bleeding Kansas," and the breakdown of intersectional politics in 1860—are arrayed in a close and inevitable series which seems to have begun when the United States unfurled its flag on the Pacific.

Of those factors in American expansionism which sought solution in the Oregon negotiations of 1846, none appeared of greater concern to the people of the United States than the disposition of Asiatic trade. Historians have detected a persistent commercial motivation in this nation's expansion to the Pacific. Foster Rhea Dulles, for example, developed the theme that Oregon and California were not ends in themselves, but rather a "point of departure" for an Asiatic commercial empire. Richard Van Alstyne held that American expansion can be only partly explained in terms of a continental domain. Frederick Jackson Turner also took the broader view of American acquisitions on the Pacific Ocean, the mastery of which, he said, "was to determine the future relations of Asiatic and European civilization."

Mercantile interests in the Pacific, however, explain more than one powerful motive in American expansionism. Maritime calculations augmented the strong inclination of American commercial interests to seek a peaceful solution of the Oregon controversy and actually defeated the movement for 54° 40' quite as effectively as the threat of war with Great Britain or Mexico. This ardent quest for ports on the Pacific, moreover, fused Oregon and California into one irreducible issue in the minds of the commercial enthusiasts and thereby played an intensely persuasive role in the eventual delineation of this nation's western boundaries.

When the 29th Congress met in December, 1845, there was still little indication that within six months the settlement of the disturbing Oregon question would be assured. Enthusiasm for the whole of Oregon, engendered by the President's message, rapidly translated United States claims to the Far Northwest into what Albert K. Weinberg has termed a "defiant anti-legalism." It no longer mattered that the American title to territory north of the Columbia was far from conclusive, and above the 49th parallel practically nonexistent. It had become, wrote John L. O'Sullivan of the New York *Morning News*, "our manifest destiny to occupy and to possess the whole of the Continent which Providence has given us. . . ." To 54° 40' proponents that seemed to settle the issue.

It quickly becomes evident from a study of the great debate that this expanding outlook was doomed from the beginning by the patent interests of American commercialism. Too many Congressional eyes were narrowly trained on ports to permit the triumph of agrarian nationalism. For almost a half century the trading empire of Boston and New York had given to Oregon's waterways a peculiar significance in America's future economic growth. Countless early spokesmen for Oregon from John Jacob Astor to Hall J. Kelley had viewed the region primarily as an American window on the Pacific. A decade of attention to trappers, missionaries, and pioneers, furthermore, had not obscured to Congressmen the strategic importance of Oregon to the trade of Asia. Samuel Gordon of New York phrased for the House in January, 1846, his district's cogent evaluation of Oregon: "It is the key to the Pacific. It will command the trade of the isles of the Pacific, of the East, and of China." Similarly Washington Hunt, also of New York, stated this repetitious theme: "Its possession will ultimately secure to us an ascendency in the trade of the Pacific, thereby making 'the uttermost parts of the earth' tributary to our enterprise, and pouring into our lap 'the wealth of Ormus and of Ind.'"

Salt spray had also conditioned New England's outlook toward Oregon. Even before the introduction in January, 1846, of the resolution to terminate the convention of 1827, Robert Winthrop of Massachusetts had defined clearly the objectives of commercial America. "We need ports on the Pacific," he shouted. "As to land, we have millions of acres of better land still unoccupied on this side of the mountains."

During the preceding year William Sturgis, the noted Boston merchant and pioneer in the Northwest fur trade, had popularized such particularistic notions in the Bay State. In his famous lecture to the citizens of Boston in January, 1845, Sturgis admitted that the Willamette Valley was both attractive and productive, but he added that he had never seen or heard of any Oregon lands which were superior to millions of uncultivated acres east of the Rockies. His three decades of intense commercial activity in the Pacific had channeled his attention to ports and not to land. Sturgis indicated, moreover, which ports in Oregon the United States would require to assure fully her future position in oriental trade. The Columbia, he warned, was always dangerous for large ships and almost inaccessible for a considerable portion of each year. Instead, this nation's maritime greatness in the Pacific would derive from the possession of the Straits of San Juan de Fuca and its numerous branches which were "easy of access, safe, and navigable at all seasons and in any weather."

Writings of such leading authorities on Oregon as Robert Greenhow, Thomas J. Farnham, and Charles Wilkes merely affirmed Sturgis' conclusions. They likewise had convinced the representatives of commerce that the Columbia, although traditionally associated with the Northwest trade, was of questionable value as an ocean port. Their writings had made axiomatic the dangers of the sand bar between Cape Disappointment and Point Adams. "Mere description," wrote Wilkes, "can give little idea of the terrors of the bar of the Columbia: all who have seen it have spoken of the wildness of the scene, and the incessant roar of the waters, representing it as one of the most fearful sights that can possibly meet the eye of the sailor."

In sharp contrast was their description of the Fuca Straits and the sea arms to the east of them. "No part of the world," wrote Farnham, "affords finer inland sounds or a greater number of harbours than can be found here. . . ." Wilkes' description was equally glowing: "Nothing can exceed the beauty of these waters, and their safety: not a shoal exists within the straits of Juan de Fuca, Admiralty Inlet, Puget Sound, or Hood's Canal, that can in any way interrupt their navigation by a seventy-four gun ship. I venture nothing in saying, there is no country in the world that possesses waters equal to these." Herein lay the primary objectives in Oregon of the commercial Northeast.

Agrarian spokesmen of the Middle West also debated the Oregon question in maritime terms, for Oregon held a special commercial significance for their constituents. The Straits of Fuca, saw these ardent expansionists, were the future link between the Mississippi Valley, with its surplus of grain, and the teeming millions of the Orient who in exchange could enrich the great valley with cargoes of tea, porcelain, silks and satins, velvets, sugar, and spices. Through possession of the Straits, moreover, the United States would challenge the commercial supremacy of England in the Pacific. Andrew Kennedy of Indiana sought to erase all doubts as to the tangible value of Oregon to the Middle West:

It is the inch of ground upon which we can place a fulcrum, giving us the lever by which to overturn the world of British commerce. It will give us a cluster of manufacturing and commerical states on the Pacific corresponding with our New England States upon the Atlantic. Then the inhabitants of the great Mississippi Valley, who have in their possession the garden of the world and the granary of the universe, will stretch out one hand to the East Indies through the Pacific chain, the other to Europe through the Atlantic channel, grasping the trade of the civilized earth, as we now hold in possession the means of subsistence of the whole human family.

What alarmed these nationalists, however, was the fact that the constant reiteration of the commercial value of Oregon bespoke compromise at the 49th parallel, for that boundary would give the United States access to the Straits. Representatives of commerce who wished to settle the issue and secure permanent title to the magnificent inlet pointed out that the United States could acquire all the excellent harbors in Oregon and still proffer an olive branch to England. Sturgis, for example, had argued effectively that a settlement at 49°, with the granting of Vancouver Island to Great Britain, would secure the maritime objectives of the United States and still not deny to England the navigation of the Fuca Straits, a right which she would not relinquish. On the other hand, Wilkes had described the Pacific coast north of the 49th parallel as being devoid of good harbors or any extensive commercial inducements. His writings simply substantiated the particularistic view that everything of value in Oregon lay to the south of that line. Bradford Wood of New York assured Congress that it "knew nothing of the country north of that parallel. All that had been said of its value and beauty were mere draughts on the imagination."

Uncompromising Democrats were driven by the logic of the commercial argument to assume the task not only of proving the value of Oregon north of 49°, but actually of doing so in realistic commercial terms. The acquisition of the Straits alone, they sought to illustrate, hardly touched the commercial possibilities of the Northwest coast. They reminded Congress that a compromise would lose the islands of Vancouver and Washington with their sturdy forests for American shipbuilding, their excellent harbors, their unparalleled fisheries, and their commanding position on the sea lanes. With such a settlement would go also other valuable islands and the bays and harbors which indented the coast. They demanded to know why the United States would voluntarily grant such enormous commercial advantages to Great Britain. John McClernand of Illinois impressed upon the commercial spokesmen of the House the fatal error of compromise when he declared:

> Commercially, indeed, by such a concession, we voluntarily decapitate ourselves upon the Pacific seaboard; we lose that portion of Oregon which bears the same relation to the Pacific, in furnishing a commercial marine upon that ocean, which New England now bears upon the Atlantic. . . . The American or British marine, which will whiten the Pacific, and carry direct trade to Asia, Polynesia, and South to the Atlantic capes, will be built, owned, and navigated by a similar people, who shall dwell north of the 49th parallel. This must naturally come to pass, because the harbors, bays, timber, and material, to give existence to a marine, exist there in combination; and there, too, are fisheries which nurse seamen.

Similarly warned Edward Hannegan, the Indiana Senator: "Let England possess Nootka Sound, the finest harbor in the world, commanding as it does the Straits of Fuca, and consequently the access to Puget's Sound, and she has all of Oregon worth possessing in a commercial and maritime point of view." He turned his abuse on men dominated by narrow commercialism. "It is the opinion of six-sevenths of the American people," he shouted, "that Oregon is ours—perhaps I should rather say five-sevenths, for I must leave out of the estimate the commercial and stockjobbing population of our great cities along the seaboard, a great portion of whom are English subjects, residing among us for the purpose of traffic. . . ."

Because of the "Bargain of 1844" and the necessity of agrarian unity in achieving the whole of Oregon, Hannegan would not write off the South or its Democratic leadership so easily. He castigated that region for losing interest in free territory after it had acquired Texas. There is more evidence, however, that southern low tariff advocates, such as John C. Calhoun, wanted to compromise the Oregon issue not only to avoid war with England, but also to facilitate the repeal of the British Corn Laws and the passage of a lower tariff in the United States. The Charleston *Mercury* gave evidence of this southern preference for free trade to the acquisition of the whole of Oregon when it declared that southern statesmen would not maintain a clear and unquestioned title to 54° 40′ at the price of two million bales of cotton per annum.

Actually the South, like the Northeast, revealed its inclination to compromise in commercial terms. No American publication called the attention to its readers to the importance of Asiatic commerce in more ebullient terms than did *DeBow's Commercial Review* of New Orleans. Declared its editor in January, 1846:

The commerce of the East Indies has for ages been a glittering object in the eyes of trading nations. They have sought it, and grown up to power and influence under its support. What, for instance, were the Italian republics, until the bounteous products of the East were thrown into their lap; and where were Venice and Genoa and Pisa, when the Portuguese, by a shorter passage to the Indies, had cut off these rich resources? Britain, too, what has been her advance since she has enjoyed an almost monopoly of this invaluable trade? If possessions on the Pacific Ocean will facilitate such a commerce—if they be necessary to its existence—then, surely, we will not be neglectful of these possessions.

Even those who believed that the trade of Oregon would accrue to the benefit of other sections insisted on the preservation of the Straits. But they would court no conflict by demanding more than 49°. To Jefferson Davis this guaranteed American interests in Oregon: "Possessed, as by this line we should be, of the agricultural portion of the country, of the Straits of Fuca, and Admiralty Inlet, to American enterprise and American institutions we can, without a fear, intrust the future."

Widening emphasis on the Fuca Straits developed public opinion for compromise in 1845 and 1846. Perhaps more significant was the role of Pacific commerce in diverting attention from Oregon to the harbors of California. Whereas the excellence of the Straits as an ocean port was widely recognized, their northern position blinded many to their potential value. All agreed that harbors were of real consequence in the development of commerce in the Pacific, but the known quality of San Francisco and San Diego harbors to the south convinced many travelers, politicians, and members of the press that the commercial growth of the United States in the Pacific was contingent upon the acquisition of the California ports. When by 1845 this ardent quest for ports encompassed the question of both Oregon and California, it increasingly motivated compromise at 49° and actually determined the fate of the Pacific coast from Lower California to Alaska.

Numerous travelers had pictured the harbor of San Francisco as the veritable answer to America's commercial dreams. Wilkes, who had also sailed the Straits of Fuca, believed that California could boast "one of the finest, if not the very best harbor in the world." It was so extensive, he added, that the "combined fleets of all the naval powers of Europe might moor in it." Farnham called it "the largest and best harbor of the earth" and "the glory of the Western world." New England's remarkable hide trade with California publicized the value not only of San Francisco but also of San Diego. Its bay, small and land-locked, free of surf, and sufficiently deep that vessels could lie within a cable's length of the smooth beach, was "tailor-made" for drying, curing, and loading hides. These facts were well known to commercial America.

Several noted writers and travelers, when they ignored the Straits of Fuca and recounted in detail the inadequacies of the Columbia, stimulated the intensive desire of Americans to acquire ports in California. Albert Gilliam warned that Oregon was so devoid of harbors that if the United States did not secure ports in California it would ultimately lack sea room. Similarly, Waddy Thompson, seeing no hope for commercial greatness in Oregon's waterways, praised San Francisco Bay in words reminiscent of Farnham and Wilkes.

It is not strange that many Americans were willing to trade off varying portions of Oregon for an opportunity to acquire California. That Daniel Webster had little interest in land empires but enormous enthusiasm for spacious ports for his Yankee constituents is well known. In 1843 he attempted to cede all of Oregon north of the Columbia in exchange for the acquisition of San Francisco from Mexico through British intercession. By 1845 the tremendous burst of enthusiasm for California which followed the passage of the Texas resolution had convinced many commercial expansionists that America's real interests lay to the south of Oregon. In March, Webster revealed his true interests in the American West: "You know my opinion to have been, and it now is, that the port of San Francisco would be twenty times as valuable to us as all Texas." In July, Thomas O. Larkin of Monterey in a letter to the New York *Journal of Commerce* found the solution of the Oregon question in the expanding commercial interest in California. He wrote: "If the Oregon dispute continues, let England take eight degrees north of the Columbia, and purchase eight degrees south of forty-two from Mexico, and exchange." The *Journal* concurred in the view that California was this nation's real objective and therefore the United States could well settle at the Columbia and still retain ten degrees of coast. John Tyler never lost the vision of Webster's tripartite proposal. He wrote to his son in December, 1845, regarding the Oregon question: "I never dreamed of conceding the country, unless for the greater equivalent of California, which I fancied Great Britain might be able to obtain for us through her influence in Mexico. . . ."

Other California enthusiasts desired to compromise the Oregon controversy but were far more sanguine in their objectives. Increasingly the American dream of empire on the Pacific included the ports of both

Oregon and California. Writing to President James K. Polk in July, 1845, Charles Fletcher, the Pennsylvania railroad booster, pictured an American union expanding from the Atlantic to the Pacific and from the 30th to the 49th degree of north latitude. The St. Louis *Missourian* demanded both the Straits of Fuca and San Francisco harbor to fulfill the maritime destiny of the United States. Quite typically William Field, a Texan, advised the President to accept the parallel of 49° and then purchase California for as much as fifty million if necessary. He wrote: "I will only remark that if you can settle the Oregon difficulty without war and obtain California of Mexico, to the Gulf of California and the river Gila for a boundary, you will have achieved enough to enroll your name *highest* among those of the benefactors of the American people." By 1846 this unitary view of the Pacific coast had penetrated the halls of Congress where Meredith P. Gentry of Tennessee observed: "Oregon up to the 49th parallel of latitude, and the province of Upper California, when it can be fairly acquired, is the utmost limit to which this nation ought to go in the acquisition of territory."

Even the British press saw the impact of American interest in California on the Oregon question. Before the news of the Mexican War had reached Europe, the London *Times* insisted that "if any incident should lead to the declaration of war against Mexico, the seizure of Port St. Francis and of Upper California, would be considered all over the Union as a sufficient pretext for adjourning the discussion of the Oregon Convention."

It was more than the desire for San Francisco Bay that caused the California issue to prompt compromise on Oregon. The pervading fear that England was negotiating for California had not only designated that province as an immediate objective of Manifest Destiny in 1845, but also it now convinced certain American observers that the United States might well compromise on Oregon to diminish British pressure in California. In urging Americans to settle the Oregon question the Richmond *Enquirer* warned: "It is clearly England which retreats. But it is too much to retreat at the same time in Oregon and California. The English annals present no example of such prudence." In one terse observation the New York *Herald* summed up the entire issue: "We must surrender a slice of Oregon, if we would secure a slice of California."

By early 1846 the metropolitan expansionist press was fostering compromise vigorously. Because of its addiction to California, the New York *Journal of Commerce* succumbed early to the desire for compromise at 49°. By January, 1846, both the New York *Herald* and the New York *Sun* had joined the trend, as had also the Washington *Union* and the St. Louis and New Orleans press. The leading compromise editors stressed the maritime significance of the Pacific coast, denounced members of Congress who still favored the whole of Oregon even at the cost of war, and minimized the worth of Oregon's soil, especially as compared to that of California. The *North American Review*, quite characteristically, after citing Wilkes, Farnham, and Greenhow to prove that Oregon was an "arid and rugged waste," inhabited only by hunters and Indians, concluded in January that "it is hardly too much to say that what Siberia is to Russia, Oregon is to the United States."

Even after the outbreak of the Mexican War, expansionist editors continued uninterrupted in their commercial outlook toward the Pacific. To them the settlement with England had been made particularly acceptable by the anticipation of adding certain Mexican ports to the American union. As war broke out in May, 1846, the New York *Herald* urged the United States to seize San Francisco so that men would forget the whole of Oregon. One California correspondent predicted the result of the speedy occupation of the Pacific ports by the American naval commander: "We shall have then a country, bounded at the North latitude by 49 degrees, to the Pacific—and the South on the same ocean by 32 degrees—and the western and eastern boundaries, being what Nature intended them, the Pacific, with China in the outline, and the Atlantic with Europe in the background." Such prospects pleased the editor of the New York *Herald*. He noted that the proposed boundaries gave the United States 1,300 miles of coast on the Pacific, several magnificent harbors, and "squared off our South-Western possessions." One writer for the New York *Journal of Commerce* in December, 1846, rejoiced that with the acquisition of New Mexico and California the territory of the United States would "spread out in one broad square belt from one ocean to the other, giving us nearly as much coast on the Pacific as we possess on the Atlantic." Obviously the imaginary line of 42° meant little to the American commercial expansionists of a century ago.

American historians have analyzed thoroughly the factors which compelled Great Britain to settle the Oregon question in 1846. In fact, in British rather than American policy is to be found the key to the several well-known interpretations of the Oregon compromise. England had long since quit her claim to the regions south of the Columbia, while the United States had traditionally offered to yield all territory north of 49°. As late as July, 1845, Polk had offered to treat on that line. Viewed from diplomatic history, therefore, a compromise at 49° was a British surrender. Melvin Jacobs has stated clearly this widely accepted assumption:

> Taking into consideration the indefiniteness and weakness of claims to new territory on the basis of discovery and exploration, in contrast to occupation and settlement, instead of raising the question as to the reasons why America

did not secure the whole of Oregon to fifty-four degrees and forty minutes, it appears to be more appropriate to raise the question as to why England lost the territory between the Columbia River and the forty-ninth parallel after she had both occupied and, apparently, possessed it.

Despite the many domestic pressures that drove Britain toward compromise, the British willingness to accept the 49th parallel, just as the American, was largely motivated by maritime considerations.

Two important streams of British trade met in Oregon waters, the commerce with the Orient and the northwest fur trade of the Hudson's Bay Company. To British officials and traders the Columbia River, therefore, presented a watercourse of peculiar significance, furnishing an ocean port as well as an access to the interior fur-bearing regions. For this reason the British during the early Oregon negotiations held to the Columbia boundary. George Canning, the British minister, giving evidence of his own commercial motivation during the 1826 negotiations, wrote that he would not care to have his "name affixed to an instrument by which England would have foregone the advantage of our immense direct intercourse between China and what may be, if we resolve not to yield them up, her boundless establishments on the N.W. Coast of America." Canning attempted unsuccessfully to quiet the early American demand for 49° by offering a frontage of isolated territory on the Straits. For the next two decades Britain continued to hold to the Columbia line. In 1846, however, only a British surrender of territory made possible a peaceful settlement.

Several American students of the Oregon question have attributed British conciliation to the pressure of American pioneers. It is unquestionably true that the British viewed their growing numbers south of the Columbia with dismay, for they endangered the peace and disrupted the fur trade. When in 1845 the Hudson's Bay Company moved its main depot to Vancouver Island because of the decline of the fur traffic and American immigrant pressure, it admitted that its perennial *sine qua non* in any treaty, the Columbia, was no longer its vital trade route. This surrender of the Columbia, says Frederick Merk, was the key to the Oregon settlement.

Lord Aberdeen, who as Foreign Secretary led the British government toward compromise, analyzed cogently his inclination to retreat in terms of Pacific ports. He wrote to Sir Robert Peel in September, 1844:

I believe that if the line of the 49th degree were extended only to the waters edge, and should leave us possession of all of Vancouver's Island, with the northern side of the entrance to Puget's Sound; and if all the harbors within the Sound, and to the Columbia, inclusive, were made free to both countries; and further; if the river Columbia from the point at which it became navigable to its mouth, were also made free to both, this would be in reality a most advantageous settlement.

A year later Aberdeen admitted that England could obtain everything worth contending for in Vancouver Island, the navigation of the Columbia, and free access to all ports between the Columbia and 49 degrees.

Aberdeen's purpose in 1845 and 1846 was to propagandize the British people into an acceptance of his view. His specific task was to convince them that British claims to Oregon were imperfect, that Oregon was not worth a dispute with the United States, that the British fur trade was dying, that the Columbia offered little security for heavy commerce, and that the United States had reasonable claims to good harbors on the Pacific. Several major British journals, especially the *Edinburgh Review*, the *Illustrated London News*, the *Quarterly Review*, and the London *Times*, spread these doctrines for him. Thus the British willingness to compromise in 1846 was in a sense a triumph for Aberdeen's maritime views.

Historians have attributed the British inclination to settle at 49° to two other factors. First, such students of the question as Thomas P. Martin and St. George Sioussat have concluded that the harvest shortage of 1845 and the corresponding need of American grain contributed to British pacificism. Merk, however, has challenged this interpretation by citing evidence that the scarcity of food in the British Isles was not sufficient to alter prices or trade considerably. A second popular interpretation, the free trade analysis, rests primarily on a variety of British statements such as one of Lord Peel: "The admission of Maize will I believe go far to promote the settlement of Oregon." Apparently certain British spokesmen believed that the opening of the British grain market would provide a market for the surplus wheat of the Old Northwest and reduce the persistent Anglophobia of the region in direct proportion. Perhaps more agrarian tempers were aggravated than soothed by this British action, however, for it removed the advantage of easy entry into the British empire trade through Canada.

The real significance of the famous British Corn Law crisis in motivating compromise rested in its creation of a realignment of British parties that brought into power in England a coalition that was willing to settle the Oregon issue for an equitable distribution of ports. The essential fact is that by May, 1846, Aberdeen, upon the passage of the resolution by the United States Congress to terminate the joint convention of 1827, was permitted by both the British government and British public opinion to proffer to the United States an acceptable treaty.

That James K. Polk without hesitation presented the British proposal to the Senate indicates that he had moved far from his December position. Historical analyses of this policy shift fall basically into two categories. Julius Pratt has developed the thesis that Polk was convinced by Minister Louis McLane early in 1846 that the British would fight and that thereafter the President was less inclined to look John Bull in the eye.

Other historians such as Albert Weinberg attribute Polk's desire to compromise to the growing threat of war with Mexico.

Although it is true that there was tremendous pressure placed upon the President to avoid war with England, it must be remembered that long before Polk forced the Oregon issue upon Congress and the British ministry in his message of December, 1845, his vision of America's future position in the West had been fashioned by the Pacific. It was largely his interest in ports that turned his attention to California in 1845. He admitted to Senator Thomas Hart Benton in October that in his desire to limit British encroachment in North America he had California and the bay of San Francisco as much in mind as Oregon. He demonstrated this interest when he attempted to purchase that port from Mexico in the Slidell mission of November, 1845. Yet at no time did the President lose sight of the Straits of Fuca. In his first message to Congress he declared that the United States could never accept a settlement in Oregon that "would leave on the British side two-thirds of the whole Oregon territory, including the free navigation of the Columbia and all valuable harbors on the Pacific." Finally, in late December, 1845, Polk noted in his diary that he would submit to the Senate for its previous advice any British offer that would grant to the United States the Straits of Fuca and some free ports to the north.

This brief analysis of the maritime objectives of the national leaders would indicate that the Oregon settlement was no compromise at all, for Polk and Aberdeen were essentially in agreement over an equitable distribution of Oregon waterways even before the great debate of 1846. For large portions of both the British and American people, however, the final settlement was viewed as a sacrifice. The task of leadership in the crisis consisted of bringing public opinion in both nations to an acceptance of the 49th parallel. Since the unequivocal language of Polk's message tied his hands, the movement for compromise in the United States had to come from Congress and the metropolitan press. For Aberdeen the task of securing support was more difficult, since Britain, unlike the United States, was forced to retreat from its traditional offer.

Both nations as a whole were content with the distribution of land and ports. During the closing argument on the Oregon treaty Benton passed final judgment on the 49th parallel: "With that boundary comes all that we want in that quarter, namely, all the waters of Puget's Sound, and the fertile Olympian district which borders upon them." The Oregon treaty brought to the business community on both sides of the Atlantic relief from the evils of suspense and uncertainty. A brief poem of America's leading expansionist press, the New York *Herald*, summed up well the attitude of the English-speaking world:

Old Buck and Pack
Are coming back
And will soon together dine.
And drink a toast
Upon their roast
To number forty-nine.

SOCIETY IN FERMENT

26 Ray A. Billington

THE FRONTIER IN ILLINOIS HISTORY

Westward expansion has been a central feature of American history. During the early decades of the nineteenth century this expansion reached a new peak. Impelled by many factors, principally the quest for land, men pushed the lines of settlement across the Alleghenies and along the Gulf of Mexico into the Northwest Territory and into a new South. In less than a decade, six new Western states were admitted to the Union: Louisiana (1812), Indiana (1816), Mississippi (1817), Illinois (1818), Alabama (1819), and Missouri (1821). In each of these a larger historical process was in motion, involving an interplay between the institutions which the new settlers brought and the frontier conditions to which they brought them.

What were the basic features of this process? An answer to this question has been the central purpose of much of the writing of Professor Ray Allen Billington of Northwestern University. Professor Billington has recently contributed a study of *The Far Western Frontier, 1830–1860* (1956) to the New American Nation Series. Before this he wrote a comprehensive account of the history of the American frontier, *Westward Expansion* (1949). Here he was guided for the most part by the premises and specific suggestions of the founder and most famous teacher of American frontier history, Frederick Jackson Turner.

In the essay which follows Professor Billington shows the frontier process in operation in Illinois at the time of its settlement. Here he finds an exemplary instance of the balance between the forces of men's traditions and those of wilderness life. In defining the balance, he poses and answers some very basic questions. How much were the inherited

Reprinted with permission from *The Journal of the Illinois State Historical Society*, XLIII (Spring, 1950), 28–45.

institutions of the pioneers altered by natural conditions? Where did
the society of settlers come from and what new amalgam did they
make up? How did man's struggle with nature affect his mechanical
ingenuity? What impact did frontier living have upon the growth of
democratic theory and practice in Illinois? How did the frontier's
faith in progress evidence itself? Finally, in what respects was the
Illinois pioneer more an opportunist than a rationalist, more the man
of practical reality than of consistent theory?

The significance of Illinois for Professor Billington therefore is
that it reveals the forces at play in westward expansion and settlement.
It is a commentary on the dynamic push which in the early decades
of the nineteenth century thrust across the Mississippi. It adumbrates
the effervescent spirit of manifest destiny which led to the farthest
reaches of the continent and to the Mexican War. In Illinois may be
heard too the early rumblings of the conflict which was to burst out
in civil war. Certainly, as Professor Billington aptly puts it, in the
Illinois frontiersman of this period one could find a perfect answer to
Crèvecoeur's question: "What then is the American, this new man?"
It would be well for the student to remember that the frontier moved
and changed and ultimately passed away. In the process there emerged
a striking succession of new Americans and new men.

The historian who attempts to isolate the unique characteristics of the people of any American region must search for clues in both their imported
traits and the environmental influences operating upon them. Of the latter,
none has been more influential than the impact of the frontier; in the continuous rebirth of civilization that occurred during the settlement process
both men and institutions were "Americanized" as inherited practices or
traits were cast aside. This mutation followed no set pattern, for in no
two regions of the West were the ingredients of the new society—man
and nature—blended in identical proportions. At times man was so influenced by tradition that he refused to bow completely to the forest environment; thus the Massachusetts Bay Puritans were too united by religious ties to respond to the centrifugal forces of wilderness life. At
other times the environment was sufficiently overwhelming to create utterly distinct behavior patterns; the Mormons who settled the deserts of
Utah exhibited few of the traits usually found on the frontier. In relatively
few areas were the two ingredients sufficiently balanced to create a completely typical result. One favored spot where this occurred was Illinois.

This can best be realized by restating several general propositions concerning the frontier process, then applying them to the early history of
the state.

First, the frontier was an area where man's inherited institutions were
significantly altered by natural conditions. Illinois offers a unique ex-

ample of this transformation, for within its borders are two differing soil areas, each of which influenced not only the settlement process but subsequent economic developments. These resulted from two of the glaciers that ground their way southward during the Pleistocene Age. One, the Illinoian Drift, covered the state as far south as the Ohio River, leaving behind as it receded a rugged hill country littered with glacial debris, and a compact clay soil marked by the absence of such essential elements as sulphur, potassium, carbon, and nitrogen. At a later day in geological history a second ice sheet pushed slowly down from the north—the Wisconsin Drift. Grinding down hills into smooth prairies, this glacier left behind a level country side and a light loam soil rich in both the humus and chemicals needed for fertility. The Wisconsin Drift, however, did not benefit all parts of the state equally. The extreme southern limit of its advance was marked by the clearly defined Shelbyville Moraine, the most important natural boundary in all Illinois. Pioneers were quick to notice the difference between lands lying north and south of this dividing line. Above the moraine the countryside was level, the soil deep, and the swamps numerous—swamps that could readily be drained to form humus-rich fields of immense productivity. Below, the rugged hills and glacier-strewn waste discouraged frontiersmen.

For a century both land prices and agricultural yields confirmed the judgment of the first settlers. In 1904, for example, lands just north of the moraine sold for from $75 to $125 an acre; those to the south for $30 an acre. In the same year fields in Coles County, lying in the glaciated area, yielded thirty-six bushels of oats or forty of corn to the acre; in Cumberland County, just to the southward, only twenty-eight bushels of oats or thirty of corn were produced. Higher yields, in turn, allowed a greater degree of population concentration; a typical county north of the moraine contained 42 per cent more people than another to the south. This reflected a more advanced stage of urbanization, on which depended cultural progress. The counties north of the Shelbyville Moraine, with more taxable wealth, could support better schools, colleges, libraries, and similar intellectual agencies. Although twentieth-century industrialization has lessened the effect of this natural boundary, Illinois' early history provides an outstanding example of that impact of nature on man, which typified the Americanization process.

Secondly, the frontier was an area where men of all sections and all nations met to form a new society, enriched by borrowings from many lands. In few other areas of the West did the accident of migration result in such a thorough blending of many racial strains as in Illinois. From the Southeast, from the Middle States, from New England, from older states of the Northwest, and from Europe came the state's pioneers, each contributing new flavor and new strength to the social order that evolved.

The first settlers were from the South. Some came from the seaboard regions, but more left homes in the uplands of the Carolinas, Virginia, Tennessee, or Kentucky, where a mingling process had already produced a mixed population from Scotch-Irish, German, and English strains. Skilled in the techniques of conquering the wilderness, these sturdy woodsmen were crowded from their old homes by the advance of the plantation frontier during the first quarter of the nineteenth century. Moving northward over Kentucky's Wilderness Road, or drifting down the Ohio River on flatboats, they reached such embarkation points as Shawneetown by the thousands, then fanned out over the trails that led to the interior: some along the Great Western Road through Kaskaskia and Cahokia to St. Louis, others along the Goshen Road toward Alton, still others northward through Carmi to Albion after that town was founded in 1818. Filling in the rich bottom lands of the Ohio and Mississippi first, they soon spread over the forested portions of southern Illinois, seeking always the dense timber that testified to good soil. There they girdled the trees, planted their corn, raised their log cabins, split rails for their worm fences, shook through regular attacks of malaria, and steadily extended their civilization over a widening area.

The predominantly southern character of Illinois' early migration cannot be overemphasized. In 1818, when the first rough survey was taken, 38 per cent of the settlers were from the South-Atlantic Seaboard, almost 37 per cent from Kentucky and Tennessee, 13 per cent from the Middle States, 3 per cent from New England, and 9 per cent from abroad. Thus 75 per cent of the people were from the South, as opposed to 25 per cent from all the rest of the United States and Europe. Nor did this ratio change during the next decade; as late as 1830 observers believed that Illinois was on its way to becoming a transplanted southern commonwealth, with all the institutions—including slavery—of its sister states south of Mason and Dixon's Line.

Then the tide turned. The Erie Canal was responsible. The opening in 1825 of that all-water route between the Hudson River and Lake Erie shifted the center of migration northward as New Englanders and men from the Middle Atlantic States found the gateway to the West open before them. Now the Great Lakes, not the Ohio River, formed the pathway toward the setting sun. From Buffalo, New York, steamboats carried pioneers to new towns that sprang up as embarkation points: Cleveland, Toledo, Detroit, and Chicago. In 1834 80,000 people followed this route westward; eleven years later the number reached 98,000. Michigan and Ohio attracted some, but Illinois, which was scarcely settled north of Alton, was the mecca of more. As they landed on the Chicago wharfs, that frontier hamlet blossomed overnight into a booming city. Such was the demand for buildings to house the newcomers that lots which sold in the spring of 1835 for $9,000 fetched $25,000 four months later. Most stayed in the cramped city only long enough to lay in supplies for the overland trip to the farm at the end of their rainbow. As they flooded over the countryside the statistics of the government land offices told a dramatic story: a quarter of a million acres were sold in 1834, two million in 1835, almost four million in 1836.

The newcomers were as predominantly northern as the earlier immigrants were southern; fully 75 per cent were from north of the Mason and Dixon Line. Some came in groups from their native New England, fully equipped with pastor, schoolmaster, and eastern ways of life. Rockwell, Tremont, and Lyons were planted in this way between 1833 and 1836; a year later Wethersfield was laid out by Yankees whose childhood had been spent in the shaded streets of that old Connecticut village. More came as individuals or in families, bringing with them the habits of their native New England and an insatiable thirst for land that did not, as one advertiser put it, stand on edge. As they came they transformed northern Illinois into a replica of the Northeast, just as southern Illinois was a duplicate of the Southeast. "Each of these two fountains of our civilization," wrote the editor of the *Democratic Monthly Magazine* in 1844, "is pouring forth its columns of immigrants to the Great Valley, forming there a new and third type that will reform and remold the American civilization."

Yet no frontier state could be typically American without the invigorating impact of European migration. Illinois benefited from the transfusion of this fresh blood during the 1840's. First to come were Irish peasants who drifted westward as laborers on canals and railroads; many eventually settled along the path of the Illinois and Michigan Canal. They were soon joined by German pioneers who had been driven from their homes by a devastating potato famine. Taking advantage of the cheap transportation offered by returning cotton ships, they reached New Orleans, then traveled up the river to the cheap lands of Missouri, Illinois, and Wisconsin. With them came a sprinkling of intellectuals fleeing the political tempests of 1848. Few in numbers but large in influence, these leaders injected German customs and thought into the Illinois social order to a degree rarely equalled in other states.

If an Illinoisan had paused to take stock of his state at the close of the settlement period he would have been proud of what he saw. In few commonwealths was acculturation so complete. Here in 1850 lived 334,000 native sons, 138,000 born in the South, 112,000 from the Middle Atlantic States, 37,000 from New England, 110,000 from the other states of the Old Northwest, and 110,000 foreign born. Each group contributed something to the composite whole; each made Illinois more completely American. "The society thus newly organized and constituted," wrote a

Westerner, "is more liberal, enlarged, unprejudiced, and, of course, more affectionate and pleasant, than a society of people of *unique* birth and character, who bring all their early prejudices, as a common stock, to be transmitted as an inheritance in perpetuity."

Illinois' good fortune was in marked contrast to the fate of its neighbor, Indiana. When the settlement of the two territories began, they seemed destined to follow a parallel course. To Indiana, as to Illinois, came the southern migratory stream, to fill the southern third of the state in the first quarter of the nineteenth century. If the frontier process had operated normally, New Englanders, men from the Middle Atlantic States, and Europeans would have moved into its northern portions. That they failed to do so was due to two unhappy circumstances.

One was the state's bad reputation. Travelers who entered Indiana from the northeast were forced to cross the elongated morass along the Maumee River known as the Black Swamp, then thread their way across the swampy tablelands of the upper Wabash where drainage was so poor that water frequently covered the trails even in periods of normal rainfall. They never forgot this first impression. In books, in newspaper articles, and in conversations they always referred to "the swamps and bogs of Indiana"—a phrase soon indelibly associated with the name of the state. In vain did Hoosiers protest that the prairies of Illinois were no drier; for decades northern pioneers passed over poorly advertised Indiana.

An even more effective deterrent to settlement was the activity of land speculators, of whom a Hartford businessman, Henry L. Ellsworth, was most prominent. Impressed with the beauty and richness of Indiana's prairies while on a western trip in the 1830's, Ellsworth moved to Lafayette in 1835 and promptly began amassing land until his holdings totaled 18,000 acres. He farmed them so profitably, even after the Panic of 1837, that other Easterners made similar investments. Ellsworth encouraged this; in his little book, *The Valley of the Upper Wabash* (1838), he promised to farm prairie land for any investor, paying the owner 8 or 10 per cent, and taking his own profit from half the remaining surplus. Numerous Easterners entered into such contracts with Ellsworth; others were persuaded to buy Indiana lands by his advertising. Within a few years their holdings blanketed the central and northern portions of the state, effectively discouraging settlement by the five-dollar-an-acre price demanded for resale. Not until the 1850's did mounting taxes force the speculators to unload; then purchasers were principally younger sons from southern Indiana who moved northward in search of land. Ellsworth's propaganda and poor advertising, by closing the gates to pioneers from the Northeast and Europe, deprived Indiana of that population blending that so benefited Illinois.

Thirdly, the frontier was a region where mechanical ingenuity was highly developed in the never-ending battle between man and nature. In Illinois settlers were forced to display a higher degree of adaptability than on most frontiers, for they faced a natural barrier that would have proved insurmountable to men of lesser stature: the vast central grassland. This was a forbidding obstacle to pioneers trained by two centuries of experience in the technique of clearing wooded areas. They had learned to judge the fertility of land by the density of its forests, to build their homes and fences from the plentiful wood supply, to secure their fuel from the wilderness, to obtain water from springs or streams, and to depend for shelter on the bands of timber left standing when fields were cleared. The habits of woodland pioneering were so deeply engrained in the average pioneer that any deviation was difficult if not impossible.

Yet that adjustment had to be made before Illinois could be settled. In the northern portions of the state vast fields blanketed by six-feet-tall grass were interlaced with forest lots or crisscrossed by the bands of timber that followed every stream, but in central Illinois the prairies stretched away to the horizon on every side. Every instinct told the pioneer to avoid these grasslands. How could soil that would not support trees grow crops? Where could he get wood for his cabin, his fences, and his fuel? How could he obtain drinking water in a region where sluggish streams were thick with silt? How could he farm fields that were turned into swamps by every rainfall? And, most important of all, how could he bring the prairies under cultivation when tough sod shattered the fragile cast-iron plows which had proved adequate in timbered areas? Those were the problems that had to be solved before central and northern Illinois could be settled.

Little wonder, in view of these obstacles, that the shift from forest to prairie was made slowly. Farmers in the wooded areas along the Fox and Rock rivers first began pasturing their cattle on near-by grasslands, then experimentally turned under some of the sod. When the land proved productive, others imitated their example, until a ring of farms surrounded the open grassland. Each year the cultivated fields were expanded until eventually they met. By 1850 all the grasslands of Illinois were under the plow save the central portions of the Grand Prairie. Not until the Illinois Central Railroad penetrated that region five years later was the last unsettled area occupied.

No simple account of the settlement of the state reveals the inventiveness, ingenuity, and boldness displayed by the Illinois pioneers. They overcame one of their most deep-seated prejudices when they learned that a soil's richness could not be determined by the density of its timber. They discovered that "stone coal" could be brought in more easily than wood for heating. They learned how to sink wells, and developed both well-drilling machinery and windmills to ease the back-breaking task of providing water. They discovered that co-operative efforts were necessary for drainage. And they invented special plows, pulled by from four to six oxen, to break the tough sod. The expense involved in the use of these cumbersome contraptions, which could be hired from a local operator at a rate of from two to five dollars an acre, created a demand for more efficient equipment which sent inventors to their drafting boards; one landmark was passed in 1837 when John Deere gave the world the steel plow. They learned to plant a "sod crop" by cutting upturned furrows at intervals with an ax, then dropping in a few kernels of corn. Although these fields could not be cultivated, the good Illinois soil produced yields up to fifty bushels to the acre, while the roots helped break up the rotting sod.

Learning new techniques and inventing new implements, the Illinois farmer not only solved one of the most troublesome problems faced in the conquest of the continent but by his very ingenuity stamped himself as a typical product of the American frontier.

Fourthly, the West was a region where democratic theory was enshrined and democratic practices perpetuated. Living in a land where all men were reduced to equality by the greater force of nature, conscious of the economic opportunity that promised to make the poor rich, and impatient of restraints from uninformed Easterners who knew nothing of western problems, the frontiersman insisted that each man's right to rule himself was as fundamental as his right to good land. The Westerner made few contributions to the mechanics of democracy, for in the realm of theory he was imitative rather than inventive, but he did show a marked tendency to adopt the most liberal practices of the East he had left behind. Illinois, as a typical frontier state, exhibited this tendency admirably.

Its people's democratic faith was first reflected in the Constitution of 1818. At this time Southerners predominated; in the constitutional convention twenty-one were from the South, two had been born in Illinois of southern parents, five came from the Middle Atlantic States, and only one from New England. Despite this influence toward conservatism, despite even the perpetuation of slavery—in the form of indentured servitude—the Illinois constitution was a model of democratic practice. Based on the frames of government already adopted in Ohio, Tennessee, and Kentucky, but going beyond them in the direction of popular rule, it vested virtually sovereign power in the legislature, while reducing the governor to a mere figurehead. True, the chief executive, together with the justices of the state Supreme Court, constituted a council of revision empowered to veto acts of the assembly, but as laws could be passed over the veto by a mere majority vote, this meant nothing. Property qualifications for voting and office holding were swept away, and all adult males who had lived in the state for six months were allowed to vote. Mounting western nationalism was reflected in a provision that the governor must have been a citizen of the United States for at least thirty years.

The Constitution of 1818, democratic as it was, only paved the way for still more liberal changes during the next years; eventually even the state judges were popularly elected. Illinois, a frontier state, believed, even before Lincoln's classic statement, in rule of the people, by the people, and for the people.

Fifthly, the frontier was a region of optimism, of boundless belief in the future. The Illinois frontiersman shared with his fellow Westerners an exuberant faith in progress; like them, too, he had a rambunctious confidence in his ability to make his dreams come true. One manifestation of this spirit was his willingness to support colleges. Although primary education was not fully established until the passage of the school law of 1855, institutions of higher learning began to multiply a quarter-century earlier, many of them church-supported schools dedicated to the task of producing intelligent congregations and learned ministers. By 1840 the thinly settled, poverty-ridden Prairie State boasted no less than twelve colleges. Pioneers unable to read and write were anxious to contribute time and money to assure their children a better opportunity, their community a richer culture. In few other states were frontiersmen willing to invest so heavily in the future.

On a less elevated plane, frontier optimism in Illinois found expression in speculative land buying. In no other wilderness commonwealth were so many acres engrossed by jobbers, so many "paper towns" laid out, so much absentee capital invested, in the years before 1850.

They were legion, the starry-eyed speculators who gobbled up the forests and prairies of the state. Many were farmers who bought more land than they could use, hoping to sell off the remainder to later comers; in 1850 seven million acres of Illinois land that had been sold but not improved was largely held by such purchasers. Others were local businessmen or politicians who accumulated strategically located lands against the price rise they believed inevitable. Still others were wealthy Easterners or Southerners whose careers were devoted to speculation. Men of this ilk engrossed 6,000,000 acres in Illinois between 1847 and 1855 by buying up soldiers' warrants at from fifty cents to a dollar an acre; others of the same fraternity bought 7,000,000 acres of rich countryside near Springfield between 1833 and 1837. A favorite occupation of all these speculators was the accumulation of prospective town sites. Scarcely a bend or fork of a stream deep enough to wade in, scarcely a bay on Lake Michigan that would shelter a rowboat, scarcely a spot on any imagined canal or railroad that might conceivably be built in the future, that was not grabbed up by some land jobber. Most of these never got beyond the "paper" stage—where maps were drawn to induce gullible Easterners to buy town lots—yet in one northern Illinois "town" that had only one house, lots sold for $2,500 each, while a Chicago observer, witnessing the mad scramble for town sites, seriously proposed reserving one or two sections in each township for farming!

Finally, the frontier was an area where opportunism, rather than an enduring belief in any one theory or system, shaped the character of economic life and thought. Students of the westward movement, failing to recognize this, have frequently insisted that the West was a region of economic radicalism, of *laissez faire*, of rugged individualism. True, the frontiersman was an economic radical on occasion, but he was just as likely to be found among extreme conservatives; he was an individualist if such a course seemed feasible, but he did not hesitate to embrace the cause of collectivism if that path promised greater profits. He did believe in *laissez faire*—some of the time—but he was ready to demand national or state aid, and even governmental ownership of essential services, if such a course seemed wiser. The frontiersman, in other words, was a practical realist who believed in following the path that promised greatest immediate returns, regardless of past precedents. An opportunist rather than a theorist, he showed no embarrassment when forced to shift his thought with the changing times. The Illinois pioneer reflected this point of view. His vacillating opinion on the question of state-operated transportation facilities and on matters of finance illustrated how well he fitted into the frontier mold.

He first became aware of the transportation problem in the 1820's and 1830's when accumulating agricultural surpluses in interior Illinois brought home the need for highways to the main trade arteries of the West: the Mississippi River system and the Great Lakes. Statisticians were everywhere present to demonstrate the profits that would go to the pioneer if these could be built. A bushel of corn, they pointed out, sold in the interior for from twelve to twenty cents; at Chicago or on the Ohio River that same bushel fetched fifty cents. As the average farmer produced sixty bushels to the acre, lead-pencil engineers needed only enough ciphering paper to prove the stratospheric profits that would be the farmer's with better outlets. For every hundred-acre farm the increased return would be $1,800 a year; for the ten million acres soon to be in production the saving would be $180,000,000! Roads and canals would transmute Illinois' poverty into luxurious affluence. So all agreed, and they were equally sure that these outlets could only be built by the state government, which alone boasted resources and credit adequate for the giant task. By the beginning of the 1830's all Illinois was advocating an important experiment in state socialism.

Thus was the stage set for the fabulous internal improvement program launched during the next decade. An approving populace watched delightedly as the legislature authorized construction of the Illinois and Michigan Canal, secured a land grant from Congress, and placed the credit of the state behind the canal bonds that were marketed in the East and England to finance the project. This simply whetted the popular appetite for more. The canal benefited only one corner of Illinois; why should the rest be neglected when state-constructed railroads and canals would not only pay for themselves and enrich shippers but assure such profits that taxes could be abolished? Swept along on this wave of enthusiasm, Illinois adopted its famous Internal Improvements Act of 1837. This fantastic measure pledged the 400,000 poverty-ridden inhabitants of the frontier state to spend more than $10,000,000 on a network of railroads and canals which would crisscross in every direction. If the program had been less grandiose, and the times more auspicious, Illinois' dreams of a state-operated transportation system might have been realized. Instead the mere magnitude of the plan, the lack of managerial skill among those entrusted with its administration, and the Panic of 1837, brought a speedy end to the whole project. By 1841 work was at a standstill.

The effect of this debacle on public opinion was great. As Illinois farmers viewed the visible remains of their wrecked hopes—half-completed road beds, untidy slashes that marked the beginning of canals, a $15,000,-000 state debt, a 50 per cent increase in land taxes, debt repudiation—a feeling of revulsion against state ownership swept across the state. During the next few years the one completed railroad, the Northern Cross, which had cost $250,000, was sold for $21,000 without a voice being raised in protest. The people wanted no more public control; private enterprise could run the risks in the future. For the next generation the citizens of Illinois advocated *laissez faire* as strenuously as they had governmental ownership a few years before.

Their frontier-like tendency toward opportunism was even better illustrated when two panics during the pioneer period brought them face to face with an age-old question: what banking and currency system would assure security and prosperity for their state? Twice they tried to solve the problem, and each time their answers differed.

The issue first arose in the era of hard times following the Panic of 1819. What was needed to stem the downward trend, all agreed, was more money. This could best be provided by local banks, backed by the faith and credit of the state, which could issue paper currency. On the crest of this pro-bank sentiment, the legislature in 1821 chartered the Bank of Illinois, capitalized at $300,000 to be subscribed by the state, and authorized to issue bank notes in small denominations to the full extent of its capitalization. The notes were made legal tender for all public and private debts; any creditor who refused to accept them was prohibited from seizing property pledged as security for at least three years. This, in other words, was an inflationary measure, designed principally to increase the amount of circulating currency. Popular meetings in Illinois and elsewhere went even farther along the path toward inflation by demanding a complete paper currency bearing no relationship to specie.

The inflationary trend was accentuated during the prosperous 1830's when money was in great demand for land speculation, business expansion, and the internal improvement program. By this time the State Bank of Illinois, with headquarters at Springfield, had joined the Bank of Illinois in catering to the state's financial needs. Both of these institutions were called upon to aid the public works program that was launched in 1837. This was done by increasing their capitalization, turning over to them state bonds in return for shares of bank stock, and then borrowing back the bank notes issued on the basis of the state's own securities. Officials honestly believed that this flimsy process would not only supply money for internal improvements but eventually pay for all construction, as the bank stock was expected to pay annual dividends of from 8 to 10 per cent. These returns, plus tolls from canals and railroads, would soon retire the entire investment and provide so much income that taxes could be abolished! This was the talk, not of wild dreamers, but of sober businessmen and state leaders.

Illinois learned its lesson when the Panic of 1837 tumbled down its speculative house of cards. With hard times antibank feeling swept across the state. Farmers who owed money to the banks grumbled that they could not continue their payments. Others who were paid for their produce in the depreciated notes of the two institutions complained that they were being swindled. Still others lost heavily when the banks finally collapsed. More were convinced that there was a direct connection between the banks and the panic. The depression, they told themselves, was a product of the wild currency fluctuations that followed the overissue of state bank notes. These might benefit eastern capitalists, but every fluctuation drove the poor man, who could never understand such financial mysteries, deeper into debt. His only protection was to abolish banks and paper money, returning to the security of a solid gold and silver currency. "A bank of earth is the best bank," wrote one, "and a plow share the best share," while another declared: "Banks to help the farmer appear to me like feudal lords to defend the people." The Illinois farmer of the post-panic era was the most conservative of all Americans on financial questions.

The reaction of the state's pioneers to the panics of 1819 and 1837 demonstrated the opportunistic nature of frontier economic thought. In one case they moved leftward along the road to inflation; in the other they swung so far to the economic right that the nation's business leaders and bankers seemed financial radicals by comparison.

Reactions such as these stamped the Illinois frontiersman as typically American. He was typical, too, in his optimism, his democracy, his ingenuity, and his faith in progress. Molded by the frontier environment and strengthened by contacts with fellow pioneers from all the western world, he served as a perfect answer to Hector St. John de Crèvecoeur's famous query: "What then is the American, this new man?"

27 *Carter Goodrich*

AMERICAN DEVELOPMENT POLICY:
THE CASE OF INTERNAL IMPROVEMENTS

Our view of the American past includes many myths, and one of the most prominent is that our great economic development was the product of a policy of laisser faire. Purportedly, there was an idyllic period of the "good old days" when government abstained from participation in economic affairs. The truth, however, as such scholars as Oscar Handlin, Louis Hartz, and Milton S. Heath have shown in recent years, is that on both the local and national levels governmental action was more than merely accepted, it was requested. By means of its fiscal policies, its tariff regulations, its financing of roads, canals, and railroads, government played a central role in the great age of business expansion between 1815 and 1860, an expansion which George Rogers Taylor has so aptly called "the transportation revolution."

Using the development of internal improvements as a case in point, Professor Carter Goodrich of Columbia University explores in the following essay the question of how and why government activity contributed to American economic growth. Having served for some three decades in various capacities in the League of Nations, the United Nations, and in administration agencies of the United States government, Professor Goodrich is eminently qualified to answer this question. His essay was originally delivered as the presidential address before the Economic History Association in 1956 and is a distillation of studies in this area over many years.

As Professor Goodrich points out, the problem of governmental participation in national economic development carries particular interest for an age such as our own, when the new and revolutionary nations of both hemispheres have thrown their energies into the cause

Reprinted with permission from *The Journal of Economic History*, XVI (December, 1956), 449–60.

of economic advance. What lesson can they learn from American development policy? What was the nature of that policy? How much did it change as development proceeded and why? In what respects was this policy similar to that of the other major industrial powers of the nineteenth century—Great Britain and Germany? In what respects was it different? What were the shortcomings of the policy we pursued? What were its unique features? From the perspective of our own experience, Professor Goodrich arrives at conclusions that are highly relevant to today's world of nascent and striving nationalities.

The root problem confronting them now, as it confronted us more than a century ago, is how to amass sufficient capital to erect a modern structure of industry and commerce. Inevitably the way they proceed is in large measure governed by the traditions of their polity and by the ratio of the advance they want to make to that which they have already made. When Americans accepted the aid of government in pursuing their economic growth, the circumstances of their acceptance were the substantial capital they had amassed on their own, the individuality of their enterprise, and the control they ultimately held over their government.

The subject I should like to discuss grows directly out of the theme of the meetings as a whole.[1] They have been concerned with the American West as an Underdeveloped Region, and the title was intended to suggest the analogy between the United States of an earlier period and the so-called underdeveloped nations of the present day. To many it would suggest a contrast in policy. These other nations are now in many cases striving to achieve economic development by national planning and deliberate measures of governmental policy. On the other hand the United States achieved its massive economic development without over-all economic planning, without five-year plans or explicit national targets of input and output, and—it is sometimes believed—without the adoption of policies deliberately intended to promote development.

Yet the contrast is not as complete as this statement would suggest. It

[1] The author's study has been carried on under the auspices of the Council for Research in the Social Sciences of Columbia University. The paper draws on the materials of articles previously published: in JOURNAL OF ECONOMIC HISTORY, "The Revulsion Against Internal Improvements," X (November, 1950), 145–169; (with Harvey H. Segal) "Baltimore's Aid to Railroads: A Study in the Municipal Planning of Internal Improvements," XII (Winter, 1953), 2–35; in the *Political Science Quarterly*, "National Planning of Internal Improvements," XLIII (March, 1948), 15–44; "The Virginia System of Mixed Enterprise: A Study of State Planning of Internal Improvements," XLIV (September, 1949), 355–387; "Local Government Planning of Internal Improvements," XLVI (September, 1951), 411–445; "Public Aid to Railroads in the Reconstruction South," LI (September, 1956), 407–442; in the *Proceedings of the American Philosophical Society*, XCII (October 25, 1948), 305–309.

is not quite true that the United States just "growed" like Topsy or that the American empire of the West was settled and developed in a fit of absence of mind. Throughout our history statesmen have been concerned with devising measures to promote economic growth, and individuals and corporations have often come to governmental agencies with demands for encouragement and assistance. Many of the great debates on political issues have turned on what would today be described as development policy. Hamilton's *Report on Manufactures* is an obvious case in point. Its well-remembered argument for protection and its almost-forgotten plea for encouraging the importation of technical improvements from abroad are both commonly duplicated in the underdeveloped nations of today. Hamilton's plea for the Funding System, that it would in effect provide a favorable climate for foreign investment, reminds us of what is so commonly urged on capital-hungry nations today. It is perhaps more difficult to disentangle explicit developmental considerations in the bitter nineteenth-century debates over monetary and banking issues. In national policy there was nothing to suggest comparison with the Development Banks, *Corporaciones de Fomento*, and National Investment Funds that play so large a role in the current plans of the less developed countries, though on the state level Milton Heath's reappraisal of the Central Bank of Georgia and Carter Golembe's study of early Middle-Western banking may suggest that we have underestimated the influence of conscious development policy.[2] With respect to land, the great decisions down through the nineteenth century were concerned with the conditions under which the national domain was to be turned over to individuals and corporations. This was the main issue of land policy, not land use, not conservation, not "land reform" in the explosive twentieth-century sense—unless you choose to regard the emancipation of the slaves as the most completely unplanned land reform in history! Yet the public domain was itself so magnificent that the manner of its disposition could not fail to be a major factor in influencing development, and explicit considerations of the rapidity and the desirable type of settlement dominated the debates from the Ordinance of 1787 to the Homestead Act, including expressions of deliberate preference for a particular type of social structure, that represented by the independent small farmer.

In an examination of American development policy, I believe that particular interest attaches to the case of internal improvements. Here the aim was directly and unmistakably developmental and the amount and variety of governmental activity quite extraordinary. Recent studies have

[2] Milton S. Heath, *Constructive Liberalism: The Role of the State in Economic Development in Georgia to 1860* (Cambridge: Harvard University Press, 1954), ch. 9. Carter H. Golembe, "State Banks and the Economic Development of the West, 1830–1844," unpublished dissertation, Columbia University, 1952.

increased our knowledge of the number of cases, and they have shown that the volume of government investment was greater than had been believed, both in absolute figures and in relation to total canal and railroad investment, to total national investment, and to the total budgets of governmental authorities.[3] Yet, half a century ago, the first modern student of the subject, Guy Stevens Callender, was able to point out that our supposedly individualistic America had had in the early and middle nineteenth century a certain world prominence as an example of the extension of the activity of the state into industry. He asked what conditions had given "rise to this remarkable movement towards State enterprise here in America, where of all places in the world"—he said—"we should least expect to find it."[4]

This movement, however, appears less paradoxical if it is examined in the light of the economics of development. The conspicuous contrast was with England. English canals and railways were built entirely by private enterprise. American canals and railways were for the most part products of governmental or mixed enterprise or the recipients of government aid. But consider the difference in economic circumstance. A railway between London and Liverpool ran through settled country and connected established centers of trade. It could expect substantial traffic as soon as completed. On the other hand, a route across the Appalachians to the largely unsettled West or a railroad running from Chicago west across almost empty plains could hardly be profitable until settlement took place along its route and at its terminus. Jerome Cranmer uses the words "exploitative" and "developmental" for these two types of enterprise.[5] Ex-

[3] Professor Lively is right in pointing out that too little has been done with the comparison with private investment. Robert A. Lively, "The American System: A Review Article," *Business History Review*, XXIX (March 1955), 81–96. He cites Heath's figures on the ante-bellum South as a notable exception. See Milton S. Heath, "Public Railroad Construction and the Development of Private Enterprise in the South before 1861," JOURNAL OF ECONOMIC HISTORY, X (Supplement, 1950), 40–53.

An approach to the comparison with total national investment has been made in Harvey H. Segal, "Canal Cycles, 1834–1861: Public Construction Experience in New York, Pennsylvania and Ohio" (unpublished dissertation, Columbia University, 1956), which relates the canal expenditures to several estimates of capital formation and construction.

Heath, *Constructive Liberalism*, ch. 15, relates improvement expenditures to the state budget of Georgia; and Goodrich and Segal, "Baltimore's Aid to Railroads," relate them to the city budget.

[4] Guy Stevens Callender, "The Early Transportation and Banking Enterprises of the States in Relation to the Growth of Corporations," *Quarterly Journal of Economics*, XVII (November, 1902) 111–162. Reprinted in Joseph T. Lambie and Richard V. Clemence (eds.), *Economic Change in America* (Harrisburg: The Stackpole Co., 1954), pp. 552–559. The quotation is from p. 554.

[5] Jerome Cranmer, "The New Jersey Canals: A Study of the Role of Government in Economic Development," unpublished dissertation, Columbia University, 1955.

ploitative canals or railroads were built to take advantage of an existing opportunity. With them early returns could be expected and private enterprise could operate without subsidy. On the other hand the developmental undertaking depended for most of its traffic on the settlement that its own construction was to bring about. But such development could not in the nature of the case be immediate, and substantial early returns on the investment were hardly possible. The ultimate benefits might be very large but they were certain to be deferred and likely to be widely diffused. Such undertakings, therefore, could hardly be carried to success by unaided private means. They required either government enterprise, subsidy to private enterprise, or else extraordinary illusions on the part of the original investors.[6]

A survey of the history of railroad building around the world illustrates this distinction and tends to confirm these observations. Few countries copied the British example. Certainly it was seldom followed where the problem was one of opening up unsettled areas or of achieving economic development in a preindustrial region. The railroads of Australia and New Zealand are state enterprises. Throughout most of the rest of the world the greater part of the railroad network has been built either on government account or with different forms of government aid or subsidy. One variant of the latter, government guarantee of return on the private investment, which Daniel Thorner has described as "Private Enterprise at Public Risk," was employed in India and Brazil as well as in France.[7] The purely private enterprises have been typically those that exploited obvious economic opportunities—to carry the produce of the pampas to Buenos Aires, or sugar from Cuban fields to the ports, or coffee to Santos. In Bolivia, for example, the pattern is precisely illustrated. The two railroads that take the tin from the great mines to the coast were built and are still owned and operated by private British interests, while the others are entirely governmental.

Nineteenth-century America displayed a similar pattern. There were certain railroad companies, particularly on the Atlantic seaboard, exploiting the opportunities of trade between established centers, which were profitable from the beginning and neither asked nor needed government aid. For New England, Kirkland described these as "dowager railroads" and cited the Boston and Lowell as one of the examples.[8] The Camden

---

[6] This last alternative is noted in Frank W. Fetter, "History of Public Debt in Latin America," *American Economic Review*, XXXVII (May, 1947), 147–148.

[7] Daniel Thorner, *Investment in Empire: British Railway and Steam Shipping Enterprise in India, 1825–1940* (Philadelphia: University of Pennsylvania Press, 1950), ch. 7. Julian Smith Duncan, *Public and Private Operation of Railways in Brazil* (New York: Columbia University Press, 1932).

[8] Edward C. Kirkland, *Men, Cities and Transportation: A Study in New England History, 1820–1900* (Cambridge: Harvard University Press, 1948).

and Amboy was a similar case, and its partner the Delaware and Hudson might be described as a dowager canal—both exploiting the trade between New York and Philadelphia. But these were exceptions. Most of the canals and early railroads depended for their traffic on the growth of the areas into which they were extended. They were developmental in character and, like developmental undertakings almost everywhere, they were in considerable part built with government funds and credit.

The same distinction supplies one important clue to the understanding of the complex and apparently irregular timing of internal improvements activity. In this there were, to be sure, many cross currents. Reversals of state policy sometimes resulted, though less often than is sometimes believed, when power shifted from Whigs to Democrats, or vice versa, or when "Redemption" ended Reconstruction regimes in the South. More often improvements policy varied with the phase of the business cycle. Ambitious programs were abandoned in depression years, and failures were followed by "revulsion" and constitutional prohibitions. The collapse of the Illinois railroad program gave a lesson of caution to neighboring Iowa. On the other hand, New York's success with the Erie Canal had earlier inspired imitation up and down the entire Atlantic seaboard. Aid was given by local authorities, in varying amounts, in every state that formed part of the Union before 1890;[9] and in some fourteen states it continued to be given after the abandonment of state programs.[10] It may be said that governmental participation at one level or another persisted in most sections of the country as long as "developmental" conditions continued to exist, and perhaps in some cases beyond that point.

In general the relationship between developmental conditions and the various waves of government activity can be readily traced. For the Federal Government the building of the National Road and the formulation of the comprehensive internal improvement plans of Gallatin and Calhoun took place when the geographical obstacle to development was the Appalachian Mountains; and the major extension of actual aid to the transcontinental railroads took place when the obstacle was that of the Rocky Mountains and the Great Plains. Government activity in internal improvements was in large measure a frontier phenomenon, a great instance of frontier collectivism. In any given area it tended to diminish and die out as settlement and traffic became more dense and also as the business corporations themselves grew in strength and in the ability to raise large

[9] In Colorado only during the territorial period.

[10] States of which this was substantially true include Georgia, Illinois, Indiana, Maryland, Michigan, Minnesota, Mississippi, Missouri, Nebraska, New York, North Carolina, South Carolina, Tennessee, and Virginia. Local aid was also given in states that had not had state programs. On the other hand, Alabama, Arkansas, Colorado, Ohio, and Pennsylvania adopted constitutional prohibitions against local aid at the same time as against state aid.

sums of money and commit them for long periods. As early as the 1850's, the *American Railroad Journal* was emphasizing this distinction. "In the infancy of our railroads," it said, "it was frequently necessary for the community to aid them in its collective capacity." Such a need continued in the South and in the West, declared the *Journal*, but in the North and East there was "abundant capital . . . for all legitimate enterprise," and public aid was no longer required.[11] To this doctrine it was not a real exception that Maine should vie with Oregon in furnishing some of the very latest cases of local government aid, since eastern Maine remained no less of a frontier than the Far West. Somewhat more surprising were the large amounts of money that Massachusetts poured out after the Civil War for the construction of the Hoosac Tunnel route and the extraordinary outpouring of municipal bonds for the building of the New York Midland. Yet in each case this represented an improvement for the less developed part of a highly developed state; and it may be added that in the case of the latter a new bankruptcy and the failure of plans for reorganization, occurring since the publication of Harry Pierce's book, tend to confirm his account of the selection of the route![12]

If, then, we think of nineteenth-century America as a country in process of development, the experience of other countries in a similar situation suggests that extensive government investment in the means of transportation was not paradoxical but something entirely to be expected. What would really have been surprising would have been the spectacle of communities eager for rapid development but waiting patiently for their canals and railroads until the way was clear for prudent private investment to go forward without assistance. Yet neither an analysis of the economics of development nor analogy from foreign experience would account for all the peculiar forms and shapes taken by the American movement for internal improvements. Among its characteristics were three general shortcomings that would at once be obvious to anyone attempting to advise the underdeveloped countries of today on the organization of their programs of public improvement.

The first of these deficiencies was the failure to develop a workable economic criterion for the selection of projects for government support. Perhaps the sheer abundance of developmental opportunities made the question seem less crucial than it is for countries with more limited resources. There was, to be sure, no lack of statements of the reasons why short-run return on the investment itself was not a sufficient test. In addition to arguments based on the political advantages of closer connection between sections, which would strike a familiar note in many under-

[11] *American Railroad Journal*, XXVII (1854), 449; XXVIII (1855), 281.
[12] Harry H. Pierce, *Railroads of New York: A Study of Government Aid, 1826-1875* (Cambridge: Harvard University Press, 1953).

developed countries, expenditure on developmental transportation was defended on economic grounds. These statements called attention, often in thoroughly sophisticated terms, to its various benefits, not all of which could be appropriated by the collection of tolls or fares and freight charges. These included gains to the government itself in the enlargement of its tax base and the enhanced value of its lands, the diffused gains to the population at large in opportunities for income and employment, and in general the external economies provided to business as a whole by the provision of adequate transportation. But how should these broader and vaguer benefits be balanced against the expected costs? How were expenditures on unnecessary projects to be prevented? If prospective profit was not to be the conclusive test, how much immediate loss—and under what conditions—should the public authorities be prepared to incur in order to obtain these general advantages? On these questions I have so far found no serious contemporary statement.

A second shortcoming was the failure to develop and apply criteria for the assignment of projects to the different levels of government authority—federal, state, and local. Gallatin's admirable attempt to define a national project had little or no practical effect, and his program of federal action foundered largely on unresolved conflicts of state and regional interests. Within the several states, the problem of competing local interests was hardly less acute. Virginia attempted to operate on the theory of state support on equal terms to all local projects meeting certain specified conditions. In Pennsylvania and elsewhere there were bitter conflicts between proponents of a main or trunk line development and the advocates of aid to miscellaneous minor projects. Ante-bellum Georgia offered the unique example of confining its contribution almost entirely to a single strategically located state railroad, leaving connecting lines to local aid and private enterprise.[13] The extensive resort to the agencies of local government, the several thousand cases of railroad subscriptions and subsidies on the part of cities, counties, towns, and villages, can hardly be explained as the result of the application of any reasoned criteria as to which authorities were best fitted to make the necessary decisions. Aside from the early projects of the ambitious eastern seaports, each eager to carve out its part of the western empire, the recourse to local aid was in most cases a final expedient adopted after state aid had been prohibited, but when public demand for improvements, skillfully abetted by the companies themselves, still remained irrepressible. The extreme example of this type of causation is that of the citizenry of Cincinnati who, discovering that prohibition against *aiding* a railroad did not prevent them from *building* one, proceeded to construct the Cincinnati Southern as a successful municipal enterprise.

[13] Heath, *Constructive Liberalism*, ch. 11.

The third shortcoming lay in the nature of the government agencies themselves. They were sometimes subject to corruption, the danger of which increased as the railroad corporations graduated from the stage of infant enterprises. Moreover, they were in most cases poorly equipped to discharge the responsibilities of planning programs of internal improvement and of operating the undertakings effectively or of protecting the public interest in those that received public support. There were, to be sure, a considerable number of notable exceptions. The Gallatin Plan, prepared by the Secretary of the Treasury and a few clerks, would stand comparison with any twentieth-century plan for the development of a nation's communications. The present location of the trunk line railroads is eloquent testimony to its geographic foresight. New York's state enterprise, the Erie Canal, was both a financial and a technological success. The engineers who learned the job on the Erie carried their technique to other undertakings. The United States Army Engineers gave technical assistance to a large number of railroads;[14] and, in its early days, the Virginia Board of Public Works furnished engineering services to local enterprises. Georgia's state railroad, the Western and Atlantic, not only earned a good return on its investment but also provided for the other railroads of the state their indispensable connection with the West. Baltimore's City Council made serious and persistent efforts to guard its railroad investments. Cincinnati's success has already been cited. Other examples could of course be named. Yet it can hardly be denied that in general the governments of the time, with small budgets and small staffs, with little expert personnel and without civil service traditions, lacked what would now be regarded as the essential means for the effective supervision of improvement programs. The deficiency became more glaring as public aid came more and more to rest on the decisions of local authorities. Little planning could be expected of village or township boards deciding whether to recommend "whacking up" the contribution demanded by the railroad agent, or to risk letting the road go through the neighboring crossroads instead. Their chance to protect the public interest consisted mainly in making sure that the company really ran cars through their village in exchange for the contribution.

To contemporaries the lightness or feebleness of the supervisory hand of government did not always appear a disadvantage. Shortly after the Federal Government had begun the practice of making land grants to railroads, a British official, reporting enthusiastically to the Privy Council's Committee for Trade and Foreign Plantations, suggested its adoption in the British colonies precisely on the ground that it gave needed assistance without imposing the penalty of interference with management. The

[14] Forest G. Hill, "Government Engineering Aid to Railroads before the Civil War," JOURNAL OF ECONOMIC HISTORY, XI (Summer, 1951), 235–246.

American Railroad Journal often advocated public aid but consistently argued that governments should not take a direct part in improvement enterprises. As president of the Baltimore and Ohio Railroad, John W. Garrett protested indignantly against what he regarded as interference by the public directors at a time when a substantial majority of the company's stock belonged to the State of Maryland and the City of Baltimore. If these attitudes are to be discounted as *ex parte*, there is evidence that legislators often shared these views and argued for them on grounds of public interest.

Virginia's system of mixed enterprise was explicitly based on the principle that the purpose of the state subscription was to draw out individual wealth for purposes of public improvement, and that the Commonwealth's control over the enterprises should extend no further than the correction of obvious abuses. With this in view, the state's participation in stock and voting rights was first limited to two fifths of the whole. When it appeared necessary to raise the state contribution to three fifths, the voting power of the state proxy in the stockholders' meeting was deliberately limited to two fifths, in accordance with the philosophy of the original law. A similar attitude was illustrated in the local aid statutes of a number of states that provided that the shares of stock subscribed to by the local governments should be distributed pro rata to the individual taxpayers. It was believed inexpedient to leave the administration of this stock in the hands of the local authorities, and that its distribution to private individuals would stimulate them to a vigilant supervision of the conduct of the work.[15]

As long as the common purpose was that of getting the much-desired improvement made, those who took part in the movement were not very much concerned if in many cases the method employed came close to being public enterprise under private management. To the Missourians on whom James N. Primm reports, as to many other Americans of the period, "The details of ownership and control were secondary . . . to the principal objective, the establishment of a comprehensive system of public improvement in the interests of the general welfare."[16]

Popular interest in this objective was very widely diffused. This was conspicuous in the support given to the many state programs and perhaps even more clearly in the willingness of the citizens to vote to assume local taxes in so many local elections. In these campaigns the appeals were typically couched in terms of public spirit and local patriotism. "Call

[15] An alternative explanation, that of evading a constitutional prohibition against government stock ownership, has been suggested for the Iowa statute. See Earl S. Beard, "Local Aid to Railroads in Iowa," *Iowa Journal of History*, L (1952), 1–34.

[16] James Neal Primm, *Economic Policy in the Development of a Western State: Missouri, 1820–1860* (Cambridge: Harvard University Press, 1954), p. 113.

meetings," urged a Mississippi paper. "Vote county, city, corporation and individual aid in bonds, money and land." A newspaper from a neighboring state added its plea: "Let the Mississippians come up strong to the work" on election day.[17] Projects were planned and campaigns organized in state or regional railroad conventions and in innumerable local railroad meetings. Boards of trade and chambers of commerce took leading parts in the movement. In a number of cases, after local government aid had been made illegal, unofficial bodies like these raised subscriptions in the same spirit and by appeal to the same arguments. It was they who took over the function of negotiating with the railroads over the location of their lines, shops, or roundhouses.

Throughout the developmental period individual citizens donated land for railroad rights of way, permitted the use of stone and timber from their lands, and supplied the labor of their slaves or their teams—occasionally even their own labor—to what was considered the common cause. Often, though not always, these services were paid for in shares of the stock of the enterprise. Appeals for cash subscriptions to canal or railroad stock were frequently based on grounds of civic duty as well as on prospects of financial return. Citizens were urged to bear an honorable part in what was often described as a great state or national work. In 1857 the president of a North Carolina railroad reproved his private stockholders for clamoring for dividends as if they had invested as capitalists rather than as citizens eager to promote the development of their state. As late as 1870, the editor of a Nashville paper declared that "no individual in this country outside of the Lunatic Asylum ever subscribed to the capital stock of a railroad expecting to receive a profit on the investment in the way of dividends." This is of course not to be taken as literal truth. By the time the editor wrote, many investors had received good returns on railroad stock, and no doubt others were bitterly disappointed that they had not done so. But it remains true that for many private subscribers, as well as for those who urged government action, "the object," as he said, or at least one great object, "was to develop the country, enhance the value of their lands, and create cheap transportation of their produce."[18]

I am sure that no one would urge the underdeveloped countries of today to pattern their programs of transportation development upon the very disorderly history of American action in the field. One may hope that they will succeed in avoiding the three shortcomings I have noted, though they will not find it easy to do so. Most students believe that they will need to use the powers and the borrowing power of government even more than in the American case. But they would be fortunate indeed if

[17] Jackson *Mississippi Daily Pilot*, May 15, 1871. Mobile *Register*, October 24, 1871.

[18] Nashville *Union and American*, February 11, 1870.

they found their citizens as ready to support the undertakings with their own savings and the forced savings of taxation and, if they could enlist as widespread an interest and participation in transportation development as was taken by the people of the United States. In this the local governments, for all their mistakes and inadequacies, and also the voluntary associations, played a considerable part. The building of the American network of transportation gained support from the local patriotism and the booster spirit of the city, town, and small community. It may be pointed out that the Communist practice of carrying regimentation and the party apparatus down into the smallest units, and the very different methods of "community development" of India and other countries, represent deliberate efforts to obtain popular participation at the local level in the processes of economic development. In the United States, vigorous local participation took instead the spontaneous forms that have been described.

On this occasion it is customary to consider The Tasks of Economic History. May I suggest that one such task is the examination of the economic effects of this American "boosterism," of this local civic pride, and to ask how much of its rather noisy activity canceled out in cross purposes and duplication of effort,[19] and to what extent its energy made a positive contribution to economic development. Since a large part of this activity has been carried on by voluntary and unofficial organizations, the subject has rather fallen between the stools of the historians of politics and the historians of business. The records of these bodies are less accessible than those of governments, and their accomplishments are less measurable than those of business firms. Yet exploration of the subject, whatever the difficulties, seems to me essential for the understanding of a unique characteristic of American life.

My discussion of internal improvements began by citing the comment that the amount of government activity and expenditure in this field appeared astonishing in so individualistic a country. It ends on a quite different note, by suggesting that the nature and manner of this extensive government activity have been in close conformity with certain special characteristics of American development. Our record demonstrates a preference, though by no means universal or doctrinaire, for government partnership or subsidy rather than for purely public enterprise, and for leaving management largely in the hands of individuals and corporations. In this American experience differs from that of many foreign countries

---

[19] The effect of local rivalries in impeding the formation of a fully connected national railroad system, by perpetuating differences in gauge and delaying physical connections between lines, is discussed in George Rogers Taylor and Irene D. Neu, *The American Railway Network, 1861–1890* (Cambridge: Harvard University Press, 1956). The text refers to the "long continued parochialism of the cities" (p. 51) and quotes a comment on "village peevishness" (p. 53).

but not of all. Our record also shows that a large amount of this government action was taken by local governments, often of small communities. In this American experience is unique. In our case, moreover, governmental effort has been accompanied and abetted by the voluntary activity of a host of unofficial civic organizations, for which I am sure no parallel can be found in the history of other developing countries. Our policy with respect to internal improvements has thus been profoundly affected —for better or worse—by the traditional American characteristics of individualism, of localism, and of the habit of voluntary association.

28 *Arthur E. Bestor, Jr.*

PATENT-OFFICE MODELS OF THE GOOD SOCIETY: SOME RELATIONSHIPS BETWEEN SOCIAL REFORM AND WESTWARD EXPANSION

America during the ante-bellum decades was in a ferment of reform. Education, from the elementary level to the college, was caught up in the zeal for change. The temperance movements, through meetings, tracts, songs, and hundreds of societies, argued the sinfulness of drinking and the need for moral restraint. Abolitionists by the thousands, radical and moderate, clamored for the end of slavery. Reformers pleaded for the rights of women, for a more humane treatment of the insane, for the improvement of prison conditions, for the permanent termination of war. In this active and multifarious world of reform belonged the communitarians, secular and religious, the Shakers, the Rappites, the Owenites, the Fourierists, and others, with their small-scale experiments in model communities and their many plans for the good society.

But just how did they belong? Were they Utopians? What was their place in early nineteenth-century social thought? What in particular was their relevance to the westward movement, considering that so many of them took root in the area of the Middle West? These are questions which Professor Arthur E. Bestor, Jr., of the University of Illinois answers in the following essay. Professor Bestor has long studied the communitarian movements and is the author of *Backwoods Utopias* (1950), which is concerned in the main with the ideas of Robert Owen and the attempt to realize them in America. In two other volumes, *Educational Wastelands* (1953) and *The Restoration of Learning* (1955), Professor Bestor has also distinguished himself as a critic of

Reprinted with permission from *The American Historical Review*, LVIII (April, 1953), 505–26.

certain tendencies in modern American education and as the proponent of a wide program of educational reform.

Professor Bestor's essay makes the important point of placing communitarian thought in the context of the expanding society of the early nineteenth century. His comments will inevitably evoke questions which, though it is beyond the scope of his essay to answer them, will demand the attention of the student. What was the substance of the plans to establish the good society? In what way was the good society good? How did communitarian thought relate to other reform movements of the period? In what way did it share with them qualities that were pragmatic, individualistic, sectarian, and moral? How did these various movements spring from a society undergoing a major redefinition of social and economic values and institutions? How do the reform movements of the ante-bellum decades fit into the larger pattern of American reform?

Of course it is a matter of interest to us to know our place in that pattern and to understand why the surge of reform has been nowhere apparent in our own age. Perhaps reform is, as Professor Arthur M. Schlesinger has suggested, cyclical in American development and we are presently at the low point of a cycle. Perhaps we have been in a mood of conservatism in response to the Communist and Afro-Asian challenge to our institutions. Perhaps what is apparent is not real; perhaps reform is currently proceeding but in less dramatic and conspicuous ways, and past reform movements have made our institutions ever more plastic and accommodating to the needs for change that accrue from decade to decade.

In the mechanical realm, nineteenth-century American inventiveness left as its most characteristic record not a written description or a drawing but a working model, such as the Patent Office then required. In somewhat similar fashion, the societal inventiveness of the first half of the nineteenth century embodied itself in a hundred or so co-operative colonies, where various types of improved social machinery were hopefully demonstrated. Patent-office models of the good society we may call them.

To build a working model is not the same thing as to draw a picture. Hence it is necessary, at the outset, to distinguish between communitarianism, or the impulse which constructed these hundred model communities, and utopianism, or the impulse to picture in literary form the characteristics of an ideal but imaginary society. The distinction is more than verbal. A piece of utopian writing pictures a social order superior to the present, and it does so, of course, in the hope of inspiring men to alter their institutions accordingly. But a utopian work (unless it happens also to be a communitarian one) does *not* suggest that the proper way of going about such a reform is to construct a small-scale model of the desired society. Edward Bellamy's *Looking Backward*, for example, was a utopian novel, but definitely *not* a piece of communitarian propaganda, because the social transformation that Bellamy was talking about could not possibly be inaugurated by a small-scale experiment; it could come about only through a great collective effort by all the citizens of the state.

The communitarian, on the other hand, was by definition the apostle of small-scale social experiment. He believed that the indispensable first step in reform was the construction of what the twentieth century would call a pilot plant. The communitarian was not necessarily a utopian; few of the religious communities, for example, attempted to visualize an ideal future society this side of heaven. When the communitarian did indulge in utopian visions, the characteristic fact about them was that they always pictured the future as something to be realized through a small-scale experiment indefinitely reduplicated. The communitarian conceived of his experimental community not as a mere blueprint of the future but as an actual, complete, functioning unit of the new social order. As the American communitarian Albert Brisbane wrote:

The whole question of effecting a Social Reform may be reduced to the establishment of one Association, which will serve as a model for, and induce the rapid establishment of others. . . . Now if we can, with a knowledge of true architectural principles, build one house rightly, conveniently and elegantly, we can, by taking it for a model and building others like it, make a perfect and beautiful city: in the same manner, if we can, with a knowledge of true social principles, organize one township rightly, we can, by organizing others like it, and by spreading and rendering them universal, establish a true Social and Political Order.

This is a fair summary of the communitarian program.

Historically speaking, the idea of undertaking social reform in this particular way—by constructing a patent-office model or a pilot plant—is not a common idea but a distinctly uncommon one. No other period comes close to matching the record of the first half of the nineteenth century, which saw a hundred communitarian experiments attempted in the United States alone. The vogue of communitarianism can be delimited even more sharply than this. During a period of precisely fifty years, beginning in 1805, when the first communitarian colony was planted in the Old Northwest, at least ninety-nine different experiments were actually commenced in the United States. Nearly half of these—forty-five to be exact—were located in the Old Northwest, strictly defined.[1] Another twenty-eight were in areas which belonged to the same general cultural region—that is, western New York, the parts of the Ohio River valley outside the Old

[1] That is, twenty-one in Ohio, eleven in Indiana, eight in Wisconsin, four in Illinois, and one in Michigan.

Northwest, and certain adjoining areas on the other side of the upper Mississippi.[2] A total of seventy-three communities—roughly three quarters of the total—thus belonged to what can be described, without undue geographical laxness, as the Middle West.

Such a clear-cut localization of communitarian ideas in time and place can hardly be fortuitous. It is the kind of fact that cries aloud for explanation in terms of historical relationships. What, then, were the unique elements in the historical situation of the Old Northwest that help to explain why communitarianism should have reached its peak there during the first half of the nineteenth century?

Twenty years ago an answer would have been forthcoming at once, and would probably have gone unchallenged: *the frontier*. If, however, the frontier is given anything like a satisfactorily limited definition—if, in other words, the term is taken to signify primarily that "outer margin of the 'settled area'" which figured in Frederick Jackson Turner's original essay—then a close relationship between the frontier and communitarianism is hard to find.

In the first place, communitarian ideas cannot be said to have arisen spontaneously among any groups living in actual frontier zones. The leading communitarian philosophies, in point of fact, were elaborated in Europe—not only those of Robert Owen, Charles Fourier, and Etienne Cabet but also those of most of the religious sects. The Moravians in the eighteenth century found their "general economy" well adapted to new settlements, but its principles were ones the sect had worked out and partially practiced before they came to America. The Shakers faced frontier conditions when they first arrived in America, but they worked out their communistic polity later. It was, in fact, their way of settling down after the frontier stage had passed. The nonreligious communitarianism of the nineteenth century drew its ideas from sources even more obviously unconnected with the frontier. Robert Owen's plan was a response to conditions which the factory system had created in Britain, and it made no significant impression in America until Owen himself brought it to this country. Americans did take the initiative in importing certain communitarian theories, but here again frontier motivation was absent. Albert Brisbane, though the son of a pioneer settler of western New York, became aware of social problems gradually, first in New York City, then in the ancient but impoverished realms of eastern Europe. He finally brought back from the Continent the most sophisticated social theory of the period, Fourierism, and made it the leading American communitarian system of the 1840's, by dint of propaganda directed largely from New York and Boston.

[2] That is, eleven in western New York, seven in western Pennsylvania, one in what is now West Virginia, two in Kentucky, two in Missouri, and five in Iowa.

If the ideas of the communitarians did not arise on the frontier, neither did the impulse to put them in practice. The handful of communities that were actually located in or near true frontier zones were all planted there by groups from farther east or from Europe. They were not established there with the hope or expectation of gaining recruits from among the frontiersmen; on the contrary, communitarian leaders were often warned against accepting local settlers. Finally, communitarians were misled if they expected greater toleration of their social nonconformity in the West than in the East. The mobs who attacked the Shakers in Ohio, at any rate, were indistinguishable from those who attacked them in Massachusetts.

Nothing created by the frontier contributed positively to the growth of communitarianism. Only as a passive force—as an area of relatively cheap land or relatively few restrictions—could the frontier be said to have had anything to do with the communitarian movement. These passive advantages of the frontier were, as a matter of fact, almost wholly delusive. The Shakers afforded an excellent test case, for their villages were to be found in regions of various types. The most successful were in long-settled areas, reasonably close to cities. The one Shaker settlement on the actual frontier—at Busro on the Wabash River above Vincennes—had a dismal history of discontent, hostility, and failure, from the time of its founding in 1810, through its evacuation at the time of the War of 1812, until its abandonment in 1827. The withdrawal of the Rappites from their westernmost outpost—in the very same region and at the very same time—may be taken as evidence that they too felt the frontier to be basically unfavorable to communitarianism. Thomas Hunt, a British Owenite who led a colony to Wisconsin in the 1840's, had to admit that whatever physical advantages the frontier might offer could "be secured, not only by bodies of men, but by private individuals." This fact was quickly discovered by members of co-operative communities which moved to the frontier. "On their arrival here," Hunt observed, "they . . . find many opportunities of employing their labour *out of the society they are connected with.*" Though Hunt saw advantages for communitarianism in the cheaper lands of the frontier, he saw none in the state of mind which the frontier engendered. Among the factors prejudicial to success, he listed, with emphasizing italics, "the *influence which the circumstances of this country may exert over their minds, in drawing them again into the vortex of competition.*"

Hunt was probably wrong in regarding even the cheap lands of the frontier as a real economic boon to communitarianism. They proved to be the exact opposite, according to the shrewdest of all the nineteenth-century historians of the movement. This was John Humphrey Noyes, himself founder of the successful Oneida Community (located, incidentally, far from the frontier), who reached the following conclusions after carefully analyzing the history—particularly the record of landholdings—of communitarian ventures contemporaneous with his own:

Judging by our own experience we incline to think that this fondness for land, which has been the habit of Socialists, had much to do with their failures. Farming is . . . the kind of labor in which there is . . . the largest chance for disputes and discords in such complex bodies as Associations. Moreover the lust for land leads off into the wilderness, "out west," or into by-places, far away from railroads and markets; whereas Socialism, if it is really ahead of civilization, ought to keep near the centers of business, and at the front of the general march of improvement. . . . Almost any kind of a factory would be better than a farm for a Community nursery. . . . Considering how much they must have run in debt for land, and how little profit they got from it, we may say of them almost literally, that they were "wrecked by running aground."

The frontier, then, did not generate communitarianism. It did not inspire its inhabitants to join communitarian ventures. It did not show itself particularly hospitable to communitarian ideas. It did not even offer conditions that could contribute substantially to communitarian success. Communitarianism, in other words, cannot be explained as an outgrowth of the conditions of frontier life.

In point of fact, communitarianism developed in a fairly normal environment of settled agricultural and commercial life. The foreign-language sectarian communities, it is true, were not indigenous to the localities in which they were established. The Rappites, for example, were conducted as a body from Germany to Harmonie, Pennsylvania, then to Harmonie, Indiana, and finally back to Economy, Pennsylvania. None of the original members had any previous connection with these places, and the number of members recruited in the neighborhood was negligible. The same could be said of communities like Zoar, Ebenezer, and Amana. In the history of the communitarian movement as a whole, however, this pattern was the exception rather than the rule. The Shakers illustrated a more typical development. Each village of theirs was "gathered" (the phrase was a favorite one with them) from among the converts in a given locality, and was established upon a farm owned by one of the group or purchased with their combined resources. When communitarianism assumed a secular character, beginning in the 1820's, this local pattern became even more characteristic of the movement.

Of the thirty-six Owenite and Fourierist communities established in the United States during the half century under consideration, only one—Hunt's colony in Wisconsin—represented an immigrant group comparable to the Rappites or Zoarites. Only ten others involved any substantial migration of members, and in many of these the recruits from the immediate vicinity clearly outnumbered those drawn from a distance. At least two thirds of the Owenite and Fourierist communities were experiments indigenous to the neighborhood in which they were located. Sometimes groups in a small village or on adjoining farms threw their lands together or traded them for a larger tract nearby. Sometimes groups in a larger town moved to a domain which they acquired a few miles out in the country. It is difficult to distinguish between the two processes, and unnecessary. In neither case did the moving about of men and women constitute anything like a true migration to a new environment. Clearly enough, communitarianism as a secular doctrine of social reform made its impact in already settled areas and it inspired its adherents to act in their own neighborhoods far more frequently than it led them to seek the frontier.

Yet the fact remains that the great outburst of communitarian activity occurred during the period when the frontier of agricultural settlement was pushing ahead most rapidly, and it tended to concentrate in the area lying in the wake of that forward thrust. Some connection obviously existed between the idea and the situation. The true nature of that relationship must be explored.

In his original statement of the so-called frontier thesis, Frederick Jackson Turner enumerated certain ideas and habits of mind that he deemed characteristically American. "These," he exclaimed, "are traits of the frontier, or traits called out elsewhere because of the existence of the frontier." The latter half of the sentence has a rather off-hand air about it, suggesting that Turner did not fully recognize how radically different were the two types of causation he was bracketing together. Indeed, if the implications of the second part of the statement had been followed out fully and carefully by Turner and his disciples, the frontier thesis itself might have been saved from much of the one-sidedness that present-day critics discover in it. Be that as it may, the second part of the quoted sentence does describe the kind of relationship that existed between westward expansion and the vogue of such an idea as communitarianism. The latter was one of the "traits called out elsewhere because of the existence of the frontier."

This paper purposes to explore the process through which communitarianism—and, by extension, a variety of other social ideas—were "called out" by the mere existence of the frontier. The statement we are using is, in part, a figurative one. For the sake of precision it ought to be restated at the outset in completely literal terms. Three points require brief preliminary discussion. In the first place, ideas are not produced by the mere existence of something. They result from reflection upon that something, reflection induced either by direct observation or by knowledge derived at second hand. We are, by definition, interested in the reflections of men and women who did not participate in, and did not directly observe, the frontier process. In the second place, ideas rarely, if ever, spring into existence fresh and new. Reflection upon a new occurrence does not produce a set of new ideas. It exercises a selective influence upon old ones. It represses some of these. It encourages others. It promotes new combinations. And it may infuse the whole with deeper emotional feeling. The resulting complex of ideas and attitudes may be new, but the newness lies in the pattern, not in the separate elements. Finally, though we have adopted Turner's phrase, and with it his use of the word "frontier," we will find that it was really the westward movement as a whole, and not the events at its frontier fringe, that the men and women "elsewhere" were meditating upon.

With these three considerations in mind, we are ready to restate the subject of our inquiry in distinct, if prosaic, terms. The rephrasing will be clearer if cast in the form of a series of questions, although these will not have to be taken up in order or answered separately in the discussion that follows. How, then, did the expansion of population into unsettled areas, and the planting of civilized institutions there, strike the imaginations of those who took no direct part in the process? What ideas of theirs about the nature of social institutions were confirmed and amplified by their reflections upon this continuing event? Which of their hopes were encouraged, which desires rendered more certain of fulfillment, by what they conceived to be taking place? And how did this new pattern of ideas and aspirations correspond to the pattern embodied in a doctrine of social reform like communitarianism?

Now, communitarianism involved, as we have seen, certain very definite convictions about the way social institutions are actually created. It assumed the possibility of shaping the whole society of the future by deliberately laying the appropriate foundations in the present. And it called upon men to take advantage of this possibility by starting at once to construct the first units of a new and better world.

In this set of beliefs can we not immediately detect certain of the ideas that took shape in the minds of men as they contemplated—from near or far—the upbuilding of a new society in the American West?

First among these ideas, certainly, was the sense of rapid growth and vast potentiality. No theme was so trite in American oratory and American writing; quotations of a general sort are not needed to prove the point. But one particular aspect of this belief in the future greatness of the United States requires special notice. The point in question was enshrined in a couplet which was composed in New England in 1791 and which quickly became one of the most hackneyed in the whole of American verse:

Large streams from little fountains flow;
Tall oaks from little acorns grow.

American civilization, to spell out the interpretation which hearers instinctively gave to these lines, was destined for greatness, but this greatness was growing, and would grow, out of beginnings that were small indeed.

The converse of this idea formed a second important element in the reflections which the westward movement induced. The habit of tracing greatness back to its tiny source, led easily to the conception that every beginning, however casual and small, held within it the germ of something vastly greater. In a stable society, small happenings might have no consequences. But to men who pondered the expansion going on in the West, there came a sense that no event was so insignificant that it might not affect the future character of an entire region—perhaps for evil (if men lacked vigilance), but more probably for good.

A third idea, closely linked to these others, provided the most distinctive element in the entire pattern. Human choice could play its part in determining the character of the small beginnings from which great institutions would in future infallibly grow. But—and this is the uniquely important point—an organized effort to shape them would be effective only during the limited period of time that institutions remained in embryo. This concept is not, of course, the obvious and quite unremarkable idea that what one does today will affect what happens tomorrow. On the contrary, it assumed that there was something extraordinary about the moment then present, that the opportunity of influencing the future which it proffered was a unique opportunity, never to be repeated so fully again.

The corollary to all this—the fourth element in the complex of ideas— was a moral imperative. Men and women were duty-bound to seize, while it still existed, the chance of building their highest ideals into the very structure of the future world. When men spoke of "the mission of America," it was this particular idea, more than any other, that imparted to their words a sense of urgency. This moral imperative applied to the transplanting of old institutions as well as the establishment of new. The link between reformer and conservative was their common belief that institutions required positively to be planted in the new areas. Naturally the *best* institutions were the ones that should be so planted. For most men and women this meant the most familiar institutions, or at least the most respected among the familiar ones. Consequently the greater part of the effort which this concept inspired went into reproducing old institutions in the new West. A few men and women, however, always sought these best institutions not among those that already existed but among those that might exist. Hence the concept gave scope for reform as well as conservation.

Even when it assumed a reformist character, however, this concept must not be equated with reform in general. That it is to say, it was not identical with the sense of duty that urges men to remedy social injustices and to remake faulty institutions wherever they find them. The present concept was much narrower. Without necessarily overlooking abuses hoary with age, those who thought in this particular way concentrated their attention upon institutions at the rudimentary stage, believing that the proper shaping of these offered the greatest promise of ultimate social reformation.

The group of four concepts we have been considering formed an altruistic counterpart to the idea of the West as a land of opportunity for the individual. The dreams of wealth, of higher social station, and of greater freedom were doubtless the most influential ideas which the West generated in the minds of those who reflected upon its growth. The action which such dreams inspired was participation in the westward movement. But all men who thought about the West did not move to it. There were also dreams which men who remained in the East might share, and there were actions appropriate to such dreams. Throughout the world, as men reflected upon the westward movement, they grew more confident that success would crown every well-intended effort to create a freer and better society for themselves and their fellows. And many of them felt that the proper way to create it was to copy the process of expansion itself, by planting the tiny seeds of new institutions in the wilderness.

What men thought about the West might or might not conform to reality. But in the fourfold concept we have analyzed, there was much that did correspond with developments actually taking place in America. At the beginning of the nineteenth century the vast area beyond the Appalachians was in process of active settlement, yet its future social pattern was still far from irrevocably determined. Different ways of living existed within its borders: aboriginal, French, English, Spanish, Southern, Yankee, the ways of the fur trader and the ways of the settled farmer. The pressures from outside that were reinforcing one or another of these patterns of life were vastly unequal in strength, and this fact portended ultimate victory to some tendencies and defeat to others. But the victory of no one of the contending social systems had yet been decisively won. And the modifications which any system would inevitably undergo as it spread across the region and encountered new conditions were beyond anyone's predicting. Half a century later this indeterminateness was no longer characteristic of the West. Many of the fundamental features of its society had been determined with such definiteness as to diminish drastically the range of future possibilities. Just as the surveyors had already laid down the township and section lines which fixed certain patterns irrevocably upon the land, so the men and women of the region, in subtler but no less certain fashion, had by the middle of the nineteenth century traced and fixed for the future many of the principal lines in the fundamental ground-plan of their emergent society.

The consciousness that they were doing this was stronger in the minds of Americans during the first fifty years of the nineteenth century than ever before or since. The idea had found expression earlier, of course, but never had it been validated by so vast a process of institutional construction as was taking place in the Mississippi Valley. The idea might linger on after the middle of the nineteenth century, but every year it corresponded less with the realities of the American scene, where social institutions were being elaborated or painfully reconstructed rather than created fresh and new. The first half of the nineteenth century was the period when it was most natural for Americans to assert and to act upon the belief that the new society of the West could and should be shaped in embryo by the deliberate, self-conscious efforts of individuals and groups.

This conviction received clearest expression in the pulpit and in the publications devoted to missions. An eastern clergyman, addressing the American Home Missionary Society in 1829, called upon the imagination of his hearers, asking that they place themselves "on the top of the Alleghany, survey the immense valley beyond it, and consider that the character of its eighty or one hundred million inhabitants, a century hence, will depend on the direction and impulse given it now, in its forming state." "The ruler of this country," he warned, "is growing up in the great valley: leave him without the gospel, and he will be a ruffian giant, who will regard neither the decencies of civilization, nor the charities of religion."

The tone of urgency increased rather than diminished as the great valley filled up and men sensed the approaching end of the time during which its institutions might be expected to remain pliant. "The next census," wrote the editor of *The Home Missionary* in 1843, "may show, that the majority of votes in our national legislature will belong to the West." The myriads there, in other words, "are soon to give laws to us all." The conclusion was obvious: *"Now is the time when the West can be saved; soon it will be too late!"*

Friends of our Country—followers of the Saviour—[the editor continued] . . . surely the TIME HAS COME . . . when the evangelical churches must occupy the West, or the enemy will. . . . The way is open—society in the West is in a plastic state, worldly enterprise is held in check, the people are ready to receive the Gospel. . . .

When the present generation of American Christians have it in their power, instrumentally, to determine not only their own destiny and that of their children, but also to direct the future course of their country's history, and her influence on all mankind, they *must* not be—we hope they *will not be*—false to their trust!

If one is tempted to regard this as the attitude only of easterners seeking to influence western society from outside, listen for a moment to a sermon preached before the legislature of Wisconsin Territory in 1843:

It will not answer for you to fold your hands in indolence and say "Let the East take care of the West. . . ." The West must take care of itself—the West *must* and *will* form its own character—it must and will originate or perpetuate its own institutions, whatever be their nature. . . . Much as our brethren in the East have done, or can do for us, the principal part of the task of enlightening and evangelizing this land is *ours;* if good institutions and virtuous principles prevail, it must be mainly through our own instrumentality. . . . In the Providence of God, you have been sent to spy out and to take possession of this goodly land. To *you* God has committed the solemn responsibility of impressing upon it your own image: the likeness of your own moral character—a likeness which . . . it will, in all probability, bear through all succeeding time. Am I not right then in saying that you . . . occupy a position, both in time and place, of an exceedingly important nature?

The same evangelical fervor began to infuse the writings of educational reformers in the second quarter of the nineteenth century, and the same arguments appeared. When Horace Mann bade his "official Farewell" to the school system of Massachusetts, he too spoke in terms of "a futurity rapidly hastening upon us." For the moment this was "a futurity, now fluid,—ready, as clay in the hands of the potter, to be moulded into every form of beauty and excellence." But, he reminded his fellow citizens, "so soon as it receives the impress of our plastic touch, whether this touch be for good or for evil, it is to be struck into . . . adamant." "Into whose form and likeness," he asked, "shall we fashion this flowing futurity?" The West was explicitly in his mind. In settlements already planted, the lack of educational provision posed problems of peculiar exigency, for "a different mental and moral culture must come speedily, or it will come too late." Nor was this all.

Beyond our western frontier [he continued], another and a wider realm spreads out, as yet unorganized into governments, and uninhabited by civilized man. . . . Yet soon will every rood of its surface be explored. . . . Shall this new empire . . . be reclaimed to humanity, to a Christian life, and a Christian history; or shall it be a receptacle where the avarice . . . of a corrupt civilization shall . . . breed its monsters? If it is ever to be saved from such a perdition, the Mother States of this Union,—those States where the institutions of learning and religion are now honored and cherished, must send out their hallowing influences to redeem it. And if . . . the tree of Paradise is ever to be planted and to flourish in this new realm; . . . will not the heart of every true son of Massachusetts palpitate with desire . . . that her name may be engraved upon its youthful trunk, there to deepen and expand with its immortal growth?

Religious and educational ideals were not the only ones which Americans cherished and whose future they were unwilling to leave to chance. In establishing their political institutions, they were weighed down with thoughts of posterity, and of a posterity that would occupy lands as yet almost unexplored. At the Constitutional Convention James Wilson of Pennsylvania spoke to the following effect: "When he considered the amazing extent of country—the immense population which is to fill it, the influence which the Govt. we are to form will have, not only on the present generation of our people & their multiplied posterity, but on the whole Globe, he was lost in the magnitude of the object."

Such ideas as these found embodiment in the great series of documents which provided for the extension of government into the American West. Usually the purpose was so self-evident as to require no explicit statement. The Northwest Ordinance of 1787, for example, was without a preamble. It proceeded directly to the task of providing frames of government for the Northwest Territory, through all the stages up to statehood, and it concluded by setting forth certain "articles of compact" which were to "forever remain unalterable" and whose manifest purpose was to determine irrevocably for the future certain institutional patterns of the region. The framers of this and similar constitutional documents were proclaiming, by actions rather than words, their adherence to the set of beliefs under discussion here, namely, that the shape of western society was being determined in their own day, and that they possessed both the opportunity and the responsibility of helping to direct the process. "I am truly Sensible of the Importance of the Trust," said General Arthur St. Clair in 1788 when he accepted the first governorship of the Northwest Territory. He was aware, he continued, of "how much depends upon the due Execution of it—to you Gentlemen, over whom it is to be immediately exercised—to your Posterity! perhaps to the whole Community of America!"

Economic and social patterns, Americans believed, could also be determined for all future time during a few crucial years at the outset. Nothing was of greater concern to most inhabitants of the United States than the pattern of landownership which was likely to arise as a consequence of the disposal of the public domain. In this as in other matters, the present interests of the persons involved were naturally more compelling than the prospective interests of unborn generations. Nevertheless, concern for the latter was never pushed very far into the background. "Vote yourself a farm" was doubtless the most influential slogan of the land reformers. But not far behind in persuasiveness were arguments that dwelt upon the kind of future society which a particular present policy would inevitably produce. The argument was often put in negative form; propagandists warned of the evils that would inescapably follow from a wrong choice made during the crucial formative period.

> The evil of permitting speculators to monopolize the public lands [said a report of the land reformers in 1844], is already severely felt in the new states. . . . But what is this evil compared with the distress and misery that is in store for our children should we permit the evil of land monopoly to take firm root in this Republic? . . .
> Time rolls on—and in the lapse of a few ages all those boundless fields which now invite us to their bosom, become the settled property of individuals. Our descendants wish to raise themselves from the condition of hirelings, but they wish it in vain . . . and each succeeding age their condition becomes more and more hopeless. They read the history of their country; they learn that there was a time when their fathers could have preserved those domains, and transmitted them, free and unincumbered, to their children.

If once lost, the opportunity could never be regained. But if seized upon "by one bold step," the report continued, "our descendants will be in possession of an independence that cannot fail so long as God hangs his bow in the clouds."

Certain aspects even of the slavery controversy grow clearer when examined in the light of this characteristic American belief. One central paradox, at least, becomes much more understandable. "The whole controversy over the Territories," so a contemporary put it, "related to an imaginary negro in an impossible place." This was in large measure true. Even the admission of new slave states or of new free ones—and such admissions were occurring regularly—aroused no such controversy as raged about the exclusion of slavery from, or its extension to, unsettled areas where no one could predict the possible economic utility of the institution or its ability to survive. The violence of this controversy becomes explicable only if one grasps how important in the climate of opinion of the day was the belief that the society of the future was being uniquely determined by the small-scale institutional beginnings of the present.

From the Missouri crisis of 1819–21 onwards, practically every major battle in the long-continued contest was fought over the question of whether slavery should go into, or be excluded from, territories whose social institutions had not yet crystallized. So long as both sides could rest assured that the existence or nonexistence of slavery was settled for every inch of territory in the United States, then the slavery controversy in politics merely smoldered. Such a salutary situation resulted from the Missouri Compromise, which drew a geographical dividing line across the territories. But when the Mexican War opened the prospect of new territorial acquisitions, the controversy burst into flame again with the Wilmot

Proviso, which aimed to nip in the bud the possibility that slavery might ever become an institution in the new areas. The Compromise of 1850 composed the dispute with less definitiveness than had been achieved thirty years before, for the question of slavery in New Mexico and Utah was left open until those territories should be ripe for statehood. Though the Compromise was, for this reason, intrinsically less stable than the earlier one, the uncertainties that it left were in areas which settlement was hardly likely to reach in the near future. Comparative calm thus ensued until the Kansas-Nebraska Act of 1854. By opening to slavery the territories north of the old Missouri Compromise line, this measure threw back into uncertainty the character of the future social order of an area now on the verge of rapid settlement. Bleeding Kansas resulted from the effort to settle by force what could no longer be settled by law, namely, the kind of social institutions that should be allowed to take root in the new territory and thus determine its future for untold ages to come.

Abraham Lincoln in his speech at Peoria on October 16, 1854, made perfectly clear his reasons for opposing the doctrine of popular sovereignty embodied in the new act:

> Another important objection to this application of the right of self-government, is that it enables the first FEW, to deprive the succeeding MANY, of a free exercise of the right of self-government. The first few may get slavery IN, and the subsequent many cannot easily get it OUT. How common is the remark now in the slave States—"If we were only clear of our slaves, how much better it would be for us." They are actually deprived of the privilege of governing themselves as they would, by the action of a very few, in the beginning.

Four years later Lincoln restated the argument in a letter to an old-time Whig associate in Illinois. His point of departure was a statement of Henry Clay's. "If a state of nature existed, and we were about to lay the foundations of society, no man would be more strongly opposed than I should to incorporate the institution of slavery among its elements," Clay was quoted as saying. "Exactly so," was Lincoln's comment.

> In our new free ter[r]itories, a state of nature *does* exist. In them Congress lays the foundations of society; and, in laying those foundations, I say, with Mr. Clay, it is desireable that the declaration of the equality of all men shall be kept in view, as a great fundamental principle; and that Congress, which lays the foundations of society, should, like Mr. Clay, be strongly opposed to the incorporation of slavery among it's [*sic*] elements.

These statements come as close as any to explaining the true nature of the issue which neither side was willing to compromise in 1860–61. In the midst of the crisis, it will be remembered, Congress passed and transmitted to the states for ratification a proposed constitutional amendment forever prohibiting any alteration of the Constitution that would permit Congress to interfere with slavery in the states. This provision was acceptable to Lincoln and the Republicans even though they were refusing to concede a single inch to slavery in the territories. On the other hand, the complete guarantee of slavery where it actually existed was insufficient to satisfy the southern leaders, so long as permission to extend slavery into new areas was withheld. For both sides the issue was drawn over potentialities. But this does not mean that it involved unrealities. In the mid-nineteenth-century climate of opinion, potentialities were among the most real of all things. The issue of slavery in the territories was an emotionally potent one because it involved a postulate concerning the creation and development of social institutions, and a corresponding ethical imperative, both of which were woven into the very texture of American thought.

How communitarianism fitted into this tradition should now be clear. The communitarian point of view, in simplest terms, was the idea of commencing a wholesale social reorganization by first establishing and demonstrating its principles completely on a small scale in an experimental community. Such an approach to social reform could command widespread support only if it seemed natural and plausible. And it was plausible only if one made certain definite assumptions about the nature of society and of social change. These assumptions turn out to be precisely the ones whose pervasive influence on American thought this paper has been examining.

A belief in the plasticity of social institutions was prerequisite, for communitarians never thought in terms of a revolutionary assault upon a stiffly defended established order. To men and women elsewhere, the West seemed living proof that institutions were indeed flexible. If they failed to find them so at home, their hopes turned westward. As Fourierism declined in the later 1840's, its leaders talked more and more of a "model phalanx" in the West. George Ripley, founder of Brook Farm in Massachusetts, defended this shift, though it belied his earlier hopes for success in the East:

There is so much more pliability of habits and customs in a new country, than in one long settled, that an impression could far more easily be produced and a new direction far more easily given in the one than in the other. An Association which would create but little sensation in the East, might produce an immense effect in the West.

But it was more than pliancy which communitarians had to believe in. Their doctrine assumed that institutions of world-wide scope might grow from tiny seeds deliberately planted. Such an assumption would be hard to make in most periods of history. The great organism of society must usually be taken for granted—a growth of untold centuries, from origins wrapped in obscurity. Rarely does experience suggest that the little projects of the present day are likely to develop into the controlling institutions of the morrow. Rarely has society been so open and free as to make plausible a belief that new institutions might be planted, might mature, and might reproduce themselves without being cramped and strangled by old ones. In America in the early nineteenth century, however, men and women believed that they could observe new institutions in the making, and they were confident that these would develop without check and almost without limit. Large numbers of Americans could be attracted to communitarianism because so many of its postulates were things they already believed.

Large numbers of Americans *were* attracted to communitarianism. If the experimental communities of the Middle West had been exclusively colonies of immigrants, attracted to vacant lands, then communitarianism would have had little significance for American intellectual history. But for the most part, as we have seen, communitarian colonies were made up of residents of the region. Though such experiments did not arise spontaneously on the frontier itself, they did arise with great frequency and spontaneity in the settled areas behind it. There men possessed a powerful sense of the plasticity of American institutions but were at the same time in contact with the social ideas circulating throughout the North Atlantic world. One strain of thought fertilized the other. In a typical communitarian experiment of the Middle West, men might pay lip service to Owen or Fourier, but their central idea was the conviction that a better society could grow out of the patent-office model they were intent on building.

On the whole, the fact that communitarianism stood in such a well-defined relationship to a central concept in American thought is perhaps the most important thing which the intellectual historian can seize upon in attempting to assess the significance of the communitarian movement. This movement has been looked at from many different points of view: as part of the history of socialism or communism, as a phase of religious history, as one manifestation of a somewhat vaguely defined "ferment" of democratic ideas. Communitarianism was relevant to these different categories, of course, but its true nature is hardly made clear by considering it within the limits of any one of these classifications. The only context broad enough to reveal the true significance of the communitarian point of view was the context provided by the early nineteenth-century American way of thinking about social change.

This way of thinking was summed up and applied in the manifesto with which Victor Considerant launched his ambitious but ill-fated colony of French Fourierites in Texas in 1854:

If the nucleus of the new society be implanted upon these soils, to-day a wilderness, and which to-morrow will be flooded with population, thousands of analogous organizations will rapidly arise without obstacle and as if by enchantment around the first specimens. . . .

It is not the desertion of society that is proposed to you, but the solution of the great social problem on which depends the actual salvation of the world.

The last sentence stated an essential part of the true communitarian faith. A remaking of society, not an escape from its problems, was the aim of communitarian social reform during the period when it exerted a real influence upon American social thought. The dwindling of the ideal into mere escapism was the surest symptom of its decline. Such decline was unmistakable in the latter half of the nineteenth century. By 1875 a genuinely sympathetic observer could sum up in the following modest terms the role which he believed communitarian colonies might usefully play in American life:

That communistic societies will rapidly increase in this or any other country, I do not believe. . . . But that men and women can, if they *will*, live pleasantly and prosperously in a communal society is, I think, proved beyond a doubt; and thus we have a right to count this another way by which the dissatisfied laborer may, if he chooses, better his condition.

In the late nineteenth century, it is true, numerous communitarian experiments were talked about and even commenced, and their prospectuses echoed the brave old words about planting seeds of a future universal social order. But such promises had ceased to be credible to any large number of Americans. Industrialism had passed beyond the stage at which a community of twenty-five hundred persons could maintain, as Owen believed they could, a full-scale manufacturing establishment at current levels of technological complexity and efficiency. Before the end of the nineteenth century, even communitarian sects like the Rappites and Shakers were in visible decline. The impulse to reform had not grown less, but it had found what it believed were more promising methods of achieving its ends. Men and women who were seriously interested in reform now thought in terms of legislation, or collective bargaining, or organized effort for particular goals, or even revolutionary seizure of power. Rarely did they consider, as so many in the first half of the century instinctively did, the scheme of embodying their complete ideal in a small-scale experimental model. When they did so, it was almost always a temporary move, a way of carrying on in the face of some setback, or a way of organizing forces for a future effort of a quite different sort. Such revivals of the communitarian program were apt to be sternly denounced as escapism by the majority of up-to-date socialists. In America, as in the world at large, communitarianism had become a minor eddy in the stream of socialism, whose main channel had once been defined by the communitarian writings of Robert Owen, William Thompson, Charles Fourier, Albert Brisbane, Victor Considerant, and Etienne Cabet.

The decline of communitarian confidence and influence paralleled the decline of the cluster of beliefs or postulates which this paper has been exploring. These intellectual assumptions faded out, not because the so-called free land was exhausted nor because the frontier line had disappeared from maps of population density but simply because social patterns had become so well defined over the whole area of the United States that the possibility no longer existed of affecting the character of the social order merely by planting the seeds of new institutions in the wilderness.

How quickly and completely the old set of beliefs vanished from the American mind was revealed by certain observations of James Bryce in 1888. In a speech to a western legislature Bryce reminded his hearers of "the fact that they were the founders of new commonwealths, and responsible to posterity for the foundations they laid." To his immense surprise, he discovered that this point of view—"trite and obvious to a European visitor," so he believed—had not entered the minds of these American legislators. In this instance it was not Bryce but his hearers who showed the greater perception. The idea he expressed had once been held with tenacity. In the end, however, it had grown not trite but anachronistic. No longer did it state a profound reality, as it might have done half a century before. By the 1880's there was no point in talking about laying the foundations of new commonwealths within the United States. The reforms in American life which Bryce thought necessary were not to be achieved that way. Serious social reformers in the later nineteenth century were faced with the task of altering institutions already firmly established. Henry George and Edward Bellamy recognized this in their writings; Grangers and trade unionists in their organizations; opponents of monopoly in the legislative approach they adopted. For most American reformers in an industrialized age, communitarianism was a tool that had lost its edge, probably forever.

29 *Samuel Rezneck*

THE SOCIAL HISTORY OF AN
AMERICAN DEPRESSION, 1837–1843

Every generation moves in concern about its destination and in doubt about its means of getting there. Times of crisis inevitably heighten the concern and the doubt. Social purpose, which is always under discussion, comes under intense review in an age of war, natural catastrophe, or depression. Since the basic question confronting any generation is one of defining what is the good society, the basic answer is perforce one that is moral. But morality is no simple thing; it is differently construed by different groups, in different places, at different times. Into the view that a generation takes of its purpose and problems enter, moreover, components of a psychological and political nature.

Here is the great interest that attaches to the following article by Professor Samuel Rezneck of Rensselaer Polytechnic Institute. Professor Rezneck is concerned with presenting the portrait of a depression, one drawn for us in contemporary colors by the generation which passed through it. In presenting it, Professor Rezneck answers three basic questions. How did the men of the time respond to the advent of the depression? To what causes did they attribute it? What solutions did they propose to end it? It will be clear enough from reading the contemporary record that to regard a depression as simply economic is simple indeed. It must be regarded rather as a heightening of social experience, one in which all groups in society are sensitized to all aspects of experience.

The depression of 1837–43 was, as Professor Rezneck indicates, a commentary on the particular problems of its times. It bespoke the advent of large-scale manufacturing, the increasing urbanization of the economy, and the growth of an urban working class. It concluded almost two decades of great credit expansion, enthusiastic building of transportation facilities, and universal land speculation. It signified a wide disparity between supply and demand and a general feeling of insecurity about the disparity.

The depression of 1837–43 serves also as a commentary on the larger problems facing every age, including our own. It poses for us the questions it posed for its contemporaries. What is the sense we have of the direction of American society, what is the national purpose,

Reprinted with permission from *The American Historical Review*, XL (July, 1935), 662–87.

how is it to be achieved? What are the different answers given by the different groups composing American society? Through the answers we shall understand the self-consciousness of our own generation as it addresses itself to its most critical problems. The student must seek out the self-consciousness of every generation, avoiding the facile simplicity which the perspective of history sometimes leads to, but understanding it instead in all its complex motives, its heterogeneous groups, its manifold purposes, its unresolved difficulties.

The year 1835 was once characterized as the most prosperous the United States had ever known. To Harriet Martineau it seemed "as if the commercial credit of New York could stand any shock short of an earthquake", since it had recovered so rapidly from the losses of the Great Fire in that year. Within two years, however, not only New York but the whole country was convulsed by a shock as devastating as any earthquake could have been. Its depressing effects were felt for several years, and even 1843 was described as "one of the gloomiest years in our industrial history". Between 1837 and 1843 American society was passing through the deep hollow of a great economic cycle, and the air became heavy with doubt and distress. Contemporary opinion regarded it as no mere "pressure in the money market", but, on the contrary, as "a national pay day. The Nation has been drawing on the Future, and the Future dishonors the draft. The forcing process is then applied, widespread ruin is the result, and a long period of paralysis ensues."

As early as 1840 the estimated losses due to depression were added up to a total of six billion dollars, but even more important were those losses incapable of measurement, as one writer pointed out:

> Let every individual calculate for himself what he, personally, has lost, what chances have been sacrificed by him, what he might have done, and what he might have been, if the prosperity of the country had not been arrested. . . .

And before prosperity was restored, he predicted a "reckoning of misfortune . . . sufficiently astounding".

Depression came quickly and catastrophically, ushered in by panic; but there had been ample warning. Already in April, 1836, Niles had sounded the alarm, which was repeated in succeeding months, as disaster approached. The notes of warning alternated, however, with the call to renewed confidence in the continuance of the era of universal prosperity. Even in the midst of the general gloom and panic during the early months of 1837, the wish fathered the thought that the worst would soon be over. It was "now time for people to thank God and take courage. Down with the panic makers, and down with the prevalent distrust. . . . A bright sun will soon dispel the remaining darkness, and days of prosperity and glory will be ours." Two years later, Greeley was still mourning over the "corpse of poor, defunct Speculation" as the unfortunate victim of undeserved slander.

The collapse of business and banking, early in 1837, was, however, only the beginning of a long and severe process of purgation. The purging extended beyond the complicated and congested mass of credits and debits which was the major proof of preceding prosperity. Every class in the community was affected, and economic interests were deeply stirred. As distress spread, political strife became embittered. Social thought, as well as public sentiment, came under the whiplash of depression. The whole pattern of American life thus mirrored the prevailing mood and state of depression.

The propertied classes felt the immediate pinch of the general depreciation of values, and were especially articulate in voicing their grievances. Their plight is recorded poignantly, year after year, in the diary of a man like Philip Hone, merchant, mayor, and *bon vivant* of New York. During 1838 he wrote that half his friends were, like himself, deeply in debt, with no prospect of getting out. A year later, Hone reported that he was now out of debt, but at the cost of two thirds of his fortune. Living was high, and Hone wondered "how the poor man manages to get a dinner for his family". In closing a volume of his diary, in June, 1840, he grieved that he had three grown sons out of work. "Business of all kinds is completely at a stand . . . and the whole body politic sick and infirm, and calling aloud for a remedy". He took comfort chiefly in the fact that a new national administration was in sight.

Not only individuals, but whole communities were involved in the general collapse. There was the case of Buffalo, which Captain Marryat found in a stagnant state, following a period of phenomenal growth. Its leading promoter and benefactor, Benjamin Rathbun, was in jail, while all of his vast enterprises were involved in a series of fraudulent endorsements. With the collapse of prices, the tide of bankruptcy rose, engulfing nearly everything and everyone. "Failures, numberless and without limit, and hardly create a sensation." In the few months of its operation the Federal Bankruptcy Act of 1842 finally wiped out four hundred and fifty million dollars of debts, affecting one million creditors. Philadelphia derived amusement from a spurious message of the governor, which recommended the project of a special railway to Texas for defaulters.

Labor, as well as property, suffered from the prolonged process of contraction and liquidation, although it is impossible, of course, to measure comparably the degree and kind of loss which each class incurred. Labor's loss came chiefly from want of employment and from lowered wages, which created an immediate problem of relief, particularly in the larger Eastern cities. Labor, however, was also subjected to other more general stresses. Class consciousness was intensified, while current doctrines of class antagonism received a sharper definition in theory, and even some application in practice.

The hardships of labor began to command early notice. Already in April, 1837, a call was issued for a meeting of the unemployed in Greenwich Village in order to petition the city for work. An early estimate reported that fifty thousand were unemployed, and two hundred thousand without adequate means of support in New York City. In August, a New York journal carried the story that five hundred men had applied in a single day, in answer to an advertisement for twenty spade laborers to do country work at four dollars a month and board. While announcing somewhat prematurely that the country was now at the bottom of the hill, Greeley[1] added that fully "one-fourth of all connected with the mercantile and manufacturing interests are out of business, with dreary prospects for the coming winter".

Similar conditions prevailed at other points in the country. A correspondent wrote that two thousand were out of work at Lynn, while wages were reduced to half the earlier rates. In Boston as in Lowell the mills were lifeless, many going only "in mercy to the workmen and all were living on their savings". In the fall of 1837, nine tenths of the factories in the Eastern states were said to be closed. In New York "the markets began to look gaunt, and the theatres are deserted . . . Winter and starvation are yet some months off".

As winter approached, house renters in New York were planning mass action against the coming quarter rent day. The landlords were advised to wait and to take what they could get, while the unemployed should go rent free. The Erie Railroad offered to employ three thousand men, if the city would lend its credit for supplies. An editorial in the *New Era*, under the caption of "The Poor! The Poor!", warned that some foresight was necessary, or "a civil volcano may explode." Greeley's comment was: " 'Hard Times!' is the cry from Madawaska to Galena." He advised the wealthy and the benevolent-minded to provide work for all who wanted it. To the workers he offered the caution to keep their jobs if they had any. Those without work should stay away from the cities. The South presented little hope, and "the West doubtless offers the fairest inducement to the emigrant. . . . But even Western emigration may be overdone." New York was too crowded, and the city factory had been overbuilt, but there was room within the pale of civilization, and it was not necessary to go "beyond sun-down." In any event, Greeley's advice was, "Fly, scatter through the country, go to the Great West, anything rather than remain here. . . ." The thousands already migrating westward might,

[1] Horace Greeley, founder of the New York *Tribune*.

however, have to move as far as the Rockies in order to escape the malice of the "Van Buren party".

As predicted, the first winter of the depression was a hard one, taxing the resources of the larger communities in the organization of relief. The problem was relatively new, and relief was largely haphazard. In New York there was a central committee for the relief of the suffering poor, which sponsored lectures and concerts as a means of raising money, but it was generally complained that hordes of beggars thronged the streets and knocked at doors. All that could be done was to see that none froze or starved. Once winter was over, the poor were expected to "subsist on the milder state of the atmosphere." Greeley's sympathy went out especially to the respectable mechanics, "whose cry was, not for the bread and fuel of charity, but for Work! . . . Work! . . .".

Only in certain New York wards, such as the sixth and the seventh, was the organization of relief relatively effective. Here a central executive committee regulated the solicitation of gifts, and everything was strictly accounted for. Orders for food and fuel were drawn upon a common store in the ward, while in the smaller districts visitors were assigned to every block or two. But even this was not enough, and Greeley, whose personal interest in relief was more than casually journalistic, recommended a permanent organization of all the charitable people in the city, as well as a union with similar associations all over the country, "for the extinction of mendicity and suffering from want". Primarily its purpose should be to provide work, and an intelligence office ought to be set up for this.

Greeley's experience with the depression left deep scars upon him and directed his attention permanently to theories of general social reform. He also returned frequently to the specific problem of relief for unemployment. In this he was like a prophet crying in the wilderness. He pleaded for the continuance of public works, which alone kept wages from falling lower. Even if mistakes had been made, it was necessary to go on, especially since prices were down. A year later Greeley again turned to his favorite theme, "to furnish honorable and suitable Employment to every waiting, wanting son and daughter of Adam within its limits". He advocated the creation of an "Exchange of Labor", where purchaser and seller might meet, but it must not be allowed to depress other labor. Greeley had arrived at the doctrine of Man's Right to Work, and insisted that it was only the sound "principle of Mutual Insurance". During the last four years, he added, the loss from unemployment and misdirection of labor had averaged one hundred million dollars a year, and was, therefore, a vital question, "of more importance than any ruling political topic . . .".

Philadelphia, like New York, had its problem of relief, for which it resorted to the familiar method of the soup house. At a public meeting in 1837, a committee reported that prices were high and suffering great. It was recommended that the state set up public granaries and coal yards, where the miner and farmer could be assured a fair price, and the consumer might buy "at cost". Another committee of sixty was appointed to beg for the poor, who were "dying of want". In Boston the Society for the Prevention of Pauperism became alarmed at the spread of beggary and, in 1838, set up an office for finding work or inducing the unemployed to leave the city. Even in 1844, when work was said to be abundant, the Employment Society had a list of some seven hundred, for whom it was unable to obtain work. At this early date the thought was dawning that some permanent unemployment was perhaps unavoidable in the larger city. In 1845 the estimate was made for New York that "there are at no time less than twenty thousand persons vainly seeking work in this city". Three hundred thousand others lived on approximately a dollar a week per person.

Greeley's plea that the depression must not be allowed to injure labor was, of course, unheeded. In the boom years preceding 1837, labor activity had increased greatly; unions and strikes were the order of the day. The inevitable reaction had followed, and a symptom of it was suggested in the advertisement of a hat manufacturer who offered his services, with those of his workmen, "all of whom are little affected with . . . the moral gangrene of Trades' Union principles". They worked without "the inconveniences, injustice . . . regular combinations, and periodical strikes . . .". The depression favored the further progress of the reaction. In 1837, a journal welcomed the offer of the trade societies to reduce wages, but added that "the labor of voting was quite lost". Wages would come down in any event, and it was hoped that "the employers will to the full adopt the English policy and employ no men who do not forever abjure the unions. . . . The rules of the unions as to hours, pay, and everything else ought to be thoroughly broken up." At a time when there was little work to be had, the advice seemed rather gratuitous that "to work only ten hours in the summer and eight hours in winter is to waste life".

The ills of depression were obviously many, and they called for prompt diagnosis and some cure. Here, however, a familiar dilemma presented itself, such as has, in fact, appeared in every American depression. The doctor was also the patient, and neither the diagnosis nor the proposed remedy could, therefore, have the necessary degree of dispassionate and clearheaded deliberation. The ailments, moreover, were at a crisis and could scarcely wait; yet there were many clashing interests. Already in 1840, it was aptly remarked, in reference to the current controversy over banking, that the question had "very little attraction for the generality of men, except at moments of difficulty and distress, moments when they are least of all qualified to form a sound and discriminating judgment . . .".

[Now, however, like drowning men, they catch at any straw, and] readily adopt any theory which tends to relieve them from all responsibility for the misfortunes which they suffer, and which holds out . . . the splendid vision of a sudden restoration of that prosperity and wealth which they feel to be slipping from their grasp.

Many were the straws thus grasped at in these years; and, if their ability to support and to supply cause or cure was small, they are at least useful in pointing the direction of the wind. It matters little now whether the diagnoses offered were good or true; the important thing is that they represent contemporary judgment. Taken together they constitute a complex pattern of speculation and controversy reflecting the manifold social interests involved.

Of causes to account for the depression there was a prolific abundance, ranging from the trivial and purely incidental to the most impressively profound. What was often only a mere circumstance in the general situation was magnified into a central and vital cause. In this almost mythical age of rugged individualism, the sins of government were too often regarded as an adequate explanation of all social ills. Many of the alleged causes served merely as weapons in the fierce battle of incrimination and recrimination. On the one side, it was charged that the failure to recharter the Bank, the distribution of the Surplus, and particularly the Specie Circular had brought on the catastrophe. As against that, the panic of 1837 was laid to a deliberate conspiracy of the opposition. Already in the fall of 1836, the Whigs were accused of calling on the merchants to close their stores and offices and to go into the streets as missionaries. Webster's appearance in New York at a critical moment, early in 1837, was "the first formal public step which was to inaugurate the new distress, and organize the proceedings for shutting up the banks . . .". Its ulterior purpose was to coerce the government into submission to the Bank "and its confederate politicians".

The prevailing distress obviously called for a scapegoat upon which public passion might vent itself, and the Democratic administration was not the only victim available for sacrifice. England, in one way or another, was joined with it. Here also what was merely a circumstance was magnified into a major cause and became a theme for angry recrimination. It was held that England was greatly to blame for America's indebtedness, and the obligation, therefore, rested upon her to wait, or worse might follow: "Sustain what you have built." As conservative a man as Philip Hone complained that, in spite of our independence, we were plunged into a new thraldom: "All we undertake to do is predicated on the chance of borrowing money from John Bull . . . and the Bank of England becomes the arbiter of the fate of the American merchant". The more radical view is, therefore, understandable; the issues at stake were patriotism and independence. "General Jackson . . . was fighting in the same cause in which he fought at New Orleans, and against the same enemy."

A shrewd insight into the world's financial interrelations, sensitive to the faintest note of disturbance even in remote China, offered a truer, because less bitter, basis for diagnosis. But this idea also lent itself to the purposes of the partisan and the agitator. The moralist inveighed against the wasteful extravagance and the love of tawdry display which swelled American imports and thus exposed us to the mercies of the international balance of trade. In a more practical way, the protectionist rose to his opportunity in casting the responsibility for the prevailing distress upon the policy of the Compromise Tariff. The American Institute of New York was prepared to lead the country back to prosperity by a return to protection. It promptly issued a call for a Business Men's Convention which met at Philadelphia during the summer of 1837. A four-day meeting of delegates, said to represent all parties and half the country's business, adopted resolutions deploring the recent haste "to be rich" and the excess of imports and foreign debt. It recommended a return to industry and economy and the payment of duties in cash.

The agitation for the revival of protection mounted and culminated, in 1841, in the formation of a Home League Association, which addressed an appeal to the people to consider "the difficulties prevailing among the productive classes . . . since 1836, and the still greater difficulties apprehended after the final reductions of duties, in 1842 . . .". The American worker must not be reduced to the European level, "underfed and overworked." Local home leagues sprang up in many places, and conventions were held, which issued fresh appeals. The crisis was affecting thousands of people, who were now idle "because no man has hired them." Clay's great authority supported the theory that free trade was always linked with depression, while protection brought prosperity. The agitation promised to bear fruit as the issue was carried into Congress. In 1842 Hone welcomed the tariff bill then pending as the "last hope of our suffering people," but was afraid it would be vetoed. After months of manipulation, however, it passed, and its reviving effects on business were soon widely proclaimed. American labor, in particular, had been rescued from "sinking rapidly into the gripping fist of European despotism, by the approximation of its prices to the European standard . . .". The tariff of 1842 was now to put it "on the true American basis, with the prospect of a fair reward."

Every specific explanation of the depression thus tended to develop into a case of special pleading. On one diagnosis, however, there was nearly general agreement among doctors and patients. It had a moral

aspect which offered ample opportunity for indignation and severe casti-
gation. From the President down, it was admitted there had been an "over-
action in all departments of business . . . the rapid growth among all classes
. . . of luxurious habits . . . detrimental alike to the industry, the resources,
and the morals of our people". The government could do something; but
in the main, nature must take its course, and it was not the business of
government to offer relief. The governor of Pennsylvania condemned
even more strongly "that desire which is now so ravenous of acquiring
wealth without labour". The "gambling spirit" was responsible for most
of the frauds which are being discovered. These have not even startled the
public.

They heard the stories with the most stoical indifference; and if any ex-
clamations were uttered, they conveyed rather a sentiment of commiseration
for the criminals, than one of detestation for their stupendous crimes.

To the clergy also the depression offered the opportunity for moraliz-
ing upon the evils of speculation. It was God's punishment for our greed
and recklessness. Even ministers and religious institutions had embarked
upon wild speculations, justifying them as a "means to great usefulness".
Now, as a result, false social principles were abroad, and there was a lack
of respect for property. The judgments of the courts were disregarded;
incendiarism and lawlessness were widespread. The remedy must, of
course, come from a spiritual reform. There must be patience in suffering
without resort to violence, for there are more important things than
wealth: "Lay up treasure in Heaven. All this may be done on a small
income . . . Godliness with contentment is a great gain." The depression
might even bear good fruit. To be sure, there has been some depreciation,
but

The world stands the same. . . . We are much richer in experience, much
more humble, much more frugal, and much more prudent already; and, if the
reformation proves permanent, then will even the pressure have proved a good
speculation.

Only Brownson, preaching on the text "Babylon is Falling", announced
the start of a revolution. Two armies, arrayed under different banners,
were "waiting but the signal to rush to the terrible encounter, if indeed
the battle have not already begun".

Speculation, however, had its rare apologists, in the very midst of the
havoc which was laid at its door. A philosophically minded foreign observer traced its roots to the American character. Less apt than the European for penny trade, the American launches upon daring enterprise.
The American credit system was personal and more democratic, hence
more speculative. Another traveler believed that a frequent periodic
"blow-up" was unavoidable in America; it occurred here once in about

every seven to ten years, as against one in every twenty years in England. But even the crash had its utility; it served as a warning, slowing up expansion; and, after subtracting losses, the net gain was still considerable. Greeley likewise argued there was no reason "to be doleful about the matter." Speculation was a phase of the natural growth of the country; it did not produce the scarcity of money. On the contrary, the scarcity checked speculation and further growth. Even its "miscalculation is on the right side". The shrewdest, if not the most eloquent, defense of speculation came from Richard Hildreth, who remarked sensibly that when it succeeds, we call it enterprise. Only when it fails, does opinion stamp it as a bubble. Thus do fashions change; the real difficulty lies in human nature, which always dodges responsibility for its mistakes. "Public opinion rushes from one extreme of blunder to another. It seldom stops half way". Government cannot regulate opinion; it must be the other way around. The best safety valve would be greater freedom from such things as the usury laws and from politics itself.

With the search for the true causes of depression went, of course, the desire to find and apply the right remedy. This released a vast amount of both deliberation and agitation. Much of it was a kind of aimless milling, expressing at most the vague discomfort which derived from real distress. Some of it broadened into the general stream of class disaffection and class conflict, while a large part of it flowed into the channels of concrete program and specific relief. Of these the most important was the chronic issue of banking and currency, but there were also the lesser ones, including the usury laws, imprisonment for debt, stay and exemption laws. For several years both state and national politics were centered upon the problem of relief in its many, often trivial forms. The evils of a preceding boom and inflation had their counterpart in the evils of the depression, in which old animosities were sharpened and new ones created. The underlying riddle, which puzzled everyone, was aptly framed by the author of a pamphlet, under the title of *Common Sense,* and "Especially Addressed to the Most Suffering Portion of our Fellow Citizens . . . the Mechanics". How is it, asked this self-styled Mechanic, that a country as rich as ours is "yet pinched for the common necessaries of life? A vigorous, healthy, and intellectual population, yet bowed down with gloom and despair . . . with ruin and starvation before their eyes?"

The cloven hoof of the partisan, however, soon appeared in its proposal that only a restored Bank of the United States "can relieve us." Only the Bank made all men equal, saving them from shavers and brokers. The controversy over banks and currency embraced, as was clearly understood at the time, the general question of price inflation or deflation. Curiously enough, the relation of the creditor and debtor classes to this issue was not the conventional one, nor was their attitude wholly consistent. The radicals, presumably reflecting the debtors' position, clamored for hard money and were against banks and credit, at least in their present familiar form. In vain did the other side, favoring the credit system and its extension, point out that more, and not less money, was needed to save the debtors from disaster. They protested that "the cures of the ignorant are themselves diseases". Hard money and the treasury system would depreciate labor and property by at least two thirds. "All the gain would be to the rich, and all the loss to the poor." Debtors would be forced to pay three times as much, and this country would cease to be the haven of the poor man. Greeley added his dread warning that to destroy the credit system was to throw a million men out of work, enabling "grasping wealth to secure [labor] for a bare trifle . . .". He urged "all sober and reasonable men" to unite "against the quack notions of the day". Protect and extend the credit system, and high prices will bring high wages. A year later Greeley argued that a metallic money "may be made a far more perfect instrument of monopoly and oppression". He was prolific in recommendation and suggestion. The national government might issue and distribute one hundred million dollars in Treasury notes bearing one per cent and receivable for all public dues. New York State should incorporate a gigantic loan and trust company, and thus add fifty million dollars to the circulation, on the security of real-estate mortgages.

None of these arguments and pleas seemed to weigh against the wide distrust of banks and their irredeemable paper money. Even the Hamiltonian advocate of a new national bank admitted that the banks must not be allowed in the future "to grind the very substance from the indebted". A more radical critic warned the workers not to be "deceived about banks and the credit system. Banks to help farmers appear to me something like feudal lords to defend the people." They have only "enabled speculators . . . to seize upon all the great branches of national industry . . . wrest them from the hands of the real manufacturer and put them into the hands of corporations . . .". One of these victims of the engrossing process in industry, Thomas Brothers, was bitter against the new "go-ahead men", but added that even they "are no other than mere slave-drivers to the bankers . . .".

The case against banks and paper currency rested on both moral and practical grounds. To Ingersoll, who prepared a minority report against banks for the constitutional convention in Pennsylvania, which refused it publication, "the paper money mongers are at once suicides and fratricides. They destroy money, morals, law, order, industry, liberty, equality and property." The ancient prejudice of country against city was invoked.

The countryman, with his dirty acres, is richer than the tradesman on paper pinions. . . . and if country people could but unite against the disorganizers, as they greatly outnumber them, they could put them down with ease at once.

A mass meeting in New York condemned the paper system as neither honest nor Christian.

The credit system did not even supply a steady and reliable medium, as was its boast. On the contrary, its practical effect was "mischievous and ruinous to the permanent prosperity of the country . . .". It kept "the whole country in a complete state of uncertainty and derangement". Actually it was an "anti-credit system", which is generous with loans when money is at three per cent a year, but "demands them back with more than Shylock sternness, when it is at three *per cent* a month . . .". Elsewhere Brownson urged that credit should not be allowed to extend beyond the rock bottom of actual resources. He admitted that such a policy would bear hard on debtors, but they could have justice done them. He proposed calculating the percentage of currency appreciation due to the deflation, which could then be subtracted from the debts. The creditor would have exactly what he lent, but no more. Brownson argued that such deflation, while bold, was yet sound. "It is better to take a medicine, which will expel a lingering disease and restore us to health. . . . It is better to feel the full shock of the evil at once . . .".

This factor of fluctuating uncertainty in the credit system also troubled as conservative an economist as H. C. Carey, who examined it in a series of articles during 1840. He concluded that "restriction cannot give steadiness", but was, in fact, responsible for increased unsteadiness. The remedy lay in complete freedom of association, subject only to a requirement of "perfect publicity . . . of all associations claiming to limit their liability . . .". This solution of full freedom of association, with its implication of more rather than fewer banks, also appealed to the radical anti-monopolist, who insisted on adding, however, a further requirement of unlimited liability. Such inconsistency of attitude was the symptom of a mental confusion, which earned the pointed censure of a contemporary critic.

[In spite of our bitter experience with a banking system which many condemn as] the very worst of all possible banking systems . . . yet how fondly do we see the minds of a large portion of the people clinging to it as the ark of our salvation. . . . Banks, more banks,—is the constant clamor at every session of every legislature.

The movement for free banking developed in New York, and led to the enactment of a law for that purpose in 1838. Its opponents complained that the existing banks were adequate for all needs, and that the new ones were merely an incentive to fresh speculation. It was reported that Wall Street was much excited over the measure, and that one third of New York's real estate was free to be turned into new bank capital. Within two years it will "produce expansion, speculations, fortunes, and efforts, such as few at this day can realize". This dire prediction did not come true in

New York, but in Michigan a similar free banking law produced disastrous results after 1837. In the next two years it seemed as if "every village plot with a house . . . if it had a hollow stump as a vault, was the site of a bank". By 1839 forty-two of these new banks had passed into insolvency, and a million dollars in worthless notes had entered into circulation. In the face of the strong sentiment for free banking the demand for a new national bank had too clear an implication of monopoly to make any headway. Although a writer, signing himself Aladdin, claimed for Boston a prior right to such a bank as late as 1841, there was no longer any magic in the idea; it had become purely academic.

Under the pressure of general distress alarming symptoms of mass disaffection appeared, and the threat of social disorder loomed large at the moment. There never was a time like this, wrote an observer in 1837. From everywhere "comes rumor after rumor of riot, insurrection, and tumult". The public is ready to explode, "and it matters not what is applied to the train—abolition, Grahamism, high prices of food, bank frauds, or gambling . . .". He trembled for the security of the country, should its chief props, respect for the law, the belief in God, and the like, be removed. The plan of action proposed was to fight the infidels and the agitators, among other ways, by means of a "Cheap Repository" of tracts, on the model of Hannah More's, for enlightening the people.

In 1841, another writer called "Ours . . . the age of suicide and mysterious disappearance". The restless spirit of the time gathered men into "noisy and tumultuous masses—shouting for change, reform, and progress. The world lives abroad. . . . The domestic feeling—households—are in a measure abrogated . . .". As for the remedy, there was a great need for "apostles of peace and tranquility". There were too many "alarmists and preachers of agitation. . . . It is necessary that the heart of the age should be soothed and calmed . . .".

The prevailing "hostility to indebtedness" was a source of apprehension to many, and it was especially deplored that even in respectable quarters there was "an amiable sympathy with what is called 'the masses' ". Already the tangible consequences have been such things as the repudiation of state debts, rebellion in Rhode Island, and a repudiation of debts and rents in New York State. The cry of feudalism was spreading to the western territories, where land offices have been in danger of attack. The anti-rent disputes, troubling upper New York State after 1839, shocked Philip Hone, who described them as "of a piece with the vile disorganizing spirit which overspreads the land like a cloud and daily increases in darkness".

There was an alarming tendency toward urban disorder as well, for even Hone noted the near-famine prices in the New York food markets early in 1837 and wondered, "What is to become of the laboring classes?"

A series of meetings held in New York during 1837 under Loco-foco auspices revealed the scope and direction of current mass discontent. The very first of these meetings culminated in an attack on several flour stores and created particular alarm. The others were limited to the usual resolutions and addresses but inspired fear in those more timid.

[In language reminiscent of Carlyle, one of these gatherings was described as] standing in ominous darkness, save for the lurid light shed upon their cadaverous-looking faces from twenty or thirty flambeaux. . . . Over their heads, floating in the dark and poisoned breeze, were a variety of banners . . . underneath these stood the managers and orators, who were straining their lungs to swell the sounds of their cracked voices. . . . We might and should probably have laughed, but for the recollection of the lamp-posts, the . . . Jacobins, and the Guillotine.

Actually the resolutions adopted at these meetings were tame enough. They demanded salary reductions in the city government and economy generally; they asked for employment on public works, and they recommended that the destitute immigrants and others be removed to the country. Their strongest resentment was voiced against the "legalized robberies" of the credit system; at the fifth in the series of meetings, it was proposed "to let credit alone", neither to enforce nor to annul debts by law, but to let them rest on honor only. Such a free system of credit would be "simple, efficient, and just". Finally, a call was issued, amid great cheers, for a "New Constitution, based . . . upon the broad and eternal basis of Right". In September, 1837, a Loco-foco convention at Utica adopted a program of constitutional revision, in which the principal issues were embodied. There should be no forcible collection of debts, nor was the state itself to incur a new debt without the people's sanction. These, with other recommendations covering the incorporation of banks and the principle of unlimited liability, became the main features of the movement for constitutional revision which spread into a number of states in succeeding years.

Loco-focoism thus reached its climax in New York in a year of severe depression; its final triumph perhaps was to see the name extended and applied thereafter to the whole Democratic party, although its die-hard leaders protested that it should continue an independent existence as the ideal of Christian democracy. The alarming spread of what was loosely labelled Loco-focoism was, however, reported from other sections of the country. In Cincinnati it was some "English natives, mustard dealers, Penny petticoat lecturers, of questionable sex, and a few American natives", who organized a celebration of Tom Paine's anniversary. The Charleston *Courier* rejoiced that an incendiary call for a mass meeting against the banks had failed. The respectable and the orderly had taken possession of the proceedings. Elsewhere, however, in Virginia, at Philadelphia and at Baltimore, such meetings had been more successful, and the "Panacea Loco-fociensis" had been approved. From the Southwest came reports of more serious disorder. In Mississippi sheriffs had been removed by force, and a courthouse had been attacked. The *Scioto Gazette* rebuked all those who were engaged

in the diabolical work of arraying one portion of the community against another, the poor against the rich, the laborer with the hands, against the laborer with the head . . . as though the farmer of this year may not be a lawyer next, or the mechanic may not also be a banker.

In the reaction which followed, nativism, a persistent factor in American social and political life, gathered fresh strength and entered upon a period of new growth. A nativist association at Germantown, in 1837, protested that the paupers and malcontents of Europe were spreading radicalism. During the next few years, petitions to Congress, from many quarters, expressed a fear for the safety of republican institutions and complained that a foreign party was being formed. It was charged that the election of 1844 had been decided by an appeal to Europe against America.

Such broad social grievances requiring large general remedies could not, of course, provide adequately for the particular stresses and strains which had developed. Here more specific measures of relief were needed, and many were adopted in proportion as group pressures began to make themselves felt. A close-knit group like the New York merchants was quick to formulate its demands in concrete form. Already in May, 1837, they asked the state to lend its credit to distressed merchants up to six million dollars for a period of ten years. A committee was also dispatched to Washington to demand a special session of Congress, the revocation of the Specie Circular, and the suspension of suits against defaulters on customs bonds. When Congress met in special session in September, it granted relief to merchants, among other provisions, by extending their customs bonds until 1839. In the meantime, on all sides "Relief was the cry—regulation of the currency—a National Bank!" Party conflicts were waged keenly with weapons forged in the existing state of depression. It was the misfortune of the Van Buren administration that its career began just before the panic broke. Thereafter it labored under a great handicap; "the single cry of the opposition is 'turn out the rogues'", which in the end succeeded. To their own needs and to those of others the legislatures of states and nation addressed themselves, pouring forth a mass of relief legislation, which defies complete enumeration or even classification.

The immediate danger of financial stringency in the Federal government was averted by an issue of ten million dollars in one-year Treasury notes, while the distribution of the fourth installment of the now theoretical surplus was postponed, never to be made. The issue of the Independent Treasury was brought to the front, and remained crucial for several years. Federal finances generally entered upon a period of growing deficiency as revenues fell from a peak of forty-eight millions in 1836 to fifteen millions in 1838 and an estimated twenty-three millions in 1839. In four years the Van Buren administration was charged with an accumulated deficit of fifty millions, and the Secretary of the Treasury made the desperate, if rather academic, suggestion that the states return a part of the surplus on deposit with them. An apologist for the government shrewdly observed that retrenchment had not failed for want of an earnest desire to "reduce expenses, and thus gain the credit with the people of loving economy". But "expenditures do go on, and will go on increasing", and the beginning of a new national debt was unavoidable.

Under a new administration, in 1841, a special session of Congress authorized a loan of twelve million dollars, and five millions more in 1842. Special duties were added to provide more revenue. A critic appraised the policy of "Whig Retrenchment and Reform" as meaning more taxes, more expenditures, a new debt, and continuing deficits. A more friendly writer, however, reviewed the solid achievements of what he described as the diligent and disciplined body of honest men comprising the Twenty-seventh Congress (1841–1843), which had really tried to restore prosperity by enacting a record number of bills in three sessions of unprecedented length. In all there were 514 laws, including a new tariff and a Federal bankruptcy act.

Like the Federal government, few states escaped without a deficit in their ordinary budgets. Pennsylvania had a shortage of one million dollars in 1839, and resorted to rather questionable methods in raising a loan to cover arrears. New York, with better credit, was able to borrow three millions in 1841. Massachusetts pledged itself to meet future expenses by means of "taxation and retrenchment". Maryland adopted new taxes in 1841; Kentucky, Indiana, and Illinois increased their land taxes by as much as fifty per cent. Many of the states were further embarrassed by the heavy burden of their debts, which in 1840 amounted to nearly two hundred million dollars. More than half of it was held abroad, and the suspension of specie in 1837 presented the immediate question of how current interest was to be paid. Pennsylvania and Maryland at first demurred but eventually fell into line and agreed to pay in specie or its equivalent, by adding the prevailing premium.

Especially serious, however, was the fact that after a time some of the states could not meet the interest requirements at all; between 1841 and 1842 eight states went into default, and two or three even repudiated part of their debts. For several years default and repudiation supplied the occasion for international recrimination and embittered public opinion on both sides. As early as 1840 the Senate lectured the states on their extravagance and rejected the proposal to transfer the state debts to the Federal government. Various schemes of this kind received currency, however, but were met with the objection, among others, that only the Rothschilds and the Barings would really be relieved by them. As late as 1843 the movement for Federal assumption of state debts was again stopped in the Senate.

In the meantime, however, even Federal credit suffered abroad. In 1842, the Treasury was unable to negotiate a loan in Europe, and the agent reported that the bankers did not now dare to offer American bonds to their clients. Partly it was because the bankers hoped to force the government into assuming the state debts, but also "partly, perhaps, from real doubts of the solidity of our institutions, and, partly, probably, with a view to make us all feel discredit . . . sensibly". In vain did one writer protest that such discredit was not deserved. The Federal government had virtually no debt; two thirds of the states were paying theirs, but Europe persisted in misunderstanding us, even in such a matter as the recent failure of the Bank of the United States. Europe now believed it was a national establishment, only because they "wish it to be believed so . . .".

With its roots back in 1837, a broad movement for the revision of state constitutions was traced by a contemporary chronicler to "one single cause—the improvidence of the Legislature in contracting debts on behalf of the State". In New York, although far from being the worst offender, the spirit of reform grew "after the State had been threatened with bankruptcy". Other forces contributed to it, of course, and by 1847 states as far apart as New York and Louisiana, Iowa and New Jersey, Texas and Missouri had framed new constitutions. It was predicted that before long this cycle of constitutional revision would have reached one third of the states. With many variations in detail, the new constitutions agreed particularly in curbing the economic powers of the legislature. In general, it might not lend its credit to or acquire stock in any private enterprise, nor could the legislature incur a new debt beyond a certain amount, often set as low as fifty thousand dollars, without the people's sanction and without ample provision for its repayment. In addition, stringent rules were imposed upon the legislature in the incorporation of banks and other enterprises. Where not forbidden entirely, banks were to bear full, unlimited liability; in New York, however, only double liability. New York also abolished all feudal tenures. The most advanced of these new constitutions, in Louisiana, received the tribute that "up to this day, it is doubtless the wisest political Constitution in force over any nation or people in the world".

The private citizen, as well as the state, needed protection against past abuse and present hardship. If the banks were permitted to suspend specie payments, some form of stay for the ordinary debtor would be only a just equivalent. Besides authorizing a five million dollar loan for the benefit of debtors, Alabama provided for the deferred repayment of bank debts. Illinois had a similar stay law, while Virginia required the creditor to accept current bank notes, or wait. In a number of states the collection of debts was linked up with the principle of appraisal. In Ohio, Indiana, Michigan, Mississippi, and Illinois property could not be sold at a forced sale, unless it brought a minimum price, usually two thirds of the appraised value. When the Supreme Court declared the Illinois appraisal law unconstitutional, in 1843, a local meeting recommended that the verdict should be resisted. The debtor's right to the exemption of a portion of his property from a forced sale was also reinforced and extended in many states. Under a law of 1842, New York allowed the householder and mechanic to retain furniture and tools worth one hundred and fifty dollars. Michigan protected the lumberman's oxen, the farmer's implements, and the housewife's furniture against seizure for debt. Mississippi exempted as much as one hundred and sixty acres, together with the necessary livestock and provisions.

Imprisonment for debt was a grievance of long standing, but the movement for its abolition received a fresh impetus after 1837. Between 1837 and 1842, Ohio, Vermont, Indiana, New Hampshire, Louisiana, Connecticut, and Mississippi left fraud as the only legal ground for imprisoning the debtor. An act of 1840 placed the non-resident debtor on the same basis as the resident of New York in respect to imprisonment. In 1839 Congress instructed the Federal courts to conform to the law of the state in which suit was made as regards the imprisonment of debtors. There was even a proposal that a constitutional amendment take the remnant of that barbarous power away from the states altogether. As in 1819, during an earlier depression, so now there was a new effort to bring the whole process of bankruptcy under a Federal law. It was urged that the eagle of prosperity, having soared, "has since fallen, with broken pinions, to the earth". Many had failed, through no fault of theirs. Only men with hearts of stone, who want their pound of flesh, oppose this reform, as they have also opposed the abolition of imprisonment for debt. "Such men were born an age too late."

First offered as an emergency measure by the Van Buren administration, the Federal bankruptcy bill was held up until 1841. It was then revived under Whig auspices and passed, but was repealed in the following year. It lasted long enough, however, to afford a large measure of relief; according to one estimate, twenty-eight thousand debtors freed themselves from nearly a half billion dollars of debt at an average cost of little more than ten per cent in assets surrendered.

Still another question affecting debtors, theoretically if not practically,

aroused considerable controversy at this time. The New York legislature
rejected a proposal to repeal the existing usury laws and, in fact, adopted
a more stringent act in 1837. In the discussion which accompanied it,
credit was given primarily to a timely pamphlet by John Whipple, who
refuted Jeremy Bentham's *Defence of Usury*. Whipple's essay became
the classic American defense of the usury laws, and was reprinted during
later periods of depression. Whipple warned that free trade in money
would lead to extortion, and "if we do not in twenty years produce a
revolution against property, then there is nothing in history and experience". In 1840 the attack on the usury laws spread to Massachusetts
and Pennsylvania, where it was argued that free trade in money was most
needed in hard times in order to ease credit; otherwise the industrious
person was driven to the usurer. Unfortunately, however, the

[American community had] a strange and mawkish sensibility for every rogue
who comes under the lash of the law . . . and for every debtor who is pressed
for the performance of his promises. The ingenuity of the present time is
exerted to prevent murderers and robbers from being made too uncomfortable
in their confinement; and to encourage debtors in a total and reckless disregard
of their . . . engagements. . . .

Not only genuine group needs but political partisanship as well waxed
strong in this period of depression and exploited it in the strategy of campaigning. Already in 1838, a Whig journal, in reviewing the course of
events since Jackson had announced he was leaving the people "prosperous
and happy", reported gleefully the turn in both the economic and political
tide. Elections were everywhere going against Van Buren. Only a complete change in the government could bring real relief, and with this sentiment the ground was prepared for the colorful and unprecedented campaign of 1840. In the Whig victory of this year, a contemporary writer
believed that the most effective cause "has undoubtedly been the depressed
prices of agricultural produce and labour". The promise of returning
prosperity was heralded in the magic slogan of an election transparency:

> Little Van's policy, fifty cents a day and French soup;
> Harrison's policy, two dollars a day and roast beef.

Hope was also held out to those who still had "masses of property bought
at speculative prices . . . through the process of a re-inflation of the bubble
. . .". The administration, on the other hand, had spoken out "in accents
of severity and rebuke . . . that they must resign themselves to their past
losses. . . . Who can be surprised at the result?" When prosperity did
not come promptly, at the mere bidding of the Whigs, they were exposed
in their turn to the taunt that the promised "better times" were actually
"bitter times". Instead of roast beef and two-dollar wages, it was now only

"ten cents a day and bean soup". A Democratic reaction was reported to have set in.

In the campaign of 1840 the Whigs were charged with spending "fabulous" sums, supplied by the banks, and used in ways "such as history blushes to record". One of these uses was undoubtedly a deliberate effort to woo the laborer and mechanic with such pamphlets as "Facts for the Laboring Man. By a Laboring Man". It became the fashion to play the democrat, and even Webster, addressing merchants in Wall Street, was indignant that anyone should have called him an aristocrat. At Saratoga he boasted of the ancestral log cabin in New Hampshire and demanded the American standard for the laborer. With some inconsistency, therefore, the same Whig pamphleteer who courted the laborer and debtor in his *Crisis of the Country*, also dragged the red herring of Jacobinism across the political trail in his *Sequel to the Crisis*. Already in 1838 Greeley had issued a warning against the recent increase of converts to "ultra radicalism", and he himself was soon to be won over to Albert Brisbane's version of Fourierism and social reform. In 1840, however, it was charged that not only had the administration nearly broken "the spirits of the most elastic and buoyant people on earth . . . but civilization itself . . . is to be broken down, and Christianity rooted from the land!"

The provocation to this indictment came from an article in a current periodical which contained one of the earliest and most trenchant statements of the doctrine of class conflict ever made in this country. Its author, Brownson, whose tortuous career was to run from radicalism to reaction, later defended himself that, "born and reared in the class of proletaries", he had only said what he knew and felt, and would stand by it, "at least, until the laboring classes . . . rise up and accuse us of misrepresenting them". His purpose had been to explode certain American myths. One was that in America every man may become rich, but nobody has grown rich by his own labor. Somewhat prematurely, Brownson announced that "the wilderness has receded, and already the new lands are beyond the reach of the mere laborer, and the employer has him at his mercy". Precisely at this time George Evans was beginning his agrarian agitation for free land, which was to culminate in the Homestead Act. Brownson also insisted that to the worker bread was more important than Channing's program of education and moral elevation. "It is no pleasant thing to go seeking work and finding none . . .". Priests and pedagogues have had their chance and can do nothing. "They merely cry peace, peace, and that too when there is no peace, and can be none." The master too is "in these times . . . shedding crocodile tears over the deplorable condition of the poor laborer, while he docks his wages twenty-five per cent . . .". And so, finally, "You must abolish the system or accept its consequences".

[But it will not be done] without war and bloodshed. We or our children will have to meet this crisis. The old war between the King and the Barons is well nigh ended, and so is that between the Barons and the Manufacturers . . . and now commences the new struggle between the operative and the employer, between wealth and labor. What or when the end will be only God knows.

In a second article Brownson enlarged upon the idea of change by violence. While he hoped his prophecy might prove to be false, he, nevertheless, believed that

If a general war should now break out, it will involve all quarters of the globe, and it will be in the end more than a war between nations. It will resolve itself into a social war, a war between . . . the people and their masters. It will be a terrible war! Already does it lower on the horizon. . . . Stay it, ye who can.

While less extreme, the Workingmen of Charlestown, Massachusetts, were addressing similar warnings "to their Brethren throughout the Union". Their distress was due to the paradox of an overproduction which forced their wages down. There was nothing to hope for from the politicians or the reformers. "Our salvation must . . . come from ourselves." The workers must organize and become a power in the state. In this respect also Brownson offered the workers practical political advice. The election of 1840 had been a victory for property; the party of 'Man' could not prevail over property unless it took advantage of the division in the opposite camp. He, therefore, urged a political union of labor with the Slave South, on the basis of a strict constitutionalism. Now, more than ever, was the time to rally to the ultimate goal of abolishing the "proletaries" and establishing equality. Brownson censured "the laissez-faire doctrine, so much in vogue . . .". But the state, rather than the Federal government, must be relied upon to "maintain between all the members of society that equality . . . which does not exist among men by nature".

The decade of the 1840's passed beyond such doctrines and eventually plunged into Utopian thought and experimentation. These included among others, agrarianism and Fourierism, as well as an elaborate, if embryonic, proposal for a kind of social planning, on a national scale, which the author, Clinton Roosevelt, presented as *The Science of Government*. All these belong, of course, to another and a different theme, and yet cannot wholly be separated from the background of preceding depression. The latter had begun in 1837 when the pressure of an inflated prosperity proved too great, and certain strains and stresses developed in the American economic and social structure. The immediate and acute emergency created the need for repair work, which was supplied by a mass of relief legislation. But depression was also reflected in the thought and action of both classes and masses. It produced a harvest of ideas which seem not so much immature as premature, at least when a more normal state of social well-being was restored. They perhaps brought a forewarning of America's later ripening and aging. Certainly there was more romance than reality in the reminiscence of one who harked back to this very period as one "of innocence and integrity . . . and equality . . . when there were no millionaires and no Standard Oil or other combines. . . . When the rich helped the poor, and the poor helped the great."

30 *Charles S. Sydnor*

THE SOUTHERNER AND THE LAWS

Historians have long been concerned with knowing about the Old South, the South, that is, of the ante-bellum decades. What kind of society was it? Was it a nation, as some historians have called it, and if so, what was its nationalism? Was it a region, as others have called it, and if so what was its regionalism? What were the purposes that moved it in its course and what were the institutions that gave expression to its purposes? To what extent were its purposes and institutions similar to those of the North and to what extent were they different? And, by knowing these similarities and differences, how far have we come toward explaining the ultimate rift between the sections?

In trying to arrive at the essence of an earlier society, the historian proceeds by a variety of institutional routes. Among these, law and the attitude toward law are certainly of great importance. One thinks immediately of the studies in the sociology of law by such masters as the English historian Frederic William Maitland, the German sociologist Max Weber, and the American jurist Roscoe Pound. Regrettably, there have been far too few such studies in American history and, as yet, no comprehensive work on the whole period. The following essay by Charles Sackett Sydnor is therefore a most welcome contribution to this field of study.

At the time of his death in 1954, Sydnor was dean of the Graduate School of Duke University and chairman of the University's Department of History. He had taught summer sessions at several universities, including the Salzburg Seminar of American History, and in 1950–51 had been Harmsworth Professor of American History at Oxford University. He was the author of several distinguished books, including *The Development of Southern Sectionalism, 1819–1848,* one of the most notable contributions to *The History of the South* series.

In the following essay, Sydnor comes to the Southern case neither to accuse nor to defend. He comes, as every historian must, to under-

Reprinted with the permission of the managing editor from *The Journal of Southern History,* VI (February, 1940), 3–23.

stand. He uses the Southerner's attitude toward the laws as a window for gaining a wider vista upon Southern society. The various bodies of law that he considers include the federal law, especially the Constitution of the United States, divine law, the laws of the states, and the unwritten code of laws. Sydnor discloses how sharp a contrast there was between the South and the North in their views of the law, so sharp indeed that the dialogue between them about their mutual problems must have proceeded in terms that were mutually unintelligible. If law is the language of order, if it articulates the process by which society operates, if it is the means by which social ends are achieved, then, one may conclude from having read Sydnor, North and South were talking different languages, articulating different processes, pursuing different ends by different means.

In seeing law and the attitude toward law as "a natural outgrowth and reflection of the social order of the region," Sydnor is of course opening up to us the wider expanse of history. From his thoughts about the Old South we may proceed to thoughts about the integration of social forces and values characterizing other areas and other ages. From what he says, moreover, we may proceed to wonder whether the dialogue between the West and the East, between the liberal and the communist worlds, is not being conducted in terms of mutual unintelligibility. If so, the time may be growing short for redefining terms. It were best spent in understanding and reconciling the different purposes that our respective regions are, without any great understanding or reconciliation, intent on pursuing.

The student of southern history constantly faces the fact that the South is not a political entity with boundaries clearly marked by treaty, constitution, or law. From this circumstance flow two consequences: historians disagree about the metes and bounds of the South, and, what is of more importance, they are compelled to seek unifying principles of southern history in social, economic, and cultural fields rather than in governmental history. Therefore, historians have concerned themselves chiefly with unique southern characteristics and, to some extent, with the causes of these characteristics. Some of them believe that the distinctiveness of southern society can be traced to an inherited cultural pattern such as that of the English gentry. Others emphasize environment: high temperature, heavy rainfall, coast line, river systems, forests, and soil types. Yet others find the common denominator of the South in such characteristics as slavery, malaria, hookworm, staple crops, lynching, tenancy, state rights advocacy, and mockingbirds. It is even true that some students believe that the unifying principle of the South is the prevalence of some intangible quality: its state of mind, way of life, attitude, loyalty, or viewpoint. Into this twilight realm this essay ventures, for this is an attempt to set forth the Southerner's attitude toward law, using that word in a broad sense to include several of the imperatives that control man and society.

But before going into this subject, one word of explanation and another of warning are in order. The explanation is that the Southerner's attitude toward law is not being offered as the outstanding unifying principle of southern history; for it was but a secondary characteristic, a natural outgrowth and reflection of the social order of the region. The warning is that from the very nature of the subject this paper must deal with probabilities and trends rather than with absolute certainties. From some examples and a few indications the attempt will be made to arrive at the prevailing opinion of the dominant element in the Old South toward certain bodies of law. Opinion was not as unanimous as this paper may indicate because in brief space due consideration cannot be given to dissenting voices.

The Southerner was aware of the authority of Federal law, especially the Constitution of the United States; of divine law as it is stated in the Bible; of those laws, most of which are made by the states, that regulate the dealings of man with man; and of the unwritten laws of society. His attitude toward each of these will be appraised, after which some comments will be ventured about the relationships between these attitudes.

The fact that the Southerner chose to make comparatively few changes in the Constitution of the United States before adopting it as the Constitution of the Confederate States of America indicates his high regard for the older of these documents. Implicit in this decision and very clearly stated by many southern spokesmen is this distinction: the South liked the Constitution but it disliked the North's misuse and disregard of it. While it is true that the South was chiefly zealous for the defensive values of the Constitution, just as other sections have been when they have suffered from hostile legislation, the fact remains that for thirty years or so before 1861—years when the South was declining in its share of national population and wealth—it found that the Constitution was a very valuable asset. Naturally, its emphasis was upon state rights and those parts of the Constitution that recognized the existence of slavery. During these same years the North sometimes found that the Constitution stood in its way as it tried to gain political power proportional to its growing population. Therefore, some Northerners began to state that the Constitution was not the highest authority in American government; above it they placed other imperatives which were variously designated as the higher law, the laws of nature, the laws of God, the moral law, the spirit of the age, and the law of majority rule. Other and less radical Northerners did not go so far as to deny the supremacy of the Constitution, but they nevertheless insisted that it had changed with changing times and that its words could no longer be taken in their original and literal meaning.

Not unnaturally, the South affirmed that the Constitution continued to be the supreme law of the land and that its words had not changed their meaning. Through repeated insistence upon the Constitution's supremacy in its original, literal meaning the South came to regard itself as the special custodian and defender of this great legal document; its attitude toward the Constitution was one of great respect.

In regard to the law of God, the South felt equally as well pleased with the orthodoxy of its own views. The barest outline of its reasoning was as follows: The Bible is the supreme revelation of God's law for man's guidance, and its validity is unchanged through the centuries; in the Bible are many passages recognizing the existence of slavery; therefore, slavery is sanctioned by the law of God. To such reasoning, antislavery theologians answered not with chapter and verse but with appeals to the broad teachings of Scripture: brotherly love, the Golden Rule, the equality of all men before God; and with nonbiblical ethical and social arguments. The South retorted that it was unorthodox to set up standards of conduct, no matter how plausible, contrary to the literal words of the Bible; it denied the propriety of the church committing itself to any program of social reform; and it added that northern reasoning about slavery was but part and parcel of northern religious anarchy evidenced by the rise of new cults, and the trend toward liberal theology, higher criticism, skepticism, and atheism.

From the one Book defenders and opponents of slavery reached opposite conclusions, partly by antagonistic criteria of selection and partly by dissimilar principles of exegesis. The North usually appealed to the teachings of the New Testament, the South to verses of the Old. The North used what might be described as a liberal, modernistic interpretation; the South denied the existence of any authority in religious matters other than the Bible, and it insisted on word for word literalism. Although a very small part of the Bible was marshaled in the slavery controversy, the vehemence and volume of the dispute were so great that there seemed to be sectional differences in interpretating the entire Book. The South became convinced that it was adhering to the strict letter of religious law. Its attitude toward the Bible was like its attitude toward the Constitution; it claimed to respect the form of the law in both cases, and it charged the North with disregard for Christian as well as constitutional law.

The apologists of the Old South seem to have exhausted their legal energies interpreting and defending the Constitution and the Bible, for they wrote very little about the Southerner's attitude toward the body of common and statutory law that regulates man's daily relations with man. Because of this lack of a body of expressed opinion, other indices must be sought. An important indication of attitude is, of course, action; and, according to a number of witnesses, the Southerner's life was made exciting by a high proportion of street fights, duels, harsh treatment of slaves, quickness to resent insults, and the common practice of carrying pistols and other weapons. But it is unwise to accept all this evidence as unqualified proof of southern lawlessness. Some Southerners have been known to give free reign to imagination when entertaining gullible strangers, and antisouthern abolitionists have shown equal and less innocent inventiveness in circulating atrocity stories concerning the land of slavery. Because of these streams of misinformation it is difficult to tell whether the Southerner acted more or less lawlessly than other Americans.

Waiving any attempt to determine the Southerner's attitude toward state law by the quantity of his illegal acts, there yet remain certain forces that must be reckoned with. In the first place, the South doubtless inherited its share of the frontier trait of personal law enforcement, which is sometimes called lawlessness. Some parts of it had been settled less than a generation when the Civil War began, while older settlements in pine barrens and mountain coves were in a sense retarded frontiers, relatively out of reach of sheriff and court. But in this respect the South was not unique. The frontier is supposed to have a lawless effect on all American society, and, generally speaking, the South at any given time was neither nearer to nor farther from the frontier than other parts of the United States. It is therefore difficult to suppose that the South had inherited more than its share of frontier lawlessness.

But what of those parts of the South where the frontier influence had faded into the relatively distant past, areas such as the Carolina low country, tidewater Virginia, the Kentucky bluegrass, and the lower Mississippi Valley, where age and conservatism and the accumulation of economic wealth and of political influence had created the way of life that has been accepted as most typical of the Old South? Were the legal attitudes of these plantation regions different from those of the commercial, industrial, and urban areas that symbolized northern progress? I think the answer must be affirmative because ruralness, slavery, the plantation system, and the existence of a strong unwritten code operated in the plantation areas of the Old South to restrict the power of ordinary law and to enlarge the area of life in which man acts without reference to legal guidance. This is to say that the segment of life that was controlled by law was reduced in these dominant regions of the Old South; it is not equivalent to saying that law, within its restricted zone, was held in disrespect. Nevertheless, one can readily understand how a citizen of another civilization could fall into the error of thinking that law was held in disrespect because its jurisdiction was not as large as he was accustomed to in his own community.

But before generalizing it will be well to consider the influence of these forces on law and legal attitudes.

Ruralness was not considered the equivalent of backwardness by the Southerner, who might have summed up his ideal of social progress in the phrase "from frontier to plantation." In the realm of ideas as well as in actuality, the acme of southern civilization was rural. It is generally accepted that the countryman is something of an individualist who shapes his actions according to local custom and his own notions of how he should behave rather than according to the dictates of law books. Like the frontiersman, he is physically remote from law-enforcing agencies. If it be true that ruralness lightens the weight of law, the South was subjected to this influence not only because of the high per cent of its agricultural population but also because of the prominence of countrymen in economic, social, and political life. Furthermore, the planters probably had less contact with commercial law than did the business men of the cities. The reading of extant plantation records and communications between planters and factors makes one wonder whether any other business of equal size has been run with as few precise records and as little commercial and legal paper as was the southern plantation.

Slavery also affected legal customs and attitudes. Although attention is being directed in this paper to those years shortly before the Civil War, when the southern mind had long felt the influence of distinctive southern institutions, it is significant that the influence of slavery upon those who owned slaves was recognized very early. It was the opinion of eighteenth century observers that the introduction of slavery had made Virginians "haughty and jealous of their liberties, and so impatient of restraint that they could hardly bear the thought of being controlled by any superior power." George Mason, one of the wisest sons of Old Virginia, declared in the Federal Constitutional Convention that "every master of slaves is born a petty tyrant." According to Thomas Nelson Page, the Virginia gentleman was imbued with "a certain pride based on self-respect and consciousness of power." Horace S. Fulkerson, who was thoroughly familiar with life in the lower Mississippi Valley, stated that the planters of that region were "arbitrary, self-willed, and dictatorial," and that even from their equals "they could illy brook contradictions and opposition." And Alexis de Tocqueville concluded that slavery "has modified the character and changed the habits of the natives of the South. . . . The citizen of the Southern States of the Union is invested with a sort of domestic dictatorship, from his earliest years; the first notion he acquires in life is that he is born to command."

Slavery must have affected the planter's attitude toward law, for in a measure slavery put him above the law. On his own estate he was law-giver, executive, and judge. In respect to the economic and social life of his slaves—work, food, clothing, housing, marriage, divorce, and religion—his word was final. He possessed the power normally exercised by the state in many kinds of cases, such as slander, assault and battery, larceny, and burglary. Law books gave him no guidance in settling important questions. But this silence of the law does not seem to have disturbed him, for even when it spoke clearly the slaveholder sometimes paid no heed. For example, if a slave stabbed a Negro belonging to another master, the neighboring planters might settle the difficulty without going to any court. This illustrates the fact that the slaveowner, while exercising the great power granted to him by the state, sometimes took yet more power. Occasionally the state even gave its blessing to such encroachments upon the state law. The South Carolina Court of Appeals once remarked, " 'A judicious freedom in the administration of our police laws for the lower order must always have respect for the confidence which the law reposes in the discretion of the master.' " A disapproving Southerner summed up the whole process by saying that slavery was " 'degrading the law by putting the authority of the master above it.' " This was correct, for southern states left the slaveowner free to exercise some of the powers that usually belong to the state, and even where there was law the planter sometimes either paid it scant attention or interpreted it with marked liberality.

The fact that Negroes could not bear witness against white men excluded a large number of cases from the courts of the South; in such instances reparation had to be sought, if sought at all, beyond the pale of law. As the critics of slavery pointed out, this rule compelled Negroes to suffer illegal treatment in silence. Less often recalled is the fact that white men, both individually and as a social order, suffered unredressed injuries because of this prohibition. For example, a tobacco planter might have a part of his crop stolen by the white boatman to whom it had been entrusted for transportation from Lynchburg to Richmond, and the boatman's Negro assistants might tell all that had happened; yet, the planter knew that it would be useless to enter suit because the Negroes could not testify in court against the white thief. Similarly, when a Mississippi slave was dangerously wounded by a white man, his master could not get legal redress either for his slave's physical suffering or for his own economic loss unless he could secure some evidence other than the word of the wounded Negro. If Negroes and white men joined in an insurrectionary plot, as they did in Louisiana in 1840, and if the conspirators were discovered and frightened into testifying against each other, the courts could sentence the slaves to death. In fact, at least three were executed. But because Negro testimony could not be admitted by the court, the white conspirators could not be convicted.

These are three instances of the kinds of injuries that white men and white society could not redress through court action because the available testimony was not admitted to the courtroom. When it is remembered that one third of the South's population was thus incompetent, one may well suppose that a multitude of similar injuries created a constant urge toward the discovery of some means, which had to be extralegal, for securing substantial justice. Thus, the exclusion of Negro testimony, the rural pattern of life, the great authority of the planter, and, as will be noted presently, certain characteristics of the southern social order, and its code, all united to restrict the segment of life ruled by state law, thereby creating within the South, even in the oldest and most cultivated parts of it, an attitude toward law that was much like that of the frontiersman. Geographical distance kept the full force of the law from touching the Westerner; the social order diminished the force of law in the South. But the resulting attitudes toward law were too similar for easy distinction. For instance, was Andrew Jackson's mother speaking from a western or a southern pattern of thought when she gave her son the following advice: " 'Never tell a lie, nor take what is not your own, nor sue anybody for slander or assault and battery. *Always settle them cases yourself!*' "

How did the Southerner's attitude toward the laws of his state compare with his insistence upon a literal, close observance of the Constitution and the Bible? While he did not profess disrespect for state law, neither did he praise it. The planter simply went through life under the assumption that a relatively large number of his deeds had to be performed out past the margin of written law in what might be called a state of nature. To northern eyes this condition looked like an approach to anarchy and chaos; but planters thought their actions were no more lawless than the operations of a court of equity. Although it might be debated whether the Southerner's life was much better or worse than contemporary life in the most litigious parts of New England, it is more profitable at the moment to remark that the extralegal, though usually not illegal, areas of life in the South convinced many onlookers that here was a land where law was frequently broken and commonly held in contempt. It is not surprising that these observers were puzzled by the contrast between the Southerner's reverence for the Constitution and the Bible and his apparent disdain for some of the laws of his state.

In those relatively large expanses of life that were not ruled by the written law the Southerner did not live in a legal vacuum. Instead he found guidance, particularly in the field of personal relationships, in a fourth kind of law: his unwritten code. Some of the sources of this body of compulsive rules were ideas of social organization imported into Virginia and the Carolinas by colonists who were familiar with the pattern of life of the English gentry of the seventeenth and eighteenth centuries; contacts with the military punctilio of French and British army officers, especially at the time of the American Revolution; the remembrance of chivalric ballads; the reading of romantic novels such as those of Sir Walter Scott; and the tradition, which evolved in later years, that southern planters were descended from the aristocracy of Europe and should therefore live in the manner of their legendary ancestors. In addition to these European heritages and influences, the social customs and mores of the Old South were affected by vestiges of the frontier practice of personal law enforcement and by certain characteristics of the planters. They were a dominant class, they were accustomed to the exercise of great authority, and some of them had the means to live like aristocrats. In parts of the Old South, more than anywhere else in the United States, countrymen had the wealth requisite for living on a high level of civilization.

A thorough understanding of the code of the Old South is difficult for several reasons. It has been much romanticized, especially by postbellum writers of fiction and memoirs, it varied somewhat from place to place, its tenets were not the same for all classes of society, it suffered infractions like other laws, and it was too complex to be learned except by a lifetime of living under its sway. It is possible that those who knew it best did not explain it because they thought it would survive longer if the uninitiated were left in their ignorance. When Thomas Nelson Page wrote: "To be a Virginia gentleman was the first duty; it embraced being a Christian and all the other virtues," he was suggesting the existence of knowledge rather than revealing it. An old family retainer once condemned a recently employed tutor with the remark: "Lord, what sort of a man is this master is got to teach his children! He don't even know how to get on a horse!" Now, although riding a horse was not in itself supremely important, it was an outward symbol of a way of life. The old Negro's remark was but a way of saying that this tutor was ignorant of other things that were exceedingly important. As one of the pupils later remarked more directly but no more informatively about this pedestrian teacher, he was "very ignorant of a thousand things we thought a gentleman ought to know."

While each of the social groups in the Old South had customs and rules of conduct, the code became more complex and emphatic among the planters and their associates. Here was a relatively small group of men maintaining a superior position out of all proportion to their numerical power. They were not only claiming and holding a place of economic, social, and racial superiority above the millions of Negro slaves, but economic and to some extent social superiority above the poor whites, small farmers, artisans, and schoolteachers. Furthermore, they were exercising in national councils greater power than the population of the South warranted.

Each of these superior positions was held in the face of a constant threat by the subordinate forces. The planter class could have been destroyed by revolt of the slaves, by votes of the nonslaveholding Southerners, or by the North. Nor were the planters blind to these dangers. The potential hostility held them together and required each member to defend the group and to conceal dissensions within it from envious and critical eyes. Self-interest as well as *noblesse oblige* required the planter to live in accordance with certain unwritten rules.

Although it is impossible to state the code of the Old South with either fullness or precision, and although the code was imperfectly obeyed, perhaps some of its rules should be set forth because, being the ideals of a society, they indicate something of the nature of that society. Among the things that a gentleman of the Old South was expected to be, to understand, and to perform were these. He must uphold the southern way of life by close observance of a complex body of rules of social and racial relationships. For example, even when performing acts of kindness to subordinates, familiarity must be shunned. Toward an equal a gentleman should be courteous. He professed no knowledge of how to behave toward superiors, for he denied the existence of any with the exception of the ladies. To these he must show perfect courtesy and always defer to their opinions. The gentleman's deference, however, was protected from too great strain because the ladies were expected to avoid expressing opinions on all subjects, such as politics, that lay in the realm of masculine jurisdiction.

Believing the southern life was well-nigh perfect, a southern gentleman was under no compulsion to change things. From this it followed that he had no public duty other than to keep society going in its accustomed way. Lacking the New Englander's zeal for improvement and reform, he could enjoy rest with a clear conscience. Thus it is that the Southerner was the only American of his and possibly any generation to whom leisure was not a sin. He was interested in being rather than in becoming. He thought it was more important in the business world for a man to maintain poise than to sacrifice dignity for wealth. Increasing mortgages and other evidences of economic failure were no disgrace even when brought about by gross inattention to business. According to his code it was bad form to intrude business matters into social life as by boasting of hard work in pursuit of wealth or by discussing money and prices except of such quasipublic commodities as cotton, tobacco, and slaves. When his leisureliness and contentment with things-as-they-were were characterized as laziness, he countered by scorning the aimless bustle and hurry of urban life. There was satire rather than kindly humor in his remark that New Englanders could not wear frock coats because they whisked around corners so fast the tails were snapped off.

The southern gentleman was expected to be truthful, an obligation that was not difficult of fulfillment by one who denied being accountable to superiors. The code required him to be brave, and skilled in managing horses and handling firearms. He must be willing to risk life itself in defense of his own good name or that of a member of his family. As long as the Old South lived, duels were fought despite criticism by prominent Southerners, abuse of the institution by adventurers, and a decline in dueling elsewhere in the United States.

The nondemocratic form of southern society was partly responsible for the survival of the duel, which is a phenomenon of aristocratic rather than democratic societies. Men may fight on the frontiers of Texas or California before law has arrived in full force. But these combats in the democratic society of the frontier are usually not conducted according to the code duello. In contrast, the duel is usually found in the upper classes of a complex society; it is found not in the broad base of the social pyramid but in the small apex—landed gentry, feudal barons, army officers—that towers above the cloud of laws that blanket and hold in place the lower orders. Therefore, gentlemen would challenge only gentlemen. To punish an insulting inferior, one used not a pistol or sword but a cane or a horsewhip.

In the practice of the duel certain cardinal ideas were implicit. First, a man's good name was more important than physical well-being, which is to say that in the South it was considered as brutal and uncivilized to call a man a liar as it was to bruise or cut his body. Secondly, questions of personal honor and integrity could not be decided by the judicial processes of democratic government; hence, slander, libel, and some other indignities could be better adjudicated with pistols in a quiet grove in the presence of only a few gentlemen than in the courtroom before a jury of small farmers, clerks, and mechanics. Furthermore, since the duel was restricted to gentlemen, a challenge carried along with its danger a certain recognition of social superiority and responsibility.

The fighting of duels and the imposition of other penalties sanctioned by the code was indeed looked upon as something of a social responsibility. A man fought because society demanded that certain issues be so adjudicated; and if one refused to obey this social demand, society would apply such complete ostracism that the offender would "never again be permitted to join gentlemen even in a fox hunt. He's utterly out of it." Doubtless many a man decided that he must fight because he was conscious of this social pressure. The upper crust of society demanded the duel because it dared not submit all of its controversies to the adjudication of a democracy.

This characteristic of the Old South, namely, that a man was conscious of belonging to and being a part of a thing larger than himself, has impressed such novelists as John Esten Cooke, Thomas Nelson Page, George Cary Eggleston, Joseph Hergesheimer, Stark Young, and Ellen

Glasgow more than it has historians. It is natural that novelists should be sensitive to the organic nature of southern society because, as Henry Seidel Canby has written in an essay about Miss Glasgow: "The great subject for the novel since its beginning in the eighteenth century has been manners, and when the novels have been also great these manners have been no superficies of behavior, but a code, a habitual philosophy of living according to which men and women proceed."

This sense of belonging to a definitely ordered society may have been the reason why Southerners were the first Americans to make much use of the word "sociology." But most of the citizens of the Old South instead of speculating about the nature of their society found their places within it and lived in harmony with its conventions. Naturally, those who enjoyed the favored places in society were most opposed to change. Their supreme patriotism was to their social order. Their highest law was the body of customs and rules that maintained this way of life. This was their code; this was the unwritten constitution of the Old South.

Most of the actions required of the Southerner by his code were the host of undistinguished and innocuous deeds that make up the fabric of everyday life. But now and again the code required a man to requite a personal insult either by a duel or by some less ceremonious form of violence. This tendency to defend personal honor extralegally, and indeed illegally, seems to have been more prevalent in the South than in the North; it does not necessarily follow that Northerners were more prone to take such questions into court. Although Northerners declared that dueling was proof of southern lawlessness, Southerners who approved this custom reasoned otherwise. Their statement of the case might be reconstructed as follows: in case of insult the code of honor required action; the state code enjoined submission. Here was a conflict of law. Therefore, the individual had to decide which body of law applied to the case, and if he decided in favor of the code of honor he was simply transferring the case from state jurisdiction to the jurisdiction of the unwritten code.

What then is the meaning of the Southerner's legal attitudes? In the first place, they were reflections of important aspects of southern history. They might be described as rationalizations in legal terms of fundamental southern interests both national and local. The Southerner's attitude toward the Constitution and the Bible was produced by his conflict with the North over slavery and kindred issues. His attitudes toward the written laws of the state and the unwritten code evolved out of southern domestic history. For instance, the occasional conflict between these two imperatives over questions of honor may be viewed as a product of the struggle of an aristocratic social order to maintain its position and power against the enlarging power of the democracy; a conflict of laws arose where the customs of the few clashed with the laws of the many.

In the second place, the Southerner's set of legal attitudes distinguished him to some extent from other Americans. The Northerner, for example, living in a different social system and possessing dissimilar economic goals from those of the South, arranged the imperatives in a totally different order. To him a literal interpretation of the biblical sanctions of slavery and of the constitutional sanctions of slavery and of state rights were undesirable; to him the meaning and the potency of the code were incomprehensible; but, on the other hand, he emphasized the sanctity of ordinary law because of its importance in the equalitarian democracy of the North.

In the third place, the Southerner did not defend all forms of law with equal vigor nor did he place them all on the same level of importance. Neither did the Northerner. But here the similarity ends; for in deciding which bodies of law deserved literal interpretation and strict application and which ought to be loosely interpreted and imperfectly enforced, North and South were in complete disagreement. Because men of both sections praised certain laws, all could consider themselves as law-abiding and therefore good men; but because they disagreed over the laws that ought to be given most respect, each thought that the other was peopled with lawless and therefore bad men. To the Northerner the Southerner seemed to be dishonest, and the reverse was also true, because each was boasting of his respect for some laws while he was actually showing disrespect for other laws. Naturally, then, each concluded that it was futile to continue negotiations with a people who refused to respect legal obligations. By such means sectional differences in legal attitudes became something more than passive reflections of basic divergencies; these attitudes became active in increasing the antagonism between the sections.

Examples of sectional differences in legal attitudes can be seen in a number of critical points in American history. For instance, when John C. Calhoun framed his powerful proslavery resolutions for presentation in the Senate in 1837 he was conscious of the fact that slavery could be and indeed was being judged by reference to several different authorities such as divine law, the moral law, and the Constitution. In his resolutions he therefore insisted that congressional legislation respecting slavery in the territories and in the District of Columbia should be framed with reference solely to the Constitution and that considerations of its alleged sinfulness or immorality should be excluded. The implications of this pronouncement could be discussed at much length, but such a discussion would be a digression from the point that is here of most significance. Calhoun was saying, in effect, that Federal legislation must be framed with reference to no more than one ultimate authority which was neither moral law nor divine law but the Constitution of the United States.

One other illustration must suffice, and it will consist in a hurried review of the Brooks-Sumner affair. The first part of this sensational episode was a speech delivered in the Senate on May 19–20, 1856, by Charles Sumner, senator from Massachusetts, denouncing slaveowners in general and South Carolinians in particular. It was a studiously learned speech, replete with classical and historical allusions; at the same time it abounded in such coarse and opprobrious terms as harlot, mistress, rape, pirate, tyrant, falsifier, assassin, thug, swindler, and criminal. Much of the abuse was directed personally to Andrew Pickens Butler, senior senator from South Carolina, who was absent from the Senate while Sumner was making his attack. Certain aspects of this speech are significant. Sumner grossly and without provocation insulted Butler; in so doing he acted deliberately, for he had prepared his speech carefully with the purpose of making it "the most thorough philippic ever uttered in a legislative body"; finally, he was accusing slaveholders of being lawless.

The sequel to this tirade occurred two days later. Following an early adjournment, Sumner remained in the Senate chamber writing letters when Preston S. Brooks, a congressman from South Carolina, walked up to him and said: "Mr. Sumner, I have read your speech carefully, and with as much calmness as I could be expected to read such a speech. You have libeled my State, and slandered my relation, who is aged and absent, and I feel it to be my duty to punish you for it." Thereupon, with a cane, he struck Sumner over the head, and he continued with rapid, hard blows until the cane was broken and Sumner was bloody and insensible. This action of Brooks also deserves close scrutiny. Deliberation rather than quick anger is indicated by the fact that after hearing oral reports of Sumner's speech he took time to examine the printed record, he discussed the question with his friends, and he sought, though vainly, an encounter outside the Senate chamber. During the two days that were thus consumed he seems to have felt no uncertainty as to whether he should punish Sumner, nor is there an indication that he at any time considered challenging him to a duel. He felt that he ought not to call Sumner to account in the presence of ladies, and because some were present in the Senate gallery he waited until they departed before attacking Sumner. A question to which he gave some thought was whether he should use horsewhip, cowhide, or cane, all of which were weapons of dishonor. Citizens of Massachusetts, judging from their subsequent remarks, did not understand as thoroughly as did South Carolinians the delicate shades of meaning implicit in Brooks' decisions.

Undoubtedly, the Brooks-Sumner affair was an expression of the angry passions of 1856 and a forerunner of yet more hatred in the years to come. But it was more than this, for the form in which anger is expressed often indicates much about the characteristics of the actor and about the mores of the society in which he lives. Brooks and Sumner were each viewed by their respective constituencies as worthy representatives: Sumner of the culture and learning of Massachusetts; Brooks of the chivalry of South Carolina. Following this encounter, the part that each had played was applauded by his people. The words "lawful" and "lawless" seemed to change their meaning as one crossed the boundary between North and South; for acts that the Northerner branded as lawless were approved by South Carolinians, words that the Southerner considered lawless met with no apparent disapproval in Massachusetts.

While peoples of all ages have faced the alternative of the ancient Hebrews: "Choose you this day whom ye will serve," this question presented itself on certain occasions to individual men in the Old South. At such times those who had never worn judicial robes had to decide which of the various imperatives they ought to obey, and at these moments of decision they often acted as if every man had been empowered to act as a court of last resort for determining certain types of questions. Perhaps, then, it was fitting that the Southerner should have found the issue of 1861 stated in the form of legal alternatives. The ordinances of secession placed the laws of state and of nation in such diametric opposition that no man could obey both. Facing this great conflict of laws each Southerner assumed full power of judicial review and rendered his own decision as to which law he should obey.

31 *John Hope Franklin*

SLAVERY AND THE MARTIAL SOUTH

In seeking the causes of the Civil War, historians have generally found that there was a growing cultural separation between the South and the North, and in explaining that separation, they have tended to settle upon the peculiar institution of slavery as a major determinant of Southern culture. The distinctiveness of the South, wrote Ulrich B. Phillips, an outstanding student of its history, was not the product of language, religion, geography, or agriculture. It was the product, rather, of the related premises of Negro slavery and white supremacy. Slavery was, of course, a central feature of the Southern economy. Inevitably, as the middle decades of the nineteenth century wore on, it began to define for the South a unique pattern of group relations, legal codes, social mores, and intellectual interests.

Slavery was certainly a factor in the growing militancy of the

Reprinted by special permission from *The Journal of Negro History*, XXXVII (January, 1952), 36–53.

South during this period. Such is the thesis, in the following essay, of Professor John Hope Franklin, chairman of the Department of History of Brooklyn College, author of a number of studies dealing with the ante-bellum and Reconstruction periods, and best known for his *From Slavery to Freedom* (1947, rev. 1956), a history of American Negroes. His thesis regarding the impact of slavery he has sustained more amply in a recent volume entitled *The Militant South, 1800–1861*, in which he explains why and how aggression and violence became increasingly prominent features of Southern life.

Professor Franklin's essay will lead the reader to some vital questions regarding Southern culture. How did slavery affect the whole complex of Southern institutions? To what extent was Southern militancy the product of factors other than slavery? Was Southern militancy a major cause of the Civil War? What was the extent of Northern militancy and to what factors could it be attributed?

The essay, indeed, will lead the reader to some significant questions regarding the history of any culture. Why and how does a peculiar institution, any peculiar institution, pervade and bind together a culture, giving it a distinctive tone and rationale? What, moreover, is the course followed by a society committed to such an institution? At what point does the commitment become irreversible and what are the consequences of that irreversibility? The immediate applicability of such questions is apparent. They are important for understanding what led to the coming of the Civil War, the militancy of Negro-white relations during the postwar decades, and their mutual aggressiveness even today. Such questions are no less important for analyzing the process of change in any society; the Union of South Africa is an obvious example in our own times, where the commitment to a peculiar institution seems to have gone beyond the limit of reversibility.

When Southern sectionalism emerged as a powerful force in the third decade of the nineteenth century, the aggressive belligerency of the people of the South became one of their outstanding attributes. In their relationships among themselves and with others, accusations, threats and challenges were a part of the general conduct; while duels, fights and other forms of violence became almost as common as the most ordinary pursuits of daily life. The atmosphere of the entire South seemed charged with a martial spirit; and pugnacity achieved a respectability, even among the upper classes, that doomed any moves toward gentility and mutual understanding. There were, perhaps, many factors that contributed to this martial spirit, and there were many aspects of life in the South that reflected its numerous manifestations. Among them were the conditions of frontier living, the Indian danger, the strong attachment of the people to military

organizations, and the widespread preparedness movement in the two decades preceding the Civil War. Few of them, however, had the profound
effect that slavery had both in shaping the martial tradition of the South
and in illustrating the ways that the spirit of belligerency could manifest
itself.

Slavery was not only a central feature in Southern commercial agriculture; it was also a major factor in the development of those traits of
Southern character that produced a domineering spirit and a will to fight to
defend its position. Thomas Jefferson recognized and deplored this condition as early as 1782. In his *Notes on Virginia* he observed that the whole
relationship between master and slave was a "perpetual exercise of the most
boisterous passions, the most unremitting despotism on the one part; and
degrading submissions on the other." What was even worse, Jefferson continued, the slave owner's child learns to imitate it. Seeing the parent storm,
the child "catches the lineaments of wrath, puts on the same airs in the
circle of smaller slaves, gives loose to the worst of passions, and thus
nursed, educated, and daily exercised in tyranny, cannot but be stamped
by it with odious peculiarities."

These views were not confined to the period of the Enlightenment.
Countless observers of a later day saw what Jefferson had seen, and were
of the view that slavery had a most deleterious effect on the owners and
their children. Captain Basil Hall reported in 1828 that even the slaveowners themselves lamented the "evil influence" that slavery was having
on the character of their children. It was a curious and instructive fact, he
declared, that the slaves themselves delighted in "encouraging 'young master' or even 'young mistress' to play the tyrant over them!" Tocqueville
made some significant remarks regarding the effect of slavery on the
character of the master. In part, he said:

The citizen of the Southern states becomes a sort of domestic dictator from
infancy; the first notion he acquires in life is, that he was born to command,
and the first habit he contracts is that of ruling without resistance. His education tends, then, to give him the character of a haughty and hasty man,—
irascible, violent, ardent in his desires, impatient of obstacles but easily discouraged if he cannot succeed in his first attempt.

When James S. Buckingham visited Columbia, South Carolina, in 1839
he saw the same thing. White children of four to seven years of age played
about the streets under the care of Negro boys and girls but little older
than themselves, the mode, he thought, by which parents evaded the responsibility of looking after their children. "But the little whites soon learn
their own superiority, and make great progress in the art of tormenting
and abusing their black guardians; laying, thus, in their very first steps in
life, the foundations of that irascible temper and ungovernable self-will,

which characterize nearly all the white inhabitants of the Slave States."

Fanny Kemble saw in slavery an even greater evil in this connection than Buckingham, if such were possible. She was greatly disturbed over what her oldest child's superior position was doing to the child. She saw with dismay how the little girl's "swarthy worshippers . . . sprang to obey her little gestures of command. She said something about a swing, and in less than five minutes head man Frank had erected it for her, and a dozen young slaves were ready to swing little 'missus'; think of learning to rule despotically your fellow-creatures before the first lesson of self-government has been well spelt over!" Miss Kemble said that the habit of command developed so early among Southerners seemed to give them a certain self-possession and ease. This, she believed, was rather superficial, and upon closer observation the vices of the social system would become apparent. The "haughty, overbearing irritability, effeminate indolence, reckless extravagancy, and a union of profligacy and cruelty" of the slaveholders were the "immediate result of their irresponsible power over their dependents." This became apparent upon intimate acquaintance with Southern character, she asserted.

That slavery tended to create a reign of tyranny in the South was no mere abolitionist prattle. It was the considered judgment of some responsible Southerners, from the eighteenth to the twentieth centuries, that a powerful socio-political absolutism was a significant consequence of the institution of slavery. In the debate on the question of the importation of slaves, Colonel George Mason of Virginia told the Federal Convention in 1787 that slaves produced "a most pernicious effect on manners" and that every master was a "born petty tyrant." The description of slavery by Ulrich B. Phillips was along a similar line. In part, Phillips said:

The actual regime was one of government not by laws but by men. In fact each slave was under a paternalistic despotism, a despotism in the majority of cases benevolent but in some cases harsh and oppressive, a despotism resented and resisted by some . . . but borne with lightheartedness, submission and affection by a huge number of blacks.

How much benevolence there was in the despotism, or whether there was any benevolence at all depended on the individual master and his relationship with his slave or slaves. What is important is that the system provided the despot with almost unlimited prerogatives and with ample opportunities for their extensive abuse. The owner had an unlimited amount of personal authority over his slaves as long as the slaves were guilty of no flagrant violations of the rights of other whites or of the feebly enforced laws of the state. For all practical purposes the master was the source of law on the plantation; and, in the infrequent instances when he resorted to the law of the state to invoke his right over his human property, its interpretation and enforcement were at his hands. If, then, the government of the plantation was not by laws, but by men, the stability of such an institution rested on the use of force, or the threat to use it. If owners felt that slavery could be sustained by force and violence against the slave or against the free men who challenged it, they had no qualms about resorting to force and violence.

The planter was forced to regard arms as a necessary adjunct to the machinery of control. The lash might be used generously or sparingly, depending on the temperament of the master and the tractability of the slave. There was always the possibility, moreover, of resorting to more deadly weapons. If the slave resisted the "mild" discipline of the lash or undertook to return blow for blow, how else could the master maintain his complete authority except through the use of, or the threat to use, the weapons whose possession was forever denied the slave?

Going about armed with knives and guns became the daily habit of many masters and overseers. And if the armed conquerors, in moments of anger, sometimes turned their weapons against each other, it was no more than was to be expected among an aggregation of armed men. The rule of tyranny by which they lived naturally fostered an independence and self-sufficiency—one is tempted to call it an individual sovereignty—that would, on occasion, burst out in all its fury in their quarrels with each other.

If the relationship between master and slave was that of a superior and a subordinate, a despot or tyrant and a powerless subject, or an armed victor and a vanquished foe, it can almost be described as a state of war. At least it is possible to recognize the martial spirit that pervaded the entire plantation atmosphere. The conduct of the master toward the slave was determined by rules and considerations not unlike those that characterized a military situation. Slaves enjoyed no well-defined body of rights; for their infractions there was summary punishment; and there was, of course, no appeal. As Richard Hildreth pointed out in a vigorous antislavery tract, the plantation might be viewed "as the seat of a little camp, which overawes and keeps in subjection the surrounding peasantry." The master was in a position to claim and exercise over his slaves all the rights that he, as a warrior, could exercise over a vanquished foe. Hildreth's rather apt analogy found its counterpart in a statement by a New Orleans editor who declared that "every plantation is a small military establishment or ought to be."

Thus, the connection between slavery and the martial spirit was apparent and was almost universally recognized by friend and foe of Southern civilization. If the observer were an implacable foe like Charles Sumner, he could see only the totally bad effects of the martial spirit growing out of slavery. To Sumner the result was criminal distortion of the values and notions regarding the fighting spirit. Thus in the South, the

swagger of the bully was called chivalry; a swiftness to quarrel was regarded as courage; the bludgeon was adopted as a substitute for argument;
and assassination was lifted to a fine art. If the observer were an apologetic
friend like the Mississippi planter, H. S. Fulkerson, he could be proud of
the fact that Southerners had been bred under the influences of the institution of slavery, "which, with its admitted evil, was calculated to foster
the martial spirit and give force of character."

The slave was never so completely subjugated as to allay all fears that
he would make a desperate, bloody attempt to destroy the institution to
which he was bound. Fear and apprehension were relative matters in the
ante bellum South; but they were always present. If the slaves seemed
satisfied and did not appear to be up to some deviltry, such as running
away or revolting, the fears, while still present, were not easily discernible. But if there was even the slightest rumor of an uprising, the entire
countryside was not only terrified, but the alarm was sounded. All whites—
loyal Negroes, too—were expected to do their share to prevent death
and destruction from stalking through the land and to restore the natural
foe to his natural condition.

The kind of dread fear that prevailed even in periods of relative calm
greatly impressed Olmsted during his visit to the lower Mississippi Valley
in 1856. At the place where he secured accommodations for the night, his
roommate, a Southern white, insisted on barricading the door of the
rather small, windowless room. He explained that he would not feel safe
if the door were left open. " 'You don't know,' he said, 'there may be
runaways around.' He then drew two small revolvers, hitherto concealed
under his clothing, and began to examine the caps. He certainly was a
nervous man," Olmsted concluded, "perhaps a mad man."

Southern slaveholders could never be quite certain that they had established unquestioned control over their slaves. A moment's relaxation
always raised new fears, like those of the night watchman who awoke
with a start, wondering how long he had been asleep. The better judgment insisted on the strictest vigilance, with no relaxation. This policy
was the only one consistent with the maintenance of the institution. As
one Southerner pointed out, a policy of carelessly widening the sphere of
freedom for the slave "would have virtually destroyed the institution.
The policy pursued by the slave states was consistent with the *fact* of
slavery, and it was an inexorable necessity that the policy should be
maintained."

The responsibility for maintaining control rested, first of all, on the
shoulders of the owner and his staff. Neither the laws of the state nor
those imposed by the slaveholder himself were of any avail unless they
were enforced by the plantation constabulary. The importance of the
owner's role was indicated by Judge Thomas Ruffin of the North Caro-

lina Supreme Court who said, "The power of the master must be absolute, to render the submission of the slave perfect." The owner, his overseer—if he had one—and other subordinates were dedicated to the task of maintaining the kind of discipline that would preserve the institution. Such a policy called for action resembling a declaration of war on the slaves. An overseer told Olmsted that if a slave resisted a white man's chastisement, he should be killed. On one occasion, a slave whom he was about to whip struck him in the head with a hoe. The overseer "parried the blow with his whip, and drawing a pistol tried to shoot him, but the pistol missing fire he rushed in and knocked him down with the butt of it." While deadly weapons might be used in disciplining slaves only in extreme cases or by singularly cruel masters and overseers, such instruments were, nevertheless, a part of the pattern of control which even the mildest owners did not entirely overlook.

Despite the fact that the plantation sought to be self-sufficient and succeeded in many respects, the maintenance of a stable institution of slavery was so important that owners early sought the cooperation of the entire community. This cooperation took the form of the patrol, which became an established institution in most areas of the South at an early date. There were many variations in the size and organization of the patrol. Rather typical was the South Carolina patrol that was established by law in 1690. The law set up patrol detachments of ten men under the captain of a militia company. All white men were eligible for patrol service. In 1819 all white males over eighteen were made liable for patrol duty, the non-slaveholders being excused from duty upon reaching the age of forty-five.

The patrol was to ride its "beat at night for the purpose of apprehending any and all Negroes who were not in their proper places." Alabama empowered its patrols

to enter, in a peaceable manner, upon any plantation; to enter by force if necessary, all Negro cabins or quarters, kitchens and outhouses, and to apprehend all slaves who may there be found, not belonging to the plantation or household, without a pass from their owner or overseer; or strolling from place to place, without authority.

There were variations in the disposition of offenders taken up by patrols. If the violators were free Negroes or runaways, they were to be taken before a justice of the peace. If they were slaves, temporarily away from their master's plantation, they were to be summarily punished by a whipping, not to exceed thirty-nine lashes.

The patrol system was essentially a military agency, and it tended to strengthen the position of the military in the Southern community. In most instances there was a substantial connection between the patrol and the militia, either through control of one by the other or through identity of personnel. In South Carolina, for example, the patrol system was early merged into the militia organization, "making it a part of the military system, and devolving upon the military authority its arrangement and maintenance." In Mississippi the structure of the patrol was but an "adaptation of the militia to the control of slaves." Under such circumstances the patrol system appeared to be an arm of the military.

Nor was the military support of slavery confined to plantations. In the towns and cities, where slaves frequently enjoyed a measure of freedom seldom conceded to persons of that status in rural areas, there was considerable military protection of the whites from the possible dangers inherent in such an arrangement. When Captain Basil Hall visited Richmond in 1828, he thought that the sentinel marching in front of the capitol building was part of an honor guard for the legislature. His guide corrected this impression by pointing out that the soldier was part of a guard to keep order among the Negroes.

It is necessary [he continued] or at all events it is customary in these states to have a small guard always under arms; there are only fifty men here. It is in consequence of the nature of our coloured population; but it is done more as a preventive check than anything else—it keeps all thoughts of insurrection out of the heads of the slaves, and so gives confidence to those persons amongst us who may be timorous.

The sight of this guard at the capitol "had almost the startling effect of an apparition" on William Chambers when he visited Richmond in 1853. It was the first time that he had seen a bayonet in the United States, and it "suggested the unpleasant reflection, that the large infusion of slaves in the composition of society was not unattended with danger."

Charleston likewise felt the need for special guards to keep order among the slaves. In 1839 the city constructed a guard house for the military on the important corner of Meeting and Broad Streets. Strategically located across from the city hall, the court house, and St. Michael's Church, it housed soldiers whose "chief duty was to watch and crush any attempt at insurrection by the slaves!" When Benwell, the English traveler, visited the city several years later, he arrived during an Independence Day celebration. His first impression was that "a sense of happiness and security reigned in the assembled multitude." But he found this to be "a notion quite fallacious" upon observing troops stationed at the guard house and sentinels pacing in front of the building, "as if in preparation or in expectation of a foe." Each evening at nine o'clock the roll of drums at the guard house announced the departure of the patrol, armed with muskets and bayonets, to make its rounds through the Negro quarters.

As early as 1787 a militia company patrolled the streets of Savannah.

The group, composed of a commanding officer, a sergeant, a corporal, and fifteen privates, was under orders to mount guard each evening at eight o'clock at the court house and patrol the outskirts of the town. During the spring months they were to patrol throughout the night. The guard was instructed to be particularly careful not to offend persons walking the streets in a peaceable manner, "but to challenge with Decency." Seventy years later, with the state of Mississippi well-populated, Natchez was facing her problem of law and order among the slaves in much the same way that Savannah had done. The citizens of that growing town were pleased that the Christmas holidays of 1856 had passed off without incident. They were quick to credit the proper persons for this good fortune: the "careful and prescient mayor who had taken the precaution to double the night guard" and "the voluntary military companies" which had been unusually on the alert to see that there was no disorder among the slaves.

The South's greatest nightmare was the fear of slave uprisings; and one of the most vigorous agitations of her martial spirit was in evidence whenever this fear was activated by even the slightest rumor of revolt. Fear easily and frequently mounted to an uncontrollable alarm in which the conduct of some citizens could hardly be described as sober or responsible. "We regard our Negroes as 'JACOBINS' of the country," Edwin C. Holland of Charleston declared in 1822. The whites should always be on their guard against them, and although there was no reason to fear any permanent effects from insurrectionary activities, they "should be watched with an eye of steady and unremitted observation. . . . Let it never be forgotten, that our Negroes are freely the JACOBINS of the country; that they are the ANARCHISTS and the DOMESTIC ENEMY; the COMMON ENEMY OF CIVILIZED SOCIETY, and the BARBARIANS WHO WOULD, IF THEY COULD BECOME THE DESTROYERS OF OUR RACE."

The farmer who told Olmsted of how the fear of revolts completely terrified some Alabama whites suggests either the extent of fear or the impact of fear upon the mind. The farmer said that when he was a boy "folks was dreadful frightened about the niggers. I remember they built pens in the woods," he continued, "where they could hide, and Christmas time they went and got into the pens, 'fraid the niggers was risin'. . . . I remember the same thing when we was in South Carolina . . . we had all our things put in bags, so we could tote 'em, if we heerd they was comin' our way." This does not seem to have been the usual reaction of whites to threats of slave insurrections. To be sure, such grave eventualities threw them into a veritable paroxysm of fear, but they moved swiftly and with determination to put up a joint defense against the common foe. Committees of safety would spring into existence with little prior notice, and all available military resources would be mobilized for immediate action.

These were not the times to entrust the lives of the citizens to the ordinary protective agencies of government. If a community or a state had any effective military force, this was the time for its deployment. Military patrols and guards were alerted, and volunteer troops and regular militia were called into service. It was a tense martial air that these groups created. For all practical purposes, moreover, even the civil law of the community tended to break down in the face of the emergency, while something akin to martial law, with its arbitrary searches and seizures and its summary trials and executions, prevailed until the danger had passed.

When Gabriel attempted to revolt in Richmond in 1800 the Light Infantry Blues were called into immediate service, the Public Guard was organized and drilled to help avert the calamity, and Governor Monroe instructed every militia commander in the state to be ready to answer the call to duty. In 1822, when Charleston was thrown into a panic by rumors of Vesey's plot, all kinds of military groups were called into service. A person unfamiliar with the problem might well have thought that such extensive mobilization was for the purpose of meeting some powerful foreign foe. The Neck Rangers, the Charleston Riflemen, the Light Infantry, and the Corps of Hussars were only some of the established military organizations called up. A special city guard of one hundred and fifty men was provided for Charleston. The cry for reinforcement by federal troops was answered before the danger had completely subsided.

The attempted revolt of Nat Turner in 1831 brought military assistance to Southampton County, Virginia, not only from the governor of the state, but from neighboring North Carolina counties, and from the federal government. Indeed, more troops reached Southampton County than were needed or could be accommodated. With artillery companies and a field piece from Fort Monroe, detachments of men from the warships *Warren* and *Natchez,* and hundreds of volunteers and militiamen converging on the place, there was every suggestion of an impending battle on a rather large scale.

There was a strong show of military force not only when the large-scale plots like those of Gabriel, Vesey and Turner were uncovered, but also whenever there was any suggestion or intimation of insurrection, however slight. The rumor of revolt in Louisiana in January, 1811, caused Governor Claiborne to call out the militia. A contingent of four hundred militiamen and sixty federal troops left Baton Rouge for the reported scene of action. Two years later the Virginia militia was ordered out to quell a suspected revolt in Lancaster. In 1816 the South Carolina militia took summary action against a group of Negroes suspected of subversive activities. The militia of Onslow County, North Carolina, was so tense during a "Negro hunt" in 1821 that its two detachments mistook each other for the Negro incendiaries and their exchange of fire caused considerable damage.

Alabama pressed its militia into service in 1841 to search for slave outlaws and to put down rumored uprisings.

Few ante bellum years were completely free of the rumors of slave revolts; and, consequently, there were few years when the South was free of at least some mobilization of its military strength. Agitation for stronger defenses against slave depredations was almost constant, with some leaders advocating a state of continuous preparation for the dreaded day of insurrection. Governor Robert Hayne of South Carolina told the legislature, "A state of military preparation must always be with us, a state of perfect domestic security. A period of profound peace and consequent apathy may expose us to the danger of domestic insurrection." The editor of a New Orleans daily called for armed vigilance, adding that "The times are at least urgent for the exercise of the most watchful vigilance over the conduct of slaves and free colored persons."

Slavery strengthened the military tradition in the South not only because owners found it desirable and, at times, necessary to build up a fighting force to keep the slaves under control, but also because they felt compelled to oppose outside attacks with a militant rationale of the institution. As the abolitionists began to attack slavery, the leaders of the South evolved a defense of slavery that was as full of fight as a state militia called out to quell a slave uprising. They began to re-state the theory of social organization that prevailed in the South and out of it came a racism that could find congenial reception only in an emotion-charged, militant, unreasoning atmosphere. They vigorously rejected the principles of liberty and equality, and one of them, Thomas Cooper, said that talk about the rights of man was a "great deal of nonsense. . . . We say that man is born free, and equal to every other man. Nothing can be more untrue: no human being ever was, now is, or ever will be born free." They also rejected political democracy, "An unmixed democracy," said one Mississippian, "is capricious and unstable, and unless arrested by the hand of despotism, leads to anarchy . . . as much of the aristocracy of England as would have been retained in America would have leavened the mass and purified the whole."

The South's society, as described by its proponents, was to rest on the inequality of men in law and economics. Slavery was a positive good. South Carolina's James H. Hammond said that slavery was "the greatest of all blessings which a kind providence has bestowed upon the South." It gave to the white man the only basis on which he could do something for a group of hopelessly inferior human beings. The view of the inferiority of the Negro was organized into a body of systematic thought by the scientists and social scientists of the South and out of it emerged a doctrine of racial superiority that justified any kind of control that the owner established and maintained over the slave. The racial basis of slavery gave Southern leaders an effective means of solidifying the economically divergent elements among the whites. At the same time, it strengthened the ardor with which most white Southerners were willing to fight to preserve slavery. The sharp cleavage between slavery and freedom was made even sharper by the factor of race. All slaves belonged to a degraded, "inferior" race; and, by the same token, all whites, however wretched some of them might be, were superior. In a society where race was so important, the whites at the lowest rung could satisfy themselves because they could identify themselves with the most privileged of the community. "Color alone is here the badge of distinction, the true mark of aristocracy," said Thomas Dew, "and all who are white are equal in spite of the variety of occupation."

White Southerners were, thus, among the first people of the world to develop a militant race superiority. As in other parts of the world where such a notion evolved, these frontier aristocrats sought support for their position by developing a common bond with the less privileged. The obvious basis was race, and outside the white race there was to be found no favor from God, no honor or respect from man. By the time that Europeans were reading Gobineau's *Inequality of Human Races* Southerners were reading Cartwright's *Slavery in the Light of Ethnology*. In admitting all whites of the South into the pseudo-nobility of race, Cartwright won their enthusiastic support in the struggle to preserve the integrity and honor of *the* race. This was a concept of social organization worth fighting for, and the white people of the South entered upon the grim task of exterminating persons and ideas hostile to their way of life.

This state of affairs and the anxiety accompanying it transformed the South into an armed camp. One seeking military activity did not have to wait for war with Britain or Mexico. He could find it in the regular campaign against the subversion of slavery. He could go with General Youngblood to annihilate a group of suspected slaves in South Carolina, or with Brigadier General Wade Hampton in the march from Baton Rouge to an infected plantation in St. John the Baptist Parish. The citadels, sentries, "grapeshotted cannon," and alerted minute men became familiar and integral parts of the Southern scene and came to be regarded by many as indispensable for the preservation of the "cornerstone" of Southern civilization. It would seem, then, that the South's first Armageddon was with her own slaves.

32 *Ralph Henry Gabriel*

EVANGELICAL RELIGION
AND POPULAR ROMANTICISM
IN EARLY NINETEENTH-CENTURY AMERICA

In the first half of the nineteenth century, the soil of European society was being pierced by lively shoots of reform. This helps to explain why citizens from the Old World were particularly interested in visiting the New to examine at close hand a society which seemed—all of it—to be a landscape of reform. Many things impressed the visitors, and none perhaps so much as the religious ways of the Americans. To some they were admirable, to others repugnant, to all interesting. The interest is eminently understandable. Here was a people splintered into a myriad of Protestant sects, and the number of these was ever increasing. In doctrine and organization the sects had differences, yet they were (and this the outsider could see from his vantage) bound by a larger unity. What, one could not help wondering, was this early nineteenth-century religion of the Americans all about?

A very perceptive answer is given in the following essay by Ralph Henry Gabriel, Professor Emeritus of History at Yale University. Professor Gabriel is one of our foremost scholars in the field of American social and intellectual history. He has written many books in this field, including the familiar *Course of American Democratic Thought* (1940, rev. 1956), has edited *The Pageant of America* Series, and is currently editing *The Library of Congress* Series in American History. Professor Gabriel has some noteworthy points to make regarding early nineteenth-century Protestantism. It was a people's religion. It was the counterpart of the American democratic creed, sharing with that creed several basic doctrines, each of which had both religious and secular expressions. Emotional and individualistic, it contributed significantly to the dominance of romanticism in mid-nineteenth-century America.

Both what Professor Gabriel says and the subject of his comments will inevitably elicit further inquiry. What, to begin with, do we mean by romanticism? We know enough, certainly, from Arthur O. Lovejoy's famous essay on romanticism to understand that the word and the historical development are not susceptible of easy definition. In what ways was American romanticism similar to European, in what ways different, and why? What explains the newer pattern of Amer-

Reprinted with permission from *Church History*, XIX (March, 1950), 34–47.

ican religion that emerged by mid-century? What is its relevance to
Western expansion, to urbanization, to the great developments in industry, transportation, and communication during this period? What
is the relevance, moreover, of the change in religion to the multifarious
reform movements of the ante-bellum decades? And, finally, viewing
the problem in the larger perspective which Professor Gabriel suggests,
what is the nature of American religious experience today?

Arnold Toynbee has described our western civilization in the twentieth
century as a rationalistic and secular culture. In the sense that an awareness of the importance of science is the starting point of the thinking of
our day the generalization seems true. We prize the realism of the objective, analytical approach of science. In a turbulent and swiftly moving
age we have substituted relativism for older values once confidently assumed
to have universal validity. We have seen scepticism, born of twentieth-
century events, erode an old and dynamic belief in progress. We observe
Protestantism, its old orthodoxy shaken, striving to make the Christian
tradition meaningful and significant for a materialistic generation. We
watch the protagonists of democracy striving to hold fast to essential human values and to protect basic freedoms in an age of fear and power.

The twentieth-century man looks back with a certain wistfulness upon
his forerunner in the eighteenth. Newton's mechanistic cosmos, symbolized
by the ordered swinging of the planets about the sun, provided the starting point of eighteenth-century thought. The concept of the order of
nature was central to the climate of opinion of eighteenth-century England
and France, the provinces of the British crown in North America. The
order of nature expressed itself in eighteenth-century America in a stable
society of aristocrats and commoners, a society that in America produced
leadership of sufficient quality to carry out a successful war of independence and to create an enduring federal republic. The order of nature,
called into being by nature's God, to use Jefferson's phrase, emphasized the
virtues of restraint and balance, the importance of reason, and the fundamental character of natural law. Washington expressed its norms in his
self-restraint, after Yorktown, in the use of the vast personal power that
came to him with victory. The eighteenth century prized realism and
decorum. Its mood and values fitted well the life of small ordered communities east of the Appalachians, conscious of their past and confident of
the future. In these communities Protestantism had lost much of the drive
and power it had had in seventeenth-century New England. Even that
restored by the Great Awakening had declined in the revolutionary years.
A deistic humanism provided the philosophy of the upper classes and had,
through Tom Paine's *Appeal to Reason*, a wide influence among common
men.

Between the rationalism and the realism of the eighteenth century and that of the twentieth lies the period dealt with in the present inquiry. The first half of the nineteenth century saw the decline of deism, the rise of evangelical Protestantism, and the final formulation of that cluster of ideas and values that made up the American democratic credo. The American revolution, through the achievement of eighteenth-century men and the product of eighteenth-century thought, looked forward to the nineteenth. The Declaration of Independence, with its emphasis on liberty and its doctrine of equality, was to be accepted by later generations as the classic formulation of democratic theory. Before he went to France as minister of the United States, Jefferson wrote the Virginia statute of religious liberty, a liberty guaranteed and extended by the first amendment to the Federal Constitution. In America, the eighteenth century ended in the triumph of freedom. The men of that age, in harmony with their predilection for balance, linked freedom and responsibility. They had won freedom both for the political state and for religion; they made both the state and religion the responsibility of the people.

In western Europe the French Revolution separated the nineteenth from the eighteenth century. In the United States the surmounting of the Appalachian barrier and the establishment of a fluid and rapidly moving frontier west of the mountains marked the boundary between the two epochs. In the first half of the nineteenth century Americans streamed westward. They filed through the passes of the Alleghenies on horseback and in Conestoga wagons. They took the leisurely boat passage on the Erie Canal. They moved westward singly, in families, and by companies. They subdued to cultivated fields the rich soils of the Ohio and Mississippi valleys. Refusing to be balked by dry plains, mountains, or deserts, they pushed on to the shores of the Pacific, where they supplanted the descendants of the Spanish conquerors. Moreover, as covered wagons jolted toward the Pacific, other Americans harnessed Atlantic streams to new machines in new factories that multiplied in size and number with each passing decade. "It was our first great period of exploitation," remarked Vernon Parrington writing beside Puget Sound in 1927, "and from it emerged, as naturally as the cock from the mother egg, the spirit of romance, gross and tawdry in vulgar minds, dainty and refined in the more cultivated. But always romance. The days of realism were past, and it was quietly laid away with the wig and the smallclothes of an outworn generation." The nineteenth-century frontier, sub-literate, undisciplined and materialistic, tested the ability of the common people of the United States to measure up to the responsibility, placed upon them by religious freedom, to preserve that ancient Christian tradition that had come to America from Europe.

Timothy Dwight, leader of Connecticut Congregationalism and president of Yale College, journeyed about the turn of the century to the back country to observe at first hand the ways of the frontiersmen. "The business of these men," he wrote in 1810 in a passage destined to become famous, "is no other than to cut down trees, build log-houses, lay open forested ground to cultivation, and prepare the way for those who come after them. These men cannot live in regular society. They are too idle, too talkative, too passionate, too prodigal, and too shiftless to acquire either property or character. They are impatient of law, religion, and morality. . . . At the same time they are possessed, in their own view, of uncommon wisdom; understand medical science, politics, and religion better than those who have studied them through life; and, although they manage their own concerns worse than any other men, feel perfectly satisfied that they can manage those of the nation far better than the agents to whom they are committed by the public." Dwight, austere gentleman of the tie-wig school, found the rough folk of the frontier log cabins and stump lots given to passion and to exaggeration in talk and behavior. An oral literature of tall tales about those mythical heroes, Mike Fink, Davy Crockett and Paul Bunyan, enlivened social gatherings from the Great Lakes forests to those of the Gulf coast. These extravagant and earthy narratives of the bunkhouse, the flatboat, and the tap room glorified the individual. Davy Crockett became a cosmic figure who twisted the tails of comets as well as catamounts. These Brobdingnagian yarns, whose humor lacked any discipline of wit, reflected a society in which ability and readiness to use his fists was frequently the primary factor in determining the status of the individual. Dwight's staid Connecticut had no counterpart for the frontier gouging fight where no holds were barred. Dwight inevitably looked with a jaundiced eye upon the unkempt population of the frontier. What he did not realize was that the future lay with that rowdy, illiterate, yet fundamentally creative, frontier.

Unlike Connecticut, where the separation of church and state was not finally effected until 1818, religion on the frontier became from the beginning the full responsibility of the common people organized into voluntary congregations. The people of the back country, selecting what they could understand of the Christian tradition, turned that tradition to their own purposes. They transformed those meager elements of western civilization that trans-Appalachian migrants brought from eastern communities into folk culture. North of the Ohio this culture was a short transitional phase in the evolution of civilization. South of that river, due in part to the tardy emergence of public schools, a folk culture persisted for generations. In this western country evangelical Protestantism became a folk religion, expressing the attitudes of the people and providing for their intellectual and emotional needs. Among a population whose principal literature was the remembered tale, the Bible became the one important book. Its narrative gave to this culture its historical perspective. The precepts and admonitions of the Old and New Testaments established authoritative norms for the governing of human conduct, norms that were nothing less than the fixed and eternal laws of God established for the ordering of society. But, though the Bible spoke with authority, its words had to be interpreted, and no established church provided a single authoritative interpretation. Herein lay the essence of that religious liberty which had been guaranteed by the First Amendment to the Constitution. Among this frontier population existed many individual minds of great native capacity, but they were walled-in by ignorance and isolated from the world of thought by the lack of educational opportunity. Such minds, making use of the only intellectual materials at hand, acquired, many times, a prodigious biblical learning and even advanced to a homespun variety of philosophical and theological speculation. These individuals, often becoming leaders of local groups, played an important part in that splintering of Protestantism that was so pronounced a phenomenon of the nineteenth century.

The extravagance and individualism of the tall tales appeared again in the emotional experiences of converted sinners of the frontier camp meetings. Back country folk invented this form of religious association and in it created not only a pattern for public worship but a means for expressing those emotions so fundamental to human life. Emotions are called up out of the depths of human nature by conflict and by rhythm. Evangelical Protestantism provided both. It presented the drama of the conflict of the Lord with the Devil for mastery in a world of sinners. It managed its greatest climax in the conflict of the individual sinner with his sin. The hysterical phenomena associated with the revival type of conversion are one of the commonplaces of frontier history. Unlettered exhorters preached what they understood to be the Christian message to country folk assembled from widely scattered cabins. In clearings lighted by flickering campfires, the preaching continued far into the night. The religious song, however, more than the spoken word, moved the mourner to grief for his sin and exaltation at his escape therefrom. The white spirituals, like the tall tales, were the creation of the folk culture of the back country. In these spirituals evangelical Protestantism, as a folk religion, came to focus.

These songs evolved out of older materials carried to the frontier by emigrants from eastern communities. Eighteenth-century Methodist and Baptist hymns underwent transformation. An unknown author of the time of Wesley wrote the stately hymn that ran:

> A few more days on earth to spend
> And all my toils and cares shall end,
> And I shall see my God and friend
> And praise his name on high.

Transformed by frontier influences, the stanza emerged as a refrain in the vernacular of the back settlements for a swiftly moving camp meeting song:

> I pitch my tent on this camp ground,
>> Few days, few days!
> And give old Satan another round,
>> And I am going home.
> I can't stay in these diggings,
>> Few days, few days!
> I can't stay in these diggings,
>> I am going home.

Other white spirituals were modifications of popular songs of the day. Many were sad and mournful songs dealing with farewell and death and set in a minor key. Through practically all ran a rhythm that lent itself to handclapping, stamping, and marching. Back country worshipers called the clapping, swaying accompaniment "the shout." The shout reinforced the emotional experience derived from these songs and from the worship of which they were a part. Ecstasy was the end sought, the supreme good, a good that could be enjoyed in the here and now. The men and women of the settlements were proud of the shout; they sang about it. Referring to the Judgment Day in one song the swaying, clapping mourners chanted:

> Sweet morning, sweet morning
> And we'll all shout together
>> In the morning.

They thought of Heaven as a place where the shout continued. In these spirituals of evangelical Protestantism, untutored men and women could forget for a moment the drabness and squalor, the pains and sorrows, of poor and isolated communities in a dazzling, romantic vision of pearly gates and golden streets. People whose place was near the bottom of the social hierarchy of the age sang of personal triumph and glory in the spirit of the aggressive individualism of the frontier.

> I want to see bright angels stand
> And waiting to receive me.

The folk religion of the exuberant, optimistic, and undisciplined frontier represented a bizarre, but nonetheless genuine, expression to the spirit of romanticism. This religion had power. It helped to subdue the grosser evils of the frontier. It made an impress on American society that persisted far into the twentieth century.

New England in the first half of the nineteenth century looked at frontier society with apprehension and with a fear that expressed itself politically in the Hartford convention at the end of the War of 1812. New England, moreover, deeply resented the condescending generalizations of such foreign visitors as Mrs. Trollope who insisted that frontier uncouthness provided the true picture of American character. "There is no literary atmosphere breathing through the forests or across the prairies," declared Horace Bushnell as late as 1847. This Congregational clergyman and theologian of Hartford, Connecticut, had before this date challenged the conservatism of his New England colleagues. He had, in fact, become a prophet who was pointing out a new way that was ultimately to lead to the social gospel of the latter years of the century. In 1847, however, Bushnell was not immediately concerned with theology. He was stumping the East from New York to Boston in the cause of home missions. He chose for the title of his address, "Barbarism the First Danger." Affirming that frontier colleges, "if they have any, are only rudimental beginnings, and the youth a raw company of woodsmen," he solicited money to rescue westerners from the darkness of ignorance and sin. "Be it also understood," he concluded in a peroration that mirrored a blend of New England practicality and complacency, "that the sooner we have railroads and telegraphs spinning into the wilderness, and setting the remotest hamlets in connection and close proximity with the east, the more certain it is that light, good manners and Christian refinement will become universally diffused. For when the emigrant settlements of Minnesota or of Oregon feel that they are just in the suburb of Boston, it is nearly the same thing, in fact, as if they actually were." The tendency of Europeans to see American culture in terms of western "barbarism" spurred eastern men of letters to attempt to create what was, in effect, a derivative culture. Longfellow, the translator, was the most important in this group. Emerson, however, refused to follow the intellectual fashions of his day. He rejected sterile imitation. He would have no truck with a culture that "fed on the sere remains of foreign harvests."

Emerson and the Concord transcendentalists stood at the opposite pole of intellectual sophistication from contemporary camp meeting exhorters and from the creators of the white spirituals. Transcendentalism, together with the folk religion of the frontier, enables us to set early nineteenth-century Protestantism in perspective. In New England a liberal movement called Unitarianism in the first half of the century tried to modify an older Puritanism, to reconcile theology with Newtonian science, and to subdue to reason the thorny doctrine of the Trinity. Emerson began his adult career as a Unitarian preacher. When he became convinced that the new liberalism had become little more than the urbane philosophy of upper class respectability, he walked out of the pulpit. Emerson sympathized with the ethical emphasis of Unitarianism, for he, together with the colleagues of William Ellery Channing, inherited the ethical seriousness of seventeenth-century Puritanism. But in Emerson's eyes Unitarianism had lost its drive; its ethic had declined into a cult of respectability. For Emerson, Unitarianism was like the conch shell he picked up on the sand and in which, when he held it to his ear, he could hear only the distant echo of the sea. He craved an immediate experience of the crash of the breakers on the shore. As he moved away from Unitarian rationalism, Emerson, however, did not take the road to orthodoxy. His trail led, rather, in the opposite direction toward what his outraged Protestant contemporaries called the new infidelity. Ethics remained his preoccupation; he sought a faith that would be a dynamism giving ethics significance in society. The discovery by Emerson and Thoreau of nature as a source of inspiration is one of the most familiar of American stories. Nature brought them into contact with that infinite and immanent God that these Transcendentalists called the Over-soul. Through mystical experience Emerson discovered what William James, in a later generation, described as "that peace abiding at the heart of endless agitation." Emerson's lines to the tiny purple Rhodora, blooming in solitude, express better than almost any other among his writings the transcendentalist mood and the transcendentalist affirmation of the unity of nature, man and God.

> Why thou wert there, O rival of the rose
> I never thought to ask, I never knew:
> But, in my simple ignorance, suppose
> The self-same Power that brought me there brought you.

Mystical experience convinced Emerson that deity dwells in the human heart, a belief that led on his conviction that the individual man has vast potential powers, that every man has a unique mission in the world, a contribution that he alone can make and which the world needs. Emerson's definition of individualism as uniqueness and non-conformity surpassed even that of the frontier.

Between New England transcendentalism and the folk religion of the frontier ran the main current of American Protestantism in an age in which cities were growing swiftly but whose outlook was still dominated by that of the countryside and the rural village. As the century rolled forward, New England theology lost some of that granite hardness of Puritan Calvinism and took on the adaptable rationality of Scottish common sense. Jonathan Edwards in the eighteenth century, moreover, had introduced the idea of the importance of emotion into what had been a coldly logical intellectual structure. Emotion had made its way in the churches despite a somewhat stubborn conservatism of theologians. The significance of religious feeling ultimately found its greatest exponent in

Horace Bushnell. As "the ideal of Greeks was beauty," he remarked in 1843, "and that of the Romans law, so this new age shall embrace an ideal more comprehensive, as it is higher than all, namely love. . . . . This love is no partial ideal, as every other must be; it is universal, it embraces all that is beneficent, pure, true, beautiful—God, man, eternity, time." In such an outlook and philosophy the social gospel was born. Bushnell also, like Emerson, had his moments of emotional exaltation. Early in December in 1852, returning from the West, the Hartford preacher paused to look at Niagara Falls. His was the familiar pilgrimage of the early nineteenth-century Americans to the natural wonder. Thousands who could not make the journey knew the Falls through published engravings made from the romantic canvases of the landscapists of the Hudson River school. "I was never so deeply impressed with them before," commented Bushnell in a letter he posted to his wife, ". . . one ocean plunging in solemn repose of continuity into another . . . a power that is the same yesterday, today, and forever . . . I could hardly stand, such was the sense it gave me of the greatness of God. . . ." Though Bushnell attacked the nature-worship of the transcendentalists six years later in a volume he called *Nature and the Supernatural*, his thought, in spite of the fact that he used the phrases of the familiar Protestant orthodoxy, disclosed close kinship to that of Emerson. Both men found nature the source of inspiration, and both looked upon man as the culmination of nature. Both exalted the individual and emphasized the importance of the free expression of his emotions. At this point it is useful to recall that early nineteenth-century romanticism emphasized just these things—the importance of nature as a manifestation of beauty and a source of inspiration, the value of the individual, and the significance of the emotions of men. Whatever their intellectual differences, Bushnell and Emerson both belonged to that international company of romantics so important in the early nineteenth-century world.

Looking backward from our day we can see that Bushnell was primarily important for the second half of the nineteenth century as his thought led out into the social gospel. A much simpler man than he pioneered in eastern communities in the development of emotional expression in early nineteenth-century Protestantism. Lowell Mason, hymn-writer, emerged in a period in which all of the United States, with unimportant exceptions, was little better than a musical wilderness. His greatest secular achievement came when he persuaded the educational authorities of Boston to lead the nation in putting musical instruction into the schools of that city. The state of early nineteenth-century American music is suggested by the fact that as late as 1837, the year of Emerson's Phi Beta Kappa address at Harvard, Mason's *New Collection of Church Music* devoted twenty-four opening pages to instruction in the "elements of vocal music." Mason did not merely collect and make available the religious songs of Europe and older America. He became the most important American creator of hymns of the first half of the nineteenth century. While he still lived, his songs became the household possessions of millions of his fellow country men. There were few Americans who did not know "My Faith Looks Up to Thee," "From Greenland's Icy Mountains," or "Nearer My God to Thee." They became what Mason intended them to be, songs of the people. He combined simple poems of aspiration with melodies that were equally simple. He rose on occasion to moderate heights of emotional expression and at times declined into sentimentality. Toward the end of his life, Mason set down the philosophy that governed him in the creation of those songs that moved the men and women of his day. Congregational singing, he remarked in 1859, "is nature's method of praise. It is, in a great degree independent of art culture, being indeed above art. It is adapted alike to the voices of the young and the old, the uncultivated and the cultivated. It engages all in the simultaneous exercise of the same emotions. . . . It belongs . . . to the sublime in nature rather than in art. It may be compared to the mountains, which owe their majesty, not to their fertile soil, nor to any architectural skill, but to the Power which commanded the light to shine out of darkness, and brought up from the depths the rough and diversified materials in which consists 'the strength of the hills.' " The character of this affirmation and the choice of metaphor make clear that Mason selected his word, nature, from the vocabulary of mid-nineteenth-century romanticism. Mason was as much affected by the romantic spirit as Bushnell or Emerson. What the white spirituals contributed to the folk religion of the frontier Mason's hymns gave to the worship of the churches of more developed communities. When the folk culture of the early settlements gave way before the advance of civilization, Mason's hymns replaced the spirituals. With their frank appeal to emotion these songs of the people played a part in the softening of the craggy theology of older New England and in preparing the way for Bushnell's manifesto concerning the law of love.

"Upon close inspection," commented Alexis de Tocqueville as he surveyed the society of early nineteenth-century America, "it will be seen that there is in every age some peculiar and preponderant fact with which all others are connected; this fact almost always gives birth to some pregnant idea or some ruling passion, which attracts to itself and bears away in its course all the feelings and opinions of the time; it is like a great stream toward which each of the neighboring rivulets seems to flow." Tocqueville seems to have thought that individualism, born of freedom in the American environment, was such a ruling idea. "*Individualism*," he noted, "is a novel expression to which a novel idea has given birth." Early nineteenth-century Protestantism, whether that of frontier folk religion or that of the more sophisticated denominations, focused on the individual, as did also

New England transcendentalism. Both Protestantism and transcendentalism, moreover, emphasized the importance of the emotions of the individual man and woman. Though the ecstasy of frontier revivalistic religious experience has been labeled a manifestation of sect tradition and practices while such communion with nature as that of Bushnell and Emerson has been called mysticism, the similarities between the two types of individual emotional experience outweigh the differences. Nineteenth-century Protestantism as a people's religion and transcendentalism as a faith for the more cultivated few were both, at bottom, romantic religions. Though such influences cannot be measured, it is a reasonable guess that Christianity had as much to do with giving romanticism its dominant position in the climate of opinion of mid-nineteenth-century America as did literary and artistic importations from across the Atlantic.

As Tocqueville suggested, there is an alchemy at work in every climate of opinion that tends to dissolve inconsistencies and to establish fundamental agreements. The concept of the order of nature was such an agent in the eighteenth century. In the first half of the nineteenth century, romanticism provided the solvent. It permeated the arts and literature. It expressed itself in the South in the cult of chivalry and in the romantic nationalism of the dream of the confederate States of America. It created the fundamental similarities between religious and secular thinking. The eighteenth century had bequeathed to the common man of the nineteenth responsibility for organized religion on the one hand and for the political state on the other. Inevitably the citizen expressed similar ideas as his thinking moved back and forth between these two realms.

The first half of the nineteenth century, as Parrington affirmed, was a time of conquest and of exploitation. As the decades advanced, Americans achieved a deepening understanding of the nature and significance of the evils that were poisoning their society—unintelligent and often cruel treatment of the mentally ill, urban slums that grew more rapidly than the cities, chattel slavery whose continuous existence mocked the pretensions of democracy. A somber realism appeared, expressing itself in the early writings of Parke Goodwin of New York City and in the hard-hitting sermons of Theodore Parker in Boston. The realism, however, was not well done by twentieth-century standards of social science, for early nineteenth-century Americans still lived in what was, in reality, a pre-scientific age. The two greatest tracts of a golden age of tracts, "Uncle Tom's Cabin" and "Ten Nights in a Barroom," fell short of achieving even literary realism. Their vast success in their own time lay not in an artistic recreation of human life distorted by social evils but rather in the fact that they frankly laid siege to the emotions of a generation brought up on the emotionalism of evangelical Protestantism. Romanticism emphasized the nobility of feelings of concern for suffering humanity. In the

varied humanitarian movements that grew to significance in early nineteenth-century America, a generous sympathy for the less favored, the
unfortunate, and the oppressed made up for inadequate knowledge of
society and of the forces that move within it. In spite of inadequacies in
scientific knowledge, however, the drive toward betterment of society and
the realization of democratic ideals brought concrete results—universal
manhood suffrage in Jackson's day, the establishment on a sure foundation
of the public school system, and the abandonment of the legal theory of
the English common law that labor unions are conspiracies. Romantic emotionalism had power in humanitarian undertakings as well as in religion.

Above the humanitarian crusades and the concrete social advances a
cluster of democratic norms emerged that Whitman, before he became the
poet of American democracy, called the American faith. It was a credo
announced on every ceremonial national occasion from public platforms.
It inspired a literature that ran the gamut from Bancroft's history to Whitman's "Leaves of Grass." Although the statements of the pattern of democratic idealism were only seldom couched in the analytical vocabulary of
logic, they have been broken down into specific doctrines. The primary
doctrine was that of the fundamental law not made by man underlying
society and making human association possible, the natural law of the
Declaration of Independence and the moral law of Christian tradition. The
emphasis was on permanence in the time and universal validity among men.
The second doctrine was that of the free and responsible individual, responsible not only for contributing to the management of the political
state but ultimately to the fundamental law before which all men are equal.
This doctrine was the secular counterpart of the religious affirmation of
the ultimate responsibility of the individual to God. In the same first half
of the nineteenth century, when American Protestants moved outward to
establish mission stations on the frontier and in non-Christian lands, the
doctrine of a national mission to stand before the world as a witness for
democracy came into being. The parallels between this early nineteenth-
century democratic faith and the romantic Christianity of the people seem
clear. To the similarities in ideas must be added similarity in emotional
emphasis. "Not in an obscure corner, not in feudal Europe . . ." said
Emerson voicing the hope that democracy would one day bring peace to
the world, "is this seed of benevolence laid in the furrow with tears of
hope, but in the broad America of God and man."

The democratic credo was also a romantic formulation. It came to
focus in its concept of the dignity of the individual—a concept which had
also been central to the rationalistic and generous humanism of the eighteenth-century "enlightenment." In the nineteenth century, though experience and logic provided important reinforcement, the essential dynamism of this doctrine of the dignity of man, when it expressed itself in

humanitarian undertakings, was not reason but rather emotion born of desire and faith. This democratic credo, this American dream, was the greatest achievement of an age that, in retrospect, we see as but an interlude between two periods of rationalism and realism, an age, moreover, that came to wreck when mid-nineteenth-century Americans abandoned rational debate and, surrendering to their hates and fears, marched off to fratricidal war.

33 *Roy F. Nichols*

AMERICAN DEMOCRACY AND THE CIVIL WAR

34 *Allan Nevins*

THE NEEDLESS CONFLICT

In the history of the national state there is often a turning point, a point of crisis at which two ideas come into conflict. Although the conflict in a superficial sense is resolved, it passes, on a deeper level and in subsequent redefinitions, into the current politics of the state. In France, the turning point came with the Revolution of 1789; in England, with the Puritan Revolution of the 1640's; in the United States, with the Civil War. In each instance, the issue to be decided was the relevance of the polity to the people. In each instance, the source of sovereignty, and therefore the very nature of the state, was being redefined. In this sense, every great revolution has been a civil war and every civil war a great revolution. Crises of such profundity become part of the mythology of the state. They are mirrors in which the changing face of the real present is variously seen, by different groups, in different ages, and for different purposes.

This is why historians have failed to come to any agreement on a very basic question about the American Civil War—what caused it? From the time of the war until the present day, opinions on this question have differed widely and, often indeed, have clashed harshly. The war has been attributed to a conflict between a ruthless "Slave Power" in control of the South and an aggressive Northern group of "Black

Republicans," intent on inflicting their views upon the South. It has been attributed to antagonistic economies and class struggles, to irreconcilable theories concerning the nature of the Union and the rights of the states, to the whipping up of sectional passions by irresponsible and selfish leaders.

While a final analysis of what caused the Civil War is therefore beyond the hope of historical scholarship, for the present certainly, some very excellent suggestions have been made. Two of these are presented in the following essays by Professors Roy F. Nichols of the University of Pennsylvania and Allan Nevins of the Huntington Library, both of whom we have had occasion to read before (see pp. 3–13 and pp. 32–52). Professor Nichols is one of our foremost authorities on the period before the Civil War. The conclusion at which he arrives in his highly important work, *The Disruption of American Democracy* (1948), is the one which he presents in the essay below. It is, essentially, that the prewar system of politics could not accommodate and adjust the divisive attitudes lying deep in American life and that, indeed, the political system tended to intensify the conflict of attitudes.

Professor Nevins's portrait of the nation in the years before and during the Civil War (six volumes have thus far appeared) is probably, in the field of American history, the outstanding work of our times. It is history in the grand manner, on a theme of epic dimensions. Professor Nevins's conclusions on the causes of the war are certainly noteworthy.

"The war, when it came, was not primarily a conflict over State Rights, although that issue had become involved in it. It was not primarily a war born of economic grievances, although many Southerners had been led to think that they were suffering, or would soon suffer, economic wrongs. It was not a war created by politicians and publicists who fomented hysteric excitement; for while hysteria was important, we have always to ask what basic reasons made possible the propaganda which aroused it. It was not primarily a war about slavery alone, although that institution seemed to many the grand cause. It was a war over slavery *and* the future position of the Negro race in North America. Was the Negro to be allowed, as a result of the shift of power signalized by Lincoln's election, to take the first step toward an ultimate position of general economic, political, and social equality with the white man? Or was he to be held immobile in a degraded, servile position, unchanging for the next hundred years as it had remained essentially unchanged for the hundred years past? These questions were implicit in Lincoln's demand that slavery be placed in a position where the public mind could rest assured of its ultimate extinction." (*The Emergence of Lincoln,* New York: Charles Scribner's Sons, II, 470–1.)

The issue which lay at the bottom of the war cannot, to the mind of Professor Nevins, be separated from the men who were called upon to make important decisions about that issue. Weak presidents were leading the nation when it most needed men of strength. Lacking in statesmanship, unimaginative, irresolute—Fillmore, Pierce, and Buchanan were incapable of facing up to the great demands of the presidency; and of the three, Buchanan was the weakest. At a time of great trial, submits Professor Nevins in the essay below, when the struggle in Kansas over slavery dramatized the national problem, Buchanan failed dismally. If leadership had been in the hands of men of conviction and strength, the war might have been averted. In this sense, Professor Nevins feels, it was a needless conflict. This argument, it will be seen, is related to the one advanced by Professor Nichols. Both cite the failure of political leadership at perhaps the most critical period of American history, the one at the level of the localities, the other at the very top.

However the question of what caused the war is ultimately resolved, there can be little doubt that the whole subject of the war is the most commanding point of interest in our history for both the professional historian and the general public. The centenary celebrations in which we are presently participating are merely quickenings of a concern which has always been there. The issues which dominated the war continue, in newer forms, to have vitality; the myth we have made of the war is very much alive. For one thing, the Old South, despite its defeat, continues to have meaning for us: in that efficient remembrance of things past by which we remember what we will and how we will, we have remade the Old South from a transient and divided society into one that is resolved and permanent; we have restyled it in feudal garb and invested it with what we consider to be the romance and simplicity of a pre-industrial age; we are caught in the paradox of applauding the triumph of the Northern ideal while regretting the defeat of the Southern one, which, in the national myth, represents aristocracy, order, chivalry, and the uncomplicated love of mannered men for beautiful women. Moreover, if the North won the war, the South, in a distinct way, won the peace; and the Civil War sustained itself long after Appomattox because the Northern ideal would have to triumph again. Another reason for interest is that the real civil war is being fought today, not so much in a clash of arms or legal decisions as in the impact of deeper economic and social forces upon the mind of the South; it is being fought internally, in individual and group consciences, in a scene of rapidly changing institutions and values. Finally, the Civil War has its meaning for an age of international struggle between two systems and two worlds. It signifies two ideas in conflict, and the shorthand of the phrases "free world" and "unfree world" may aptly summarize both the American conflict of the 1860's and the world conflict of a century later.

Roy F. Nichols

I

The United States has always been a laboratory and experiment station for political scientists, of both amateur and professional standing. Its research program has been the invention and perfection of mechanisms of self-government, designed to enable a growing society to enjoy liberty, equality, and unlimited opportunity, and at the same time to maintain a reasonable amount of order. The output of this laboratory has been of constant interest to the many observers who have been particularly concerned with the inventions in federalism designed to enable democracy to operate.

The history of some of these experiments is of particular moment today, when mankind is struggling with the great political problem of world federalism. The current effort to create the United Nations is the center of universal attention, for the dangers which confront humanity make this an experiment which may be crucial. The nature of American experience therefore should be an object of careful study and no incident more so than the Civil War of 1861–1865, for it clearly demonstrated certain federal weaknesses, weaknesses that contemporary architects of federalism should carefully seek to avoid.

Unfortunately historians have had a difficult task in discovering the truth about the Civil War and in interpreting its causes and its significance. So much of the record is clouded by obscurantism, made the murkier by nationalistic and patriotic folk interpretations and traditions, which are among the most difficult classes of evidence with which the historian has to deal. In every nation's history the spokesmen of the populace make up a canon of historical interpretation as crises occur. Also a vested interest often appears shortly after such cataclysms and devotes much energy to establishing an interpretation which is generally too simple to have much validity for the scientific scholar of later day. Such interpretations pose a difficult problem to all students of political experience, a problem which is of interest to anyone concerned with the use of evidence.

During the Civil War, Lincoln and his associates made superb statements of the causes and purposes of the conflict as they saw them with their contemporary northern vision. Their official version was that a righteous and indignant people was struggling to prevent the destruction of the Union by a group of ardent, misguided secessionists who sought to break

Reprinted with permission from *Proceedings of the American Philosophical Society*, XCI (April, 1947), 143–9.

up the American political experiment because they feared—quite mistakenly and willfully—that their civilization was in danger. A more radical faction of Lincoln's party added that the war was fought to destroy the curse of slavery. The Republican party, the G.A.R., school-book writers, and historians in general wove these two purposes into a composite and repeated them frequently enough to make them traditional. The military and political phases of the war attracted attention, especially as the generals and politicos fought it over again in their memoirs. For years the scholars spent their time in working out such details, discussing political issues and military strategy, and endeavoring to solve "scientifically" the controversies over reputation.

Just about the time when, under the old rules, historians would have begun to be really concerned with questioning tradition, namely about two generations after the event, the problem of the discovery of the truth was further complicated. A Southern interpretation emerged which was the more convincing because it seemed to be "scientific." I refer to the Southern reinterpretation which has been appearing in monographs, articles, and comprehensive works during the last fifteen years, and has been no mean part of a Southern renaissance.

The essence of this analysis is that cultured, civilized people were driven to fight in order to protect their superior institutions from attacks which a swiftly growing industrialized northern capitalism was directing against them in the name of liberty, hypocritically denouncing Negro slavery while itself creating a wage slavery more inhumane and degrading. According to this theory, the Southern "cause" was "lost" because borne down by the weight of superior numbers and resources; and the implication is that this defeat destroyed the best possible effective check on the oligarchic power of industrial capitalism. Further it is maintained that Negro slavery had reached its natural limits and had the North been better mannered, less grasping, abusive, and hypocritical there would have been no war. The fault lay north of the Mason-Dixon line.

This thesis has won such wide acceptance that one historian has declared "in song and story it is the South that has won the decision at Appomattox." Another, much concerned at this, believes that these "revisionist dogmas are carrying historians further from an explanation year by year."

This later type of interpretation has been made by very able scholars, trained in the best graduate schools, several of them born in the North and most of them educated there. They have been activated by that great and worthy ambition of modern scholarship to correct ancient errors, discover new truth, and perchance to hang the scalp of a "find" on the belt of the scholar. Nevertheless, the result is a "scientific" blessing of a folk-legend long current in the land where the "Lost Cause" has never been forgotten.

Despite the obfuscations of these nationalistic folklore interpretations, efforts have not been lacking to produce a more objective explanation. Much research and writing have brought to light new data, particularly regarding social and cultural factors. The war has been described as a contest between economic interests, namely the agrarian South and the industrialized North; or as a clash between cultures when the people of the sections living in different physiographic environments developed separate ways of life and patterns of thought. Psychological complexes and antagonisms have been emphasized in line with recent interest in psychiatry.

Much of the work represents a retreat from political interpretation. Such a broadening of the base of analysis was desirable; there had been too great a preoccupation with the political. But the pendulum has swung too far in the other direction and has left an unfortunate blind spot. For political behavior is an important and often decisive factor in a cultural interpretation of history, particularly among a people so politically minded as the inhabitants of this Republic. It should be remembered that the various economic, social, and psychological factors, which figure so largely in more recent theories of causation applied to the Civil War, have existed elsewhere without causing wars. Why did they do so here? What was the peculiar catalytic agent in the United States? I am about to maintain that it is found in the nature of our political behavior.

II

When the Founding Fathers met, . . . in Independence Hall, to create the United States of America they were remarkably wise but at the same time much limited by the narrow bounds of contemporary social knowledge. Their political wisdom moved them to prescribe a federal system, rather than to attempt to force the establishment of a centralized national government. They failed, however, to foresee how the processes of national growth were to affect their handiwork. They created a system without sufficient mechanism to operate it. Their successors, without their wisdom or purposefulness, had to create this machinery.

The crux of the problem of government, for which machinery was necessary, presented by the federal system in operation, was the method of registering the popular will. All laws, all executive acts, all judicial determination were to be made by representatives of the people, or their appointees. How were these representatives to be chosen?

The makers of the Constitution were used to a state system of elections which was the product of colonial custom and experience rather than the result of comprehensive planning. In the main the drafters accepted these electoral customs and added but little to them. The two popularly-elected groups, the members of the lower house of the Federal Congress, and that part of the Electoral College chosen by direct vote rather than by state legislatures, were to be selected at such times and by such voters as the states might prescribe. The only federal requirement was that the Congressmen must be chosen in time to assemble on the first Monday in December of the odd years, and the Presidential electors so that they could meet in their respective state capitols in the December of every leap year. The result was that from the beginning each state determined its own times and seasons and as late as 1861 there had been little progress on the road to uniformity among the then thirty-four states. State and Congressional elections were held here and there in all months of every year, save January, February, June, and July. Election activity was never ending.

A second mechanism for registering the popular will—the system of parties—was not envisioned by the gentlemen next door when they did their work in 1787, nor did it emerge quickly, as historians generally assume. Machine politics was of slow growth and developed only after a phenomenal increase in the population. Political leaders in the 1820's and 1830's saw that elections could be carried most effectively by careful organization, and so a group of them created the Democratic party between 1828 and 1836. They were clever and did their work so well that, barring accidents, they seemed destined to control permanently; they actually did rule this country, with the exception of two brief intervals, from 1829 to 1861—thirty-two years.

This Democratic party, and the various less successful organizations which attempted to oppose it, were in reality not national parties, as we understand such a term; in fact even our Republican and Democratic groups of today are not as national and centralized as people commonly assume. They are really federations of state machines, and these machines are generally very independent and often hard to handle, as any national chairman can testify. In the period just before the Civil War there was hardly any central organization at all, but some sixty-eight state parties acting with great individual independence.

III

Those chosen by the voters, in such a haphazard series of elections operated by parties so disorganized, must then direct the federal system and must do so ostensibly as representatives of the states. As such they must apportion patronage and appropriations as well as answer legislative demands as federal legislators and officials. They constantly employed diplomatic negotiating and bargaining. Legislation was more like treaty making than statute writing, and it often was done in an atmosphere of bad temper and antagonism, especially as the capital city, Washington, was so badly equipped and so unhealthful.

Their task was the more difficult because federal relations among the states were so difficult. Few of the states were coherent or integrated units of opinion and a large proportion of them were confused by various and conflicting internal interests and views. Such differences often crossed state lines. Even today, understanding of the true nature of the federal system is hampered by the earlier emphasis on state rights and by the fact that certain states once seceded and formed a Southern republic. The North and the South, as the antagonists were then labelled, went to war. This eventual narrowing of the interest to two easily defined belligerents also gives a false impression of simplicity which is projected back into the ante-bellum years. The federal system and its relation to the Civil War need a more penetrating analysis than can be had by concentrating on states and their rights and on the growing antagonism between two entities described as North and South.

Those chosen by the people to operate the federal system were not only confused by the factors just mentioned but they were most handicapped because they failed to understand what sort of federalism they were representing. Before the Civil War the political leaders were deceived because they were thinking of federalism not in terms of the basic cultural situation; rather they were absorbed by an accidental political combination, a union of states. In fact the people of the new republic were not so much the citizens of the several states, or dwellers in two distinct sections growing continually more incompatible, as they were people activated by a series of attitudes. They were living within a cultural federalism, in which men and women of different attitudes were pooling their interests in the operation of a political federal system. The basic fact is the cultural federation of attitudes rather than the political federation of states.

The men and women exhibiting these different attitudes were not isolated and separated by boundaries, they dwelt side by side and on occasion the same person might be moved by more than one attitude, or by different ones at different times. The emotional complex which was created by the variety of these attitudes and the tension which their antagonisms bred added such confusion to that already provided by the chaotic electoral customs and poorly organized parties, that the total precipitated a resort to arms. The baffling problem was not how to maintain a balance among states but how to preserve a balance among a number of emotional units or attitudes. It was this that proved beyond the political capacity of the time.

Of the multitude of attitudes within this cultural federalism discernible during the ante-bellum days, there were five which were particularly dangerous in their conflict-breeding potentialities. Most prominent among them was a state of mind and emotion best called Southernism, which dominated not only many within the South but numerous migrants from that region as well as sympathizers with its situation who dwelt in the North. Its chief characteristic was its increasing defensiveness, its praise of slavery, its fear that Southern culture was in danger of destruction or degradation. A second divisive attitude was that dominating those eager to see the nation wax in wealth and power, who were anxious to exploit national resources, develop industry, provide transportation, and promote commerce and banking. These interests of the metropolis make it appropriate to speak of this attitude as Metropolitanism. It was characteristic of the era and was found everywhere, but it was less common in the South where the fear grew that such swift development might come at the South's expense. A third attitude, for convenience called Territorialism, was characterized by an intense interest in frontier development, in the organization of territories and the admission of new states. Here fortunes, financial and political, could be made and interest was feverish. The urge for political growth vitally affected state and national politics during the ante-bellum years between 1815 and 1860, as sixteen new states were created. Most of them emerged from territorial status through political turbulence, in which men from various regions had fought furiously to control the pattern of development in the new communities.

The confusion was worse confounded by two other attitudes which injected a combination of hatred and moral indignation into the turmoil, by Anti-Slaveryism and New Englandism. The existence of slavery in the Southern states troubled many people, as both anachronistic and sinful. Particularly in the Middle West many hated slavery and were moved by an intense desire to abolish it or at least to prevent its extension. Their hatred of slavery often was combined with antagonisms bred of struggles against persons dominated by Southern ways of thought and behavior, over the political and business problems of their states. Furthermore many people in New England were activated by a variation of Anti-Slaveryism. That region had been losing ground politically and people of ambitions or pride felt thwarted. They found that the dominant Southern politicians stood most in their way and their bitterness at their inferiority easily could be translated into hatred of the sin of slavery and into attacks upon the slave power.

This complex series of divisive attitudes—Southernism, Metropolitanism, Territorialism, Anti-Slaveryism, and New Englandism—was underlined, emphasized, and exaggerated by two prevailing attitudes which had no suspicion of sectional location. They were found everywhere and their nature was such as to intensify the emotional stimulus which the divisive attitudes projected. These attitudes were the prevailing Protestantism and Romanticism so characteristic of the time. The first of these two emphasized morality and duty and caused many consciences to be concerned over sin in the community. Because of it there was in the free labor states therefore much hatred of slavery as a sin and a very active and militant group of abolitionists. Sensitive conscience caused people to fight Southern political power in the name of a crusade against a national shame. In the South, on the other hand, the same Protestant attitude prevailed, but slavery was praised as a blessing because it enabled African heathen to secure Christian salvation. There, attacks upon the institution by abolitionists and opponents of slavery-extension were countered by denunciation of Northern materialism, wage slavery, general servitude to Mammon, and hypocrisy, all sins.

The intensity of these feelings was strengthened by the prevailing Romanticism of the period. A rosy optimism precluded a realistic view of the perplexing problems. Virtues and vices stood unqualified. Few people would admit any dangers and most went on sublimely with the most naive concepts of contemporary trends. This romantic state of mind placed a premium upon exaggeration; ideas and emotions that were attractive were embraced without critical appraisal of their validity. There was therefore a minimum of that commodity labelled "common sense." Too few could be convinced that concerted efforts should be made to encourage cohesive attitudes which would counteract the divisive tendencies.

The few who were endeavoring to encourage such cohesive attitudes sought to stimulate Nationalism. They stressed the increasing strength of the nation, natural pride in the creation and maintenance of free institutions. The growing sense of the success of the United States gave some confidence that Nationalism might counteract the divisive attitudes enough to overcome the disrupting tendencies. Others felt that the saving formula should be an appeal to fair play under the classic theory of Democracy. Government should be by the rule of the majority. That majority which ruled in town meeting and county council, in state legislature and Congress, should rule everywhere. The people could be trusted; by and large the majority in the greatest number of cases was bound to be right. All vexed questions of dangerous import should be referred to the people and everyone should be bound to submit to the will of the majority. Yet neither Nationalism nor Democracy could satisfy the South. Both attitudes assumed that the Southern people as a minority must be subject to the will of others, an intolerable assumption. Yet, since some reconciling formula was necessary, their political philosophers must suggest an alternative. They began to encourage a concept of Regionalism, an autonomy designed to make the enactment of certain types of legislation dependent upon some form of regional consent.

The strength of those leaders endeavoring to encourage the cohesive attitudes was entirely inadequate for the task and they were further hampered by the general lack of understanding of the cultural federalism which was conditioning their problems. They thought they were dealing with a controversy which was primarily legal involving merely a harmonization of rights, state and federal. They sought—just as if they were settling a case at law—to achieve a legal formula which would reconcile states to federal exercise of power and sovereignty. It was an era that throve on legal and political theory, on countless hours spent in oratory and in the writing and reading of those long, theoretical debates which we now think to have been so unrealistic. Unrecognized behind the oratory were the prevailing attitudes, giving direction to such dynamics as moral indignation (which some present-day blasé historians seem inclined to discount), thwarted ambition, fear of loss of face and power, and the countless confusions of a growing state.

The political leaders failed as they were bound to fail because they oversimplified their problem and tried to stop a flood with a sand pile. And this flood reached its crest because they themselves fed it by the constant agitation which rose out of the chaotic electoral system. Contests were waged not only continually but also on two levels, local and federal. The same party organizations had to maintain themselves in power in the states and in Washington; and it was generally more important to maintain their local controls. They frequently brought national issues into state contests because of the greater potential interest. The people of one locality could easily be whipped into political fury about the sins of omission or commission of others in a distant region, and with little risk to the local agitators. This possibility bred irresponsibility about playing with emotional dynamite. Dangerous divisive attitudes were encouraged for local purposes by agitators of narrow vision, heedless of the consequences.

Thus the prime factor that made conflict irrepressible was political. The divisive and pervasive attitudes provided inexhaustible material for political controversy, and the will and the strength to carry it on vigorously whenever opportunity demanded. These controversies reached the blood-letting pitch because the chaotic election program called for contests somewhere nearly all the time. Issues were never allowed to rest. Political oratory, pamphleteering, inflammatory journalism, and more important, corner store and tavern argument, were going on all the time.

The swift growth of population brought a constant demand for the recognition of new political units to be fitted into the federal government and the federal party organizations. Controversy over these political realignments became more intense as the conflicting attitudes became stronger. The control of government was more sought after as the growth of the country made federal functioning more vital particularly through subsidy, "protection," and the opening of new territory. The stakes of power were constantly growing higher, with many more men becoming politically ambitious and seeking office more intensively. So the contests were more vigorously waged. Popular interest in them could generally be captured more effectively by predictions of calamity and danger; so, quite heedlessly, literally hundreds of persons seeking public office stirred up increasing apprehension among the voters.

IV

This rising tide of crisis agitation wracked the political machinery operating the federal system. The Democratic party had been in power almost continuously through three decades. Its strength lay in its appeal as a people's party, in the heroic Jackson legend, in a swash-buckling, expansionist, foreign policy, in its effective political organization, but particularly in its laissez-faire philosophy in domestic affairs. On questions of subsidy the party leaders, sensing some of the variety of interests and attitudes endangering the party's control, had avoided such issues by maintaining the federal government as one of very limited powers. It attempted to encourage Nationalism by its aggressive foreign policy. In domestic policy it was more and more sympathetic to regionalism.

But no party in this country has ever remained in power for much more than the life of a generation. As the 1860's approached the ruling Democratic party was more and more cursed by the resentments of those who had been thwarted by its laissez-faire policy, those disappointed in their ambitions for leadership and office, and of course by the rising generation inevitably at feud with its elders. The stage was set for schism and it came.

A new political group was ready to take advantage of these signs of discontent and rebellion. The old opposition party, the Whigs, had never been very effective, in part because it took little advantage of the controversial issues of conflicting attitudes and merely tried to promote the cohesive idea of Nationalism. It was now pushed aside by a new party, the Republicans, who capitalized division. They saw that the majority of the voters lived in regions where metropolitan, territorial, anti-slavery, and New England attitudes existed in profusion and confusion. Heedless of danger they made a catch-all appeal. Combining moral indignation against slavery with promises to various promotional interests, and stressing the theoretical concept of the right of the majority to rule, they had an appeal strong enough to break the long-continued power of the South and of the Democratic party.

The Democratic leadership saw this opposition swiftly rising but were incapable of coherent action to meet it. They were faced with a dilemma. The free state Democrats saw the need of concessions to save their ranks from the onslaught of the Republicans but their Southern associates refused these concessions for they themselves were in danger. They had as their local opponents the Southern branch of the Whig party, which had lost most of the Northern wing to the Republicans and therefore could go all-out for Southern interests. If the Southern Democrats agreed to concessions in the national platform to placate free state opinion, they would be accused by their local opponents of betraying the South and might well be driven from the state governments. Rather than lose local control the Southern Democratic leaders sacrificed their national power, a phenomenon not unusual in American political history. The result was the split of the Democratic party at the national convention in 1860. The delegations from the Gulf states took a walk probably expecting thereby to force a compromise which would restore unity. But then it appeared that the Northern state machines refused harmony because any concessions would destroy their slim chances of maintaining power. Indeed the intricacies of a local feud in New York may have been the immediate cause of the failure of compromise. The system of federally organized parties had resulted in the exaltation of the local over the national and had so hindered the growth of nationally-minded leaders that there were none powerful enough to meet the crisis.

This schism made the election of 1860 unique in American political history. Hitherto there had never been more than two parties, or at most two major and one minor organization, at any one of the Presidential elections since 1824. Now however there were four substantial parties in contest: the Republicans, the Regular Democrats, the Bolting Democrats (largely though by no means exclusively from the South), and the Whig organization transformed by a new name into the Constitutional Union party. In this four-cornered contest the Republicans won, though garnering only forty per cent of the votes, because their minority of the popular votes was sufficient to gain a majority of the electoral ballots.

Then the constant agitation bore its fruit. There were enough Southerners so angered and fearful, after years of alarmist campaigning in their own and in the free labor communities, that they demanded and secured secession by eleven states in the interest of preserving their freedom. In the free states indignation at this attempt to break up the great democratic experiment led to a resort to arms, to preserve the Union against these secessionists.

Thus war came when the American people for the first time refused to abide by a national election. The parties which had been promoting the cohesive attitudes had broken down and their disorganization had permitted the new Republican organization to win through direct appeal to the divisive attitudes. The constant heat generated in the frequent elections brought an explosion. The social, economic, and cultural differences had been so used by the political operators as to produce secession and civil war.

The war came because no means had been devised to curb the extravagant use of the divisive forces. Statesmanship seemed poverty stricken. The work of the nationalists who sought to find the formula with which to overcome the divisive attitudes was vain. Too few even saw the need for the formula; they ran heedlessly down the path to disruption. In the last analysis the war was the product of the chaotic lack of system in ascertaining the public will, a chaos exploited by irresponsible and blind operators of local political machinery without adequate central organization.

The Civil War fortunately did not spell destruction to the republic. It left its lessons behind it. Growing social coherence, the nationalism accelerated by the war, at length produced more orderly democratic procedures. Elections are now concentrated in the autumn of the even years; there are long breathing spells between campaigns. Parties were better organized with more centralized management. Isolated, irresponsible action became somewhat less frequent. The two party system was resumed. Although there have been a score of small parties and upon occasion three large enough to become major, the disintegration of 1860 has never been repeated.

It is to be hoped that the architects of world federation study carefully the lessons of American experience. Woeful are the results of irresponsible exploitation of divisive attitudes. Strenuous effort is essential to invent political machinery effective enough to keep cohesive attitudes dominant.

Allan Nevins

When James Buchanan, standing in a homespun suit before cheering crowds, took the oath of office on March 4, 1857, he seemed confident that the issues before the nation could be readily settled. He spoke about an army road to California, use of the Treasury surplus to pay all the national debt, and proper guardianship of the public lands. In Kansas, he declared, the path ahead was clear. The simple logical rule that the will of the people should determine the institutions of a territory had brought in sight a happy settlement. The inhabitants would declare for or against slavery as they pleased. Opinions differed as to the proper time for making such a decision; but Buchanan thought that "the appropriate period will be when the number of actual residents in the Territory shall justify the formation of a constitution with a view to its admission as a State." He trusted that the long strife between North and South was nearing its end, and that the sectional party which had almost elected Frémont would die a natural death.

Two days after the inaugural Buchanan took deep satisfaction in a decision by the Supreme Court of which he had improper foreknowledge: the Dred Scott decision handed down by Chief Justice Taney. Its vital ele-

Reprinted with permission from *American Heritage, The Magazine of History*, VII (August, 1956), 5-9, 88-90.

ment, so far as the nation's destiny was concerned, was the ruling that the Missouri Compromise restriction, by which slavery had been excluded north of the 36°30' line, was void; that on the contrary, every territory was open to slavery. Not merely was Congress without power to legislate *against* slavery, but by implication it should act to protect it. Much of the northern press denounced the decision fervently. But the country was prosperous; it was clear that time and political action might change the Supreme Court, bringing a new decision; and the explosion of wrath proved brief.

Buchanan had seen his view sustained; slavery might freely enter any territory, the inhabitants of which could not decide whether to keep it or drop it until they wrote their first constitution. In theory, the highway to national peace was as traversible as the Lancaster turnpike. To be sure, Kansas was rent between two bitter parties, proslavery and antislavery; from the moment Stephen A. Douglas' Kansas-Nebraska Act had thrown open the West to popular sovereignty three years earlier, it had been a theater of unrelenting conflict. Popular sovereignty had simply failed to work. In the spring of 1855 about five thousand invading Missourians, swamping the polls, had given Kansas a fanatically proslavery legislature which the free-soil settlers flatly refused to recognize. That fall a free-soil convention in Topeka had adopted a constitution which the slavery men in turn flatly rejected. Some bloody fighting had ensued. But could not all this be thrust into the past?

In theory, the President might now send out an impartial new governor; and if the people wanted statehood, an election might be held for a new constitutional convention. Then the voters could give the nation its sixteenth slave state or its seventeenth free state—everybody behaving quietly and reasonably. Serenity would prevail. Actually, the idea that the people of Kansas, so violently aroused, would show quiet reason, was about as tenable as the idea that Europeans would begin settling boundary quarrels by a quiet game of chess. Behind the two Kansas parties were grim southerners and determined northerners. "Slavery will now yield a greater profit in Kansas," trumpeted a southern propagandist in *De Bow's Review*, "either to hire out or cultivate the soil, than any other place." He wanted proslavery squatters. Meanwhile, Yankees were subsidizing their own settlers. "I know people," said Emerson in a speech, "who are making haste to reduce their expenses and pay their debts . . . to save and earn for the benefit of Kansas emigrants."

Nor was reason in Kansas the only need. Impartiality in Congress, courage in the presidential chair, were also required. The stage was dressed for a brief, fateful melodrama, which more than anything else was to fix the position of James Buchanan and Stephen A. Douglas in history, was to shape the circumstances under which Lincoln made his first national reputation, and was to have more potency than any other single event in deciding whether North and South should remain brothers or fly at each other's throats. That melodrama was entitled "Lecompton." Douglas was to go to his grave believing that, had Buchanan played an honest, resolute part in it, rebellion would have been killed in its incipiency. The role that Buchanan did play may be counted one of the signal failures of American statesmanship.

To hold that the Civil War could not have been averted by wise, firm, and timely action is to concede too much to determinism in history. Winston Churchill said that the Second World War should be called "The Unnecessary War"; the same term might as justly be applied to our Civil War. Passionate unreason among large sections of the population was one ingredient in the broth of conflict. Accident, fortuity, fate, or sheer bad luck (these terms are interchangeable) was another; John Brown's raid, so malign in its effects on opinion, North and South, might justly be termed an accident. Nothing in the logic of forces or events required so crazy an act. But beyond these ingredients lies the further element of wretched leadership. Had the United States possessed three farseeing, imaginative, and resolute Presidents instead of Fillmore, Pierce, and Buchanan, the war might have been postponed until time and economic forces killed its roots. Buchanan was the weakest of the three, and the Lecompton affair lights up his incompetence like a play of lightning across a nocturnal storm front.

The melodrama had two stages, one in faraway, thinly settled Kansas, burning hot in summer, bitter cold in winter, and, though reputedly rich, really so poor that settlers were soon on the brink of starvation. Here the most curious fact was the disparity between the mean actors and the great results they effected. A handful of ignorant, reckless, semi-drunken settlers on the southern side, led by a few desperadoes of politics—the delegates of the Lecompton Constitutional Convention—actually had the power to make or mar the nation. The other stage was Washington. The participants here, representing great interests and ideas, had at least a dignity worthy of the scene and the consequences of their action. James Buchanan faced three main groups holding three divergent views of the sectional problem.

The proslavery group (that is, Robert Toombs, Alexander H. Stephens, Jefferson Davis, John Slidell, David Atchison, and many more) demanded that slavery be allowed to expand freely within the territories; soon they were asking also that such expansion be given federal protection against any hostile local action. This stand involved the principle that slavery was morally right, and socially and economically a positive good. Reverdy Johnson of Maryland, in the Dred Scott case, had vehemently argued the beneficence of slavery.

The popular sovereignty group, led by Douglas and particularly strong among northwestern Democrats, maintained that in any territory the issue of slavery or free soil should be determined *at all times* by the settlers therein. Douglas modified the Dred Scott doctrine: local police legislation and action, he said, could exclude slavery even before state-making took place. He sternly rejected the demand for federal protection against such action. His popular sovereignty view implied indifference to or rejection of any moral test of slavery. Whether the institution was socially and economically good or bad depended mainly on climate and soil, and moral ideas were irrelevant. He did not care whether slavery was voted up or voted down; the right to a fair vote was the all-important matter.

The free-soil group, led by Seward and Chase, but soon to find its best voice in Lincoln, held that slavery should be excluded from all territories present or future. They insisted that slavery was morally wrong, had been condemned as such by the Fathers, and was increasingly outlawed by the march of world civilization. It might be argued that the free-soil contention was superfluous, in that climate and aridity forbade a further extension of slavery anyhow. But in Lincoln's eyes this did not touch the heart of the matter. It might or might not be expansible. (Already it existed in Delaware and Missouri, and Cuba and Mexico might be conquered for it.) What was important was for America to accept the fact that, being morally wrong and socially an anachronism, it *ought* not to expand; it *ought* to be put in the way of ultimate eradication. Lincoln was a planner. Once the country accepted nonexpansion, it would thereby accept the idea of ultimate extinction. This crisis met and passed, it could sit down and decide when and how, in God's good time and with suitable compensation to slaveholders, it might be ended.

The Buchanan who faced these three warring groups was victim of the mistaken belief among American politicians (like Pierce, Benjamin Harrison, and Warren G. Harding, for example) that it is better to be a poor President than to stick to honorable but lesser posts. He would have made a respectable diplomat or decent Cabinet officer under a really strong President. Sixty-six in 1857, the obese bachelor felt all his years. He had wound his devious way up through a succession of offices without once showing a flash of inspiration or an ounce of grim courage. James K. Polk had accurately characterized him as an old woman—"It is one of his weaknesses that he takes on and magnifies small matters into great and undeserved importance." His principal characteristic was irresolution. "Even among close friends," remarked a southern senator, "he very rarely expressed his opinions at all upon disputed questions, except in language especially marked with a cautious circumspection almost amounting to timidity."

He was industrious, capable, and tactful, a well-read Christian gentleman; he had acquired from forty years of public life a rich fund of experience. But he was pedestrian, humorless, calculating, and pliable. He never made a witty remark, never wrote a memorable sentence, and never showed a touch of distinction. Above all (and this was the source of his irresolution) he had no strong convictions. Associating all his life with southern leaders in Washington, this Pennsylvanian leaned toward their views, but he never disclosed a deep adherence to any principle. Like other weak men, he could be stubborn; still oftener, he could show a petulant irascibility when events pushed him into a corner. And like other timid men, he would sometimes flare out in a sudden burst of anger, directed not against enemies who could hurt him but against friends or neutrals who would not. As the sectional crisis deepened, it became his dominant hope to stumble through it, somehow, and anyhow, so as to leave office with the Union yet intact. His successor could bear the storm.

This was the President who had to deal, in Kansas and Washington, with men of fierce conviction, stern courage and, all too often, ruthless methods.

In Kansas the proslavery leaders were determined to strike boldly and unscrupulously for a slave state. They maintained close communications with such southern chieftains in Washington as Senator Slidell, Speaker James L. Orr, and Howell Cobb and Jacob Thompson, Buchanan's secretaries of the Treasury and the Interior. Having gained control of the territorial legislature, they meant to keep and use this mastery. Just before Buchanan became President they passed a bill for a constitutional convention—and a more unfair measure was never put on paper. Nearly all county officers, selected not by popular vote but by the dishonestly chosen legislature, were proslavery men. The bill provided that the sheriffs and their deputies should in March, 1857, register the white residents; that the probate judges should then take from the sheriffs complete lists of qualified voters; and that the county commissioners should finally choose election judges.

Everyone knew that a heavy majority of the Kansas settlers were antislavery. Many, even of the southerners, who had migrated thither opposed the "peculiar institution" as retrogressive and crippling in character. Everybody also knew that Kansas, with hardly thirty thousand people, burdened with debts, and unsupplied with fit roads, schools, or courthouses, was not yet ready for statehood; it still needed the federal government's care. Most Kansans refused to recognize the "bogus" legislature. Yet this legislature was forcing a premature convention, and taking steps to see that the election of delegates was controlled by sheriffs, judges, and county commissioners who were mainly proslavery Democrats. Governor

John W. Geary, himself a Democrat appointed by Pierce, indignantly vetoed the bill. But the legislature immediately repassed it over Geary's veto; and when threats against his life increased until citizens laid bets that he would be assassinated within forty days, he resigned in alarm and posted east to apprise the country of imminent perils.

Along the way to Washington, Geary paused to warn the press that a packed convention was about to drag fettered Kansas before Congress with a slavery constitution. This convention would have a free hand, for the bill just passed made no provision for a popular vote on the instrument. Indeed, one legislator admitted that the plan was to avoid popular submission, for he proposed inserting a clause to guard against the possibility that Congress might return the constitution for a referendum. Thus, commented the *Missouri Democrat*, "the felon legislature has provided as effectually for getting the desired result as Louis Napoleon did for getting himself elected Emperor." All this was an ironic commentary on Douglas' maxim: "Let the voice of the people rule."

And Douglas, watching the reckless course of the Kansas legislators with alarm, saw that his principles and his political future were at stake. When his Kansas-Nebraska Act was passed, he had given the North his solemn promise that a free, full, and fair election would decide the future of the two territories. No fraud, no sharp practice, no browbeating would be sanctioned; every male white citizen should have use of the ballot box. He had notified the South that Kansas was almost certain to be free soil. Now he professed confidence that President Buchanan would never permit a breach of fair procedure. He joined Buchanan in persuading one of the nation's ablest men, former Secretary of the Treasury Robert J. Walker, to go out to Kansas in Geary's place as governor. Douglas knew that if he consented to a betrayal of popular sovereignty he would be ruined forever politically in his own state of Illinois.

For a brief space in the spring of 1857 Buchanan seemed to stand firm. In his instructions to Governor Walker he engaged that the new constitution would be laid before the people; and "they must be protected in the exercise of their right of voting for or against that instrument, and the fair expression of the popular will must not be interrupted by fraud or violence."

It is not strange that the rash proslavery gamesters in Kansas prosecuted their designs despite all Buchanan's fair words and Walker's desperate efforts to stay them. They knew that with four fifths of the people already against them, and the odds growing greater every year, only brazen trickery could effect their end. They were aware that the South, which believed that a fair division would give Kansas to slavery and Nebraska to freedom, expected them to stand firm. They were egged on by the two reckless southern Cabinet members, Howell Cobb and Thompson, who sent an agent, H. L. Martin of Mississippi, out to the Kansas convention. This gathering in Lecompton, with 48 of the 60 members hailing from slave states, was the shabbiest conclave of its kind ever held on American soil One of Buchanan's Kansas correspondents wrote that he had not supposed such a wild set could be found. The *Kansas News* termed them a body of "broken-down political hacks, demagogues, fire-eaters, perjurers, ruffians, ballot-box stuffers, and loafers." But before it broke up with the shout, "Now, boys, let's come and take a drink!" it had written a constitution.

This constitution, the work of a totally unrepresentative body, was a devious repudiation of all the principles Buchanan and Douglas had laid down. Although it contained numerous controversial provisions, such as limitation of banking to one institution and a bar against free Negroes, the main document was not to be submitted to general vote at all. A nominal reference of the great cardinal question was indeed provided. Voters might cast their ballots for the "constitution with slavery" or the "constitution without slavery." But when closely examined this was seen to be actually a piece of chicanery. Whichever form was adopted, the 200 slaves in Kansas would remain, with a constitutional guarantee against interference. Whenever the proslavery party in Kansas could get control of the legislature, they might open the door wide for more slaves. The rigged convention had put its handiwork before the people with a rigged choice: "Heads I win, tails you lose."

Would Buchanan lay this impudent contrivance before Congress, and ask it to vote the admission of Kansas as a state? Or would he contemptuously spurn it? An intrepid man would not have hesitated an instant to take the honest course; he would not have needed the indignant outcry of the northern press, the outraged roar of Douglas, to inspirit him. But Buchanan quailed before the storm of passion into which proslavery extremists had worked themselves.

The hot blood of the South was now up. That section, grossly misinformed upon events in Kansas, believed that *it* was being cheated. The northern freesoilers had vowed that no new slave state (save by a partition of Texas) should ever be admitted. Southerners thought that in pursuance of this resolve, the Yankees had made unscrupulous use of their wealth and numbers to lay hands on Kansas. Did the North think itself entitled to every piece on the board—to take Kansas as well as California, Minnesota, Iowa, Nebraska, Oregon—to give southerners nothing? The Lecompton delegates, from this point of view, were dauntless champions of a wronged section. What if they did use sharp tactics? That was but a necessary response to northern arrogance. Jefferson Davis declared that his section trembled under a sense of insecurity. "You have made it a political war. We are on the defensive. How far are you to push us?" Sharp threats of secession and battle mingled with the southern denunciations. "Sir," Senator Alfred Iverson of Georgia was soon to assert, "I believe that the time will come when the slave States will be compelled, in vindication of their rights, interests, and honor, to separate from the free States, and erect an independent confederacy; and I am not sure, sir, that the time is not at hand."

Three southern members of the Cabinet, Cobb, Thompson, and John B. Floyd, had taken the measure of Buchanan's pusillanimity. They, with one northern sympathizer, Jeremiah Black, and several White House habitués like John Slidell of Louisiana, constituted a virtual Directory exercising control over the tremulous President. They played on Buchanan's fierce partisan hatred of Republicans, and his jealous dislike of Douglas. They played also on his legalistic cast of mind; after all, the Lecompton constitution was a legal instrument by a legal convention—outwardly. Above all, they played on his fears, his morbid sensitiveness, and his responsiveness to immediate pressures. They could do this the more easily because the threats of disruption and violence were real. Henry S. Foote, a former senator from Mississippi and an enemy of Jefferson Davis, who saw Lecompton in its true light and hurried to Washington to advise the President, writes:

It was unfortunately of no avail that these efforts to reassure Mr. Buchanan were at that time essayed by myself and others; he had already become thoroughly *panic-stricken;* the howlings of the bulldog of secession had fairly frightened him out of his wits, and he ingloriously resolved to yield without further resistance to the decrial and villification to which he had been so acrimoniously subjected.

And the well-informed Washington correspondent of the New Orleans *Picayune* a little later told just how aggressively the Chief Executive was bludgeoned into submission:

The President was informed in November, 1857, that the States of Alabama, Mississippi, and South Carolina, and perhaps others, would hold conventions and secede from the Union if the Lecompton Constitution, which established slavery, should not be accepted by Congress. The reason was that these States, supposing that the South had been cheated out of Kansas, were, whether right or wrong, determined to revolt. The President believed this. Senator Hunter, of Virginia, to my knowledge, believed it. Many other eminent men did, and perhaps not without reason.

Buchanan, without imagination as without nerve, began to yield to this southern storm in midsummer, and by November, 1857, he was surrendering completely. When Congress met in December his message upheld the Lecompton Constitution with a tissue of false and evasive statements. Seldom in American history has a chief magistrate made a greater error, or missed a larger opportunity. The astute secretary of his predecessor, Franklin Pierce, wrote: "I had considerable hopes of Mr. Buchanan—I really thought he was a statesman—but I have now come to the settled conclusion that he is just the damndest old fool that has ever occupied the presidential chair. He has deliberately walked overboard with his eyes open—let him drown, for he must."

As Buchanan shrank from the lists, Douglas entered them with that *gaudium certaminis* which was one of his greatest qualities. The finest chapters of his life, his last great contests for the Union, were opening. Obviously he would have had to act under political necessity even if deaf to principle, for had he let popular sovereignty be torn to pieces, Illinois would not have sent him back to the Senate the following year; but he was not the man to turn his back on principle. His struggle against Lecompton was an exhibition of iron determination. The drama of that battle has given it an almost unique place in the record of our party controversies.

"By God, sir!" he exclaimed, "I made James Buchanan, and by God, sir, I will unmake him!" Friends told him that the southern Democrats meant to ruin him. "I have taken a through ticket," rejoined Douglas, "and checked my baggage." He lost no time in facing Buchanan in the White House and denouncing the Lecompton policy. When the President reminded him how Jackson had crushed two party rebels, he was ready with a stinging retort. Douglas was not to be overawed by a man he despised as a weakling. "Mr. President," he snorted, "I wish you to remember that General Jackson is dead."

As for the southern leaders, Douglas' scorn for the extremists who had coerced Buchanan was unbounded. He told the Washington correspondent of the Chicago *Journal* that he had begun his fight as a contest against a single bad measure. But his blow at Lecompton was a blow against slavery extension, and he at once had the whole "slave power" down on him like a pack of wolves. He added: "In making the fight against this power, I was enabled to stand off and view the men with whom I had been acting; I was ashamed I had ever been caught in such company; they are a set of unprincipled demagogues, bent upon perpetuating slavery, and by the exercise of that unequal and unfair power, to control the government or break up the Union; and I intend to prevent their doing either."

After a long, close, and acrid contest, on April 1, 1858, Lecompton was defeated. A coalition of Republicans, Douglasite Democrats, and Know-Nothings struck down the fraudulent constitution in the House, 120 to 112. When the vote was announced, a wild cheer rolled through the galleries. Old Francis P. Blair, Jackson's friend, carried the news to the dying Thomas Hart Benton, who had been intensely aroused by the crisis.

Benton could barely speak, but his exultation was unbounded. "In energetic whispers," records Blair, "he told his visitor that the same men who had sought to destroy the republic in 1850 were at bottom of this accursed Lecompton business. Among the greatest of his consolations in dying was the consciousness that the House of Representatives had baffled these treasonable schemes and put the heels of the people on the neck of the traitors."

The Administration covered its retreat by a hastily concocted measure, the English Bill, under which Kansas was kept waiting on the doorstep—sure in the end to enter a free state. The Kansas plotters, the Cobb-Thompson-Floyd clique in the Cabinet, and Buchanan had all been worsted. But the damage had been done. Southern secessionists had gained fresh strength and greater boldness from their success in coercing the Administration.

The Lecompton struggle left a varied and interesting set of aftereffects. It lifted Stephen A. Douglas to a new plane; he had been a fighting Democratic strategist, but now he became a true national leader, thinking far less of party and more of country. It sharpened the issues which that summer and fall were to form the staple of the memorable Lincoln-Douglas debates in Illinois. At the same time, it deepened the schism which had been growing for some years between southern Democrats and northwestern Democrats, and helped pave the way to that disruption of the party which preceded and facilitated the disruption of the nation. It planted new seeds of dissension in Kansas—seeds which resulted in fresh conflicts between Kansas free-soilers or jayhawkers on one side and Missouri invaders or border ruffians on the other, and in a spirit of border lawlessness which was to give the Civil War some of its darkest pages. The Lecompton battle discredited Buchanan in the eyes of most decent northerners, strengthened southern conviction of his weakness, and left the Administration materially and morally weaker in dealing with the problems of the next two and a half critical years.

For the full measure of Buchanan's failure, however, we must go deeper. Had he shown the courage that to an Adams, a Jackson, a Polk, or a Cleveland would have been second nature, the courage that springs from a deep integrity, he might have done the republic an immeasurable service by grappling with disunion when it was yet weak and unprepared. Ex-Senator Foote wrote later that he knew well that a scheme for destroying the Union "had long been on foot in the South." He knew that its leaders "were only waiting for the enfeebling of the Democratic Party in the North, and the general triumph of Free-soilism as a consequence thereof, to alarm the whole South into acquiescence in their policy." Buchanan's support of the unwise and corrupt Lecompton constitution thus played into the plotters' hands.

The same view was taken yet more emphatically by Douglas. He had inside information in 1857, he later told the Senate, that four states were threatening Buchanan with secession. Had that threat been met in the right Jacksonian spirit, had the bluff been called—for the four states were unprepared for secession and war—the leaders of the movement would have been utterly discredited. Their conspiracy would have collapsed, and they would have been so routed and humiliated in 1857 that the Democratic party schism in 1860 might never have taken place, and if it had, secession in 1861 would have been impossible.

The roots of the Civil War of course go deep; they go back beyond Douglas' impetuous Kansas-Nebraska Bill, back beyond the Mexican War, back beyond the Missouri Compromise. But the last good chance of averting secession and civil strife was perhaps lost in 1857. Even Zachary Taylor in 1850 had made it plain before his sudden death that he would use force, if necessary, to crush the secessionist tendencies which that year became so dangerous. A similar display of principle and resolution seven years later might well have left the disunionist chieftains of the Deep South so weakened in prestige that Yancey and his fellow plotters would have been helpless. The lessons of this failure in statesmanship, so plain to Douglas, ought not to be forgotten. The greatest mistake a nation can make is to put at its helm a man so pliable and unprincipled that he will palter with a clean-cut and momentous issue.

35 *James G. Randall*

LINCOLN AND JOHN BRIGHT

36 *David Donald*

ABRAHAM LINCOLN AND THE
AMERICAN PRAGMATIC TRADITION

What is it in our great political leaders that makes us regard them as great? They are, in one sense, the demigods of a national worship. American religious experience has, in the long-range pursuit of a libertarian ideal, always been political; and American politics has, in the absence of any other unifying creed, always been religious. Our patron saints are canonized by popular vote. Each of our great political leaders, moreover, represents a desirable quality of the national character in what, to the popular mind, is the grand and continuous morality play of American politics. Washington is the granite figure of manly virtue, Jefferson the lofty protagonist of abstract liberty, Wilson the prescient and inflexible man of principle, Franklin D. Roosevelt the smile triumphant over personal tragedy and national despair.

Where in this pantheon is the place of Lincoln? Why does he seem to be the greatest? He is, for one thing, the only one who does not come from the patrician class or from a background of privilege. He fulfills our egalitarian myth of opportunities open to talent. His universal appeal lies also in his humanity. He does not preach, he understands. He has all the virtues of the great leader without expecting everybody else to have them too. His premises seem clear and simple, his politics has the conviction of a creed. Himself the incarnation of all that is best in American political values, he forgives others their failure to observe them. The Gettysburg Address and the Emancipation Proclamation sum up his achievement in the popular mind. They make men free, they define purpose in a time of travail, they speak their pithy and almost Biblical words in a spirit of humility. His tragic death enhances both his humanity and his stature. Lincoln, if anyone, is the American folk hero.

To the professional historian, aware as he is of the hard facts about the leader and not only of the legend, Lincoln nonetheless remains a great political leader, though perhaps for somewhat different reasons. This can be seen from the following essays by Professors James G. Randall and David Donald. The late Professor Randall, who died in 1953, after some three decades at the University of Illinois, was probably the foremost Lincoln scholar of recent years. It was a position which he well earned, through such major studies as *Constitutional Problems Under Lincoln* (1926), *Civil War and Reconstruction* (1937), *Lincoln the Liberal Statesman* (1947), and above all *Lincoln the President* (4 volumes, 1945–55: the last volume was completed by Richard N. Current). Professor Donald, a student and assistant of Professor Randall, has taught at Columbia University, served as Harmsworth Professor of American History at Oxford, and is presently at Princeton University. He has rapidly established himself as a first-rate scholar in the field of Civil War and Lincoln studies. His works, each of them a signal contribution, include a biography of Lincoln's law partner (*Lincoln's Herndon*, 1948), an edition of the Civil War diaries of Salmon P. Chase (*Inside Lincoln's Cabinet*, 1954), a biography of Charles Sumner in two volumes (of which the first appeared in 1960), and a book of thought-provoking essays on the Civil War era (*Lincoln Reconsidered*, 1956), from which the essay below has been selected.

The Lincoln portraits drawn by Professors Randall and Donald are contrasting but in no wise contradictory. They complement each other in representing Lincoln as the protagonist and practitioner of American liberalism. Individually and together they suggest a series of questions. What exactly do we mean by the world liberalism? In what ways are liberalism and democracy similar in their premises, in what ways are they antipathetic? What is the common ground between the values of Lincoln and Bright and what forces in the larger Atlantic world of the mid-nineteenth century defined this common ground? Wherein do Bright and Lincoln go their separate ways and why? Does Lincoln's pragmatism impinge on his liberalism or may one argue, paradoxically, that it insures it?

Both essays, it will be seen, agree that Abraham Lincoln was a great statesman, though each offers a different explanation of the greatness. To Professor Randall it is to be found in Lincoln's political values, in his ideology, in his adherence to the liberal tradition of the Anglo-Saxon world. To Professor Donald, it is to be found in Lincoln's conscious adjustments to political realities, in "his tragic realization of the limitations of human activity," his understanding that whatever his own liberal convictions were, they were subject to the judgment of the people and ultimately to the will of God.

Concerning the greatness of the Lincoln of folklore, the Lincoln who remains outside the tangible realm of scholarship, some suggestions have already been made. He is the log-cabin Lincoln, the Great Emancipator, the Great Martyr, the splitter of rails, the leader of the Republican party but at bottom no less a good Democrat, the true and devout Christian, the self-made man, the man of humor, sympathy, and heroism. What is interesting about the greatness of the Lincoln of folklore and the Lincoln of the scholars, of course, is the different basis for estimating greatness in each case. There can be little doubt, however, as David Donald has well noted in another of his essays, that "the Lincoln of folklore is more significant than the Lincoln of actuality."

To someone seeking to fathom the popular sense of American purpose and direction today, the Lincoln of folklore offers an abundance of information. He is the most important personage in the drama of American politics. He is the protagonist of our cause in a continuing struggle with alien causes. More than being the articulator of American democratic values, he is himself the American democrat.

James G. Randall

The dramatic meetings between President Roosevelt and Prime Minister Churchill are without precedent. Nevertheless, from a momentous past one may recall another example of a deeply significant Anglo-American friend-

Reprinted with the permission of Mrs. James G. Randall and the publishers, Dodd, Mead & Company, from *Lincoln the Liberal Statesman*, by James G. Randall. Copyright 1947 by Dodd, Mead & Company, Inc. Originally appeared in the *Yale Review*.

ship of two great political figures in war time. While Abraham Lincoln was President he enjoyed a community of understanding with the English leader John Bright, which being interpreted throws a flood of light upon human influences that leaped across the ocean eight decades ago. The story of the Lincoln-Bright friendship is important because in treating the subject one is not merely considering the "clothes and buttons" of a man, as Mark Twain said; one is dealing here with a topic of dominant significance for Lincoln, for Bright, and for the essential harmony and unity of Britain and America.

Bright and Lincoln never met, for the British leader never visited the United States, thus forgoing not only the ovations he would have received, but also the opportunity to talk face to face with the homely President whose aspirations were essentially his own. His relations with Lincoln were indirect. His American correspondence was with Charles Sumner, who showed the letters to Lincoln; other matters pertaining to the friendship came through Thomas H. Dudley, American consul at Liverpool. This indirectness may have been largely a matter of position in office: Lincoln's foreign relations were handled through diplomatic channels, and Bright was so prominent a British leader that direct communication with him by the American President might have been deemed irregular.

Few friendships so indirect have been so real. Its essence was to be understood in terms of the lack of personal contact or face-to-face association. It was a friendship not of men who see each other and grasp hands but of kindred minds. Lincoln and Bright were not alike in manners, habits, or personality. Perhaps they might not have enjoyed the same jokes. Their likeness was in essential views. It was precisely their similarity of approach to political and social questions that made their relationship significant.

It is not to be thought, however, that the relation was distant nor altogether impersonal. Mementos and symbols played their part; affection was not absent. Goldwin Smith, describing the anteroom leading to Lincoln's office, noted how "a large photograph of John Bright" struck his eye. The story of this photograph, noted in diverse sources—including manuscripts in the British Museum, the Huntington Library, and the Library of Congress—would make a chapter in itself. The portrait did not come from Bright to Lincoln, but indirectly by the kindness of an English admirer of the two leaders. A bust of Bright, donated by one Thomas G. Blain of Manchester, was sent to the United States. It had been intended for Lincoln, but was presented after his death to President Johnson as a gift to the American nation. A cane once carried by Lincoln became a treasured heirloom in the Bright home.

There was also the episode of Alfred Rubery—an adventuresome British youth who became the beneficiary of one of Lincoln's most notable pardons. Participating in a privateering escapade against the United States, Rubery had been convicted in a federal court in California and sentenced to a fine of $10,000 and imprisonment of ten years. Interesting himself in the case as that of a young man of his Birmingham constituency who was foolish and thoughtless rather than vicious, Bright brought the matter to Lincoln's attention through Sumner, and on December 17, 1863, Lincoln issued a pardon for Rubery in a formal and carefully worded proclamation, in which he took pains to mention that in addition to other considerations the act of clemency was done "especially as a public mark of the esteem held by the United States of America for the high character and steady friendship of . . . John Bright." On January 22, 1864, Bright wrote beautifully to Sumner expressing both his own appreciation of Lincoln's act and the heartfelt gratitude of Rubery's mother and sister. He referred to the matter as one that "produced a kindly feeling towards the President and towards the . . . United States." The incident was fully treated by F. Lauriston Bullard in the American Bar Association "Journal" for March, 1939. Carl Sandburg noted it in his "War Years"; "Lincoln," he said, "believed John Bright was entitled to one pardon and no questions asked."

The Lincoln-Bright friendship was not related to any particular setting nor confined to a special episode. Its reference was to great and enduring values. Its concern was the essential attitudes of whole peoples towards each other; its bearing was even broader, for it touched problems of world significance. We are dealing here not alone with men but with nations and destinies. Since it is the weakness of men that they live in the midst of such destinies without rising to a full contemplation of them, the friendship of these great minds has the more meaning because this contemplation was not lacking.

On this side of the Atlantic in the Civil War period, there were groups who served their own short-sighted ends by misrepresenting and denouncing Britain. Within England also the forming of attitudes towards the American struggle was a matter of classes and groups, or rather of a small element against the great majority. Those groups that were most class-conscious, by which is meant British "society," clubland, and the Tories, wanted the United States adventure to fail and for that reason favored the Confederacy. Liberals in England, and with them the masses of the people, favored the American Union, despite what Bright called the "folly" of the tariff in contrast to the Confederacy's gesture towards free trade.

It was the great English nation, rather than the few, who had their way. Britain's relation to Washington was not only unbroken, but grew notably more friendly in the latter half of the war. It is important that this fact be understood, the more so since misconceptions in this field of history are all too common. It has even been mistakenly said that Britain "intervened" for the Confederacy. Such statements have appeared in American newspapers. This is the exact opposite of the truth. It is true that there were tensions; there were disputes; on two or three occasions there came what were called "crises." It is precisely in such situations that the friendship of nations is tested. Peace does not depend upon the lack of dispute or difference; it depends upon the basic common sense of statesmen and the fundamental harmony of peoples when faced with disputes and confronted with international problems.

The fundamental question was whether Britain would offend the government of the United States by recognizing the independence of the Confederacy; whether it would attempt mediation between the opposing sides, thus promoting a termination of the war on the basis of a broken American nation; and whether it would throw its military and naval power on the side of disunion. Britain did none of these things. Belligerency of the Southern government was recognized, but never its independence. As to episodes that involved serious tension, there were two: the matter of the *Trent* late in 1861, in which a naval officer of the United States had removed Confederate envoys from a British ship, and the *Alabama*, which, with several other ships, was built in Britain and delivered to Confederate hands with the alleged "connivance," though it was more like delay or inaction, of the British government. When one speaks of these two matters, one has told the worst, yet both of these issues were peaceably adjusted. The American government released the Confederate envoys, Mason and Slidell, in January of 1862, and the further delivery of British-built ships for service against the United States was decisively stopped midway in the war. Strenuous efforts of the Richmond government to get additional warships from England were unsuccessful, as in the case of the *Alexandra* and the Laird rams in 1863; and the sequel of this failure, as also of the British government's refusal to receive Confederate diplomats and deal officially with them, was the total disillusionment of the Confederacy in its frustrated contact with Britain.

This frustration, which is insufficiently understood, amounted to nothing less than a complete breach between Richmond and London, if one can speak of a breach between governments that never had regular relations, or anything approaching them. The Southern envoy Mason withdrew from England, and British consuls, whose status was irregular, were expelled from Confederate cities by the government of Jefferson Davis. This was but a natural result of the aloofness of the British foreign minister towards Southern representatives and the disappointment of Confederate hopes for mediation, recognition, and support. Thus it was not Washington but Richmond that broke with England, and that in 1863, the middle year of the war.

It seemed natural and inevitable that Southerners should command the admiration of many English minds. That admiration has become a long-standing tradition, but it needs to be rightly viewed. Where friendliness to the South was motivated by willingness to see the United States fail as a nation and as a democratic experiment—such motivation being not entirely absent—it became only a complicating war-time factor. This, however, leaves much to be said, for in the long run, in its healthier aspects, British interest in the South has managed to transcend or by-pass the political implications of the American controversy. If Britons have admired Lee and Jackson, that does not mean that they have turned against Lincoln. Governmentally, their unbroken amity was with the United States. In the sense of American reunion, that amity embraces both North and South. One is not disregarding Southerners as Americans when one emphasizes British friendship for that government which survived the American struggle.

In the days of this struggle it would be a fair judgment to say that in the Anglo-Saxon world the two most prominent liberals were Lincoln in the United States and Bright in England. Bright was an industrialist; yet his great contribution was that of economic liberal and friend of workingmen. With Richard Cobden (for the names Cobden and Bright were inseparable) he had promoted a whole school of thought in terms of free trade, opposition to militarism, and relief from those hated "corn laws" which were associated with landed privilege and monopoly. Instead of conceiving of England in terms of the school tie, the aristocracy, the martial spirit, and the Tory's raised eyebrow, he was concerned for the rights of sturdy millions of fellow humans whose sufferings and aspirations he knew at first hand. He had that feeling for the people which was matched by Lincoln's expressed wish to "lift artificial weights from all shoulders." If this be idealism, make the most of it, was Bright's view. Though popular at times, he sometimes felt almost wholly alone. He was caricatured in "Punch" and endured the scorn that idealists suffer; yet, in considerable part, England did the things he asked. He was more than a voice of protest, though he was often that.

It has been said that he "stood before his audience like a tower," never hiding behind a pulpit, for he thought that "no man can move an audience that does not see his boots." His portraits show a leonine head with a countenance of remarkable handsomeness and distinction. His combination of Quaker simplicity with electrifying eloquence should cause no wonder, for it was said of him, "If he hadn't been a Quaker, he would have been a prize-fighter." His speeches read well today, but to the words themselves one must add the magnetism of his appeal to popular audiences and the effortless ease with which his bell-like voice filled the largest hall. There was the further fact of his religion, for with the devotion of a forthright nature Bright was a Christian and a Friend. In his biography of Bright, George Macaulay Trevelyan writes: "He practised the silence of his sect, and drew thence the strength of his soul, the purity of his heart, and the quality of his speech." As a boy he had sat in the Quaker meeting house at Rochdale, "where silence spoke in the heart." His phrases became popular slogans. One epigram would have the carrying power of a whole discourse, as when he caricatured a few political malcontents under the biblical analogy of the Cave of Adullam, a comparison which Lincoln also used, or when he remarked with regard to Irish disturbances, "Force is not a remedy."

His public activity was that of reform leader, Member of Parliament, and unafraid champion of the British masses; in personal affairs he was owner of a textile mill at Rochdale in industrial Lancashire. In the superficial sense in which economic motive is supposed to color all history, he might have been expected to favor the Confederacy, for he found his business threatened with ruin by the Union blockade which shut off the supply of Southern cotton. It was precisely this economic dislocation, widespread and disastrous in British manufacturing districts, on which leaders of the secessionist government banked in their drive for foreign intervention.

Despite this business motive, Bright emphatically favored the Union cause, including the blockade, because to him it was the cause of broad economic opportunity and political liberalism. Thousands of English laborers were thrown out of work, including employees of Bright, but British self-help and American good will came handsomely to their relief. Trevelyan records that "all England came to the rescue with abundant generosity"; then he adds that three large ships brought American flour as a token of friendship "tangible to eye and hand and mouth."

The economic thesis of "King Cotton"—the doctrine that this master crop would control the affairs of governments including international relations—broke down, and the colossal tragedy of war between the great English-speaking nations was averted. A significant chapter was added to the history of peace, whose economic basis is more fundamental than the overadvertised material "causes" of war, these often being mere excuses for an aggressive war party whose economics is as unsound as its jingoism.

To take the measure of this one man's influence one must remember factors and overtones that escaped formal diplomacy. One cannot adequately write the story of that time without due contemplation of Bright in England writing letters of passionate intensity to Sumner, waiting in suspense for news of Union victory, mustering all his oratorical power so that the Union cause would be fairly presented and the acts of the Lincoln Administration not misunderstood, acting as friend, counsellor, and interpreter, finding England, as he wrote the American Senator, "almost as much interested in your conflict as if it was raging in . . . our own country." "Don't allow *temper*," he wrote, "in any of your statesmen to turn his judgment." "At all hazards you must not let this matter [the *Trent* case] grow into a war with England, even if you are right and we are wrong." He would not have it said by Americans "that in the darkest hour of their country's trials England, the land of their fathers, looked on with icy coldness, and saw unmoved the . . . calamities of their children." In the mass of Englishmen he saw no such indifference. "Our working-class is with you," he wrote. All parties, he said, had "a high respect for Mr. Lincoln." In the period when tension was most acute because of the *Trent* controversy, he declared: "I dread the consequences of war quite as much for your sakes as for our own. So great will be my horror of such a strife that I believe I shall retire from public life entirely . . . should war take place between your country and mine."

There were other leaders in Britain who befriended the United States: they included George Thompson of anti-slavery fame, W. E. Forster, Prince Albert, the Duke of Argyll, Goldwin Smith, Leslie Stephen, the evangelist Spurgeon, and John Stuart Mill. None, however, was so eminent as Bright; none took so much time from a busy life for this "foreign" matter; none brought to it such high-calibre leadership. By his eloquence in Parliament he effectively opposed a motion looking towards a recognition of the Confederacy; by his contact with Sumner he kept in touch with the man who was chairman of the committee on foreign relations of the United States Senate. The importance of this contact was impressively shown on Christmas day of 1861—one of those occasions when deliberation on matters of high policy brought practical results. Lincoln's Cabinet met; Sumner was invited in, this being most unusual for one who was not of the Cabinet; friendly letters just received from Bright and Cobden constituted a unique feature of this important consultation; the *Trent* affair was settled then and there; the Cabinet decided that the envoys must be released and that war with England was to be avoided. Bright's contribution to this fortunate outcome was one of the most significant acts of his life.

The mind of Lincoln as it touched public questions was closely similar to that of Bright. Conservative though he was in some respects, Lincoln was fundamentally a Jeffersonian liberal in his emphasis upon human rights and his clear sense of equity and justice. He took the Declaration of Independence seriously, stressed equality of men, cherished Anglo-Saxon civil justice, and on one occasion spoke for woman suffrage far ahead of his time. To broaden political rights, befriend the colored race, and relieve the underprivileged, came naturally to the man whose Emancipation Proclamation was one of the milestones of the century.

Liberalism, indeed, was the essence of Lincoln's thought. Confessing that he had himself been "a hired laborer," he remarked in one of his speeches that he wanted "every man to have a chance." "To secure to each laborer the whole product of his labor," he said, "is a worthy subject of any good government." He considered that the "strongest bond of human sympathy, outside of the family relation, should be one uniting all work-ing people, of all nations, and tongues, and kindreds." Repeatedly he em-phasized the dignity of labor, urging that workingmen are the basis of all government.

He gave thought to the farmer as a man, to the farmer's pride in his work, to the relation of labor and capital. He held that "labor is prior to . . . capital; that . . . capital is the fruit of labor." He disliked the "mud-sill" theory, "that whoever is once a hired laborer, is . . . fixed in that condition for life." He was concerned for the "prudent, penniless be-ginner," anxious that he should acquire a surplus and one day own his land and tools. Not alone untutored folk, he thought, but men with education must work. The country could not sustain them in idleness; the laborer should not be "a blind horse upon a tread-mill."

While still a youth living close to the frontier, Lincoln had reasoned these things out. One of his most thoughtful and mature pronouncements was his address before the Young Men's Lyceum of Springfield, Illinois, January 27, 1838 (misdated 1837 in his "Works"), in which he interpreted American institutions in the light of "a system . . . conducing more es-sentially to the ends of civil and religious liberty than any of which the history of former times tells us." He thought destruction of "that fair fabric" could come only from within, and in this connection, at the age of twenty-nine, he issued a stinging warning against men setting themselves up as bigger than the government, descending to lynch law, regarding government as a bane and making "a jubilee of the suspension of its operations."

In this notable address the young Lincoln was referring to some of the uglier manifestations of his day. Frontier vigilantism had degenerated into lawless violence. "Regulators," seeking at first to enforce law and order against horse thieves and desperadoes, had taken a downward trend till their irregular military force, trials, and executions had developed into private warfare, gang against gang; finally, the legislature and governor had to step in, tone up the courts, and put down the regulators. To those who naïvely think of the purity of that early age, it is a shock to realize the turbulent conditions that caused so much concern to one who believed in democracy. Lincoln, however, was not naïve; he realized that democ-racy is not a thing to prate about, or a possession guaranteed for all time. It is rather a heritage transmitted in trust, a thing whose value depends on the manner of its use, a legacy that requires eternal diligence if, as young Lincoln said, it is to be kept "unprofaned, . . . undecayed . . . and un-torn by usurpation."

Lincoln did not merely burble about Americanism. He had the courage and the insight to speak of "danger" and "ill omen" in discussing his own times. Viewing the tendency to substitute "wild and furious passions" (the kind of thing that fascism in our day has promoted) in lieu of law and order, he realized that vicious inner forces existed, and that it is only by determined purpose that freedom can be kept. One must think, therefore, not only of the eloquent idealism of Lincoln's democratic and liberal concepts, but of the toughness and the rude alarm of his warning against that arrogant disposition which, he said, "is awfully fearful in any community" and which "now exists in ours."

In the whole range of social questions Lincoln was found on the liberal side. In a day when intolerant nativism claimed thousands of America's prominent politicians, and even such a distinguished citizen as Samuel F. B. Morse, Lincoln was friendly towards foreigners, avoided denunciation of alien groups, and declared that when he saw a people borne down by tyranny he would do all in his power to raise the yoke. He did not overlook America's larger opportunity. He saw enduring values, was impatient of unenlightened politics, and refused to surrender to cynicism.

One topic above others was President Lincoln's basic theme: the concept of identifying the American experiment with the broad cause of democracy in the world. Early in the war he remarked to John Hay that the central idea of the struggle was "proving that popular government is not an absurdity." He advised that it would be "a great lesson of peace" to prove that ballots, not bullets, were the rightful appeal, "teaching all the folly of being the beginners of a war." In the Gettysburg Address this again was the central idea: the world significance of democracy's testing, the enduring importance of proving that govenment of the people is no failure. In his magnanimity, friendship for the soldier, humor, tolerance, readiness to reason with his people, and careful effort to keep the Union cause free from abuse, Lincoln showed not only leadership but statesmanship in liberal terms. His regard for Bright was no accident; it signified union of thought; it offered a commentary on the political and social attitudes of congenial spirits. The sympathy of these men for each other belongs to the very history and definition of liberalism.

It is noteworthy that after eighty years an English reformer of our own time, whose ideals are similar to Bright's, has given us a most eloquent and understanding appreciation of Lincoln. In "London Calling" (1942) Mr. Harold J. Laski has shown that "Lincoln is America, and America is democracy." "Everyone," he writes, "knew that Abraham Lincoln cared passionately for freedom; that he wanted an America in which humble folk found happiness, that he wanted courts of law to be temples of justice, that he thought it wrong that anyone, black or white, should be hungry or illiterate or miserable. . . . When he was assassinated, they knew . . . that his death was his own 'last full measure of devotion' to that idea of America which can never die."

It was not as if Bright's championship of Lincoln's cause had brought him into opposition to the British ministry of the time. Certainly among the men who kept Britain friendly were Palmerston the Prime Minister and Earl Russell the foreign secretary, both Liberals. The Tory Lord Derby led the opposition, and it was Derby who tried unsuccessfully to get England to side with the South against the Union and who sought on this issue to force a ministerial crisis. That Bright did not have to disagree with the ministry on this point detracts not at all from his work for the American cause. The fact that a ministry did not have to be overthrown in order to preserve British friendship for the American Union serves to point up the solidity of that friendship. In stressing Bright, therefore, one must not forget the work of Charles Francis Adams, of Earl Russell, of Lincoln and Seward, indeed of all who controlled events and caused the harmony of nations to become vocal and dominant.

That the masses of the British working people recognized as did Bright the identity of their cause with Lincoln's, was impressively shown in a notable series of popular meetings all over England in January of 1863. The Emancipation Proclamation was the cue for these meetings, which were held in London, York, Halifax, Birmingham, Sheffield, Coventry, Manchester, Bristol, Bath, Glasgow, Cobham, Carlisle, Chesterfield, and in many other places. In all these gatherings, economic liberalism and political democracy were prevailing notes. It is no disparagement of these demonstrations to say that in hailing Lincoln, British workingmen were promoting their own cause. In reply, Lincoln sent his famous letter to the workingmen of Manchester in which he spoke eloquently of human rights while expressing sympathy for the sufferings which laboring people in Britain were enduring.

People did not realize the part that Lincoln himself had in these assemblages. Through Sumner he had sent to Bright in his own handwriting the draft of a resolution expressing the views which he wished to have adopted in British public meetings. The gist of the resolution was that civilized states ought to deny recognition to a nation constructed with the "fundamental object to maintain . . . and perpetuate human slavery." This Lincoln autograph, published by Trevelyan, not only offers another illustration of Lincoln's connection with Bright; it shows what was not known at the time, namely, that in his own discreet manner Lincoln was a conscious factor in the interplay of public opinion between nations. The memorandum through Sumner to Bright would now be called "propaganda," but the shaping of sentiment is the business of statesmen, and such a memorandum was the kind of propaganda that wise leaders do not fail to use.

These popular demonstrations in England, which seemed a kind of tidal wave, are matters of voluminous record. In the National Archives at Washington one finds the original "Address of the Inhabitants of Birmingham to His Excellency Abraham Lincoln, President of the United States of America." It is a gigantic scroll, a huge paper carrying at least ten thousand signatures, in which the men of Bright's constituency conveyed to Lincoln their "deep and heartfelt sympathy" and assured him of the "good wishes of all Men who love liberty."

To know the harmony of views between such a Briton as Bright and such an American as Lincoln is to do more than make clear the solid ground of understanding between two great nations. It is characteristic of Anglo-American collaboration that its objectives do not conflict with the true interests of other peoples. Not only for English-speaking countries but for the United Nations today, the theme that the cause of democracy is of world importance, that it lives because of its deep human significance, and that it is inseparable from its international aspects, presents a stirring challenge. In meeting it, to use Lincoln's phrase, we shall "nobly save or meanly lose the last, best hope of earth."

David Donald

I

Everybody admits that Abraham Lincoln was a great statesman, but no two writers seem to agree upon the basis of his greatness. Some think he merits immortality as the spokesman of Republican principles—whatever they may be—but others give him most credit for being a kind of crypto-Democrat. In recent years major historians have debated whether Lincoln was the embodiment of the American conservative tradition or the personification of American liberalism.

Such arguments on the whole reveal more about their authors than about Lincoln, and often they evidence more an inclination to annex a major folk hero to some current cause than a desire to accept the past upon its own terms. To most men of his own day Lincoln seemed neither liberal nor conservative statesman; he was simply a rather ineffectual President. It is hard to remember how unsuccessful Lincoln's administration appeared to most of his contemporaries. He was, as J. G. Randall has pointed out in a brilliant essay, "The Unpopular Mr. Lincoln," a man censured and distrusted by all parties. Friendly critics viewed him as honest, well intentioned, but rather lacking in force; hostile ones, as weak, vacillating, and opportunistic. They agreed in sensing an absence of direction in Lincoln's administration, a seeming and puzzling lack of policy.

As President, he appeared not to take hold. Before he was inaugurated,

Reprinted from *Lincoln Reconsidered*, pp. 128–43, by David Donald, by permission of Alfred A. Knopf, Inc. Copyright 1947, 1950, 1951, 1956 by David Donald.

seven worried states of the Deep South seceded, but Lincoln did little to avert a crisis. He issued no public statements, announced no plans for peace, and apparently spent his time growing a set of whiskers. On his way to Washington in February 1861 his speeches bore the obviously erroneous refrain: ". . . There is nothing going wrong. . . . There is nothing that really hurts anybody." After he was inaugurated, war broke out and four more states deserted Lincoln's government for the Confederacy. The President called for 75,000 nine-month volunteers to fight a war that was ultimately to enroll more than 2,000,000 soldiers on both sides and to cost $20,000,000,000. Northern newspapermen and politicians demanded a prompt advance against the Confederate armies, and under their pressure the President yielded and ordered the army "On to Richmond"—and on to Bull Run. Other disasters followed with monotonous regularity—the Peninsula campaign; Second Bull Run; Fredericksburg; Chancellorsville—and the few Federal victories were as costly as the defeats.

The President seemed unable to cope with the crisis. As an administrator, he appeared hopelessly incompetent. He was a born enemy of rules. His secretaries fought a constant and losing battle to systematize his schedule. For a long while he refused to put any restrictions upon the throngs of visitors, petitioners, and office-seekers who besieged his White House office. "They do not want much," he explained, "and they get very little. . . . I know how I would feel in their place." Finally, under the pressure of urgent war business, the President was persuaded to limit these tiring visitors' hours, but even then he was constantly making exceptions for needy cases.

His Cabinet was of little help in organizing the war effort. For a while he held no regular Cabinet meetings at all. Then, when they were held, they seldom dealt with serious matters of policy. As a usual thing, Lincoln permitted each Cabinet officer to run his own department without control, guidance, or interference. When Secretary Chase presented proposed financial measures for his consideration, the President agreed without a question, saying: "You understand these things. I do not." But along with this aloofness, Lincoln also had a fondness for what seemed to be random meddling with his administrators. Just when a Cabinet officer had worked out some systematic plan for handling his department's business, he would unexpectedly be greeted by petitioners bearing brief but authoritative notes signed by the President: "Let this woman have her son out of Old Capital Prison." "Attorney-General, please make out and send me a pardon in this case." "Injustice has probably been done in this case, Sec. of War please examine it."

As the war dragged on : 1d defeat followed defeat, nearly every segment of Northern opinion showed distrust of the unsuccessful President. Copperheads, Radicals, War Democrats, Conservative Republicans—all attacked Lincoln. Day after day indignant Senators and irate Representatives stalked into the White House, blustering, threatening, cajoling, all demanding that the President take a firm stand and do something—indeed, do almost anything—positive. "Let him," wrote Lincoln's disillusioned law partner, Herndon, "hang some Child or woman, if he has not Courage to hang a *man*." "Does he suppose he can crush—squelch out this huge rebellion by pop guns filled with rose water."

II

To such critics Lincoln amiably gave the often repeated reply: "My policy is to have no policy." To men with plans, to men with axes to grind or hatchets to use, the President's remark was incomprehensible. Self-righteous Secretary Salmon P. Chase snorted that it was an "idiotic notion." But Lincoln was not being flippant or evasive; he was enunciating the basic premise of his political philosophy and at the same time expressing the fundamental pragmatic element in the American political tradition.

The President's statement sounded simple, and if it had come from another man, it might have revealed nothing more than simple-mindedness. But when Lincoln said: "My policy is to have no policy," he was enunciating, either directly or by implication, a series of fundamental political principles.

(1) He was rejecting the doctrinaire approach to problems, declining to become attached to inflexible solutions or to ideological labels. Consistency meant little to Lincoln, and he refused to measure his associates by rigid tests of doctrinal purity. He was concerned with results. Long before the war, in 1844, he had energetically supported Henry Clay for President, believing that the Kentuckian, though himself a slaveholder, would not permit the further expansion of slavery. Simon-pure abolitionists took the opposing view—how could a real antislavery man vote for a slaveholder?—and they wasted their votes on the doctrinally pure but politically hopeless third-party candidate. Their vote helped elect James K. Polk and to bring on the Mexican War. To Lincoln the abolitionists' way of thinking seemed "wonderful." To their contention that "We are not to do *evil* that *good* may come," he countered with another, more apt Biblical injunction: "By the *fruit* the tree is to be known."

A decade later, ironically enough, the situation was reversed, for conservative Whigs hesitated to oppose Stephen A. Douglas's Kansas-Nebraska scheme because they disliked to join the suspected abolitionists. "Good humoredly" Lincoln told his Whig friends that they were being "very silly," and he gave them some practical advice: "Stand with anybody that stands RIGHT. Stand with him while he is right and PART with him when he goes wrong. Stand WITH the abolitionist in restoring the Missouri Compromise; and stand AGAINST him when he attempts to repeal the fugitive slave law."

So pragmatic an attitude was, of course, shocking to those Americans who lived by dogmas, by the hoary certainties of the past. No one could have exceeded Lincoln in his admiration for the founders of the Republic. "I have never had a feeling politically that did not spring from the sentiments embodied in the Declaration of Independence," he declared, and he spoke reverently of the "great authority" of the Revolutionary Fathers. But he warned his own age not to be bound by history. "The dogmas of the quiet past," he wrote, in an annual message to Congress, "are inadequate to the stormy present. The occasion is piled high with difficulty, and we must rise with the occasion. As our case is new, so we must think anew, and act anew. We must disenthrall ourselves, and then we shall save our country."

(2) Rejecting ideological labels, Lincoln tried to face political reality as it was, not as he would have it become. No man more carefully distinguished between "is" and "ought to be." On slavery, for example, Lincoln's personal views had long been a matter of public record. "If slavery is not wrong," he said simply, "nothing is wrong." But the President of the United States could not act as Abraham Lincoln wished. He was President not of the antislavery forces but of a disunited and divided people, and he must serve the general welfare. "I am naturally antislavery," the President declared. "And yet I have never understood that the Presidency conferred upon me an unrestricted right to act officially upon this judgment and feeling."

As a man he wished to eliminate slavery everywhere, but as President it became his official and painful duty to rebuke his subordinates who took extralegal steps to uproot the peculiar institution. When Generals John Charles Frémont and David Hunter issued edicts liberating the slaves in their military commands, Lincoln promptly overruled both commanders. Their hasty action would have cost the Union the support of the loyal slaveholders of Kentucky, and if Kentucky seceded, Missouri and Maryland might well follow. "These all against us," Lincoln explained, "and the job on our hands is too large for us. We would as well consent to separation at once, including the surrender of this capitol."

While Radical antislavery men grumbled about Lincoln's subservience to "negrophobic" counsels, the President was realistically warning his Southern friends that the war meant death for slavery. As Federal troops advanced into the South, flocks of Negroes left the plantations and fled to freedom. Whenever a raiding party returned from Virginia or Tennessee, it had behind it "an outlandish tatterdemalion parade of refugees, men and women and helpless children, people jubilant and bewildered and wholly defenseless, their eyes on the north star." It was not possible, the President

advised their owners, to reduce these people again to slavery; there was no
law that could remove the idea of freedom from the heart of a Negro.
Earnestly Lincoln advised the border states to move toward gradual, compensated emancipation while there was still time.

Equally realistic was Lincoln's advice to the Negroes themselves. The
President himself was color-blind; he shared neither the antislavery man's
idealization of the Negro as God's image in ebony nor the slaveholder's
view of the Negro as an inferior race. He had warm friends and countless
admirers among the Negro people, and he thought of the black man first
of all as a man. But again he separated his personal feelings from what he
regarded as his official duty when he summoned a group of Northern free
Negro leaders to the White House in August 1862. Plainly and painfully
he told them the facts of life: "You and we are different races. We have
between us a broader difference than exists between almost any other two
races." Right or wrong, he continued, the difference meant that the Negro
was unassimilable in American society. Freedom would not solve their
problems. ". . . Even when you cease to be slaves, you are yet far removed from being placed on an equality with the white race. You are cut
off from many of the advantages which the other race enjoy." If the
Negroes wanted to avoid a future of menial subjection, they should think
of colonizing, under United States protection, say in Haiti or in Central
America. "It is better for us both," the President concluded, "to be
separated." Such advice seemed inhuman to the idealists of the time, and it
is unpalatable to the present-day liberal as well; yet clearly Lincoln had
correctly analyzed the current state of American popular sentiment.

(3) Refusing to force reality to fit a formula, Lincoln insisted that
every problem was unique, that issues could only be decided one at a time,
that conflicts need be resolved only when they actually arose. Again and
again he told anecdotes to illustrate his view. "The pilots on our Western
rivers steer from *point to point* as they call it—setting the course of the
boat no farther than they can see," he said, "and that is all I propose to
myself. . . ." He was not, he told a questioner, going "to cross 'Big
Muddy' until he reached it."

War-torn and politics-ridden Missouri presented to President Lincoln
a never-ending source of problems. Radicals and Conservative Republicans
fought the secessionists, each other, and also the Federal military commanders in that state with about equal ferocity. All factions kept sending deputations to Washington, calling upon Lincoln to take a firm stand
and commit himself to a clear-cut solution. The temptation must have
been almost irresistible to take sides, to apply some simple formula to the
Missouri problem in order to end the strife. Lincoln rejected the temptation. The governor of Missouri demanded that the President recognize his
right to appoint the commanding officers of the state militia; his political

opponents urged that, as the militia was now in the Federal service, the appointments must be made by Washington. Quietly Lincoln bypassed the issue. He permitted the Missouri governor to commission the officers first —and then he re-commissioned them himself. "After a good deal of reflection," he explained to the governor, "I concluded that it was better to make a rule for the practical matter in hand . . . than to decide a general question, . . . which, while it might embrace the practical question mentioned, might also be the nest in which forty other troublesome questions would be hatched. I would rather meet them *as* they come, than *before* they come, trusting that some of them may not come at all."

(4) The ability to face reality means, of course, a willingness to change with events. Lincoln willingly admitted that his opinions and his actions were shaped by forces beyond his control. His shifting position on emancipation clearly illustrates his flexibility. At first Lincoln and his administration were committed to the Crittenden Resolution, declaring that the purpose of the war was simply to restore the Union without disturbing slavery at all. Then the pressures for emancipation began mounting. By 1862 American diplomats warned that only a firm antislavery stand would check the pro-Confederate sympathies of France and England. Northern governors bluntly told the President that their antislavery young men were unwilling to enlist in an army still legally bound to preserve the hated institution. Military leaders like General Grant demanded more men and pointed to the large numbers of Negroes who would willingly serve for their freedom.

As events moved, so moved the President. He was not going to act blindly, he assured a group of antislavery churchmen; there was certainly no point in issuing proclamations that "must necessarily be inoperative, like the Pope's bull against the comet." But he did act when ends and means were fitted, and the Emancipation Proclamation was a masterpiece of practical political sagacity. Lincoln rightly regarded the Proclamation as his chief claim to historical fame, but he was always careful to insist that it was a product of circumstances. He had responded to the changing times. In 1864 he wrote to an admirer: "I claim not to have controlled events, but confess plainly that events have controlled me."

(5) As a pragmatic politician, Lincoln was careful not to make irredeemable pledges against the future. Characteristically, he approached the difficult problems of reconstruction with an open mind and an absence of commitment. When Federal troops overran Louisiana and Arkansas, some sort of civil government had to be re-established, and the President, as commander-in-chief, had to act. He offered a lenient program of amnesty and reconstruction, under which the states would be restored to the Union if only ten per cent of the 1860 voting population assented. He did not attempt to set up loyalty tests that would disqualify former Confeder-

ates from participating in the elections. "On principle I dislike an oath which requires a man to swear he *has* not done wrong," he told Secretary Stanton. "It rejects the Christian principle of forgiveness on terms of repentance. I think it is enough if the man does no wrong *hereafter.*"

Lincoln's hopes for generous amnesty and quick restoration in the South have often been distorted by historians, who speak of "Lincoln's plan of reconstruction" as though the President had a blueprint for peace. It is true that later, in the unskillful hands of Andrew Johnson, Lincoln's suggestions were converted into dogmas, but it is important to remember that while Lincoln was alive his views on reconstruction were constantly changing. A shrewd observer like James G. Blaine felt "that Mr. Lincoln had no fixed plan for the reconstruction of the States."

The President did not take his own "ten per cent plan" too seriously as a program for action. To the military officials who supervised the Southern elections, he gave the pragmatic advice: "Follow forms of law as far as convenient, but at all events get the expression of the largest number of the people possible." The whole condition of the conquered South he thought "so new and unprecedented, . . . that no exclusive and inflexible plan can safely be prescribed as to details and colatterals [*sic*]." He himself, therefore, had one reconstruction program for Louisiana, another for Virginia, and yet another for Tennessee.

Lincoln repeatedly refused to commit himself to any theoretical position about the nature of reconstruction. The whole moot question of whether the seceded states were legally in or out of the Union he dismissed as "a merely pernicious abstraction." When extreme antislavery men urged that the Negro be given the vote, he did not, as did Andrew Johnson later, reply with a reminder that the Constitution left suffrage in the hands of the states. Doubtless Lincoln realized that the whole issue of reconstruction was by its nature extra-constitutional, that that venerable document no more contemplated the appointment of military governors for Southern states than it did the enfranchisement of the Southern Negroes by Federal enactment. As the case was unprecedented, so the action had to be unprecedented, without ritualistic invocation of constitutional sanctions. Very practically, Lincoln tried to solve the issue by writing to Southern leaders and urging that the ballot be given to some, at least, of the more intelligent freedmen, especially those who had served in the Union army.

Throughout all the discussion of reconstruction, Lincoln showed no pride of authorship. As he had been obliged to take some action in a conquered area like Louisiana, he explained, he had issued a proclamation outlining "*a* plan of reconstruction," but it was "not the only plan which might possibly be acceptable." The alternative, congressional proposals for reconstruction, embodied in the Wade-Davis bill of 1864, he pocket-vetoed—because he was "unprepared to be inflexibly committed to any single plan of reconstruction" and because he had not sufficient time to study so important a measure in the ten days after the adjournment of Congress. When he did examine it, he took the unprecedented step of recording his opinion of the Radical measure. It was not exactly what he himself preferred, he explained, but, he said, "I am fully satisfied with the system of restoration contained in the Bill, as one very proper plan for the loyal people of any State choosing to adopt it."

In the last public speech of his life, Lincoln once again turned to the difficulties of peace and urged bold and pragmatic facing of issues as they arose. Any "exclusive, and inflexible plan," he kept insisting, "would surely become a new entanglement." And he himself offered a practical example of what he meant by freedom from *a priori* commitments. His word was out to the government recently organized in Louisiana and now seeking congressional approval, and on the whole he believed that recognition of this government would be the surest way to secure peace in that state. But he was not blindly bound by his own words. ". . . As bad promises are better broken than kept, I shall treat this as a bad promise, and break it, whenever I shall be convinced that keeping it is adverse to the public interest."

III

Absolutists thought that Lincoln's "no policy" theory was nothing but untrustworthiness, indecisiveness, and opportunism, and it is clear that pragmatism, misapplied, can be a polysyllabic synonym for drift. In Lincoln's case it meant something very different; it was an expression of his tragic realization of the limitations on human activity.

As a statesman, he was leader in a democratic society, and he firmly believed that such a free government represented "the last, best hope of earth." He knew that the successful democratic leader must not be too far ahead of his following. "Public opinion in this country," he had said before his election, "is everything." He did not have a naïve confidence that identified the popular voice with God's; he knew that the popular will was slow, blundering, and often mistaken. But no one could deceive all the people all the time, and, rejecting the flashy notion of authoritarian leadership with its claim to superior wisdom, Lincoln felt "a patient confidence in the ultimate justice of the people." In a free society one had to believe in the soundness of their final judgment. "Is there," Lincoln asked in his first inaugural, "any better, or equal hope, in the world? In our present differences, is either party without faith of being in the right? If the Almighty Ruler of nations, with his eternal truth and justice, be on your side of the North, or on yours of the South, that truth, and that justice, will surely prevail, by the judgment of this great tribunal, the American people."

Such a trust in the people could easily deteriorate into cosmic optimism, into Pollyanna's philosophy of history. But Lincoln did not mean it so, and his reference to "the Almighty Ruler" in connection with the popular will is significant. For, just as the President of a democratic country could only act within the limitations of a free society, so all men were restrained by forces and patterns larger than themselves. Back in Illinois Lincoln had often quoted fatalistically:

> *There's a divinity that shapes our ends,*
> *Rough-hew them how we will.*

As wartime President, he had greater reason to learn that man's plans are not always God's plans, that, in the haunting words of the second inaugural, "The Almighty has His own purposes."

In his own distinctively American way, then, Abraham Lincoln possessed what John Keats called the "quality [that] went to form a Man of Achievement," that quality "which Shakespeare possessed so enormously— . . . *Negative Capability*, that is when a man is capable of being in uncertainties, Mysteries, doubts, without any irritable reaching after fact and reason. . . ." Lincoln knew that there were limits to rational human activity, and that there was no virtue in irritably seeking to perform the impossible. As President, he could only do his best to handle problems as they arose and have a patient trust that popular support for his solutions would be forthcoming. But the ultimate decision was beyond his, or any man's, control. "Now, at the end of three years struggle," he said, "the nation's condition is not what either party, or any man, devised, or expected. God alone can claim it."

37 *Bruce Catton*

UNION LEADERSHIP AND
DISCIPLINE IN THE CIVIL WAR

If the prelude to the Civil War poses many problems for the historian, so too does the drama of the war itself. There are important questions to be asked about the resources of the combatants, their external relations, their internal policies, the lives they led behind the front, their economies, and their politics. Perhaps the most salient question is about the two great armies which grappled with each other for four long years. Who were these men? What did they think they were fighting

Reprinted with permission from *Marine Corps Gazette*, XL (January, 1956), 18–25. Copyright 1956 by *Marine Corps Gazette*.

for? How were they organized, trained, equipped? Who were their leaders? What were the larger campaign tactics of the war and how were they pursued?

Centering his attention on the leadership and discipline of the Union army, Bruce Catton affords some interesting clues to the answers insofar as the Northern armies were concerned. There is no one better qualified than Mr. Catton to do so. He has established his position as the foremost writer today of Civil War military history through a series of significant volumes, including the trilogy on the Army of the Potomac: *Mr. Lincoln's Army* (1951), *Glory Road* (1952), and *A Stillness at Appomattox* (1953). He won the Pulitzer Prize in History in 1954 and is the editor of *American Heritage*. The essay which follows was delivered as a lecture before the Marine Corps Association at Quantico, Virginia.

What Mr. Catton says is revealing and thought-provoking. One need not necessarily agree with him, however, that an army of volunteers has perforce virtues that are lacking in an army of conscripts. Does it not depend on the cause for which the army is fighting? The Union soldier, as Mr. Catton himself indicates, volunteered for reasons which hardly could have insured his victory. But the Confederate soldier, as Professor David Donald of Princeton University suggests in an interesting essay (*Journal of Southern History*, May, 1959), was himself trammeled in a cause which preached democracy but practiced aristocracy. Thus, to the degree that the outcome of the war depended on a sense of cause and the discipline it would command, it may be suggested that the North won because Johnny Reb had less of that sense and of that discipline than Billy Yank.

What is the relevance of Mr. Catton's analysis of men at war to our own military ways and values? What is the nature of an institution which is relatively new in American history—peacetime conscription? Is our army any different for having been organized at a time of peace and for having been conscripted? How do leadership and discipline today differ from those of the Civil War? The basic question, one suspects, concerns the cause for which armies are summoned and for which they would pay with their lives. Here is what needs examination when one compares the American soldier in the Armageddon of the 1860's with his counterpart in the cold war of today.

The American soldier has been much the same, probably, from the Revolutionary War down to the present day. He reflects the national character, and the national character has not changed a great deal. Weapons, tactics, strategic concepts, equipment—all of these may have changed enormously; yet the human material of which American armies are made is today very much like it was generations ago. As the battle record of many wars attests, this material has uniformly been pretty good.

Yet the ways in which this material has been used have undergone many changes. It may be instructive to note some of these changes, to see what happened in an earlier, more informal period, and to reflect on some of the lessons which can be deduced.

The Civil War was fought nearly a century ago. At this distance it is apt to look like a romantic museum piece. It was fought by men who went into battle in close formation, with waving flags and beating drums. Generals went about on horseback in those days, they frequently rode into the middle of the fighting line, and their contacts with private soldiers tended to be direct and intimate. It is easy to think of the Civil War as a story-book affair which was not really very much like modern warfare, and in which officer and enlisted man alike somehow operated under much less pressure than is the case today.

Yet the fact remains that when the total number of casualties caused by that war are matched against the country's total population, the Civil War emerges as the costliest, deadliest war America ever fought. Five hundred thousand soldiers lost their lives, in a country whose entire population, north and south together, numbered less than 30 millions. If battle losses in the Second World War had been in proportion, we would have 2,500,000 men killed—exclusive of those wounded and missing. Some of the individual battles of the Civil War cost each army engaged more than 25 per cent of its total numbers, including the men in non-combat details. Individual tactical units met even more appalling losses. In a surprising number of cases, a regiment might lose as many as 75 or 80 per cent of the men engaged; and the fight in which such losses were incurred might last no longer than an hour or so.

All of this took place, furthermore, in the era of muzzle loaders. With rare exceptions, infantrymen used muzzle-loading muskets—usually rifled, but by no means invariably so—with which the best man could hardly get off more than 2 shots a minute. Artillery was equally primitive. Indirect fire was unheard of; the gunner had to see his target with his own eyes in order to fire at it, and shell fuses were so unreliable that it was often an even chance whether the shell he fired would burst over the enemy or over his own infantry. To all intents and purposes there were no rapid fire guns. Land mines, known then as torpedoes, were used only in a very few cases and were no more than minor nuisances.

The contrast between the primitive nature of the weapons and the deadly character of the fighting is striking. It is worth emphasizing because it proves that that far-off war was as deadly and as frightening, for the man engaged in it, as any war ever fought. And what makes the case even more astounding is the fact that the system of drill and discipline which took Civil War soldiers into action had nothing like the hard, impersonal tautness with which we are familiar today. The Civil War army tended to be loose-jointed, informal, almost slap-dash. Yet somehow it got results. Any system of discipline which would hold men together through the impact of a battle like Gettysburg or Chickamauga must have had its virtues.

So it may pay us to have a close look at the way in which the basic tactical unit of the Civil War armies, the regiment, was brought together and led.

The very way in which the ordinary Civil War regiment was organized was an obstacle to strict military discipline. While the Federal government, of course, controlled the raising of troops, and had complete supervision over them once they were mustered-in, the matter of raising and organizing the regiments was up to the state authorities. Most regiments were recruited locally. In the ordinary course, some citizen would be commissioned by the governor to raise a regiment. He would open recruiting offices, deputize a number of men to help him, and go about looking for volunteers. If one of his helpers brought in a substantial number, that man would possibly be rewarded with a commission as lieutenant or captain; and the man in charge of the whole effort would, of course, become the colonel. In a great many cases, the individual companies would elect their own officers; very often, the colonel himself was elected by the men.

What all of this meant was that in the average regiment the officers were people whom the enlisted men had known all of their lives. The colonel or the major might, indeed, be a "leading citizen" of such stature that few of the recruits had ever been intimate with him, but the company officers had usually been on a first-name basis with their men for years. The same, of course, was true of the NCOs.

It goes without saying thus, that the private soldier was not likely to treat his officers with any undue amount of military formality. Perfectly typical is the account of a New York regiment toiling at infantry drill on a dusty field on a hot summer day. Presently one of the soldiers turned to his captain and said: "Say, Tom, let's quit this dern foolin' around and go over to the sutler's." An Illinois veteran wrote after the war: "While all of the men who enlisted pledged themselves to obey all the commands of their superior officers, and ought to have kept their word, yet it was hardly wise on the part of volunteer officers to absolutely demand attendance on such service, and later on it was abandoned." An Indiana soldier was even more explicit about it, declaring: "We had enlisted to put down the rebellion and had no patience with the red-tape tomfoolery of the regular service. Furthermore, the boys recognized no superiors, except in the line of legitimate duty. Shoulder straps waived, a private was ready at the drop of a hat to thrash his commander—a thing that occurred more than once."

It is perfectly obvious that an army organized in this way required rather special qualities of leadership from its officers. In general terms, the Civil War officer led his men, not because he wore shoulder straps, but because the men came to recognize and accept him as a qualified leader. This meant, above everything else, that in battle the officer had to be absolutely fearless. Even a major general would immediately lose control over his men if they found reason to suspect his courage. From army commander on down, he had to show physical courage rather ostentatiously. If he could not do this he could not do anything.

The officer also had to realize that he was dealing with citizen soldiers who, even after 2 years of war, would insist on remaining more citizen than soldier. They could be led anywhere, but they could hardly be driven at all. West Point training seemed to work 2 ways, in this connection. At its best, it turned out officers who knew instinctively how to induce obedience; at its worst, it produced officers who simply could not command volunteers at all.

It is interesting to look at U. S. Grant himself, when in the early summer of 1861 he became colonel of a rowdy Illinois regiment which had just run one colonel out of camp and which was doing so much drinking, fighting and chicken-stealing that it was known all around its training camp as "Governor Yates' Hellions." One of Grant's first jobs was to get his regiment over from Springfield to a point on the Mississippi River. Trains were available, but there was plenty of time and Grant decided to take his men over on foot. The march would take 4 or 5 days.

The first day's march was a shambles, with no more than half a dozen miles accomplished. That evening, Grant announced that the regiment would resume the march at 6 the next morning. Morning came, reveille was sounded—and at 6 o'clock most of the men were just starting to cook breakfast, no tents had been struck and no wagons had been loaded, and all in all it was an hour and a half longer before the march could begin.

That evening, again, Grant announced that they would march at 6 in the morning. Again, when 6 o'clock came two-thirds of the regiment was still frying bacon, tying its shoes or otherwise engaged. No matter: Grant ordered the regiment paraded and got the march started, leaving most of the men behind, frantically trying to get organized. After marching a few miles he had the men who were on the road fall out for a breather, and he extended this breather until the rest of the regiment could catch up. That evening, as before, he announced that the march would begin at 6 the next morning.

And on this morning, when 6 o'clock came, the regiment was pretty largely ready to go. It got on the road at the proper time, with only a few stragglers and the rest of the way to the Mississippi it moved on schedule. After that Grant had no trouble with it.

Now the common sense quality that enabled Grant to get this regiment in hand may seem too obvious to be worth mentioning; but not all professional soldiers had it, and those who did not failed miserably. There is something instructive about the case of Major General C. C. Gilbert, a soldier in one of the western armies who in the fall of 1862 was jumped from captain of regulars to corps commander of volunteers, and who lasted in that high position only for a few weeks.

Gilbert was one of those starchy, take-his-name-sergeant old regulars who never understood the volunteer soldier. While Buell's army was pursuing Bragg's in Kentucky, that fall, making long forced marches day after day and driving on at a man-killing pace, an Indiana regiment late one evening fell out by a dark roadside for a 5-minute rest. The men dropped in their tracks, naturally, and went sound asleep. Past this sleeping regiment, presently, came General Gilbert and his staff, clanking along on horseback; and Gilbert was incensed by the regiment's failure to stand up and salute. He grabbed the first officer he could find awake—a company commander—and demanded:

"What regiment is this?"

"12th Indiana."

"Humph. Damn pretty regiment. Why in hell don't you have your men line the road and salute when I pass by?"

"Who in hell are you?"

"Major General Gilbert, by God, sir. Give me your sword—you are under arrest."

At this point the regiment's colonel woke up and came over to take a hand in the game. Gilbert repeated his demand, and the colonel announced that his men had marched 15 hours that day and he "wasn't going to hold a dress parade at midnight for any damn fool living." Most of the regiment was awake and listening by now, and Gilbert spotted the color bearer. He reached for the flag, announcing that he was going to seize it and disgrace the regiment.

Now the color bearer told him to keep his hands off the flag or he would be killed. Someone fired a musket in the air; someone else called out "Shoot the SOB!" and a third party jabbed a bayonet into the haunch of General Gilbert's horse, which caused the beast to take off down the road at a gallop, bearing a fuming general, his staff trailing out behind him. He never did get the salute, and he lasted as a general only a few weeks after that.

It is simple enough to remark that Grant was an officer with common sense and that Gilbert was not, but the two anecdotes do tell something about the state of discipline in Civil War armies. It was a discipline which rested largely on the officer himself. It was not something he could very easily enforce; it had to come out of his own qualities of leadership. If he lacked those qualities, he had no discipline.

There were points on which the Civil War soldier simply refused to submit to restraint no matter what the source. This was especially true in respect to the matter of foraging and looting civilian property in occupied territory.

The Northern soldier was pretty much unindoctrinated, when he enlisted. He usually joined up because it seemed like an adventurous, romantic thing to do, or because everybody else was doing it—or, in a great many cases, simply for fun. Mostly he liked camp life, once he got into it. A Massachusetts soldier recalling his career early in the war wrote that "Our drill consisted largely of running around the Old Westbury town hall, yelling like devils and firing at an imaginary foe." A Chicago boy wrote home from training camp: "It is fun to lie around, face unwashed, hair uncombed, shirt unbuttoned and everything uneverything-ed. It sure beats clerking." Another Illinois boy wrote to his parents: "I don't see why people will stay at home when they can get to soldiering. A year of it is worth getting shot for to any man."

Yet if he tended to enjoy camp life—right at first, anyway—the northern soldier usually had no very clear notion of what he was fighting for, except that he believed he was fighting to save the Union. As he figured it, that meant that all southerners were trying to destroy the Union; were, in other words, traitors, to whom the worst that could happen was far too good. Figuring that way, he resolutely refused to respect southern farmers' rights to their chickens, hogs, green corn, fence rails or other property. It is interesting to note that the ravages northern soldiers inflicted on southern territory came much more from the impulse of the common soldier than from the orders of men like Sherman and Sheridan.

Indeed, Sherman himself, during the first 2 years of the war, worked himself almost to a frazzle trying to keep his men from stealing Confederate hams and burning Confederate barns. He tried all sorts of ferocious disciplinary measures to stop it, including ordering enlisted men tied up by the thumbs, but without the slightest success. His men simply did not feel that there was anything wrong with what they were doing. Furthermore, the regimental officers, as a rule, felt the same way the enlisted men did, and flatly refused to enforce orders against looting and foraging. It was common for a colonel, as a regiment made camp, to address his men, pointing to some nearby farm, and say: "Now boys, that barn is full of pigs and chickens. I don't want to see a one of you take any of them" —upon which he would fold his arms and resolutely look in the opposite direction. It is equally common to read of a colonel, imposing punishment on men who had been caught looting, saying sternly: "Boys, I want you to understand that I am not punishing you for stealing but for getting caught at it, by God!"

The point of course is that Civil War discipline was never tight enough to keep the men from doing something which the men themselves believed to be justified. Sherman's orders could not be enforced, partly because the men were not disposed to obey them, and partly because the regimental officers who were primarily responsible did not try to enforce them. In broad areas of conduct the Civil War soldier tended to go his own way regardless of what the man at the top had to say.

As a matter of fact, it was this rowdy approach to southern property which, as much as any other single thing, killed slavery.

The average northern soldier was not fighting to free the slaves. He did not care about slavery one way or the other, and he had very little fondness for the colored man as such. But he did have the feeling that when he got down south it was up to him to put a heavy hand on the men who had rebelled against his government. He would destroy the property of such men whenever he got a chance—and the most obvious, visible, easily-removed piece of property of all was the slave. He might have very little sympathy with the Emancipation Proclamation—some of the western regiments, as a matter of fact, came very close to mutiny when the thing was read to them—but he did understand that the institution of slavery supported the Confederacy, and so he went to work to dismantle it, chattel by chattel, in precisely the same spirit that he killed pigs and burned corncribs. It is hardly an over-statement to suggest that if all northern armies had operated under strict discipline, so that orders against interfering with southern property had been rigidly obeyed, the institution of slavery would have had a much better chance to survive the war.

Perhaps the most surprising part about the defective discipline of the Civil War regiment is that it nevertheless sent to the front a great many fighting regiments of amazing effectiveness.

Partly this was because the men did, after all, know each other well. They had a solid feeling that they could count on one another—and, no doubt, a reluctance to show fear or hesitancy before men they had known all their lives. If a man was wounded, he knew perfectly well that even if the stretcher parties missed him some of his pals would hunt him up, if they possibly could. There was a powerful feeling of comradeship in most of these regiments, and it was a prodigious factor in battle.

In addition, many of those Civil War units built up a very high esprit de corps. The soldier identified himself first of all with his regiment, and he tended to be very proud of it. If his brigade or division had made a good name in some battle, he was equally proud of that. General Phil Kearny, the one-armed soldier who was killed in the summer of 1862, started something when he made all the men in his division wear a diamond-shaped patch of scarlet flannel on their caps. He did this simply in order that when he saw stragglers in the rear areas he could tell at once whether the men belonged to his outfit; but in no time at all the red patch became a badge of honor, Kearny's men felt they were something special because they wore it, and when a new regiment was assigned to the division the men in the other regiments refused to warm up to it until they had a chance to see it in battle—and, as one veteran put it, see "whether the regiment was worthy of belonging to the red diamond division." Six months later, Joe Hooker had similar patches made for each army corps in the Army of the Potomac, and before long the idea had spread to the western armies. Today's shoulder patches are direct descendants of those devices.

The eastern armies adopted the corps badge ahead of the westerners. In 1863, when eastern troops were sent west to bolster Grant's army in front of Chattanooga, some of the westerners in the XV Corps looked in wonder at General Slocum's XII Corps boys, whose badge was a red star. A XV Corps Irishman finally accosted one of the easterners:

"Are you all brigadier generals, with them stars?" he asked.

"That's our corps badge," explained the easterner loftily. "What's yours?"

"Badge, is it?" snorted the Irishman. He slapped his cartridge box. "Here it is, be Jazus—40 rounds!"

His corps commander heard the story and promptly adopted the device; and for the rest of the war, the XV Corps wore for its badge a replica of a cartridge box with the words "40 rounds" printed under it.

Soldiers would quickly take their tone from a commanding officer, if the officer had enough force and leadership. There was an old Regular Army man, General Charles F. Smith—tall, slim, straight as a ramrod; with long flowing white mustachios—who knew instinctively how to lead men in action. He showed up at Fort Donelson with a division of green troops who had never before been under fire, and he had to lead them up a hill, through tangled woods and underbrush, in a charge on a Confederate line of trenches. He stuck his cap on the point of his sword, got out in front of his frightened greenhorns and started off. Confederate bullets began to come through pretty thickly and Smith's men wavered. He turned about in his saddle and called out:

"Damn you, gentlemen, I see skulkers. I'll have none here. Come on, you volunteers, come on. This is your chance. You volunteered to be killed for love of your country and now you can be. You damned volunteers— I'm only a soldier and I don't want to be killed, but you came to be killed and now you can be!"

The line went on up the hill and captured its objective. One soldier wrote: "I was pretty near scared to death, but I saw the Old Man's mustache over his right shoulder and I kept on going."

Discipline or no discipline, enough men would respond to that sort of leadership to put up an excellent fight.

Old Man Smith, incidentally, was an interesting soldier. He had been Commandant of Cadets when both Grant and Sherman were in West Point, and although both of them later out-ranked him—he was a division commander under Grant at Fort Donelson—both confessed that they always felt like school boys in his presence. He seems to have led his volunteers by storming at them, so that they were scared to death of him, and by going in ahead of them when there was danger.

One very junior officer in his division told how, in that spring of 1862, his regiment was camped on a farm where a lot of mint was growing. He and another officer plucked a lot of it, got some commissary whiskey, obtained ice from the farmer's ice house, and made some excellent mint juleps. Then it occurred to them that "Old Smith" would like one, so they took one and went to his tent. The tent flaps were closed, but there was a light inside; Old Smith was propped up in his cot, reading.

One of the officers rapped on the tent pole. Out came Smith's rasping voice: Who was it, and what did he want?

These officers were so much in awe of the old soldier that they did not dare announce themselves. But the one who carried the julep finally worked up his nerve and without saying a word thrust his arm through the tent flaps, the julep glass in his fist.

Inside there was a dead silence. Then the beautiful truth dawned on the old general, and they heard him rumble: "Well, by God, this is kind!" He took the glass, they could hear him sniffing and tasting, and his voice repeated: "Kind, indeed!" Then he drained the glass at a gulp, put the empty glass in the officer's still-extended hand and relaxed. The two officers went away without having said a word, and to the end of his days Old Smith never knew where he got that drink.

From whatever source he got his battle morale, the Civil War soldier somehow learned how to handle himself under fire. Sometimes he had to learn the hard way, for he was often thrown into action almost totally untrained. Perhaps the best illustration of this comes in the terrible battle of Shiloh, where 2 completely green armies ran into each other head-on and fought for 2 days.

It is almost impossible nowadays to understand how pathetically unready for battle were the men who were pushed into the great fight at Shiloh. A Confederate brigadier general confessed afterward that until the moment the fight began he had never heard a gun fired, nor had he ever read a book or heard a lecture on tactics. There were Confederate batteries in that battle which had never fired their guns before; ammunition had been too short to allow practice firing. Many Union infantry regiments received their muskets on the way to the field, and loaded and fired them for the first time in action.

There is one revealing picture of a pea-green Ohio regiment which was in that fix, drawn up in line of battle under a heavy fire. The colonel had run for the rear at the first shock; the men were leaderless, not knowing what they were supposed to do or how they were supposed to do it, but game enough to want to stick around and find out. From somewhere there came a private soldier from another regiment. He had fought at Fort Donelson, and compared with these recruits he was a veteran. He carefully went along the firing line, showing the boys how to load these muskets and how to use them; and as he went, he kept explaining: "It's just like shooting squirrels, only these squirrels have guns—that's all."

And the regiment stayed there, unled, and fought all day long.

Civil War officers quickly learned one thing about green troops which were shoved into battle that way. They would either run away quickly, after the first volley—or they would not run away at all.

At Shiloh, a great many did run; after the battle was a couple of hours old, probably a fourth of Grant's army was huddled under the shelter of the river bank in the rear, completely leaderless and useless. But the rest stayed and fought, and few soldiers have ever fought in a more vicious battle. All military order and tactical formation was quickly lost. A battle line might contain elements from half a dozen different regiments, huddled together, somehow drawing from one another's presence the courage to stay and fight. An advance would be a rush forward by a mob; a retreat would be the same, with the men sticking close to whoever seemed to show the qualities of leadership. We read of one Indiana lad who got a flesh wound in his arm, showed it to his colonel, and was told to drop his rifle and go to the rear. He started off, found Rebel troops in the rear, and presently came back to his colonel.

"Gimme another gun, Cap," he said. "This blame fight ain't got any rear."

Some of these undisciplined private soldiers developed strong qualities, as the war wore along. In the battle of Champion's Hill, during the Vicksburg campaign, General John A. Logan, commanding a Federal division, was sitting on his horse on a hill-top, watching the fight, when a lanky enlisted man—who seems to have been prowling around more or less on his own hook—sauntered up to him and said:

"General, I've been over on the rise yonder, and it's my idea that if you'll put a regiment or 2 over thar, you'll get on their flank and lick 'em easy."

Logan looked where the man pointed, decided that the advice was good, sent a couple of regiments over—and, as the man had predicted, won his fight.

One of the most striking things about the average Civil War regiment was the high degree of manpower wastage that afflicted it. Every regiment contained a certain number of men who would fade back to the rear when the fighting began. No colonel could count on all of his men; there was a steady leakage back from the firing line, even in the veteran regiments, from the beginning of the war to the end.

Worse yet was the toll taken by disease. Medical examinations for recruits were very sketchy. Some regiments got in without any medical examinations at all; and in any case, medical care was so imperfect that there was a steady, remorseless drain on combat strength, month after month. The Civil War regiment had a paper strength of 1,000 men; the regiment that could bring as many as 500 to the field, after 6 months in camp, was very lucky, and the average strength of a veteran regiment would usually be between 200-300. One veteran remarked that a third of a regiment's strength would usually be lost by desertion or straggling, and another third by sickness. The remaining third—the men too stout to run away and too tough to get sick—had to do the fighting. It was right there, probably, that the loose discipline and informal organization of the volunteer army proved most costly.

Yet in the long run these odd combat organizations did what they were supposed to do. If it is possible to dredge up any number of stories revealing slipshod organization and peculiar military habits, it is also possible to show fantastic instances of solid bravery and endurance which no professional soldiers could have improved upon.

On the second day of the battle of Gettysburg, for instance, when the left end of the Union line on Cemetery Ridge had more or less dissolved, and Confederate troops were swarming up the slopes with nothing much to stop them, the 1st Minnesota came marching up from the rear to get into the fight. General Winfield Scott Hancock, corps commander in charge of that part of the line, saw a Confederate assault wave coming, and galloped over to the Minnesota's colonel. This colonel had been under arrest for several days; on a forced march to Gettysburg he had halted his troops, against Hancock's orders, so that they could take off their shoes and socks before fording a little stream, and Hancock had punished him for it. The colonel was feeling rather bitter about it.

Hancock pointed toward the oncoming Confederates, whose battle flag was visible.

"Do you see those colors?" he demanded. The colonel nodded. "Well, take them!" demanded Hancock belligerently.

The 1st Minnesota went in, head on. It numbered only 262 men, but it swung into line and made its fight. It stopped the Confederate charge, captured the battle flag, and an hour later it had just 47 men left—for a loss of 82 per cent, which seems to have been a record for the Union army for the entire war. Next day, incidentally, those 47 who remained stayed in line and helped repel Pickett's charge.

Any military system which can produce combat units that will stay and fight after a loss of 82 per cent seems to me to be a pretty good system, no matter how many surface defects it may have.

And the military system that prevailed in the Civil War was, with all of its defects, a pretty good system. The worst thing about it, probably, was that it gave the willing horse all of the load. It never controlled the stragglers and the faint-hearts. The good men got all the worst of it, and the gold-bricks mostly got off easy. But a tremendous job of fighting did get done.

At bottom, the system drew its strength from several things.

The comradeship that prevailed in the ranks was a prime element. The men knew each other; regiments were pretty largely homogeneous; out of this they built a very high morale. Pride in the regiment, and sometimes in the brigade, division or army corps grew up naturally and became an immense stimulus to good performance. And the very looseness of army organization seems to have brought forward uncommon qualities of leadership in the officer corps. There was an enormous amount of wastage, to be sure, as the test of battle weeded out the unfit, but in the end those regiments were extremely well led.

Last of all, the human material was very, very good. By and large, I think, it was the same sort of material we have nowadays; I don't think the American people have changed a great deal. And the great lesson of the Civil War, to me, is simply this: that with volunteer American soldiers, the right leadership can do anything.

38 *Bernard A. Weisberger*

THE DARK AND BLOODY GROUND
OF RECONSTRUCTION HISTORIOGRAPHY

The years which followed Appomattox were no less dramatic or important than those which had preceded it. Appomattox meant an end to the trials of war and a beginning to the problems of peace. How would the victory of the North be translated into deeper economic and social terms? Would the triumph in arms also be a triumph in peace? Would the South lose the war but win the peace? What commercial and industrial policies would the new nation pursue? What

Reprinted with permission of the managing editor from *The Journal of Southern History*, XXV (November, 1959), 427–47.

would be the status of the freedman? What would the defeat of the Southern aristocracy mean for the social structure of the new America? How much had the compound of American society been altered by the chemism of war? Whatever the deeper problems resulting from the war, the most immediate one was that of Reconstruction. How were the defeated states to be governed? On what terms were they to be brought back into the Union?

Because Reconstruction dealt with problems which had been central to the war, its history has been as much a matter of controversy as the war itself. For the most part, historians have viewed Reconstruction politics as the rule of Radical Republicans in Congress and of "Carpetbaggers," "Scalawags," and Negroes in the Southern States. Despite recent modifications of this view, a general re-appraisal of the postwar decade has not yet been made. The reason is suggested by Dr. Bernard A. Weisberger in the following essay. Dr. Weisberger has taught at Wayne State University and at the University of Chicago and is the author of *Reporters for the Union* (1953), an account of the war correspondents, and *They Gathered at the River: The Story of the Great Revivalists and Their Impact Upon Religion in America* (1958). With regard to what he calls "the dark and bloody ground of Reconstruction historiography," his viewpoint is that it will remain so until historians come to terms with some basic problems in the American past.

To understand the age of Reconstruction, submits Dr. Weisberger, we must answer questions which go to the root of all American history. What, to begin with, is our view of the Negro, his nature, his potentialities, his personality? How far, moreover, does the corruption that seems to have been so widespread during Reconstruction tend to be part of the American democratic process? In what way were postwar relations between the federal government and the states merely a step in the road of a long-term evolution? To what extent are we still interpreting Reconstruction in the light of economic and social concepts whose validity is questionable and which we no longer apply to other areas of American history? What, in general, are the deeper personal values by which we construe the American past and what, in particular, are the values of those whose interpretations have dominated Reconstruction historiography? It is the sum of Dr. Weisberger's suggestion that our views on a part of American history ought to be consistent with our views on the rest of it.

The South is today in a state of radical transition; it is being made over by powerful internal forces and by the impact on American policy of the opinion of a largely non-white world. Industrialization and desegregation are two significant commentaries on the restyling of Southern life. In this sense, we are witnessing a second and more profound Reconstruction. It is imperative for an honest consideration of what is occurring today that we reconsider the first Reconstruction and that we understand what its men and its problems really were.

Twenty years ago, as the exciting thirties drew to a close, the dry bones began to stir in that notable valley of historical skeletons, the Reconstruction period. In February 1939, the *Journal of Southern History* carried an article by Francis B. Simkins describing a number of "New Viewpoints of Southern Reconstruction."[1] Frankly facing the fact that "the main issue of the Reconstruction period, the great American race question," like Banquo's ghost, would not down, Simkins asked for a fairer analysis of Reconstruction's achievements and failures and an end to the notion that encouraging the Negro in voting and officeholding was somehow a crime of crimes. By adopting a more "critical, creative and tolerant attitude," he said, historians of the South could better discharge their "great civic obligation."

In the following year, Howard K. Beale took up this theme with a brisk, provocative essay, "On Rewriting Reconstruction History," in the *American Historical Review*.[2] Forthrightly, Beale asked if it were "not time that we studied the history of Reconstruction without first assuming, at least subconsciously, that carpetbaggers and Southern white Republicans were wicked, that Negroes were illiterate incompetents, and that the whole white South owes a debt of gratitude to the restorers of 'white supremacy'?" He then posted a list of questions previously ignored except in scattered numbers of the *Journal of Negro History* and in W. E. B. Du Bois' 1935 volume, *Black Reconstruction*. What was the *whole* story of popular government in the South from 1865 to 1900? What were the economic connections of the so-called Redeemers? How much of the famed Reconstruction debt went for gilt spittoons and legislative boodle, and how much for social, educational, and industrial rebuilding? Where did the poor white fit into the picture? What lessons could be learned by considering Reconstruction anew, this time as a short-lived revolution which placed power in inexperienced hands?

These questions struck to the heart of the prejudiced version of Reconstruction laid down around the turn of the century by Rhodes, Burgess, and Dunning, developed by Fleming and some of the individual state historians of the period, and widely popularized, in 1929, by Claude Bowers' zestful work of imagination, *The Tragic Era*.[3] That story is familiar. It

[1] *Journal of Southern History*, V (February 1939), 49–61.

[2] *American Historical Review*, XLV (July 1940), 807–27.

[3] Claude G. Bowers, *The Tragic Era; the Revolution after Lincoln* (Boston, 1929). To particularize individual monographs on Southern Reconstruction here would involve the compilation of a virtually complete critical bibliography of works on the subject up to 1939, whereas this article aims at a detailed examination only of studies appearing since that date. Accordingly, the reader's familiarity with the earlier works is assumed. They are conveniently listed in a number of places, notably in James G. Randall, *The Civil War and Reconstruction* (Boston, 1953), 881–935.

told of how "Vindictives" and "Radicals" in Congress shouldered aside Johnson and the Supreme Court and imposed "Carpetbag" and "Scalawag" and "Negro" governments on the South by the bayonet. These new governments debauched and plundered a proud but helpless people until finally, desperately harried whites responded with their own campaigns of violence and persuasion. These respectable folk at last took advantage of mounting Northern disgust with "carpetbag crimes" to restore "home rule" unopposed.

The Beale and Simkins articles seemed to indicate that professional historians were ready to overhaul this operatic version of events—perhaps to use the perspective gained at the end of one decade of swift social change in the careful examination of an earlier period of upheaval. Yet now, twenty years after these premonitory signs, the indicated tide of revision has not fully set in. Certainly the work still needs to be done. The New Deal, the Second World War, and the Cold War have all set in motion what some have called a "New Reconstruction" of the South—with fresh patterns in industry, urban life, population movement, agrarian practice, social and political leadership, and capitalization forming almost faster than the census takers can reveal them. The school desegregation crisis has, since 1954, moved the race question into disturbing but unescapable prominence. It is more important than ever that progress be made towards understanding the issues raised in the "old" Reconstruction of 1865 to 1877. Yet something seems to have blunted the purpose of the historical guild, and the discovery of what this something is deserves professional attention.

Certainly it is no lack of revisionary work on the monographic level. There is plenty of that, some of it brilliant. One is almost tempted to cite the leading journals *passim* for fear of overlooking meritorious pieces, but short of that, one may point to at least half a dozen books and twice that many articles of genuine significance. There are, for one thing, three pathbreaking books by C. Vann Woodward dealing with economic leadership, political organization, and racial adjustment in the post-Appomattox South.[4] Among articles on more specialized topics, there is, to begin with, an outstanding survey of the attitudes dominating the historical approach to Reconstruction by T. Harry Williams, fit to stand in the good company of the Beale and Simkins articles.[5] David Donald gave impetus to a study of Southern Republicans, in 1944, with a piece on Mississippi "scalawags," and he has since given fresh scrutiny to the relationships between the Radicals,

[4] *Reunion and Reaction; the Compromise of 1877 and the End of Reconstruction* (Boston, 1951); *Origins of the New South, 1877-1913* (Baton Rouge, 1951); *The Strange Career of Jim Crow* (New York, 1955).

[5] "An Analysis of Some Reconstruction Attitudes," *Journal of Southern History*, XII (November 1946), 469-86.

Lincoln, and Johnson.[6] Thomas B. Alexander surveyed the role of the Whigs in Tennessee Reconstruction and found a more complex story than had hitherto been suggested.[7] The oft-maligned agents of the Freedmen's Bureau have been made the subjects of a judicious plea in defense by John and LaWanda Cox.[8] Northern philanthropists and educators, alternately hailed as agents of progress and damned as Yankee marplots, have also undergone dispassionate examination by such scholars as Henry L. Swint and Ralph Morrow.[9] Both Swint and Morrow have published full-dress books on the subjects of their articles, and, indeed, monographs continue almost regularly to break up the fallow ground.[10] George R. Bentley has brought up to date Paul Pierce's half-century-old work on the Freedmen's Bureau.[11] Otis Singletary has submitted the fullest report so far on Negro militiamen in the occupied states of the South.[12] Vernon Wharton has, it may be hoped, provided a pilot project for the studies of the Negro as voter and officeholder in his book on Negroes in Mississippi during and after the Radical heyday.[13] Fresh biographies, both of major and minor actors, have also appeared. Robert Durden has revealed the paradox of a Negro-hating Radical in his life of James S. Pike, and Jonathan Daniels has

[6] "The Scalawag in Mississippi Reconstruction," *Journal of Southern History*, X (November 1944), 447–60; "Why They Impeached Andrew Johnson," *American Heritage*, VIII (December 1956), 20–25; "The Radicals and Lincoln" in *Lincoln Reconsidered* (New York, 1956), 103–27.

[7] "Whiggery and Reconstruction in Tennessee," *Journal of Southern History*, XVI (August 1950), 291–305.

[8] "General O. O. Howard and the 'Misrepresented Bureau,'" *ibid.*, XIX (November 1953), 427–56. The Coxes believe that "even the most friendly studies of the Bureau have exaggerated its weaknesses and minimized its strength." LaWanda Cox has also contributed fresh material on the motivation of postwar reformers in "The Promise of Land for the Freedman," *Mississippi Valley Historical Review*, XLV (December 1958), 413–40.

[9] Henry L. Swint, "Northern Interest in the Shoeless Southerner," *Journal of Southern History*, XVI (November 1950), 457–71; Ralph Morrow, "Northern Methodism in the South during Reconstruction," *Mississippi Valley Historical Review*, XLI (September 1954), 197–218.

[10] Henry L. Swint, *The Northern Teacher in the South, 1862–1870* (Nashville, 1941); Ralph Morrow, *Northern Methodism and Reconstruction* (East Lansing, 1956). Before leaving the subject of periodical articles, it is well to note that this sampling takes no note of articles in the journals of various state historical societies or of professional associations for the study of economics, sociology, and political science. Nor is any attempt made here to list new works of which the author is aware on subjects related to Reconstruction indirectly—studies of pardon, amnesty, and loyalty oaths after the war, of railroad financing in the Southern states, or of aspects of the national battles over land, currency, and tariff reforms. Such a listing would unduly prolong this article, but would also add support to one of its contentions, that abundant material for a fresh synthesis of the period is available.

[11] George R. Bentley, *A History of the Freedmen's Bureau* (Philadelphia, 1955).

[12] *Negro Militia and Reconstruction* (Austin, 1957).

[13] *The Negro in Mississippi, 1865–1890* (Chapel Hill, 1947).

contributed a portrait of a "carpetbagger," Milton S. Littlefield, the delicious wickedness of which should not obscure its real importance.[14] At least two writers have grappled, since 1940, with the contradictions of Thaddeus Stevens: Richard Current in a sharply critical book, and Ralph Korngold in a rather saccharine tribute.[15] Two recent biographies of Benjamin F. Butler also bear witness to the dangers of attempting to "typecast" an important Radical.[16] Still more light on Reconstruction may be expected when David Donald's forthcoming life of Sumner appears.

Varied as are all these works in quality, aim, and scope, their total impact clears the air. They show, first of all, that the so-called "scalawags" were not all the ragged underlings of Southern society, but included—at least early in the period—many erstwhile Southern Whigs, high in status and thoroughly baptized in the church of the Lost Cause. The nucleus of a Southern Republican party, they were displaced by extremist pressure from overardent Radicals, both Negro and white, on the one hand, and die-hard "white line" supporters on the other. Often, however, the issues on which they were challenged had as much to do with patronage and with profit as with race.[17] Secondly, the Republican state governments chosen under the operation of the Reconstruction Acts of 1867 were not composed exclusively of corruptionists, white or Negro, and achieved a number of praiseworthy social and educational reforms.[18] Thirdly, such corruption as did

[14] Robert F. Durden, *James Shepherd Pike: Republicanism and the American Negro, 1850–1882* (Durham, 1957), a significant part of which appeared as "The Prostrate State Revisited: James S. Pike and South Carolina Reconstruction," *Journal of Negro History*, XXXIX (April 1954), 87–110; Jonathan Daniels, *Prince of Carpetbaggers* (Philadelphia, 1958).

[15] Richard N. Current, *Old Thad Stevens; A Story of Ambition* (Madison, 1942); Ralph Korngold, *Thaddeus Stevens; A Being Darkly Wise and Rudely Great* (New York, 1955).

[16] Robert Holzman, *Stormy Ben Butler* (New York, 1954); Hans L. Trefousse, *Ben Butler, the South Called Him Beast!* (New York, 1957).

[17] Evidence for this statement is scattered widely through the works already referred to. Donald, "Scalawag in Mississippi Reconstruction," 60, declares that in that state, "the importance of the former Whigs has generally been neglected." Alexander, in "Whiggery and Reconstruction in Tennessee," 305, suggests "the possible value of reviewing Reconstruction in all southern states to appraise the role of persistent Whiggery." Insofar as the business community of the South was identified with the Whigs, this view finds support in T. Harry Williams' study, "The Louisiana Reunification Movement of 1873," *Journal of Southern History*, XI (August 1945), 349–69, wherein he finds in Reconstruction "still another group whose importance has not been recognized—the business men, not closely affiliated with politics, who saw the strife of parties and races destroying the stability they desired. . . ." (369). Woodward, in *Reunion and Reaction*, significantly entitles one chapter "The Rejuvenation of Whiggery," and begins his *Origins of the New South* with a quotation from a contemporary Southern source concerning a marriage whose "high contracting parties were Whiggism and Democracy," and whose presumable offspring was Conservatism.

[18] This point was so widely conceded as early as 1939 as to require little docu-

exist was shared in by many white and respectable Southerners, later to become "Bourbons," who did not scruple to profit by the lavish gifts of the sinful "carpetbag" governments to Southern development companies. Moreover, when restored to control, these "Conservatives" continued to keep the doors of the state treasuries hospitably open to businessmen who had formerly supported the Radicals.[19] Fourthly, the restored "Conservatives" were willing to live with Negro suffrage, provided they could control its outcome. The "sin" of enfranchising the illiterate freedman was apparently washed whiter than snow, once he switched to the Democratic ticket.[20] Fifthly, life somehow went on under "bayonet rule." Crops, capital, and order *were* restored, after all, and there were cakes and ale as well as heartbreak and ugliness. Violence there was; but the legend of Negro militiamen's "atrocities," perpetuated in Thomas Dixon's *The Klansman*, is as baseless as the implication in Albion Tourgée's *A Fool's Errand* that every square Southern mile contained a secretly buried victim of the Klan.[21] Lastly, neither in Congress nor in the South were the Radicals the

---

mentation here. It is cogently stated in Simkins, "New Viewpoints of Southern Reconstruction," Beale, "On Rewriting Reconstruction History," and Williams, "An Analysis of Some Reconstruction Attitudes," already cited. Vernon Wharton, after a close study of one "reconstructed" state, reaches a conclusion probably applicable to most of the former Confederate commonwealths: "Altogether, as governments go, that supplied by the Negro and white Republicans in Mississippi between 1870 and 1876 was not a bad government." *The Negro in Mississippi*, 179.

[19] This point forms almost the entire thesis of Woodward's *Reunion and Reaction*, and is explored in depth in *Origins of the New South*, 1–74, as well as in the opening chapters of the same author's *Tom Watson, Agrarian Rebel* (New York, 1938). Daniels' *Prince of Carpetbaggers* is an excellent detailed account of the financial relationships between white Democrats and "carpetbaggers" in North Carolina and Florida.

[20] Negroes "continued to vote in large numbers in most parts of the South for more than two decades after Reconstruction." Woodward, *Strange Career of Jim Crow*, 35.

[21] E. Merton Coulter, who most certainly believes Reconstruction to have been a severe time of trial for the South, nevertheless thoroughly documents the return to normal life in *The South during Reconstruction, 1865–1877* (Baton Rouge, 1947). He declares (ix): "There were . . . with all the political and constitutional abnormalities of the times, the ordinary activities of the people, as they sowed and reaped, went to church, visited their neighbors, sang their songs, and sought in a thousand ways to amuse themselves." As for the question of placing the role of the Negro militia in its true proportions, Singletary observes that the Radical governors rarely used the troops available to them under state law, and notes that the real affront, for white Southerners, was the simple presence of Negroes in uniform. "For even had the militia refrained from committing a single act antagonistic to the whites, in all probability they would still have been destroyed." *Negro Militia and Reconstruction*, 152. The use of Federal troops is a matter deserving greater study, and as for riots and incidents not involving the use of uniformed soldiery, the responsibility is not easily pinned on one side or the other.

purposeful and unified group of conspirators that they have been made out to be by friendly biographers of Andrew Johnson.[22] Johnson himself, pilloried though he was by his enemies, added to his own woes by personal hardheadedness, political stumbling, and a blind belief that the incantation of constitutional formulas could change the brute facts of power distribution.[23]

This is a good record of piecemeal accomplishment. Yet in two significant areas, the professional record remains poor. For one thing, there has been no synthesis of this material in a good general history of Reconstruction. The one full-scale treatment by an academic historian since 1940 is E. Merton Coulter's *The South during Reconstruction, 1865–1877*. Regrettably, Professor Coulter chose to begin with a veteran's indignant rejection of the entire notion of revision. There could be, he said, "no sensible departure from the well-known facts of the Reconstruction program as it was applied to the South. No amount of revision can explain away the grievous mistakes made in this abnormal period of American history."[24] This attitude seems excessively conservative. If modern historical scholarship teaches anything, it teaches that "well-established" facts are constantly changed in implication as new facts are unearthed, and that there are sev-

[22] David Donald notes, in *Lincoln Reconsidered*, 103–27, that the concept of the "malevolent Radical" comes in part from the need to find new antagonists, in every generation, for the noble figure of Lincoln in the Lincoln-myth. Certainly close study of the lives of eminent Radicals reveals plenty of dissension among them; as for the Southern Radicals in the statehouses, their factional feuds in every state suggest, in the words of a recent article, "a much more complex social, economic and political evolution than is found in partisan accounts." Jack B. Scroggs, "Southern Reconstruction: A Radical View," *Journal of Southern History*, XXIV (November 1958), 428. Both Williams and Donald warn against facile generalization. "Southerners differed among themselves on the issues of Reconstruction in about the same degree as did groups in the North," says Williams in "An Analysis of Some Reconstruction Attitudes," 486, while Donald reports that the "difficulties of making an adequate study of a Reconstruction election in the South have seldom been realized." "The Scalawag in Mississippi Reconstruction," 458. James M. Dabbs, a temperate Southerner of today, also underscores the complexity of the story in *The Southern Heritage* (New York, 1958), 105.

[23] The most intelligent critical discussion of Johnson to appear recently is David Donald's "Why They Impeached Andrew Johnson," *American Heritage*. A good, new biography of the impeached President is needed. The two most frequently cited nowadays suffer from the vigor of their efforts to defend him unreservedly. They are, George F. Milton, *The Age of Hate; Andrew Johnson and the Radicals* (New York, 1930) and Lloyd P. Stryker, *Andrew Johnson; A Study in Courage* (New York, 1929). An interesting minor revision of the Johnson story has lately been contributed by Ralph J. Roske, "The Seven Martyrs?" *American Historical Review*, LXIV (January 1959), 323–30, who challenges the view that the seven Republicans who voted for his acquittal were "relentlessly persecuted . . . until they were forced altogether from the American political scene" (323). He denies that their later careers were marked by "unrelieved martyrdom."   [24] Coulter, *South during Reconstruction*, xi.

eral sensible departures from any set of facts, depending upon whose definition of "sensible" is employed.[25] Rich though it may be in material, *The
South during Reconstruction* is no contribution to understanding. In point
of fact it is something of a setback. Appearing as it does in the *History of
the South* series published by the Louisiana State University Press—a set of
works which must long remain the standard repository of Southern history—it would have been more enduring had it maintained a more judicious
attitude. Since 1947 the only other general book on Reconstruction is
Hodding Carter's *The Angry Scar; the Story of Reconstruction*.[26] Carter, a
literate and "moderate" Mississippi editor, provides a book which is a distinct improvement in fairness on the earlier "nonprofessional" study of
Bowers. Yet it is still marked by a defensive spirit, and more to the point,
its incorporation of fresh research is at best uneven.

The other failure of historians to deal adequately with Reconstruction
is evident in textbooks, many of which play old tunes on worn keys. This
is especially lamentable since the text is so often the college graduate's only
exposure to the literature of history. Some volumes designed for classroom
use attempt balanced discussions—notably (though not exclusively) the
works of Freidel, Current, and Williams, of Hofstadter, Aaron, and Miller,
of Billington, Loewenberg, and Brockunier, and of Leland D. Baldwin.[27]
Others lean heavily on stereotyped reactions. For one thing, the terms
"Carpetbagger" and "Scalawag" are sometimes used as if they were genuine
proper nouns and not cartoonists' labels. It is true that they are now so
familiar as perhaps not to need quotation marks, and yet by the same token

[25] A searching critique both of Coulter's "facts" and his deductions therefrom is
John Hope Franklin's "Whither Reconstruction Historiography," *Journal of Negro
Education*, XVII (February 1948), 446–61. For a briefer statement of Coulter's conventional view of Reconstruction, see A. B. Moore, "One Hundred Years of Reconstruction of the South," *Journal of Southern History*, IX (May 1943), 153–80.

[26] New York, 1959.

[27] Frank Freidel, Richard N. Current, and T. Harry Williams, *A History of the
United States* (2 vols., New York, 1959), II, 23–27; Richard Hofstadter, Daniel Aaron,
and William Miller, *The United States: The History of a Republic* (Englewood Cliffs,
N.J., 1957), 404–405; Ray A. Billington, Bert J. Loewenberg, and Samuel Brockunier,
The United States; American Democracy in World Perspective (New York, 1947),
261–85; Leland D. Baldwin, *The Stream of American History* (2 vols., New York,
1953), I, 911–15. The first two of these books stress economic turmoil as the basis for
a good deal of political misbehavior usually imputed to "carpetbag" villainy or Negro
ignorance. Baldwin declares that one "can find what he seeks when he examines the
role of the Negroes in the reconstruction period. . . . If it was Negro votes that made
some astonishing steals possible, it should be remembered that it was white men who
got the bulk of the swag." Billington, Loewenberg and Brockunier point out that the
"reconstruction record, written under the tutelage of scholars of Bourbon lineage seeking a gentlemanly road to reunion, has long demanded reappraisal." Another sympathetic and careful presentation of the Reconstruction period is to be found in Carl
N. Degler, *Out of Our Past* (New York, 1959).

we should expect to find Jacobin, Doughface, and Gold Bug in current and unqualified usage to describe certain groups in our history. Negro suffrage is generally deplored and credited only to opportunistic, if not openly base, motives. Thus, John D. Hicks traces "an infinite amount of abuse" to "premature" voting by the freedmen, while Morison and Commager explain that it was instituted by the Radicals "to secure the colored vote at the earliest opportunity," which is partly true but does not explain why the Fourteenth Amendment offered the South the opportunity to reject Negro enfranchisement if Southerners were willing to pay the price of reduced representation in Congress.[28] Riegel and Long deplore the handiwork of the "ill-trained Negro freedman, intoxicated by his first breaths of liberty," while Carman and Syrett, generally fair, nevertheless ring the changes on the gross extravagance of the "black and tan" legislatures.[29] Thomas A. Bailey's *The American Pageant*, a highly popular one-volume text, belongs to the Burgess era. "The Radicals," it declares, "would 'Republicanize' the South by making the freedman an unwitting tool of their own schemes, and ride into power on his lash-scarred back." The "gun-supported reconstruction of the South, begun so brutally in 1867 . . . under the stern eye of bayonet-bearing Union soldiers," resulted in Southern legislatures which sometimes "resembled the comic opera."[30] No doubt this is as stirring, for students, as a showing of *The Birth of a Nation*, but it is not much more accurate.

In sum, although the foregoing survey does not pretend to cover the textbook situation completely, teachers of American history have not taken into account the newest modifications of the "Carpetbag–bayonet rule–Negro domination" legend either in general works for the broad public or in texts designed for college students. The question of "why" is a challenging one. Part of the answer appears to lie in a professional conservatism which we historians of America too often permit to close our minds to new approaches in the entire range of our work. "He that is unjust in the least," Scripture says, "is unjust also in much." If we have been unjust to some actors in the Reconstruction story, it is because we have not come to terms with some larger problems of United States history.

In the first place, white historians have shied away from grasping the nettle of race conflict, mainly because of the difficulty of recognizing their own emotional involvement in the problem. Yet this unwillingness to dwell

[28] John D. Hicks, *The American Nation; a History of the United States from 1865 to the Present* (Cambridge, 1955), 30; Samuel E. Morison and Henry S. Commager, *The Growth of the American Republic* (2 vols., New York, 1950), II, 38–43.

[29] Robert E. Riegel and David F. Long, *The American Story: Volume One: Youth* (New York, 1955); Harry J. Carman and Harold Syrett, *A History of the American People* (2 vols., New York, 1952), II, 20–31.

[30] Thomas A. Bailey, *The American Pageant: A History of the Republic* (Boston, 1956), 467–74.

on the almost universal nineteenth-century conviction of the Negro's innate inferiority often leads to a slipshod evaluation of materials. It is proper to take account of the frankly political motives of many Radical defenders of the Negro voter. It is equally proper to bear in mind the frankly racial motives of some of the Radicals' opponents. A glance at source materials of the sixties, for example, shows that many so-called conservatives opposed the Radical program for the South not because they were devoted to states' rights, or agrarianism, or the Constitution, or the Democratic party alone, but plainly and simply because they thought it was sinful to give so-called Africans the right to share in governments framed by a clearly superior Anglo-Saxon race. In combing the Civil War files of such northern Democratic papers as the New York *World*, Chicago *Times*, and Cincinnati *Enquirer*, one finds diatribes against "niggers" and the "Republican niggerocracy" quite as fulsome as anything ever concocted by today's racists.[31] Instincts of decency as much as anything else prompt the suppression of such material, but silence on the subject covers up some of the ignobler motives of men who are now and then lauded as brave opponents of "Radical tyranny." It is hardly correct to judge "Radicals" by their worst motives and "Redeemers" only by their best.

Negro historians, from the venerable days of George Williams to the modern times of John Hope Franklin, Rayford W. Logan, and others, have had, perforce, to recognize a conflict between the status conservatism of a dominant white race and the aspirations of the Negro people. Reviewers sometimes tend to patronize their works as restricted by adherence to a minority point of view. But white historians, naturally enough, write from a majority point of view which is sometimes confused with objectivity— and which leads even the fairest of them on occasion into unrecognized value judgments. Take, for example, the simple matter of suffrage. Many textbooks deprecate the enfranchisement of freedmen almost immediately after emancipation. While by no means "naturally" inferior, they argue, the victims of slavery were as yet too ignorant and irresponsible to be trusted with political power. The statement is true in part, but the historian who demands intelligence and responsibility as prerequisites for the ballot is, wittingly or not, making the Federalist and Whig case against universal suffrage. Unique as was the experience in slavery, it would be difficult to prove that the freedman was inherently less ready to vote than the illiterate backwoodsman or the freshly-arrived immigrant. Yet the same historian who has doubts about the freedman as voter often votes in earlier chapters *for* the Jacksonians and *against* the Know-Nothings. It would be a good thing, in fact, if more historians examined critically the libertarian and

---

[31] Abundant documentation of this statement is available in the newspapers mentioned. For a brief sample drawn from the news columns only, see Bernard A. Weisberger, *Reporters for the Union* (Boston, 1953), 265-70.

equalitarian assumptions, both romantic and rationalistic, which have governed our experiment in democracy, but the examination ought to extend to all groups, localities, and periods, and not merely to Reconstruction Negroes. The members of the James Ford Rhodes school of historians were more consistent in this regard. Often they *did* distrust the immigrant as a voter, and if they supported universal suffrage, it sometimes seemed to be on the ground that illiterate Anglo-Saxons were by nature better citizens than men of lesser breeds without a "genius for self-government." Their views should not be perpetuated nowadays by mixing them with the base alloy of hypocrisy. It would be better to discuss the Negro vote in terms of public resistance to it and of what parties gained by it—in terms of motive and expediency—rather than by Olympian judgments on how "good" a voter the Negro made. Evaluations of the political records of entire groups of citizens are at best difficult, and at worst dangerous.

Historians are not obliged, of course, to support the Negro's case unreservedly wherever it appears. They ought, nonetheless, to walk humbly when talking of the American Negro as slave, freedman, voter, or worker. He is known to us almost exclusively through the writings of white men, who, whether well-intentioned or not, were interested parties to a conflict.[32] Conflicts may be solved peaceably, but not wished away. The conflict between white Southerners' determination to be the architects of their own society and black Southerners' desire for a place of dignity in that society did not disappear in 1877. It was "solved" by Northern acquiescence in the subordination of the Southern Negro. Paul Buck's well-known "road to reunion" was paved with the broken ambitions of the freedmen.[33] If Reconstruction is to be correctly branded as a failure, it is just to point out that its aftermath also represented a great failure of democracy. But American historians do not, to judge by their works, like

[32] One basic historiographical problem, in fact, revolves around the question of whether "the Negro" revealed by the documents is the true image of himself or the man whom whites want him to be. One may hope that not all Negroes feel like the grandfather in Ralph Ellison's *Invisible Man* (New York, 1952), whose dying words were: "Son . . . I never told you, but our life is a war and I have been a traitor all my born days, a spy in the enemy's country ever since I gave up my gun back in the Reconstruction" (13-14). But considering the Negro's position in American society, one may also wonder if there is not a certain applicability to him in words used by a president of the Southern Historical Association to describe white ex-Confederates in Reconstruction: "Southerners were being forced, like the peoples in any conquered and occupied country, to resort to deception, violence, and intrigue. Double standards and non-moral attitudes were inevitable results." Avery Craven, "The Price of Union," *Journal of Southern History*, XVIII (February 1952), 11.

[33] This fact is underscored by contrasting the optimistic and conciliatory statements reported in *Road to Reunion* (Boston, 1937) with the unpleasant facts noted in Rayford W. Logan, *The Negro in American Life and Thought: The Nadir, 1877–1901* (New York, 1954).

the word "failure" any better than the word "conflict." Neither fits the textbook myths of underlying unity, of unceasing progress, of all problems ultimately coming out right, somehow, in the pendulum swings of time. In the case of the knotty race problem, however, only a hardheaded approach to distasteful truths will yield real understanding.

Secondly, it is time for a fresh look at the "abnormal corruption" of Reconstruction, which has long colored the period's image. True, it is now often palliated by comparison with the general fraudulence of the Grant era—the grafting of a Tweed, the gaudy robberies of the Erie gang, the copious cheats practiced by the appointees and favorites of the Hero of Appomattox. Yet this does not get at the *basic* historical question. Where does "corruption" begin and "lawful business" end in our society, which has encouraged unlimited gainfulness and freedom from restraint as legitimate goals, and insisted meanwhile that these characteristics can readily be combined with public virtue and civic responsibility. Tocqueville, acute as usual, saw the catch. "When the taste for physical gratifications" among a democratic people outgrew their wisdom and experience, he prophesied in warning of dangers to democratic states, some men would "lose all self-restraint. . . . In their intense and exclusive anxiety to make a fortune they [would] lose sight of the close connection that exists between the private fortune of each . . . and the prosperity of all."[34] From the beginning, the United States has liberally rewarded enterprise and industry—one form of the pursuit of private fortune—and assumed that the public prosperity would flourish in consequence. But with unerring periodicity some businessmen have run so far and so fast in their quest that they have found even our few legal safeguards of the public weal in their way. Then they have tried to evade, hurdle, or destroy them, producing, in consequence, what is called "fraud."

Let the judicious historian of Reconstruction consider the widespread land frauds involved in the sale of portions of the public domain in the old Northwest. Let him recall the fragrant Yazoo scandals, and reflect on Joseph G. Baldwin's description of the Southwest of Jackson's day:— "What country could boast more largely of its crimes? What more splendid role of felonies! . . . What more magnificent operations in the land-offices! . . . And in INDIAN affairs!—the very mention is suggestive of the poetry of theft—the romance of a wild and weird larceny!"[35] Let those who read Reconstruction history recall the banking swindles and internal improvement bubbles and repudiations of the period just before 1837, and then, skipping ahead five or six decades, dwell on the state house gangs and

---

[34] Alexis de Tocqueville, *Democracy in America*, tr. by Henry Reeve, revised by Francis Bowen, ed., by Phillips Bradley (2 vols., New York, 1945), II, 140–41.

[35] Joseph G. Baldwin, *The Flush Times of Alabama and Mississippi* (New York, 1853), 238.

municipal rings with whom the Progressives did battle. Let all American scholars contemplate the Harding regime, and then ponder soberly our own society, with its expense-account millionaires, its depletion allowances, its licensing scandals, its much-advertised union corruption, its much *less* well-advertised business corruption and tax evasion, its paid "amateur" university athletes, its call girls hired to "entertain" key "accounts," and its numerous other evidences of the conflicts that can arise between "good business" and "good morals." In the face of all this, can the Reconstruction legislatures which showered the resources of their states on promoters and developers be properly called "abnormal"? What manner of historical "abnormality" is it which recurs every twenty years or so, if not oftener?

This is not to suggest that students of the national past should now turn to the writing of a running record entitled *Main Currents in American Larceny*. The matter is not that simple. Yet it has been made so; our use of the word "corruption" in connection with Reconstruction and other periods supports the faith that our institutions are fundamentally whole and sweet, and that only when "dishonest men" get control of them are the times out of joint. We could do with a rereading of Lincoln Steffens. And we could do more good by asking ourselves questions than by condemning rascals. Is this cycle of so-called "corruption" and "purification" inherent in our marriage, during the last century, of the acquisitive mentality and the liberal state? Did we thus, to borrow from Shaw's definition of marriage, combine "the maximum of temptation with the maximum of opportunity?"

Certainly the "carpetbaggers," for example, deserve a fresh look. Remarkably few of them are well-known to history. Mostly they were young men winging into undeveloped territory in search of profitable opportunities, with a light load of moral as well as of personal baggage. Such enterprise was praised when it carried "civilization" into the West, where only aborigines were dispossessed of their birthright. It was condemned in the South when it resulted in the impoverishment of disfranchised whites. Yet was not the "carpetbagger" as much a product of nineteenth-century America's values of "get" and "build" and "hustle" as was, say, the frontiersman? Or the industrial tycoon? Or the "Bourbon" who took over where the "carpetbagger" left off—without bothering to plow back some of the loot into vote-getting social services as the "carpetbagger" had done? There is no need to rehabilitate the "carpetbagger"—although it may be unjust to leave him in outer darkness when some historians are telling us once more that his counterparts in Northern business circles were creative capitalists. But chroniclers of America will do American democracy better service if they examine it with true impartiality and do not dismiss its contradictions as merely accidental, or as the work of powers of darkness.

A third error in compiling the Reconstruction record has been its treatment as an almost isolated episode in federal-state relations. The national fetish of Constitution-worship is partly to blame here. "Constitutional history" is not valid as a study of inviolable principles, but rather as an examination of how men adapt their principles to the actual shifts of power within a political system. Thus, to talk of Reconstruction's "constitutionality" is not very useful except as theoretical exercise. The real question is one of just how the Constitution itself was reconstructed. Historians ought to beware of the snare which entangled Andrew Johnson. Some of his supporters have praised his "realism" in contrast to the alleged Radical bemusement with the "abstraction" of Negro equality. Yet it was Johnson and some other "conservatives" who believed that the victors, after the bloodiest civil war of modern history, would restore the defeated enemy to a share in national power immediately —and out of respect for a compact whose interpretation had been one of the very causes of the war. This is a high order of abstraction! Yet it was fundamentally American. Even the Radicals showed a surprising concern for the maintenance of the forms of the federal system, whatever the realities, and for the appearances of constitutionalism. Otherwise why did this "united" and "vindictive" group not choose to protect "its" national program by simply occupying and running the South as conquered territory for a dozen years, as some suggested?[36] Why, otherwise, were they so ready to undertake the bothersome (and ultimately unworkable) business of building Republican machines in the defeated states and then readmitting them?

The perspective of the present day should give us, as historians, a clearer view. We can see that throughout the modern world a massive centralization of power and a corresponding decline in localism and provincialism were in process. We need to spend less time in praising the Jeffersonian dream and more in analyzing the forces that eroded it. In 1787 the state governments were the nurseries of national statesmen. Today they are often enough, in Harry Ashmore's phrase, "the happy hunting grounds of the interests," and a state legislator is frequently "a small-town lawyer who makes no secret of the fact that he has accepted a part-time job that pays little . . . in order to run errands for his clients."[37] We need to know the extent to which this transition has taken place and how it came about. Yet there are few state studies that analyze problems and forces as

[36] Such a policy would have appeared logical to twentieth-century nationalism. Even John W. Burgess, no friend to the racial policies of Radicalism, defended the Wade-Davis bill, considered the idea of restoring the South to territorial status to be "sound political science," and considered the theory of Congressional (as opposed to Presidential) reconstruction "in the right, logically, morally, and legally." John W. Burgess, *Reconstruction and the Constitution, 1866–1876* (New York, 1902), 17–18, 60, 111.

[37] Harry Ashmore, *An Epitaph for Dixie* (New York, 1958), 111.

probingly as those of Shugg on Louisiana, Hartz on Pennsylvania, or the Handlins on Massachusetts, to name three outstanding examples.[38] There are many "narrative" state histories—many of them monuments to local patriotism—designed to serve the needs of required courses in state history at public universities, courses too often thrust upon the most defenseless member of the department. This creates a fundamental weakness, for good history of the United States must rest on sound historical knowledge of each of them. A sound beginning would be the study of Reconstruction as an episode in the decline and fall of the states, and not as a conspiracy to overthrow a wise and good constitutional arrangement.

A fourth barrier to the writing of a sound, modern history of Reconstruction lies in the fact that historians as a group are too often bounded, when dealing with economic and social matters, by obsolete, unsophisticated, and intellectually isolated viewpoints. A few examples will readily illustrate this point. Reconstruction is still frequently taught as the story of how "the North" attempted to remold "the South." But the sectional approach so well employed by historians of a past generation has exhausted most of its utility. Beyond a certain point, the theory of sectionalism fails to explain similarities of pattern clearly visible in "North," "South," and "West," and what is more, it stumbles over the widespread cultural and economic differences among regions *within* each section. Nowadays, the use of a purely sectional analysis is a triumph of mere habit over critical thought.

Also noticeable is a lack of refinement in economic as well as geographical thought. Textbooks cling yet to the well-known view—once a "radical revision" in itself—that the Civil War and Reconstruction sealed the triumph of "industry" over "agriculture," the process christened by Charles A. Beard as the "second American revolution."[39] Yet this conflict

[38] Roger Shugg, *Origins of Class Struggle in Louisiana; a Social History of White Farmers and Laborers During Slavery and After, 1840–1875* (Baton Rouge, 1939); Louis Hartz, *Economic Policy and Democratic Thought: Pennsylanvia, 1776–1860* (Cambridge, 1948); Oscar and Mary F. Handlin, *Commonwealth; a Study of the Role of Government in the American Economy: Massachusetts, 1774–1861* (New York, 1947). The selection of these three works is not meant to imply that they are our only valuable state histories, but to illustrate the type of analysis too rarely undertaken.

[39] Charles A. and Mary Beard, *The Rise of American Civilization* (2 vols. in one, New York, 1930), II, 52–121. It is interesting to note how "revisionists" are themselves revised. Both Beard and Howard K. Beale (in *The Critical Year; a Study of Andrew Johnson and Reconstruction*, New York, 1930) assumed the triumph of "business" to be evident in the Radical plan of Reconstruction. Yet this view is undergoing new scrutiny. In a recent article on the money question, Irwin Unger shows an abundance of evidence to support his contention that it is "clearly not valid to speak of a single business attitude toward the money question after the Civil War." "Business Men and Specie Resumption," *Political Science Quarterly*, LXXIV (March 1959), 46–70. Stanley

cannot be neatly packaged. Richard Hofstadter reminds readers in an article lately published that Americans in sentimental championship of the yeoman as the staunch foe of Mammon, only pay tribute to "the fancied innocence of their origins," and Henry Nash Smith has dealt elaborately with a national image of the farming West which he calls "the myth of the garden."[40] The facts are less picturesque. The American farmer, perennially in search of a cash crop, had never, in Parrington's words, "been a land-loving peasant, rooted to the soil and thriving only in daily contact with familiar acres. He had long been half middle-class, accounting unearned increment the most profitable crop, and buying and selling land as if it were calico."[41] In him we can see already outlines of today's businessman-farmer, private plane, automatic feeder, and all. As for the agrarian South in 1860, it was neither the "feudal" empire of Marxist historians (who have been as obtuse as anyone about Reconstruction), nor yet the physiocratic paradise envisioned by Jefferson, Nathaniel Macon, or John Taylor. Its prosperous planters with their wide holdings and great labor gangs were farmer-capitalists, curiously modern in some ways as they were archaic in others. Reconstruction's real economic story is in the emergence of a new *kind* of agrarian-industrial capitalism in the South, and the need of history is for studies of how this came about, to what end, and to whose advantage—not for lamentations on the disappearance of a fancied Arcadian way of life.

A last example of overly restricted outlooks among historians is in the charge that Reconstruction made the South a victim of colonialism.[42] This is a valuable insight, but its value is diminished sharply by the failure to take cognizance of comparable world developments. "Colonialism" is a complex term, describing a relationship which brings about vast changes in class structure, local leadership, resource exploitation, social mobility, and even religious belief in both colony and mother country. Few writers who employ "colonialism" as a key to Reconstruction show much familiarity

---

Coben, in "Northeastern Business and Radical Reconstruction: A Re-examination," *Mississippi Valley Historical Review*, XLVI (June 1959), 67–90, concludes from an examination of tariff and currency debates that "factors other than the economic interests of the Northeast must be used to explain the motivation and aims of Radical Reconstruction."

[40] Richard Hofstadter, "The Myth of the Happy Yeoman," *American Heritage*, VII (April 1956), 43; Henry Nash Smith, *Virgin Land: The American West as Symbol and Myth* (Cambridge, 1950), 123–260, but especially 123–33.

[41] Vernon L. Parrington, *Main Currents in American Thought* (3 vols., New York, 1930), III, 26.

[42] Thus Coulter declares that Reconstruction "riveted tighter upon the South a colonial status under which it had long suffered," *South during Reconstruction*, 1, while Walter P. Webb made this complaint the basis of an entire book, *Divided We Stand; the Crisis of a Frontierless Democracy* (New York, 1937).

with the best comparative studies of the subject by European historians, or by economists, sociologists, and geographers. Rather, they applaud or, more often, condemn on the basis of emotional reactions aroused by the word itself.

Finally, the historical profession is not likely to revise its notions concerning Reconstruction or any other phase of the American experience unless it subjects itself to the same discriminating analysis which it applies to the documents of history. Historians themselves work from implicit assumptions, measurable in the light of sociology and psychology, and it is a legitimate duty of scholars to examine those assumptions. It is surely no disparagement to the historians of the generation of Rhodes, Burgess, Dunning, and Fleming to point out that their background predisposed them towards a dim view of so-called "Black Reconstruction." The success of Rhodes in the coal business is well known. Dunning was the son of a New Jersey manufacturer. Burgess was trained to be a lawyer and studied abroad, an option not open to the lesser classes of mankind in the years just after the Civil War. Fleming's father had been a "well-to-do farmer" in Alabama before the war ruined him. It might be noted, too, that the authors of at least six of the "standard" monographs on Reconstruction in individual states—Garner, Hamilton, Lonn, Patton, Ramsdell, and Staples— had reached the age of twenty-one by 1901.[43] These are in no sense submitted as hostile suggestions. These men and women were fair-minded and thorough. We who write history today will do well to be as scrupulous within our own limitations. What is more, these students of sixty years ago unearthed materials which must form the basis of any future judgments on Reconstruction. Yet they *did* come from an "old-stock" background; they *were* the children of small property-owners and professional men, and in entering academic life they were themselves joining a genteel profession; they *were* taught, in the formative years of adolescence, to believe that Civil Service, a low public debt, stout constitutions, and Anglo-Saxon leadership were the pillars of a great and enduring republic which was naturally perfect, though it might sometimes be tainted by the work of wicked plutocrats or ignorant foreign voters.[44] We need not wonder that these men and their students identified themselves with the displaced and respectable leaders of the "white South," and not with the adventurers, social climbers, and black and white laborers who wielded power for what must

[43] Biographical data and dates of birth are from the *Dictionary of American Biography* and its two supplements and from the 1942 and 1951 editions of the *Directory of American Scholars*. Information on Thompson, Fertig, Ficklen, and Eckenrode, not available at the time of this writing, might increase the list of writers on Reconstruction in individual states who were born before 1880.

[44] Hofstadter has sharply etched a similar group mentality in his analysis of the Progressives in *The Age of Reform; from Bryan to F. D. R.* (New York, 1955).

have seemed, retrospectively, a brief and unpleasant hour. But we ought to recognize that the Reconstruction story which they left arose in part out of identification with a supposed natural aristocracy of ownership and talent.

These observations are only the framework of an answer to the question of why Reconstruction represents a challenge not met by academic historians. Underlying the problem is the fact that Reconstruction confronts American writers of history with things which they prefer, like other Americans, to ignore—brute power and its manipulation, class conflict, race antagonism. Yet these things make it an essentially modern period. Reconstruction cannot be properly "gotten at" by the well-worn roads of agrarianism, sectionalism, or constitutional analysis. It cannot be approached without perhaps requiring of American historians that they yield up some of their marvelous ability to read unity, progress, and patriotism into every page of the American record—that they face problems which all their piety and wit cannot dismiss or solve with credit to all. Yet those who teach and write the American story cannot be a mere priesthood of patriotism, unless they wish to invite the dominion of the second-rate. If they do not confront tragedies, paradoxes, tidal forces in the culture—if they do not show the forces eroding the compromises of the post-Civil War period and illustrate the frustrating complexity of the problems now awakened again—then Reconstruction will have added the historical guild to the list of its "victims."

CORRELATION OF *AMERICAN HISTORY: RECENT INTERPRETATIONS*, BOOK I, WITH AMERICAN HISTORY TEXTS

	Hofstadter, Miller, and Aaron THE UNITED STATES: THE HISTORY OF A REPUBLIC	Hofstadter, Miller, and Aaron THE AMERICAN REPUBLIC, VOL. I	Williams, Current, and Freidel AMERICAN HISTORY: A SURVEY	Williams, Current, and Freidel A HISTORY OF THE UNITED STATES [TO 1876]
Text Chapters	*Related selections in* AMERICAN HISTORY: RECENT INTERPRETATIONS			
Preface	1	1	1	1
1	3	3	2, 3, 4	2, 3
2	2, 4, 6, 11	2, 4, 6, 11	5, 6, 7, 8, 9, 10	4, 5
3	5, 7, 8, 12	5, 7, 8	11, 12, 13	6
4	9, 10	9, 10	14	7, 8, 9, 10
5	13, 14	12, 13	14	11, 12, 13
6	15, 16, 17	14	15, 16, 17	14
7	18, 19	15	18, 19	14
8	20, 21	16, 17	26, 27	15, 16, 17
9	26	18, 19		18
10	22, 23, 24		20	19
11	28, 32	20, 21	21	
12	25	26	22, 23	
13	30, 31	22, 23	24	20
14	29	28, 32	27, 29	26
15	33, 34	25	28, 32	21
16	35, 36, 37	24, 30, 31	30, 31	27, 29
17	38	27, 29	25	
18		33, 34	33, 34	23
19		35, 36, 37	35, 36, 37	22
20		35, 36, 37	35, 36, 37	28, 32
21			38	24
22				25
23				
24				30, 31
25				33, 34
26				33, 34
27				33, 34
28				35, 36
29				35, 36
30				37
31				38

	Carman, Syrett, and Wishy	Parkes	Malone and Rauch	Morison and Commager
	A HISTORY OF THE AMERICAN PEOPLE, VOL. I	THE UNITED STATES OF AMERICA	EMPIRE FOR LIBERTY, VOL. I	THE GROWTH OF THE AMERICAN REPUBLIC, VOL. I
Text Chapters	*Related selections in* AMERICAN HISTORY: RECENT INTERPRETATIONS			
Preface	1	1	1	1
1	2	2, 3		2
2	3, 4	4, 5, 6	2	3
3	6, 7	11, 12	3, 4	4, 5
4	5, 8, 9, 10	7, 8, 9, 10	5	6, 11
5	11	13, 14	6	7, 8, 9, 10
6	12, 13	15, 16, 17	7, 8, 9, 10	12, 13
7	14	18, 19	11, 12, 13	14
8	15, 16, 17	20, 21	14	14
9	18, 19	26	14	14
10		24, 30, 31	14	
11	20	27, 29	14	
12	26	22, 23	15	15, 16, 17
13	21	28, 32	16, 17	15, 16, 17
14	22, 23		18	
15	27, 29	25		18
16	28, 32	33, 34		
17	25	35, 36, 37	19	19
18	24, 30, 31	38		
19	33, 34			
20	35, 36, 37		20	20
21	38		21	26
22			26	21
23				22, 23
24			22, 23	27, 29
25			22, 23	28, 32
26				30, 31
27			28	24
28			32	
29			25	25
30				33
31			27, 29	33
32			24, 30, 31	34
33				35, 36, 37
34			33	35, 36, 37
35			34	35, 36, 37
36			35, 36, 37	35, 36, 37
37			35, 36, 37	35, 36, 37
38			35, 36, 37	
39			35, 36, 37	
40			35, 36, 37	

	Kraus THE UNITED STATES TO 1865	Hicks THE FEDERAL UNION	Bailey THE AMERICAN PAGEANT
Text *Chapters*	*Related selections in* AMERICAN HISTORY: RECENT INTERPRETATIONS		
Preface	1	1	1
1		2, 3	2, 3, 4
2	2, 3	4, 5	5, 6
3	4, 5		12, 13
4	6	6, 7, 8, 9, 10	7, 8, 9, 10
5	7, 11	11	11, 14
6	9	12, 13	
7	12, 13	14	15, 16, 17
8	8, 10	14	18
9	14		19
10	14		
11	16, 17	16, 17	20
12	15, 18, 19	15, 18	21
13	20		
14	21	19	22, 23, 24
15	22, 23, 28		25
16	32	20	29
17	24, 27, 29, 30	20	26, 27, 32
18	25, 26		28
19	31, 33	21, 26	30, 31
20	34	27	33, 34
21	35, 36, 37	23	33, 34
22		22	37
23		24, 29	35, 36
24		28, 32	38
25		30, 31	
26		25	
27		33	
28		33	
29		34	
30		35, 36, 37	
31		35, 36, 37	
32		35, 36, 37	
33		38	

Index